THE PAPERS OF
Andrew Johnson

Sponsored by
The University of Tennessee
The National Historical Publications and Records Commission
The National Endowment for the Humanities
The Tennessee Historical Commission

Commemorative medal struck in 1867 at the
U.S. Mint in Philadelphia in honor of President Johnson
Photograph Courtesy Special Collections,
University of Tennessee Library

THE PAPERS OF
Andrew Johnson

Volume 12, February-August 1867

PAUL H. BERGERON

EDITOR

PATRICIA J. ANTHONY   GLENNA R. SCHROEDER-LEIN

MARION O. SMITH   LISA L. WILLIAMS

RICHARD M. ZUCZEK

THE EDITING STAFF

1995

THE UNIVERSITY OF TENNESSEE PRESS

KNOXVILLE

Library of Congress Cataloging in Publication Data
(Revised for volume 12)

Johnson, Andrew, 1808–1875.
        The papers of Andrew Johnson.
        Vols. 8—edited by Paul H. Bergeron.
        Includes bibliographical references and indexes.
        Contents: v.1. 1822–1851.—v.2. 1852–1857—[etc.]—
v.12. February–August 1867
        1. United States—Politics and government—1849–
1877—Sources. 2. Johnson, Andrew, Pres. U.S., 1808–1875.
3. Presidents—United States—Correspondence.
I. Graf, LeRoy P., ed.   II. Haskins, Ralph W., ed.
III. Bergeron, Paul H., 1938–   . IV. Title.
E415.6.J65   1967   973.8'1'0924 [B] 67-25733
ISBN 0-87049-896-7 (v. 12)

TO
Dean Lorman A. Ratner
and
Associate Dean Charles O. Jackson
Historians both, as well as administrators,
they have faithfully supported and encouraged
the Andrew Johnson Papers Project.

Contents

Illustrations

Introduction

An exasperated Conservative Republican congressman, Henry L. Dawes of Massachusetts, declared in July 1867: "The President . . . *does* continue to do the most provoking things. If he isn't impeached it wont [*sic*] be his fault."[1] Indeed the shadow of possible impeachment lay across the presidential administration from early 1867 through the late summer months. It clouded any hopes that Andrew Johnson and the congressional leadership might effect a mutually-beneficial relationship. The collision course that they had charted earlier simply could not be altered.[2]

It is perhaps fitting that the very first document published in this volume refers to the threat of impeachment.[3] Introduced thus at the outset, this theme recurs throughout the seven months covered herein. While it is undeniably true that the President provoked certain members of Congress, it is likewise true that they provoked him. The remarkable activities of Benjamin F. Butler and James M. Ashley, for example, should not be ignored or condoned. Perhaps not surprisingly, the House Judiciary Committee engaged in unconscionable behavior in 1867. Its inability to uncover the hoped-for evidence of criminal wrongdoing by Johnson merely fed its determination to go to almost any extremes to snare the President. Meanwhile the politically maladroit Johnson played into the hands of his would-be impeachers by his vetoes, his removal of officials, and his steadily worsening relations with a majority of Congress. Regrettably, there seemed to be little sanity on either side during these months of intense conflict.

The shadow of the Fourteenth Amendment lay across the entire nation but particularly the South and thereby hastened further difficulties. The obstinance of the former Confederate states (Tennessee excepted) with regard to ratifying this Amendment sent signals to the Northern leadership that Reconstruction would not be concluded conveniently. The President himself encouraged animosity toward the Amendment and its ratification, to be sure. But even without his defiant stance, it is not likely that the Southern states would have endorsed the Amendment. The reality of Rebeldom's refusal to accept this formula for readmission forced the

---

1. As quoted in Michael Les Benedict, *A Compromise of Principle: Congressional Republicans and Reconstruction, 1863–1869* (New York, 1974), 253.

2. This essay is based upon documents published in this volume as well as upon several very able monographs: Hans L. Trefousse, *Andrew Johnson: A Biography* (New York, 1989); Albert Castel, *The Presidency of Andrew Johnson* (Lawrence, Kans., 1979); Benedict, *Compromise of Principle*; Eric L. McKitrick, *Andrew Johnson and Reconstruction* (Chicago, 1960); James E. Sefton, *Andrew Johnson and the Uses of Constitutional Power* (Boston, 1980); and Michael Perman, *Reunion Without Compromise: The South and Reconstruction, 1865–1868* (Cambridge, England, 1973).

3. See Anne M. Deen to Johnson, Feb. 2, 1867.

hand of Republican leaders, regardless of conservative, moderate, or radical views. Flowing from this was a series of Reconstruction acts which imposed further requirements upon the South.

The First Military Reconstruction Act emerged in late February after a rather tense dispute within Congress that momentarily divided various factions of Republicans. With its intended establishment of military (and congressional) control over the South, the long-awaited and long-feared punishment of the belligerent region seemed to have arrived. The new law established five military districts for the South, instructed the states to write new constitutions (with black suffrage), and mandated ratification of the Fourteenth Amendment. With such provisions it is no wonder that one historian has labelled this act "the most ambitious and far-reaching piece of domestic legislation in the history of the United States."[4] Certainly the President held a similar view; and although he could have easily pocket-vetoed the bill, he chose instead to issue a formal presidential veto.[5] But indicative of the widespread support which the bill enjoyed in Congress, despite the disagreements surrounding it, the House and Senate easily overrode Johnson's rejection of this legislation.

Because of questions that arose shortly thereafter about the specifics of registering voters in the South and holding constitutional conventions, Congress enacted a Second Military Reconstruction Act in March. This new measure authorized the military district commanders to handle all such matters. The President was quick to veto this bill and just as quickly Congress set aside his action.[6]

In the meantime Congress had taken two other steps to demonstrate its tightening grip on Reconstruction and, one might say, on Johnson's presidential neck. The Army Appropriations bill, which should have been a routine enactment, contained the extraordinary requirement that the President and the secretary of war must transmit all military orders through the general of the army (U. S. Grant). Johnson rightly protested against such an invasion upon his executive prerogatives but reluctantly agreed to sign the bill, lest the military be denied its funds.[7]

On the same day that Johnson vetoed the First Military Reconstruc-

4. Perman, *Reunion Without Compromise*, 270. In his study, Castel has called the act "the single most drastic piece of legislation to emerge from Congress." Castel, *Presidency of Johnson*, 108.

5. See Veto of the First Military Reconstruction Act, Mar. 2, 1867. Prior to the veto, several correspondents gave Johnson the benefit of their opinions about this bill. See, for example, Isaac D. Jones to Johnson, Feb. 22, 1867; Francis P. Blair, Sr., to Johnson, Feb. 24, 1867; and Montgomery Blair to Johnson, Feb. 26, 1867—all of whom opposed the bill and urged the President's veto of it. Henry A. Smythe wrote a somewhat muted request that Johnson sign the bill; Smythe to Johnson, Feb. 25, 1867. Probably the most perceptive advice came from George P. Este to Johnson, Feb. 27, 1867, who informed him about Moderate Republican support of the bill.

6. See Veto of the Second Military Reconstruction Act, Mar. 23, 1867.

7. See Johnson's "protest" against the appropriations bill: To the House of Representatives, Mar. 2, 1867.

tion Act he also rejected the Tenure of Office Act.[8] A blatant attempt to diminish the President's executive powers, this latter measure prohibited him from removing anyone unless the Senate concurred, provided that official's appointment had originally been approved by that body. Johnson's entire cabinet, including Edwin Stanton, agreed with his decision to veto the bill. Stanton's endorsement may have been a cagey bit of strategy, for had the secretary opposed the veto the President could have summarily removed him before the new legislation became law. In any event, Johnson issued a strong rejection, but Congress had little difficulty overriding it.

The Third Military Reconstruction Act, enacted in July, grew out of continuing controversy over carrying out various provisions of the first two Reconstruction laws, such as the far-reaching powers of the military district commanders. General Sheridan in the Fifth District, for example, demonstrated little inhibition about removing civil officials. Johnson therefore asked for restraints upon the general's actions and requested the attorney general to render an interpretation of the Reconstruction acts. Henry Stanbery moved with deliberate speed and finally issued an opinion by mid-May.[9] It was exactly what the President had hoped for and exactly what the Radicals had feared. In the document Stanbery declared, among other things, that the military commanders could not remove officials, could not deny voting rights to persons who had taken the oath of eligibility, and could not alter the laws of the various states. In response to the document, Radicals in Congress vehemently protested. More important, they passed the third act which overruled Stanbery and gave the district commanders full removal powers and virtually any other ruling powers. Ironically, what Republican leaders had attempted to take away from the President they eagerly conferred upon the military commanders. Johnson vetoed the new act and Congress immediately overrode his veto.[10] The legacy of rejection of the Fourteenth Amendment proved to be a bitter one for the Southern states in 1867—and also for the President.

Having suffered greatly at the hands of his tormentors, so he believed, Johnson determined in the late summer to fight back. In compliance with the First Military Reconstruction Act he had dutifully, albeit unenthusiastically, appointed the five commanders recommended to him by General Grant. But the subsequent activities of Generals Sheridan and Sickles disturbed the President immensely, as did the continuing conflict with Secretary Stanton. Thus, Johnson reasoned, he either had to exert some control over the situation or else concede that he no longer possessed any real powers or influence. He therefore launched an auda-

8. See Veto of the Tenure of Office Act, Mar. 2, 1867.
9. See Henry Stanbery to Johnson, May 24, 1867. See also Stanbery to Johnson, June 12, 1867.
10. See Veto of the Third Military Reconstruction Act, July 19, 1867.

cious strategy, an August triple-play: throw out Stanton, Sheridan, and Sickles. It has been labelled by one historian as "Johnson's rampage"—language reminiscent of the Radicals themselves.[11] As a matter of fact, the President had long been urged by friends to revamp his cabinet and particularly to get rid of Stanton.[12] Johnson succeeded with his removal of the "Triple-S team"—partly because Congress was not in session in August. Howls of protest and indignation greeted the President's actions, as did renewed impetus to the impeachment drive. Numerous documents published herein treat the story of the controversial August removals and the replacements which immediately followed.[13] The President demonstrated that despite his lack of political power, he still retained some institutional power.

In the midst of these nearly cataclysmic struggles, the President and his enemies continued to wage patronage wars. It is no surprise then that documents concerning patronage in this volume stretch from the very first date, February 2, through the last date, August 31.[14] But there is a heavy concentration of patronage-related material in the months of February through April, for the conflicts between Congress, the President, and their rival constituencies were at their peak. The Republican leadership in the Senate attempted, with considerable success, to block many of Johnson's nominations, no matter how seemingly inconsequential the post. Skirmishes over assessorships and collectorships, for example, were everywhere, geographically and ideologically. Along the way the President sought to accommodate his friend George Bancroft, first with the Boston collectorship (which Bancroft refused) and then with the Berlin diplomatic appointment.[15] Prominent persons seeking to influence the patronage landscape included all three Blairs, Reverdy Johnson, Charles Halpine, James R. Doolittle, Samuel J. Tilden, John Sherman, and most interestingly, Daniel E. Sickles, who corresponded about minor internal revenue posts as well as a military promotion for himself. Of the three letters from family members in this volume, one is from nephew James Johnson, an assessor at Galveston, who wrote about a possible removal

11. Benedict, *Compromise of Principle*, 255. Evidently historians have not applied the term, "Sheridan's rampage" to the general's ouster of governors, mayors, and other civil officials in Louisiana and Texas.

12. See, for example, Francis P. Blair, Sr., to Johnson, Feb. 12, 24, 1867.

13. There are at least twenty-six documents published in this volume, beginning with August 1 and continuing through August 30, that deal with the Stanton and Sheridan removals. Strictly speaking, Johnson "suspended" Stanton rather than removed him in these August maneuvers. To complicate matters further, Secretary Seward submitted his resignation to the President, but Johnson immediately refused to accept it. See Seward to Johnson, Aug. 23, 1867.

14. See Arno Wiswell to Johnson, Feb. 2, 1867, and Thomas W. Egan to Johnson, Aug. 31, 1867.

15. George Bancroft to Johnson, Feb. 11, May 18, 1867. Bancroft was not averse to seeking a military promotion for his step-son. See Bancroft to Johnson, Feb. 22, 1867.

and vacancy in the collector's position there.[16] In the evident frustration that Secretary McCulloch shared with the President over the efforts to appoint persons to office he declared to Johnson in April, "some of your bitterest enemies desire that important offices should remain un-filled. . . ."[17] Yet as the President had known even before 1867, the dis-tribution of the loaves and fishes afforded very little opportunity to build support.

Two of the Southern states, Louisiana and Tennessee, demanded Johnson's attention more than did the others. Approximately seventy documents are published in this volume which directly address the situa-tions in these two states. Not only was there the usual array of concerns over patronage but also there were other pressing matters. Regarding Louisiana, two correspondents in particular, William H. C. King and R. King Cutler, kept a steady flow of information and requests coming into the White House. Others joined them to complain about scandals among certain officials but mainly to protest vigorously against Sher-idan's removals of prominent Louisiana officeholders.[18] The paramount focus in Tennessee during these months revolved around the forthcom-ing gubernatorial and legislative elections scheduled for August. Friends from that state kept Johnson apprised of Governor Brownlow's activities, especially as the campaign unfolded. They furthermore alerted the Presi-dent to the scenes of domestic disturbance and violence that marred the landscape.[19]

There were at least two pieces of good news for Johnson during these turbulent months. One was the diplomatic breakthrough with Russia, engineered by Secretary Seward, concerning the purchase of Alaska. The President supported Seward's negotiations which bore fruit at the end of March; fortunately for the administration, Senator Sumner en-dorsed the purchase treaty. There were skeptics, to be sure, but generally the agreement with Russia was deemed a smart move on the part of the United States. Johnson, however, reaped little political advantage from it. Encouraging news came from Connecticut, where in April the Demo-crats swept the governor's election and three out of the four congressional seats. Understandably, the President interpreted these results as vindica-tion of his policies and as evidence of the Democratic trend that he had long predicted. The fall months would bring even better news as Demo-crats elsewhere carried important elections.

Like many other presidents, Johnson was able to "escape" the tribula-

16. Sickles to Johnson, Feb. 26, Mar. 5, 13, 1867; James Johnson to Johnson, July 5, 1867.
17. Hugh McCulloch to Johnson, Apr. 17, 1867.
18. Over thirty documents (stretching from March through August) published in this volume, including those from King and Cutler, deal with various Louisiana matters.
19. Approximately thirty-five documents are published which treat Tennessee matters.

tions of office temporarily by traveling outside of the nation's capital. In early June, for example, he embarked upon a sentimental journey to North Carolina. There he visited Raleigh and participated in the dedication of a monument to his father.[20] Afterwards, he moved on to Chapel Hill, where he took part in commencement exercises at the University of North Carolina. Near the end of the same month, the President went to Boston to participate in dedication ceremonies for a new Masonic temple.[21] In the course of his travels he visited several other cities, including New Haven, where he spoke to the Yale students. En route back to Washington he delivered speeches or remarks at both Baltimore and Annapolis.[22] These presidential travels in June seemed to have provided a recuperative time for him; surely he needed such.

But personal rejuvenation and political restoration are not the same thing. Amazingly, Johnson did persevere throughout the turmoil of the February-August period. Physically and emotionally he did not collapse, whereas a person of lesser fortitude might have. Part of Johnson's strength was rooted in his belief that his cause would eventually prevail; he stubbornly clung to that conviction. Certainly letters of support from friends far and wide encouraged the President's determination. He also drew sustenance from his passionate faith that he must defend both the Constitution, as he understood it, and the office of the presidency. The latter concern had considerable merit in 1867, for clearly not only Johnson but also his office were under attack—as various congressional acts and the House Judiciary hearings indicated.

By the end of the summer Johnson was nearly politically bankrupt; but the institution of the presidency, though damaged, was not. That offered him a glimmer of hope. Nevertheless, he did "continue to do the most provoking things."

ACKNOWLEDGMENTS

With each passing year and with each new volume the Johnson Project acquires additional indebtedness. We gratefully acknowledge our obligations to friends and supporters, archives, libraries and historical societies, and federal and state agencies. Without the variety of ways in which these individuals and groups have assisted us we could not maintain our active publishing schedule.

20. Documents concerning the North Carolina trip include: Johnson to William D. Haywood, May 22, 1867; John M. Schofield to Johnson, May 26, 1867; Speech at Raleigh, June 3, 1867.
21. Regarding the Boston and New England trip, see: Johnson to Otis Norcross, June 11, 1867; James E. English to Johnson, June 12, 1867; Johnson to Samuel A. Parker, June 21, 1867. Thomas Ewing warned Johnson not to go to Boston but approved plans to travel to North Carolina; see Ewing to Johnson, May 24, 1867.
22. See Remarks at Reception at Baltimore, June 28, 1867, and Speech at Annapolis, June 29, 1867.

Once more several libraries and archives have provided copies of Johnson documents as well as research assistance. We wish to single out the Library of Congress, the National Archives, the Lawson McGhee Library (Knox County Public Library), and the University of Tennessee Library, especially its Special Collections Department. Furthermore, our list of repositories that immediately follows the Editorial Method section, as well as numerous repositories referred to in our footnotes, give indication of our widespread obligations.

Needless to say, financial support of our editing enterprise is indispensable. We continue to be grateful to the National Historical Publications and Records Commission, the National Endowment for the Humanities, and the Tennessee Historical Commission—all governmental agencies. These have provided more than monetary support, for they have assisted us in several important ways. We are particularly beholden to Richard N. Sheldon and Timothy D.W. Connelly of the NHPRC, to Douglas M. Arnold of the NEH, and to Herbert L. Harper, executive director of the THC.

A vital part of our operations is the monetary and moral support given by the University of Tennessee, Knoxville. Primary among our backers here are Dean Lorman A. Ratner and Associate Dean Charles O. Jackson of the College of Arts and Sciences. Our dedication of this volume to them is only a modest recognition of their incalculable importance to us. Professor Russell D. Buhite, head of the History Department, continues to endorse our endeavor in direct and indirect ways—all of which are greatly appreciated. The University of Tennessee Press as always has been a valuable partner in our joint effort to produce worthy Johnson volumes. Finally, we continue to benefit from our relationship with our neighbors at the Tennessee Presidents Center; namely, Dr. Harold D. Moser and his staff at the Andrew Jackson Papers and Dr. E. Wayne Cutler and his staff at the James K. Polk Correspondence.

Andrew Johnson's hometown of Greeneville is well represented among the Johnson Project's friends and supporters. Principal among them is, of course, Ralph M. Phinney, a longtime benefactor. Moreover, personnel at the Andrew Johnson National Historic Site have aided us over the years. We acknowledge two staff persons, Elaine Clark and Jim Small, who have rendered special assistance.

This new volume, like all previous ones, owes its publication to the amazingly effective and efficient Johnson Project staff. An observant reader will note some changes on the title page's listing of the editing staff. Missing this time are the names of Dr. LeRoy P. Graf, who died in May 1993 about the time that Volume 11 went to press; and Dr. Randall B. Rosenberg, who left our staff in August 1993 to accept an academic appointment at another university. Dr. Graf was associated with the Johnson Project from its inception in 1956 until the time of his death, serving as Editor until the summer of 1987 and thereafter as Consulting

Editor. Our dedicatory statement in Volume 9 summarizes still our indebtedness to him.

In February 1994 we had the good fortune to add Dr. Richard M. Zuczek to our staff. This is his first volume with us and we are much appreciative of his contributions in this short span of time. The other four names on the list represent the backbone of our enterprise; these persons combined have contributed nearly forty years of labor to the Johnson Project. There is simply no way to calculate the significance of this continuity. Although Mrs. Ruth P. Graf has not worked with us on Volume 12, we remain grateful for her years as a volunteer here. To all of the persons who have served on the staff I again express my profound gratitude; together we have accomplished much.

As has been my custom, I conclude with my acknowledgment of the immeasurable debt I owe to my family. My wife, Mary Lee, and our three sons, Pierre, André, and Louis, cannot fully comprehend the role they have played in my professional accomplishments, but it has been of utmost importance.

Paul H. Bergeron

Knoxville, Tennessee
July 1994

Editorial Method

Inasmuch as we offered a fairly extensive discussion in Volume 11 of our methodology and procedures, it seems unnecessary to do so here. In this volume we have not deviated from our previously outlined policies, except for a few very minor stylistic changes in some footnote citations (such as the rendering of newspaper titles). Once again selectivity has been demanded by the simple fact that for the February-August 1867 period we have far more documents than could possibly be included in Volume 12. We have published approximately five hundred documents in full and have referred to hundreds of others in our footnotes. The extant documents compel us to admit once again that Johnson's world was primarily political (with the various ramifications of that word).

Like previous volumes this one is marked by a paucity of documents directly *from* Johnson. To offset these lacunae we have sought and published herein his speeches and interviews, as well as official messages and proclamations, so that the President's own views are represented to a much fuller extent.

A careful reader will note the diligence and creativity with which we have gone about the task of providing explanatory footnotes and identifications of persons and things. As always, however, there are a few instances where we have been unable to uncover a person's identity or to explain a particular reference in a document. We wish to remind our readers that persons previously identified in earlier volumes are *not* identified again in this volume. The Index indicates whether and where an individual has been identified elsewhere. The Index also tells if a particular person has either corresponded with Johnson or else has received a communication from him.

In this volume we have not strayed from the well-worn (by us and others) middle path of editorial methodology. Our goal remains to offer a faithful and accurate rendering of all documents published in the volumes. But in this regard we acknowledge that we have transformed handwritten nineteenth-century documents into published ones.

SYMBOLS AND ABBREVIATIONS

Repository Symbols

CSmH	Henry E. Huntington Library, San Marino, California
CtY	Yale University, New Haven, Connecticut
DLC	Library of Congress, Washington, D.C.
DNA	National Archives, Washington, D.C.

RECORD GROUPS USED*

RG45	Naval Records Collection of the Office of Naval Records and Library
RG48	Records of the Office of the Secretary of the Interior
RG56	General Records of the Department of the Treasury
RG59	General Records of the Department of State
RG60	General Records of the Department of Justice
RG75	Records of the Bureau of Indian Affairs
RG92	Records of the Office of the Quartermaster General
RG94	Records of the Adjutant General's Office, 1780s–1917
RG105	Records of the Bureau of Refugees, Freedmen, and Abandoned Lands
RG107	Records of the Office of the Secretary of War
RG108	Records of the Headquarters of the Army
RG153	Records of the Office of the Judge Advocate General (Army)
RG233	Records of the U.S. House of Representatives

*We have also used a number of microfilm collections from the National Archives, all of which are parts of the various Record Groups listed here.

MeB	Bowdoin College, Brunswick, Maine
MHi	Massachusetts Historical Society, Boston, Massachusetts
NNPM	Pierpont Morgan Library, New York, New York
OClWHi	Western Reserve Historical Society, Cleveland, Ohio
OFH	Rutherford B. Hayes Library, Fremont, Ohio
RPB	Brown University, Providence, Rhode Island

MANUSCRIPTS

AD	Autograph Document
ALI	Autograph Letter Initialed
ALS	Autograph Letter Signed
ALS draft	Autograph Letter Signed, draft
Copy	Copy, not by writer
Draft	Draft
L	Letter
LBcopy	Letter Book copy
L draft	Letter, draft
LS	Letter Signed
PD	Printed Document
Pet	Petition
Tel	Telegram

ABBREVIATIONS

ACP	Appointment, Commission, and Personal Branch
Adj.	Adjutant
Appl(s).	Application(s)
Appt(s).	Appointment(s)
Arty.	Artillery
Asst.	Assistant
Atty. Gen.	Attorney General
Bk(s).	Book(s)
Brig.	Brigadier
Btn.	Battalion
Bty.	Battery
Bvt.	Brevet
c/ca.	circa
Capt.	Captain
Cav.	Cavalry
Cld.	Colored
Co.	Company
Col.	Collection/Colonel
Commr.	Commissioner
Comp(s).	Compiler(s)
Cong.	Congress
Corres.	Correspondence
CSA	Confederate States of America
CSR	Compiled Service Records
Dept.	Department
Diss.	Dissertation
Dist(s).	District(s)
Div.	Division
Ed(s).	Editor(s)
Enum.	Enumeration
Ex.	Executive
fl	flourishing
Gen.	General
Gov.	Governor
Inf.	Infantry
JP	Johnson Papers
Let(s).	Letter(s)
Lgt.	Light
Lt.	Lieutenant
Maj.	Major
Mil.	Military
Misc.	Miscellaneous
No(s).	Number(s)

n.d.	no date
n.p.	no page; no publisher
p./pp.	page/pages
Pet(s).	Petition(s)
Prec.	Precinct
Pt.	Part
Recd.	Received
Recomm.	Recommendation(s)
Regs.	Regulars
Res.	Reserve
Rev.	Revised/Reverend
Rgt.	Regiment
Sec.	Secretary
Ser.	Series; Serial
Sess.	Session
Subdist.	Subdistrict
Subdiv.	Subdivision
Tel(s).	Telegrams(s)
Trans.	Transcriber(s)/Translator/Translation
Twp.	Township
USCT	United States Colored Troops
Vet.	Veteran
Vol(s).	Volume(s); Volunteer(s)

SHORT TITLES

BOOKS

Alexander, *Reconstruction*	Thomas B. Alexander, *Political Reconstruction in Tennessee* (Nashville, 1950).
American Annual Cyclopaedia	*American Annual Cyclopaedia and Register of Important Events* (42 vols. in 3 series, New York, 1862–1903).
Appleton's Cyclopaedia	James G. Wilson and John Fiske, eds., *Appleton's Cyclopaedia of American Biography* (6 vols., New York, 1887–89).
Bancroft, *Nevada, Colorado, and Wyoming*	Hubert H. Bancroft, *History of Nevada, Colorado, and Wyoming, 1540–1888* (San Francisco, 1890).
Bancroft, *Washington, Idaho, and Montana*	Hubert H. Bancroft, *History of Washington, Idaho, and Montana, 1845–1889* (San Francisco, 1890).

BDTA   Robert M. McBride et al., comps.,
                                Biographical Directory of the Ten-
                                nessee General Assembly (5 vols.,
                                Nashville, 1975–).

BDUSC   *Biographical Directory of the United*
                                States Congress, 1774–1989,
                                Bicentennial Edition
                                (Washington, D.C., 1989).

Beale, *Welles Diary*   Howard K. Beale, ed., *Diary of*
                                Gideon Welles (3 vols., New York,
                                1960).

Brown, *Am. Biographies*   John H. Brown, ed., *The*
                                Cyclopaedia of American
                                Biographies (7 vols., Boston,
                                1897–1903).

Conrad, *La. Biography*   Glenn R. Conrad, ed., *A Dictionary*
                                of Louisiana Biography (2 vols.,
                                New Orleans, 1988).

DAB   Allen Johnson and Dumas Malone,
                                eds., *Dictionary of American*
                                Biography (20 vols., supps., and
                                index, New York, 1928–).

Dawson, *Army Generals and*   Joseph G. Dawson, *Army Generals*
    Reconstruction   *and Reconstruction: Louisiana,*
                                1862–1877 (Baton Rouge,
                                1982).

Dorris, *Pardon and Amnesty*   Jonathan T. Dorris, *Pardon and*
                                Amnesty Under Lincoln and
                                Johnson (Chapel Hill, 1953).

Everly and Pacheli, *Records of* Elaine Everly and Willna Pacheli,
    Field Offices   comps., *Preliminary Inventory of*
                                the Records of the Field Offices of
                                the Bureau of Refugees, Freedmen,
                                and Abandoned Lands (3 pts.,
                                Washington, D.C., 1973–74).

Guide to U.S. Elections   *Guide to U.S. Elections* (Washington,
                                D.C., 1975).

Hanchett, *Lincoln Murder*   William Hanchett, *The Lincoln*
    Conspiracies   *Murder Conspiracies* (Urbana, Ill.,
                                1983).

Hill, *Indian Affairs*   Edward E. Hill, *The Office of Indian*
                                Affairs, 1824–1880: Historical
                                Sketches (New York, 1974).

Holli and Jones, *American*   Melvin G. Holli and Peter d'A.
    Mayors   Jones, eds., *Biographical*

	1789–1978 (4 vols., Westport, 1978).
Taylor, *La. Reconstructed*	Joe Gray Taylor, *Louisiana Reconstructed, 1863–1877* (Baton Rouge, 1974).
Trefousse, *Johnson*	Hans L. Trefousse, *Andrew Johnson: A Biography* (New York, 1989).
U.S. Off. Reg.	*Register of the Officers and Agents, Civil, Military and Naval in the Service of the United States . . .* (Washington, D.C., 1851–).
Van Deusen, *Seward*	Glyndon G. Van Deusen, *William Henry Seward* (New York, 1967).
Wakelyn, *BDC*	Jon L. Wakelyn, *Biographical Directory of the Confederacy* (Westport, 1977).
Warner, *Blue*	Ezra J. Warner, *Generals in Blue* (Baton Rouge, 1964).
West Point Register	*Register of Graduates and Former Cadets of the United States Military Academy: Cullum Memorial Edition* (West Point, 1970).

JOURNALS

AHR	*American Historical Review*
ArHQ	*Arkansas Historical Quarterly*
LHQ	*Louisiana Historical Quarterly*
MdHM	*Maryland Historical Magazine*
OHQ	*Oregon Historical Quarterly*
PHR	*Pacific Historical Review*
PNQ	*Pacific Northwest Quarterly*
Records CHS	*Records of the Columbia Historical Society*
THQ	*Tennessee Historical Quarterly*
WHQ	*Western Historical Quarterly*

Chronology

1808, December 29	Born at Raleigh, North Carolina
1826, September	Arrives in Greeneville, Tennessee
1827, May 17	Marries Eliza McCardle
1829–35	Alderman, then mayor
1835–37, 1839–41	State representative
1841–43	State senator
1843–53	Congressman, First District
1853–57	Governor
1857, October 8	Elected to U.S. Senate
1862, March 3	Appointed military governor of Tennessee
1864, November 8	Elected Vice President
1865, March 4	Inaugurated as Vice President
1865, April 15	Sworn in as President
1865, May 29	Amnesty Proclamation
1865, December 4	First Annual Message to Congress
1866, February 19	Vetoes the Freedmen's Bureau Bill
1866, March 27	Vetoes the Civil Rights Bill
1866, April 2	Proclamation *re* End of Insurrection
1866, May 15	Vetoes the Colorado Statehood Bill
1866, July 16	Vetoes the Freedmen's Bureau Bill
1866, August 28– September 15	Trip to the Northeast and Midwest
1866, December 3	Second Annual Message to Congress
1867, January 5	Vetoes the District of Columbia Franchise Law
1867, January 28	Vetoes the Colorado Statehood Bill
1867, January 29	Vetoes the Nebraska Statehood Bill
1867, February 21	Interview with Charles Halpine
1867, February 23	Meets at White House with Indian delegation
1867, March 2	Vetoes the First Military Reconstruction Act and the Tenure of Office Act
	Approves the Army Appropriations Act
1867, March 5	Interview with Charles Halpine
1867, March 11	Appoints the five military district commanders

THE PAPERS OF
Andrew Johnson

February 1867

From Anne M. Deen [1]

New York City   Feby 2. 1867.

Dear Sir

Dr. Burchard[2] wrote the enclosed letter[3] some time since, and as I expected to visit Washington, handed it to me to deliver to you, but circumstances prevented my doing as I intended, and I have delayed forwarding it sooner because of the deep grief you must experience at the course of the House—in reference to the unwarrantable and cowardly attack of some of its members in threatening "Impeachment." The voters of New York my dear sir will adhere to you—endorsing your acts, and feeling contemp for the imbecile traitors, who after trying all other manner of means to seduce you from your patriotic course, have resorted to the meanest and most contemptible of all acts, to attempt to frighten you into concilliating them by threatening a measure which any sane man would repudiate—a measure which your official acts deny, but which if investigation follows will result in the entire country endorsing you as a self-sacrificing patriot and statesman the type man of the age.

Mr Deen[4] and myself fully sympathize with you in the troubles which beset you, and pray that you may speedily confound your enemies, and that the entire nation may joy with you, in your deliverance from them.

I hope Mr President—you will give that attention to the enclosed letter, I have the honor to transmit, which you may deem it merits.

We pray that Wisdom may continue to guide you in your official and private acts.

Mrs A M Deen   4. East 30th St

ALS, DLC-JP.

1. A New York native, Deen (c1825–fl1870) was a housewife who had one daughter living with her at the time of the 1870 census. 1870 Census, N.Y., New York, New York, 21st Dist., 21st Ward, 10.

2. The Rev. Dr. Samuel D. Burchard (1812–1891) was a Presbyterian clergyman in New York until 1879. *NCAB*, 11: 473–74.

3. No letter was found enclosed. However, there is extant a January letter written to Johnson in which Burchard refers to an interview he had with the President regarding the appointment of John Deen as naval officer. See Burchard to Johnson, Jan. 8, 1867, Appts., Customs Service, Naval Officer, New York City, John L. Deen, RG56, NA.

4. John L. Deen was not successful in the search for appointment as naval officer.

From Duff Green

Southern Hotel, N York   2nd Feby., 1867

I arise from a sick bed to thank you for your efforts in behalf of the public liberty and of the constitution, and to suggest that, inasmuch as Congress cannot deprive a state of proportionate representation in the Senate, the refusal of the Radical Senators, to admit the Senators from the Southern States to thier seats is a sufficient cause why you should refuse to recognise, as the congress of the United States, a body from which the Senators and Representatives from the Southern States are excluded.

Yet it may well be urged that a quorum of the whole is a congress, if the absentees are voluntarily absent. Permit me therefore to suggest that, upon the organisation of the next Congress, the Senators and Representatives should all be present, and from day to day ask to be admitted to thier seats; and that in addition to this, they should protest against thier exclusion—denying that any act passed by the body, from which they are excluded will be valid. Let this action of the excluded members of the Senate & of the House also, be from day to day repeated. Let the Conservative members of the Senate and of the House unite in these protests and refuse to recognise the authority of the majority to act as a congress, placing on the journals of each House, from to day thier protests against all attempts to act as the regularly organised Congress so long as the Southern members are Excluded.

If you and the conservative members take this ground we can organise the people and bring a controlling cooperation in support of the action thus suggested.

The proposed convention, to meet in this city on the 4th of March[1] can, and under such circumstances, doubtless would make an appeal to the people, in support of the constitution—of the Union, & of Peace and Public Liberty which would rally a large and overwhelming majority against the revolutionary movement of your Enemies.

Belive me my dear Sir ever ready to cooperate with your friends.

Duff Green

P S. It may be objected to the course suggested that you have recognised the existing congress. You had no right to assume in advance that they would exclude the Southern members and the question had not arisen when you recognised them as a Congress. It seems that the proper time for raising that question will be upon the organisation of the next Congress.

Duff Green

ALS, DLC-JP.
1. Not identified.

From Arno Wiswell [1]

Ellsworth, Maine,   February 2, 1867.

Sir,

Pardon me for writing you with regard to the Frenchman's Bay Collection District.

You may remember I called on you the latter part of December, and had some conversation about it. I then supposed that our representative, Mr. Pike,[2] would again urge the appointment of N. K. Sawyer,[3] the editor of a radical newspaper here, in case Mr. Young the present collector[4] should be rejected by the Senate. In consequence of Sawyer's personal abuse of yourself in his paper, I presume Mr. Pike has little hope of procuring Sawyer's appointment, and in case he fails, he will ask the appointment of Mr. H. M. Hall.[5] An arrangement has been made between Sawyer and Hall for the latter to take the appointment and to give Sawyer the emoluments, and not to stand in Sawyer's way for the appointment two years hence.

Mr. Hall, if possible, is a more bitter radical than Sawyer, and he has frequently and publicly been heard to say that, you were a d—d traitor— that you deserved to be impeached and hung and if this could be done, he was willing for Jeff. Davis to go free.

The fact that he has repeatedly used this and similar language can be abundantly proved, by many of our most reliable citizens.

Now it would not be agreeable to your political friends in this district to see such a man holding office under you, and we have no fears of it, if the facts are understood by you.

I hold myself personally responsible for the truth of the above statement with regard to Mr. Hall, and will obtain the concurrence of Mr. young, the Collector of this District, to whom the facts are well known.

Arno Wiswell.

ALS, DNA-RG56, Appts., Internal Revenue Service, Collector, Maine, Frenchman's Bay, H. M. Hall.

1. Wiswell (b. *c*1819) was a notary, justice of the peace, and attorney in Ellsworth. Wiswell himself was nominated by the President as collector of customs on February 5, but was rejected by the Senate near the end of the month. 1860 Census, Maine, Hancock, Ellsworth, 974; Maine directory (1856); Ser. 6B, Vol. 4: 2, Johnson Papers, LC.

2. Frederick A. Pike (1816–1886) was a lawyer, former member of the state legislature, former mayor of Calais, and a U.S. representative (1861–69). *BDUSC.*

3. Nathaniel K. Sawyer (*c*1816–*fl*1872) was editor of the *Ellsworth American* (1855–72). Sawyer was listed as a temporary inspector at the Frenchman's Bay customs office in 1867. Two years later Johnson nominated him to be collector of customs and the 1870 census listed him as the collector. 1870 Census, Maine, Hancock, Ellsworth, 1; Harrie B. Coe, ed., *Maine Resources, Attractions, and Its People: A History* (4 vols., New York, 1928), 2: 749; *U.S. Off. Reg.* (1867); Ser. 6B, Vol. 4: 3, Johnson Papers, LC.

4. Monroe Young (*c*1822–*fl*1870) was listed as a "gentleman" in the census reports. By the time of Wiswell's letter, Young had already been rejected by the Senate. In the 1850s he

had been a deputy sheriff. 1860 Census, Maine, Hancock, Ellsworth, 986; (1870), 49; Ser. 6B, Vol. 4: 2, Johnson Papers, LC; Maine directory (1856).

5. Henry M. Hall (*c*1830–*fl*1870) was in the lumber business in Ellsworth. On two occasions, once in late February and again in early March, Secretary McCulloch forwarded to the President the name of Hall to be appointed collector at the Frenchman's Bay district. Each time the President's secretary returned the nomination to McCulloch with the suggestion of a different person to be considered for the appointment. The second man, William B. Peters, was indeed nominated and then confirmed by the Senate. 1870 Census, Maine, Hancock, Ellsworth, 117; Ser. 6B, Vol. 4: 2–3, Johnson Papers, LC; McCulloch to Johnson, Feb. 25, 1867, Appts., Customs Service, Collector, Ellsworth, George W. Buckmore, RG56, NA; McCulloch to Johnson, Mar. 8, 1867, ibid., William B. Peters, RG56, NA.

From Francis P. Blair, Sr.

Wash: 4 Feb '67

My Dear Mr. President—

The Editor of the Nat: Int:[1] desired me to ask you to appt. Wendell[2] Superintendent of Public printing. I told him that I had an opinion of his character that would not justify it. He insisted however that he would be under the supervision of those who wd. take care of the public interest— that he knew & could expose all the abuses to which the work had been subjected and that it would have a good effect to employ him under the control he would have over him.

I recommended him[3] to employment as Gen Jackson employed Lafitte[4] the pirate. He knew the intricacies of the mouth of the Mississippi & would be able to detect the approaches of the enemy. I understand that Wendell has joined the Knaves whom he supplanted & therefore trust that he may not be retained by you and write this note to say I committed a fault in suggesting his appointment & send this note as a recal of my recommendation.[5]

F. P. Blair

ALS, DLC-JP.

1. John F. Coyle.
2. Cornelius Wendell.
3. Blair, Coyle, and Rousseau had called upon Johnson on July 30 asking for Wendell's appointment. In August Johnson offered the position to Wendell, who then served from September 1, 1866, to February 22, 1867. Coyle to Johnson, July 31, [1866], *Johnson Papers*, 10: 766; Charles Lanman, *Biographical Annals of the Civil Government of the United States, During Its First Century* (Detroit, 1976 [1876]), 511.
4. Jean Laffite or Lafitte (*c*1780–*fl*1821), a privateer and native of France, operated for many years around New Orleans before disappearing. *DAB*.
5. On February 22 Congress passed "An Act providing for the Election of a Congressional Printer," which abolished the appointed position of superintendent and replaced it with a Senate-elected congressional printer. The Senate then on February 26 unanimously elected to the new position John D. Defrees, the man whom Wendell had replaced. *Congressional Globe*, 39 Cong., 2 Sess., Appendix, pp. 187–88; Lanman, *Biographical Annals*, 511.

From William T. Dowdall

Office National Democrat
Peoria Ills   Feby 4th 67

You may think it stepping aside for me to go out of my District to make reccommendations for office and too when I myself am an applicant for a similar position in my own Dist but knowing the facts as I do and feeling great solicitude for the final success of your principles and party in this State and nation can not remain silent when I know there is a movement on foot to probably cause you (unless notified of the true facts in the case) to remove a good and efficient officer and one of your stronger political supporters for personal spite.

It is this the *Copperhead* portion of the Democracy of the 8th Dist are petitioning the removal of David T. Littler[1] Internal Revenue Collector of the Dist because he will not permit that wing of the party to run his Office. I know Mr L. to be a reliable man as a politician and officer and hope you will find it concistent with the public interest to retain him in office.[2]

W. Dowdall

ALS, DNA-RG56, Appts., Internal Revenue Service, Collector, Ill., 8th Dist., David Littler.

1. Littler (1836–1902), a lawyer, was admitted to the bar in 1860. During his political career he served as justice of the peace, master in chancery, internal revenue collector (1866–68), and state representative (1882–90) and senator (1894–98). Newton Bateman and Paul Selby, eds., *Historical Encyclopedia of Illinois* (3 vols., Chicago, 1912), 1: 341.

2. Littler remained in office until early 1868 when he resigned. He was eventually replaced by Edwin McCook the following July. Ibid.; Ser. 6B, Vol. 4: 305, Johnson Papers, LC.

From David M. Fleming

Piqua, Feb. 4th 1867

Sir:

Permit me at this juncture of affairs to remind you of the promise made me in your note to me of the 15th of October last.[1] It may be possible that the Senate will not confirm the appointment of John E. Cummins, the person who succeeds me as Assessor of this, the 4th District of Ohio, and in that case it would leave you free to act on your own judgement.[2] I have no influential friends to urge my claims and will ask none. When I came to the conclusion Oct 14, 1863, that you were the gentlemen among all others, the most entitled, by your patriotism and devotion to the country during the existence of the rebellion, for the 2d office in the gift of the people, I did not consult the prominent men in the party for their consent to present you for that position. Instead of this I said to Rev. Granville Moody that you were the man for the place, and acted on the suggestion at once by announcing you for Vice President eight months in advance of the Convention and at least four months in advance of all other announcements. My removal last August was a hardship, and I am sure at that time you had not a better friend in America. My only sin was that while I gave you a firm and cordial support, as you yourself acknowledged to me, I demanded that in the elections we should not be compelled to forswear our every act during the war by giving our support to men who had used their influence to break up our glorious Union by aiding the rebels in their warfare against the Government. I demanded as candidates for the offices Union men, and had my wish been complied with the result would have been vastly different.

In the letter alluded to you say to me, "*I need hardly assure you that had I, at the time, fully understood all the facts in your case, the change would not have been made*." And in conclusion, "*when opportunity occurs, I hope to be able to give you evidence of my appreciation of your friendliness*."

I have often heard that the "*true Southern*" was a *chivalrous, magnanimous gentleman*, and never disabused the confidence reposed in him or the friendship manifested in his behalf. If this is true, ANDREW JOHNSON will yet do justice to his old friend by restoring him to the position he says himself he was removed from by mistake.

With my best wishes for your continued health, and that the day is not far distant when the animosities of the past two years may disappear, and that you will be regarded by the people of this nation as pure a patriot as when nominated and elected . . .

D. M. Fleming.

This is of course private.

ALS, DNA-RG56, Appts., Internal Revenue Service, Assessor, Ohio, 4th Dist., D. M. Fleming.

1. See Johnson to Fleming, Oct. 15, 1866, *Johnson Papers*, 11: 354.

2. While Cummins, nominated on January 21, 1867, was rejected February 6, Fleming did not immediately regain the assessorship. James H. Hart received the commission on March 14; upon Hart's death, Fleming was eventually nominated and subsequently confirmed July 1, 1868. Ser. 6B, Vol. 4: 257, 259, 262, Johnson Papers, LC.

From William H. Seward

Department of State,
Washington, February 4th 1867.

To the President,

The Secretary of State, in answer to the Resolution of the Senate, of the second instant requesting him to report to the Senate what steps have been taken by him to obtain from the Republic of Colombia the right for the United States to make necessary surveys for an interoceanic ship-canal through the territory of the Republic.[1] I have the honor to submit the following statement.

On the 16th of March, last, the Minister of the United States of Colombia[2] to this country, submitted to the State Department a memorandum[3] of the following purport.

The United States of Colombia, offer to the United States the privilege to explore and survey any portion of the Isthmus of Darien for the purpose of ascertaining the most suitable location for an interoceanic ship-canal.

2nd.   Colombia will zealously co-operate in the undertaking, by granting all the necessary authorizations aid and comfort within its power to facilitate the object.

3rd.   In view of obstacles which might arise from the hostility of Indians, the United States may unite with the Expedition, a force sufficient for its protection, which shall enjoy the privileges usually conceded to an army passing by permission through a friendly State, with the addition of the right of self defence. The said force not to exceed one hundred and fifty men, rank and file, unless actual forcible resistance by hostile Indians or others, should render an increase necessary, in which case the additional force is not to exceed five hundred men. The whole force is not to remain in the country any longer than the said survey may render it necessary, nor be employed for any other object whatsoever.

4th.   The Government of Colombia will supply the Expedition with all the maps, charts, surveys, reports and plans or information in its possession, which the Engineers may deem calculated to facilitate their labors, unless where it should be deemed incompatible with any of its existing obligations.

5th.   The expenses of the Exploration and Survey except as otherwise stipulated are to be defrayed by the United States.

6th.   In consideration of the premised, the United States of Colombia grant to any organized company of citizens of the United States of America or its agents or assigns the right of priority or preference to construct and use, an interoceanic ship canal within and across the aforesaid territory with all the necessary lands and collateral privileges to render the same effective that may be hereafter agreed upon as satisfactory to the United States of Colombia, and the company aforesaid.

So that, if by virtue of said survey, said work is to be undertaken upon the same terms any company as aforesaid shall have the preference over any other company whatsoever. But, if after the expiration of the three years assigned for the completion of the survey in the next article, the said survey has not been made or if it does not favor the undertaking, or, if another survey be on such account deemed necessary and executed by the direction of the Colombian Government, then, and in any one of such cases, this privilege of priority or preference in favor of citizens of the United States shall cease.

7th.   The Exploration and survey is to be commenced within a year and to be finished within three years from the date of the acceptance of the proposition contained in the memorandum by the two Governments.

8th.   The Engineers in charge of the Expedition shall make the same identical reports upon the progress and result of their labors to the Government of Colombia, as they shall make to the Government of the United States accompanying them with the same illustrations, maps, charts drawings &c.

The above propositions are made subject to the approval of the Congress of Colombia and the minister of Colombia undertakes to transmit them at once for the action of that body on the receipt of their conditional acceptance by the Executive Department of the United States.

On the 19th March 1866, this Department addressed a note to the Minister of Columbia, in reply to his memorandum in words of the following effect. "Having taken the President's views on your memorandum, I beg to inform you that if the propositions in the form in which you have presented them shall be sanctioned by the Government of Colombia through the requisite treaty stipulations, the United States will accede to them, subject however to the ratification of the Senate.["]4

No further information has been received from the Government of Colombia, on the matter, and, on the 23d of last November the Department again addressed the Minister of Colombia asking him what action, if any, had been taken in the premises by the Congress of Colombia.

No reply has, as yet, been received, to that communication.5

William H. Seward

LBcopy, DNA-RG59, Reports to President and Congress, Vol. 9.

1. *Congressional Globe*, 39 Cong., 2 Sess., p. 958. The Colombian-controlled Panamanian isthmus was only one of many proposed sites; for more on this issue, see Henry Wikoff to Johnson, Oct. 25, 1866, *Johnson Papers*, 11: 387–88.

2. Gen. Eustorjio Salgar (1831–1885), soldier and statesman, began his political career in 1852; he eventually was elected president of the Republic of Colombia (1870–72). *Enciclopedia Universal Ilustrada* (1926).

3. Memorandum from Eustorjio Salgar, Mar. 16, 1866, Notes from the Colombian Legation, 1810–1906 (M51, Roll 5), RG59, NA.

4. William H. Seward to Eustorjio Salgar, Mar. 19, 1866, Notes to Foreign Legations, 1834–1906 (M99, Roll 15), ibid.

5. Despite Caleb Cushing's negotiated agreement by 1868, the Colombian Senate rejected the treaty and the U.S. Senate consequently dropped its consideration. Van Deusen, *Seward*, 517–18.

From Joseph A. Wright

U S Legation   Berlin   Feb 4th 1867

My Dear & Kind President,

Allow me to thank you heartily for the leave of absence granted in your Secretary's last dispatch1 (doubtless coming from you).

I will not, however, leave home until spring advances, as I am improving daily since I submitted to an operation, (deemed necessary by my physicians,) and which they hope, will be attended with perfect restoration.[2] Yet notwithstanding my critical situation for weeks, I was not confined to my bed or room, but was able every day to keep a general oversight over all the business of the Legation, leaving the details and labor to be attended to by Son, (the Secretary[ )].[3]

I assure you, that in the midst of my sickness, and while you were passing through your arduous duties & trials I have *not failed to Sympathize* with you deeply. *You are right*—and time will demonstrate it.

And I fully agree in the opinion expressed in all the leading Journals of Europe, that the late movement of the Radicals will end in signal failure. God bless you, dear President, for this renewed expression of kindness to me; and for all the unchanging tokens of friendship shown me. You know I am ever at your service.

Kindest regards to your Lady & family from Mrs. Wright and myself.

Joseph A. Wright

P.S. When I avail myself of the leave of absence, I shall not be far from my post of duty, as the watering places are within a few hours travel of Berlin.

ALS, DLC-JP.

1. Not found.

2. Despite his hopes and predictions, Wright did not improve; in March a Washington newspaper indicated that his recovery was "considered doubtful." Wright died on May 11. *Washington Evening Star*, Mar. 11, 1867; *BDUSC*.

3. John C. Wright.

From Nathaniel G. Taylor

House of Reps.   Washington D.C.
Feb 6th 1867

Sir:

I have the honor to enclose to you the within note[1] from Hon. W. B. Stokes which is an *endorsement* of one to him from some one in the Senate stating that the Senate "Books" satisfy him that Col Stokes' name has not yet been sent to the Senate as Brevet Brigr. Genl.

I venture to suggest that, if a mistake has been made in this matter,— your Excellency have it immediately corrected.

This correspondence results from my having informed Col Stokes upon your Statement to me that his name had been sent in for Brevet— nearly a month since.

Please respond in such form that I may exhibit your reply to Col. Stokes.[2]

N G Taylor

ALS, DLC-JP.

1. Found enclosed are two notes. One from Stokes to Taylor transmits a note from an anonymous writer who testified that Stokes's nomination had not yet been forwarded to the Senate. Although the second note bears a signature, the page has been torn, thereby obliterating the name.

2. Attached is a note from William G. Moore which claims that the nomination of Stokes was presented to the Senate on January 14. Another source which bears Johnson's recommendation of the Stokes nomination indicates that he was nominated on December 24, 1866. Evidently that date is correct, for a Senate document confirms it; apparently Stokes's name was actually presented to the Senate on February 8, 1867, and was approved on February 21—with the appointment to date from March 13, 1865. File cover sheet, ACP Branch, File S-1558-CB-1866, W. B. Stokes, RG94, NA; *Senate Ex. Proceedings*, Vol. 15, Pt. 1: 95, 180, 240; Hunt and Brown, *Brigadier Generals*.

From Allen A. Bradford

Washington D.C.   Feby 7. 1867

Mr. President.

I respectfully ask for the removal of Alexander Cummings the Governor and Ex. Officio Superintendent of Indian Affairs of Colorado from the position he now occupies, for the following reasons.

He has misapplied a large portion of the fund appropriated for the Indian service in Colorado. I find on examing his returns now on file in the office of the Commissioner of Indian Affairs,[1] an item showing that the sum of $1800. purports to have been paid one M B. Cummings as Clerk of the Superintendency for the year ending Dec 31. 1866, the said M B. Cummings being a resident of the city of Philadelphia, and it is a well know fact that this assumed Clerk has not been in Colorado since April last.[2]

On further examining his returns I find an item in which one John Wanless[3] appears to have received the sum of $2342.00 for transporting 19,600 lbs of freight from Denver to Middle Park at 12 cts per lb when it is well known that the distance is less than 80 miles, and it believed that said Wanless performed no service whatever; I find many other items in his returns equally dishonest.

I charge him with malfeasance in office as Governor in appointing a Territorial Treasurer[4] and directing the territorial revenue to be placed in his hands before he had given the bond required by law. I charge him with neglecting the duties of his office and with unwarrantable assumptions in violation of the rights of the people.

I therefore in behalf of the people of Colorado ask for the removal of said officer and the appointment of some citizen of the Territory who possesses the qualifications of "capability and honesty."[5]

signed   Allen A Bradford
Delegate from Colorado

Copy, DNA-RG59, Territorial Papers, Colorado (M3, Roll 1).

1. Dennis N. Cooley.

2. No likely M. B. Cummings has been located. It is possible, however, that this was a cover for nepotism, since allegedly Governor Cummings's daughter and son, May and Boyd, were receiving government salaries as Indian clerks. Howard R. Lamar, *The Far Southwest, 1846–1912: A Territorial History* (New York, 1970 [1966]), 263.

3. Canadian native Wanless (c1835–1886), a stock dealer and capitalist, moved from Illinois to the territory in 1859. He served as provost marshal of Denver from 1863 to March 1865, when he became lieutenant colonel of the 5th U.S. Inf., a post he held for about a year. Wanless was Colorado territorial treasurer and ex officio superintendent of public instruction in 1866. In 1870 he was defeated in the election for territorial delegate of Wyoming. Denver directories (1871–76); Bancroft, *Nevada, Colorado, and Wyoming*, 440, 441, 749; Pension File, Mary E. Watson, RG15, NA; CSR, John Wanless, RG94, NA.

4. Probably Bradford is referring to the appointment of Wanless because the successor, Columbus Nuckolls, is unlikely to have been an Alexander Cummings appointee. Bancroft, *Nevada, Colorado, and Wyoming*, 440.

5. This letter was a continuation of the lengthy effort to remove Cummings, who resigned in April 1867. See Frederick J. Stanton to Johnson, June 9, 1866, *Johnson Papers*, 10: 576–77.

From William P. Fessenden

Senate Chamber   Feb. 7. 1867

Sir—

I have known for many years the parents of Appleton Oaksmith,[1] who formerly resided in Portland, Maine, and feel an interest in their happiness. I am therefore induced to address you in their behalf.

I know that the absence of their son against whom I have heard no charge except that for which he was indicted, and on account of which he became a fugitive, has been to them a source of great distress. They firmly believe in his innocence. But whether guilty or not, I am of the opinion that considering the punishment he has endured by long absence from his native country, his family & friends, the fact that all necessity for further examples by way of punishment for such offences, has apparently ceased, and the previous respectable standing of the accused, no good can accrue by keeping the indictment longer hanging over him, compelling him longer to remain an exile and a wanderer.

Executive clemency in his case will not, I think, be misplaced.[2]

W P Fessenden

ALS, RPB-Lincoln Coll.

1. Oaksmith (c1825–1887) was a businessman, shipowner, and adventurer, whose exploits included outfitting a filibuster against Cuba in the 1850s. He was arrested in 1861 for "complicity in the slave trade" but escaped to Europe before his trial. Oaksmith was the son of Seba Smith and Elizabeth Oakes Smith (1806–1893), a poet, author, and lecturer. *New Orleans Times*, June 12, 1867; *NUC*; *DAB*; *New York Tribune*, Nov. 19, 1861; Record of Pardon Cases, File B-312, Appleton Oaksmith, RG204, NA.

2. In June 1867 Johnson rejected an application for pardon made by Oaksmith on his own behalf. Although the ultimate outcome of the case is not clear, there is evidence that Oaksmith had returned to the South by 1873. *New Orleans Times*, June 12, 1867; *NUC*.

From Simon P. Hanscom

Private.

Wash.   Feb. 8th 1867

Dear Sir;

A conversation occurred yesterday, at the Capital, which I take the liberty to state to you, in writing, as I have not the time to give which it requires to gain an interview to state it to you. It may or may not be of importance.

Mr. Rice,[1] of Massachusetts, stated that the reason why Couch[2] was not confirmed was because he would not agree to keep certain of his subordinates in office. The fact that he had not removed them was cited as an evidence that he might continue them. Rice said there were two reasons why they were not *yet* removed, first because he (Couch) wished to secure his confirmation, second because they, (the radicals) had "fixed the matter" with Mr. McCulloch! Mr. Rice then said, to use his own language, "We have one man at the other end of the Avenue, in the Treasury, who agrees with us; *we shall have things to suit ourselves*. McCulloch has got some bills up here that he wants passed and he wants our votes, and will give us the control of the patronage of his Department in our Districts." &c, &c.

Now, Mr. President, as I have before intimated as much to you I send this as a confirmation of the "selling out" policy of the Secretary of the Treasury to gain *for himself popularity with the financial community*, at your expense and the expense of your friends. Mr. Rice made the statement yesterday to one of your friends who authorized me to *tell* you of it but did not authorize me to *write* it to you. I suppose it makes no difference, therefore I inform you that Gen. John L. Swift[3] is the gentleman. He will make the statement to you. If you want further proof that such trading is going on, to the great injury of yourself and those who have been your faithful friends, *I can give you an abundance of it*. In sending you this letter I feel that I am only doing my duty. The cost to me for the performance of that duty I have not estimated and care nothing about. I believe in telling the truth let what will come. One thing is certain, after the radicals get what they want they will never thank you for it. They will denounce you the very next day *and already say so*. Mr. Rice said as much to Mr. Swift. I think the best thing you can do for yourself is to keep them at bay by refusing to make a single appointment until the very last moment of recorded time allowed you by the law.[4]

S. P. Hanscom

ALS, DLC-JP.
  1. Alexander H. Rice.
  2. Darius N. Couch. See McCulloch to Johnson, Sept. 19, 1866, *Johnson Papers*, 11: 245–46. The Senate rejected Couch's nomination as collector of Boston on February 6.

3. The Senate rejected Swift's nomination as Boston's naval officer on February 6. Ser. 6B, Vol. 4: 24, Johnson Papers, LC.

4. The President evidently ignored this advice from Hanscom, for he immediately sought to fill both the collector and the naval officer slots and succeeded within a few weeks.

From Henry W. Harrington

Madison   Feb 8th 1867

Sir,

I observe from the telegrams that the Senate has refused to confirm my appointment.[1] This I anticipated at the time I received it. I have found the office less remunerative than I expected, and after my term under your appointment expires I would not desire it again. The time required in the performance of official duties devoted to professional labors would far exceed the emoluments of the office. I respectfully recommend as my successor, Charles A. Korbly Esq.[2] of Madison, and earnestly request that he may receive the appointment. He is conservative and would be likely to receive confirmation. Mr. K. has been my law partner and is eminently qualified to discharge all the duties of the office. I found that the office in this district, had been carried on without system and its affairs were very much deranged. Mr. K. acted as my assistant, and to him I am entirely indebted for the complete order and business like system to which the business in this District has been reduced. For the manner in which the business has been transacted and accounts kept I respectfully refer you to the Internal Revenue Department and to Mr. Lawrence[3] Rev. Agt. of Chicago Ills., who has visited my office in his tour through Indiana.

I can say that Mr. K. is honest and reliable and I know of no one in the District so well qualified to discharge the duties of the office. The office ought to be located at Madison for the interests of the public as well as for the Rev. Dept. Jefferson County in which it is situated and Switzerland County adjoining pay 3/4 of the revenue of the entire district, comprising eight counties. The distilling and manufacturing interests of the district are situated in those two counties; and the delay in getting permits and transacting business while the office was located in the interior, at Columbus, was frequently vexatious and detrimental to commercial interests.

If Mr. K. is appointed the business of the office will be carried on entirely by himself, that I desire to have nothing to do with it after my successor is appointed.[4]

Permit me to take this opportunity of acknowledging my gratitude to you for the confidence which you have placed in me, and of expressing my confidence in Your Excellency and the final triumph of your policy.

H. W. Harrington

ALS, DNA-RG56, Appts., Internal Revenue Service, Collector, Ind., 3rd Dist., Charles A. Korbley.

1. Temporarily appointed collector of the Third District in October 1866, he was formally nominated January 27, 1867, but rejected February 6. Ser. 6B, Vol. 3: 552; Vol. 4: 285, Johnson Papers, LC.

2. Korbly, Sr. (1842–1900), a Union veteran and prominent lawyer, practiced with Harrington for nearly thirty years in Jefferson and surrounding counties. Jacob P. Dunn, *Indiana and Indianans* (2 vols., Chicago, 1919), 2: 1640–41.

3. H. C. Lawrence served as a special revenue agent of the Treasury Department sometime between June 1866 and February 1868, and may have been the Chicago bookkeeper Henry C. Lawrence. *House Ex. Docs.*, 40 Cong., 2 Sess., No. 144, p. 7 (Ser. 1337); Chicago directories (1865–67).

4. Smith Jones replaced Harrington, being nominated February 20, 1867, and commissioned March 2. Ser. 6B, Vol. 4: 286, Johnson Papers, LC.

From Francis C. LeBlond

Washington, D.C.   Feb 8th 1867

Sir

Before the close of the last session of Congress Genl Steedman Myself and others recomended the appointment of Col Neibling[1] for assessor of the 5th Congressional District of Ohio. I had the promise of the Hon Mr. Cooper[2] your then private Secty that the appointment should be made as soon as Congress should adjourned and authorized me to so Write to Col Neibling which I did. To my surprise after the Phila. Convention I saw the appointment of T E Cunningham.[3] The appointment was a good one and I have no complaints to make other than it put me in a very awkward position. I very much regret his appointment will not be confirmed. Senator Sherman[4] informed me yesterday that it would not be.

It is my desire that the name of Col Neibling should be sent in when Cunningham is rejected.[5] The papers are on file I suppose in the proper Department. He was a soldier in the late war and lost an arm in the service. He is believed to be well qualified for the place.

Genl Robinson[6] is here seaking the appointment. He has not been acting with us but against us in the late Contest.

The Senate I think will not dare reject Col Neibling. At any rate he comes within their rule for he has been a consistant democrat all his life.

F. C. LeBlond

ALS, DNA-RG56, Appts., Internal Revenue Service, Collector, Ohio, 5th Dist., James M. Neibling.

1. James M. Neibling.

2. Edmund Cooper.

3. Theodore E. Cunningham (1830–1889), a prominent Ohio lawyer, first worked in newspapers, owning the *Lima Argus* in 1852–54. He was appointed assessor in August 1866; formally nominated in January 1867, he was rejected by the Senate the following month. Charles C. Miller and Samuel A. Baxter, eds., *History of Allen County, Ohio, and Representative Citizens* (Chicago, 1906), 345–46; Ser. 6B, Vol. 3: 494; Vol. 4: 257, Johnson Papers, LC.

4. John Sherman.

5. Neibling was nominated February 12, 1867, but rejected February 25. Ibid., 258.

6. James S. Robinson (1827–1892) edited and owned the *Kenton Republican* from 1847 until 1861. He served with the Union army, attaining the rank of brigadier general in January 1865. Following the war he served as Ohio's commissioner of railroads and telegraphs, as U.S. congressman (1881–85), and as Ohio secretary of state (1885–89). He was nominated as Fifth District assessor on March 16, 1867, and commissioned three days later. Ibid., 259; Warner, *Blue*.

From Hugh McCulloch

Treasury Department, February 8th, 1867.

My dear Sir:

I have received the letter of Hon. John Q. Adams,[1] recommending Col. Joseph M. Day for appointment as Collector of Internal Revenue, 8th District of Mass., and referred by you for special attention.

Major Church Howe[2] very earnestly recommends the appointment of Genl. Charles Devens[3] and states that Col. Day is not a resident of the District. Major Howe also protests against the appointment of Genl. Sprague,[4] whom he says is opposed politically to the Administration.

Will you please indicate to me your preference for appointment if you decide not to send in the nomination of Col. Sprague, now before you.[5]

H. McCulloch, Secy., &c.

You will bear in mind that Sprague is strongly recommended by Baldwin,[6] the member, who I think it will be well for you to oblige.

H. McC.

Copy, DNA-RG56, Lets. Sent *re* Internal Revenue Service Employees (QD Ser.), Vol. 1.

1. Evidently a reference to Adams to McCulloch, Feb. 2, 1867, Appts., Internal Revenue Service, Collector, Mass., 1st Dist., Joseph M. Day, RG56, NA.

2. Howe (1839–1915) saw action during the Civil War as an officer of the 15th Mass. Vol. Inf. and resigned in 1863. He returned to his native Massachusetts, but six years later headed west to Wyoming. In 1871 he settled in Nebraska, became a successful farmer and community leader, and remained there until his death. *History of the State of Nebraska* (Chicago, 1882), 1167; CSR, Church Howe, RG94, NA; Pension File, Church Howe, RG15, NA.

3. Charles Devens, Jr. (1820–1891), a successful antebellum Massachusetts lawyer, served extensively with the 15th Mass. during the war. He commanded the Charleston, South Carolina, district immediately after the war ended. In 1867 he became a judge of the Massachusetts superior court; six years later he became a state supreme court justice. He served as attorney general during the Hayes administration. Warner, *Blue*.

4. Augustus B.R. Sprague (1827–1910), a merchant, was an officer in several different Massachusetts regiments and brevetted brigadier general in March 1865. Afterwards he was internal revenue collector, a county sheriff, and mayor of Worcester in the 1890s. Hunt and Brown, *Brigadier Generals*; Ellery B. Crane, ed., *Historical Homes and Institutions and Genealogical and Personal Memoirs of Worcester County, Massachusetts* (4 vols., New York, 1907), 1: 43–45.

5. Howe had been given a recess appointment as Eighth District collector of internal revenue earlier in 1866. The President recommended Howe in December 1866 for permanent appointment; the Senate rejected him in late January 1867. A few days later Johnson submitted Sprague's name as collector. The Senate received the nomination one day after McCulloch's letter and on February 21 it approved Sprague's appointment. *Senate Ex. Proceedings*, Vol. 15, pt. 1: 41, 139, 190, 240.

6. John D. Baldwin (1809–1883) was a Congregational minister before launching his political and newspaper career in Connecticut. He moved to Massachusetts in the early 1850s and was affiliated with the *Worcester Spy* from 1859 until his death. He served three terms in the U.S. House (1863–69). *BDUSC*.

From John Atkinson[1]

Washington   Feb. 9. 1867

Sir:—

I have the honor to enclose the application of Edgar G. Spalding[2] asking to be appointed Collector of Customs at Port Huron to fill vacancy occasioned by my rejection.[3] Mr. Spalding is a young man of ability and integrity and his appointment would be better than that of any other applicant. He was a gallant soldier and is thoroughly acquainted with his duties as a Revenue Officer.[4] He will be confirmed by the senate if nominated. Of this there is no room for doubt. He has never been active as a politician but has authorized me to speak for him in saying that he will give your policy an honest support.

The Congressional delegation will present John P. Sanborn, William Sanborn or John W. Thompson.[5] They are all bitter political enemies of yourself and the two Sanborns have been bitter personal assailants. None of them is as competent as Mr. Spalding, and aside from mere politicians none command as much influence in the Republican party. Those who have yielded your policy an honest and hearty support Democrats and Republicans alike ask as a special favour to them that neither John P. Sanborn nor William Sanborn be appointed and are satisfied they cannot be if you are fully acquainted with their antecedents.[6]

I thank you sir for your kindness to myself and ask your pardon for this paper which is urged from a strong sense of duty.

John Atkinson   Collector of Customs
Port Huron Michigan

ALS, DNA-RG56, Appts., Customs Service, Collector, Port Huron, Edgar G. Spalding.

1. Atkinson (1841–1898), a native of Canada, went to Port Huron in 1854 and studied law before serving with the 22nd Mich. Inf. and ultimately as lieutenant colonel of the 3rd Mich. Inf. during the Civil War. In 1870 he moved to Detroit where he continued his law practice. In 1897–98 he served in the state house of representatives. *Michigan Biographies* (2 vols., Lansing, 1924), 1: 30; *History of St. Clair County, Michigan* (Chicago, 1883), 416; Pension File, Lida Atkinson, RG15, NA.

2. Spalding (1843–1912) enlisted in the 22nd Mich. Inf. as a private and rose to the rank of lieutenant before being wounded and captured at the Battle of Chickamauga on September 20, 1863. He was a prisoner of war until March 1, 1865. *History of St. Clair County*, 380, 595; Pension File, Leonora B. Spalding, RG15, NA. See Spalding to Johnson, Feb. 5, 1867, Appts., Customs Service, Collector, Port Huron, Edgar G. Spalding, RG56, NA.

3. Atkinson served briefly as customs collector from some time in 1866 until March 4, 1867. On January 23, 1867, he had been rejected by the Senate for the second time, the first rejection having occurred in July 1866. *Michigan Biographies*, 1: 30; Ser. 6B, Vol. 4: 274–75, Johnson Papers, LC.

4. Spalding had been serving as deputy collector and inspector since the fall of 1865. *History of St. Clair County*, 595; Spalding to Johnson, Feb. 5, 1867, Appts., Customs Service, Collector, Port Huron, Edgar G. Spalding, RG56, NA.

5. John P. Sanborn (1833–*fl*1881), a native of Maine, was a merchant and lumberman, as well as deputy collector of customs at Port Huron (1862–66). William Sanborn (1834–1876), probably John's brother, was a lumberman who had been deputy commissioner of the state land office before he enlisted in the 22nd Mich. Inf. While lieutenant colonel of the regiment, he was wounded at Chickamauga and medically discharged in June 1864. He later received the brevets of colonel and brigadier general and served as state senator (1867–68). Thompson (1817–*fl*1881), a Scotsman, was an agent for a variety of steamship and other transportation companies in addition to serving as deputy collector and inspector of customs until at least 1881. *History of St. Clair County*, 593, 598; *Michigan Biographies*, 2: 261; *U.S. Off. Reg.* (1881); Hunt and Brown, *Brigadier Generals*.

6. Johnson nominated Spalding to be collector on February 19, 1867, but, contrary to Atkinson's assurances, the Senate rejected Spalding on February 25. Two days later Johnson nominated John P. Sanborn, whom the Senate confirmed on March 2. Sanborn held the post of collector until at least 1881. Rejection for the collectorship did not sever Spalding's connection with the customs office, for, in addition to running a prosperous insurance business, he remained a deputy collector and cashier until at least 1885. Ser. 6B, Vol. 4: 275, Johnson Papers, LC; *U.S. Off. Reg.* (1881–85); *History of St. Clair County*, 593, 595.

From William Bigler

Private

Phila   Feb 9th 1867.

My dear Sir.

Preliminary steps have been agreed upon for a terrific demonstration against the Military Bill of Mr Stevens[1] should it pass the House by 2/3d vote. There is less agitation than for two days past for the reason that the belief is general that the bill must fail in the Senate if not in the House. The more abortions the better for the conservative.

Wm. Bigler

ALS, DLC-JP.

1. On February 6 Thaddeus Stevens of the Joint Select Committee on Reconstruction delivered to the House "An act to provide for the more efficient government of the insurrectionary States" (the First Military Reconstruction Act). The House passed the measure on February 13, 1867. *Congressional Globe*, 39 Cong., 2 Sess., pp. 1036, 1215.

From George Bancroft

New York, 11. Feb. '67.

Dear Mr. President,

I see in the papers, that you, in your friendly regard for me, have sent my name to the Senate for the office of collector of Boston.[1] The law makes residence in Boston a condition of the tenure, & I am not willing to transfer my home to that city, even if otherwise the office were agreeable to me.[2]

I have delayed thanking you for the copy of your annual message, which you were so good as to send me; partly because I thought I might be in Washington, & so talk over with you the present state of affairs & the new obstacles to peace & union. I remain firmly attached to the opinions which I expressed to you a year & a half ago.

Present my best regards to Mrs. Johnson, & remember me most kindly to your daughters, who made my visit to you so pleasant by their charming hospitality.

Geo. Bancroft

ALS, DLC-JP.
    1. A few days after the rejection of Darius Couch's nomination, the President forwarded Bancroft's nomination as collector. Ser. 6B, Vol. 4: 24, Johnson Papers, LC; *Senate Ex. Proceedings*, Vol. 15, pt. 1: 190. A newspaper account of Bancroft's nomination is found in the *National Intelligencer*, Feb. 12, 1867.
    2. On February 12 Bancroft sent two telegrams to Johnson, entreating him to withdraw his name from the collectorship nomination. Bancroft's nomination was withdrawn the following day. Bancroft to Johnson, Feb. 12, 1867, Johnson Papers, LC; Ser. 6B, Vol. 4: 24, ibid.; *Senate Ex. Proceedings*, Vol. 15, pt. 1: 204.

From Charles S. Cary [1]

Olean [N.Y.],   February 11th 1867

Sir

I beg leave to respectfully call your attention to the matter of Collectorship of this District.

In September last you did me the honor to confer that appointment upon me. I took possession of the office and removed it from Jamestown to this place on the 1st of November.

In consequence of my earnest support of your policy I incurred the bitter hostility of the Fenton men[2] whose headquarters for this District is at Jamestown where the Govr. resides. They have procured my rejection by the Senate[3] solely upon the ground of political differences and I suppose it now becomes necessary that you should appoint some one else in my place.

It is understood here that an effort is to be made to procure the nomination or reinstatement of Milton Smith[4] the former incumbent and a blatant Radical. If this could be accomplished it would be a complete Radical triumph and a bitter pill for your friends to swallow. I of course do not believe any such nomination will be made unless the position of Smith is misrepresented to you.

The opposition having so unjustifiably procured my rejection and been so bitter in their hostility to me personally and politically I feel that the appointment should be given to a friend of mine who will retain the office here and thus defeat the principal object in rejecting me. I have consulted with our leading friends in this section of the state and they entirely concur in this view. On the 5th inst I sent to Honl. J M Humphrey papers signed by Honl. A P Laning Chas. H Lee Lemuel Jenks[5] and myself asking that the appointment of Thos. Edgerton[6] should be made. Mr E possesses superior qualifications for the place and can probably procure a confirmation. I earnestly request his appointment. My official and professional engagements are such that I am unable to visit Washington just now and I take this method of calling your attention to the matter and, then I supposed that under the circumstances, with the strong recommendations sent Mr Humphrey it would be unnecessary. If I am mistaken in this I desire delay until I can fully represent the matter to your Excellency.

Chas. S Cary

ALS, DNA-RG56, Appts., Internal Revenue Service, Collector, N.Y., 31st Dist., Thomas Edgerton.

1. Cary (1827–*fl*1893) was a longtime Olean lawyer who, in the 1880s, served in the New York state legislature. William Adams, ed., *Historical Gazetteer and Biographical Memoirs of Cattaraugus County, N.Y.* (Syracuse, N.Y., 1893), 348–49.

2. Reuben E. Fenton, New York governor.

3. As Cary's letter indicates, he had been appointed as collector of the Thirty-first District in September 1866. President Johnson nominated him to a permanent post in mid-December 1866; the Senate rejected the nomination on January 26, 1867. Ser. 6B, Vol. 3: 94; Vol. 4: 51, Johnson Papers, LC.

4. Smith (*fl*1875), a resident of Mayville, had earlier been supervisor and sheriff of the county. He evidently held the collector's post from 1865 until he was removed in the summer of 1866. Andrew W. Young, *History of Chautauqua County, New York* (Buffalo, N.Y., 1875), 281; *U.S. Off. Reg.* (1865); *Senate Ex. Proceedings*, Vol. 15, pt. 1: 40.

5. Albert P. Laning (1819–1880) was a lawyer in Buffalo from 1855 until his death. He served in the state legislature and also was an attorney for the New York Central Railroad. Lee (*c*1819–*fl*1875), the son of Oliver Lee, became a business partner with his father in 1840. Lemuel S. Jenks (b. *c*1815) was a farmer in Cattaraugus County. H. Perry Smith, ed., *History of the City of Buffalo and Erie County* (2 vols., Syracuse, N.Y., 1884), 2: 478–79; *New York Times*, Sept. 5, 1880; *New York Tribune*, Sept. 5, 1880; Young, *Chautauqua County*, 421; 1860 Census, N.Y., Chautauqua, Silver Creek, 28; (1870), Cattaraugus, Persia, 15.

6. Edgerton, not further identified, had served as managing clerk in the collector's office during Cary's tenure and evidently ran the office for a while after the rejection of Cary. There is no evidence, however, that Johnson nominated Edgerton. Instead, he submitted the name of Charles Kennedy in early March and the latter was immediately approved by the Senate and commissioned as collector. Lemuel S. Jenks et al. to Johnson, Jan. 31, 1867, Appts., Internal Revenue Service, Collector, N.Y., 31st Dist., Thomas Edgerton, RG56, NA; Ser. 6B, Vol. 4: 53, Johnson Papers, LC.

From Tennessee Citizens [1]

Nashville Tennessee   Feb. 11th 1867.

The undersigned beg leave to recommend to your favorable notice for the office of "Commissioner of Education" the Hon: Henry Barnard L.L.D formerly of Connecticut & now of Maryland.[2]

Dr. Barnard by his long and most successful labors in behalf of Public and general education has won the esteem, respect and admiration of all educators & friends of education not only in America, but literally throughout the civilized world. He combines in a peculiar degree all the qualifications requisite for success in the new and important position of "Commissioner of Education."

Many years of distinguished usefulness in administering the Public Systems of the Schools of Connecticut and Rhode Island render him perfectly familiar with the details of educational schemes in their most efficient & celebrated forms. Other years of laborious toil in the Western States give him a practical acquaintance with the wants and capacities of the great communities so rapidly springing up between the Mississippi River and the Pacific Ocean: while personal observation in, and a wide correspondence throughout the Southern States have made him well and favorably Known to all the friends of education in the vast region occupied by those States.

The appointment of Dr. Barnard as "Commissioner of Education" will be hailed with delight by the friends of education from end to end of this great Republic, and will confer lasting honor upon the source whence it emanates.

Pet, DNA-RG48, Appts. Div., Misc. Lets. Recd.

1. This petition was signed by some twenty-six prominent citizens, including Governor Brownlow, Secretary of State A. J. Fletcher, two state supreme court judges (including Sam Milligan), and several important education leaders. In addition, on February 21 James Dixon attached his endorsement of the recommendation.

2. The congressional act establishing the Department of Education cleared at the end of February and the President nominated Barnard in early March 1867 to be the first commissioner of education. See James Dixon to Johnson, July 8, 1866, *Johnson Papers*, 10: 655.

From Francis P. Blair, Sr.

Washn.   Tuesday Morning 12 Feb 67

My Dear Mr. President

I talked last night with you of a "*Coup d'etat*" and my head throbed about it all night. I put it on paper now to rid my self of the *one idea* that haunts me.[1]

	John A Andrew—	Sec of State
	George Peabody[2]	Sec of Treasury
	Horace Greely	Post Master Genl.
	Govr. Cox of Ohio—	Sec of Interior
	Cowan of Pa	Attorney Genl.
ad interim	Admiral Farragut	Sec of Navy
do. do.	General Grant	Sec of War

No Patriot can refuse to you his aid in your effort to lift the Govt. above revolutionary factors—to save the constitution & put in place the dislocated members of the Union.

An universal Amnesty to all involved in the rebellion, except the members of Congress, who begot the conspiracy & who Seceded from the

National Councils to give it birth, together with the North Carolina program would put down the lame Devil of the House[3] & crew. Pardon & burn this impertinence, which I am afraid you will consider audacity & folly, and no one will ever know I have been guilty of it.

F. P. Blair

ALS, DLC-JP.

1. The Blairs tried, during Johnson's presidency, to persuade Johnson to make changes in his cabinet. It was public knowledge that this subject was being discussed in official circles. However, despite Blair's continued argument for a completely new cabinet, Johnson took no such action. Following his acquittal in the impeachment trial Johnson admitted that maybe he should have followed some of Blair's suggestions for the cabinet. William E. Smith, *The Francis Preston Blair Family in Politics* (2 vols., New York, 1933), 2: 331–33; *Philadelphia Public Ledger*, Feb. 11, 1867.

2. Peabody (1795–1869), merchant, financier, and philanthropist, settled permanently in London, England, in 1837. He was greatly respected in America and England for his monetary gifts aiding educational pursuits and the working class. Johnson had visited Peabody at Willard's Hotel on the 11th. Ibid.; *DAB*.

3. Probably a reference to Thaddeus Stevens.

From Hugh McCulloch

Treasury Department. Feby. 12, 1867.

Dear Sir:—

My engagements in the Department are so pressing that I will not attend the meeting of the Cabinet to-day unless my presence is necessary. If it is be so good as to send a messenger for me.

I sent you yesterday the name of Mr. J. H. Alexander[1] for Director of the Mint. Mr. Randall[2] strongly recommends a Mr. Page[3] for the place. I sent the name of Mr. A. to you because, in my judgment, he would fill the office with as much ability as it ever has been filled, and because no appointment would reflect more credit upon yourself.[4]

Hugh McCulloch

LS, DNA-RG56, Appls., Asst. Treasurers and Mint Officers, Philadelphia, John Alexander.

1. Professor John H. Alexander (1812–1867) was a renowned scientist who achieved recognition on the subject of standardization of weights and measures. He held several different academic appointments over the years, the last being professor of natural philosophy at the University of Maryland. On February 7 McCulloch had informed the President of his favorable recommendation of Alexander's appointment. *DAB*; McCulloch to Johnson, Feb. 7, 1867, Appls., Asst. Treasurers and Mint Officers, Philadelphia, John Alexander, RG56, NA.

2. Samuel J. Randall.

3. James Page (1795–1875), a Philadelphia lawyer for many years, had served in the prewar years as postmaster and port collector at Philadelphia. *Philadelphia Evening Bulletin*, Apr. 6, 1875. For an example of a letter of support in behalf of Page's nomination, see Henry Phillips to Johnson, Feb. 22, 1867, Appls., Asst. Treasurers and Mint Officers, Philadelphia, James Page, RG56, NA.

4. The plans to place Alexander in the director's office were upset by his death on March 2. McCulloch informed the President of Alexander's death and recommended the

nomination of Henry R. Linderman. The latter was eventually confirmed on April 1, 1867. McCulloch to Johnson, Mar. 4, 1867, Lets. Sent *re* Customs Service Employees (QC Ser.), Vol. 6; *Senate Ex. Proceedings*, Vol. 15, pt. 2: 454, 592.

From Samuel C. Pomeroy

Senate U. S   Washington D C
Feb. 12th. 1867

Sir

Maj. Snow,[1] Agt. of Osage Indians in Kansas, called the "Neosh Agency"[2]—was commissioned in Aug. last, during the recess of the Senate. And his name has not been sent to the Senate for confirmation.

I shall be glad to have it sent up immediately—as the session will soon close. Mr. Snow is believed to be a good agent, and a good man.

This appointment will gratify me, very much, be satisfactory I trust to the Indian and the Government.[3]

S. C. Pomeroy U.S.S

ALS, OFH.

1. George C. Snow (*c*1820–*fl*1869) was postmaster at Bellmore, Indiana, from 1855 until late 1861. On January 7, 1862, he was appointed agent to the loyal Seminole Indians who had fled from the Indian Territory to Kansas. He was appointed to the Neosho Agency on March 16, 1865. 1860 Census, Ind., Parke, Union Twp., 113; *U.S. Off. Reg.* (1863–67); Hill, *Indian Affairs*, 106, 107, 168, 169.

2. Neosho Agency.

3. Johnson endorsed the missive, "Attention is called to this letter." His private secretary, William G. Moore, noted on the same day, "Mr. Pomeroy informed by note of this date, that nomination was sent to the Senate Dec. 19/67 [1866]." Snow's nomination was referred to the Indian Affairs committee on December 20, 1866; the Senate approved the nomination on March 2, 1867. Hill, *Indian Affairs*, 107; *Senate Ex. Proceedings*, Vol. 15, pt. 1: 64–65, 332.

From Sylvester H. Rosecrans[1]

Cincinnati O.   Feb. 12, 1867

Dear Mr. President

My brother has, I am sorry to find, sent in the resignation of his commission. I beg you for the sake of the country, and for his sake to refuse to accept it. You knew him in Tennessee—And do you not think the country can afford to keep him out of the California mines the balance of his days?[2]

S. H. Rosecrans   Aux. Bp of Cincinnati

ALS, DNA-RG94, ACP Branch, File R-160-CB-1867, William S. Rosecrans.

1. Rosecrans (1827–1878) was ordained a Roman Catholic priest in 1852 and was consecrated a bishop in 1862. His years of service in Cincinnati and Columbus (1868–78) established him as a greatly respected priest. *DAB*.

2. William S. Rosecrans's resignation was accepted by Johnson on March 28, 1867, following the termination of his leave of absence. Endorsements, William S. Rosecrans to

From Henry Stanbery

February 13th 1867.
MEMORANDUM FOR THE PRESIDENT.

The act hereunto appended[1] has for its object the prevention of the payment to disloyal persons of claims for property destroyed, used, or appropriated by the U.S. Army during their operations in the States in insurrection. It also cuts off claims of loyal persons of similar character and origin. The intention is right; for it may well be seen how easily large claims might be established by fraud and perjury; how the disloyal might be made to appear loyal, and how impossible it would be to protect the United States from such frauds, were claims for *all* losses sustained by loyal citizens in *any portion* of the immense arena of our late military operations allowed to be adjudicated by a bureau of the government. The mischief which might arise under the law as it stands is great and a remedy should be applied. But in providing against the apprehended mischief, it seems to be unnecessary and it is harsh and unjust to truly loyal citizens whose claims could be paid without incurring the risk of the mischief alluded to, that the act—should exclude all loyal citizens, no matter where resident, from relief. By joint resolutions Congress has extended to loyal citizens of Tennessee and West Virginia the benefits of the law,[2] and this wise enactment ought, it seems to me, to be extended to citizens of all cities and parts of a State declared in insurrection by any Proclamation of President Lincoln, possession of which was recovered by the United States and which remained permanently under its dominion,— as for instance New Orleans and the portions of Louisiana adjacent thereto, New Bern, N.C., and other portions of territory forming parts of any State which had been so declared in insurrection. That such would be just toward our loyal citizens who had the good fortune to fall again under the protection of the United States no one will deny. They had suffered oppression and ought not to be deprived of the "just compensation" which the Constitution secures, having done nothing to forfeit their right thereto, but rather, by their fidelity under trial, having made their claim to compensation stronger. It seems to me that the places which ought to be excepted from the operation of the act now under consideration, should be designated so as to comply with the views expressed by Chief Justice Chase in the case of Mrs. Alexander (2 Black),[3] who defines the occupation which confers on the inhabitants of such territory as is recovered from hostile occupation the character of friends. He says it must not be "brief and precarious."

We must bear in mind that the Supreme Court of the United States in the case of Mitchell vs. Harmony,[4] and the Court of Claims in the case of

Grant vs. United States (Octo. Term 1863)[5] have decided that private property taken for public use by military authority must be paid for. This rule of law is not universal, for in the "Prize Cases" in the case of Mrs. Alexander (2 Black) the Courts have held that those who inhabited the portions of the insurrectionary States (not in occupation of the United States) were to be treated as enemies, and as such their property was by the laws of war and the Acts of Congress passed in pursuance thereof liable to be taken, used, and appropriated by the armies of the United States without compensation.

What effect is produced upon the status of a citizen by the renewed occupation by the United States of the place in which he dwells and the restoration therein of the laws and constitution of the United States, we find declared in the case of the "Venice," (2 Wallace)[6] the opinion in which was delivered by[7] and concurred in by the whole Court.[8] The Court thus defines the law: "There was no hostile demonstration and no disturbance afterwards, and we think that the military occupation of the City of New Orleans may be considered as substantially complete from the date of this publication" (Proclamation of Genl. Butler)[9] "and that all the rights and obligations resulting from such occupation * * * * may be properly regarded as existing from that time." The proclamation declared the city to be under martial law and announced the principles by which the commanding general would be guided in its administration. Two clauses, only, have an important bearing upon the case before us. One of them is in these words: "*All the rights of property of whatever kind will be held inviolate* subject only to the laws of the United States * * * * *." These clauses only re-iterated the rules established by the legislative and executive action of the national government in respect *to the portions of the States in insurrection, occupied and controlled by the troops of the Union.*

"Military occupation and control must be actual * * not illusory, not imperfect, not transient, but substantial, complete and permanent. Being such it draws after it the *full measure of protection to persons and property consistent with a necessary subjection to military Government.*" The effect on the property of *all citizens* of New Orleans was thus declared to be to give it protection.

In the particular case, the cotton of a foreigner, found on a vessel, was restored to him—not declared forfeit as was Mrs. Alexander's—and the difference was owing to the restored authority of the United States at New Orleans. If then all persons in New Orleans were thus protected by the occupation of the city, it seems that to enact a law by which a loyal citizen shall not be permitted to prosecute a claim for property taken, used or occupied by the army of the United States after the city was so occupied, would be to deprive him of a remedy given to other citizens and to deny him the right to compensation secured to him by the Constitution, and to the full enjoyment of which the Supreme Court has by the decision last quoted declared he became entitled, by the fact that New

Orleans was captured and the National authority restored. The right to compensation gives a right to the existing remedy provided by law, and to deny the remedy is to deprive of the right to the property. To give a remedy to some and to withhold it from others is forbidden by the very first principles of a free country—contrary to Magna Charta, which provides that the Courts shall always be open to all men alike, excepting, only, that felons, outlaws and traitors may be deprived of the right.

It follows from what has preceded that the act in question, so far as it denies to loyal persons compensation for their property taken, used or occupied by the armies in the city of New Orleans after its capture, is repugnant to the Constitution as defined by the Supreme Court, and cruel and harsh to those who fidelity to the Union entitles them to especial favor. The same remarks apply to citizens of other portions of the States which were in insurrection over which the dominion of the United States was permanently established by the armies of the Union.

Many cases have been submitted to the Executive where the loyalty of the parties is attested by officers of the highest rank, including the Commanding General; where the claim is for supplies voluntarily furnished, and where the fact that the party did furnish the supplies is established and their value ascertained by commissions ordered by Generals commanding—all appearing upon the certificates of officers of the highest rank. The claimants are often destitute, they have not only experienced loss of property but have suffered social persecution by reason of their known union proclivities; yet such claimants are debarred compensation for such supplies furnished by them, because they resided, say, at Vicksburg after its capture by the U.S. forces, where the supplies were furnished, whilst other persons, of doubtful loyalty perhaps, will receive compensation because they furnished the supplies in Tennessee or in West Virginia.

D, DLC-JP.

1. Attached was H.R. 902 as sent to the Senate, which referred it to the Committee on the Judiciary—"An act to declare the sense of an act entitled 'An act to restrict the jurisdiction of the Court of Claims, and to provide for the payment of certain demands for quartermaster's stores and subsistence supplies furnished to the army of the United States.'"

2. See various resolutions in *U.S. Statutes at Large*, 14: 350, 358, 364, 370–71.

3. The Supreme Court case referred to here is: *United States v. Elizabeth Alexander*, 2 Wallace 404 (1865). Stanbery evidently erred when citing the case as being in Black, rather than Wallace.

4. Here Stanbery left an open space, apparently intending to place the case citation in it, but failed to do so. The case is: *David D. Mitchell v. Manuel X. Harmony*, 13 Howard 115 (1852).

5. *William S. Grant v. United States*, 1 Court Cl. 41 (1863).

6. *United States v. David G. Cooke*, 2 Wallace 258 (1865).

7. Here Stanbery left an open space, evidently intending to insert the name of the justice, Salmon P. Chase.

8. For reasons not altogether apparent, Stanbery left an open space before the words, "the Court thus . . ."

9. Proclamation of Major General Butler, May 1, 1862. *OR*, Ser. 1, Vol. 6: 717–720.

From Ethan A. Allen[1]

National Hotel.   Washington City D.C.
Feby. 14, 1867.

Dear Sir.

Since I had the honr. of seeing you this morning I have had the pleasure of seeing Honl. Reverdy Johnson who thinks a report, from personal observations by myself in the Southern States may be productive of good. I mentioned to him the nature of my interview with you relative to such trip. He promises to communicate with you on the Subject.[2]

I expect to reach Charleston, S.C. on or about the 22d. Inst.

Should you wish to write me on any subject, after that time please address me at the St. Charles Hotel—New Orleans, from which point my letters will reach me promptly after their arrival there, through the directions which I shall forward there from time to time.

Of course Sir *all* communications which you may think proper to make to me shall be held *Sacredly, private, & Confidential.*

I leave here at 11.15. A M tomorrow morning for Norfolk Va. via Baltimore Md.

Ethan A. Allen

ALS, DLC-JP.
1. Allen (*fl*1884), grandson of the famed Revolutionary War leader Ethan Allen, had resided in Norfolk, Virginia, before working in New York City as a dry goods merchant, publisher, and broker. During the early 1880s he lived in North Carolina where he apparently owned a gold mine. Ethan A. Allen to James A. Garfield, May 22, 1881, Garfield Papers, LC; *New York Times*, Nov. 15, 1868; J. Montgomery Seaver, *Allen Family History* (Philadelphia, 1929), 27; New York City directories (1848–84).
2. No Reverdy Johnson correspondence has been found which discusses Allen's proposed southern tour. The trip was made and by early June 1867 Allen had written Johnson at least seven letters, several of which are published in this volume. Allen to Johnson, Mar. 8, 11, 19, Apr. 9, May 17, 28, June 3, 1867, Johnson Papers, LC.

From William M. Daily

Private

New Orleans, Louisiana   February 14th, 1867.

Mr. President:

Once more, I ask *another office,* at your hand for myself.

If you have nothing for me here, in New Orleans, where I have asked so often you now have an opening for me in Indiana. I see the U.S. Senate have rejected *H. W. Harrington,*[1] as Collector of Internal Revenue for the *Third District* in *Indiana.* Now as that is my old Congressional District— and the home of my family, and where my friends are "*legion,*" I respectfully ask you to *nominate me,* to the *Senate* as *Collector* of *Internal Revenue,* for the *Third District* of *Indiana.* And I have strong faith, that my *confirmation*, by the *Senate*, would be certain. For, while I am *everywhere known*, as the *devoted friend* and *zealous advocate, of the President*, and his *Administration*, in all its length and breadth, yet such are my personal relations, with many Senators, that they would gladly vote for my *confirmation*, as a personal favor to me. I am peculiarly situated in this respect—And if you desire to *confer a lucrative appointment* on one of the very *best*, and *most devoted friends*, you ever had with a certainty of having the appointment *confirmed*, you can certainly do so by *nominating me*, for the place above referred to, or any other lucrative position.

Now, surely, while so many of your friends are being rejected, you will find a place for me, where I can make a living for myself and family, either in Louisiana, or in Indiana. I call your attention to the present opening in my old Congressional District in Indiana—the Third—And trust you will give me the place—Or, something down here. For I am still *hopeful*, though pressed with poverty, and feeling the want of sufficient means for a support.[2]

You will not forget me. Always rely upon me, as your ever faithful and true friend.

Wm. M. Daily

P.S. Do not forget that I have now lived in Louisiana eighteen months or more, which makes me elligible to office here or in Indiana either.

W.M.D.

ALS, DNA-RG56, Appts., Internal Revenue Service, Collector, Ind., 3rd Dist., William M. Daily.

1. Henry W. Harrington was rejected by the Senate on February 6, 1867. Ser. 6B, Vol. 4: 285, Johnson Papers, LC.

2. Smith Jones was nominated for the collectorship of Indiana's Third District on February 20, 1867, followed by confirmation and commissioning on March 2. Daily continued to importune Johnson for a post in letters of March 23 and April 20, 1867. Ibid., 286. See Daily to Johnson, Mar. 23, Apr. 10, 1867, Johnson Papers, LC.

From Thomas Swann

Annapolis   Feb: 14, 1867

My Dear Sir,

Since my interview with you yesterday, in reference to the appointment of Mr. L. P. Ashmead,[1] to the Naval Office in Philadelphia, I am informed that Mr. McCulloch, is still undecided, although I left him with a *firm* belief, that he would concur in this nomination; and so stated to you. I feel interested in the success of Mr. Ashmead, because I know what he has done to serve you. I shall feel greatly disappointed if he should not succeed in this application. Mr. Ashmead is a conservative, war Democrat, and is backed by the strongest support from a class of friends, whose cooperation in the future I look upon as essential to the success of the conservative platform on which I stand, and to which you have given your support. I sincerely trust that you will not suffer his claims to be ignored, in view of his manly efforts to sustain you.[2]

Tho: Swann

ALS, DNA-RG56, Appts., Customs Service, Naval Officer, Philadelphia, L. P. Ashmead.

1. Lehman P. Ashmead (*fl* 1901) was a merchant and publisher in Philadelphia. At the turn of the century he was employed in the Post Office. Philadelphia directories (1867–1901); *U.S. Off. Reg.* (1901).

2. A month later, March 13, the President sent Ashmead's nomination as naval officer to the Senate. It was immediately referred to the commerce committee, which one day later reported adversely on the nomination. The Senate then rejected Ashmead's nomination on March 14. *Senate Ex. Proceedings*, Vol. 15, pt. 2: 435, 438, 452.

From A. McLean White[1]

New York, Feby. 14 1867

Hon Sir

The troubles that now disturb our Country, are many and of great magnitude, and it becomes us all as patriotic citizens, to waive all matters of minor importance, in order to bring about a consolidation of our Government.

With the most profound respect for your position as the head of this great Nation, let me ask, in the most sincere way that my heart is capable of expressing—a favor—the greatest I could possibly solicit at you hands—the noblest the grandest gift you ever bestowed.

Andrew Johnson, I beg, I implore you to waive any objections you may well have against the Reconstruction Amendment,[2] and to recommend its passage by the Southern States, as the quickest shortest way to present adjustment & harmony between the North & South.

Do this and we will all be grateful to you, more we will love your memory as long as our National name shall be spoken in ages to come, and we will all say truthfully that none was abler, more just, or self sacrificing that ever ruled our glorious Republic.

A McL. White.

ALS, DLC-JP.

1. Not identified.

2. By February 6 every state of the former Confederacy, with the exception of Tennessee, had rejected the Fourteenth Amendment, due in part to Johnson's prompting.

From John Williams, Jr.

Knoxville Tennessee   Feby. 14, 1867

Dear Sir:

It is stated here that the Senate has rejected Mr. James T. Abernathy as Collector for this Congressional District.[1] If such is the fact, it has been

done simply because he is a defender of your Administration against the
vile slanders of corrupt & designing men.

Mr. Abernathy is a gentleman whose moral character cannot be impeached. He has conducted the affairs of his office thus far with a degree
of fidelity unsurpassed by any officer of the Government. Then I cant
imagin any reason for his rejection, except the one stated above, & this
being the case, I hope you will not allow him to be set aside for any such
reason, & I trust you will reappoint him at your earliest convenience.

An effort is on foot here, to get you to nominate some one in his stead,
who is *perhaps a nominal supporter* of your Administration. This I hope
you will not do, for the movement as I have reason to believe, originated
with your enemies.

From this stand point, things look somewhat improved at the Capitol.
From the Congressional proceedings, I infer that a diversion has been
made, & I hope you will come out triumphant yet. Banks, Bingham[2] &
others, seem to have moderated considerably. They begin to look upon
you as being a little more important personage than merely the "head
clerk" of their *august body.*

While in Washington,[3] I desired to talk with you in reference to the
claims of the people of East Tennessee for supplies furnished the Federal
Army in 1863, 64 & 65. It seems to me if you would send a short special
message to Congress upon this subject, that it would be of infinite advantage to us.[4] After doing this, should Congress reject a bill for our relief, I
am confident it will be a blow to the Radical, or negro party in East Tennessee, from which they will not very soon recover. Should Congress
pass the bill, having recommended it, you will share at least equal benefits with them. The Government has paid every body in the North, for
every thing furnished the Federal Army, & also for all damage done by
the Rebels. Now we do not ask to be paid for any thing taken by the Rebels, but simply ask them to pay our people what they justly owe us. We
are quite as worthy as gentlemen of the North, and are certainly not behind them in devotion to the Gov. It is worse than useless to try to get any
thing through the Quarter Masters Department in Washington, & unless
we can get Congress to authorize the President to appoint a Commission
in East Tennessee for the settlement of accounts, we had just as well
abandon all hope of being remunerated for our losses. Your assistance in
this matter, will confer an everlasting favor upon thousands of the people
of your own East Tennessee.

John Williams.

ALS, DLC-JP.
    1. Concerning the appointment of Abernathy, see Williams to Johnson, Oct. 23, 1866,
Johnson Papers, 11: 381–82. There seems to be no evidence of a Senate rejection of Abernathy, who had been appointed in October 1866 and continued serving until 1868. In
fact, on January 14, 1867, the Senate received Johnson's nomination (dated January 2) of

Abernathy for permanent appointment. A month later, February 21, the Senate approved Abernathy's appointment. *Senate Ex. Proceedings*, Vol. 15, pt. 1: 79, 240.

2. Nathaniel P. Banks and John A. Bingham.

3. Perhaps a reference to his visit in August 1866. See Williams to Johnson, Oct. 23, 1866, *Johnson Papers*, 11: 381–82.

4. President Johnson evidently did not heed this advice, for in 1867 he issued no message or speech regarding East Tennessee claims.

From Nathaniel Boyden and Lewis C. Hanes

Raleigh N C   Feb 15 1867

The new plan of adjustment is hanging fire in our legislature.[1] A dispatch from you strongly urging it may secure its passage. Let us hear from you at once.[2]

N. Boyden
Lewis Hanes

Tel, DLC-JP.

1. This was no doubt the "North Carolina Plan" put forth by Boyden and Hanes as an alternative to any new congressional reconstruction act. The main points were a constitutional amendment similar to the proposed Fourteenth Amendment and an amendment to the various state constitutions calling for all suffrage to be based on certain property and educational requirements, thereby giving limited voting rights to freedmen. The North Carolina legislature had not yet voted on this measure when Congress passed the First Military Reconstruction bill of March 2, 1867, effectively killing any compromise. Horace W. Raper, *William W. Holden: North Carolina's Political Enigma* (Chapel Hill, 1985), 90–91; *American Annual Cyclopaedia* (1867), 546; Richard L. Zuber, *Jonathan Worth: A Biography of a Southern Unionist* (Chapel Hill, 1965), 251–52.

2. The next day William G. Moore wired Boyden and Hanes in Johnson's behalf: "It was hoped that there would be prompt action. It would do good at this time. A friend will be at Raleigh without delay, to confer with you, if no action shall have been had before this reaches you." The unnamed "friend" started south on February 17. Moore to Boyden and Hanes, Feb. 16, 17, 1867; Boyden and Hanes to Moore, Feb. 16, 1867, Johnson Papers, LC.

From William F. Johnston

Private

Philadelphia.   Collector's Office,
15' Feby, 1867

My dear Sir

Pardon this intrusion. My great repugnance to annoy by personal interview or *even* by letters I trust will be accepted, as an apology for the lateness of this Note, returning my sincere thanks for the kindness & confidence I have received at your hands.

I am aware of the constant & worrying pressure, that is made upon your time & patience, as well as of the more important cares and duties, that surround you at the present moment & hence to intrude, unnecessarily, I have neither the disposition or desire.

I consider it however, a duty as your devoted friend, to speak frankly, in reference to rumors that are afloat.

It is alleged, that the Senate, has determined to reject, without regard to qualification or otherwise, any & every person, who formerly belonged to the Republican party, but who dared to vindicate their manhood by a support of yr. Administration. That, in order to *discourage* and *distract* your friends, the Senate had further determined to confirm all nominations made from a party which had uniformly & bitterly opposed the views & purposes of the Republican Union party. To this extent I suppose there is truth in the rumors. It is further stated that no name will be submitted for any position to the Senate, whom it has or is likely to reject.[1] This latter statement altho I cannot believe, it has caused to me, much distress.

Being a victim of the Senate's ostracism,[2] & now virtually disconnected from official position by the *nomination* of my successor[3] I hope to be permitted without being subject to the charge or imputation of selfishness—to enter an earnest protest against this great wrong, by which without cause, your *early friends* are deprived of all hopes of official station simply for an independent expression of opinion & for active friendship and support of your self in the past fierce contests.

I am confident among the early Republican Johnson men, there are friends to Yr. Excellency, whom neither defeat or outrage will estrange or deter from sustaining & defending your Administration. These men in my humble judgment ought to be made the recipients of yr. kindness. I speak this frankly, without aiming in the slightest degree to be benefitted personally, as I am prepared to return to private life—whenever it is deemed proper to give me the necessary orders.

With sincere respect, and with the hope, that anything here in stated, that ought not to be written, will be attributed to my warm friendship and regard . . .

Wm. F Johnston

ALS, DLC-JP.

1. The President responded to Johnston's concerns two days later. See Johnson to Johnston, Feb. 17, 1867.

2. Johnston, who had held a recess appointment as collector at Philadelphia, had been rejected by the Senate for a permanent appointment in late January 1867. Samuel J. Randall to Johnson, July 12, 1866, *Johnson Papers*, 10: 683; *Senate Ex. Proceedings*, Vol. 15, pt. 1: 72, 124, 136–37.

3. Apparently Johnston's information was incorrect, for a successor was not nominated by the President until mid-March. The nominee, William Goodwin, was eventually rejected by the Senate in early April. Ibid., pt. 2: 490, 648, 680.

From Hiram Ketchum, Jr.

private

New York   Feby 15" 1867

Dear Sir:

Upon consultation with Senator Dixon I have suggested that all your Messages to Congress on the subject of reconstruction, including all the Vetoes, should be published in pamphlet form and widely circulated gratuitously. It is very inconvenient for me to collect these documents here, and if not asking too much of your Excellency—will you direct your Secretary to collect them, and communicate with me; I will instruct him to whom to send them, and the work shall be forthwith begun and prosecuted with vigor. They will be stereotyped, and if there be any verbal corrections required please have them made, for many copies will be published, and it would be well to have them verbally accurate. I shall consult friends here to day, and, if approved, propose to publish the enclosed CHALLENGE.[1] Would you suggest any alterations in this document?

My purpose is, if I am able to accomplish it, to have the proposed pamphlet, as soon as it can be got out, first circulated in N Hampshire, and Connecticut where we find popular elections are to be held. My most earnest desire is that the radicals shall be defeated in *Connecticut* and for this purpose, my limited influence to its full extent, shall be exerted. If Connecticut can be carried for the Administration it will be a significant testimony that the popular tide is turning, and will have an important influence upon the proceedings of the next Congress. What the prospects in this State are I know not but, in my judgment all the efforts of Conservative men should be directed to this point without delay.

Please regard this as *strictly private*, and excuse me for troubling your Excellency with the matter. I have communicated with no person in Washington but Senator Dixon with whom you are at liberty to confer.

Hiram Ketchum

ALS, DLC-JP.
1. The enclosed "Challenge" was a pamphlet containing the acts and resolutions of Congress, together with the messages and vetoes of the President. Ketchum hoped to distribute the pamphlet nationally in order to aid citizens "in forming a right judgment" regarding the Reconstruction controversies.

From Edwin M. Stanton

Washington City, Feb. 15th 1867.

Sir:

I have the honor to acknowledge the receipt of Senate Resolution January 8th 1867 requesting the President to inform the Senate "if any violations of the Act of Congress entitled 'An Act to protect all persons in the United States in their civil rights and furnish the means of their vindication,' have come to his knowledge and if so what steps, if any, have been taken by him to enforce the law, and punish the offenders"[1] together with a report of the Attorney General on the condition of the Act referred to, which papers were referred to me by you for report on the 23d of January. In answer to said reference I have the honor to report.

First, that in relation to the steps taken by this Department to enforce the Act of Congress referred to in the said resolution, so far as its execution devolved upon military authorities, it was promulgated in General Orders No. 50[2] July 21st 1866 to all commanders of Military Departments, Districts and Posts, a copy of which order is hereto attached. The enforcement of said Act of Congress is also one of the general regulations of the Bureau of Refugees, Freedmen and Abandoned Lands. And a General Order hereto attached was also issued from the Army Head Quarters.[3]

No instance has been reported to this Department of any neglect or refusal by Military officers or employees of this Department to enforce to the extent of their legal authority the provisions of the aforesaid Act of Congress within their respective commands and stations and I have no knowledge of any such neglect or refusal having been reported to the President.

Second: The following cases of alleged violation of the said Act of Congress were officially reported to the President, to wit:

1st.   The case of Dr. Watson[4] for the murder of a negro in the Department of Virginia, who after his discharge by civil tribunal was put on trial before a Military Commission, which was dissolved on the ground of want of jurisdiction, under the decision of the Supreme Court.

2d.   The case of Wm. Fincher[5] a person of color sentenced to the chain-gang in Georgia as a vagrant which was referred to the Attorney General and is under his direction and charge.

3d.   The case of Perkins[6] in the State of Texas when protection to a colored man from alleged illegal acts under color of civil authority was afforded by the Assistant Commissioner of the Freedmen's Bureau and his action approved by this Department. Full reports of these cases are hereto annexed.

No other reports of violation of the Act aforesaid have been made to you by me. Reports by military commanders of crimes and offenses committed against freedmen and others in their respective commands have been made to this Department[7] and referred to the Attorney General for his opinion on the appropriate remedy. Whether they or any of them constitute violations of the Civil Rights Law I am unable to state.

(Signed)   Edwin M. Stanton, Secretary of War.

Copy, DNA-RG107, Lets. Recd., Executive (M494, Roll 96).
1 *Congressional Globe*, 39 Cong., 2 Sess., p. 326.

2. See *Senate Ex. Docs.*, 39 Cong., 2 Sess., No. 29, pp. 13–16 (Ser. 1277).

3. General Orders No. 44. Ibid., pp. 16–17.

4. James L. Watson (1814–*fl*1867), a physician, was acquitted by the civil authorities of the murder of a black man. Subsequently, however, Watson was arrested for the same offense by military authorities by the direction of General Schofield. On December 22, 1866, the military commission which convened to try Dr. Watson was dissolved by order of the President as the commission was deemed not to have jurisdiction. *Richmond Dispatch*, Dec. 7, 8, 10, 17, 24, 1866; 1860 Census, Va., Rockbridge, 3rd Dist., Natural Bridge P.O., 202.

5. See Henry Stanbery to Johnson, Jan. 21, 1867, *Johnson Papers*, 11: 621–23.

6. See James W. Throckmorton to Johnson, Dec. 23, 1866, *Johnson Papers*, 11: 560.

7. Found in *Senate Ex. Docs.*, 39 Cong., 2 Sess., No. 29, pp. 1–43 (Ser. 1277).

From George C. Tichenor [1]

Strictly *Confidential*

Des Moines, Iowa, Feby 15 1867

Mr President

Although I am an humble citizen, occupying an obscure station in life, I have felt much solicitude with refference to the condition of our country since the cease of the war & now as heretofore feel great interest in measures having in view the practical re union of the states. As an Army Officer I served the Government for near four years[2] believing my efforts were devoted to the purpose of maintaining the integrity of that Government in compelling refractory States to acknowledge themselves irrevocably obligated to the Federal Union. I believed that when we had compelled the peoples of these States to lay down their arms & acknowledge the federal authority we had accomplished the purpose for which we had taken up arms. Viz obedience to the Governmental Authority & and an acknowledgement of their obligations to the federal Union, as parts thereof on the part of the rebellious states. I cannot now see but that to assume that these states are not a part or parts of the Union, entitled to representation & all the other privileges & immunities of states in the Union, is to declare to the world that on our part we have utterly failed to accomplish the purposes of the war. If these States are not *in* the Union, they are of course *out* of it, and to assume that they are not in it, is to recognize the success of rebellion.

While such are & have been my opinions I have cooperated earnestly with the Radical party of the North believing that the success of that party was necessary in order to intimidate the southern people into such reforms in their local fundamental & statutory laws &c as would make them conform more nearly to those of the Northern states & by a general harmonizing of condition destroy the land marks of sectional differences.

I acknowledged assent to the radical policy of the present Congress during its past session of refusing the admission of representatives from the late rebellious states, satisfied however that by so doing the provisions of the Constitution & laws were contravened, but believing that the same would be justified in the permanent beneficial results to be accomplished. Believing now that the experiment has been amply tried & that to press it further would tend most certainly to divide instead of unite—to exasperate the southern people instead of intimidate them—to fasten a sentiment of dis union alike upon the people of the two sections instead of increasing fraternal feelings. I am in favor of such measures as will speedily secure the admission in Congress of the representatives of all the late rebellous states, and the removal from those states of all disabillities affecting their rights & privileges as States in the Union. I have strong hopes that it lies within *your* power, in a great measure at least, to accomplish this result. The public pulse about me indicates unmistakably a growing feeling of conservatism, a feeling inclining toward concession, not strong but susceptable of successful cultivation, not to such an extent as to produce rebellion against the radical party but to such an extent as to moderate & largely revolutionize the sentiment & policy of that party within itself. Now this can be effected Sir, by moderating the tone of *your* feeling & conduct toward that party, by overtures of peace & show of sentiments of more kindly feeling toward that party. Invite earnest & candid consultations with the leading representatives of the party especially those most moderate & honest. Receive their recommendations for appointments to offices within your gift favorably. Accept their suggestions kindly. Counsel them as well as southern men, to moderation. Assume the attitude, not of an open enemy of the Republican party, but of a *leader in* that party, differing in opinion on some questions only with other leaders of the party.

The radical party of the North is now under the control of Army men—they hold & govern it. So far as in your power appoint to office prominent Army men who have been & are identified with the radical party. By so doing you make them your friends & their friends your friends, thus concilliating enemies & making friends of enemies.

Time will not serve to eradicate the prejudice of the people of the North against that weak organization known as the Democratic or Copperhead faction. Republicans who would be conservative vote with the radicals because their *hate* forbids fellowship with "Copperheads"—& radicalism is strengthened, kept alive & made triumphant by simple hatred of "Copperheads"—& your appointment of these men to federal offices and your thereby apparent fellowship with them did more to strengthen the radical party & intensify its more dangerous sentiment than four years of War had done.

You can moderate this sentiment by appearing to sympathize with it but never by open hostility. The Republican party can be made conservative, but its strength can never be impaired by the conversion of its members to the "Copperheads."

The recent action of Congress with refference to the plan of adjustment understood to have your sanction,[3] evinces a spirit of concession &

of a tendency toward conservatism on the part of the Republican party. Now my advice to you is to encourage the development of this friendly symptom by a reciprocal show of friendliness & if I mistake not you will find a decided change of attitude in the 40th Congress.

In conclusion permit me to say that although a young man I have for some years taken an active part in politics, have been a close observer of public sentiment, am in correspondence with leading politicians in my State & with some of our representatives in the present Congress & some who will be in the next—& what I have written is the result of convictions thereby reached. I have been more readily encouraged to write this by the hope that you will remember me as having met you at times in Nashville, when I was serving as a Staff Officer in Tennessee.[4]

I think I need not hesitate to refer to Senators Grimes & Kirkwood[5] of this State.

I ask that this may be treated as a confidential communication to yourself and that the *fact* even of its having been *written* may not be known beyond yourself—or at least become public.

Geo C. Tichenor   late Bvt Col U.S.V

ALS, DLC-JP.

1. Tichenor (1838–1902) moved to Iowa about 1857 where he held various jobs, including clerk of the U.S. district court. After the Civil War he had a lumber business and served as postmaster of Des Moines (1867–72). He became a grain and provisions merchant in Chicago, at several times held special treasury agent posts, served as assistant secretary of the treasury during Harrison's presidency, and finally became president of the board of appraisers for the port of New York. *New York Times*, July 12, 1902.

2. Tichenor enlisted as a private in 1861 but was soon made adjutant of the 39th Iowa Inf. He was an aide-de-camp on the staff of Gen. Grenville M. Dodge for several years. In 1864–65 he was acting judge advocate for the Department of the Missouri. Eventually ranking as a major, Tichenor was mustered out of the service in January 1866. Ibid.

3. Congress, at this time, was working on the First Military Reconstruction Act which Johnson vetoed on March 2. Eric Foner, *Reconstruction: America's Unfinished Revolution, 1863–1877* (New York, 1988), 273–76.

4. General Dodge and his troops, including Tichenor, were in Tennessee in November 1863 at least. *OR*, Ser. 1, Vol. 31, Pt. 3, passim.

5. James W. Grimes and Samuel J. Kirkwood.

From Nelson J. Waterbury [1]

(For the President's own perusal only)

New York   15 February 1867

Mr President

Allow me as a warm admirer, friend and political supporter of yours to make a suggestion as to your interest here in having your friends—take the place of your secret enemies—in *the subordinate places in our custom Housses.* If you intimate such to be your wish & determination to the Collector[2]—it will of course be done. Those Mr Smythe has appointed are Administration men (Johnson men)—the others your secret foes—disguising perhaps for the moment their real sentiments as disunion Radicals. No political engine is so potent as our Custom House properly wielded—it is all potent in our City Canvasses.

I say not one word against the Collector or any of the Revenue Officers—only 'tis due to you that those recommended by the Congressmen and others of your supporters should take the places of the Chase-Radicals appointed by Ex-Collector Barney[3] (all abolition-disunionists). This whole thing is—so to say in a nutshell do you or do you not want to sustain your own friends and party here, or those who are bent upon your ruin—if it were a possible thing.

It must be borne in mind that Mr. Smythe is totally inexperienced in politics—a mere Dry Goods merchant—unknown before in public matters, tho' doubtless a good officer. I believe he desires to carry out your view if so instructed.

If things go on as they have this Conservative stronghold will I fear be overborne. Pardon my freedom. I write from deep conviction of your interest now & in the Campaign of 1868.[4]

Nelson J. Waterbury

ALS, DLC-JP.
1. Waterbury (1819–1894), a New York City lawyer, was quite active in local politics and, in fact, was chosen head of Tammany in 1862. He served as judge advocate general on the staff of Gov. Horatio Seymour. *NCAB*, 12: 383–84; *NUC*.
2. Henry A. Smythe.
3. Hiram Barney (1811–1895), a lawyer, was collector during the first three years of Lincoln's administration. He had been a delegate to the Republican national conventions of 1856 and 1860. Brown, *Am. Biographies*, 1: 199.
4. For further information regarding Smythe's abilities, see Smythe to Johnson, Mar. 6, 28, 1867.

From Henry Liebenau [1]

No. 4. Hamilton place
West 51st Street, near 8th Ave:
New York   Feby: 16th, 1867.

Honored Sir.

Permit me most respectfully to submit for your perusal, the enclosed "Platform and Address" of an organization composed of "*Conservative men*,"[2] from all the old and modern parties, and, if it meets your approval, allow me the pleasure of naming you, as one of our "*Honorary*" members.

Greatly admiring your true Patriotism and Statesmanship, sincerely appreciating your valuable services during the late desperate struggle for national existence, as well as the exposure and sufferings yourself and family have been subjected to; and, the very noble and generous manner which you have in a Christian-like spirit manifested towards your oppressors, gives me assurance that the principles enunciated in the enclosed document, will be graciously received by Your Excellency.

Watching with fearful forebodings the course of our national events, and closely scrutinizing the sayings and doings of our public men, I feel more than convinced that the hand of Providence placed your Excellency at the head of our affairs, for the special preservation of our Union,— Your high regard for the Constitutional rights of all,—Your invaluable firmness at this important crisis, are the only hopes of redemption from the recklessness and fanaticism which surround us.

As a "War democrat" and one of the fast friends of your generous and patriotic "Restoration" policy, having been a member of the "Conservative Convention" of our state, that met at Saratoga,[3]—Also, a member of the National Convention of Conservatives who met at Philadelphia, and at which my old personal friend General Dix,[4] presided, and knowing as I do, that every member of our Association highly approve your policy and admire your inflexability, they would be much gratified to number Andrew Johnson as one of their "Honorary" members, and this organization is a true and loyal one to the Union, many of them having like myself as well as yourself proved their loyalty in the bloody and dangerous fields of the insurrection.

Regarding Your Excellency as the only reliance for our National existance, and having enjoyed the personal friendship of the Great Jackson who but a few months before his death, enclosed to me a lock of his hair, as a souvenir; and you will pardon me for soliciting a lock of yours, that I may have it placed side by side, with that of the Great departed Hero and statesman Andrew Jackson, for I am convinced future historians will place to your credit the salvation of our Union, if it survives this most serious and most dangerous trial.

Henry Liebenau.

ALS, DLC-JP.

1. Liebenau (c1803–fl 1875) was the corresponding secretary for the pro-Johnson "Constitutional Union Club" based in New York City. Before the war he had been a portrait artist and inspector at the customs house, but resigned to assist General Daniel Sickles in raising a brigade. See also Liebenau to Johnson, Aug. 13, 1867. *U.S. Off. Reg.* (1859–61); Liebenau to Johnson, Jan. 7, 1875, Johnson Papers, LC; Appts., Customs Service, Inspector, New York, Henry Liebenau, RG56, NA; 1870 Census, N.Y., New York, New York, 1st Dist., 12th Ward, 1st Enum., 11.

2. Not found.

3. New York supporters of the National Union movement held a preliminary convention at Saratoga on August 9, 1866, but there is no evidence that Liebenau was an official delegate. *New York Tribune*, Aug. 9, 10, 1866.

4. John A. Dix.

To William F. Johnston

Private

Washington, D.C., Feby 17 1867.

Dear Sir:

I am in receipt of your note of the 15th instant,[1] and, in thanking you for your friendly expressions, beg to assure you that the rumor to which you refer is without the slightest foundation whatever.[2] I will be governed in the future, as I have been in the past, by the interests of the Government and the facts connected with each individual case.

Andrew Johnson.

Copy, DLC-JP.

1. See Johnston to Johnson, Feb. 15, 1867.
2. It was rumored that the administration would not submit any nominations to the Senate that were likely to be rejected. Ibid.

From James L. Orr

Columbia, 17th February 1867

My Dear Sir:

I have been surprized to learn that some effort is being made to effect the removal of C. C. Neil Esqr Surveyor of the Port of Charleston.[1] By recurring to the testimonials on file in your office you will see he was a Soldier in the Union Army through the War, that he was recommended by most of the large importing houses in Charleston, and has recommendations of the most complimentary character from many northern men including Congressmen. I have just returned from Charleston and desire to assure you that he is administering the duties of his office to the entire satisfaction of the business men of Charleston.

I think if the business men were consulted they would unanimously sustain him.

The only opposition I could hear of to him came from the Collector[2] and I am satisfied it originates rather in personal antipathy than in official delinquency on Neils part.

I should regret very much to hear of his removal unless specific charges are made against him & proved, he being allowed the privilege of making his defence when the proofs against him are furnished.

James L. Orr   Govr. of SC

ALS, DNA-RG56, Appts., Customs Service, Surveyor, Charleston, Cecil C. Neil.

1. Cecil C. Neil (c1834–1889) had served in both the navy and army from 1862 to 1865. For approximately the next five years he was surveyor at Charleston, after which he rejoined the navy and served in a variety of posts until his death. Johnson nominated Neil as

surveyor in June 1866 and the Senate approved the nomination one month later. There is
no evidence that he was removed; in fact, when he wrote to Johnston in October 1867, he
was continuing as surveyor. Pension File, Annie F. Neil, RG15, NA; *Senate Ex. Proceedings*, Vol. 14, pt. 2: 877, 907, 921–22; Neil to Johnson, Oct. 28, 1867, Appts., Customs
Service, Surveyor, Charleston, Cecil C. Neil, RG56, NA.
    2. Ironically, the collector, Albert G. Mackey, was himself removed from office in 1868.
Ser. 6B, Vol. 4: 153, Johnson Papers, LC.

From Allen A. Bradford

Washington, D.C.   Feb 18 1867

Mr President

Learning that the office of Superintent of the Branch Mint and Assistant Treasune of the United States at Denver Colorado Territory will
soon be vacant I take pleasure in recommending Hon Amos Steck[1] as a
suitable person to occupy that position. Mr Steck is one of the earliest of
the Territory. He has been a member of the Legislative Council and
Mayor of the City of Denver.[2] He is a gentleman of the strictest integrity
and of superior business qualifications. His appointment would be
highly satisfactory to the people I have the honor to represent.[3]

Allen A. Bradford   Delegate Colorado

ALS, DNA-RG56, Appls., Asst. Treasurers and Mint Officers, Denver, Amos Steck.
    1. Steck (*c*1822–*fl*1881), a lawyer and banker, went to Denver in 1860. He was re-
ceiver of the U.S. land office (1874–75) and a probate judge (1876–79). 1870 Census,
Colo., Arapahoe, Denver, 27; *History of the City of Denver, Arapahoe County, and Colorado*
(Chicago, 1880), 587–88; Denver directories (1873–81).
    2. Steck was a member of the first (1861), seventh (1867), and eighth (1870) council
and was elected mayor of Denver in April 1863. Ibid. (1863); Bancroft, *Nevada, Colorado,
and Wyoming*, 416, 442.
    3. Steck was not appointed; the incumbent, George W. Lane, remained in office. *U.S.
Off. Reg.* (1865–67).

From Joseph R. Flanigen

Naval Office, Philadelphia, Feby 18 1867

My dr Mr President

I hear it stated frequently that Mr Ancona[1] will be appointed to this
office. You know my opinion as to the *im* policy of appointing democrats,
and I do hope you will avoid doing so. But independent of this I have to
request that *no* appointment may determined on for this place untill I can
see you which I hope to do on Wednesday.[2] Would have done so last week
but for the illness of my Deputies. As I have said to you on previous occasions it is not posible to continue the Daily News without some outside
help and I submit to you, that I ought to be allowed to name my successor
with a veiw to make the office render such assistance.[3]

J R Flanigen

ALS, DLC-JP.

1. Sydenham E. Ancona (1824–1913) was about to go out of office as a U.S. representative, a post he had held since 1861. Both before and after his congressional career he was involved in a number of business activities. *BDUSC*.

2. It has not been determined if Flanigen met with Johnson as he had planned.

3. On March 9 the President nominated Ancona as naval officer, but three days later the Senate rejected the recommendation. In fact, the naval office appointment seemed jinxed as the Senate turned down several of Johnson's nominations. *Senate Ex. Proceedings*, Vol. 15, pt. 1: 136–37, 388, 426. For further information on the naval post, see Swann to Johnson, Feb. 14, 1867.

From Charles Milne [1]

Stanhope. N J.   Feb 18th 1867.

Great & Worthy Sir.

A note from the Hon A J Rogers M C[2] informs me that you have put my "case into the hands of the Secy of State the Hon Wm. H Seward, to find me a place if possible."[3]

At this I rejoice, and thank you; for him, next to yourself, I honour most of all men in this broad land. What he will select will likely save me from the unpleasant arena of *competition*.

Mr Rogers also makes this remark, "I suppose you would not be confirmed by the Senate."

I have noticed with pain how that body deals with many men of noble records.

Yet, should it be your pleasure to nominate me to the Senate, I have a hope that there is a possibility of my being not so ruthlessly dealt with by them.

Ministers are in some respects different from others. Prudent ministers usually have friends on both sides. *Political ministers* are not so popular here as in some parts. I am not known as a *politician*. Outside of this community my sentiments are not known, and I have been gratified to see how many friends I have in both parties since my disability became known.[4] Especially have I the sympathy of ministers and their friends.

Now, I believe that, through relatives of mine, and relatives of his, and especially through *his pastor*, the influence in the Senate of the *Hon F T Freelinghyson*,[5] senator from New Jersey, could be obtained on my behalf. Perhaps that also of Mr Cattell[6] through Mr Freelinghyson. I think influences can be brought to bear to convince these gentleman, and the Senate through them, that this is not a party measure, but an act of noble generosity on your part in a very trying case.

Therefore, should the Hon Secretary of State fail to find me a place, or should you feel disposed to nominate me to the Senate, and let me know that you will do it, and *when*, I will apply to my friends at once to prepare my way in the Senate. I will address some of them to day.[7]

Praying for your preservation and success . . .

Charles Milne.

ALS, DNA-RG59, Lets. of Appl. and Recomm., 1861–69 (M650, Roll 33), Charles Milne.

1. Milne (c1820–1882), a Presbyterian minister, served various congregations in New Jersey from 1855 to his death. *Minutes of the General Assembly of the Presbyterian Church in the United States of America*, 14 (1854): 358; 15 (1857): 101; 16 (1860): 139; 17 (1863): 143; New Series, 2 (1872): 347; New Series, 7 (1882): 122.

2. Andrew J. Rogers (1828–1900), a clerk, teacher, and lawyer, served two terms as a U.S. representative from New Jersey (1863–67). In the 1890s he was police commissioner of Denver, Colorado. *BDUSC*.

3. In response to a Milne letter of late December, Wright Rives informed him, "The President desires me to say that he will be happy to do all in his power to obtain for you any office that you may desire. You will please make your application, (enclosing your recommendations) and specify the office to which you wish to be appointed." Milne requested a consulship in the West Indies. Rives to Milne, Dec. 31, 1866; Milne to Johnson, Feb. 5, 1867, Lets. of Appl. and Recomm., 1861–69 (M650, Roll 33), Charles Milne, RG59, NA.

4. Milne reported that "For two years I have been afflicted with *bronchial disease*. This winter I have had so many acute paroxisms of it that, I am disabled, and physicians advise a cessation at once from professional duties, and a removal to a less severe climate." Milne to William H. Seward, Feb. 17, 1867, ibid.

5. Frederick T. Frelinghuysen (1817–1885), lawyer and longtime trustee of Rutgers College, was attorney general of New Jersey (1861–66). He served in the Senate twice (1866–69, 1871–77) and as secretary of state for President Chester A. Arthur (1881–85). *BDUSC*.

6. Alexander G. Cattell.

7. Rather than being sent to the West Indies, Milne was confirmed and commissioned consul to Cobija, Bolivia (on the Brazilian border), in late March 1867. Yet by April 25 he had not yet received official notice of his appointment or his commission. He apparently served in that post until at least late 1869. By 1872 he had returned to the U.S. and the Presbyterian ministry. Milne to Johnson, Apr. 25, 1867, Lets. of Appl. and Recomm., 1861–69 (M650, Roll 33), Charles Milne, RG59, NA; *U.S. Off. Reg.* (1867–69); *Minutes of the General Assembly of the Presbyterian Church*, New Series, 2 (1872): 347; *Senate Ex. Proceedings*, Vol. 15, pt. 2: 489, 496.

From William E. Robinson

Brooklyn New York   Feby 18th 1867.

Dear Sir.

His Grace, Archbishop McCloskey[1] by Letter to Your Excellency of 5th Ins't[2] asks, as a *special* favor; that you will appoint his friend Capt John Foley,[3] Collector of Int Rev for the *Eighth* District, City of New York. This being the Archbishop's District & the only appointment asked for by his Grace, and the fact of his being a Powerful friend both of yourself & your administration I deem it to be, most important that his request be complied with.

I would also respectfully call your attention to the fact, that the much larger portion of your supporters in New York City *are wholly unrepresented here* in the distribution of Federal Patronage[4]—hence the *urgent request* of Archbishop McCloskey.

I need not say that I most cordially unite in commending the claim of Mr. Foley. I have Known him several years—& a resident of the 8th District over 20 years. He is well qualified & worthy of the Place. His appointment would give credit to your administration. Nearly all of our best people have signed for him. His success would be well received—with great satisfaction to a large body of Citizens now without acknowledgement who so firmly sustain your policy.[5]

W. E. Robinson M.C. Elect 3rd Dist.

ALS, DNA-RG56, Appts., Internal Revenue Service, Collector, N.Y., 8th Dist., John Foley.

1. John McCloskey (1810–1885) of New York was a Roman Catholic priest, bishop (1844–64), archbishop (appointed 1864), and the first American cardinal. *DAB.*

2. McCloskey to Johnson, Feb. 5, 1867, Appts., Internal Revenue Service, Collector, N.Y., 8th Dist., John Foley, RG56, NA.

3. Foley (1835–1903), a gold pen manufacturer, had served as captain, commissary of subsistence, with the Union volunteer forces, November 1, 1862-June 25, 1863. Pension File, Guliaelma B. Foley, RG15, NA.

4. Newspaper editor Charles Halpine, who also recommended Foley for the position, said that seven-eighths of Johnson's supporters in New York were not represented. Charles G. Halpine to Johnson, Mar. 5, 1867, Johnson Papers, LC. For Halpine's recommendation, see Halpine to Johnson, Feb. 25, 1867.

5. Johnson nominated Foley for assessor rather than collector on April 9, but the Senate tabled the nomination on April 19 and no further action was taken. *Senate Ex. Proceedings,* Vol. 15, pt. 2: 676, 765.

To the Senate

WASHINGTON, *February 18, 1867.*

To the Senate of the United States:

I have received a resolution of the Senate dated the 8th day of January last, requesting the President to inform the Senate if any violations of the act entitled "An act to protect all persons in the United States in their civil rights and furnish the means of their vindication" have come to his knowledge, and, if so, what steps, if any, have been taken by him to enforce the law and punish the offenders.[1]

Not being cognizant of any cases which came within the purview of the resolution, in order that the inquiry might have the fullest range I referred it to the heads of the several Executive Departments, whose reports are herewith communicated for the information of the Senate.

With the exception of the cases mentioned in the reports of the Secretary of War and the Attorney-General,[2] no violations, real or supposed, of the act to which the resolution refers have at any time come to the knowledge of the Executive. The steps taken in these cases to enforce the law appear in these reports.

The Secretary of War, under the date of the 15th instant, submitted a series of reports from the General Commanding the armies of the United States and other military officers as to supposed violations of the act alluded to in the resolution, with the request that they should be referred to the Attorney-General "for his investigation and report, to the end that the cases may be designated which are cognizant by the civil authorities and such as are cognizant by military tribunals." I have directed the reference so to be made.

ANDREW JOHNSON.

Richardson, *Messages*, 6: 468.
  1. *Congressional Globe*, 39 Cong., 2 Sess., p. 326.
  2. See *Senate Ex. Docs.*, 39 Cong., 2 Sess., No. 29, pp. 1–43 (Ser. 1277).

From John T. Tanner [1]

Athens, Ala., Febry 18 1867

Sir,

It is beleived here that the opposition to me in the United States Senate[2] has been brought about by interested parties in North Alabama wanting the place for themselves, through a Mr Bingham[3] once a resident of this place, but now filling an office in Washington, charging me with disloyalty.

It is a well known fact here, where I have lived for forty years, that I am no political man, having followed Commercial and financial pursuits for thirty years, and have endeavored to be strictly a business man.

Those who know me will testify that no one was more opposed to secession than myself. I remained at home during the war with a large family of young children,[4] and hundreds of Union soldiers will bear testimony to my kindness and hospitality to them, from the occupation of this place in 1862 down to the evacuation in 1865. I might refer to Genl. Dodge, Genl. Rousseau, Genl. Steadman Genl. Garfield, Genl. Thomas,[5] and by reference to my recommendations to you in 1865, now on file in the Office of Commissr. Int Rev at Washington, you will find quite a number of Military gentlemen who certified to my loyalty and fitness for the office, and now after nearly two years have elapsed I should be charged with disloyalty is a little singular.

I defy any one to shew a single act of mine in opposition to the Government of the United States. I never sought nor accepted office at the hands of the Confederate Govt. nor never cast a vote for Mr Davis, and if I am disloyal there are none loyal in the Southern States.

For your confidence and kindness manifested for me I shall ever be grateful, and hope you may have a long life of happiness & usefullness, and abundant success politically or otherwise.

Jno. T. Tanner

ALS, DNA-RG56, Appts., Internal Revenue Service, Collector, Ala., 3rd Dist., John T. Tanner.
    1. Tanner (1820–1899), a longtime Athens businessman, was collector of internal revenue for the Third District of Alabama. Later he became actively involved with the Athens Female Institute, of which he served as president, and with the temperance movement. *Northern Alabama Historical and Biographical Illustrated* (Birmingham, 1888), 81–82;

Limestone County, Alabama Cemeteries (3 vols., Athens, Ala., 1977–79), 3: 15; Henry S. Marks, comp., *Who Was Who in Alabama* (Huntsville, 1972), 172.

2. Perhaps Tanner did not know that at the time of his letter he had already been rejected by the Senate (January 26) and the President had submitted the nomination of Robert Johnson. *Senate Ex. Proceedings*, Vol. 15, pt. 1: 78, 138, 139, 181, 240. For other comments and observations by Tanner about his appointment, see Tanner to Johnson, Feb. 12, Feb. [Mar.] 1, 1867, Appts., Internal Revenue Service, Collector, Ala., 3rd Dist., John T. Tanner, RG56, NA.

3. Daniel H. Bingham.

4. By 1867 Tanner had four daughters, aged eight to eighteen, and three sons, aged two to sixteen. 1860 Census, Ala, Limestone, Athens, 82; (1870), 3.

5. Grenville M. Dodge, Lovell H. Rousseau, James B. Steedman, James A. Garfield, George H. Thomas.

From William W. Peck

Salisbury—N. C.   Fy 20/67.

Dr Sir.

If the Bankrupt Bill[1] has been sent to you for approval, let me urge you to veto it without delay: or, if you are disposed in favor of it, to delay for consideration. A few in the South want the law: the *great majority* of southern debtors oppose it:—& because they own the bulk of the real estate, have sufficient but unavailable resources: are now protected only by home stay-laws. There is no extravagance in saying that, were the Bill to become a law, the Bulk of the Landed Interest at the South would under its *involuntary provision* be forced to change hands in 12 months. A more cruel measure towards the South could hardly be devised.

The parties, whose interests would mainly be advanced by the law, are northern speculators.[2]

William Ware Peck

ALS, DLC-JP.

1. The bankruptcy bill cleared both houses of Congress and on March 2 was signed by Johnson, who ignored Peck's plea for a veto. *Congressional Globe*, 39 Cong., 2 Sess., Appendix, pp. 228–36. For a discussion of the background of the bill and its eventual passage, see Charles Warren, *Bankruptcy in United States History* (Cambridge, Mass., 1935), 104–9.

2. Some credence was given this claim by a column in the *New York Times* which asserted: "The demand for relief grows in force every day. The insolvent record of the past year alone shows that for one trader of the South that could benefit by the operation, eight at least would profit at the North." In his study of the bankruptcy bill, Warren notes that "the chief pressure for the bill came from Northern creditors of Southern debtors." *New York Times*, Feb. 18, 1867; Warren, *Bankruptcy*, 106.

From Andrew M. Frantz[1]

E. Lampeter Twp. Lan. co Pa.   Feby 21, 1867.

Dear Sir:

I address you by permission of the custom of regarding public official Gentlemen as familiar friends. Like many other American customs it exists in spite of Etiquette. Your name and character, as President of the U.S. I have freely used and very often approved, both in public and private, ever since you assumed the high office you now have the honor to fill. You will already anticipate my object in writing to you. I shall not be embarressed in candidly acknowledging that I address you in reference to official appointment. We are anticipating the nonconfirmation on part of the U.S. Senate of the Revenue officers (Collecter & Inspecter) in this district.[2] In the event, that such proves the case, I can see no reason why I should not solicit the Collectorship. I do, however, not feel disposed to resort to any sort of dishonorable means, simply announcing the fact that I desire to be nominated by you. I will promise you to produce any recommendation you may be pleased to require—as to family connexion, reputation for integrity and fitness. I will furnish my endorsements from the most respectable citizens—the Democratic party and conservative republicans from any source it may be desired. One thing I may be permitted to mention and that is—that in the race of professional party politicians I shall be left far in the rear. I may mention that in me *you* have a devoted adherent and had it not been your misfortune to have your *case* in our (the Steven's) district in the care of the most bitter Copperheads and Anti war Democrats Andrew Johnson would have had a great many more friends. A few men of that class of politicians got control, through Senator Cowan, of the appointments here and it was very unfortunate. On the stump last fall I was accosted with such attacks as this, for instance; Andrew Johnson has turned traitor or he would not have avowed sympathizers to manage for him the appointments. What could we say. It was only too true. How Senator Cowan could be thus imposed upon I cannot conceive. These very men had no kind word for you until they got control of the appointments. I must confess regardless of consequences that the confirmation of the appointments as they now stand are not desired by the real *Johnson* party in this district which means the *War democrats* and a few Johnson Republicans but the latter are very few—do not number 200 in the county. I must close—what I say I will and can do at any time and adduce the requisite proof &c. If you will give me any inducement, I shall marshall my friends and character before you.

Andrew M. Frantz   Lancaster City Pa.

ALS, DNA-RG56, Appts., Internal Revenue Service, Pa., 9th Dist., Andrew M. Frantz.

1. Possibly Frantz (*c*1830–*fl*1875), a farmer who was justice of the peace in 1854 and became an attorney in 1861. He was not nominated by Johnson for either collector or assessor. 1860 Census, Pa., Lancaster, East Lampeter Twp., 33; Franklin Ellis and Samuel Evans, *History of Lancaster County, Pennsylvania, with Biographical Sketches of Many of Its Pioneers and Prominent Men* (Philadelphia, 1883), 246, 901, 958; Lancaster directory (1875).

2. Matthew M. Strickler and David A. Brown, both recess appointments, were nominated by Johnson on January 14 for collector and assessor, respectively. Strickler (b. *c*1836) was a well-to-do farmer with a wife and daughter in 1860. On February 23, 1867, his nomination was rejected by the Senate. Not until April 18 was a candidate, Wil-

liam M. Wiley, finally approved for the Ninth District collectorship. Brown (1830–
*fl*1903), also a farmer who had taught school and would later serve as a justice of the peace,
was rejected the same day as Strickler. *Senate Ex. Proceedings*, Vol. 15, pt. 1: 80, 83, 246–
47; pt. 2: 715, 758; 1860 Census, Pa., Lancaster, West Hempfield Twp., 24; *Biographical
Annals of Lancaster County, Pennsylvania* (Chicago, 1903), 501.

Interview with Charles G. Halpine

WASHINGTON, D.C., February 21.

"The trouble is," said the President, "that instead of inquiring what
we are and our present powers, we insist on making ourselves something
else, and inventing new powers which it cannot be for our benefit to
yield. We make the mistake of becoming inventors, instead of applying
ourselves to become discoverers.

There are now a score of plans for reconstructing the Southern States
before the country, and the public mind is unduly agitated as to which
shall be adopted. Amendments are proposed to the Constitution, amendments of every possible character; whereas, if people, instead of inventing
new things, would seek to discover what already exist, they would find
all the powers they need to accomplish their legitimate wishes in the
Constitution as it stands.

The Constitution guarantees a Republican form of government to every State, and says that no State shall be deprived of its representation in
Congress without its own consent. Well, on the other hand, some of our
people say that they will not allow men who participated in the rebellion
to be their peers and to have voices in the great council of the nation.
They therefore demand a Constitutional Amendment on his head; and so
likewise for every other evil that they can find or fancy to be existing.

But does not the Constitution itself provide a remedy for this very evil,
where it says that each House of Congress shall be absolute judge of the
elections, returns and qualifications of its own members? May not each
House, under this, while rejecting any prominent ex-rebel or man obnoxious for disloyalty, who shall be sent from any of the so-called Confederate States, at the same time not deprive the State of representation, but
merely says: 'This man we reject under our constitutional prerogative.
We do not, however, deny the right of your State to representation whenever you shall send us a proper man?[']

See, for a moment, what would be the effect of this course. We at once
divide the public opinion of the State so treated—at present made a unit
under the ban of indiscriminate exclusion. We hold out a great reward for
the election of loyal men, and attach a penalty, which the people of the
State must themselves impose, for the restraint of active participants in
the late rebellion. There are scores and hundreds of ambitious men of
loyal record in every State who would then be naturally forced to the surface, but under the present system of indiscriminate exclusion it can

make no difference whether loyal or disloyal Senators and Representatives shall be sent.

Even let us take an extreme case. Suppose the State of Georgia should send Alexander H. Stephens to the Senate, and that the Senate should say: 'We acknowledge the right of Georgia to representation; we acknowledge that the credentials of Mr. Stephens are made out in the proper form; but in view of his connection with the rebellion, and former connection with the United States, we—in the exercise of our constitutional privilege—do not choose to accept Mr. Stephens as our peer, and must insist that some man of loyal record shall be sent in his place.'

Would not the Georgians at once commence looking around for some one who could satisfy these conditions? And would not an immediate impetus be given toward building up a loyal sentiment in that State? The wounds our country has suffered are not vital, though the depletion of blood was great. There were none of the great bones broken, for the framework of the Constitution still remains, and is sufficient, if we could only abstain from further irritating surgery. The best healing in surgery is that which the doctors describe as by 'the first intention,' or force of nature; but our violent doctors in Congress—and this is spoken with no disrespect to that body, but as a fact of observation—will still insist on tearing open the wounds afresh, in order to force a faster healing by caustic applications and the actual cautery.

What we need—what we vitally need, both for payment of the national debt and to enable us to assume a proper foreign policy, too long, I confess, delayed—is harmony, internal peace, and a condition of restored confidence that will draw capital to develop the industrial resources of the South, and to assist the Southern planters in reorganizing the shattered relations of labor. We need all this to make the national burdens endurable. Every bale of cotton, every barrel of sugar, every tierce of rice, every hogshead of tobacco raised in the ex-rebel States, must furnish a proportionate reduction to the taxation of the North; and must go, so far as it may be worth, toward restoring an equilibrium in our foreign exchanges, which must be the first fundamental step towards a return to the hard money basis, instead of paper currency.

As for myself, my convictions in politics are things that I cannot change to suit the expediencies of this or any other moment. They have grown with my growth, they have strengthened with my strength, and they are to me only less sacred, and as much to be preserved, as my religious faith. Attempts are made to make it appear that my words at different times have been inconsistent; but were not the circumstances inconsistent under which the apparently contradictory words were spoken or opinions given? During the high storm of the rebellion, or in the first heat of its subsidence, words were proper to be said which would be utterly improper in time of peace. We put a broken limb in splints to hold it quiet, whether the patient will or no; but to insist on holding the splints there when the limb is restored, or when a further examination shall have proved that the wounds though deep were only flesh wounds, leaving the bones uninjured—this would not be wise surgery, but cruelty; not states-manship, but barbarous usurpation.

I am accused of usurping power, when my whole life has been one con-tinual battle against the tendency of bureaucracy or aristocracy—the concentration of power in the hands of the few. I was accused of usurping power for my veto of the first Freedmen's Bureau bill; although that was a voluntary putting away from me of a patronage and power more unlim-ited than was ever previously offered to any President! I am for holding all possible power in the hands of the people permanently; I am in favor of always finding the minimum of power necessary to be delegated to any officials, or to the General Government, and only allowing that mini-mum to be given.

But look, even at this bill of Senator Sherman's,[1] and see what it does, or proposes doing? It is only less objectionable than the House bill, in that it does not openly supersede the President, representing the civil power, in favor of the General commanding the armies of the United States. But it violates the Constitutional provision guaranteeing a Re-publican form of government, and substitutes a military despotism over the lately revolted States. It disfranchises nearly all the intelligent whites, and gives universal suffrage to the ignorant blacks, thus overriding the provision that each State shall determine who shall be entitled to its suf-frage. It also nullifies the Constitutional Amendments, by practically de-claring the existing governments of the Southern States illegal, so that their adoption of the Amendments must be without validity.

Everywhere there is a tendency to substitute the 'Government' as the source of power, instead of the 'people;' and it is against this tendency I am at issue. The Sherman bill denies the writ of *habeas corpus*, whenever such shall be the pleasure of an arbitrary military commander, in whose power to rule over them the people of the subjugated district shall have no voice. It also strikes down the right of early trial by a civil court and by a jury of the peers of the accused. In fact it fundamentally uproots all those popular and constitutional guarantees of freedom which were extorted from King John by the barons of England in the signature of *Magna Charta*—that basis of our common law.

It is for the principles of our common law and common justice and for the rights of the whole people as against what is called the 'Government,' that I am to-day contending. It is for this I am called a 'usurper,' while the fact is it is because I will not usurp power, nor have excessive power thrust upon me, if I can help it, that this war has been made upon me. I challenge the production of a single act in my whole administration which has aimed to increase my authority as President. Even in con-structing provisional governments for the Southern States—also de-nounced as one of my 'flagrant usurpations'—the object evidently was to divest the National Government of its centralizing power and restore that power as nearly and promptly as circumstances would permit to the people of the various ex-rebel States.

The South is to-day in our hands, a beaten, helpless, well nigh hopeless country, and the power we wield should be held as a sacred trust. We should not use it vindictively. I will not argue because we profess to be Christians, and these men are our brothers; but, if on no higher ground, then upon the ground of self-interest. All the legislation proposed for the South proposes to multiply offices at the expense of the General Government, while not adding the productions of Southern industry to the general stock for the redemption of our national debt and the support of our annual burdens. My object is to reduce the assumed and really usurpational powers forced on the General Government during the war, powers that were then essential to meet a desperate emergency, but which cannot much longer be continued without vitiating the whole fabric and theory of our representative and popular system.

What Congress in its wisdom may see fit to do, I cannot say; but my own course is clear. I shall exercise every function of my office in defense of the people and their rights according to the best judgment that Heaven has endowed me with. I shall execute all laws scrupulously, and perhaps most scrupulously those which have been passed against my judgment and over my veto. But for all such legislation, Congress must bear the undivided responsibility; and the days cannot be far distant in which the terrible logic of events will force the people to ask themselves seriously, and not in passion: On which side lay the tendency to usurpation?"

Augusta Constitutionalist, Feb. 28, 1867.
1. The First Military Reconstruction Act which Congress passed and Johnson vetoed on March 2.

From Fernando Wood

New York   Feby 21 1867.

Dear Sir

Your own position in history—your consistent defence of the Constitution, and the welfare of our common country demand that you should *not* permit the Military Reconstruction bill to become a law. Its fate is in your hands & the people will hold you responsible. *Let it die the death*, and to the next Congress March 4th you can discuss the question, & once more endear yourself to the friends of Constitutional liberty by maintaining you position as the great defender of their cause. This can be done in your annual message. What ever else you lose preserve your manhood.

Fernando Wood

ALS, DLC-JP.

From George Bancroft

New York   22 Feb. 1867.
Dear Mr. President.

Counting on your friendly regard, I venture to ask of you an act, which would be most grateful to me, & I believe right & proper in itself. It is

In the new army corps to grant to my step-son Brevet Col. Alexander Bliss promotion to the rank of Major in the regular army, in the quarter master's department.[1] He is now a captain in the regular army, in the quarter master department.

His merit is well known to Mr. Stanton.

If this promotion can be properly made, you could do nothing that would gratify me more.[2]

Geo. Bancroft

ALS, DLC-JP.

1. Bliss (1829–1896) was a lawyer and businessman prior to military duty during the war which included service as quartermaster of the Eighth Army Corps, headquartered in Baltimore. He did not receive promotion from captain to major in the regular army. Powell, *Army List*, 198; *NUC*; Bancroft to Lorenzo Thomas, Dec. 23, 1861, Jan. 1, 1864, Aug. 1, 1865, ACP Branch, B-1160-CB-1863, Alexander Bliss, RG94, NA.

2. In July 1867 the President nominated Bancroft as minister to Berlin and Bliss as secretary to the legation there; the Senate quickly approved both nominations. In 1868 Bliss resigned his military commission, in order to remain at Berlin; Congress had enacted legislation forbidding military personnel from holding diplomatic assignments. *Senate Ex. Proceedings*, Vol. 15, pt. 2: 788, 794; Bliss to Edward D. Townsend, June 30, 1868, ACP Branch, B-1160-CB-1863, Alexander Bliss, RG94, NA; *Washington Evening Star*, Aug. 18, 1868.

From Jane Deringer[1]

[Washington, February 22, 1867][2]
Dear Mr President:

The Senate rejected Mr Deringer yesterday.[3] It was supposed that he was right but we found the Senate bitter against Johnsons appointments and I having held up so strong for our president that I suppose that they went against us and because of my advocating you and yours. A more faithful and conscientious officer never held the place and I have been told that the most fearful letters have been written to the different Senators. That I heard before I came down. Dear Mr. President you I have much to thank you for. I know that they the Enemies of Mr. D have been the means of causeing you much trouble but for you what light would we have stood in this world. Dear Mr President I will never forget you. You have indeed been a true Friend and I never as long as God gives me breath I will never forget you. I knew that Mr. Cuttell[4] was determined to throw Mr. D over. I myself went to him before his D death and askked his attention to Mr D. confirmation. He did not speak like a gentleman but screamed out no. I was going to ask him the reason and he said hold your tongue. I know your politicks and I dont wish to see or hear you either. Go go. I dont want to see you. And he turned his back. I went right away and told Gov and Mrs. R.[5] They said he might have treated me civily. Now Dear Mr President I did not never intend to tell you how badly he treated me but now he has rejected I want to ask you for the last time if you will reappoint Mr Deringer in March when the New Senate Convenes. Pennsylvania will then be represented and Mr D has many Friends who will come in. He has been so persecuted. Never allow either of us to say fail. I believe you are a true Friend of (Me and Mine) & although I do not know you so well only that you have stood by. I will tell you confidentially that Simon Cameron is a bosom friend of Theopholis Mr Deringer brother[6] and always has professed to be a Friend of Mr Deringer. I tell you only in great confidence that Mr Cameron said he would go for Mr Deringer but not a soul must know. I hope that this will be confidential with you. Do Dear Mr. President see if you cannot do what I ask. I shall keep perfectly quiet—not a living soul shall know. Mr Deringer lost so much money in speculations that it almost made us poor. I would never tell this to the world to gratify them but to you I will. When I go home I am going to write a long letter to you if you will allow and then I hope it will be the last.

Mrs. Deringer

ALS, DLC-JP.

1. Deringer (b. c1825), like her husband Calhoun, was a native of Ireland. The 1860 census reported four children living in the household. 1860 Census, Pa., Philadelphia, Philadelphia, 8th Ward, 372.

2. Although the writer of the letter provided no provenance or date, we suggest Washington, for the letter appears to have been hand-delivered to Martha Patterson at the White House. We suggest the date, because of the reference to the rejection of Deringer's nomination which occurred on February 21.

3. Deringer's nomination for Pennsylvania's Second District assessorship had always been controversial, dating from his fall 1866 recess appointment. The culmination of the difficulties came with the February rejection. See Edgar Cowan to Johnson, Oct. 25, 1866; Joseph R. Flanigen to Johnson, Nov. 15, 1866, *Johnson Papers*, 11: 385, 460.

4. Sen. Alexander G. Cattell of New Jersey, formerly a Philadelphia resident. *BDUSC*.

5. Possibly former Pennsylvania governor Joseph Ritner and his wife Susanna. Ritner (1780–1869), governor from 1835 to 1839, was noted for his anti-Masonic and anti-slavery stances, as well as his life-long efforts in support of public education. Susanna Ritner (nee Alter), not otherwise identified, was the mother of four boys and three girls. *DAB*; Sobel and Raimo, *Governors*, 3: 1302–3.

6. Theophilus T. Deringer (c1811–1874), formerly a gunsmith at his father's pistol factory and Philadelphia County's deputy register of wills (1850), later engaged in the marble business. *Philadelphia Evening Bulletin*, Feb. 16, 1874; John E. Parsons, *Henry Deringer's Pocket Pistol* (New York, 1952), 229; Philadelphia directories (1867–71).

From William F. Johnston

Washington City   February 22. 1867

My dear Sir

I shall be greatly obliged by the appointment of Gen Tho. E. Rose (now a Capt. in the Regular army[ )], as Professor of Military instruction, in the Western University of Penna. located at Pittsburg under the provisions of 26 Sect. of Art No 187 to "increase & fix" the military peace establishment of the United States.[1]

Gen Rose is eminently qualified—an excellent & worthy citizen.[2]

The Western University is an old established, well managed & successful literary institution and, I humbly, conceive, that there is no portion of the country more justly entitled to the [care?] of Governmt, in the distribution of any aids for the increase of military knowledge.[3]

Wm. F Johnston

ALS, DNA-RG94, Lets. Recd. (Main Ser.), File 79-R-1867 (M619, Roll 577).

1. The "Act to increase and fix the Military Peace Establishment of the United States" was signed by Johnson on July 28, 1866. It authorized the President to appoint an army officer to a college (with not less than 150 male students) for purposes of promoting knowledge of military science. The act also required the school to request such an appointment, no more than twenty officers could be serving in this capacity at any one time, and they had to be distributed throughout the country. *Congressional Globe*, 39 Cong., 1 Sess., Appendix, pp. 420–22.

2. Evidently, Rose did not go to Western University as a professor in 1867 since he remained in the regular army until his retirement in 1894. Hunt and Brown, *Brigadier Generals*.

3. As early as August 1866 the president of the board and the trustees in separate letters asked Johnson for an officer to be assigned to Western University. Their request was followed by a letter from Pittsburgh bank president John Harper to the secretary of war. Assistant adjutant general Townsend informed the school officials about various situations that influenced the selection of an army officer but also encouraged the college to make application. W. D. Howard to Johnson, Aug. 10, 1866; Trustees to Johnson, n.d.; Harper to Stanton, Aug. 29, 1866; Edward D. Townsend memorandum, Sept. 5, 1866, Lets. Recd. (Main Ser.), File 565-H-1866 (M619, Roll 481), RG94, NA.

From Isaac D. Jones [1]

Annapolis, Md.   22nd. Feb. 1867

My dear Sir,

As one of the delegates of Maryland on the committee to present to you the proceedings of the Phila. Convention, in August last,[2] I had the honor to take you by the hand, in the midst of the throng that surrounded you on that occasion, & that is my sole claim to your acquaintance. I had hoped ere now to see you again, but since my arrival here, my engagements in the Ho. of Delegates have not allowed me to visit Washington. I write now to assure you again, as I did when I had the honor to take you by the hand, that the Hope of the Country is upon you—now more than ever. If others fail, I trust in God, that you will not falter; that nothing will induce you to approve the bill passed by Congress to usurp the Governments of the Southern States, & to establish over them, a military despotism.[3]

It is not pretended that a pretext for such power can be found in the Constitution. To call them *States*, to invite their ratification of an amendment to the Constitution, which implies necessarily a free grant of additional powers by the States to Congress, & in the same bill to assume to exercise not only the powers sought by the amendment, but others which can never be delegated without totally destroying the present form of Government, seems to my mind nothing short of absolute insanity. I beg you to maintain at all hazzards, your firm stand in defense of the Constitution, you have sworn to support, whoever else may surrender to the madness of the times. The people want a rallying point, when radicalism now unveiled, awakens them to a sense of the danger to all Constitutional Government, in this land. We feel a deep sense of disappointment at the vote of Senator R. Johnson. He has not a friend in the world who can sustain him.

As Chairman of the Committee on Federal Relations, I am about to begin the report on the Constitutional amendment. It will be a firm & unequivocal protest against it, in every form—& against all the usurpations of Congress. It will counsel patient endurance; in the faith that at the next return to the ballot box, the awakened people, who have been deceived & betrayed, will right the wrongs to the cause of Constitutional Government in this land. The enclosed slip[4] will indicate the views entertained of the legality of this Congess. If their successors in wrong attempt the threatened impeachment, they will incur the excited & aroused indignation of the whole civilized world.

I beg a thousand pardons for the liberty I have taken in these suggestions, but I could not resist the impulse to make them.

Isaac D. Jones.

ALS, DLC-JP.

1. Jones (1806–1893), a lawyer, served in the Maryland house of delegates (1832, 1835, 1840, 1866), the U.S. House (1841–43), was state attorney general (1867), and served as director of the Maryland State School for the Deaf (1867–93). *BDUSC*.

2. The committee visited Johnson on August 18. For a report of their visit, see the *Washington Evening Star*, Aug. 18, 1866.

3. See "An Act to provide for the more efficient Government of the Rebel States," in *U.S. Statutes at Large*, 14: 428–30, and Johnson's Veto of the First Military Reconstruction Act, Mar. 2, 1867.

4. The cover sheet indicates that the enclosed "slip" was a newspaper clipping. It is now missing.

From William V. Barr

Topeka   Feb 23d 1867

Dear Sir

I have just learned that you are about to appoint an Assessor for the State of Kansas. You will probably reccognise my name as one of the old LAND REFORMERS of New York. You may also remember it as the name of one, who at one time urged you to make YOURSELF a candidate for the presidency; declaring my self a democrat, under your leadership; but under any other a Republican. I have remained a Republican; But one of the few, who knowing your devotion to the intrest of the masses of the people, have never ceased to defend that devotion when attacked by friends or foes. Believeing that I can give entire sattisfaction; I take this method of applying for the position. Refer to J L. McDowell Levenworth, F. E. Spinner U.S. Treasurer, Hon E. G. Ross[1] on whom I Should rely for confermation haveing to the best of my ability opposed Pomeroys election also to Gov R. B. Mitchell.[2] Should you do me the faivor to confer this appointment or any other of equal proffit it would be thankfully recieved and its duties faithfully performed.[3]

Wm. V. Barr

Box 157 Topeka

ALS, DNA-RG56, Appts., Internal Revenue Service, Assessor, Kans., 1st Dist., William V. Barr.

1. James L. McDowell, Francis E. Spinner, and Edmund G. Ross. McDowell (c1827–fl1870) was postmaster at Leavenworth City (as distinguished from Ft. Leavenworth which also had a postmaster) from March 1866 until sometime in 1869. By 1870 he was a cattle dealer. Spinner (1802–1890), a banker, served as auditor for the port of New York before his election to three terms in the U.S. House of Representatives. Lincoln appointed him treasurer of the United States in 1861, a post he held until 1875. Ross (1826–1907), a Wisconsin newspaper printer and editor with vehemently anti-slavery opinions, moved to Kansas about 1856 where he was involved in journalism and politics. He served during the Civil War with troops on the Missouri border. Appointed and then elected to fill James H. Lane's Senate seat in 1866, Ross was a radical but voted against Johnson's conviction during the impeachment trial, for which Ross was vilified. He later moved to New Mexico and was governor of that territory (1885–89). 1870 Census, Kans., Leavenworth, Leavenworth, 3rd Ward, 377; Ser. 6B, Vol. 4: 353, Johnson Papers, LC; *U.S. Off. Reg.* (1867–69); *DAB*.

2. Samuel C. Pomeroy and Robert B. Mitchell.

3. There is no indication that Johnson appointed Barr to any post.

Indian delegations at the White House, February 23, 1867.
Photo probably taken by Alexander Gardner.
Courtesy State Historical Society of Wisconsin [WHi(X3)18548]

From Francis P. Blair, Sr.

Washington   24. Feb. '67

My Dear Sir:

I hope the expression of opinion on the impending crisis, may not be unwelcome to you. My devotion to the cause you maintain through a long life and a regard for you personally will excuse me.

I think the veto of the Bill to establish military Govt. by the overthrow of the constitutions, state & national in the South, supplanting them by the omnipotence of a congress in which neither those states nor their people have a representative, is *in effect* to make the Bill a law by *Executive action*. The Bill was rushed through congress under duresse. Every delay that the constitution makes possible ought to be interposed to arrest such proceeding. It ought to be suffered to slide into non-entity with the broken congress that gave birth to the monster—the begotten of an illegitimate caucus. Could the party in power impeach your refusal to act sooner than you are required to act, when the only consequences are to give the new congress to meet the next day an opportunity to apply "a sober second thought" to such a transcendant measure and also to obtain for yourself an appropriate occasion for submitting your views to a new congress in regard to it, in connexion with all the other momentous questions with which it is associated. The purpose of urging this scheme— sacrificing the constitution & the South together—& our white to the black race—with impeachment hanging over your head is a flagrant attempt at intimidation. The Revolutionists have concentrated their strategy to this point. If you aid it in any way, the subjugation of the South is accomplished by you. The humiliation will never be forgotten nor forgiven. If you stand firm, you and our cause will stand together. If you remove the obstacle to the passage of the Bill by submitting it again to the power of those who passed it, you throw down your bulwark. It is in effect submission, whatever may be said—and this will not satisfy the men who would make the Govt. their prey. To retreat before furious dogs, invites pursuit. That man only is safe who confronts them & stands upon his defence. You have ambition—avarice—revenge & party phrenzy at your heels if any shunning is attempted instead of that *negative* action, which alone can balk, by defeating them.

I think the true plan to meet the exigency is a clean sweep of the present cabinet as a concession to the discontents of the country. This is done by the Head of all free Govts. in such a state of affairs. The appointment of the most important, impartial & patriotic men of the leading states of the North, complying as far as possible with the popular will in each, would save the constitution. To impeach you after such concession, would be to impeach you for it, and those who came to the rescue of the constitution.

This movement would at once vindicate your constitutional right to make a Cabinet which is called in question & surround yourself with increased moral stregth, to resist the overthrow of the Govt.

If there is any value in my suggestion ought not the places in the Departments, *be made vacant by your positive order before or at the close of this session,* so that a new cabinet might be nominated immediately on the opening of the next session of the Senate of the new Congress? The Chief clerks or assistants might become locum tenens of the vacated secretary's places until the cabinet you select is confirmed by the Senate.

F. P. Blair

ALS, DLC-JP.

From Fanny M. Jackson

Pulaski Tennessee   Feb 24th [1867][1]

My Dear Mr. President!

My heart was made glad—and to feel, Oh! so proud, when Judge Walker[2] returned to our little village, and told me that you *still* remembered me, and *inquired* after me! And I felt that amidst all your trials and tribulations of Office, you would take time to read a note from one, whose heart would ever beat so kindly and gratefully towards you. Your proud high-toned honorable course, has forever endeared you to your people, and given you a position in our hearts equal to Washington, and encouraged us to give vent, to affectionate rememberance, and heart-felt approval, of the many great and noble acts of heroism, which have adorned your Administration.

May God bless you, my dear Mr. President, and sustain you in your course. We in Tennessee, have been disappointed in our state government, our hopes blighted, and are now moaning, and brooding over the ruin of our peace. I know your patriotic heart must bleed, when you read the acts of the Legislative body in your old home, made dear, doubly dear to you, by suffering!

Some of the leading radicals of this state, and *other* states, have written us repeatedly, and visited us, deploreing our obstinacy in adhering to your policy—a policy they denounce as "the ruin and d———— of Union people in the South": but they always get from us—if you will pardon the expression—"a flea in their ear"—for their advise! We can never forget what is due to you, and our suffering Country, in straying after Brownlow radicals, the despots of the crushed and fallen, the evil arbiters of our state, the destroyers of our peace!

Remember me kindly to Judge Patterson and his estimable lady,[3] also to Maj Morrow,[4] and accept for yourself my most profound esteem and grateful acknowledgement for many kindnesses. . . .

Mrs. John A. Jackson

P.S. Since I visited you in Washington, I have visited many of the northern cities,—and the proudest day of my life was the one upon which I stood upon Broadway New York, and looked upon *your face*, as you passed down, receiving the adulations of a justly proud people![5] Yet, as much as my heart yearned to approach my countryman, and beloved President, I dared not, in the vast throng which surrounded him.

Mrs. Jackson

ALS, DLC-JP.
1. The year is supplied based upon the clerk's file cover which gives 1867 as the date and upon the presumed reference in the letter to the appearance in New York by Johnson in August 1866.
2. Perhaps John C. Walker, a Pulaski attorney.
3. David T. Patterson and Martha Johnson Patterson.
4. Robert Morrow.
5. Although Fanny Jackson visited Washington on more than one occasion (see Jackson to Johnson, Sept. 2, 1865, *Johnson Papers*, 9: 15), this is probably a reference to her summer visit which coincided with Johnson's tour of New York City in August 1866— near the beginning of his Northeastern-Midwestern trip.

From Charles G. Halpine
Private & Confidential

City & County of New York.
Feby. 25th 1867

My dear Sir:

You were pleased to intimate at the close of our conversation last Wednesday afternoon that you would be glad to see some gentleman possessing the public ear putting forward the views of policy & your position with which you then honored me. This I have done, as the enclosed extracts will show you—first in my paper "The Citizen";[1] from which the Article was immediately Copied into the "Sun," "World," "Post," "Brooklyn Eagle," &c &c, & will probably be more widely copied than any newspaper article of recent date,—thanks to the excellent wisdom & justice of the words which you placed in my mouth to speak. I was very much pressed for time when writing the article; but when I see you next, will (if you honor me with another conversation;) endeavor to report it more fully & in a manner to command more attention. The *Tribune*, I may add, copies the article tomorrow. Very often a semi-official paper such as this, when vouched by any well-known signature, can attract more attention, because more at liberty to place the matters it touches in *a popular form*, than if the same facts had been directly put forth in dry official shape by the Prest.

It is my hope that this article may do good; and if you regard it as a fair statement of your views, a note from you to that effect, or from your private Secretary, might help to confirm the evidently wide & deep impression the article has created. Marble, Sam Tilden and Seymour[2] are highly pleased with it, and say it makes out a strong case against the Radicals,—all the stronger because so quiet.

I wish to devote my best energies to the service of the country; and shall hope to have the honor of seeing you again next Saturday or Monday at the farthest.[3]

Archbishop McCloskey[4] has written to Secretary McCulloch and this letter (his FOURTH in this connection, all now on file,) urging that Captn. John Foley be appointed Collector of Internal Revenue 8th Congressional District, & I am to see his grace on the subject tomorrow morning. Beyond any doubt he takes deep interest in the matter, as I do also; and I fear he will be sadly disappointed if Foley be not the man.

The two other candidates are Thos. E. Smith,[5] a veteran republican place holder, now Asst. Depty. Collr. of the Bureau of Assessts., who is pressed by WEED,[6] & by nobody else,—I care not how many names may be moved across the desk of the Camera Obscura.[7] I would not think Tom Smith, or "Red Headed Tom" as he has been called in local politics for a dozen years, worth a janitor's place in my office, salary $800; & I would not give him that place for all the names he has on his recommendation together. It is notorious that money is used to secure certain of the influences which are in his favor; & I believe Foley's appointment would be (without exaggeration) five or ten thousand times more to your interest in its popular effect.

The other candidate is Charles W. Baker,[8] a broken down Democratic politician—a good fellow, formerly a great friend of Douglas[9] in an humble way; but one whose name has been fatally mixed with the transactions known in our city politics as the "Commissioners of Records Swindle," the "Baker and McSpeden bills"[10] and so forth. He is a good hearted, gay, fellow—very loose in money transactions; & one who cannot, I believe, be confirmed, in consequence of the WILD HOWL his name will create in the papers here when he is spoken of for so important a pecuniary post. It is said, Mr. Johnson, and said openly, that he has offered certain men (of our city) $10,000 for his appointment; and certainly their zeal in his behalf can be explained in no other way. I once wrote a letter for him[11] at the earnest request of Hugh Smith Esqr,[12] & because I was told when writing it that M. L. Harris's appointment was sure,[13] & that my letter would gratify Smith & Baker without doing any injury. I regret having placed that letter on file, for, while it was of no use at that time (as I expected) I hear it is now being used as a practical endorsement, for which purpose it was never given.

John Foley, is a gold pen manufacturer worth $150,000 in real estate, & of as high character (as appears from the mercantile signatures to his papers)[14] as any man in this City. He is an IRISH CATHOLIC, and ex-soldier, & no Irish Catholic holds an appointment under you in this city. He is pressed with surprizing zeal by the Cath Archbishop; & I, as a Protestant, specially desire to be instrumental in having his Grace gratified. I pledge myself & Mr. Greeley[15] for his confirmation by the Senate; & I think his appointment may help toward righting the injury which Mr. Seward is doing you with the Irish Cath. & Fenian vote. Beyond, this, I pledge my honor I have no motive of interest for urging Foley's appointment; and I need not point out the injury it does a party in a city, where bribes are taken (or even believed to be taken,) for securing offices for worthless candidates. I earnestly hope the Mr. Foley may be appointed to gratify Bishop McCloskey; and I send you a letter from Member of Congress Elect, John Fox,[16] in his favor. Wm. E. Robinson, Member Elect is now at Washn. urging him,[17] & I know that John Morrissey would join if I could only lay my hands on him.

Chas. G Halpine

Also copies of letters from Arch Bishop McCloskey & Edwards Pierrepont—the pencilling on the back of this being the names of some of our first merchants who recommend Mr. Foley,[18] & whose original papers are on file with Secretary McCulloch.[19]

C.G.H

ALS, DLC-JP.
1. Not found enclosed. For the article as it appeared in the *Augusta (Ga.) Constitutionalist*, see Interview with Charles G. Halpine, Feb. 21, 1867.
2. Manton Marble and Horatio Seymour. Marble (1835–1917) was the editor and publisher of the *New York World* (1862–76). *DAB*.
3. Halpine met with Johnson on Tuesday, March 5. William Hanchett, *Irish: Charles G. Halpine in Civil War America* (Syracuse, 1970), 163.
4. John McCloskey to Hugh McCulloch, Feb. 19, 1867, Appts., Internal Revenue Service, Collector, New York, 8th Dist., John Foley, RG56, NA.
5. Smith (c1818–fl1868) was a bookseller and commission merchant as well as collector of street opening and repair assessments. *New York World*, Apr. 29, 1867; New York City directories (1860–68).
6. Thurlow Weed.
7. A camera obscura, literally a dark chamber, was a darkened box with an opening through which an image was projected on the wall opposite to the opening. It could be used for taking photographs or making exact drawings.
8. Baker (fl1868) was a New York City stationer and merchant. New York City directories (1860–68).
9. Stephen A. Douglas.
10. Not found.
11. Charles G. Halpine to Johnson, Sept. 18, 1866, Johnson Papers, LC.
12. Not identified.
13. Morgan L. Harris (fl1870) held a number of positions including measurer, assessor, and president of a company. He was nominated for the collectorship of the Eighth District on December 13, 1866, and rejected on January 26, 1867. New York City directories (1860–70); Ser. 6B, Vol. 4: 51, Johnson Papers, LC.
14. Numerous New York City bankers and merchants signed a petition requesting the appointment of Foley as collector or assessor for the Eighth District. New York City Bankers and Merchants to Johnson, July 21, 1866, Appts., Internal Revenue Service, Collector, New York, 8th Dist., John Foley, RG56, NA.
15. Horace Greeley.
16. John Fox to Johnson, Feb. 14, 1867, ibid.
17. See William E. Robinson to Johnson, Feb. 18, 1867.
18. John McCloskey to Johnson, Feb. 5, 1867, with undated endorsement from Ed-

wards Pierrepont; list of letters relating to Foley, Appts., Internal Revenue Service, Collector, New York, 8th Dist., John Foley, RG56, NA.

19. Johnson's endorsement on the McCloskey and Pierrepont letter referred it to the secretary of the treasury. Despite the enthusiasm of the various promoters of Foley, Johnson nominated Thomas E. Smith for collector of the Eighth District on February 27, 1867. Although the nomination was then withdrawn, Smith was again nominated on April 10 and confirmed and commissioned the same day. On that day also Johnson nominated Foley for assessor of the Eighth District; however, the Senate seems to have taken no action on the nomination. Ser. 6B, Vol. 4: 52, 55, Johnson Papers, LC. For one interpretation of Johnson's actions on this appointment, see Hanchett, *Irish*, 163–65.

From William C. Jewett

For the special national & *personal*
attention of the President & Cabinet

[Washington]   Feby 25th [186]7

At our interview,[1] I had the honor to state—my opinion—that as well recognize the dead-body of Abraham Lincoln—President—as recognize the existence of the Constitution—at the same time urging you to sign the military bill, as the corner stone of a new Republic. While declaring a few days would settle that point—*You requested my views in writing—expressed upon the opinion of European Capitalists—as to the instability of the American Republic.* I beg in response to state that I am in possession of letters showing want of confidence in our Republic—upon the part of leading Capitalists—on the Continent of Europe in one case—in which I am interested as President of a Land Co[2]—retarding progress—in a transaction involving 10,000,000$ & more—that its tendency—is to impare the credit of our securities abroad—& to retard emigration. I ask—you to refer to the subject in your coming message & at least take the ground that whatever be the action of American Statesmen, on the position of the Country—the spirit of the people will protect American Liberty & sustain the national debt.

In conclusion—permit me to thank you for the kind & magnanimous spirit in which you received me & to hope that should you not sign the military bill & thereby take no part in a harmonious reconstruction—that you will yield to the incoming Congress their right to mark out the future of our Republic—through the majority of the people—if not under your (care) appeal to the people to sustain, or condemn your policy.

Wm. Cornell Jewett

ALS, DLC-JP.
1. The interview was on February 25 according to an attached printed version of this letter which begins "At our interview to day."
2. Unknown.

From Augustus Pleasonton [1]

Washington City D.C.   Feby 25th 1867.

Sir

I have the honor to inform you that the Secretary of War will decide my case today. I have served both in the army and Navy[2] during the War, and you appointed me a 2nd Lieut 6th Regt. U.S. Cavalry—was rejected by the Surgeon[3] of "Cavalry Board" in consequence of blemish on my right collarbone, which blemish does'nt affect the action of my sabre arm in the least. Surgeon Bliss and A. K. Smith[4] of U.S.A. consider me fit for any duty, and this blemish was developed by my horse falling on me while enroute to a Brigade Drill. *I have sacrificed my all* by endeavouring to return to the army, and at present *my wife, my children*,[5] and *myself* are financially ruined. My family and friends have centered their hopes upon my success, and I hope they may not be disappointed. If you will do me the honor to send a line to the Secretary of War desiring my appointment at once to some old Regt. and to place me upon duty at as early a period as possible, you will do me the greatest honor, and will render my family the greatest kindness.[6] Hoping that these few lines may meet with your approbation . . .

Augustus Pleasonton
Late 2nd. Lieut. 6th U.S. Cavalry
No 365 C St. bet. 4 1/2 & 6th Sts Washington.

ALS, DNA-RG94, ACP Branch, File P-76-CB-1867, Augustus Pleasanton.

1. Pleasonton (b. 1836), a native resident of Philadelphia, served during the war with the 1st Drag. and 1st Cav. as a second and first lieutenant, retiring in August 1862. Powell, *Army List*, 532; Pleasonton to Adjutant General, Dec. 28, 1866; Pleasonton to President and Members of the Board of Examiners for the U.S. Infantry, Jan. 7, 1867, ACP Branch, File P-76-CB-1867, Augustus Pleasonton, RG94, NA.

2. Save for his statement that, following his retirement, he was appointed clerk to his brother-in-law, Capt. John Guest, USN, commanding the U.S. steam sloop of war "Galatia" on duty in the West Indies, no evidence of naval service has been found. Ibid.

3. William Thomson (1833–*fl*1900), a Philadelphia physician, was an assistant surgeon with the Army of the Potomac from 1861 to 1863. By 1864 he had been named medical inspector of the Department of Washington. He resigned in 1868 as a brevet major and full surgeon, and returned to his practice in Philadelphia becoming a noted authority on ophthalmology. Thomson to Maj. Gen. David Hunter, Feb. 3, 1867, ibid.; William B. Atkinson, ed., *The Physicians and Surgeons of the United States* (Philadelphia, 1878), 344–46; Philadelphia directories (1890–1900).

4. Probably D. Willard Bliss (*c*1827–*c*1889), a New York native and Grand Rapids, Michigan, resident in 1861, who served as a Union surgeon from September 1861 to late 1865. He later practiced in Washington, D. C. Andrew K. Smith (*c*1825–1899), career army surgeon, entered the service in 1853 as a first lieutenant. He retired in 1890 with the rank of colonel and resided in New York City. D. Willard Bliss to Lorenzo Thomas, Sept. 9, 1861, ACP Branch, File B-886-CB-1865, D. W. Bliss, RG94, NA; Personal Papers of Medical Officers and Physicians, D. W. Bliss, ibid.; Washington, D. C., directories (1889–90); Powell, *Army List*, 592; *New York Tribune*, Aug. 15, 17, 1899.

5. Unidentified.

6. According to Pleasonton, Johnson had appointed him a second lieutenant, 25th Inf., on December 1, 1866, but the examining board rejected him on January 10, 1867, on the grounds of not having two years' service in the volunteers. Subsequently, in late January, Johnson requested Pleasonton's appointment per a vacancy. Appointed to the 6th Cav., Pleasonton was rejected on February 4 by the cavalry board on the physical and moral grounds that a tumor, which had developed on his collarbone near the point of an earlier injury, was the result of a long-standing, pre-existing syphillitic condition. The board refused to reconsider. No evidence has been found of further action by Johnson. Pleasonton to Lorenzo Thomas, Jan. 21, 1867; David Hunter to Adjutant General, Feb. 4, 1867; R. H. Montgomery to Pleasonton, Feb. 8, 1867, Pleasonton to Johnson, Feb. 11, 1867, ACP Branch, File P-76-CB-1867, File P-88-CB-1867, Augustus Pleasonton, RG94, NA.

From Henry A. Smythe

New York, 25 Feby 1867

My dear Sir.

I have just been called upon by Messrs. Beecher, Claflin[1] & others, who desire me to write in their behalf, & to use my influence urging you *to sign the reconstruction bill now before you*. Of course it is with reluctance that I comply—but in response to their appeal, with great respect & delicacy—I would say from all I hear & see—it will be regarded nothing short of a *calamity* if you do not sign it—this being regarded by people of all parties as the most sane & reasonable bill likely to be passed—& it is naturally hoped by your friends, that you will give this your signature—with all its objections—in the hope of its being one step—towards reconciliation, & better feeling.

I see by the telegrams published in the papers today[2]—that I am "*to be removed*"—for which I am quite ready—& resigned too—if it will help matters, and render the atmosphere around you more balmy & agreeable.

My present Secretary Mr. Wilbur[3]—is an applicant for Secy of Legation at Paris—which capacity he filled many years—creditably & to the satisfaction of all who knew him. I saw him many times when abroad, & like him so well, appointed him my Secy—at the commencement of the year.

He is a well educated gentleman—& an excellent french scholar.

Hoping you will pardon any seeming intrusion on my part . . .

H. A. Smythe

ALS, DLC-JP.

1. Henry Ward Beecher and Horace B. Claflin. Claflin (1811–1885) began as a dry goods merchant in Massachusetts before moving to New York City in 1843. His company became one of the biggest and most profitable wholesale firms in the country. Claflin was also a trustee of Plymouth Church, Brooklyn, in Beecher's pastorate. *DAB.*

2. *New York Herald*, Feb. 24, 25, 1867. For further information on the attempted removal of Smythe, see Smythe to Johnson, Mar. 6, 28, 1867.

3. John B. Wilbur, Jr., son of the U.S. consul at Nice, spent much of his life abroad, including serving as temporary secretary to the American legation at Paris in 1851. Despite numerous requests spanning several presidencies, Wilbur never received a permanent

foreign appointment. *U.S. Off. Reg.* (1859); Lets. of Recommendation, 1845–53, (M873, Roll 95), RG59, NA.

From Montgomery Blair

Washn.   Feby 26, 1867

My dear Mr. President

The prevailing rumor is, that you are about to return the Reconstruction bill with your objections. I hope you will not do this. The bill was hurried through in such a manner that the friends of the Constitution and even those most moderate in opposition were trapped in to supporting the most ultra measure ever presented instead of supporting the less objectionable measure originally introduced by Stevens. As the measure now stands it authorizes the military to reconstruct the whole South so as to vote the Radical ticket in '68. As Stevens introduced it, it was a bill to prevent the States from voting at all. I trust you will not allow this bill to be passed this Session so as to allow our friends to cooperate in the next congress with those who will keep 80 votes out of the Electoral College agnst. the Constitutional party.[1]

M Blair

ALS, DLC-JP.

1. Johnson vetoed the bill the day it was passed, March 2, 1867. See Veto of the First Military Reconstruction Act, Mar. 2, 1867.

From William J.C. Duhamel

Washt D.C.   Feb 26th 1867

Mr President:

I was yesterday approached by the Rev W. B. Matchet[1] (No. 444. 8th St) who says he is connected with the Judiciary Com'te and asked if I often saw John H Surrat. I replied I did in a professional way (as physician to the U.S. Jail).[2]

He Mr. Matchet then requested me to mention to Surratt *that there was a means* by which he could save his neck have the shackles struck from his arms and his mother's name[3] rescued from odium if he would give the name of some one high in position who might have prompted the assasination as he and his party were no doubt mere tools in the hands of other more important personages and that he need not look to Andrew Johnson as he dare not interfere or pardon him.

He Mr. Matchett said he had approached Miss Surratt[4] but old Bradley[5] her brothers lawyer had prevented his communicating with her. He said many other things which I have also taken note of.

W.J.C. Duhamel

ALS, DLC-JP.

1. William B. Matchett (c1830–fl1900) was apparently not a practicing clergyman as no association with a specific church has been discovered. He was apparently a clerk to the House Judiciary Committee. 1870 Census, D.C., Washington, 2nd Ward, 5; Washington, D.C., directories (1866–1900); Randall, *Browning Diary*, 2: 153.

2. Surratt had been arrested in Alexandria, Egypt, in November 1866. He arrived back in the United States in early February 1867 and was in prison awaiting trial for the assassination of Lincoln. Thomas R. Turner, *Beware the People Weeping: Public Opinion and the Assassination of Abraham Lincoln* (Baton Rouge, 1982), 227, 229. See also Johnson to Ward H. Lamon, Apr. 16, 1861, *Johnson Papers*, 4: 471.

3. Mary E. Surratt.

4. Anna E. Surratt (1843–1904) was educated at St. Mary's Female Institution, a Catholic school in Bryantown, Maryland. After the assassination of Lincoln and the execution of her mother, Anna taught school in Baltimore. In 1869 she married William P. Tonry, a chemist and toxicologist. Louis J. Weichmann, *A True History of the Assassination of Abraham Lincoln and of the Conspiracy of 1865*, ed. by Floyd J. Risvold (New York, 1975), 20, 465–66; Alfred Isacsson, ed., "Some Letters of Anna Surratt," *MdHM*, 54 (1959): 310, 311; *Washington Evening Star*, June 18, 1869; *New York Times*, Oct. 4, 1905.

5. Joseph H. Bradley, Sr. (1802–1887), was city attorney (1834–50, 1862–67) and practiced law in Washington, D.C., for many years. Often involved in "stormy" cases, he had a fight with the judge during John H. Surratt's trial and was temporarily disbarred. Vernon E. West, "History and Function of the Office of the Corporation Counsel," *Records CHS*, 48–49 (1946–47): 118; Allen C. Clark, "More About the Fourth Ward," Ibid., 33–34 (1932): 79; *NUC*, 71: 548.

From Daniel E. Sickles

Metropolitan Hotel

Tuesday   [February 26, 1867][1]

My dear Mr President

The vacancy made in the grade of Brigadier General in the Army, by the recent resignation of Gen'l Rosecrans,[2] opens the way for a promotion I venture to ask at your hands. For my Military record and professional qualifications I feel authorized or rather justified in refering to the Secretary of War & the General in Chief of the Army.

In desiring Civil Office, I confess my ambition to deserve and attain a rank in the permanent Military Establishment Corresponding to the grade I reached as a Volunteer Officer by service in the field during the War for the suppression of the rebellion.[3]

D. Sickles

ALS, DLC-JP.

1. This date has been assigned by the Library of Congress.

2. William S. Rosecrans submitted his resignation in December 1866, and it was accepted by Johnson on March 28, 1867. See Sylvester H. Rosecrans to Johnson, Feb. 12, 1867.

3. Sickles was brevetted brigadier general and major general on March 2, 1867. He retired two years later a major general in the regular army. Powell, *Army List*, 586–87; Warner, *Blue*.

From John Bigler

U.S. Assessors Office
Sacramento   Feby 27 1867

Dear Sir

Surrounded as you have been and still are, by an intollerant and even vindictive majority, I was prepared to cheerfully acquiesce in any action you might deem it necessary to take in my case after my rejection by the Senate.[1] As you know, I did not wish a second nomination to be followed by rejection. I therefore desire you to understand that I do not complain that another has been selected in my place.

I now as in the past cordially endorse your policy as far as known to me and will remain your True friend.

But, you will pardon me for troubling you with the pointed evidence that B. N. Bugbey,[2] appointed as he states at the instance of that bad man Senator Conness[3] *is your enemy*. The card enclosed and signed by B. N. Bugbey, was published here[4] after he had been nominated to the Senate, and after he beleived the appointment was beyond your reach.

He then declared *for* Congress and *against* you.[5]

Renewing to you assurances of my friendship for you personally and your policy . . . [6]

John Bigler

ALS, DNA-RG56, Appts., Internal Revenue Service, Assessor, Calif., 4th Dist., John Bigler.

1. Bigler was rejected for the post of internal revenue assessor for the Fourth District of California on January 22, 1867. Ser. 6B, Vol. 4: 347, Johnson Papers, LC. See also Bigler to Johnson, Mar. 14, 1866, *Johnson Papers*, 10: 253–54; Bigler to Johnson, Dec. 1, 1866, ibid., 11: 501–2.

2. Benjamin N. Bugbey (c1827–fl1870), a wine producer and former sheriff of Sacramento County (c1861–63), resided in Folsom and was involved in Republican/Union politics. He had been nominated to the assessorship of the Fourth District on February 9, 1867, and had been confirmed and commissioned on February 21. *Sacramento Union*, Feb. 25, 1867; Ser. 6B, Vol. 4: 347, Johnson Papers, LC; Sacramento directories (1863); 1870 Census, Calif., Sacramento, Granite Twp., 25.

3. John Conness did indeed recommend Bugbey in letters to E.A. Rollins of Aug. 9, 1866, and to Andrew Johnson of Jan. 24, 1867. See Appts., Internal Revenue Service, Assessor, Calif., 4th Dist., Benjamin N. Bugbey, RG56, NA.

4. Bugbey's letter addressed "To the Public" appeared in the *Sacramento Union* on Monday, February 25, 1867. He was protesting the comments of James McClatchy, editor of the *Sacramento Bee*, which implied that Bugbey was not a Union man. Bugbey intended to disabuse everyone of this notion by giving examples of his Union sentiments and actions.

5. Bugbey said he had not applied for the position of assessor nor did he see any reason why Johnson should give it to him. "I have consistently supported a radical Congress as against the President's policy. . . . I would not give up my principles for this or any other place." *Sacramento Union*, Feb. 25, 1867.

6. Bigler's letter could not have arrived in Washington in time to affect Johnson's decision; obviously something influenced the President because Bugbey's nomination was withdrawn on March 2, the day on which Thomas J. Blakeney was nominated, confirmed, and commissioned for the post. Ser. 6B, Vol. 4: 347, Johnson Papers, LC.

From George P. Este

Wednesday Ev   [Washington, February 27, 1867][1]

Mr. President

Lest I may not see you I write this note. Probaly before this your action in regard to the Military Reconstruction Bill has been determined upon. Nevertheless you might like to know my observations of the past few days.

I find that *all* the more moderate Radicals desire you to sign the Bill. I mean those who dont wish to follow the lead of Stevens, Boutwell & Co.[2] *They say* your signing the Bill will forever kill the extreme wing of the Party and give you the Control of the situation.

Most of them (and I believe sincerely) think a veto, however worded, will result in yet more Extreme measures And your ultimate Impeachment. A few of them are of the opinion that a veto of temperate tone, with suggestions as to the Common ground on which you could meet Congress might prevent any more extravagant measures.

Among those who are with you on Principle—there is some difference of opinion as to the Course you should take. Many of your sincerest friends desire you to sign the Bill under protest. The majority probaly think you ought not to. What Democrats as a whole would advise you of course know. *All* agree though that if you Conclude to veto, you ought if possible to send it in to-morrow.

I dare not offer any advice. The situation is too grave to do it lightly. You know that I regard the measure as atrocious. Yet bad as it is, if your signing it—would bring the States in and put an End to the domination of Stevens & Co—I would say it would be clearly your duty to do it. If a veto should precipitate Impeachment—& your approval would prevent it—then you ought to sign the Bill—for no man can tell the injury your Country would receive if you should be deprived of your high Office. The mere personal consequences are nothing. But the public are grave beyond calculation. As I said before I wont presume to offer advice. If even asked I should hesitate to give it. The occasion is a grave one Mr President, and he is a presumptuous man who would presume to give an opinion without the most serious thought. May God give you Wisdom to decide aright. I may add that in my opinion the Butler, Stevens wing desire a veto.

Geo. P. Este

P.S. Whatever you do, I shall be with you.

ALS, DLC-JP.

1. We have assigned this date as internal evidence clearly indicates that this is an 1867 letter. It appears from the contents also that the letter was written sometime between the Senate's initial passage of the First Military Reconstruction Act on February 20 and

Johnson's March 2 veto. February 27 fell on a Wednesday in 1867. Este, who was practicing law in Washington, probably wrote his letter from the nation's capital.
   2. Thaddeus Stevens and George S. Boutwell.

From Hannibal D. Norton[1]

Goldsboro', N.C., Feb. 28, 1867.

Sir:

I have the honor to address your Excellency upon a subject which is of vital importance to me; and only take this liberty for the reason that I have failed, in every other way, to obtain what I desire.

In Nov. last I applied to the Adjutant General[2] for an appointment in Co. "H." 8th U.S. Inf'y. With my application I forwarded all the recommendations I could then obtain, and referred, also, to testimonials on file in the War Dep't. This was all I could offer. I had no political influence. Having been a resident of South Carolina for two years previous to the war, and an officer in Mass. Vols. since Apl. 1861, I was comparatively unknown in my own State—Mass.

Inasmuch as I have not succeeded in obtaining an appointment through the ordinary channel, I now appeal to your Excellency, and respectfully submit my claims to one.

I entered service as Lieut. in 5th Mass. Inf'y, Apl. 17. 1861. Was wounded at 1st Battle of Bull Run. In 1862 was promoted to Captain, and assigned to 32d Mass. Inf'y. Was wounded at "Antietam" and "Fredericksburg." Was appointed in V.R.C. in 1863. I am now Capt. V.R.C., and Bt. Major U.S. Vols., but expect to be mustered out of service very soon. The War has rendered me poor. I have lost my all. I have a wife and four children;[3] and, unless I can obtain an appointment in the Army, or a Gov't position of some kind, I know not how I can support them. Being without capital, and the general stagnation of business rendering it almost impossible to obtain a clerkship, at a living salary, I shall be in a poor situation to maintain a family. I am 28 years of age. My family reside in Chelsea, Mass.

With the hope that my case will be favorably considered, and that your Excellency will deem me worthy of an appointment in the Regular Army, . . .

Hannibal D. Norton,   Capt. V.R.C. & Bt. Maj. U.S.V.
Ass't Sup't Bureau R. F. & A. L.,   Sub-Dist. of Goldsboro'.

ALS, DNA-RG94, ACP Branch, File N-77-CB-1867, H. D. Norton.
   1. Norton (1838–1921), an accountant before the war, was given a medical discharge from the 32nd Mass. Vols. in March 1863. In 1867 he was subassistant commissioner of the Freedmen's Bureau at Morganton, North Carolina; through 1868 he continued to hold a position with the Bureau in North Carolina. Following his discharge in December 1868, Norton moved frequently, living for a time in New York, Ohio, Texas, and Missouri, often working in post offices. He did not receive the appointment to the U.S. infantry. Pension

File, Nellie A. Norton, RG15, NA; Everly and Pacheli, *Records of Field Offices*, Pt. 2: 333, 344.

2. Gen. Lorenzo Thomas.

3. Nellie A. Williams (c1838–1924) and Norton were married in Boston in December 1858. By 1867 they were the parents of three girls, born between 1860 and 1864, and one son, born November 1866. Pension File, Nellie A. Norton, RG15, NA.

From Unknown

Philadelphia   Feby 28th 1867

Dear Sir

This mode of addressing you no doubt will seem novel, but circumstances are such that such a measure alone seems posible. To undertake to reach our object through a paid and truckling press would be fruitless, and when we see the same old grim visage that fought so savagly against our forefathers, again standing arrect and defying the great life giving principles of Eternal liberty we feel it our duty to speak as a body in some way that we may be heard, (in effect only) and that to our Honorable President, The great center, from whom we now above look in the hour of our Countrys perrel.

We see a bill passed both houses of the National Congress under the assumed name of a reconstruction bill, superceding the civil by a military power, Thus destroying the primates of our Constetution, and striking a deadly blow at the root of the great Tree of Liberty, and with the shameless hardihood to ask the President to indorse it, The object of said bill solely partisan, To force peacble citizens of ten states to accept of Negro sufferage The object to well understood by your Excelency to need our comment. Now we would propose for the benefit of the Negro, a seperate political organisation, With a right to patition, and a right of appeal. Let them be the Executors of all laws the same as the white man, but let them have no Legislative powers. They have their spirituel organisations, they worship after Luther, Calvin, Wesley, &c without any Legislative authority of their own, and they are in harmony with the white church organisations. They grow and flourish under such conditions, and are respected. Then is not the higher law of Church Christianity worthy of a precident? It has shurly cost enough blood and treasure to make it such. If God is to weak to protect the physical world, The Legislation, and the vast and expensive Church extention is a great blunder, and should amedietly be cast asside, and in the absence of that, Universal Negro Sufferage would be useless. We would propose to give the colored race their own Courts with all the lawfull ability to conduct them, a right to all schools and school appropriations, exccept the Military. We would bind them in their processes of law to their own color, But would allow Them the right of appeal to the white Courts, even to the highest, with the prvalege of a Lawyer of their own color and race, to represent them, and see that they are accorded thei full and unrestricted rights. Without some

such law the civil rights bill lately passed by Congress, and partially ac-
knoledged by the South, can never be carried out for the benefeit of the
Colored race, and with the organisation herein refered to. The race
would soon grow into respect and usefulness. They are imitative in ther
nature, and an incentive like we have refered to, would stimulate them to
an emulation of the higher and better morals and habits of the white man,
and no doubt before the lapse of many years, examples of the black man
would be shoun the world, proving again that statuts, when connected,
and in working conjointly in harmony with the laws of nature, are alone
the great propelling powers that lifts humanity from the miry pit of clay,
and places him on the grand smoothe highway leading to Eternal peace,
prosperity, and happiness. Now before we close we wish to say somthing
in regard to the National Congress.

This body eminating as it has from an excited people, and usurping the
power of the Constetution, claiming their authority from the people, propose to strip the Executive of the powers given him by the Constitution
and laws of the Nation, also the same in regard to the supreme Court,
thus throwing the whole Govenment into the hands of a powerfull poli-
ticl faction. We would sujest if this people have this power claimed by this
usurping Congress, have they not the power to do away with themselves,
and let the legislative power revert back to the people, and let all laws
eminate direct from the people, With a National elected counsil similar to
the President and Cabinet? We have the Press, and Tellegraph, and by
disposing with a Congress would save the nation countless millions and
save a world of strife and bad feeling, besides being the first and a grand
step towards breaking down political parties, and turn the mind from its
presant inharmonious conditions, to one of fillial affection, the great palladium that alone can propel mankind on the greased smooth highway
leading to peace, prosperity, and happiness.

Respetfully by order of the Committe

L, DLC-JP.

March 1867

From G. B. Wright[1]

Respected Sir.

In behalf of the people of Our beloved State of Tennessee, I would state that I have resided in Sumner Co. One of the strongest *Rebel* Counties in the State in former days, and that I have always had the character and reputation of a Union man in every sense of the Word. And I would further state that I have had *no* Occassion to call on U.S. Troops to protect my life limb or property. And I would also state that no mans life or liberty is in danger because of his Union sentiments provided he act honestly and uprightly with all men and claim no proviledge politicaly the he would not grant his neighbors under the laws of the Land.

Registration In this state is decidedly a hum-bug of the most magnificient species. Ex United States Officers who fought so hard to maintain the Union of the States during the late war are refused Certificates. Civil officers of the U.S are also refused in like manner. I will give you an Instance of this kind within my own observation to wit Mr C. H. Hatcher[3] late of Illinois a Union man during the war and P.M at Castallian Springs applied to the Commissioner of Registration for a Certificate to vote and was refused on the ground that a Commission as P.M. signed by Ex. P.M.G. Wm. Dennison was not sufficient evidence of loyalty to obtain a Certificate in this state according to the acts of the Tennessee Legislature;[4] and he had to go out and hunt up some of Brownlows pets to vouch for his loyalty before he procured a Certificate.

Union Leagues etc Brownlows pets have organized various societies throughout the state styling themselves "The Loyal Men &c.["][5] These midnight assassins are evidently trying to bring about a conflict between the white and Colored people. Therfore I would suggest to your Excellency the propriety of puting a stop to the meetings of such bodies as tend to disturb the peace and harmony of our beloved state and bring utter destruction upon the heads of the poor Colored people who are misled by their teachings in to these midnight Conclaves of Thieves and Murderers. I say thieves and murderers because no honest well meaning man is associated with them and their teachings are purely of the kind above mentioned.

Hoping you will carefully consider the condition of affairs in Tennessee. It is useless for me to say that you have an eye single to the restoration of Peace and harmony in this state.

G. B Wright   Gallatin Tenn

ALS, DLC-JP.

1. Probably Gideon B. Wright (1825–*fl*1870), a well-to-do farmer who served as post-

master at Gallatin from 1864 until April of 1869. 1850 Census, Tenn., Sumner, 12th Dist., 579; (1870), Gallatin, 20; *U.S. Off. Reg.* (1865–69).

2. The reference to the February act, as well as other internal evidence, suggests this approximate date.

3. Charles H. Hatcher (*fl*1868) was postmaster of Castalian Springs from 1867 through December 1868. Ibid. (1867–69).

4. A reference to the acts of May 3, 1866, and February 25, 1867, which established the criteria for voting eligibility. Although the laws set forth elaborate categories and qualifications, they also placed an inordinate amount of power in the hands of the commissioners of registration. These officials, appointed by the governor, had the final say on an applicant's eligibility to vote. *Tennessee Acts, Public and Private* (1865–66), 42–48; (1866–67), 26–33.

5. Probably a reference to the Tennessee state guard, organized under "An Act to Organize a State Guard, and for other purposes," passed February 20, 1867. As a safeguard to insure Governor Brownlow's control of the force, only "loyal men" were to be enlisted. Ibid., 24–25; Robert H. White et al., *Messages of the Governors of Tennessee* (10 vols., Nashville, 1952–), 5: 551–55.

From Virginia C. Clay

First Spring day!   1st March 1867

Mr. President,

I came to say farewell to you, & say a few parting words.

Regret I cannot see you, but you know & feel, *all* I wd. say to you. God give you grace to do your *duty* to yourself—your country & your God, & if you *perish*, perish with a clear conscience.

I will write you from Huntsville. GEN. HOWARD says he will order *rent* paid Mr. Clay, if *you* will order it.[1] Can you not do it?

Trusting to hear cheering accounts from you & your veto . . .

V. C. Clay.

ALS, DLC-JP.

1. In late November 1866 Johnson had given an order for the release of Clay's property in Alabama. This was challenged by local authorities until Virginia Clay secured an order in mid-January from Attorney General Stanbery to dismiss a suit against Clay. Evidently this action set in motion the circumstances that, by April 1867, enabled the Clays to collect rent on their office building previously under control of the Freedmen's Bureau. Ruth K. Nuermberger, *The Clays of Alabama* (Lexington, 1958), 302–3.

From John A. Turley [1]

Portsmouth, Scioto Co., March 1, 1867

It is with deep humiliation that I address you. You were pleased to appoint me Assessor of the Eleventh Dist of Ohio. Although I had served my country faithfully for three years & until discharged, having my leg broken by a musket ball, the senate refuses to confirm your appointment, of me to that office. It may be reconsidered yet and if so, I hope you will do me the favor to consider my claim as I am totally incapacited for active duty. If necessary thousands of petitions will be forwarded in my behalf.

If the senate will not reconsider their action, then I hope you will send in the name of *Alva F Kendall*[2] one of my assts. who is an excellent man was a Lieut during the war was the mustering officer in the Dpt. of West Va & mustered out nearly all the troops in that Depart and is fully competent to discharge the duties of the office. I ask this of your excellency as a speial favor not only to a soldier but as a Brother Mason. I am worthy Sir Warder of Encampment No 3 Knights Templar. I am also Prin Sojourner of Mt. Vernon Chapt. No 23 and of course am not a drone, but a working member. I have been a mason for 23 years. This sheet is for none but your eyes. The fist [illegible] may make any disposition you please or with this among Brother Masons. Mr Bundy[3] our member is a mason and I have written to him today as such. I hope he will agree to have my appointment reconsidered. If you will hold the appointment, until I could visit Washington I think I could get the senate to reconsider.[4] I was Col 91st OVI when wounded.

John A Turley

ALS, DNA-RG56, Appts., Internal Revenue Service, Assessor, Ohio, 11th Dist., John A. Turley.

1. Turley (1816–1900), a farmer, served in the Ohio Vol. Inf. during the war and was brevetted brigadier general in 1865. Johnson had given him a recess appointment as assessor on August 24, 1866. He was nominated for a regular appointment on January 21, 1867, and rejected by the Senate on February 8. Hunt and Brown, *Brigadier Generals*; Ser. 6B, Vol. 3: 494; Vol. 4: 258, Johnson Papers, LC.

2. Kendall (1832–1901) spent the prewar years in Ohio and California operating a grocery and mining. During the war he served with the 91st Ohio Vol. Inf., mustering out with the rank of captain. Afterwards he served as assistant assessor to Turley and deputy collector under Benjamin F. Coates. Later he returned to work in the revenue service until his death. Nothing has been found to indicate that Johnson nominated him for office. Nelson W. Evans, *A History of Scioto County, Ohio, Together with a Pioneer Record of Southern Ohio* (Portsmouth, 1903), 1021–22.

3. Hezekiah S. Bundy (1817–1895) practiced law before and after his terms in the Ohio house (1848, 1850) and senate (1855) and U.S. House of Representatives (1865–67, 1873–75, 1893–95). *BDUSC.*

4. Bundy believed that the rejection of Turley had been a mistake and that, with some additional time, support for him would emerge and enable Turley to be approved. Therefore, Bundy urged McCulloch to stall before sending forth a new nomination. Bundy to McCulloch, Mar. 1, 1867, Appts., Internal Revenue Service, Assessor, Ohio, 11th Dist., John A. Turley, RG56, NA.

To the House of Representatives

MARCH 2, 1867.

The act entitled "An act making appropriations for the support of the Army for the year ending June 30, 1868, and for other purposes"[1] contains provisions to which I must call attention. Those provisions are contained in the second section,[2] which in certain cases virtually deprives the President of his constitutional functions as Commander in Chief of the Army, and in the sixth section,[3] which denies to ten States of this

Union their constitutional right to protect themselves in any emergency by means of their own militia. Those provisions are out of place in an appropriations act. I am compelled to defeat these necessary appropriations if I withhold my signature to the act. Pressed by these considerations, I feel constrained to return the bill with my signature, but to accompany it with my protest against the sections which I have indicated.

ANDREW JOHNSON.

Richardson, *Messages*, 6: 474.
   1. For the text of the act, see the *Congressional Globe*, 39 Cong., 2 Sess., Appendix, pp. 217–18.
   2. The second section required that all orders from the president or secretary of war must pass through the general of the army, and that the general of the army could not be removed without prior Senate approval.
   3. Section six formally disbanded the militia forces in the South that had been organized under President Johnson's provisional governors.

From Reverdy Johnson

Senate Chamber   2 March '67

My dear sir

If you would delay sending in another nomination for the Collectorship in Boston, for today I have reason to believe, that the Senators from Massts. would recede from their objections to Genl. Couch, the present incumbent.[1] The General served the Country so faithfully & gallantly during the war, & is so well fitted for the office that in Common with all your friends, I feel very solicitous in regd. to him.

Reverdy Johnson

ALS, OFH.
   1. On the very day of Reverdy Johnson's letter, the President submitted the name of Thomas Russell as collector to replace Darius N. Couch, who had been rejected on February 6. Ser. 6B, Vol. 4: 24, Johnson Papers, LC. For information about the attempt to place George Bancroft in this collector's post, see Bancroft to Johnson, Feb. 11, 1867.

From Reverdy Johnson

Senate Chamber   2 March '67

My Dear Sir

Mr Price[1] is rejected as Dist' Atty, tho' I Did all I could to prevent it.

I beg leave therefore again to recommend Mr Andrew Sterritt Ridgely[2] of Baltimore for an office.

He is, I know *Eminently* fit for the office & that he *will be confirmed.*

Redy Johnson

ALS, DLC-JP.
　　1. William H. Price (c1794–1868), a Baltimore lawyer, was nominated December 14,
1866, as U.S. district attorney for Maryland. However, the Senate rejected the nomination
on March 2. *NUC*; Ser. 6B, Vol. 4: 106, Johnson Papers, LC; Baltimore directories
(1858–69).
　　2. Ridgeley (1826–1877), an attorney, was Reverdy Johnson's son-in-law. He was
nominated and confirmed as district attorney on March 2, 1867. Ser. 6B, Vol. 4: 107,
Johnson Papers, LC; *NUC*; Beale, *Welles Diary*, 3: 55–56, 58–59; *Washington Evening
Star*, Mar. 5, 1867.

From Hugh McCulloch

Treasury Department. Mch. 2, 1867.

Dear Sir:—

　　I notice that you instructed me this morning to send you names for the
Collector of Internal Revenue and Naval Officer at San Francisco;[1] and
I deem it proper to say that while these nominations have been doubt-
less recommended by Mr. Conness they will not be very agreeable to Mr.
Cole.[2] Neither of these gentlemen are in sympathy with the adminis-
tration, but my opinion is that Mr. Cole stands much nearer to it than
Mr. Conness.

　　It is undoubtedly the desire of Mr. Conness that these nominations
should go to the Senate before Mr. Cole takes his seat;[3] and I submit to
you whether in this matter he is inclined to treat his colleague fairly.

H McCulloch.

ALS, OFH.
　　1. Frank Soulé was the collector of internal revenue at San Francisco at this time and
there is no indication of an attempt to replace him. Naval officer Noah Brooks had been
removed and his first potential replacement, Thomas Gray, had been rejected on March 1.
McCulloch then recommended Andrew J. Bryant. *U.S. Off. Reg.* (1865–67); Ser. 6B,
Vol. 4: 347, Johnson Papers, LC.
　　2. California's U.S. senators John Conness and Cornelius Cole.
　　3. Cole began serving his Senate term on March 4, 1867. Evidently McCulloch believed that Conness wanted to hurry the nominations through the Senate before Cole could
vote. Bryant was nominated, confirmed, and commissioned on March 2, 1867, and retained the post until late 1868 or early 1869. *BDUSC*; Ser. 6B, Vol. 4: 347, Johnson Papers, LC; San Francisco directories (1867–69).

From Hugh McCulloch

Treasury Department. Mch. 2, 1867.

My Dear Sir:—

　　Enclosed I hand you a telegram from Boston to which I *invite your
especial attention*.[1] If you are not inclined to send in Gov. Clifford's
name,[2] I advise the nomination of Judge Russell,[3] whose appointment
would, I think, be more satisfactory to the people generally than that of
Gov. C.

I also enclose a note from Mr. Buckalew[4] in regard to the assessorship of the 2nd. Dist. of Penn.

H McCulloch

ALS, OFH.
1. Not found.
2. The reference here is to John H. Clifford (1809–1876) who had applied for the position of collector of the port of Boston. Clifford had served one term as governor of Massachusetts in the 1850s. Subsequently, he served in the state senate until 1867, when he became president of the Boston and Providence Railroad. Sobel and Raimo, *Governors*, 2: 704–5.
3. Thomas Russell (1825–1887), a Boston lawyer who became justice of the state superior court in 1859. In the 1870s he served as minister to Venezuela. Russell was nominated as Boston collector and confirmed on March 2. *NCAB*, 13: 446; Ser. 6B, Vol. 4: 24, Johnson Papers, LC.
4. Charles R. Buckalew. The note has not been found.

From James W. Nesmith

Washington.   March 2d 1867

Sir,

On yesterday the Senate rejected Elwood Evans[1] for Secretary of Washington Territory, and George E Cole[2] for Governor of the same Territory. Those gentlemen were both good Union men during the war. They were rejected because they attended the Philadelphia convention.[3]

Efforts will be made by the present Delegate—Denney[4]—to secure the appointment of some two men who are your enemies to those places, and I desire in advance to caution you, and to protest against the appointment of—*Pickering* or *Calvin Hale*,[5] *to any position* in that Territory.

I would be obliged if you would nominate *Benjamin F Yantes* for Governor, and Thomas F McEllroy[6] for Secratary. They are both Conservative honest men, and your friends. They are old residents of Washington Territory.[7]

J W Nesmith

ALS, DNA-RG59, Lets. of Appl. and Recomm., 1861–69 (M650, Roll 31), Thomas F. McEllroy [*sic*].
1. Pennsylvania native Evans (1828–1898), a lawyer, went to the Oregon Territory in 1852 as deputy collector of customs for Puget Sound. He was appointed Washington territorial secretary in 1862 and was still holding the post in 1867, when his renomination was rejected by the Senate. He later served in the territorial house of representatives and as its chief clerk, and in 1889 published his important *History of the Pacific Northwest: Oregon and Washington*. John MacEachern, "Elwood Evans, Lawyer-Historian," *PNQ*, 52 (1961): 15–16; Hubert H. Bancroft, *History of Washington, Idaho, and Montana, 1845–1889* (San Francisco, 1890), 54, 219, 288; Pomeroy, *The Territories*, 120.
2. Cole (1826–1906) had mercantile and railroad interests. After living in Oregon for about ten years, where he was a member of the territorial legislature, clerk of the U.S. district court, and postmaster at Corvallis, he moved to the Washington Territory in 1860. A Democrat, Cole was elected territorial delegate and served from 1863 to 1865. Appointed territorial governor by Johnson on November 21, 1866, he served several months until his

rejection by the Senate. After this debacle he moved back to Oregon and eventually served as Portland's postmaster (1873–81). Thomas A. McMullin and David Walker, *Biographical Directory of American Territorial Governors* (Westport, 1984), 317–18; Bancroft, *Washington, Idaho, and Montana*, 264–66.

3. Evans did attend the National Union Convention. Elizabeth M. Allison and W. A. Katz, "Thornton Fleming McElroy—Printer, Politician, Businessman," *PNQ*, 54 (1963): 61.

4. Arthur A. Denny (1822–1899), Washington territorial delegate (1865–67), had moved from Illinois to the Pacific Northwest in 1851. He was a member of the Washington territorial house of representatives (1853–61), as well as the territorial council (1862–63), and held the post of register of the land office in Olympia (1861–65). After completing his term as delegate he became involved in banking. *BDUSC.*

5. William Pickering (1798–1873) moved from England to Illinois in 1821, where he engaged in farming, civil engineering, and Whig/Republican politics. Lincoln appointed him territorial governor of Washington in December 1861. He arrived in the territory in June 1862 and held office until removed by Johnson in November 1866 for criticizing Reconstruction policies. Hale (*c*1818–*fl*1870), a native of Maine and a farmer, was a member of the territorial house of representatives, a regent of the university in Seattle, and territorial superintendent of Indian affairs (1862–64). McMullin and Walker, *Territorial Governors*, 316–17; Bancroft, *Washington, Idaho, and Montana*, 73, 215, 219; Hill, *Indian Affairs*, 197; 1860 Census, Wash., Thurston, 205; (1870), Thurston, Olympia, 235.

6. Yantis (1807–1879) served as justice of the peace and Washington territorial legislator, as well as Idaho territorial legislator. Thornton F. McElroy (*c*1824–1885) was a printer and a political wheeler and dealer, especially when trying to secure the territorial printing contracts. He served in the territorial legislature, as deputy collector of internal revenue, and as mayor of Olympia (1875). Bancroft, *Washington, Idaho, and Montana*, 64; Allison and Katz, "Thornton Fleming McElroy," 54–65.

7. McElroy arrived in the Pacific Northwest in 1849 and Yantis came in 1852. Johnson did not nominate either of them. This is a prime example of the interference of Oregon officials in the affairs of neighboring territories. Ibid., 54–55; Bancroft, *Washington, Idaho, and Montana*, 64.

From Dorsey B. Thomas

Washington City D.C.   Mch 2d 1867

Respected Sir

Knowing the deep solicitude you feel for the peace of the whole country and especially for our own state I venture to write you.

Brownlow has declared his purpose to organize the militia of the State and the Legislature has by resolution called upon Gen Thomas for troops to help keep the peace of the State.[1]

Every body in Tennessee knows there is no necessity for either. The request for U.S. troops is only to secure themselves to those who complain about the expense of keeping up the malitia,—"that they could not get U.S. troops and hence are compelled to rely upon home malitia." The regular troops will be welcomed by the people of the state and will be a protection against Brownlow's faction;—the malitia will be made up of renegade rebels and thieves, under the lead of Brownlow's satrap who will seek to control by violence the coming election. This will surely lead to strife and to what extent no one can tell. Would it not be better to send the regular troops?

My earnest desire to preserve peace in our State and to afford protec-

tion to all black and white have prompted me to thus obtrude myself
upon you.

D. B. Thomas

ALS, DLC-JP.
    1. On February 28 the Tennessee legislature adopted resolutions requesting the gover-
nor to seek federal troops from General Thomas in order "to keep the peace and restore
order and quiet in our State." The governor transmitted this request to Thomas on March
1, who then replied six days later. The general indicated that his troops could assist civil
authorities in maintaining law and order at those localities designated by the governor.
General Thomas subsequently forwarded the Tennessee resolutions and Brownlow's letter
to Edward D. Townsend in Washington. Joint Resolution of the General Assembly of the
State of Tennessee, Feb. 28, 1867; Brownlow to Thomas, Mar. 1, 1867; Thomas to
Brownlow, Mar. 7, 1867; Thomas to Assistant Adjutant General, Mar. 12, 1867, Johnson
Papers, LC.

Veto of the First Military Reconstruction Act

WASHINGTON, *March* 2, 1867.

TO THE HOUSE OF REPRESENTATIVES:

I have examined the bill "to provide for the more efficient government
of the rebel States" with the care and anxiety which its transcendent importance is calculated to awaken. I am unable to give it my assent for reasons so grave, that I hope a statement of them may have some influence on
the minds of the patriotic and enlightened men with whom the decision
must ultimately rest.

The bill places all the people of the ten States therein named under the
absolute domination of military rulers; and the preamble undertakes to
give the reason upon which the measure is based, and the ground upon
which it is justified. It declares that there exists in these States no legal
Governments, and no adequate protection for life or property, and asserts
the necessity of enforcing peace and good order within their limits. Is this
true as matter of fact?

It is not denied that the States in question have each of them an actual
Government, with all the powers, executive, judicial, and legislative,
which properly belong to a free State. They are organized like the other
States of the Union, and, like them, they make, administer, and execute
the laws which concern their domestic affairs. And existing *de facto* Government, exercising such functions as these, is itself the law of the State
upon all matters within its jurisdiction. To pronounce the supreme law-
making power of an established State illegal, is to say that law itself is
unlawful.

The provisions which these Governments have made for the preservation of order, the suppression of crime, and the redress of private injuries,
are in substance and principle the same as those which prevail in the
Northern States and in other civilized countries. They certainly have not
succeeded in preventing the commission of all crime, nor has this been

accomplished anywhere in the world. There, as well as elsewhere, offenders sometimes escape for want of vigorous prosecution, and occasionally, perhaps, by the inefficiency of courts or the prejudice of jurors. It is undoubtedly true that these evils have been much increased and aggravated, North and South, by the demoralizing influences of civil war, and by the rancorous passions which the contest has engendered. But that these people are maintaining local Governments for themselves which habitually defeat the object of all government and render their own lives and property insecure, is in itself utterly improbable, and the averment of the bill to that effect is not supported by any evidence which has come to my knowledge. All the information I have on the subject convinces me that the masses of the Southern people and those who control their public acts, while they entertain diverse opinions on questions of Federal policy, are completely united in the effort to reorganize their society on the basis of peace, and to restore their mutual prosperity as rapidly and as completely as their circumstances will permit.

The bill, however, would seem to show upon its face that the establishment of peace and good order is not its real object. The fifth section declares that the preceding sections shall cease to operate in any State where certain events shall have happened. These events are—First, the selection of delegates to a State Convention by an election at which negroes shall be allowed to vote. Second, the formation of a State Constitution by the Convention so chosen. Third, the insertion into the State Constitution of a provision which will secure the right of voting at all elections to negroes, and to such white men as may not be disfranchised for rebellion or felony. Fourth, the submission of the Constitution for ratification to negroes and white men not disfranchised, and its actual ratification by their vote. Fifth, the submission of the State Constitution to Congress for examination and approval, and the actual approval of it by that body. Sixth, the adoption of a certain amendment to the Federal Constitution by a vote of the legislature elected under the new Constitution. Seventh, the adoption of said amendment by a sufficient number of other States to make it a part of the Constitution of the United States. All these conditions must be fulfilled before the people of any of these States can be relieved from the bondage of military domination; but when they are fulfilled, then immediately the pains and penalties of the bill are to cease, no matter whether there be peace and order or not, and without any reference to the security of life or property. The excuse given for the bill in the preamble is admitted by the bill itself not to be real. The military rule which it establishes is plainly to be used—not for any purpose of order or for the prevention of crime, but solely as a means of coercing the people into the adoption of principles and measures to which it is known that they are opposed, and upon which they have an undeniable right to exercise their own judgment.

I submit to Congress whether this measure is not, in its whole character, scope, and object, without precedent and without authority, in palpable conflict with the plainest provisions of the Constitution, and utterly destructive to those great principles of liberty and humanity for which our ancestors on both sides of the Atlantic have shed so much blood and expended so much treasure.

The ten States named in the bill are divided into five districts. For each district an officer of the army, not below the rank of brigadier general, is to be appointed to rule over the people; and he is to be supported with an efficient military force to enable him to perform his duties and enforce his authority. Those duties and that authority, as defined by the third section of the bill, are, "to protect all persons in their rights of person and property, to suppress insurrection, disorder, and violence, and to punish or cause to be punished all disturbers of the public peace or criminals." The power thus given to the commanding officer over all the people of each district is that of an absolute monarch. His mere will is to take the place of all law. The law of the States is now the only rule applicable to the subjects placed under his control, and that is completely displaced by the clause which declares all interference of State authority to be null and void. He alone is permitted to determine what are rights of person or property, and he may protect them in such way as in his discretion may seem proper. It places at his free disposal all the lands and goods in his district, and he may distribute them without let or hindrance to whom he pleases. Being bound by no State law, and there being no other law to regulate the subject, he may make a criminal code of his own; and he can make it as bloody as any recorded in history, or he can reserve the privilege of acting upon the impulse of his private passions in each case that arises. He is bound by no rules of evidence; there is indeed no provision by which he is authorized or required to take any evidence at all. Everything is a crime which he chooses to call so, and all persons are condemned whom he pronounces to be guilty. He is not bound to keep any record, or make any report of his proceedings. He may arrest his victims wherever he finds them, without warrant, accusation or proof of probable cause. If he gives them a trial before he inflicts the punishment, he gives it of his grace and mercy, not because he is commanded so to do.

To a casual reader of the bill, it might seem that some kind of trial was secured by it to persons accused of crime; but such is not the case. The officer "may allow local civil tribunals to try offenders," but of course this does not require that he shall do so. If any State or Federal court presumes to exercise its legal jurisdiction by the trial of a malefactor without his special permission, he can break it up, and punish the judges and jurors as being themselves malefactors. He can save his friends from justice, and despoil his enemies contrary to justice.

It is also provided that "he shall have power to organize military commissions or tribunals;" but this power he is not commanded to exercise. It is merely permissive, and is to be used only "when in his judgment it may be necessary for the trial of offenders." Even if the sentence of a commission were made a prerequisite to the punishment of a party, it would be scarcely the slightest check upon the officer, who has authority to organize it as he pleases, prescribe its mode of proceeding, appoint its members from among his own subordinates, and revise all its decisions. Instead of mitigating the harshness of his single rule, such a tribunal would be used much more probably to divide the responsibility of making it more cruel and unjust.

Several provisions, dictated by the humanity of Congress, have been inserted in the bill, apparently to restrain the power of the commanding officer; but it seems to me that they are of no avail for that purpose. The fourth section provides—*First*. That trials shall not be unnecessarily delayed; but I think I have shown that the power is given to punish without trial, and if so, this provision is practically inoperative. *Second*. Cruel or unusual punishment is not to be inflicted; but who is to decide what is cruel and what is unusual? The words have acquired a legal meaning by long use in the courts. Can it be expected that military officers will understand or follow a rule expressed in language so purely technical, and not pertaining in the least degree to their profession? If not, then each officer may define cruelty according to his own temper, and if it is not usual, he will make it usual. Corporal punishment, imprisonment, the gag, the ball and chain, and the almost insupportable forms of torture invented for military punishment, lie within the range of choice. *Third*. The sentence of a commission is not to be executed without being approved by the commander, if it affects life or liberty, and a sentence of death must be approved by the President. This applies to cases in which there has been a trial and sentence. I take it to be clear, under this bill, that the military commander may condemn to death without even the form of a trial by a military commission, so that the life of the condemned may depend upon the will of two men, instead of one.

It is plain that the authority here given to the military officer amounts to absolute despotism. But, to make it still more unendurable, the bill provides that it may be delegated to as many subordinates as he chooses to appoint; for it declares that he shall "punish or cause to be punished." Such a power has not been wielded by any monarch in England for more than five hundred years. In all that time no people who speak the English language have borne such servitude. It reduces the whole population of the ten States—all persons, of every color, sex, and condition, and every stranger within their limits—to the most abject and degrading slavery. No master ever had a control so absolute over his slaves as this bill gives to the military officers over both white and colored persons.

It may be answered to this that the officers of the army are too magnanimous, just, and humane to oppress and trample upon a subjugated people. I do not doubt that army officers are as well entitled to this kind of confidence as any other class of men. But the history of the world has been written in vain, if it does not teach us that unrestrained authority can never be safely trusted in human hands. It is almost sure to be more or less abused under any circumstances, and it has always resulted in gross tyranny where the rulers who exercise it are strangers to their subjects, and come among them as the representatives of a distant power, and more especially when the power that sends them is unfriendly. Governments closely resembling that here proposed have been fairly tried in Hungary and Poland, and the suffering endured by those people roused the sympathies of the entire world. It was tried in Ireland, and, though tempered at first by principles of English law, it gave birth to cruelties so atrocious that they are never recounted without just indignation. The French Convention armed its deputies with this power, and sent them to the Southern departments of the Republic. The massacres, murders, and other atrocities which they committed show what the passions of the ablest men in the most civilized society will tempt them to do when wholly unrestrained by law.

The men of our race in every age have struggled to tie up the hands of their Governments and keep them within the law; because their own experience of all mankind taught them that rulers could not be relied on to concede those rights which they were not legally bound to respect. The head of a great empire has sometimes governed it with a mild and paternal sway; but the kindness of an irresponsible deputy never yields what the law does not extort from him. Between such a master and the people subjected to his domination there can be nothing but enmity; he punishes them if they resist his authority, and, if they submit to it, he hates them for their servility.

I come now to a question which is, if possible, still more important. Have we the power to establish and carry into execution a measure like this? I answer, certainly not, if we derive our authority from the Constitution, and if we are bound by the limitations which it imposes.

This proposition is perfectly clear—that no branch of the Federal Government, executive, legislative, or judicial, can have any just powers, except those which it derives through and exercise under the organic law of the Union. Outside of the Constitution, we have no legal authority more than private citizens, and within it we have only so much as that instrument gives us. This broad principle limits all our functions, and applies to all subjects. It protects not only the citizens of States which are within the Union, but it shields every human being who comes or is brought under our jurisdiction. We have no right to do in one place, more than in another, that which the Constitution says we shall not do at all. If, therefore, the Southern States were in truth out of the Union, we could not treat their people in a way which the fundamental law forbids.

Some persons assume that the success of our arms in crushing the opposition which was made in some of the States to the execution of the Federal laws, reduced those States and all their people—the innocent as well as the guilty—to the condition of vassalage, and gave us a power over them which the Constitution does not bestow, or define, or limit. No fallacy can be more transparent than this. Our victories subjected the insurgents to legal obedience, not to the yoke of an arbitrary despotism. When an absolute sovereign reduces his rebellious subjects, he may deal with them according to his pleasure, because he had that power before. But when a limited monarch puts down an insurrection, he must still govern according to law. If an insurrection should take place in one of our States against the authority of the State Government, and end in the overthrow of those who planned it, would that take away the rights of all the people of the counties where it was favored by a part or a majority of the population? Could they, for such a reason, be wholly outlawed and deprived of their representation in the Legislature? I have always contended that the Government of the United States was sovereign within its constitutional sphere; that it executed its laws, like the States themselves, by applying its coercive power directly to individuals; and that it could put down insurrection with the same effect as a State, and no other. The opposite doctrine is the worst heresy of those who advocated secession, and cannot be agreed to without admitting that heresy to be right.

Invasion, insurrection, rebellion, and domestic violence were anticipated when the Government was framed, and the means of repelling and suppressing them were wisely provided for in the Constitution; but it was not thought necessary to declare that the States in which they might occur should be expelled from the Union. Rebellions, which were invariably suppressed, occurred prior to that out of which these questions grow; but the States continued to exist and the Union remained unbroken. In Massachusetts, in Pennsylvania, in Rhode Island, and in New York, at different periods in our history, violent and armed opposition to the United States was carried on; but the relations of those States with the Federal Government were not supposed to be interrupted or changed thereby, after the rebellious portions of their population were defeated and put down. It is true that in these earlier cases there was no formal expression of a determination to withdraw from the Union, but it is also true that in the Southern States the ordinances of secession were treated by all the friends of the Union as mere nullities, and are now acknowledged to be so by the States themselves. If we admit that they had any force or validity, or that they did in fact take the States in which they were passed out of the Union, we sweep from under our feet all the grounds upon which we stand in justifying the use of Federal force to maintain the integrity of the Government.

This is a bill passed by Congress in time of peace. There is not in any one of the States brought under its operation either war or insurrection. The laws of the States and of the Federal Government are all in undisturbed and harmonious operation. The courts, State and Federal, are open, and in the full exercise of their proper authority. Over every State comprised in these five military districts, life, liberty, and property are secured by State laws and Federal laws, and the National Constitution is everywhere in force and everywhere obeyed. What, then, is the ground on which this bill proceeds? The title of the bill announces that it is intended "for the more efficient government" of these ten States. It is recited by way of preamble that no legal State Governments, "nor adequate protection for life or property," exist in those States, and that peace and good order should be thus enforced. The first thing which arrests attention upon these recitals, which prepare the way for martial law, is this—that the only foundation upon which martial law can exist under our form of government is not stated or so much as pretended. Actual war, foreign invasion, domestic insurrection—none of these appear; and none of these in fact exist. It is not even recited that any sort of war or insurrection is threatened. Let us pause here to consider, upon this question of constitutional law and the power of Congress, a recent decision of the Supreme Court of the United States in *ex parte* Milligan.

I will first quote from the opinion of the majority of the Court: "Martial law cannot arise from a threatened invasion. The necessity must be actual and present, the invasion real, such as effectually closes the courts and deposes the civil administration." We see that martial law comes in only when actual war closes the courts and deposes the civil authority; but this bill, in time of peace, makes martial law operate as though we were in actual war, and become the *cause*, instead of the *consequence* of the abrogation of civil authority. One more quotation: "It follows from what has been said on this subject that there are occasions when martial law can be properly applied. If in foreign invasion or civil war the courts are actually closed, and it is impossible to administer criminal justice according to law, *then*, on the theatre of active military operations, where war really prevails, there is a necessity to furnish a substitute for the civil authority, thus overthrown, to preserve the safety of the army and society; and as no power is left but the military, if is allowed to govern by martial rule until the laws can have their free course."

I now quote from the opinion of the minority of the Court, delivered by Chief Justice Chase: "We by no means assert that Congress can establish and apply the laws of war where no war has been declared or exists. Where peace exists, the laws of peace must prevail." This is sufficiently explicit. Peace exists in all the territory to which this bill applies. It asserts a power in Congress, in time of peace, to set aside the laws of peace and to substitute the laws of war. The minority, concurring with the majority, declares that Congress does not possess that power. Again, and, if possible, more emphatically, the Chief Justice, with remarkable clearness and condensation, sums up the whole matter as follows:

"There are under the Constitution three kinds of military jurisdiction—one to be exercised both in peace and war; another to be exercised in time of foreign war without the boundaries of the United States, or in time of rebellion and civil war within States or districts occupied by rebels treated as belligerents; and a third to be exercised in time of invasion or insurrection within the limits of the United States, or during rebellion within the limits of the States maintaining adhesion to the National Government, when the public danger requires its exercise. The first of these may be called jurisdiction under MILITARY LAW, and is found in acts of Congress prescribing rule and articles of war, or otherwise providing for the government of the national forces; the second may be distinguished as MILITARY GOVERNMENT, superseding, as far as may be deemed expedient, the local law, and exercised by the military commander under the direction of the President, with the express or implied sanction of Congress; while the third may be denominated MARTIAL LAW PROPER, and is called into action by Congress, or temporarily, when the action of Congress cannot be invited, and in the case of justifying or excusing peril, by the President, in times of insurrection or invasion or of civil or foreign war, within districts or localities where ordinary law no longer adequately secures public safety and private rights."

It will be observed that of the three kinds of military jurisdiction which can be exercised or created under our Constitution, there is but one that can prevail in time of peace, and that is the code of laws enacted by Congress for the government of the national forces. That body of military law has no application to the citizen, nor even to the citizen soldier enrolled in the militia in time of peace. But this bill is not a part of that sort of military law, for that applies only to the soldier and not to the citizen, whilst, contrariwise, the military law provided by this bill applies only to the citizen and not to the soldier.

I need not say to the Representatives of the American people that their Constitution forbids the exercise of judicial power in any way but one— that is by the ordained and established courts. It is equally well known that in all criminal cases a trial by jury is made indispensable by the express words of that instrument. I will not enlarge on the inestimable value of the right thus secured to every freeman, or speak of the danger to public liberty in all parts of the country which must ensue from a denial of it anywhere or upon any pretence. A very recent decision of the Supreme Court has traced the history, vindicated the dignity, and made known the value of this great privilege so clearly that nothing more is needed. To what extent a violation of it might be excused in time of war or public danger may admit of discussion, but we are providing now for a time of profound peace, where there is not an armed soldier within our borders except those who are in the service of the Government. It is in such a condition of things that an act of Congress is proposed which, if carried out, would deny a trial by the lawful courts and juries to nine millions of American citizens, and to their posterity for an indefinite period. It seems to be scarcely possible that any one should seriously believe this consistent with a Constitution which declares, in simple, plain, and unambiguous language, that all persons shall have that right, and that no person shall ever in any case be deprived of it. The Constitution also forbids the arrest of the citizen without judicial warrant, founded on probable cause. This bill authorizes an arrest without warrant, at the pleasure of a military commander. The Constitution declares that "no person shall be held to answer for a capital or otherwise infamous crime unless on presentment by a grand jury." This bill holds every person, not a soldier, answerable for all crimes and all charges without any presentment. The Constitution declares that "no person shall be deprived of life, liberty, or property without due process of law." This bill sets aside all process of law, and makes the citizen answerable in his person and property to the will of one man, and as to his life to the will of two. Finally, the Constitution declares that "the privilege of the writ of *habeas corpus* shall not be suspended unless when, in case of rebellion or invasion, the public safety may require it;" whereas this bill declares martial law (which of itself suspends this great writ) in time of peace, and authorizes the military to make the arrest, and gives to the prisoner only one privilege, and that is a trial "without unnecessary delay." He has no hope of release from custody, except the hope, such as it is, of release by acquittal before a military commission.

The United States are bound to guarantee to each State a republican form of government. Can it be pretended that this obligation is not palpably broken if we carry out a measure like this, which wipes away every vestige of republican government in ten States, and puts the life, property, liberty, and honor of all the people in each of them under the domination of a single person clothed with unlimited authority?

The Parliament of England, exercising the omnipotent power which it claimed, was accustomed to pass bills of attainder; that is to say, it would convict men of treason and other crimes by legislative enactment. The person accused had a hearing, sometimes a patient and fair one; but generally party prejudice prevailed, instead of justice. It often became necessary for Parliament to acknowledge its error and reverse its own action. The fathers of our country determined that no such thing should occur here. They withheld the power from Congress, and thus forbade its exercise by that body; and they provided in the Constitution that no State should pass any bill of attainder. It is, therefore, impossible for any person in this country to be constitutionally convicted or punished for any crime by a legislative proceeding of any sort. Nevertheless, here is a bill of attainder against nine millions of people at once. It is based upon an accusation so vague as to be scarcely intelligible, and found to be true upon no credible evidence. Not one of the nine millions was heard in his own defence. The representatives of the doomed parties were excluded from all participation in the trial. The conviction is to be followed by the most ignominious punishment ever inflicted on large masses of men. It disfranchises them by hundred of thousands, and degrades them all—even those who are admitted to be guiltless—from the rank of freemen to the condition of slaves.

The purpose and object of the bill—the general intent which pervades it from beginning to end—is to change the entire structure and character of the State Governments, and to compel them by force to the adoption of organic laws and regulations which they are unwilling to accept, if left to themselves. The negroes have not asked for the privilege of voting—the vast majority of them have no idea what it means. This bill not only thrusts it into their hands, but compels them, as well as the whites, to use it in a particular way. If they do not form a Constitution with prescribed articles in it, and afterwards elect a Legislature which will act upon certain measures in a prescribed way, neither blacks nor whites can be relieved from the slavery which the bill imposes upon them. Without pausing here to consider the policy or impolicy of Africanizing the Southern part of our territory, I would simply ask the attention of Congress to that manifest, well-known, and universally acknowledged rule of constitutional law, which declares that the Federal Government has no jurisdiction, authority, or power to regulate such subjects for any State. To force the right of suffrage out of the hands of the white people and into the hands of the negroes is an arbitrary violation of this principle.

This bill imposes martial law at once, and its operations will begin so soon as the General and his troops can be put in place. The dread alternative between its harsh rule and compliance with the terms of this measure is not suspended, nor are the people afforded any time for free deliberation. The bill says to them, take martial law first, *then* deliberate. And when they have done all that this measure requires them to do, other conditions and contingencies, over which they have no control, yet remain to be fulfilled before they can be relieved from martial law. Another Congress must first approve the Constitutions made in conformity with the will of this Congress, and must declare these States entitled to representation in both Houses. The whole question thus remains open and unsettled, and must again occupy the attention of Congress, and in the meantime the agitation which now prevails will continue to disturb all portions of the people.

The bill also denies the legality of the Governments of ten of the States which participated in the ratification of the amendment to the Federal Constitution abolishing slavery forever within the jurisdiction of the United States, and practically excludes them from the Union. If this assumption of the bill be correct, their concurrence cannot be considered as having been legally given, and the important fact is made to appear that the consent of three-fourths of the States—the requisite number—has not been constitutionally obtained to the ratification of that amendment, thus leaving the question of slavery where it stood before the amendment was officially declared to have become a part of the Constitution.

That the measure proposed by this bill does violate the Constitution in the particulars mentioned, and in many other ways which I forbear to enumerate, is too clear to admit of the least doubt. It only remains to consider whether the injunctions of that instrument ought to be obeyed or not. I think they ought to be obeyed, for reasons which I will proceed to give as briefly as possible.

In the first place, it is the only system of free government which we can hope to have as a nation. When it ceases to be the rule of our conduct, we may perhaps take our choice between complete anarchy, a consolidated despotism, and a total dissolution of the Union; but national liberty, regulated by law, will have passed beyond our reach.

It is the best frame of government the world ever saw. No other is or can be so well adapted to the genius, habits, or wants of the American people. Combining the strength of a great empire with unspeakable blessings of local self-government—having a central power to defend the general interests, and recognizing the authority of the States as the guardians of industrial rights, it is "the sheet-anchor of our safety abroad and our peace at home." It was ordained "to form a more perfect union, establish justice, insure domestic tranquillity, promote the general welfare, provide for the common defence, and secure the blessings of liberty to ourselves and our posterity." These great ends have been attained heretofore, and will be again, by faithful obedience to it, but they are certain to be lost if we treat with disregard its sacred obligations.

It was to punish the gross crime of defying the Constitution, and to vindicate its supreme authority, that we carried on a bloody war of four years' duration. Shall we now acknowledge that we sacrificed a million of lives and expended billions of treasure to enforce a Constitution which is not worthy of respect and preservation?

Those who advocated the right of secession alleged in their own justification that we had no regard for law, and that their rights of property, life, and liberty would not be safe under the Constitution, as administered by us. If we now verify their assertion, we prove that they were in truth and in fact fighting for their liberty, and instead of branding their leaders with the dishonoring name of traitors against a righteous and legal Government, we elevate them in history to the rank of self-sacrificing patriots, consecrate them to the admiration of the world, and place them by the side of Washington, Hampden, and Sydney.[1] No, let us leave them to the infamy they deserve, punish them as they should be punished, according to law, and take upon ourselves no share of the odium which they should bear alone.

It is a part of our public history which can never be forgotten that both Houses of Congress in July, 1861, declared in the form of a solemn resolution that the war was and should be carried on for no purpose of subjugation, but solely to enforce the Constitution and laws; and that when this was yielded by the parties in rebellion, the contest should cease, with the constitutional rights of the States and of individuals unimpaired.[2] This resolution was adopted and sent forth to the world unanimously by the Senate, and with only two dissenting voices in the House. It was accepted by the friends of the Union in the South, as well as in the North, as expressing honestly and truly the object of the war. On the faith of it, many thousands of persons in both sections gave their lives and their fortunes to the cause. To repudiate it now by refusing to the States and to the individuals within them the rights which the Constitution and laws of the Union would secure to them, is a breach of our plighted honor for which I can imagine no excuse, and to which I cannot voluntarily become a party.

The evils which spring from the unsettled state of our Government will be acknowledged by all. Commercial intercourse is impeded, capital is in constant peril, public securities fluctuate in value, peace itself is not secure, and the sense of moral and political duty is impaired. To avert these calamities from our country, it is imperatively required that we should immediately decide upon some course of administration which can be steadfastly adhered to. I am thoroughly convinced that any settlement, or compromise, or plan of action which is inconsistent with the principles of the Constitution will not only be unavailing, but mischievous; that it will but multiply the present evils, instead of removing them. The Constitution, in its whole integrity and vigor, throughout the length and breadth of the land, is the best of all compromises. Besides, our duty does not, in my judgment, leave us a choice between that and any other. I believe that it contains the remedy that is so much needed, and that if the co-ordinate branches of the Government would unite upon its provisions, they would be found broad enough and strong enough to sustain in time of peace the nation which they bore safely through the ordeal of a protracted civil war. Among the most sacred guaranties of that instrument are those which declare that "each State shall have at least one Representative," and that "no State, without its consent, shall be deprived of its equal suffrage in the Senate." Each House is made the "judge of the elections, returns, and qualifications of its own members," and may, "with the concurrence of two-thirds, expel a member." Thus, as heretofore urged, "in the admission of Senators and Representatives from any and all of the States, there can be no just ground of apprehension that persons who are disloyal will be clothed with the powers of legislation; for this could not happen when the Constitution and the laws are enforced by a vigilant and faithful Congress." "When a Senator or Representative presents his certificate of election, he may at once be admitted or rejected; or, should there be any question as to his eligibility, his credentials may be referred for investigation to the appropriate committee. If admitted to a seat, it must be upon evidence satisfactory to the House of which he thus becomes a member, that he possesses the requisite constitutional and legal qualifications. If refused admission as a member for want of due allegiance to the Government, and returned to his constituents, they are admonished that none but persons loyal to the United States will be allowed a voice in the Legislative Councils of the Nation, and the political power and moral influence of Congress are thus effectively exerted in the interests of loyalty to the Government and fidelity to the Union." And is it not far better that the work of restoration should be accomplished by simple compliance with the plain requirements of the Constitution, than by a recourse to measures which in effect destroy the States, and threaten the subversion of the General Government? All that is necessary to settle this simple but important question, without further agitation or delay, is a willingness on the part of all to sustain the Constitution and carry its provisions into practical operation. If to-morrow either branch of Congress would declare that, upon the presentation of their credentials, members constitutionally elected and loyal to the General Government would be admitted to seats in Congress, while all others would be excluded, and their places remain vacant until the selection by the people of loyal and qualified persons; and if, at the same time, assurance were given that this policy would be continued until all the States were represented in Congress, it would send a thrill of joy throughout the entire land, as indicating the inauguration of a system which must speedily bring tranquillity to the public mind.

While we are legislating upon subjects which are of great importance to the whole people, and which must affect all parts of the country, not only during the life of the present generation, but for ages to come, we should remember that all men are entitled at least to a hearing in the councils which decide upon the destiny of themselves and their children. At present ten States are denied representation, and when the Fortieth Congress assembles on the fourth day of the present month, sixteen States will be without a voice in the House of Representatives. This grave fact, with the important questions before us, should induce us to pause in a course of legislation which, looking solely to the attainment of political ends, fails to consider the rights it trangresses, the law which it violates, or the institutions which it imperils.[3]

ANDREW JOHNSON.

PD, Johnson-Bartlett Col., Greeneville.

1. George Washington, John Hampden, and Algernon Sidney (or Sydney). Hampden (1594–1643), a leader in the English Parliament, was imprisoned for refusing to support various revenue schemes of Charles I. Attempts to arrest him and others precipitated events that led to the English Civil War. Sidney (1622–1683) served in the parliamentary forces during the English Civil War and was later a member of the Council of State during the Commonwealth. An opponent of Cromwell's dictatorship, Sidney left England, only to return after the Restoration. Soon he became imbroiled in plots against Charles II and was executed for treason in 1683. *The New Columbia Encyclopedia* (1975).

2. See Remarks on War Aims Resolution, July 25, 1861, *Johnson Papers*, 4: 597–99.

3. On March 30 a joint resolution of Congress authorized appropriations sufficient to implement the terms of the First Military Reconstruction Act, provided that the amount did not exceed $500,000. Johnson gave his approval to the joint resolution largely because he liked the limitation upon expenditures stipulated by the resolution. See *U.S. Statutes at Large*, 15: 29; Johnson to House of Representatives, Mar. 30, 1867, Richardson, *Messages*, 6: 521.

Veto of the Tenure of Office Act

WASHINGTON, *March 2, 1867.*

To the Senate of the United States:

I have carefully examined the bill "to regulate the tenure of certain civil offices." The material portion of the bill is contained in the first section, and is of the effect following, namely:

> That every person holding any civil office to which he has been appointed, by and with the advice and consent of the Senate, and every person who shall hereafter be appointed to any such office and shall become duly qualified to act therein, is and shall be entitled to hold such office until a successor shall have been appointed by the President, with the advice and consent of the Senate, and duly qualified; and that the Secretaries of State, of the Treasury, of War, of the Navy, and of the Interior, the Postmaster-General, and the Attorney-General shall hold their offices respectively for and during the term of the President by whom they may have been appointed and for one month thereafter, subject to removal by and with the advice and consent of the Senate.

These provisions are qualified by a reservation in the fourth section, "that nothing contained in the bill shall be construed to extend the term of any office the duration of which is limited by law." In effect the bill provides that the President shall not remove from their places any of the civil officers whose terms of service are not limited by law without the advice and consent of the Senate of the United States. The bill in this respect conflicts, in my judgment, with the Constitution of the United States. The question, as Congress is well aware, is by no means a new one. That the power of removal is constitutionally vested in the President of the United States is a principle which has been not more distinctly declared by judicial authority and judicial commentators than it has been uniformly practiced upon by the legislative and executive departments of the Government. The question arose in the House of Representatives so early as the 16th of June, 1789, on the bill for establishing an Executive Department denominated "the Department of Foreign Affairs."[1] The first clause of the bill, after recapitulating the functions of that officer and defining his duties, had these words: "To be removable from office by the President of the United States." It was moved to strike out these words and the motion was sustained with great ability and vigor. It was insisted that the President could not constitutionally exercise the power of removal exclusively of the Senate; that the Federalist so interpreted the Constitution when arguing for its adoption by the several States; that the Constitution had nowhere given the President power of removal, either expressly or by strong implication, but, on the contrary, had distinctly provided for removals from office by impeachment only.

A construction which denied the power of removal by the President was further maintained by arguments drawn from the danger of the abuse of the power; from the supposed tendency of an exposure of public officers to capricious removal to impair the efficiency of the civil service; from the alleged injustice and hardship of displacing incumbents dependent upon their official stations without sufficient consideration; from a supposed want of responsibility on the part of the President, and from an imagined defect of guaranties against a vicious President who might incline to abuse the Power. On the other hand, an exclusive power of removal by the President was defended as a true exposition of the text of the Constitution. It was maintained that there are certain causes for which persons ought to be removed from office without being guilty of treason, bribery, or malfeasance, and that the nature of things demands that it should be so. "Suppose," it was said, "a man becomes insane by the visitation of God and is likely to ruin our affairs; are the hands of the Government to be confined from warding off the evil? Suppose a person in office not possessing the talents he was judged to have at the time of the appointment; is the error not to be corrected? Suppose he acquires vicious habits and incurable indolence or total neglect of the duties of his office, which shall work mischief to the public welfare; is there no way to arrest the threatened danger? Suppose he becomes odious and unpopular by reason of the measures he pursues—and this he may do without committing any positive offense against the law; must he preserve his office in despite of the popular will? Suppose him grasping for his own aggrandizement and the elevation of his connections by every means short of the treason defined by the Constitution, hurrying your affairs to the precipice of destruction, endangering your domestic tranquillity, plundering you of the means of defense, alienating the affections of your allies and promoting the spirit of discord; must the tardy, tedious, desultory road by way of impeachment be traveled to overtake the man who, barely confining himself within the letter of the law, is employed in drawing off the vital principle of the Government? The nature of things, the great objects of society, the express objects of the Constitution itself, require that this thing should be otherwise. To unite the Senate with the President in the exercise of the Power," it was said, "would involve us in the most serious difficulty. Suppose a discovery of any of those events should take place when the Senate is not in session; how is the remedy to be applied? The evil could be avoided in no other way than by the Senate sitting always." In regard to the danger of the power being abused if exercised by one man it was said "that the danger is as great with respect to the Senate, who are assembled from various parts of the continent, with different impressions and opinions;" "that such a body is more likely to misuse the power of removal than the man whom the united voice of America calls to the Presidential chair. As the nature of government requires the power of removal," it was maintained "that it should be exercised in this way by the hand capable of exerting itself with effect; and the power must be conferred on the President by the Constitution as the executive officer of the Government."[2]

Mr. Madison, whose adverse opinion in the Federalist had been relied upon by those who denied the exclusive power, now participated in the debate. He declared that he had reviewed his former opinions, and he summed up the whole case as follows:

The Constitution affirms that the executive power is vested in the President. Are there exceptions to this proposition? Yes; there are. The Constitution says that in appointing to office the Senate shall be associated with the President, unless in the case of inferior officers, when the law shall otherwise direct. Have we (that is, Congress) a right to extend this exception? I believe not. If the Constitution has invested all executive power in the President, I venture to assert that the Legislature has no right to diminish or modify his executive authority. The question now resolves itself into this: Is the power of displacing an executive power? I conceive that if any power whatsoever is in the Executive it is the power of appointing, overseeing, and controlling those who execute the laws. If the Constitution had not qualified the power of the President in appointing to office by associating the Senate with him in that business, would it not be clear that he would have the right by virtue of his executive power to make such appointment? Should we be authorized in defiance of that clause in the Constitution, "The executive power shall be vested in the President," to unite the Senate with the President in the appointment to office? I conceive not. If it is admitted that we should not be authorized to do this, I think it may be disputed whether we have a right to associate them in removing persons from office, the one power being as much of an executive nature as the other; and the first one is authorized by being excepted out of the general rule established by the Constitution in these words: "The executive power shall be vested in the President."[3]

The question, thus ably and exhaustively argued, was decided by the House of Representatives, by a vote of 34 to 20, in favor of the principle that the executive power of removal is vested by the Constitution in the Executive, and in the Senate by the casting vote of the Vice-President.

The question has often been raised in subsequent times of high excitement, and the practice of the Government has, nevertheless, conformed in all cases to the decision thus early made.

The question was revived during the Administration of President Jackson, who made, as is well recollected, a very large number of removals, which were made an occasion of close and rigorous scrutiny and remonstrance. The subject was long and earnestly debated in the Senate, and the early construction of the Constitution was, nevertheless, freely accepted as binding and conclusive upon Congress.

The question came before the Supreme Court of the United States in January, 1839, *ex parte* Hennen.[4] It was declared by the court on that occasion that the power of removal from office was a subject much disputed, and upon which a great diversity of opinion was entertained in the early history of the Government. This related, however, to the power of the President to remove officers appointed with the concurrence of the

Senate, and the great question was whether the removal was to be by the President alone or with the concurrence of the Senate, both constituting the appointing power. No one denied the power of the President and Senate jointly to remove where the tenure of the office was not fixed by the Constitution, which was a full recognition of the principle that the power of removal was incident to the power of appointment; but it was very early adopted as a practical construction of the Constitution that this power was vested in the President alone, and such would appear to have been the legislative construction of the Constitution, for in the organization of the three great Departments of State, War, and Treasury, in the year 1789, provision was made for the appointment of a subordinate officer by the head of the Department, who should have charge of the records, books, and papers appertaining to the office when the head of the Department should be removed from office by the President of the United States. When the Navy Department was established, in the year 1798, provision was made for the charge and custody of the books, records, and documents of the Department in case of vacancy in the office of Secretary by removal or otherwise. It is not here said "by removal of the President," as is done with respect to the heads of the other Departments, yet there can be no doubt that he holds his office with the same tenure as the other Secretaries and is removable by the President. The change of phraseology arose, probably, from its having become the settled and well-understood construction of the Constitution that the power of removal was vested in the President alone in such cases, although the appointment of the officer is by the President and Senate. (13 Peters, p. 139)

Our most distinguished and accepted commentators upon the Constitution concur in the construction thus early given by Congress, and thus sanctioned by the Supreme Court. After a full analysis of the Congressional debate to which I have referred, Mr. Justice Story comes to this conclusion:

After a most animated discussion, the vote finally taken in the House of Representatives was affirmative of the power of removal in the President, without any cooperation of the Senate, by the vote of 34 members against 20. In the Senate the clause in the bill affirming the power was carried by the casting vote of the Vice-President. That the final decision of this question so made was greatly influenced by the exalted character of the President then in office was asserted at the time and has always been believed; yet the doctrine was opposed as well as supported by the highest talents and patriotism of the country. The public have acquiesced in this decision, and it constitutes, perhaps, the most extraordinary case in the history of the Government of a power conferred by implication on the Executive by the assent of a bare majority of Congress which has not been questioned on many other occasions.[5]

The commentator adds:

Nor is this general acquiescence and silence without a satisfactory explanation.

Chancellor Kent's remarks on the subject are as follows:

On the first organization of the Government it was made a question whether the power of removal in case of officers appointed to hold at pleasure resided nowhere but in the body which appointed, and, of course, whether the consent of the Senate was not requisite to remove. This was the construction given to the Constitution, while it was pending for ratification before the State conventions, by the author of the Federalist. But the construction which was given to the Constitution by Congress, after great consideration and discussion, was different. The words of the act ⟨establishing the Treasury Department⟩ are: "And whenever the same shall be removed from office by the President of the United States, or in any other case of vacancy in the office, the assistant shall act." This amounted to a legislative construction of the Constitution, and it has ever since been acquiesced in and acted upon as a decisive authority in the case. It applies equally to every other officer of the Government appointed by the President, whose term of duration is not specially declared. It is supported by the weighty reason that the subordinate officers in the executive department ought to hold at the pleasure of the head of the department, because he is invested generally with the executive authority, and the participation in that authority by the Senate was an exception to a general principle and ought to be taken strictly. The President is the great responsible officer for the faithful execution of the law, and the power of removal was incidental to that duty, and might often be requisite to fulfill it.[6]

Thus has the important question presented by this bill been settled, in the language of the late Daniel Webster (who, while dissenting from it, admitted that it was settled), by construction, settled by precedent, settled by the practice of the Government, and settled by statute. The events of the last war furnished a practical confirmation of the wisdom of the Constitution as it has hitherto been maintained in many of its parts, including that which is now the subject of consideration. When the war broke out, rebel enemies, traitors, abettors, and sympathizers were found in every Department of the Government, as well in the civil service as in the land and naval military service. They were found in Congress and among the keepers of the Capitol; in foreign missions; in each and all the Executive Departments; in the judicial service; in the post-office, and among the agents for conducting Indian affairs. Upon probable suspicion they were promptly displaced by my predecessor, so far as they held their offices under executive authority, and their duties were confided to new and loyal successors. No complaints against that power or doubts of its wisdom were entertained in any quarter. I sincerely trust and believe that no such civil war is likely to occur again. I can not doubt, however, that in whatever form and on whatever occasion sedition can raise an effort to hinder or embarrass or defeat the legitimate action of this Government, whether by preventing the collection of revenue, or disturbing the public peace, or separating the States, or betraying the country to a foreign enemy, the power of removal from office by the Executive, as it has heretofore existed and been practiced, will be found indispensable.

Under these circumstances, as a depositary of the executive authority of the nation, I do not feel at liberty to unite with Congress in reversing it by giving my approval to the bill. At the early day when this question was settled, and, indeed, at the several periods when it has subsequently been agitated, the success of the Constitution of the United States, as a new and peculiar system of free representative government, was held doubtful in other countries, and was even a subject of patriotic apprehension among the American people themselves. A trial of nearly eighty years, through the vicissitudes of foreign conflicts and of civil war, is confidently regarded as having extinguished all such doubts and apprehensions for the future. During that eighty years the people of the United States have enjoyed a measure of security, peace, prosperity, and happiness never surpassed by any nation. It can not be doubted that the triumphant success of the Constitution is due to the wonderful wisdom with which the functions of government were distributed between the three principal departments—the legislative, the executive, and the judicial—and to the fidelity with which each has confined itself or been confined by the general voice of the nation within its peculiar and proper sphere. While a just, proper, and watchful jealousy of executive power constantly prevails, as it ought ever to prevail, yet it is equally true that an efficient Executive, capable, in the language of the oath prescribed to the President, of executing the laws and, within the sphere of executive action, of preserving, protecting, and defending the Constitution of the United States, is an indispensable security for tranquillity at home and peace, honor, and safety abroad. Governments have been erected in many countries upon our model. If one or many of them has thus far failed in fully securing to their people the benefits which we have derived from our system, it may be confidently asserted that their misfortune has resulted from their unfortunate failure to maintain the integrity of each of the three great departments while preserving harmony among them all.

Having at an early period accepted the Constitution in regard to the Executive office in the sense in which it was interpreted with the concurrence of its founders, I have found no sufficient grounds in the arguments now opposed to that construction or in any assumed necessity of the times for changing those opinions. For these reasons I return the bill to the Senate, in which House it originated, for the further consideration of Congress which the Constitution prescribes. Insomuch as the several parts of the bill which I have not considered are matters chiefly of detail and are based altogether upon the theory of the Constitution from which I am obliged to dissent, I have not thought it necessary to examine them with a view to make them an occasion of distinct and special objections.

Experience, I think, has shown that it is the easiest, as it is also the most attractive, of studies to frame constitutions for the self-government of free states and nations. But I think experience has equally shown that it is the most difficult of all political labors to preserve and maintain such free constitutions of self-government when once happily established. I know no other way in which they can be preserved and maintained except by a constant adherence to them through the various vicissitudes of national existence, with such adaptations as may become necessary, always to be effected, however, through the agencies and in the forms prescribed in the original constitutions themselves.

Whenever administration fails or seems to fail in securing any of the great ends for which republican government is established, the proper course seems to be to renew the original spirit and forms of the Constitution itself.

ANDREW JOHNSON.

Richardson, *Messages*, 6: 492–98.
1. *U.S. Statutes at Large*, 1: 28–29.
2. These remarks most closely resemble those made by Theodore Sedgwick, representative from Massachusetts, on June 16, 1789. *Annals of Congress*, 1 Cong., 1 Sess., cols. 478–79.
3. William T. Hutchinson and William M.E. Rachal et al., eds., *The Papers of James Madison* (17 vols. to date, Charlottesville, 1979–), 12: 228.
4. 13 Peters 230 (1839).
5. Joseph Story, *Commentaries on the Constitution of the United States*, 2nd ed. (2 vols., Boston, 1851), 2: 343–44.
6. James Kent, *Commentaries on American Law*, 8th ed. (4 vols., New York, 1854), 1: 339–40.

From Edwin D. Morgan

Washington, Mar 3, 1867

My Dear Sir

I desire to see you previous to the signing of the partial Tariff bill[1]— which takes effect from the *date of its passage*. The Bill should not be signed *before* the 4th otherwise it will be most unjust and oppressive. It will be partial & unjust under any circumstances.

E. D. Morgan.

ALS, DLC-JP.
1. Probably the Wool and Woollens Act of 1867 which passed Congress on March 2, following the failure of the general tariff bill, and was signed by Johnson in the last minutes of the session on March 3. The act raised duties above the already high rates established during the war. While only a partial measure and viewed by many as unjustly discriminating against other industries, this act laid the foundation for the broader application of the protective principle in subsequent tariffs. Edward Stanwood, *American Tariff Controversies in the Nineteenth Century* (2 vols., New York, 1967 [1903]), 2: 154–58. For details, see *U.S. Statutes at Large*, 14: 559–62; F. W. Taussig, *The Tariff History of the United States*, 4th ed. (New York, 1898), 194–219.

From Francis P. Blair, Jr.

Washington City   March 4, 1867

It has been stated to me by gentlemen in whom I have great confidence that Colonel Murphy[1] of New Orleans is the choice of the great body of the old residents & business men of Louisiana for the place of Marshal of that District and under the circumstances I should think that their wishes should be regarded. Almost every office of any consequence in the state has been conferred upon persons living out of the state or who were but recent residents. Under these circumstances it would seem that if the state could furnish an old resident who was loyal & competent & was recommended by the old residents of the state that it would be proper to give him the place.[2]

Frank P. Blair

ALS, DNA-RG60, Appt. Files for Judicial Dists., La., Edmund Murphy.

1. Edmund Murphy.

2. Blair's letter, which was endorsed by his brother Montgomery, was probably written in response to the Senate's rejection of J. H. McKee for marshal on March 2, 1867. Murphy had applied for the post in October 1866 and did so again on March 5, but Johnson did not nominate him. Murphy to Johnson, Oct. 1866, Mar. 5, 1867, Appt. Files for Judicial Dists., La., Edmund Murphy, RG60, NA; Ser. 6B, Vol. 4: 202, 203, Johnson Papers, LC.

From Thomas F. Bowie[1]

Upper Marlbo [Md.]   March 4th 1867

The Senate having refused to confirm the appointment of William Price Esqr as District Attorney for Maryland, I am induced at the request of many of your and my political friends to solicit the appointment at your Hands.

My qualifications as a Lawyer are well known throughout the State. For seventeen years I was the assistant Attorney General of the State under the late Cheif Justice Taney and If you should require any other evidences of my fitness for the situation they can be had in abundance.

I need not say that I am and always have been your political and personal friend, and as to my Loyalty to the Government its Constitution and laws I challenge the production of one more so.

I was among the first to unite against the Doctrine of Secession as my letter to Mr Clement Hill[2] published in the Intlligener Dec. 1860 will shew, and have always taken the same ground on that subject in Maryland that you did in Tennessee.

Thomas F Bowie

ALS, DNA-RG60, Appt. Files for Judicial Dists., Md., Thomas F. Bowie.

1. Bowie (1808–1869), a brother-in-law of Reverdy Johnson, was admitted to the Maryland bar in 1829. He served in the state house (1842–46) as well as the U.S. House of Representatives (1855–59). Bowie did not receive the position as Andrew S. Ridgely had already been confirmed. BDUSC; Reverdy Johnson to Johnson, Mar. 2, 1867.

2. The letter has not been found. Hill (1813–1892), a Kentucky lawyer, served in the state house of representatives in 1839 and later in the U.S. House (1853–55). BDUSC. ˙

From S. Coffin[1]

Hudson N Y   March 4/67

Dear Sir

I am highly gratified with You at the noble position You have taken upon the Military Reconstruction Bill It being only a political measure wholy calculated to produce disunion and discord. We have the constitution our Fore Fathers fought for and it has always been good enough and if it is not now why do away with it. But do not trample it under foot as some of those wooly headed congress Men have. I would like to get in discussion with some one or two of them I could name. I would show them in a short time where their feelings for their country is. Although I am an entire stranger to You my sentiments are for the good of the Country and not for a set of Men that I know and You know are no more nor less than a lot of Political demagoges. I am a Mechanic and a worthy and good one and some few Years ago had charge as an Assistant of our Post office the time Mr Polk of Tenneese was President. And now many of our citizens are over anxious I should have the appointment of Post Master as they alledge I kept it better than any Man that ever had it as I understand it perfectly from root to branch.

S Coffin

If convenient please acknowledge the receipt of this by causing to be forwarded an interesting Public Document. I would like to go into a Political discussion in this letter about matters and things as they have been and as they now are.

S Coffin

ALS, DLC-JP.
1. Possibly Stephen I. Coffin (b. 1813), a Hudson carpenter and father of three daughters. 1860 Census, N.Y., Columbia, Hudson, 3rd Ward, 88.

From Alfred Gibson[1]

this 4th March 1867

My Dear Sir.

Your Honor, will admit the following enquiry, of which you will please answer (in haste).

I with 15 or 20 famelleys principally Freed-men is poore and wants to go North or South West to serch Out Homes. We are not able to precure Homes here, infact can scarcely live in this countary. Now in case, Your Honor can precure a Transportation for us we will severally & collectively bind our-selves &.c. to pay for the same, within such time as may be reasonable prescribed. Infact there is Hundreds of famelleys hereabout in our same situation, which never can be of any youse to our countary short of a facility of this sort.[2]

Alfred Gibson   Lenoir P.o. Office
Caldwell County   N. Ca.

ALS, DNA-RG105, Records of the Commr., Lets. Recd. (M752, Roll 43).
1. Gibson (b. c1833) is probably the farm worker who lived in Guilford County three years later. 1870 Census, N.C., Guilford, Rock Creek Twp., 2.
2. On March 8, 1867, Johnson's office routinely referred Gibson's request to Secretary Stanton. Records of the Commr., Lets. Recd., (M752, Roll 43), RG105, NA.

From William Graves [1]

Niles Michigan   March 4th 1867

I have learned that since the rejection of Mr Beckwith[2] as Collector of Internal Revenue for the Second District of Michigan, who by the way is a competent officer and an honorable man, that an effort is being made for the appointment of Dr. Bonine[3] in his stead. Dr. Bonine has no special fitness for the place and has no claim whatever upon the confidence or respect of the Executive. When the Presidential party passed through this place on their way to Chicago the past summer,[4] Dr. Bonine who was Mayor of the City, delined to participate in a Reception at the Depot, solely and avowedly on partizan grounds, and as the oldest Member of the Common Council, and at request of my fellow Citizens, I performed that agreeable duty. At a later period as a member of the Lagislature, Dr. Bonine has given a more signal expression of His animosity, by introducing a Resolution which is contained in the accompanying Journal,[5] and which his particular suporters regard as a preeminent qualification for preferment. I was appointed by Mr Beckwith Deputy Collector, and expect to be superceeded when he is, but it would be Verry painfull to us, to see our places filled by the Malignent Enemies of the President and of sound Consitutional Government.[6]

William Graves

ALS, DNA-RG56, Appts., Internal Revenue Service, Collector, Mich., 2nd Dist., Dr. Bonine.
1. Graves (1808–1881), a stagecoach agent, moved to Michigan in 1835. A Democrat, he was twice mayor and four times treasurer of Niles. *Michigan Biographies*, 1: 345–46.
2. Walter G. Beckwith (c1811–c1887), a member of the Democratic party, was nominated on January 21, 1867, but rejected on February 21. A farmer, he moved to Cass County, Michigan, about 1833, where he was elected sheriff for several years and was president of the state agricultural society. L. H. Glover, ed., *A Twentieth Century History of Cass County, Michigan* (Chicago, 1906), 607–8; Howard S. Rogers, *History of Cass County, From 1825 to 1875* (Cassopolis, Mich., 1875), 145; Ser. 6B, Vol. 4: 275, Johnson Papers, LC; 1860 Census, Mich., Cass, Jefferson Twp., Cassopolis, 169.
3. Evan J. Bonine (1821–1892), a Republican, settled in Niles in 1844 where he had a large medical practice, was twice mayor, and served as postmaster (1870–85). He was a surgeon with the 2nd Mich. Inf. during the Civil War. In addition to serving as a represen-

tative in the state legislature for four terms, he also had one term as a state senator. *Michigan Biographies*, 1: 94–95; Pension Files, Evaline Bonine, RG15, NA.

4. Johnson and his entourage were in Niles, Michigan, on Wednesday, September 5, 1866.

5. Bonine's resolution commended the action of the U.S. House of Representatives "in ordering a committee to inquire concerning the high crimes and misdemeanors alleged to have been committed by Andrew Johnson." Lansing Legislative Journal, Jan. 10, 1867, Appts., Internal Revenue Service, Collector, Mich., 2nd Dist., Dr. Bonine, RG56, NA.

6. Bonine was not nominated. After one further nominee was rejected, Fred W. Cartenius was nominated, confirmed, and commissioned on April 5, 1867. Ser. 6B, Vol. 4: 276–77, Johnson Papers, LC.

From William H.C. King

New Orleans La   Mch 4th, 1867

McKee was defeated[1] through Trumbulls[2] influence because he would not pledge himself to build up a paper against you and because his patronage came to the Times.[3] I respectfully ask you to appoint Wm. L Stanford[4] who goes to Washington with strong letters from Rosilyns Rosier Hunt Fellow & others.[5] I must be unknown in the matter. The Senate will reject any man known to be a friend of mine or the Times. Stanford starts for Washington today. He was in the Union Army.[6]

Wm. H.C. King

Tel, DLC-JP.

1. On December 14, 1866, J. H. McKee was nominated for U.S. marshal of Louisiana but rejected on March 2, 1867. Ser. 6B, Vol. 4: 202, Johnson Papers, LC.

2. Lyman Trumbull.

3. King's paper.

4. Stanford (c1834–1899) was an Auburn, New York, grocer before the Civil War. Pension File, William L. Stanford, RG15, NA; CSR, William L. Stanford, RG94, NA.

5. Christian Roselius, J. Adolphus Rozier, Randell Hunt, and John Q.A. Fellows. Rozier (c1820–1896), a lawyer, moved to New Orleans in 1839. A member of the 1861 Louisiana secession convention, Rozier voted against seceding and later was active as a conservative Unionist during the federal occupation of Louisiana and Reconstruction. Fellows (c1825–*fl*1897), a Vermont native and lawyer, owned a substantial fortune in real estate by 1870. Conrad, *La. Biography*; 1870 Census, La., Orleans, New Orleans, 1st Ward, 25; 6th Dist., Jefferson City, 106; New Orleans directories (1871–98). Letters from these and other recommenders are found in Appts., Customs Service, Appraiser, New Orleans, William L. Stanford, RG56, NA.

6. Stanford had served as captain of Co. "K", 75th N.Y. Inf., part of the time on detached duty as provost marshal in St. Bernard and Plaquemines parishes. He was apparently never nominated for marshal, but on December 6, 1867, he was nominated for local appraiser in the customs office at New Orleans, and was confirmed and commissioned for that post on March 3, 1868. Pension File, William L. Stanford, RG15, NA; Ser. 6B, Vol. 4: 203, Johnson Papers, LC; CSR, William L. Stanford, RG94, NA.

From Lucy E.W. Polk

Warrenton [N.C.]   March 4 [1867]

Dr Sir

To-day I suppose important events are agitating the Political elements of our Republic. I left Washington the Monday after the Levee on the 22d. not however, without making an effort to pay my respects to yourself & the ladies of the White House but was not so fortunate in seeing you, being informed that the President was engaged so I concluded that my Pen might accomplish what my tongue failed to do.

What I now ask is—at your earliest convenience will you do me the kindness to give me a letter endorsing my faithful adherence to the Government of the United States, during the War.[1] It may be of service to me hereafter, at all events a satisfaction—which I am sure will be granted.

I remarked in the presence of a Radical that the President would endorse my Loyalty, to which he rather sneeringly replied that such an endorsement would avail but little. Women like I must have the last word & I answered with more spirit than prudence "perhaps not sir under radical rule but reason must resume its sway & with it a proper appreciation for one who has so fearlessly & nobly dared do his duty to his country while Radicalism Fanaticism & Heaven knows what other isms threaten its destruction. I find great depression here occasioned by the passage of the Military bill & anticipations of even more stringent measures. Business dull—money scarce. "Cuffee" jubilant. Altogether a state of affairs never dreamed of. My reverses have been quite as great as most persons—but I try to keep Hope at the helm & inspire others with the same feelings. But pardon my trespassing so long. With kind regards for the Ladies & best wishes for your happiness & success in sweeping every cloud from the Political horizon.

Mrs. W. H. Polk
Warrenton N. Carolina

ALS, DLC-JP.
1. Months later, Mrs. Polk renewed her request for a letter which the President finally produced in July 1867. See Lucy E.W. Polk to Johnson, June 22, 1867.

From Nathaniel P. Sawyer

Pittsburgh   March 4th 1867

At a meeting of the National Union Men held at the Johnson Head Quarters 21 fifth Street this evening at 7½ Oclock,

The Following Preamble and Resolutions was unanimously adopted.

Whereas, We have with much regret and astonishment heard of the appointment by the President of James H. McClelland[1] a well known and noted enemy of the administration, to the Post Mastership of the city of Pittsburgh

Be it Resolved. That we the steadfast and consistent friends of Andrew Johnson and the principles he represents, Do respectfully and earnestly protest against the appointment of J H. McClelland and ask that his appointment be revoked and that Hall Patterson[2] be appointed in his place.

Be it Resolved. That we protest against the contemplated removal of Major Henry A. Weaver[3] Assessor of the twenty second District of Penna. at Pittsburgh, a warm consistent and energetic Johnson man and the appointment thereto at the solicitation of J K. Moorhead,[4] who has always opposed the President, John H. Stewart[5] one of the Presidents violent and vindictive opposers.

Resolved. That we request if not incompatible with the laws and regulations of the department the reappointment of Andrew L. Robinson the present Postmaster of Allegheny City and if he cannot be reappointed would request that Wilkins H. Robinson[6] be appointed in his place.

Resolved   That we reccommend Robert H Roach[7] for Assessor and Thomas Johnston[8] for Collector of the 23 District of Penna. at Allegheny City.

Nathl. P. Sawyer   President

ALS, DLC-JP.

1. McClelland (c1801–fl1871) had been nominated for postmaster at Pittsburgh at the end of February 1867 and was approved by the Senate on March 2. He was listed variously as architect, builder, and carpenter. He continued as postmaster at least through 1869. 1860 Census, Pa., Allegheny, Pittsburgh, 3rd Ward, 176; *Senate Ex. Proceedings*, Vol. 15, pt. 1: 285, 334; *U.S. Off. Reg.* (1867–69); Pittsburgh directories (1861–72).

2. Patterson (fl1901) was a longtime Pittsburgh attorney. Ibid. (1872–1901).

3. Weaver (1820–90), former mayor of Pittsburgh (1857–60) and an active Republican. After the war he was involved in gas and oil production and banking. Weaver continued in office as assessor; Johnson informed McCulloch that charges had to be specified against Weaver in order for him to be removed. Holli and Jones, *American Mayors*; *U.S. Off. Reg.* (1867); Johnson endorsement, July 24, 1867, Appts., Internal Revenue Service, Assessor, Pa., 22nd Dist., John H. Stewart, RG56, NA.

4. James K. Moorhead, U.S. representative.

5. Two days after Sawyer's letter was written, the President forwarded the nomination of Stewart (fl1880) as assessor. But on March 8 Johnson withdrew Stewart's nomination. Stewart was in business in Pittsburgh for a number of years and became postmaster in 1871. *Senate Ex. Proceedings*, Vol. 15, pt. 1: 349, 376; *U.S. Off. Reg.* (1871); Pittsburgh directories (1865–80).

6. Andrew Robinson was replaced as postmaster by virtue of Senate rejection. But his successor was Hugh McKelvy, not Wilkins H. Robinson (fl1871), a Pittsburgh attorney. Ibid. (1858–71). See William F. Johnston to Johnson, Aug. 2, 1866, *Johnson Papers*, 11: 8–11.

7. Roach (fl1886) was a miller and involved in real estate. There is no evidence that he was ever nominated for assessor. Instead, on March 6 Johnson nominated Jacob Ziegler as assessor, but the Senate rejected him. Afterwards, the President forwarded Daniel E. Nevin's name; on March 15 the Senate approved Nevin's appointment. Pittsburgh directories (1865–86); *Senate Ex. Proceedings*, Vol. 15, pt. 1: 347, 378, 412; pt. 2: 452.

8. On March 6 the President submitted the name of Thomas Johnston, not otherwise identified, as the nominee for the collector's post, in place of the rejected William G.

McCandless. The Senate did not approve Johnston's nomination, and it was early April
before the President succeeded with the nomination of John M. Sullivan. In the meanwhile, McCandless continued to serve under a temporary commission. Ibid, pt. 1: 349,
378; pt. 2: 455, 502, 647, 680.

From James M. Tomeny
Personal

Brooklyn   March 4, 1867

Dear Sir:

I have just read your message vetoing the Military Government bill,
and beg to offer you my heartfelt thanks.

It covers the whole ground and cannot be answered except by ignoring
the Constitution and trampling upon the liberties of the people. With the
infamous threat of impeachment hanging over you, some supposed you
would acquiesce in the measure but all who know you well were confident you could not be driven into a violation of the Constitution. In the
purity of your patriotism and your personal and official integrity, your
friends and the great majority of the American people have an *unwavering, steadfast faith*. This faith with me can never be shaken hence I have
no apprehensions as to impeachment except that your rights, the forms of
law and of justice will be wholly disregarded by your enemies. I pray
from the depths of my soul for your preservation. My wife[1] and children
constantly pray for you, as do millions of your countrymen. Everything
depends upon you. The peace and the life of the nation are in your hands.
I know you will make any sacrifice to preserve both. This is now the *only*
hope of our distracted country.

When in Washington a few days ago I endeavored to see you but failed
to get an interview. For the past twelve months the war made upon me by
the court at Mobile[2] has paralized my energies and my ambition, and
rendered me powerless to aid your friends in our own State or elsewhere.
Because you gave me the office and I exposed the cotton frauds at Mobile
the parties concerned have sought to crush and destroy me regardless of
justice or of law. My vindication is certain and will be complete.[3]

When I visit Washington again I hope to have the pleasure and the
honor of seeing you.

J. M. Tomeny

ALS, DLC-JP.
    1. Fanny Webb (c1838–1878), the mother of five children, died in the Memphis yellow
fever epidemic as did her husband. 1870 Census, Tenn., Shelby, Memphis, 7th Ward, 72;
Memphis Daily Appeal, Oct. 6, 1878.
    2. Tomeny's troubles at Mobile had a long and complicated history, a good bit of which
has been covered in the different letters to the President published in Volumes 9 and 10 of
the *Johnson Papers*. See, for example, Tomeny to Johnson, Dec. 20, 1865, *Johnson Papers*,
9: 526; Tomeny to Johnson, May 15, 20, June 12, 1866, ibid., 10: 510–11, 528, 581–82.

3. In the fall of 1866 it was reported by the press that charges against Tomeny had been dismissed. Yet, in late March 1867, the attorney general instructed the U.S. attorney at Mobile to suspend civil and criminal proceedings against Tomeny until after his arrival in Mobile. Obviously, Tomeny was exonerated at some time, because in mid-April 1867 the President nominated him as U.S. marshal for West Tennessee and the Senate approved the appointment. *Memphis Daily Post*, Oct. 2, 1866; Stanbery to L.V.B. Marlin, Mar. 29, 1867, Office of Atty. Gen., Lets. Sent (M699, Roll 11), RG60, NA; *Senate Ex. Proceedings*, Vol. 15, pt. 2: 746, 766.

From Mary J. Baldwin[1]

March 5th/67

Mr. President

This being Cabinet day, I fear I will not see you. Have you appoint the boy Frank Wilson.[2] If Alex M. McCook is not to be promoted—Have him made Commandent of Cadets—at West Point. This can be done if Genl. G—prevents his *being promoted*.[3]

Will you add to the written the Autograph letter—presented me to present to *our Ministers abroad*[4]. Please dont forget to have my family mentioned. Feeling *very very* sorry for all your troubles.

Mary J. Baldwin

Please send to 128 Penn. Ave. bet *19 & 10 Streets*.

M.J.B.

ALS, DLC-JP.

1. Baldwin (b. *c*1828) was the daughter of Daniel and Martha McCook and one of two sisters among nine brothers, all of whom, as well as their father, served in the Union army. Born in New Lisbon, Ohio, she lived in Nashville in 1864. 1850 Census, Ohio, Warren Twp., 149th Dist., 104; C. S. Speaker, C. C. Connell, and George T. Ferrell, *An Historical Sketch of the Old Village of New Lisbon, Ohio* (Lisbon, 1903), 67; Simon, *Grant Papers*, 16: 439; Mary J. Baldwin to Lincoln, [Jan.] 22, Aug. 22, Nov. 4, 1864, Lincoln Papers, LC.

2. Wilson (b. *c*1844) worked on his father's farm in Jefferson County, Ohio, before Johnson appointed him to West Point as a cadet-at-large, to enter in September 1867. He did not graduate. 1860 Census, Ohio, Jefferson, Knox Twp., 112; R. Morrow to Stanton, Mar. 7, 1867, USMA Corres. *re* Mil. Academy, 1867–1904, File W-46-1867, RG94, NA; *West Point Register*, 267.

3. Alexander McD. McCook was promoted to lieutenant colonel of the 26th Inf. on March 5, 1867. He was never commandant of West Point. Powell, *Army List*, 463.

4. Nothing has been found concerning this requested letter.

From John M. Glover[1]

La Grange [Mo.], March 5 1867

Sir:

By the unanimous wish of your political Friends of the 8th Congressional Dist. & your Kindness I was appointed Collector of 3d Revenue Dist of Mo. Took possession of office on 1st Dec. last. At very considerable cost have fitted up office. I am just now notified that my commission has expired.[2] If I am not eligible to reappointment, I shall be brought in debt by the office thus far. I am certain that no friend of yours or mine will seek the place without my consent. The former Incumbents, your *bitter enemies* & in every way unfit, are seeking it. I respectfully ask, that if I can not be renominated—please withhold action in the premises, until I confer, by letter or see you in person. But if you can not wait, for reasons unknown to me, I furnish you with the name of one of the best qualified Gentlemen in every respect, in the Dist, as my successor—William P. Moore Esq of La Grange Mo.[3]

You will know me, Mr. President as the candidate for Congress in this Dist, against J. F. Benjamin, the present usurper of a seat in Congress.[4]

My labors & pecuniary expenditures in the late Canvass, to sustain your wise & statesmanlike policy—were very lavish & If you cant renominate me, I ask it as a *special favor* to one who fought for 4 years in our army[5] & one year in the political arena for the perpetuation of free government, to appoint Mr. Moore—who is now acting as the accomplished Deputy Collector.[6] I start for St Lous tomorrow & maybe to Washington.[7]

J. M. Glover

ALS, DNA-RG56, Appts., Internal Revenue Service, Collector, Mo., 3rd Dist., John M. Glover.

1. Glover (1822–1891) moved to Missouri in 1836 where he studied and practiced law. After settling in California, he returned to Missouri in 1855. Eventually he served three terms in the U.S. House of Representatives (1873–79). *BDUSC*.

2. Glover had been nominated for the post in July 1866 and quickly rejected by the Senate. Johnson then gave him a recess appointment and renominated him on January 14, 1867. He was rejected on February 6 and his temporary commission expired on March 4. In April Johnson unsuccessfully attempted to place Glover in the collector's post. Ser. 6B, Vol. 4: 315–16, Johnson Papers, LC; *Senate Ex. Proceedings*, Vol. 15, pt. 1: 77, 180; pt. 2: 638, 644.

3. Not further identified.

4. John F. Benjamin had defeated Glover in the Eighth District by 1,532 votes out of 13,670 cast. *American Annual Cyclopaedia* (1866), 526.

5. From September 4, 1861, to February 23, 1864, when he resigned because of ill health, Glover served as colonel of the 3rd Mo. Cav. *BDUSC*.

6. Johnson did nominate Moore on March 12, 1867, but the Senate rejected him on March 14. Ser. 6B, Vol. 4: 316, Johnson Papers, LC.

7. Glover did go to Washington, as he wrote to Johnson while there. For further correspondence pertaining to this collectorship, see Smith S. Allen to Johnson, Mar. 14, 1867; Glover to Johnson, Apr. 4, 1867. See also Appts., Internal Revenue Service, Collector, Mo., 3rd Dist., William P. Moore, RG56, NA.

Interview with Charles Halpine

Washington, March 6 [March 5, 1867][1]

And now, apart from the directly political, continued the President, what is the main issue looming up in the immediate future? What issue is clearly foreshadowed to be the Aaron's rod which must swallow up all minor questions? It is the great financial issue, the issue of the national debt; whether it shall be paid or repudiated? This issue has fibres extending into the pocket of every citizen, for wherever a man has a dollar, or can earn a dollar, the Government is now compelled to go for its portion of his substance, and with the vast machinery under its control, the money is fetched.

There were four millions of slaves in the Southern States before the rebellion, representing a capital of three, or possibly four billions of dollars; but let us call it three billions, or three thousand millions, as you may please. These slaves represented that amount of property, men put their savings into purchasing or raising them, and they represented as property whatever were the surplus profits of their labor, after due allowance for food, clothing, medicine, and interest on the capital invested.

On this property in slaves gradually grew up that slave oligarchy or aristocracy, against which the leaders of the anti-slavery party so successfully thundered during the twelve years preceding the rebellion; and after the first mad plunge into rebellion the fate of that aristocracy was sealed. It is now a thing of the past. With its virtues—for it had virtues, courage, and hospitality eminently—and with its crimes of pride and lawless revolution, it has entered into history, and is a thing of the past.

But what do we now find? The aristocracy based on three thousand millions of property in slaves south of Mason and Dixon's line has disappeared; but an aristocracy, based on over two thousand five hundred millions of national securities, has arisen in the Northern States; to assume that political control which the consolidation of great financial with political interests formerly gave to the slave oligarchy of the lately rebel States. The aristocracy based on negro property disappears at the Southern end of the line, but only to reappear in an oligarchy of bonds and national securities in the States which suppressed the rebellion.

We have all read history, and is it not certain that of all aristocracies, that of mere wealth is the most odious, rapacious, and tyrannical? It goes for the last dollar the poor and helpless have got; and with such a vast machine as this Government under its control that dollar will be fetched. It is an aristocracy that can see in the people only a prey for extortion. It has no political or military relations with them, such as the old feudal system created between liege lord and vassal, it has no intimate social and domestic ties, and no such strong bond of self-interest with the people as existed of necessity between the extinct slaveholders of our country and their slaves. To an aristocracy existing on the annual interest of a national debt, the people are only of value in proportion to their docility and power of patiently bleeding golden blood under the tax-gatherer's thumb-screw.

To the people the national debt is a thing of debt, to be paid; but to the aristocracy of bonds and national securities, it is a property of more than two thousand five hundred million, from which a revenue of one hundred and eighty millions a year is to be received into their pockets. So we now find that an aristocracy of the South, based on three thousand millions of dollars in negroes—who were a productive class—has disappeared; and their place in political control of the country is assumed by an aristocracy based on nearly three thousand millions of national debt—a thing which is not producing anything, but which goes on steadily every year, and must go on for all time until the debt is paid, absorbing and taxing at the rate of six or seven per cent a year for every hundred dollar bond that is represented in its aggregation.

Now, I am not speaking of this to do anything but deprecate the fearful issue which the madness of partisan hatred and the blindness of our new national debt aristocracy to their own true interests is fast forcing upon the country. But is it not clear that the people, who have to pay one hundred and eighty millions of dollars a year to this consolidated moneyed oligarchy, must, sooner or later, commence asking each other, "How much was actually loaned to our Government during the civil war by these bondholders, who now claim that we owe them nearly three thousand millions of dollars?["] You know what the popular answer must be—I do not say the right answer: "less than half the amount they claim, for gold ranged at an average of one hundred premium while this debt was being incurred."

Just think of the annual tax of one hundred and eighty millions for payment of interest on our national debt! This Government we have, with its enormous machinery, is a pretty hefty business in itself, costing more *per capita* to the people than the Government of England, which we always heretofore regarded as the most tax-devouring on earth. But over and beyond the expenses of this Government proper, as it should standing in the scale of peace at about sixty millions a year, we have, in the one hundred and eighty millions of interest paid yearly on our national debt, enough to support three such governments as this, with all their vast machinery and disbursements! We have not only, under the present system, one Government for the people to support, but, over and beyond this, we have to raise, by taxation from the people, sufficient to support three similar establishments every year!

All property is based upon and can only be sustained by law; and it is for a return to law and the guide of fixed constitutional principles that my whole course has been contending. But so short sighted is this aristocracy of bonds and paper currency—this Plutocracy of the national debt—that my efforts in behalf of their true interests (which are certainly involved in the maintenance of law and the Constitution) have been everywhere encountered, and almost everywhere overwhelmed by the preponderating influence which they have acquired from the natural force of capital and the agency of our National banks.

And what has been the course of that Congress which has just ended, and which this blind aristocracy of national debt sustained in overriding my efforts for a return to sound principles of internal government? Look at the bill giving from four hundred and eighty to six hundred millions of dollars—nominally for back bounty, or as an equalization of bounties to the soldiers, but really, as all intelligent men must be aware, to be parcelled out as a prey among the bounty sharks and claim agents, who are the most reckless and clamorous adherents of the dominant majority in Congress. Then look at appropriations amounting to another hundred millions for internal improvements, which should properly be left to the laws governing private industry and the progress of our national development. Look also at the increase of all salaries with a prodigal hand; this virtuous Congress first setting an example against retrenchment by voting to themselves an increase of salaries. Everywhere, and in an ever-increasing ratio, the motto seems to be: "Always spend and never spare;" a fresh issue from the paper-mill over yonder (slightly pointing his pencil to the Treasury Department) being the panacea prescribed for every evil of our present situation.

Every effort to increase our annual taxation is resisted, for increased taxes might help to awaken the people from their false dream of prosperity under the sway of revolutionary and Radical ideas; but no addition to the national debt can be proposed, no further inflation of our inflated currency, which the preponderating votes of the Western States will not be certain to favor. The war of finance is the next war we have to fight, and every blow struck against my efforts to uphold a strict construction of the laws and the Constitution is in reality a blow in favor of repudiating the national debt. The manufacturers and men of capital in the Eastern States and the States along the Atlantic seaboard—a mere strip or fringe on the broad mantle of our country, if you will examine the map—these are in favor of high protective, and, in fact, prohibitory tariffs, and also favor a contraction of the currency. But against both measures the interests and votes of the great producing and non-manufacturing States of the West stand irrevocably arrayed, and a glance at the map and the census statistics of the last twenty years will tell every one who is open to conviction how that war must end.

The history of the world gives no example of a war debt that has ever been paid; but we have an exceptional country, and present an exceptional case. Our debt *might* easily be paid, provided the brakes against excessive expenditures could be turned on quickly enough—but now is the appointed time, and now or never the work must be commenced. If that debt is ever to be paid we need ecomony in every branch of the public service—the reduction, no; and increase of salaries to Congressmen and other officials; the systematic reduction of our national debt; and not its increase by such monstrous bills as this last demagogue measure for the pretended equalization of bounties. The Congress, forsooth, is so patriotic, so loyal, that it "can refuse our gallant soldiers nothing;" but you must have seen how promptly it reject the names of nearly every gallant veteran sent in by me for confirmation to any civil office—a majority of our extremely "loyal Senators" using the guillotine, without remorse, in nearly every instance.

And whither is all this drifting? To intelligent men there can be but one answer: We are drifting toward repudiation, and the moneyed aristocracy of the national debt—the very men whose interests are most jeopardized—are so blind that they are practically helping to accelerate, not check our course in this downward direction. We need the industry and enormous possible products of the lately revolted States to help us in bearing our heavy burden. We need confidence and calm—we need internal harmony; and above all, we need a return to the unquestioned supremacy of the civil laws and constitutional restraints if our debt is not to be repudiated within the next half score of years.

Financial prosperity was secured up to within a recent period; but already the delicate fabric of public credit—a house of cards at best—begins to totter under the concussion of the various revolutionary ideas which have been recently exploited on the floors of Congress. Who now talks of the Constitution with respect? Who is not now made a laughing-stock in the papers and speeches of the violent, revolutionary party, if he shall be so hardy as to claim that, being again at peace, the sway of civil over military law should be immediately resumed, if we desire to maintain our liberties? "The Constitution is played out," we hear on every hand; and every effort to advocate the just ascendancy of the civil law only furnished fresh food for ridicule.

No party as yet, and possibly no party for some years, will openly hoist the banner of repudiation. But a majority of those who shaped the legislation of this last Congress must know, unless they deceive themselves, or are too ignorant to appreciate their own acts, that we are drifting in that direction, and that it is by their votes we have been swung out into the downward stream. Doubtless, some of them would either be, or affect to feel, horrified if to-day branded as repudiationists, just as, in the infancy of the free soil agitation, it was considered a bitter slander if the "free-soiler" should be styled an "abolitionist." There are steps in everything, and the term of reproach to-day will be worn as a feather in the cap some years from now, unless the true conservative wisdom of the country can be awakened, and, rapidly, from its asphyxiating dream that our "national debt is a national blessing."

And look at the effect of the reconstruction bill just passed over my unavailing veto. I mean its peculiar effect as a step in the direction of repudiation, and not its general effect as a high-handed measure of Congressional usurpation, striking out of existence so many States, and establishing a military despotism over more than one-third of our geographical Union. This bill suddenly adds four million of ignorant and penniless negroes to the voting force of the country—an accession of just so much strength to the party whose interest it is, and must increasingly become, to favor repudiation as a policy. To secure the public creditor, our efforts should be—if that were possible—to restrict rather than to extend the right of suffrage; for money rapidly aggregates in a few hands; and whenever the men who have an interest in seeing that our national debt is paid shall have become out of all proportion few, compared with those who have an interest in its repudiation, the votes of the many will carry it, and the debt of three thousand millions will be struck out of existence by ballots, just as rapidly and utterly as the similar amount invested in Southern negroes has been abolished during the recent war under showers of bullets. At least, this is possible.

That we are to have a great financal crash this year I hold to be inevitable—though deprecating it, and having used every effort for its avoidance. To say that it can be staved off by any legislation, if the violated laws of trade and public economy call for it is to assert that water can be made to run uphill, or shall cease to seek its own level under the compulsion of a congressional enactment. Perhaps for so violent a disease, this violent cure may be the only remedy. It is like a man sustaining his strength on brandy; so long as he can increase the dose daily, he may get along in high good humor, just as we have been prospering on an irredeemable paper currency and fresh issues of public securities. But, sooner or later, the day will come in which brandy no longer can stimulate, nor can irredeemable promises to pay pass current as a circulating medium forever. To the man will come a severe fit of sickness, teaching him that the laws of temperance can only be violated under fearful penalties; and to the nation will come a financial crash, teaching it that paper is only a representative of value, not value itself; and that the only true securities for our public credit must be looked for in a system of rigidly exacted obedience to all constitutional restraints, and a thorough system of economy in all branches of the public service.

For the slights and indignities—the unconstitional curtailments and dishonors which the recent Congress has attempted to cast upon me for my unflinching and unalterable devotion to my constitutional oath, and to the best interests of the whole country, according to my best judgment and experience, I am only sorry as regards the indignities sought to be imposed on my high office, but unmoved as regards myself. Conscious of only having executed my duty—conscious of being denounced for "usurpation" only because refusing to accept unconstitutional powers and patronage—and satisfied that the day of wiser thought and a sounder estimate cannot now be far distant—I look with perfect confidence for my vindication to the justice of that future which I am convinced cannot long be delayed. Unless all the senses are deceptive, unless all truth be a lie, unless God has ceased to live, I tell you that the folly and fraud now dominating the councils of this distracted country in Congress cannot endure forever.

National Intelligencer, Mar. 11, 1867.
    1. The report to the paper was dated March 6, but the interview took place on the afternoon of the 5th.

From Hugh McCulloch

Treasury Department. Mch. 5th, 1867.

My Dear Sir:—

It is understood that *Sumner will defeat*, if he can, the nomination of Mr. Kingsbury for Naval Officer at Boston.[1] I hope you will give him an opportunity of doing it to-day by sending in Mr. K's. name.

H McCulloch

ALS, OFH.
    1. George H. Kingsbury (*fl*1881) was a Boston attorney who was deputy collector at the customhouse before being nominated as naval officer on March 7. One day after his nomination, Kingsbury was rejected by the Senate. Boston directories (1861–81); Ser. 6B, Vol. 4: 25, Johnson Papers, LC.

From Cyrus H. Mackey[1]

Sigourney Iowa   March 5 1867

Dear Sir

I see by the Newspapers that the Hon S. Harned,[2] whom you had heretofore appointed Col of Int Rev for this Dist (4th) has been rejected by the "*Senate*."[3] If no one but a *Radical* can be confirmed, *and you are under the necessity of making your reccommendations from that party*—I think it but just that your Frinds should have some *voice* in saying what Radical should have it.

I would therefore respectfully reccommend to your favorable consideration Major Alonzo J. Pope[4] of this city. There is no man in the Dist better qualified And the Radical member from this Dist[5] is pledged (by letter) to assist in his confirmation. And I am fully satisfyed they do not dare to reject him. Maj Pope is a member of the Radical Party, but notwithstanding this He is Judge Harneds Depty in this County. He is every way fully qualified for the position—and fully understands the business of the Office. It would be much more convenient to make the transfer of the office, to some person here, and who knows the exact condition of the Office.

As a matter of course I would not reccommend you to appoint a Radical if there is any chance to get one of our frinds in the position.

But if you cannot get a friend confirmed I do think your friends should be heard in making selection from the opposition.

In reccommending Judge Harned to you I was confident there could be no objections against him except that he was a friend of your Administration. And since I have seen his rejection I must say I have little hope we could get a friend in the place. There could not have been a man more *un*objectionable reccommend in the Dist.[6]

Cyrus H Mackey

P.S. I would add that Judge Harned cordially endorses the reccommendation of Maj Pope.

M

ALS, DNA-RG56, Appts., Internal Revenue Service, Collector, Iowa, 4th Dist., Alonzo J. Pope.

1. In 1855 Mackey (1837–1909) moved to Iowa, where he became a lawyer. During the Civil War he was lieutenant colonel of the 33rd Iowa Inf. He was elected to the state house of representatives in 1879. *The History of Keokuk County, Iowa* (Des Moines, 1880), 513, 627–28; Edward H. Stiles, *Recollections and Sketches of Notable Lawyers and Public Men of Early Iowa* (Des Moines, 1916), 726.

2. Sanford Harned (1814–1889), an attorney, was an early settler of Keokuk County, where he served as county judge in the 1850s. From 1864 to 1866 he was with the quartermaster corps of the Federal army. He later served in both houses of the state legislature. *Keokuk County*, 615; Pension Files, Evaline Harned, RG15, NA.

3. Harned was nominated January 21, 1867, and rejected on February 22. Ser. 6B, Vol. 4: 329, Johnson Papers, LC.

4. Pope (1837–1883), a tinsmith, went to Iowa in 1856. He enlisted in the 13th Iowa Inf. in 1861. Wounded at Shiloh in 1862 and captured at Atlanta in 1864, he rose to the rank of major by the end of the war. Afterwards he worked in the offices of the collector of internal revenue and the auditor. He was a bookkeeper at the time of his death. *Keokuk County*, 505–6, 630–31; Pension Files, Hannah A. Pope, RG15, NA.

5. Republican William Loughridge (1827–1889) served three terms in the U.S. House of Representatives (1867–71, 1873–75). By profession a lawyer, he had previously held office as an Iowa state senator, and as judge of the sixth judicial circuit of Iowa. *BDUSC*.

6. Nominated for the collectorship on March 6, 1867, Pope was confirmed and commissioned on March 11, 1867, and apparently held the office for four years. *Keokuk County*, 631; Ser. 6B, Vol. 4: 329, Johnson Papers, LC.

From Edward C. Quin [1]

611 Walnut street   Philada.   March 5. 1867

Dear Sir,

I cannot deny myself the pleasure of tendering to you my heartfelt congratulations for your two great veto messuages on the "Military reconstruction bill" and the "Tenure of Office Bill." They are the two greatest state papers in the American archives. I trembled least you should falter in the hour of your greatest trial. The Rubicon is now passed. Your enemies are now yours. They have exhausted their malignity and they are powerless. They have made themselves infamous whilst they have shown you to be the Sternest patriot and the wisest Statesman. No tampering vacilation compromise—you are right and as sure as God is just your cause must triumph.

I thank you from the bottom of my heart for what you have so nobly done for our common Country for its laws and liberties as well as for humanity.

E. C. Quin

ALS, DLC-JP.
1. Quin (c1828–c1899), a native of Ireland, was a longtime Philadelphia lawyer. 1870 Census, Pa., Philadelphia, Philadelphia, 3rd Ward, 9th Dist., 516; Philadelphia directories (1868–1900).

From Daniel E. Sickles

Washington, D.C.   5h March 1867.

My dear Mr President

I beg you will kindly Consider the claims of three Military Candidates for positions in the Internal Revenue Service, in the Cities of New York and Brooklyn—viz:

3rd Dist.—(Brooklyn)

Gen'l *Wm. R. Brewster* [1]—heretofore nominated, but *not acted* upon by the Senate.

8th Dist—New York City—for this place Sec. McCulloch has recommended my friend *Gen'l Charles K. Graham* [2]—and I hope you will send his nomination to the Senate. I believe that he will be Confirmed. The *only* objection that can be urged *there* against him is that he was a prominent member of the Cleveland Convention. [3]

In the 9th Dist.—City of N.Y.—*Gen'l Egans* friends believe the Senate will *now* confirm him. [4] Allen [5] was sent in last week & confirmed, but this *action was afterwards reconsidered* & the place is open for a new nomination. Please keep this District open for two or three days—Say until Saturday—& meanwhile we will ascertain whether Egan can be confirmed. I believe the Sec. of the Treasury will be gratified to retain Egan [6]—and he truly deserves consideration for his brilliant military record—pronounced by all his Commanders to be of "the first order of merit."

D. E. Sickles

ALS, DLC-JP.
1. Brewster (1828–1869) had served as a colonel, 73rd N.Y. Inf., during the war; he was brevetted brigadier general in 1864. For reasons not fully understood, Johnson nominated Brewster as collector of internal revenue for New York's Third District in mid-February 1867 and then renominated him on March 8. The Senate finally rejected his nomination on April 20, whereupon Johnson successfully nominated Theophilus Callicott to be the collector. Hunt and Brown, *Brigadier Generals; Senate Ex. Proceedings*, Vol. 15, pt. 1: 237, 403; pt. 2: 776, 779.
2. Graham (1824–1889) worked as an engineer before the war, eventually became colonel of the 74th N.Y. Rgt., and was wounded in action at Gettysburg. Despite Sickles's

repeated entreaties in behalf of the appointment of Graham to an internal revenue position, there is no indication that he was ever nominated. Warner, *Blue*; Sickles to Johnson, [Mar. 7, 1867], Johnson Papers, LC; Sickles to Morrow, Apr. 3, 1867, Tels. Recd., President, Vol. 5 (1866–67), RG107, NA. See also Sickles to Johnson, Mar. 13, 1867.

3. Graham was a delegate from New York at the Soldiers' and Sailors' Convention held in Cleveland on September 17, 1866. The convention endorsed the platform of the National Union Convention held the previous month in Philadelphia. *Cleveland Plain Dealer*, Sept. 19, 1866.

4. Thomas W. Egan had initially been nominated as collector, Ninth District, in mid-December 1866 but rejected by the Senate in late January 1867. The President tried again with Egan's nomination, which the Senate received on March 11 but rejected the next day. Ser. 6B, Vol. 4: 51, 53, Johnson Papers, LC; *Senate Ex. Proceedings*, Vol. 15, pt. 1: 403, 425.

5. Probably William H. Allen. The Senate received Johnson's nomination of Allen on February 25, 1867. Three days after the President forwarded Allen's nomination, McCulloch urged him to recall it, on the grounds that Egan believed he could be confirmed at the next session of Congress. Egan sent a letter to Johnson conveying the same message. The Senate approved the nomination of Allen on March 2 but immediately reconsidered its approval. This action prompted the President to resubmit the name of Thomas Egan. Ibid., 247, 325, 332, 336; McCulloch to Johnson, Feb. 28, 1867, OFH; Egan to Johnson, Feb. 28, 1867, Appts., Internal Revenue Service, Collector, N.Y., 9th Dist., Thomas W. Egan, RG56, NA.

6. On March 8 McCulloch forwarded a letter from Fernando Wood in behalf of Egan's nomination. McCulloch to Johnson, Mar. 8, 1867; Wood to McCulloch, Mar. 8, 1867, OFH. See also Fernando Wood to Johnson, Mar. 8, 1867, Appts., Internal Revenue Service, Collector, N.Y., 9th Dist., Thomas W. Egan, RG56, NA.

From Frank Smith

Private

                                 No. 48 Pine Street   New York   Mch 5/67

My Dear Sir.

Since I saw you on Saturday last I have heard frequent expressions of approval of your vetoes of the Military & tenure of office bills. A great many of the office holders here are afraid to express their opinions although they approve your course.

I leave for Alabama tomorrow and will return in about ten days when I hope I will be able to bring my matter with the Treasury Department to a close.[1] Mr Courtnay U S District Attorney[2] here informs me that the Secretary[3] has called on him for an opinion in my case and since I have had a conversation with him I think he looks upon the matter from a different stand point than that presented to him by the Secty. My last visit to Washington I think has had some effect, for Mr Drapers successors[4] inform me that they have received several letters from Mr Chandler[5] asking information in regard to the list of expenses on the cotton furnished me and which you now have. I hope you have seen the Secretary and have learned his statement of affairs. There are certainly some things surrounding the affair which does not look very well. If you should need my services a message sent here will be telegraphed to me.[6]

                                                                 Frank Smith

ALS, DLC-JP.

1. Under authority from a December 1865 appointment, Smith had confiscated several thousand bales of cotton claimed by Alexander Collie & Co. of London. Smith continued to press for compensation from the Treasury Department for his work. Eventually in 1867 he was paid some $33,000. Johnson to McCulloch, Dec. 8, 1865, *Johnson Papers*, 9: 497–98. See also Smith to Johnson, June 17, Aug. 23, 1867.

2. Samuel G. Courtney.

3. Hugh McCulloch.

4. Perhaps a reference to Simeon Draper, a cotton agent and port collector in New York City who died in 1866. His successors have not been found. *Johnson Papers*, 7: 514.

5. William E. Chandler.

6. Nearly a month later Smith informed the President that Courtney had not been able to render an opinion regarding his claims but believed that they were in order. Smith wanted to be notified when the attorney general would hear his case so that he could be in Washington to represent himself. Smith to Johnson, Apr. 2, 1867, Case Files and Suit Papers, Closed Cases, RG206, NA.

From Henry A. Smythe

New York, March 6th, 1867.

Sir:

Recommended to your favorable regard by the commercial public of New York, by your appointment in April, and in May, 1866, by the favorable vote of the Senate of the United States, I was honored with the office of Collector of the Port of New york. From that day to the present, I have discharged its duties, devoting to them all my energies, intelligence, and my most conscientious zeal. I have scrupulously sought to obey the revenue laws which it is my duty to administer; to perfect the machinery by which they are executed, to restrict disbursements at the point of efficiency, and to secure faithful and trusty subordinates in all departments of the Custom-House. These I conceived to be my first and chief duties to the people upon whom the Customs revenue falls as a tax; to you who honored me with your confidence; to the Senate which honored me with its endorsement, and to myself.

I affirm that the New York Custom-House was never more economically administered than it has been by me; I affirm that it was never more purely administered; I affirm that it was never more efficiently administered than it is today. In no department is the public business in arrears; in nearly every bureau improvement has been made in the character and competency of my subordinates. Reforms are still possible, economies are still possible—and these will be accomplished as fast as practicable whilst I continue to discharge the duties of this office. Herein I mean to imply no inculpation of my predecessors. I can claim no possible advantage over them, except in my experience as a merchant, and my freedom from political environments of every sort. But if the latter has been an advantage to the public service, it has been my personal misfortune. I am accused by the Committee on Public Expenditures of the House of Representatives, in a published report[1] handed in during the final hours of an expiring Congress:

1—Of making removals and appointments which have impaired the efficiency of the public service.

2—Of having, whilst the business of the Custom-House was decreasing, increased its expenditures by from $250,000 to $300,000.

3—Of having contemplated a distribution or farming out of the profits of the General-Order business.

These are the sum-total of the Committee's accusations. Doubtless they are decorated and padded out and ribboned off with adjectives and rhetoric and are lightened here and darkened there with surmises and probabilities, inuendoes and insinuations. To the one I oppose only the stainless record of my life; to the other, facts.

The first charge of having made removals and appointments whereby the efficiency of the Public service has been impaired, is not true. I have weeded out incompetency, ignorance, intemperance and vice from my working-force wherever found, and have filled vacancies with competent, temperate and honest men. You do not need to be informed that the applications have out-numbered a hundred to one the places in the Custom-House. In making selections from these, competency and honesty have been the condition *sine quo non*. This condition being satisfied, I have next been guided in my choice, as any other honest public-officer must be, in all cases out of the range of his personal acquaintance, by the testimony of those whom I believed worthy of trust. I have appointed men from both political parties, and men of no politics. Some men I have appointed for faithful service in the Union Armies; some, because they were destitute and deserving; some because they were highly recommended for such and other reasons by your political friends; some because they were personally known to me to be such as the public service required. I have uniformly filled vacancies by the promotion of officers of proved efficiency and fidelity. The new appointments have always been to the inferior places thus left vacant. It is by this plan, in part, that I have improved the efficiency of the Custom-house force, putting the square pegs into the square holes and the round pegs into the round holes. That inefficiency does not characterize my appointees, is best proved by the fact of efficiency in the public-service in this department—in proof of which I call to witness the head of every bureau, and the whole commerical public of New-York.

The Committee allege in evidence of my bad appointments that an indicted murderer "might have had" a place in the Custom-House.

For that saddest "might have been" I was indebted to the Surveyor of this Port[2] and to the most venerable politician in these parts. Be pleased to accept my assurances that I have not searched among thieves and murderers for Custom-House officers.

The Committee say of me, "while business decreased, he has increased expenses at the rate, *it is said*, of from $250,000 to $300,000 a year."

In the first place, the business of the Custom-House has *not* decreased. On the contrary, it has steadily increased. Indeed, the Committee itself, in the first part of this very report, had stated the fact of increased business, on the authority of the Bureau of Statistics. The enlarged and complex tariff of 1866 has obviously required a larger working force in the Customs' service, and while in no department of public service or of private industry have wages and salaries failed to rise above those which were paid two or five years ago, nevertheless, by retrenchments, reforms and the discharge of political barnacles, the necessary increase of the expenditures of the Custom-House has been so counterbalanced, that it does not amount to one-fifth of what, as the Committee allege in their "it is said," and THAT increase is chiefly made up of surplus Messengers paid $750, who have been promoted to be useful clerks at $1000, and of twelve Entry-Clerks, whose salaries the Secretary of the Treasury raised at my recommendation from $2000, to $2500. I asked the increase in order to forbid and stop their old practice of receiving fees from importers for work done after office-hours—a practice prejudicial to the interests of the Government for obvious reasons.

Finally, I am charged with a "contemplated distribution" or farming out of the perquisites or profits of the "General-Order" business. Perhaps the Committee intended to charge me not only with a "contemplated," but also an actual "distribution"; they probably intended to insinuate as much, even though the *denoument*, as they themselves have shaped it, fails to satisfy the expectations raised by the rhetorical plot. If that be their insinuation it is false and unjust. But I frankly plead guilty, whilst acquiring a knowledge of the Custom-House business to some contemplations which were never realized—some plans which were never executed—some purposes which were always inchoate. Conscious of no purpose or act which needed concealment, I plead guilty also to having concealed nothing from this Committee—not even those inchoate purposes, nor those rejected projects. I gave them the means of knowing the truth, and these are the very weapons of their injustice.

Much of my testimony they forbade their Stenagrapher to record. Part of what was recorded they have suppressed. All of it they have *distorted*.

The facts regarding the "General-Order" business are these: I found it in the hands of a nephew of one, the partner of another, and the son of another of my predecessors in this office, with certain distributive shares alloted to the proprietor[3] of the *"Independent"*—(a weekly *religious* newspaper published in this City) and to *other politicians*. These facts were presented to me at the commencement of my duties, and I was informed that the profits of the business were legally and properly distributable perquisites of my office. Having no partners nor relatives to share in these, and being satisfied with my other emoluments, I formed the purpose to divide and distribute the whole amount thus: a portion to a friend not successful in business—who had aided me to success when I was a boy, struggling for advancement as a Clerk in a New-York store; a portion to political friends who had recommended me to the Senate; a portion to one or two Assistants, whose salaries did not seem to me adequate to their services; a portion to a Member of Congress previously interested in this storage business; a portion to a woman, named Mrs. perry,[4] who presented herself to me as interested in Barr & Phelps[5] obtaining the business, who had lost her husband and sons in the War, and all her property by fire;—a portion reserved for a "political fund" to protect the Clerks in the Custom-House against the electioneering Assessments heretofore levied upon them. This purpose, as I testified to the Committee under oath, and again repeat here, was unknown to most of those whom I intended to commit the business to, was never executed— a half-formed project speedily dismissed from my mind.

My first action in the matter was to transfer the "General-order" business to E. C. Johnson & Co.[6] without payment, agreement, or undertaking as to any profits they might make from it—but this transfer disturbed so many political "rings" and interfered with so many "vested rights," that complaints from merchants of excessive charges, so soon led me to believe that a further change was as necessary for my comfort as for the public good, that after a short experiment I transferred the "General Order" business to Meyers & Smith,[7] as before without payment agreement, or undertaking expressed or implied, with orders to reduce their charges, to a basis satisfactory to the merchants, and with the distinct information that any just complaints from merchants would be deemed sufficient reason for its prompt withdrawal. But one complaint and that trivial, has been made from that day to this.

I again repeat that I never received one dollar from this source, in any form whatever, directly or indirectly, and of course never distributed what I never received. Out of my own pocket, in simple charity, I did relieve Mrs. Perry's disappointment by giving her enough money to take her home to the West—an indiscretion I have been guilty of in more cases than one—to the horror of this benevolent and pure-minded Committee.

In conclusion, suffer me to express regret that my inexperience of Star-Chamber investigations and political trickeries should have made me the instrument of possible harm to you, who appointed me to this office. I took no pains to guard against the machinations of those who sought my removal, for I believed that honesty and efficiency were alone required here. I was credulous enough to believe this Committee when they informed me that there was nothing before them which would require contradiction or refutation on my part. I was credulous enough to suppose that the testimony elicited in my favor, outweighing in quantity and quality all that which their ingenuity has garbled and distored to my discredit, would go out with it. I was not enlightened as to their real purpose till they coined calumnies against you into interrogatories to me, and ordered their stenographer to suppress the indignant truth which nailed their base coinage to the counter.

In this business I chiefly regret the wounds which have passed by me to the hearts of those who are dear to me. I have wondered if the members of this Committee have wives or children.

But a man's life-long character stands for something in this community, and I am less anxious therefore to vindicate it to the public against outrageous aspersions of this Committee, than to vindicate your appointment to a public trust of the undersigned, for no other reason than your belief in his capacity, and with no other expectations than his honesty and efficiency in the discharge of its duties.[8]

Henry A Smythe

LS, DLC-JP.

1. See the *New York Tribune*, Mar. 4, 1867, or *House Reports*, 39 Cong., 2 Sess., No. 30, pp. 1–23 (Ser. 1305).

2. Abram Wakeman.

3. Henry C. Bowen.

4. Jennie A. Perry, possibly of Cincinnati and the widow of a naval officer, but otherwise not identified, had arranged with Barr & Phelps to gain Johnson's endorsement for their getting the general order business from Smythe at the New York customhouse. Ibid., pp. 26, 78, 80, 83, 93–94, 106; *Cincinnati Gazette*, Mar. 21, 1867. See also Jennie A. Perry to Johnson, June 24, 1867.

5. Thomas J. Barr and Edward R. Phelps were only associated in connection with their attempt to obtain the general order business. Barr (1812–1881), a lawyer, had served as a city alderman (1852–53), in the state senate (1854–55), and U.S. House (1859–61). He later became police commissioner for New York City (1870–73) and worked in the city's customhouse. Phelps (*fl*1880) was a merchant and sometime broker. *House Reports*, 39 Cong., 2 Sess., No. 30, p. 79 (Ser. 1305); *BDUSC*; New York City directories (1858–80). For this and subsequently mentioned firms' part in this controversy, see the committee's report and testimony in *House Reports*, 39 Cong., 2 Sess., No. 30, pp. 4–8, 83–91, 155–59 (Ser. 1305).

6. Edward C. Johnson (1816–*fl*1878), a graduate of Dartmouth and trained in law, moved to New York City in 1845 and became involved in mercantile and storage pursuits. Rev. George T. Chapman, *Sketches of the Alumni of Dartmouth College* (Cambridge, 1867), 309; New York City directories (1858–78).

7. Henry J. Meyer (*fl*1875) and Alpheus S. [A.?] Smith (*fl*1867) had a storage business in 1867–68. Meyer, previously involved in the liquor business, remained in the storage business until at least 1875. Ibid.

8. For more on the customhouse controversy, see Smythe to Johnson, Feb. 25, Mar. 28, 1867.

From William H. Thomas [1]

Raleigh N.C.   March 6th 1867

Dear Sir.

I presume I shall be arrested in a day or two for telling the truth—a truth unknown to any one outside myself and five hundred thousand Confederate Soldiers and officers—which is that the day he surrenders the Capitol to a bush Convention under the recent act of Congress[2] it will be taken possession of by myself and followers and if the Army retake it it will be over our dead bodies. Since having been made a slave all the favor I ask is if I am imprisoned by Federal Troops while held in Confinement until liberated by my followers direct the officer in command to allow the ladies to furnish me with provisions. Please send a copy of this to the Speaker of the Senate of the United States.

Wm H. Thomas
Formerly Commander of Thomas Legion
who pulled down the last flag in Dixie.

Tel, DNA-RG107, Tels. Recd., President, Vol. 5 (1866–67).

1. Thomas (1805–1893), a North Carolina businessman and advocate for the local Cherokee, raised and led, as a civilian volunteer, a company of Cherokee and whites, before being named colonel of a Confederate legion. Though seeing action in Tennessee and North Carolina, he was seen as a political threat and a useless military commander. Court-martialed three times for taking in deserters, he was pardoned by Jefferson Davis. Following the war he was pardoned by Johnson and, beginning in March 1867, spent his remaining years in and out of mental hospitals, where he died. *Encyclopedia of the Confederacy* (New York, 1993); E. Stanly Godbold, Jr., and Mattie U. Russell, *Confederate Colonel and Cherokee Chief: The Life of William Holland Thomas* (Knoxville, 1990), 129.

2. Perhaps he is referring to the First Military Reconstruction Act or the Tenure of Office Act, both passed on March 2, 1867.

From John Alexander[1]

Flemingsburg Ky   March 7th 1867

Mr President

I have just concluded the reading of your veto message of the "military Bill"[2] and wish to present you humble as I am my sincere and heartfelt thanks for the manly patriotic and firm manner in which you so nobly vindicated not only the Constitution but also the rites of the citizens and liberties of the people against the gross usurpations and slavish and distructive policy of this majority who now have control of the Legislative department of the Government.

Your masterly vindication of the Constitution and the views of its immortal framers are held in venerated regard by all lovers of civil and religious liberty here and even the few reckless time servers who oppose, acknowledge the true statesmanlike and firm manner in which you so nobly met the issue, and in my judgement when the Historian in after years shall write the history of our now distracted and divided union your views of constitutional liberty therein expressed will be recognised as a monument of wisdom standing firmly upon the foundations which under lie the pillars of all free Government. Once again I thank you for that document Hoping the time may speedily come when the people both North and South may be once more hapy & prosperous under the Constitution of our Fathers with but one aim and object and that to restore fraternal love and to guard and protect the best Government upon which the light of Heaven has ever flashed from the anarchy and ruin which now seems almost inevitable. Accept my best wishes for your health and safety and prayers to Almighty God for a continuation of civil & religious liberty upon this Continent.

John Alexander

So Say I.
H B Franklin[3]

ALS, DLC-JP.
1. Not identified.
2. The First Military Reconstruction bill.
3. Franklin (b. *c*1814) was a local farmer who had retired by the time of the 1870 census. 1860 Census, Ky., Fleming, Dist. No. 1, 139; (1870), Flemingsburg, 24.

From Anne M. Deen

New York City   Mch 7. 1867.

Dear Sir

I have but just returned from Washington and I am constrained to write you to express my sorrow that I could not see you while I was in Wash'g. I desired an interview very much, but the pressure you had from others—Members of your Cabinet, and other high officials, and the urgent matters before the Congress which required your attention, I feel to be the only cause of my not getting an interview.

We fully sympathize with you in the unjust manner with which Congress has treated you, and we admire the statesmanlike exhibit of your deportment, and the sound constitutional objections which you offered to their clearly unconstitutional measures.

We are pleased that you have imparted to you Wisdom to guide you in the consciencious performance of your duty.

Mr Deen and myself both desire to see you to express our approbation of your firmness, and to assure you of our continued esteem and regard. We feel when in your presence, that we see an honest man, whom the wiles of party men, cannot seduce from a consciencious performance of Constitutional duty. I also desired to press upon your notice Mr Deen's name for the position of Naval-officer.[1] I am confident he would receive a confirmation from the Senate—and you would thereby secure a valuable officer to the government. Mr Deen has been endorsed by many of the leading houses in N.Y. and by others, and were it necessary further evidence could be furnished of his honesty and fitness for the position.

In a conversation yesterday with an influential and prominent politician,—one who holds an important trust under government, I was assured that if Mr Franklin[2] were not your choice, Thurlow Weed—would through his influence for Mr Deen. I feel Mr President that if you would but signify a preference for Mr Deen to the Sec'y of the Treasury, he would abandon whom he may have in his mind, and cordially endorse Mr Deen.

Mr Deen has a vast controlling influence, not only in this City, but throughout the entire States, and why would it not be expedient to place in a position, a friend of our Country? I feel Mr President that there must be a change in the Legislative branch of the country or farewell to Democratic government. The House and Senate fully realize the influence at Mr Deens command—when they pass Bills and Measures—per advice of their constituents—at Mr Deens suggestion! I refer particularly to those Bills passed at the last session in the interest of the Cigar manufactures and Tobaconists,[3] throughout the States. Members of Congress have been advised by their constituents to act upon Mr Deens suggestions, or abandon all hopes of a return to Congress. The members know and realize Mr Deens influence, and some of them have asked Mr D— to favorably report them to their constituents.

The influence of Mr Deen will always be given to his Country: to a Constitutional restoration of the States; and why not reward him for his devotedness? Why present to undecisive men the best positions? I trust Mr President you will view this matter as I do, and that men who *dare not say* "I endorse the President," will be excluded from positions in favor of those who dare and who do say I am a "Johnson man" endorsing his every act.

I shall soon visit Wash'g again, and I hope you may deem it wise to postpone any nomination for the Naval office of the Port of New York— (unless you should kindly deem it proper to send Mr Deens name to the Senate) until I see you. I feel that I can convince both yourself and the Hon Secretary of the Treasury of the Wisdom and expediency of selecting Mr Deen, and of his peculiar fitness for the position.

I trust Mr President you will not have tired perusing this, but will give it the attention which your good judgement may think it merits.

Mrs John L Deen
4 East 30th Str   New York City.

ALS, DLC-JP.

1. Since early 1866 Deen's name had been promoted for appointment as naval officer at New York City. See, for example, D. J. Shotwell to Johnson, Aug. 10, 1866; John L. Deen to Johnson, Oct. 5, 1866, *Johnson Papers*, 11: 60–61, 308–9.

2. Cornell S. Franklin, deputy and acting naval officer at New York City, had been seeking permanent appointment to the naval officer post since June 1866. Johnson nominated him in April and again in July 1867, but he did not receive the appointment. *U.S. Off. Reg.* (1867–69); Franklin to Johnson, June 22, 1866, Appts., Customs Service, Naval Officer, New York, Cornell S. Franklin, RG56, NA; Franklin to Johnson, April 13, 22, 1867, Johnson Papers, LC.

3. Evidently a reference to the law passed in July 1866 which established protective rates for tobacco products, among other items. See *Congressional Globe*, 39 Cong., 1 Sess., Appendix, pp. 418–20.

From Benjamin B. French

Washington City, Mar 7th, 1867.

Sir,

The Act making Appropriations for sundry civil expenses of the government for the year ending July 30, 1868,[1] contains the following clause—

"That the Office of Commissioner of Public Buildings is hereby abolished, and the Chief Engineer of the army shall perform all the duties now required by law of said Commissioner, and shall also have the Superintendence of the Washington Aqueduct and all the public works and improvements of the Government of the United States in the District of Columbia, unless otherwise provided by law."

In the first place I make the point that, as the Commissioner of Public Buildings has the control, by former laws and even by that law, by name, of a large number of Appropriations, that that clause of the Act cannot go into effect until the main Act goes into effect, to wit, on the 1st day of July next.

I also make this point, and it is a very grave one—can the Congress of the United States, *constitutionally*, designate any person to take charge of an office, the incumbent of which was required *by law* to be appointed by the President, in conformity with the Constitution? If this can be done, all Congress has to do is to abolish every civil office under this government, from the Department of State down, and designate whomsoever they may think proper to discharge the duties of them, thus overriding the Constitution with a single sentence in an appropriation Bill, and, virtually, destroying the Government!

I do not believe it can legally or constitutionally be done.

The office has been abolished at the outside, after June 30, 1867. But, as I believe, no power on earth can prevent The President of the United States from appointing the person who shall take charge of it, and exercise the duties that *some one must exercise*, or the great number of laws touching it cannot be carried out!

The archives of this office are invaluable. The duties of the officer having charge of it are exceedingly onerous and important. Every deed of the land on which the City of Washington is erected, is here. All the records, diagrams, & papers concerning the lots of the City are here. All the old instructions of Washington, Adams Jefferson, and other Presidents are here. The records of all the Commissioners from 1791, are here, and law after law makes the Commissioner the certifying officer & the custodian of all the valuable papers. It ought not to be that such an office should be abolished by the single stroke of a pen, and all its valuable records and papers taken from the possession of a person under heavy bonds, and handed over to whomsoever Congress, in a fit of almost lunacy, brought on by hatred of a Patriotic President, may see fit to designate.

The questions are grave ones, and ought to be settled with much care after much consideration.

Under all these circumstances, Mr. President, I hope you will think proper to continue the office in progress, for it is now *at a stand still*, by directing me to continue to exercise its duties until the matter can be investigated calmly, & then give such further orders concerning it as you may deem lawful & constitutional.[2]

B. B. French   C.P.B.

This letter is written in great haste & may be crude in expression.

ALS, DNA-RG48, Appts. Div., Misc. Lets. Recd.
1. *U.S. Statutes at Large*, 14: 466.
2. The act was passed by Congress on March 4, 1867, but dated March 2 because, according to French, Congress held a continuous session from the 2nd to the 4th. However, the discussion concerning French and the office had begun in late February. Though upset by what he perceived as a personal attack, French expressed relief at turning over the office to Brig. Gen. Nathaniel Michler on March 14. He immediately set up a law practice partnership but soon tired of it and, in July, requested appointment to some foreign post. Donald B. Cole and John J. McDonough, eds., *Benjamin Brown French, Witness to the Young Republic: A Yankee's Journal, 1828–1870* (Hanover, N.H. 1989), 531–39; French to Seward, July 20, 1867, Johnson Papers, LC; *Washington Evening Star*, Mar. 15, 1867.

From Jacob O. Jones [1]

Rushville Illinois   March the 7/67

Dr Sir

I suppose that it is nothing uncommon for you to recieve letters of this kind as there is so many men just like myself that would like to have office and I will make direct application to you as I am an old Tailor and consequently have A right to do as that is the way for A jur to obtain work in our trade. I would refer you to O. H. Browning[2] of Quincy Ills as to my Honesty as he is acquainted with me and I hope if it is within your Power to give me A lift that you will do so as I am needy and I think that I am Qualified to fill the office of assesor of this the ninth district Ills. or the Post office in this Town or Both if you Please with Honesty towards the Government.[3] Now this is all I have to say on that subject but I will tell you some few things. The man James G McCreery[4] whose name was sent to the senate for confirmation should have been rejected just as he was and why because he would sell his Savour for the Price of A Quart of whisky as I believe. I have lived in this Town for thirty years and we have had A Law against the sale of strong drink I would say for twenty and he has sold it notwithstanding and during the same time he has been *A Pillow in the Presbytery* church. I leave you to draw your own conclusion so far as he is conserned. There is A nother jintlman from our county made

application for the assesship of this district. His name is J. D. Manlove.[5]
He is as I have said a jintleman but is well off in this worlds goods and
consequently if you can find it agreeable with your feelings to give me the
appointment I shall feel much obliged to you and think there will not be
any objections raised as to my being appointed to fill that office. I have
served Eight years as justice of the Peace in this county since liveing
in this state or in other words this county. I was Born and brought up
in A slave state in Fredrick County Maryland and used to have two
Uncles liveing in Washington City D.C. There names ware Wm. & John
Martin[6] and I think perhaps they are still liveing but have not heard from
them for several years. Perhaps you would like to know my Politicks.
Well I can tell you them. I am a johnson man when he does what is right
and I give him creddit for being an Honest man self willed like they
say that I am. I used to be a whig and since have been a Republican in
Principal and expect to remain so unless they should become as corrupt
as the democratick party have become. I signed Manlovs letter and Peti-
sion for the office of assesor but that does not make any diferance. There
is not any one here but myself that know that I am makeing application
for the assesorship. Give it to me if Posable and the Post office too if not
contrary to your feeling. The man Samuel McCreery[7] that got the appoint when Scripps[8] was turned out for saying he was a johnson man said
so for Bread and butter which was contemptable although him and me
have allways been friends and belong to the same Party.

J. O. Jones

ALS, DNA-RG56, Appts., Internal Revenue Service, Assessor, Ill., 9th Dist., J. O. Jones.
    1. Jones (b. c1815) served as justice of the peace from 1840 to 1849. 1860 Census, Ill.,
Schuyler, Rushville, 338; *Combined History of Schuyler and Brown Counties, Illinois* (Philadelphia, 1882), 113.
    2. Orville H. Browning, secretary of the interior.
    3. Jones was not nominated for either position. Eventually Henry L. Bryant was com-
missioned assessor and George W. Scripps, postmaster. Ser. 6B, Vol. 4: 304, Johnson Papers, LC; *U.S. Off. Reg.* (1865–67).
    4. McCreery (1815–*fl*1882), a druggist and longtime resident of Rushville, was nomi-
nated on January 21, 1867, but rejected a month later. 1860 Census, Ill., Schuyler, Rushville, 333; *Schuyler and Brown Counties*, 243; Ser. 6B, Vol. 4: 300, Johnson Papers, LC.
    5. Jonathan D. Manlove (c1803–*fl*1882), a farmer, later moved to Fort Scott, Kansas.
1860 Census, Ill., Schuyler, Rushville, 370; *Schuyler and Brown Counties*, 59.
    6. Possibly John W. Martin (c1810–*fl*1870), a machinist and blacksmith in 1860 and
1870, respectively, or John Martin (c1798–*fl*1850), an auctioneer in 1850, and William
Martin (c1800–*fl*1870), a collector and later justice of the peace (1867–70). 1850 Census,
D.C., Washington, 4th Ward, 276; (1860), 7th Ward, 739, 744; (1870), 285, 316; *U.S.
Off. Reg.* (1867–69).
    7. McCreery (b. c1816) was a justice of the peace in 1860 and postmaster at Rushville
from August 2, 1866. 1860 Census, Ill., Schuyler, Rushville, 339; *U.S. Off. Reg.* (1867).
    8. George W. Scripps (c1826–*fl*1879), editor and owner of first the *Schuyler Democrat*
and then the *Schuyler Citizen*, was postmaster at Rushville from late 1865 to August 1,
1866. 1860 Census, Ill., Schuyler, Rushville, 342; *U.S. Off. Reg.* (1865–67); *Schuyler and
Brown Counties*, 155.

From Hiram Ketchum, Jr.

New York   March 7" 1867.

Sir

I wrote you some days ago in respect to the publication of your messages to Congress in a separate pamphlet.[1] Your Asst. private Secy.[2] send me copies of those messages. The immedate publication of this pamphlet it was thought was called for by the near approach of the Connecticut election. Our friends in Connecticut have decided that it would be more expedient to publish for wide circulation in the State, your last veto upon the military re-construction bill, *separately*, and that is to be done immediately. I saw and conferred with the democratic candidate for Gov,[3] and the democratic candidate of one Dist for Congress, Mr. Barnam—(our Barnum) and Mr. Burr[4] the editor of Hartford, yesterday, and was not less gratified than surprized to find that the prospect for the success of the Demo. candidates was very encouraging. If these gentlemen are not deceived the result of the Connecticut election will give a new aspect to public affairs.

I see it announced this morning that your Excellency has sent to the Senate the name of Col Wood[5] as your nomination to the vacancy in the Naval office department. If this be true, I would respectfully request your Excellency, at your leisure, and when entirely convenient, to direct your private Secty[6] to collect and return to me *all* the letters I have taken the liberty of writing to your Excellency respecting my nomination to this vacancy. I hope the Country will find in Col Wood a faithful officer, and your Excellency an efficient friend.

Hiram Ketchum

ALS, DLC-JP.

1. See Ketchum to Johnson, Feb. 15, 1867.

2. Possibly Robert Johnson.

3. James E. English.

4. William H. Barnum and Alfred E. Burr. Barnum (1818–1889), a manufacturer in Connecticut, served in the U.S. House (1867–76) and Senate (1876–79). Ketchum makes a distinction here, because in 1867 Barnum (Democrat) ran against Phineas T. Barnum (Republican). *DAB.*

5. Alfred M. Wood (1828–1895) was active in Brooklyn politics before the war, including terms on the board of aldermen. At the outset of the war he organized and commanded the 14th N.Y. Rgt. Severely wounded in battle, he returned to Brooklyn, where in 1863 he was elected mayor. Rumors about Wood's pending appointment as naval officer existed but no evidence has been uncovered to indicate that Johnson sent forth Wood's name. *The Civil, Political, Professional and Ecclesiastical History . . . of the County of Kings and the City of Brooklyn, N.Y. from 1683 to 1884* (2 vols., New York, 1884), 1: 491–92; Pension File, Mary A. Wood, RG15, NA; *New York Tribune*, Mar. 7, 1867.

6. William G. Moore.

From Theodoric R. Westbrook[1]

Albany   March 7, 1867

Dear Sir

I reside in Kingston, Ulster Co, NY, which is the principal village in the 13th Congressional District, & the residence of William Masten[2] the present collector of internal revenue, & *of E W Buddington,*[3] *who (according to the Albany Evening Journal of this evening) is to supersede Mr Masten.* My political past, and present is *identical* with yours. I neither hold, nor desire office, but am simply desirous to say a word, for *your good* in reference to this rumored change.

I know Masten and Buddington well. I meet them daily when at home, and expect to do so, so long as we live, and our residence is unchanged, of which latter event occurring, I see no probability. I am here temporarily attending court, and write without solicitation from any one, to let you know three things.

First: William Masten *is* your friend, and active supporter.

Second: E W Buddington is *not* your friend, but a disciple of Sumner, & Stevens. Not a moderate Republican but an ultra radical of the worst type.

Third: Thomas Cornell,[4] the Member of Congress from the 13th District is also an ultra republican, elected by many, and other causes which I have not space to mention, *who would vote for your impeachment tomorrow*, if that question were up.

Upon these facts you may rely, no matter what Cornell says. Now, if in view of these facts, you make this change, all that I can say is, that while I and others who think with me, will still say your vetoes & policy are right, we will also say that you have a queer way of making a party to support you.

Excuse plainness of speech, for the times demand it. Mastens removal will not affect *me*, but *you*.

T R Westbrook
Kingston   Ulster Co   NY

ALS, DNA-RG56, Appts., Internal Revenue Service, Collector, N.Y., 13th Dist., William Martin [*sic*].

1. Westbrook (1821–1885) had served in the U.S. House in the 1850s. He was a long-time practicing attorney in Kingston, New York, and in 1873 became a justice of the state supreme court. *BDUSC.*

2. Masten (b. *c*1808) was a harbor master at Kingston before becoming collector of internal revenue. 1860 Census, N.Y., Ulster, Kingston, 91.

3. Edward W. Buddington, not further identified, was nominated by the President to replace Masten as collector on the very day that Westbrook wrote to Johnson. The Senate approved Buddington's nomination on March 8. *Senate Ex. Proceedings*, Vol. 15, pt. 1: 351, 377.

4. Cornell (1814–1890) was engaged in the transportation business before becoming a

U.S. representative, a post he held at two different times (1867–69, 1881–83). He remained active in the Republican party until his death. *BDUSC.*

From Ethan A. Allen

Charleston, S.C.   March 8th 1867

Dear Sir.

When I had the pleasure of seeing you in Washington last Month,[1] I promised as pr agreement that I would write you from place to place what might be my observations relative to the state & feelings of the people in the Southern States. The Negroes I find quite inclined to work as a general rule, but very many will not if they can possibly help it. The general desire on their part is to crowd into Cities & Towns where they hope to get some light work to do, & after earning a few dollars, "knock off," until absolute want obliges them to do something. This I particularly observed on visiting Norfolk Va. & find the same rule holds good everywhere I have been & particularly so here. While the General Government encourages them in idleness by supplying them with rations just so long will they be a heavy tax on her coffers.

Mr. President you may depend on it that the maintanance of the "Freedmans Bureau" is a great mistake. Were that abolished the Negro would at once become *self sustaining*. They would then know that they *must work, or starve*.

Were the people of the Southern States permitted to govern themselves as are the Northern States they would at once enact proper Laws. *All* would be protected by their operations & we should hear no truthful reports of "Outrages upon Loyal Men," & I fully believe within a comparatively short time, the country would be united in sentiment & the horrors of the bloody War from which we have so recently emerged would be in a measure soon forgotten. I speak Sir as a *Nation*. Of course the Widow & the orphan in *many, many* cases would be but a living emblem of withered hopes, & crushed expectations. Then let us try & bind up those wounds, & bid the Nation live.

The people have a dread of the approaching Military rule under which they are to be placed, but Sir, relying on your patriotism, & love of justice they still look to you as their protecting Angel, placed by the Almighty in your exalted position, as a rock for their protection, & hope you will deal magnanimously, with a brave but fallen foe. I have conversed with no Gentleman during my trip who is not fully disposed to aid the Government in maintaining its authority. This Sir is the feeling, & sincere desire of the people & the general assertions which you hear in Congress of the danger of "Union Men" South is all buncomb.

I regret to say I have met with Northern men down here who feel as though they are not at home. They have no standing in the community & I have made some enquiries as to their *social* relations, & find them of the *basest* kind. The man in this City who most glories in a Military rule is a Doctor, G. R. Cutter,[2] who was formerly a Surgeon in a Volunteer Regt. (of Massachusetts I think) now practicing Medicine in this City with Negroes. He keeps a negro woman as his Mistress & has a child by her. He so far forgot a decent regard for public opinion as to drive with her in a buggy frequently through the streets of Charleston.

Again Sir, at a Negro public meeting held in Norfolk Va. a few days since several *white* Men made themselves very conspicuous in denouncing your policy.[3] I assure you those Men prior to the War could not have been elected to the position of a Town Constable, & may with propriety be denominated as *Vagabonds*.

I beg leave again to refer to the "Freedmans Bureau." An Officer in the U.S. Army *now* stationed here has just assured me (in a general conversation) that he thinks at least Four or Five Millions of Dollars could be saved to the Government by a *proper* administration of that branch of the service in this Department.

Ethan A. Allen

P.S. I shall visit various places on my way to New Orleans where I shall be within three or four weeks & stop at the St. Charles Hotel.

E.A.A.

ALS, DLC-JP.
   1. See Allen to Johnson, Feb. 14, 1867.
   2. George R. Cutter (1840–1891) entered military service in the 127th N.Y. Vol. Rgt. shortly after graduation from medical school. Evidently sometime in 1867 Cutter left Charleston to begin the practice of medicine in Brooklyn. Howard A. Kelly and Walter L. Burrage, *Dictionary of American Medical Biography* (New York, 1928), 285; William B. Atkinson, ed., *The Physicians and Surgeons of the United States* (Philadelphia, 1878), 327.
   3. Allen could be referring here to either the Monday, February 25, meeting at the Methodist church or to the Saturday, March 2, meeting at the Lyceum Hall in Norfolk. Both events were attended by a mixed crowd of blacks and whites. From the cursory newspaper accounts, however, it is not clear which one of the meetings, if either, engaged in denouncing Johnson's policy. See *Norfolk Virginian*, Feb. 26, Mar. 7, 1867.

From William H.C. King

New Orleans   March 8th, 1867

Considerable excitement here. Situation critical and similar to that preceding riot. Wells issued proclamation under Military bill.[1] Election Monday.[2] People believe Wells had no right to issue such documents. Gen Sheridan says he received no official announcement of bill and refers to District Commander Mower[3] who says he knows nothing about it but must sustain Governor if called upon. People think the actions & language of both Welles & Monroe[4] likely to lead to trouble. Welles Said to be organizing negroes under title of Grand Army of Republic.[5] We will try and get Legislature defer Election.[6] I am of opinion power should be telegraphed Gen. Sheridan at once and if he deems necessary for public safety relieve both Wells & Monroe.[7]

W H C King

Tel, DLC-JP.
   1. J. Madison Wells said in his proclamation of March 8, 1867, that all elections held in the state must conform to the provisions of the new First Military Reconstruction Act and that "all persons elected to office must be able to qualify under said law before they will be allowed to enter on the duties of the same." *New Orleans Picayune*, Mar. 9, 1867 (morning).
   2. The election was supposed to be for some New Orleans aldermen. Ibid.
   3. Joseph A. Mower.
   4. New Orleans mayor John T. Monroe.
   5. The Grand Army of the Republic was an organization of Union army veterans. It did have a branch in Louisiana and did influence the blacks there. It is not known that Governor Wells had any connection with it, however. Taylor, *La. Reconstructed*, 134–35.
   6. The resolution to suspend the election passed the state house but not the senate. As a result of this impasse, Sheridan issued a proclamation postponing the election. King to Johnson, Mar. 9, 1867, Johnson Papers, LC.
   7. Sheridan did not relieve Wells or Monroe at this time. See Monroe to Johnson, May 9, 1867.

From Francis H. Peirpoint

Richmond   Mch 8 1867

The General Assembly of Virginia has unanimously signed a petition to your Excellency requesting the appointment of Gen Schofield to the command of Virginia under the late act of Congress. The Memorial will be presented to you tomorrow.[1]

F H Peirpont [*sic*]

Tel, DLC-JP.
   1. In a cover letter dated March 8, Peirpoint presented the petition also dated the 8th. John M. Schofield, commander of the Department of the Potomac, which included Virginia, officially took command of the First Military District on March 13, 1867. Peirpoint to Johnson, Mar. 8, 1867, Johnson Papers, LC; James L. McDonough, *Schofield: Union General in the Civil War and Reconstruction* (Tallahassee, 1972), 170.

From James B. Bingham
Private

Memphis, Tenn., March 9, 1867.

Dear Sir—

As you are aware, I was induced to retire from newspaper business last fall on account of ill health. For the last five months I have devoted myself assiduously to the improvement of my general health, and with the best possible results. I have become so vigorous that I had intended running the race for Congress next August, but the adoption of negro suffrage by the legislature compels me to decline the honor.

I write now to ask your good offices in my appointment as Commissioner under the Bankrupt Law which has just passed.[1] I consider myself fully equal to the duties, and will do my divinist to confer credit on the appointing power. You know me well enough without recommendations, but if you require it, I will furnish them in any quantity or character you may indicate, always excepting Leftwich and those who with him were in *opposition* to you and myself in the reorganization of our state government in the spring of 1864. Now, Mr. President, you can easily appoint me to this commissionership, and I shall expect you to do it, and with as little delay as possible. I will add, that I think I will be as acceptable to the Radicals in this section as any man, except one of them, who could be appointed.

Negro suffrage will seriously affect us in our elections next August. Brownlow and his friends say they will carry the state, and I fear they will, unless our supreme court shall in the meantime pronounce the franchise act unconstitutional.

In this District, Leftwich will never touch bottom again. He is too *unreliable. I* shall not be in his way, as I intended. I fear the hopelessness of the contest will induce all your friends, except Leftwich, to retire, and between him and W. J. Smith, Radical, Smith will beat him out of sight.

Rolfe Saunders, our new collector, is reported as under promise to aid the Radicals in pay for his confirmation. He has little influence, however, outside of his official position, and it is not unlikely that he may disregard his pledges. He will certainly do so if he can *make* any thing by it.

Trusting that you will give my application immediate and favorable attention . . .

James B. Bingham

ALS, DNA-RG56, Appls., Positions in Washington, D.C., Treasury Offices, James B. Bingham.
1. Evidently, Bingham was confused about provisions of the bankruptcy law; presumably when he refers to commissioner, he means the bankruptcy register. In any event, said registers were to be appointed by the U.S. district court judges. See *Congressional Globe*, 39 Cong., 2 Sess., Appendix, pp. 228–36.

From Canadian Cherokee Delegation[1]

Washington, D.C.   March 9, 1867

Your memorialists, duly appointed by that portion of the Cherokee Nation known as the Canadian Cherokees[2] to represent their interests at Washington, and acknowledged in that capacity by the Government as will be seen from the enclosed letter of the Commissioner of Indian Affairs,[3] having been informed that there is now before your Excellency for consideration a convention under date of the 1st instant purporting to have been entered into between the United States and the Cherokees, most respectfully beg leave to protest against its approval for the following reasons:

1. The so-called convention has been concluded without consulting the Canadian Cherokees who comprise seven-seventeenths of the entire Cherokee Nation and who have mutual rights and interests in the matters disposed of by that convention.

2. That under the articles of said convention the neutral lands of the nation, of which the Cherokees represented by your memorialists own seven-seventeenths, being their share based on actual population, have been sold so as to subserve the peculiar ends and enure to the sole benefit of the Cherokees represented by the Ross delegation,[4] and in total disregard of the wishes and violation of the interests of the Cherokees of the Canadian district.

3. The party assuming to act for the Cherokee Nation in concluding said convention, to wit, Wm. P. Ross, Riley Keyes and Jesse Bushyhead,[5] had no power whatever to act in the premises. They profess to represent said Nation by virtue of authority derived from a so-called "National Council" that met at Talequah of October of last year, but which was composed exclusively of representatives chosen by the Ross party. By article 6 of the Treaty of July 19, 1866, the Canadian Cherokees are guaranteed "representation according to numbers," but they were wholly excluded from said council and their places filled by representatives elected by the Ross party from the Canadian district prior to the treaty and who still continue to hold their seats, thus usurping the rights to which our constituents were entitled.

4. A formal protest against any acknowledgment of the Ross delegation as representing the Cherokee Nation, they having been appointed by only a part of said Nation, and against entering into any agreement, convention or treaty with that delegation which would affect the rights of the whole Nation, without the concurrence of the delegates of the Canadian Cherokees, was filed with the Commissioner of Indian Affairs several weeks prior to the date of the convention referred to, but, as we have been reliably informed, was withheld from the President to whom it was addressed.[6]

5. A supplemental treaty is vitally important to remove the many embarrassing ambiguities of the Treaty of 19 July, 1866; to secure payment to the Cherokee Nation for the lands lying west of the 96', alienated by it under that treaty, amounting to about ten millions of acres; and to provide for a proper distribution of the proceeds of those lands as well as of the neutral lands in Kansas:—to which supplemental treaty the delegation representing the Canadian Cherokees ought of right to be a party.

For the above reasons your Memorialists respectfully request that the said convention be returned to the Commissioner of Indian Affairs with instructions to open negotiations with the Delegations representing the two parties of the Cherokee Nation, for the purpose of securing the objects set forth.

And your memorialists will ever pray.

R. Fields   (Chairman)

W. P. Adair

J. A. Scales

Delegation Canadian Cherokees

Mem, DNA-RG75, Gen. Records, Lets. Recd. (M234, Roll 101).

1. Richard Fields, William P. Adair, and Joseph A. Scales. Fields (*fl*1868), a well-known Cherokee attorney, was a captain in Drew's Confederate regiment and was captured at Pea Ridge. After his exchange he served under Stand Watie and, after the war, was an active representative of the Confederate Cherokees. Adair (*c*1828–1880), sometime assistant chief of the Cherokee Nation, was a colonel with the Confederate Cherokees. Scales (*fl*1868), a major with the same forces, had been a substantial slaveholder. William P. Thompson, "Courts of the Cherokee Nation," *Chronicles of Oklahoma*, 2 (1924): 67; W. Craig Gaines, *The Confederate Cherokees: John Drew's Regiment of Mounted Rifles* (Baton Rouge, 1989), 88, 123; *Appleton's Cyclopaedia*; Kenny A. Franks, *Stand Watie and the Agony of the Cherokee Nation* (Memphis, 1979), 127, 174; Theda Perdue, *Slavery and the Evolution of Cherokee Society, 1540–1866* (Knoxville, 1979), 116–18; Edward E. Dale and Gaston Litton, *Cherokee Cavaliers* (Norman, Okla., 1940), 260–61.

2. Those Cherokees who had supported the Confederates. William C. McLoughlin, *Champions of the Cherokees: Evan and John B. Jones* (Princeton, N.J., 1990), 439.

3. The letter from Lewis V. Bogy has not been found.

4. Northern or Unionist Cherokees who belonged to the faction supporting the late principal chief John Ross. Ibid.

5. Keyes (*fl*1874) was a circuit judge. Bushyhead (d. 1867), son of the Baptist minister and Cherokee chief justice of the same name, was operating a mercantile business at Fort Gibson at the time of his death. Ibid., 469; Gaines, *Confederate Cherokees*, 39; *Biographical Dictionary of Indians of the Americas* (2 vols., Newport Beach, Calif., 1991), 1: 103, 106.

6. Not found.

From Frank S. DeHass [1]

Balto. Md.   March 9th 1867.

Hon. Sir.—

I met with Genl. S. Berry[2] to day, a very warm friend of your Excellency, & he seemed to feel badly that his proposition to pay in your name, $5000. to our Memorial Church, had never been acknowledged. I told him you had accepted his kind offer, but was very much pressed with state affairs, & would no doubt write him soon. Please excuse me for calling your attention to this matter. Hoping that you will appreciate the General's feelings, & accept his generous gift . . . [3]

F. S. DeHass   Pastor.

ALS, DLC-JP.

1. DeHass (*fl*1875), a native of Pennsylvania, was in Washington, D.C., in 1867–69. He served as consul at Jerusalem (1873–75) and wrote about his travels in that region. *U.S. Off. Reg.* (1873–75); *NUC*; Washington, D.C., directories (1867–69).

2. Probably Adj. Gen. John S. Berry.
3. No details are known about this situation.

From William F. Lockwood[1]

Washington D.C.   March 9" 1867

To the President

During the last three years of my discharge of the duties of United States Judge of the Territory of Nebraska *Casper E Yost*[2] was Marshal of said Territory. I desire to say that I alwais found *Mr Yost* in his relations to said office & the discharge of his duties to the Government a most honest & efficient officer. I have no doubt but what he satisfied the people of the Territory. I know he did the U.S. so far as I represented it as Judge. He is an applicant for the appointment to the office of U.S. Marshal of the new District of Nebraska and I most cheerfully & earnestly reccomend him for the place.[3]

Wm. F. Lockwood   Late U S. Judge Neb. Ter.

ALS, DNA-RG60, Appt. Files for Judicial Dists., Neb., Casper E. Yost.
1. Lockwood (1822–1901), a lawyer and sometime newspaper editor, moved from Ohio to the Nebraska Territory in 1856. Lincoln appointed him a territorial associate justice there in 1861, a post he held until statehood. Unable to be confirmed by the Senate for the federal district judgeship of Nebraska, Lockwood returned to Ohio where he practiced law and served as judge of the court of common pleas for Lucas County. Harvey Scribner, ed., *Memoirs of Lucas County and the City of Toledo* (2 vols., Madison, Wisc., 1910), 1: 467.
2. University of Michigan graduate Yost (1841–1922) moved to Nebraska, where he was appointed territorial marshal in 1865. After his tenure in this position he was postmaster of Omaha (from 1872 to sometime before late 1877), part owner and president of the *Omaha Republican*, and a major telephone company executive for Nebraska and surrounding states and territories. *NCAB*, 2: 394–95; *U.S. Off. Reg.* (1873–77).
3. Since Nebraska had become a state on March 1, 1867, territorial officers were being replaced by state officials. In addition to the state courts, Nebraska would also have a federal district court. Yost had a number of recommendations from other former territorial officials as well and Johnson did nominate him for U.S. marshal on March 18, 1867. He was confirmed and commissioned on March 28 and served until sometime before late 1869. Ibid. (1867–69); Ser. 6B, Vol. 4: 362, Johnson Papers, LC. For one example of Yost's recommendations, see A. S. Paddock to Johnson, Mar. 8, 1867, Appt. Files for Judicial Dists., Nebr., Casper E. Yost, RG60, NA.

From David L. Seymour

Troy N.Y.   March 9, 1867

Dear Sir

Permit me to say as an old friend that I have read your recent veto of the Military Reconstruction Bill passed by the last Congress and am much pleased with it. You have pursued the true course of a Chief Magistrate. When a law was passed by the Legislative body overthrowing the constitutional governments of ten States of the Union & in time of profound peace establishing military governments & martial law in them, you as was your duty under the Constitutional Government bequeathed to us by our fathers; interposed your power & by the veto attempted to prevent the reckless invasion of constitutional right attempted by the radical & revolutionary majority of Congress. You have placed your veto upon record for all time to come & it is a most able & eloquent vindication of the constitution & of your own policy under it. The wild passions of a fanatical majority have for the time prevailed over constitutional rights, over reason & common sense & in spite of your efforts to save the country from this fearfull step & its sad consequences the law is passed & the Constitution violated. But the evil done lies not at your door. On the contrary in after times, every lover of freedom & the constitutional rights of the people will bless your name as their champion. Where the revolutionary tendencies of the hour will carry our country no one can tell. But whatever may await us as a people in the unknown future let me assure you that I would rather stand with you upon the battlements of the Constitution than to achieve all the temporary success which the demogogues of the day hope for. Permit me as one of the people to thank for the noble vindication of our rights & to assure you of my high regard.

David L Seymour

ALS, DLC-JP.

From Daniel E. Sickles

              298 [F?] St.   Saturday Night   9th March '67
Mr President,

I trust that no misapprehension of my actual grade in the army will exclude me from consideration, if deemed otherwise qualified, in the selection of commanding officers for the Military Districts created by the recent Act of Congress.[1]

The Act requires the District Commander to be an officer of the army not below the rank of Brigadier General. My grade in the army is that of Major General.

The act does not require the commanding officer of a District to be an officer of the *Regular* Army. Yet, if such a construction be put upon the law I am not the less eligible, inasmuch as I might then be assigned as a *Brevet* Major General in the Regular Army,—thus satisfying any construction of which the terms of the Act are susceptible.

It is my only purpose in this communication to prevent a possible misapprehension as to my eligibility, without intending to solicit one of these difficult and responsible commands,—as to which I do not need to be admonished that the action of the Executive should remain entirely unembarrassed by personal considerations.

D. E. Sickles   Maj. Gen'l

ALS, DNA-RG108, Lets. Recd. *re* Military Discipline.

1. Within a few days the President appointed Sickles to serve as commander of the Second Military District (the Carolinas).

From George D. Prentice

Louisville, Ky., March 10th, 1867.

Dear Sir,

I am informed that the patronage of the Government will be given to the party in Kentucky that now calls itself the "Conservative party."[1] That party is exceedingly small. There are very few avowed friends of yours in it. It is trying to break up the Democratic party, and the only result of its success would be to give a triumph to the Radicals. Neither the Louisville Democrat nor any other organ or leader of its party has ever endorsed you or your administration.

The policy of the Louisville Journal is to sustain you in your brave and noble course. We have constantly written for you and are writing for you as no other editors in this State have done or are doing.[2]

Our policy is to endeavor to control the Democratic party in Kentucky, bringing it to your support, and placing it in full fellowship with the Democracy of the North. We think that we are doing this effectually.

Our alternative was to go with the Democrats or with your bitterest enemies, the Radicals, and we know, that, in taking the course we have done and in pursuing it, we are doing the best possible thing we can for your administration and the country.

God bless you for your noble deeds!

Geo. D. Prentice.

ALS, DLC-JP.

1. The Conservatives in postwar Kentucky constituted something of an anomaly, for at times they functioned as a sort of third party, yet at other times they blended in with either the Democrats or the Republicans. A March 1867 meeting of Conservative leaders attempted to reestablish the group's identity in the wake of Democratic party gains in the state. By this time Prentice himself had shifted away from the Conservatives into the Democratic party fold. E. Merton Coulter, *The Civil War and Readjustment in Kentucky* (Gloucester, 1966 [1926]), 319–21.

2. For Prentice's earlier statement in support of Johnson's policies and his plea in behalf of government printing contracts for the *Journal*, see Prentice to Johnson, Oct. 5, 1866, *Johnson Papers*, 11: 310–11. Johnson responded to Prentice's March letter with a note of thanks for the Kentuckian's support and friendship. Johnson to Prentice, Mar. 13, 1867, Johnson Papers, LC.

From Lewis [Louis] Rittenhouse[1]

Philada.   March 10, 1867

Honored Sir—

Enclosing article[2] is in every respect most true of the man referred to, and is a type of the men with whom he recently associated to bring about, as was said a "Coup d'etat," that is to say—*Flanigan*—*Coggshall Welsh* and *Zulich*[3] all of Philadelphia. The two first are notorious frauds, and to put money in their pockets would sacrifice any good honest man on this earth. But little better is Welsh and Zulich—they are not to be trusted, and are only used by Flanigan that he may the better succeed in his nefarious schemes to rob and filch monies and any other favors that you may have to dispense to the end that he may be benefitted at the expense of those to those on whom you bestow your patronage. This can be proved true in every particular. It is to be hoped that he may no longer have your ear to pursue his diabolical purpose.

L. Rittenhouse   Philadelphia

ALS, DLC-JP.
1. Rittenhouse (*c*1825–*fl*1896) was for many years a carpenter in Philadelphia. 1860 Census, Pa., Philadelphia, Philadelphia, 22nd Ward, 407–8; Philadelphia directories (1861–96).
2. The clipping, which carried the byline of the *Philadelphia Sunday Mercury*, March 10, 1867, reported that Albert B. Sloanaker had allegedly removed several deputy collectors before stepping down as collector, First District. Sloanaker had been appointed during the congressional recess in 1866 but was rejected by the Senate in late February 1867. *Senate Ex. Proceedings*, Vol. 14, pt. 1: 268; Sloanaker to Johnson, May 18, 1867.
3. Joseph R. Flanigen, Henry R. Coggshall, John Welsh, and Samuel M. Zulick.

From Chauncey H. Snow

Washington, March 10 1867.

Private and Confidential

Sir.

A sense of imperative duty to myself, impels me to address you this note.

I have expended all of my private fortune in publishing the "National Intelligencer," which you will admit has steadily and faithfully sustained the measures and policy of your administration. My pecuniary resources are exhausted. A radical Congress has shorn the paper of what little Government patronage it has heretofore enjoyed, simply *because* of its support of your administration.

I have asked that in making *one single appointment* you would nominate a friend through whose official position and influence the "Intelligencer" might be sustained. Unaided I can publish it no longer, without involving myself in financial ruin.

If my interests can be thus protected by you, consistently with your sense of public duty, I shall endeavour to continue the paper as a steadfast and unfaltering friend of your administration, which it is unnessary to say, I regard as eminently patriotic. If this cannot be, I shall be *compelled*, however humiliating the necessity, to dispose of the establishment to parties who have for some time stood in readiness to purchase it, and who would undoubtedly radically change the tone and spirit of the paper—employing it *against* the wise and beneficent measures for which it has so long and so zealously labored.

I write this letter with regret, but inexorable necessity compels me to the unwelcome task.[1]

C. H Snow.

P.S. Will you oblige me by indicating at what time I can see you in reference to this matter, which to *me* is of vital interest.

ALS, DLC-JP.
  1. Snow, Coyle, & Co. had acquired the paper in 1866 upon the death of William Seaton. Though some patronage was bestowed upon the *Intelligencer* by the State and War departments, it was not enough to offset the half million in bad debts on its books. By the end of the decade the paper faltered and was moved to New York. Frederic Hudson, *Journalism in the United States, from 1690 to 1872* (New York, 1873), 259; *U.S. Off. Reg.* (1867).

From William C. Patterson

Phila.   March 11th 1867

Dear Sir

If no democrat or republican agreeing in opinion with you upon the Subject of reconstruction can be confirmed by the Senate and your choice is to be limited to radical republicans the friends of Col W B Thomas will bring his name to yr notice in connexion with the collectorship of this port.[1]

Differing in political faith very widely from Col. Thomas I have always found him a frank and manly opponent and as Such he has earned at my hands the respect due to personal worth and integrity of character.

Coming into this community a Stranger without friends he has so conducted himself as to deserve and command its entire confidence and no appointment could be made from the radical wing of the republican party which would be more generally acceptable to the business men of this city.

The patriotism of Col. Thomas differs from the obtrusive fair weather loyalty which so many found at once pleasant and profitable during the war in this that it led him to imperil his person under the old flag in vindication of the supremacy of law.

W C Patterson

ALS, DNA-RG56, Appts., Customs Service, Collector, Philadelphia, Wm. B. Thomas.
  1. While there appears to have been some discussion about the possible appointment of Thomas as collector, his name was not one of the several nominees offered by the President in March and April 1867. See *Washington Evening Star*, Mar. 14, 1867.

From Jane R. Stanton [1]

Windy Hill Plantation [Miss.]   March 11th 1867

I trust you will be induced to read this letter as it is written by a Southern woman one who has a great admiration for your character and who looks upon you as the only barrier that stands between the South and utter distruction. Your excellency can scarcely realize the condition of the Southern people. Indeed I do not exagerate when I say many very many who lived in affluence before the war are actually on the verge of Starvation. In this county (Adams Miss) one of the weathiest in the State the people are almost in a despairing condition. The almost failure of the cotton crop of last year and the heavy expenses incurred have thrown them far behind as the crop scarcely realized more than one half of expenses, and the present political aspect has so discouraged Capitalists that they will not or cannot make advances to enable Planters to make another struggle this year. The negroes are necessarily great sufferers. They are wanting the necessaries of life. Every day I have applications from old negroes for food and have not the means of supplying their wants. Our old family servants still look to us for food and shelter, and altho demanding all the rights of the white man, *expect* all the priveledges of a negro. We have large tracts of land with negroes already upon them willing to work, but we have not the means of feeding them or of providing teams for them to work. We are much discouraged and can see no way to overcome our difficulties. My Husband Dr. Stanton[2] is a graduate of Jefferson College Phia. has practised his profession only on his plantations and in his family. Soon after he graduated he fell heir to a large property in land and negroes. As the war has left him destitute he desires to practice his profession and make some efforts for a support for his family. He had the honor of taking you by the hand in the Presidents mansion last winter a year ago. My object in troubling you is to know if there is any possible chances of getting some Consolship or office to California or Sandwich Islands where we could serve the country and make a livelihood at the same time. Do not smile at my wants. I desire to get some honorable position for my Husband who is a gentleman in every respect and well qualified to fill an office with honor. He is a native Miss & nephew to one of the early Governors of the State, Gerard Brandon.[3]

Your excellency little knows with what longing hope and egerness the People of the South look to you for help, and with what apprehension and almost dismay they witness the actions of Congress. We are sustained by the hope that the genius of yourself and Mr. Seward will yet save the Republic.

Jane R Stanton

Will you be so kind as to answer direct to Mrs J R Stanton care Dr. F Stanton Natchez Miss.

ALS, DNA-RG59, Lets. of Appl. and Recomm., 1861–69 (M650, Roll 47), Jane R. Stanton.

1. Stanton (c1835–fl1870), nee Chaplin, was first married to Robert Stanton, who died in 1853, and then his brother, Fred. 1870 Census, Miss., Adams, Natchez, 465; Elizabeth and Huldah M. Stanton file, Congressional Jurisdiction Case 8731, Records of the Court of Claims, RG123, NA.

2. Fred Stanton (c1826–fl1870) owned a plantation in Louisiana. 1870 Census, Miss, Adams, Natchez, 465; Ibid.

3. Brandon (1788–1850) served as Mississippi governor from the 1820s until 1832, when he retired from public life and devoted himself to his plantation. Sobel and Raimo, *Governors*, 803.

From James S. Campbell[1]

The State of Mississippi   Kemper county
March 13/67

Dear sir

Permit me to address you which I will endeavour to do in a brief & plain manner & will state nothing but facts which I am will able to substentate. I am a citizen of this state & county & has been for the last thirty two years & Forty six years of age when this state seceded from the U S A govermet. I opposed it with all my power never cast a vote from Novr 1860 until 1865. I opposed the whole course the south took in her Rebellion. I was allways Ready & willing to comply with the Laws of the goverment. I was a small slave holder owned twenty one in no. but looked to the governmnt for protection & aid, and being so unfortunat as to be greatly damaged by the fate of War having sufferd great affliction during the Rebellion on account of my principles & actons during the whole contest, having proved myself Loyal to the government of the united states look to her for aid in this time of pressure, having a family to support by my own exertions Begs your honor the President & Congress to grant to me the appointment of Assessing or Collecting the Revinew Taxes in the State of Mississippi.

Being well qualified to attend to any business office in the state & claimg myself as being an honest & correct man and fully able to give you general satisfaction in Refernce to any thig I have stated to you I am at a great loss to no who to apply to for office but my understanding is officrs get the appoint in the southren states by the Presidnt. If out of you Power to grant to me the office I ask for please grant to me some office in the state that you think I deserve to Remunerate me for the time past & prove a blessing for the future. We do not no what officers will be in power in the states yet. Thare fore we do not no what to ask for. I hope you will Read this brief petition with sympathy & be governd by your good feelings and hope you will assign to me some office in this state or Refer me to the authorities whare I will Rech it & Should you wish a personal Interview I will present myself before you at Washington City & give you general satisfatin.

James S. Campbell

P.S. Please address me at Lauderdale Dopt Mobile & O.R.R. Miss. It is hard that the Richeous should be punished with the Wicked and we think those who choose the good part ought to be favoured in those times of trouble & famine in the south & hope the authorities that govern them will aid and assist us.[2]

J.S.C

ALS, DNA-RG56, Appts., Internal Revenue Service, Collector, Miss., 12th Dist., James S. Campbell.

1. Not identified.

2. The *Senate Ex. Proceedings* shows no appointments for internal revenue posts in Mississippi during 1867.

From James R. Doolittle

PRIVATE

Washn   March 13, 1867

Dear Sir.

We have been so anxious about the paymaster question from Wisconsin, that I hope the President can give us two.

There are two said to be appointed from Vermont, and among the appointments to the regular army Wisconsin has not received any thing like so many as Iowa, Michigan and Illinois in comparison.[1]

J. R. Doolittle

This if it could be done would disentangle some matters between our delegation and Gov Randall[2] & myself. The President understands that I am fully committed in favor of Major Ely's appointment.[3]

ALS, DLC-JP.

1. In late 1867 Iowa had one paymaster; Michigan and Vermont, two; and Illinois, three. The Iowa paymaster, as well as one each from Michigan and Vermont and two from Illinois, had been appointed as of January 17, 1867. Perhaps it was this spate of appointments which caused Doolittle and his associates to be "so anxious about the paymaster question." Only one paymaster from Wisconsin was appointed on March 13, 1867, possibly as a result of Doolittle's request. *U.S. Off. Reg.* (1867); Powell, *Army List*, 160, 231, 350, 476, 502, 605, 645.

2. Alexander W. Randall.

3. Probably George B. Ely (c1826–fl1887), a lawyer, who had served with Wisconsin troops as a captain until wounded at Antietam, and then as a paymaster of volunteers from February 19, 1863, to July 26, 1866. He does not appear to have received any further appointment. He later practiced law in New York City. Ibid., 787; *U.S. Off. Reg.* (1863–65); *Off. Army Reg.: Vols.*, 7: 164; *New York Times*, Aug. 23, 1904; CSR, George B. Ely, RG94, NA; Pension File, George B. Ely, RG15, NA; New York City directories (1880–88).

From George F. Gordon[1]

Philadelphia   March 13th 1867

Honored Sir

In my letter of the 9th inst, making application for the position of "Commissioner of Education,"[2] I said I would write you a personal letter, which I now do—and I will consider myself favored if you will READ IT.

There are times when a man may speak or write of himself without being subjected to the charge of egotism. *This is such a time for me*. When the "Johnson Movement" in Philadelphia took semi-organized form *in* the Republican party—and afterwards seperate formation as a political party—I was at the head of one of the Departments of our City government. My office was used as a sort of "Head Quarters" for the "Johnson Republicans" for some months. I Reside in the 4th Congression District (W D Kellys). After failing to defat Kelly *in* the party, I was the *first*, as the Newspapers of that day will shew—to call and organize a convention of Republicans against him. I worked to defeat him on PRENCIPLE, not INTEREST. We worked hard, but failed. *Why*, and *How?*—if given, would open to your view a state of thing here which I think you are not aware of. I took the nomination—which was unanimously given me—in the 10th Dist for state assembly—to look after Senator Cowans interests. I Reduced the previous Radical majority 400—and Received the entire vote of the democracy. It was not enough. In the meantime, the city council— the same which disgraced themselves by Refusing to Receive you and your cabnet—the same who were loud in denouncing you for Removals—had been plotting my Execution! No charges could be preferred against me, and if so it Required two-thirds to impeech, which they had not. So, with true Radical *instinct*, (not Reason) They passed an ordinance *abolishing* my office and Department, which they could do by a majority vote—and of course the Mayor,[3] who was ABSENT from the city on the occasion of your visit could see no reason for checking with his veto *such wise* and consistent legislation. The last Radical indignity put upon me, was leaving my name of[f] all the committees in the School Board of which I am a member.

I have waited patiently for some vindication at your hands. The pecularities and prominance of my case seemed to demand ON YOUR OWN ACCOUNT; and on our "National Union Partys" account, a pointed Rebuke to the City Councils—by my being Recognized by you for some prominent position at least equal to the one I lost in embracing your cause.

Which, of *all* those, who have been appointed here or who *now* press you, have been thus marked? *Not one*.

Now Mr. President, if I have Rightly apprehended your *Real nature*, I think you will be somewhat surprised to be informed—that notwithstanding all I have stated I have been straingly excluded from the least prospect of being Recognized by you. It is evident from very many broken promises, decepions and missrepresentations of false friends here —that I am not in the "Ring"—*a Ring whoes vital-life* is SELFISHNESS— with no *soul* to embrace a MAN, or grasp a cause, or buid a party. Nor am I the only National Union man here who has had to stand aside—while very many—who for five long years held the nation by the throat and tried to drink its hearts blood—walked right in to the subordinate offices here—and that to in wicked and heartless violation of solemn agreement—"that the positions *here* should be given to "Johnson Republicans" ONLY!" This, to us who had sacrificed so much to organize a party to sustain you—was not *betrayel* merely—but the political murder of men, who though poor were as true as Demascus Steele. None of us blame you, but eyes are being opened to the *Continued* deceptions practiced upon us here by those who *profess to be of us* ; as well, as by those *who keep no faith.*

As President of the "National Union Johnson Club" of the 15th Ward, I have been Requested by our Club, as well as by officers and members of others, as a *last effort*, to find out, where the *masses* of our Party stand— by presenting to you personally, the facts connected with my case, to see what action you will take. As to the truth of the statements conserning myselfe, (if doubted) I Refer you to Congressman—S J Randell, and every man holding or having held office under your appointment here— they all *profess* to be my friends and have Repeatedly promised to bring the facts of my case before you.

Now in conclusion let me say—that having been always prominent in the Republican party—10, years as a "School Director"—3 years as a Councilman—3 years as "chief clerk of Common Council"—1 year as "Registrar of Ga[?]["] and Recently as "Chief Inspector of Streets"—my acts and speeches during the last election of necesity made me prominent; and the *unprecedented and vindictive* action of the city councils in *abolishing a Department* of the City government to punish me for political acts, fixed the public eye on me.

Is all I have done and suffered, not worth a SENATE-REJECTION?

Waveing all personal considerations—would not good party management dictate that one worthy of being thus marked, should at least be Recognized?

Is the *Voice*, nearly hushed, and the heart nearly broken—of the NATIONAL UNION PARTY of this city—to be *ignored* by YOU? I will never believe it untill you say it.

My case is presented by THE PARTY here because *my* treatment is a perfect type of the *Partys* treatment;—and because the *managers* here cannot *Explain* or *satisfy* YOU in Regard to my case;—and because *you can* ACT on my individual case, when you could not in that of the PARTY.

George F Gordon

☞ PHILADELPHIA POSITIONS STILL VACANT
Collector of Customs—by Senate Rejection

Naval officer	Do	Do	
Surveyor	Do	Do	
Postmaster	Do	Do	3 times

Director of U S Mint
and many others elsewhere in your gift.

ALS, DNA-RG56, Appts., Customs Service, Subofficers, Philadelphia, George F. Gordon.
1. Gordon (c1822–fl1895) held a number of different positions: attorney, clerk, secretary, and contractor. 1860 Census, Pa., Philadelphia, Philadelphia, 15th Ward, 232; Philadelphia directories (1861–95).
2. See Gordon to Johnson, Mar. 9, 1867, Appts. Div., Misc. Lets. Recd., RG48, NA. Two days after this March 9 letter, the President nominated Henry Barnard as commissioner of education. See James Dixon to Johnson, July 8, 1866, *Johnson Papers*, 10: 655.
3. Morton McMichael.

From Charles G. Halpine
Private

City & County of New York.
March 13th 1867

My dear Sir:
I take it for granted you have seen how earnestly and cordially the *Herald* of yesterday[1] endorses your views (as imperfectly expressed in my report of your last remarks;) and I have reason to believe that the change of public opinion which I predicted, has already set in and is crystallizing around that article. The *Herald* indeed turns a complete and decisive summersault; & one, I have reason to believe, which indicates that it purposes a permanent change of point,—though one to be made gradually and in its own erratic way.

The *Boston Post* copies the report with a strong editorial endorsement, as also does the Albany *Argus*; and indeed no newspaper report for the past two years (since Lee's surrender) has created more universal criticism. I was glad to see by the *National Intelligencer*'s copying the article[2] that it was approved by your friends in Washn.; & indeed it seemed to me "a bold cure for a desperate disease." Nothing short of some startling sensation like this could have arrested the attention of the Country. One great point it has accomplished is placing the Radicals on the DEFENSIVE: they have been in the "accusative case" too long.

The *Times* correspondent hints that your Excellency feels aggrieved at not having had that report submitted for your "revision,"—but in this he must surely be wrong? To have asked you to "revise," would have involved your direct responsibility; & no one was better aware than myself that many points of the argument had been amplified & illustrated by my

own remarks as you proceeded,—things essential to be said to arrest
public attention, but which were not said by you in the manner stated.
On the whole I believe the article has set more men thinking seriously of
whither Congress has been hurrying us of late, then could have been
achieved by any less potent instrumentality.

I hope to have the honor of waiting upon you soon in person; and shall
then submit a few propositions with regard to the formation of new
issues, which have been largely discussed here and at Albany (where I
was yesterday,) by many of your leading friends,—Mr. Cassidy, Peter
Cagger[3] & others of like wisdom & experience. If any appointment for
Collector of the 8th Congl. Dist. is being made, please let me know that I
may inform Archbishop McCloskey.[4]

Chas. G. Halpine

ALS, DLC-JP.
1. The *New York Herald* of March 12 carried a printed version of Halpine's interview
with Johnson. Then, in an editorial column, it commented favorably upon the President's
concerns about the financial situation of the U.S. government. The paper advocated that
Congress "must check its reckless extravagance in appropriations of the public money."
2. The *National Intelligencer*, Mar. 11, 1867, ran a copy of Halpine's interview with
Johnson.
3. William Cassidy. Cagger (1812–1868) was a prominent and longtime member of
the Albany bar. *DAB*; George R. Howell and Jonathan Tenney, *History of the County of
Albany, N.Y., from 1609 to 1886* (New York, 1886), 146–47.
4. For further information on McCloskey and the revenue appointments, see Robinson
to Johnson, Feb. 18; Halpine to Johnson, Feb. 25, 1867.

From Daniel E. Sickles
Confidential

298 [F?] St.   13th March 1867.

My dear Mr President,

If you will send Graham[1] to the Senate to-day I am confident his friends
can secure his confirmation—Gen. Arthur[2]—a confidential friend of
Morgan's[3] so assures me.

I fear that certain influences from the Treasury proved fatal to poor
Egan[4] & gave a pretext to Conckling[5] & Morgan to break the promises
they made to Logan, Andrews, Madden, Brewer & Burns.[6]

I desire to leave Washington to-morrow en route for my Command.
Unless you desire me to return here I will go to New York for a day to
arrange some private business and start from there on *Monday* 18th inst.
for Charleston, direct.

Sickles

ALS, DLC-JP.
1. Charles K. Graham. There is no evidence that Johnson nominated Graham. See
Sickles to Johnson, Mar. 5, 1867.

2. Chester A. Arthur (1830–1886) served in a series of state posts in New York during the Civil War and as collector of the port of New York under the Grant administration. In 1880 Arthur received the nomination for vice president. He became president in September 1881 upon the assassination of James Garfield, but was unable to win presidential nomination in 1884. *DAB*.

3. Sen. Edwin D. Morgan.

4. Twice Johnson nominated Gen. Thomas W. Egan for internal revenue collector, but the Senate rejected him both times. See Sickles to Johnson, Mar. 5, 1867.

5. Sen. Roscoe Conkling.

6. The names correspond to army officers nominated for promotion by Johnson. Unfortunately, each name matches several appointees, so individual identification is impossible. See *Senate Ex. Proceedings*, Vol. 15.

From John W. Stokes [1]

Private

Philada.   March 13th 1867

Dear Sir

I feel under many obligations to you for the favour twice confered in Appointing me to offices in the Internal Revenue departmt in the 4th District of Penn; but failed in being confirmed by the Senate[2] because I would not compromise myself by secureing the favour of Judge Kelley[3] the Representative in Congress from this district. I am thefor out of office but feel it to be a duty I owe to you as one of your original supporters and friends to apprise you of any and all schemes to place your enemies and as I think the enemies to the true interest of the Country in official positions made vacant by the rejections of your friends.

Immediately upon my entering upon the duties of the office I removed about twenty offices who had been and were your open and bitter enemies and put in their places as many good true and faithful men and warm supporters and defenders of yourself and measures. But I now advise you of a scheme which is about being consumated to put these men back; which is to be done by the appointment either of HENRY LEWIS[4] the chief Clerk of the former assessor of this district who wrote an offensive letter in answer to the circular calling the August Convention which met in this district last year; or CHARLES GITHENS[5] an assistant assessor removed by me residing near Kelleys immediate residence. These are Kelly's own appointments and the object is to put these men all back so as to strengthen Kelley in his nomination again; although they may I believe have secured the aid of some democrats as a blind; but be not deceived! I am not mistaken!

There is also going on various schemes of Compromises between the radicals and democrats to divide the patronage. The result of all this will be to have the most radical in both of these parties appointed to office and all of your original and still staunch supporters and conservative men left out in the cold.

If you will pardon the suggestion I will venture to advise that you should continue till the end of the Chapter in appointing men of your own choice and from amongst your own friends who will lend a willing support to your efforts in upholding the Constitution and defend You from the vile slanders that are daily heaped upon you.

Believing that you are an honest, patriotic, and well meaning Executive and gentleman, I have never hesitated openly to say so at all times. This course has brought upon me the displeasure of the radicals whose doctrines and dogmas I cannot and will not subscribe to for the sake of office and hence my rejection.

I do not intend that my children shall have the trouble when I am dead and gone of denying that their ancestor ever held or advocated what I regard as the most monstrous of unwarentble acts of Congress towards these poor and deluded people and the states recently in rebellion (but for now nearly two years at peace) by the establishment of military governmts and other offensive measures and terms in times of professed peace; and when; to by their own recorded proceedings before the ink is dry upon the military bill that these very people are in a starving condition caling for the interposition and aid of the governmt to save them from a state of starvation.

I have troubled you with a much longer letter than I had intended; but it is so difficult to see you in person in consequence of your great press of business must be my excuse. Hoping, as I sincerely believe you will live to see your acts vindicated by a grateful people.

J. W. Stokes   1921 Green St

ALS, DLC-JP.

1. Stokes (1813–1888), a Philadelphia lawyer, held several federal appointments, including chief clerk to the U.S. purchasing agent, during the Civil War. In 1865–66 he served as chief clerk in the U.S. Department of Agriculture—a position to which he was reappointed in May 1867. Stokes resigned in 1867. *NUC*; 1870 Census, Pa., Philadelphia, Philadelphia, 15th Ward, 44th Dist., 53; *U.S. Off. Reg.* (1865–67); Philadelphia directories (1861–87); *Washington Evening Star*, May 16, Dec. 5, 1867; *Philadelphia Press*, Feb. 8, 1888.

2. In May 1866 Johnson had nominated Stokes as collector of the Fourth District, but the Senate rejected the nomination. In mid-January 1867 the President nominated Stokes as assessor of the Fourth District; on March 2 the Senate also rejected this nomination. Ser. 6B, Vol. 4: 82, 84, Johnson Papers, LC.

3. William D. Kelley.

4. Unidentified.

5. Githens (c1828–c1874) was a printer and publisher. Neither he nor Lewis were nominated for the position. 1860 Census, Pa., Philadelphia, Philadelphia, 24th Ward, 5th Prec., 44; Philadelphia directories (1867–75).

From Smith S. Allen[1]

Hannibal Mo   March 14 1867

Sir—

The office of Collector of this the 3rd Internal Revenue District in this State is now practically vacant by reason of the refusal of the Senate to confirm your nomination of Col John M Glover to that office.[2] Your Friends here and elsewhere (who are also mine) have pursuaded me to apply to you for the place. They hope that I can get your nomination, and also that I can procure the confirmation of the Senate. Letters written by your Friends to you on this subject will inform you whether I have been true to my country and true also to your policy. After more than twenty years spent in the practice of law, this is the first application that ever I made for office of any kind; and I am therefore the more anxious not to be disappointed. It is believed that Ingham[3]—the old incumbant—(and a bitter enemy of yours) is trying to get in again through his former Deputy Chas P Haywood.[4] Haywood is also a Radical. The plan is believed to be this—to get you to nominate Haywood by virtue of the recommendation of Gov Fletchers[5] appointees and a few other conservatives. They know that the Senate will confirm Haywood *just because he is a Radical*. The Radical friends of Ingham will then come forward and fill Haywoods Bond, with the understanding that Haywood is to transfer the office to Ingham, which it is supposed he will do, retaining for himself the Deputyship which he had before. And thus Ingham will be forced in again; not only against the wish of the President, but equally against the wish of the Johnson men of Mo. All this, is believed to be the plan. Whether Haywood will succeed or not we shall see.[6]

I am most intimately acquainted with both Senators from this State— Henderson & Drake[7]—and we have reason to believe that if nominated by you I will be confirmed by the Senate.[8]

S. S. Allen

I will take the liberty of sending you further Recommendations tomorrow or at least very soon; and may come to Washington with them myself.[9]

S. S. Allen

ALS, DNA-RG56, Appts., Internal Revenue Service, Collector, Mo., 3rd Dist., S. S. Allen.

1. Allen (b. c1825), an attorney, was a native of Kentucky. 1860 Census, Mo., Marion, Hannibal, 3rd Ward, 836.

2. For further information on this rejection, see John M. Glover to Johnson, Mar. 5, 1867.

3. Massachusetts native William S. Ingham (b. c1807) was a Hannibal, Missouri, grocer who was serving as collector by 1865 and had been removed by midsummer of 1866. 1860 Census, Mo., Marion, Hannibal, 2nd Ward, 171; *U.S. Off. Reg.* (1865); Ser. 6B, Vol. 4: 315, Johnson Papers, LC.

4. Perhaps Haywood was the Irish native (b. c1828) who apparently had a railroad tie business in Buchanan County, Missouri, in 1860. 1860 Census, Mo., Buchanan, Washington Twp., Western Dist., 285.

5. Thomas C. Fletcher.

6. Haywood did not succeed at that time. Johnson nominated five more candidates before the Senate confirmed John M. Cashman in April. Cashman, however, resigned in 1868 and Johnson's second, and successful, candidate was Haywood who was nominated, confirmed, and commissioned on July 27, 1868. Ser. 6B, Vol. 4: 317–19, Johnson Papers, LC.

7. John B. Henderson and Charles D. Drake.

8. Allen was not nominated as collector but as pension agent to serve at Macon City. However, two days after the nomination, on April 19, 1867, Allen's name was withdrawn from consideration. Ibid., 318.

9. Allen's files contain several recommendation letters in his behalf. Moreover, Allen did get to Washington in his quest for appointment, as indicated by Allen to Johnson, Mar. 30, 1867, Appts., Internal Revenue Service, Collector, Mo., 3rd Dist., S. S. Allen, RG56, NA.

From Henry C. Connelly [1]

Rock Island, Ill., March 14" 1867.

Dear Sir:

Permit me to thank you for the kindness done me, in designating me for the position of post-master for this City. I was not aware that my name had been sent to the Senate until it was announced as rejected.[2] To whom I am indebted for the suggestion of my name to you I am not aware. My only regret is that the Senate committee did not have my military record before them, when action was taken in my case. This record I mailed yesterday to Gen. Koontz,[3] M.C. from Pa., a boyhood friend. I took the liberty of also writing to Senators Trumbull and Cameron[4] as well as to Gen. Capron,[5] my former Colonel. I can scarcely hope for the Senate to reconsider the nomination; but presumed this action on my part could do no harm.

I shall never forget an incident which occurred in your old town of Greenville, Tenn., in September, I think, 1863. Being on duty with Gen. Shackelford,[6] I accompanied the advance. As we entered the west end the enemy passed out of the east end. Casting my eye to the left hand side I observed an old lady on her knees, with uplifted hands, supplicating, and apparently blessing us and thanking God for the safe delivery of the town. Her attitude was sublime and touching. As this old lady prayed to be delivered from the enemies of her country, thousands daily pray that *you* may overcome your enemies, and crush the conspirators who seek fame by attempting to destroy their Country.

I may say, *en passant*, if the Senate did not endorse me, my fellow citizens, (those who know me best,) of this City, last week, by a majority of 185, elected me as magistrate for the City Court. For Congress last fall, Genl. Logan[7] had 82 majority in the City. *My* friends are *your* friends. This is at least a straw.

H. C. Connelly,   Late Maj. 14" Ill. Cavy

ALS, DLC-JP.

1. Connelly (1831–1916), a native of Pennsylvania and Rock Island resident since 1855, edited and owned several papers in Pennsylvania and Illinois before taking up a legal practice in 1860. Between 1862 and 1865 he served with the 14th Ill. Vol. Cav., eventually attaining the rank of major. Following the war he served Rock Island in a variety of capacities while continuing his law practice. Pension File, Adelaide M. Connelly, RG15, NA.

2. Connelly was nominated on March 9, 1867, but rejected two days later. Ser. 6B, Vol. 4: 302, Johnson Papers, LC.

3. William H. Koontz (1830–1911), an attorney, began his legal practice in 1851 in Somerset, Pennsylvania, from which he later served as U.S. (1865–69) and state (1899–1902) representative. *BDUSC*.

4. Lyman Trumbull and Simon Cameron.

5. Horace Capron (1804–1885), farmer and agricultural authority, served as colonel and brevet brigadier general in the 14th Ill. Vol. Cav. Following the war he was U.S. commissioner of agriculture (1867–71) and agriculture adviser to the Japanese government (1871–75). Hunt and Brown, *Brigadier Generals*.

6. James M. Shackelford.

7. John A. Logan.

From John Foster[1]

Augusta   Mch 14 1867

The annual election for Mayor & Alderman takes place April eighth. The Registry of those entitled to vote closes on the first of April. Will Negroes be entitled to vote under the Military bill at said election? If so should they be registered under our present state law? Please answer by telegraph.[2]

John Foster   Mayor

Tel, DLC-JP.

1. Foster (*c*1803–1870) was a butcher by trade and helped establish the People's Savings Bank in Augusta. In the fall of 1866 he was elected to finish the term of the resigned James Gardiner. However, in May 1867 Augusta's municipal government was removed by General Pope and Foster was replaced with Foster Blodgett. 1860 Census, Ga., Richmond, Augusta, 1st Ward, 745; *Augusta Chronicle and Sentinel*, May 18, 1870; Charles C. Jones, *Memorial History of Augusta, Georgia* (Spartanburg, S.C., 1980 [1890]), 136, 187, 339.

2. A reply from Johnson to Foster has not been located. It is unknown whether the election of April 8 took place. Registration, however, continued throughout Georgia for several more months. C. Mildred Thompson, *Reconstruction in Georgia* (Savannah, 1972), 169–71.

From George P. Sewall[1]

Oldtown, [Maine]   March 14 1867

Sir:

I am credibly informed that a majority of the Maine Congressional delegation have combined to induce you, under some pretext, to remove me from the office of assessor of this district,[2] and as you might do so under a misapprehension, I beg leave to observe that the real, and only motive which can prompt such a request, is that I have refused to act with the men who have abused, and are now assailing you. I have at all times, from the first openly defended you, and I was the chairman of the first meeting held in this State at Portland, to organize a party for your support. In our late State election I voted with your friends, and I regret to say, I am the only public officer now in commission in Maine, who did so. If any man otherwise represents my position, or charges me with official misconduct, I care not who he is, I respectfully ask a hearing before you take action in relation to this office.

I am aware I am very obnoxious to your enemies, the Radicals of this State. I have been the object of their invective and calumny, because I refused to join a mad crusade against your administration; but having been with you politically, and voted the democratic ticket steadily from the days of Jackson to the breaking out of the rebellion, and with you supported the administration of Mr Lincoln during the war, I would not desert the cherished principles of former years, you are fearlessly and faithfully maintaining.

Trusting you will pardon me for troubling you upon this subject . . .

Geo: P. Sewall

ALS, DNA-RG56, Appts., Internal Revenue Service, Assessor, Me., 4th Dist., George P. Sewall.

1. Sewall (c1812–fl1882) was a lawyer in Oldtown, where he had practiced since about 1835. He had served as assessor of the Fourth District since at least 1863. *History of Penobscot County, Maine* (Cleveland, 1882), 215; *U.S. Off. Reg.* (1863–67).

2. Despite Sewall's fears, there is no indication that the President took any steps to replace Sewall as assessor. Later in 1867 his name was still listed as the Fourth District assessor. Ibid.

From Jeremiah S. Black

[ca. March 15, 1867][1]

Mr. President:

Allow me to make a suggestion. Cowan's rejection leaves a vacancy in the Austrian mission. Would it not be well to send in Dawson? He is not here—he knows nothing about it. But his appointment would give great satisfaction. If rejected by the Senate it would be on the sole ground that he is a friend of yours—and that would certainly not be a good reason for not nominating him. You know him as well as I do, or better.[2]

J. S. Black

ALS, DLC-Papers of Benjamin F. Butler.

1. This date is somewhat arbitrarily assigned because it falls between Edgar Cowan's rejection on March 12, 1867, and Blair's nomination on March 25. Ser. 6B, Vol. 2: 51, Johnson Papers, LC.

2. There is no evidence that John L. Dawson was nominated for the Austrian mission. See also John F. Coyle to Johnson, Mar. 27, 1867.

From Thomas W. Freelon[1]

San Francisco   March 15 1867.

Sir.

I see by the telegraph that L. C. Baker, formerly of San Francisco,[2] professes some knowledge, which may be sought to be used against you, by your Enemies[3]—wherein his oath may be of importance—or his character an item of consideration.

I think it my duty to inform you that his oath, here, is valueless—and his character infamous. And, if, in the course of events it should really happen that you were liable to suffer anything from his testimony, that it could be easily impeached in San Francisco.

He was obliged to leave the police force here,[4] for little less than larceny—(legal larceny, I mean) for in its moral character his offence was greater than that of larceny. Amongst others, I suffered at his hands to the amount of $500—and for that reason am conversant with his acts—and know his reputation—which is bad,—very bad.

I hope and trust that he is so well known about Washington, that he is harmless, but if it should happen otherwise—it would be easy to find proof of his infamy here.

I beg to be excused for writing you, about what I know, is in all probability an imaginary fear.

If circumstances should make this communication of any importance—Judge Field, or Ex Senator McDougal[5] will inform you that any statement of mine may be relied upon.

T W. Freelon

ALS, DLC-JP.

1. As early as 1852 Freelon (c1827–fl1872), a lawyer, was in San Francisco, where he later served as county judge of the court of sessions and presiding judge, probate court (1854–58). 1870 Census, Calif., San Francisco, San Francisco, 9th Ward, 109; San Francisco directories (1852–72).

2. Lafayette C. Baker was in San Francisco about 1858–61. Ibid. (1858–61).

3. In January 1867 Baker testified before the House Judiciary Committee "that he had seen and could obtain wartime correspondence between the president and Davis and other Confederates that proved Johnson had been a Rebel spy." But he was unable to produce the evidence and his own lies were finally exposed. Hanchett, *Lincoln Murder Conspiracies*, 83.

4. In 1858 Baker was a policeman, but by 1859 he was a "turner," and in 1860 a merchant. San Francisco directories (1858–61).

5. Stephen J. Field and James A. McDougall.

From Robert L. Martin

Private

Lenni Mills Delaware Co Penna.   March 15 1867.
Dear Sir.—

It is a duty for the nonperformance of which, I should reproach myself; to inform you of the treachery of one who owes an appointment as Assessor of the 7 Dist. Penna. to the kind partiality which you extended to an application which I was induced to recommend.

It is quite distinctly intimated by the Hon John M Broomall[1] Radical Member of Congress from this Dist: and all his friends that the Johnson men, have been completely sold out in the appointment of Captn. J L Englebert,[2] and that his confirmation was due to an arrangement by which the subordinate officers (twenty four Depy Assessors) were to be placed in the hands of the Radicals and of course under his, (Broomalls') control.

I am very much afraid that this base treachery of Englebert is unfortunately too true. It is very certain, that the Radicals confidently expect, that every one of your friends appointed by Major Martin,[3] will be turned out and the old incumbents whom he dismissed, will be reinstated.

Now this matter is in the control of the Secretary of the Treasury, whose decision against any nomination made by Englebert, of course must be final, and I earnestly entreat you therefore to take such action that no nomination made by him, shall be approved by the Secretary without the consent of Joseph R Flanigen of Phila. and myself. To permit the true friends who have sustained you, and do yet sustain you, to be proscribed and punished, would be inexpressibly mortifying to all your supporters and would swell the arrogant triumph of the Radicals to an almost unendurable entent. I write you directly on this subject, because I think it calls for prompt and decisive action. I am with sincere esteem, and a hearty sympathy with you in your arduous trials, truly your friend and supporter.

Robert L Martin

ALS, DNA-RG56, Appts., Internal Revenue Service, Assessor, 7th Dist., Penn., J. Lee Englebert.

1. Pennsylvania lawyer Broomall (1816–1894) was a state representative (1851–52) and served as a captain in the 29th Rgt., Pa. Emergency Men, during the Civil War. After three terms in the U.S. House (1863–69), Broomall briefly held a judgeship in Delaware County before returning to his law practice in 1875. *BDUSC.*

2. Englebert had been confirmed by the Senate as assessor in March 1867. See Martin to Johnson, Jan. 18, 1867, *Johnson Papers*, 11: 614–15.

3. Archer N. Martin, son of Robert L. Martin.

From Edwin O. Perrin

New York   Mch 15 1867

I learn Henry W. Eastman[1] my predecessor removed by affidavits for denouncing you as a "damned Traitor" "Drunken Renegade" & "political Judas." is about being reappointed by Treasury department.[2] All your friends here indignantly protest. I start for Washington tonight.

E. O. Perrin   Late Assessor 1st Dist   New York

Tel, DLC-JP.

1. Eastman (c1825–1882), a real estate lawyer in Queens, had served as assessor of the First District since at least 1863. *New York Times*, Apr. 1, 1882; *U.S. Off. Reg.* (1863–65).

2. Perrin's fears appear to have been unfounded. After Perrin's rejection by the Senate in early March 1867, the President submitted several other names for the assessorship; none of them was Eastman. Ser. 6B, Vol. 4: 51, 53–54, 57, Johnson Papers, LC.

From Martin Ryerson [1]

Newton N.J.   March 15, 1867

Sir

Although a stranger, I trust you will excuse the liberty I take in addressing you, as I have some statements to make which I deem it important for you to know, and I refer to my friend Mr. Seward that you may know what reliance is to be placed on them.

Last year a number of your friends tried to prevent A. J. Rogers controlling the Federal patronage in this District to secure his nomination for a 3d term, feeling that he was a very unfit & unreliable Representative, & a disgrace to the State.[2] All well informed & fairminded Democrats conceded that his nomination would lose the District. As Mr. Seward will inform you, I exerted myself, through him, to make known to you the man's true character, in order to prevent this control of patronage, & his nomination. I had no desire to participate actively in the election, & had the Democrats nominated a fair man he would have been elected by at least 1000; but I was determined if Rogers was nominated to do my utmost to defeat him, as I did. He was elected in 1862 by over 3000, reelected in 1864 by some 1900, & defeated in 1866 by some 450.

Every effort to prevent his use of patronage for this purpose was unavailing, & by a shameful abuse of it he secured a nomination, & your friends lost the District.

In a speech against him I declared my purpose of driving him from the bar of N.J. for mal-practice as a lawyer, by applying to the Sup. Court to take away his license. Since the speech, he has agreed to remove from this State if I would not prosecute the matter, & as I can thus accomplish my object I have waived the prosecution for the present.

To show you how he abused your confidence, he procured the appointment as Post Master of this town of Henry C. Kelsey,[3] for several years Editor of the Dem. paper here (the N.J. Herald) one of the bitterest opponents of the war that there was in N.J. and who in his paper publicly denounced you as the murderer of Mrs. Surrat, saying that you was more guilty than Booth,[4] & several months after her execution repeating the same denunciations in public & private, and once in the fall of 1865, at a public meeting, in my presence, avowing that he wrote the abusive articles in the Herald.

Mr. Kelsey was rejected by the Senate & thereupon the Republican Senators & Representatives of N.J. united in recommending for the place Major William R. Mattison,[5] a former Democrat, who in 1861 volunteered as a private in the Cavalry, serving through the war, & rising to a Majority, a most estimable man, & an excellent appointment. Mr. Hill,[6] Representative of this District, presented the papers to P.M. Genl. Randall, on the 7th who endorsed on them as follows "Genl. Skinner,[7] have these papers made out for the Newton office, so as to go in to the President with other papers at once," and on the next day Mr. H. was told they were sent in to you. But instead of Major Mattison, a Mr. Congar[8] was appointed, & it is the universal belief, & so stated in the newspapers, that Rogers' influence with you secured it, & it is believed that he was well paid. Mr. Hill complains that he has been similarly snubbed as to other appointments in the Department of the Treasury, & ascribes it all to Mr. Rogers' influence with you.

I mention these things, because they are producing on the mind of Mr. Hill & others an effect prejudicial to you & the public interests. He is a very upright, conscientious man, an elder in the Presbyterian Church, went to Washington with moderate & conservative views, utterly opposed to impeachment, & to following the lead of the extreme Radicals.

But to be thus snubbed through the influence of the notorious Jack Rogers is producing a very unfavorable impression on Mr. Hill & many others & in a letter to me of the 11th inst., after recounting how he had been treated in reference to appointments, he says "But one thing is certain, it will not take much more such treatment as I have received the last week to make me an *Extreme Radical*."

It is generally believed in N.J. that Jack is hanging around Washington as a paid lobby member; he may thus line his own pockets, but it can result only in injury to yourself, & the public interests. For my part I am anxious beyond measure to see harmony between the different Departments of the Government, and peace & quiet throughout the land, but to see such men as Jack Rogers in favor, & controlling the offices, will do any thing but promote harmony, & will only tend to ensure an impeachment.

If your confidence has been as much abused in other States, as in this, it is not surprising that the elections went as they did. In our 5th District,

MARCH 1867 161

Geo. A. Halsey, a very capable, efficient, & popular assessor, was removed, & a miserable appointment made;[9] the feeling excited thereby sent Halsey to Congress, when otherwise your friends would have carried the District. So, the universal conviction that Jack Rogers was your favorite, operated immensely last fall to your prejudice in every part of the State, & if you still continue to favor him you will yet see the bad effects. You ought to know that he constantly boasts of his influence with you, & he has been foolish enough to charge you with gross immoralities with the other sex. I have been credibly informed of his saying "that you was as big a whoremaster as himself," (& we all know what he is in that line.) I know a man in this town to whom in his room in Washington, Rogers last year pointed out a showily dressed woman in the Street, as one who granted you favors of that kind, in return for pardons which she sold. You may imagine how such stories injure you in public estimation, & many people say they cant explain Jack's influence except on the theory that he knows many things which he might tell, damaging to you, & that you are compelled to keep him in a good humor. Of course I do not for a moment credit such stories, & I only mention it that you may know the injury he is doing you.

I have never asked for any office & dont want any, & care very little who have them, provided they are honest, capable, & faithful to the Country, but I beg respectfully to suggest that it would be well to shake off such men as Jack, & that the public interests would be much promoted by treating Mr. Hill, & his recommendations to offices, with proper respect.

As there is nothing in this letter that I am not willing to stand by, you may, if you see proper, show it to Mr. Rogers, or any one else.

Martin Ryerson
late Judge of the Supreme Court of N.J.

ALS, DLC-JP.
1. Ryerson (1815–1875), a lawyer, served on the New Jersey state supreme court in the 1850s. He was subsequently a member of the state legislature. James P. Snell, comp., *History of Sussex and Warren Counties, New Jersey* (Philadelphia, 1881), 181; *New York Times*, June 15, 1875.
2. For Rogers's response to some of Ryerson's charges, see Rogers to Johnson, Mar. 18, 1867.
3. Kelsey (1837–1920) held a postmastership before the war, owned and published newspapers in the early years of the war, became a state judge in 1868, and thereafter served as New Jersey's secretary of state for nearly thirty years. Kelsey served as Newton's postmaster for a brief period, December 1866 through April 1867; his nomination was rejected by the Senate on March 2, 1867. Snell, *Sussex and Warren Counties*, 224; *New York Times*, May 15, 1920; Ser. 6B, Vol. 4: 75, Johnson Papers, LC; *U.S. Off. Reg.* (1867).
4. Mary E. Surratt and John Wilkes Booth.
5. Mattison (1850–1915) eventually served as a major in the 2nd N.Y. Cav. In 1869 he became postmaster at Newton. Snell, *Sussex and Warren Counties*, 106–7; Pension File, Fannie L. Mattison, RG15, NA.
6. John Hill (1821–1884), a bank clerk, bookkeeper, and prewar local postmaster, served in the New Jersey legislature during the war. He later served in the U.S. House (1867–73, 1881–83). *BDUSC*.

7. Beginning in the early 1850s, St. John B.L. Skinner (c1797–1872) served several presidential administration as first assistant postmaster general. *New York Times*, July 11, 1872; *U.S. Off. Reg.* (1867).

8. John F. Conger (b. c1829), a longtime resident of Newton, replaced Kelsey as postmaster in May 1867. His nomination was confirmed by the Senate in mid-March. 1860 Census, N.J., Sussex, Newton, Newton Twp., 32; Ser. 6B, Vol. 4: 75, Johnson Papers, LC; *U.S. Off. Reg.* (1867).

9. Conrad M. Zulick. See R. V. Wright to Johnson, Sept. 27, 1866, *Johnson Papers*, 11: 275–76.

From William H.C. King

New Orleans La   March 17th 1867

Have taken lead with "Times" recommending legislature to call convention and by taking all the weapons we can from opponents eventually strip them of political power. Astonished to find people with us and believe great Majority South will acquiesce in any means left of extrication. Believe you would recommend such course. People will never forget you, and say you have nobly stood by them and Constitution. They will now place themselves in position to be of service to you—depend upon them and me. Genl Granger[1] telegraphs me to recommend Herron.[2] To do so would be false to you and myself.

W.H.C. King

Tel, DNA-RG107, Tels. Recd., President, Vol. 5 (1866–1867).

1. Gordon Granger.

2. Francis J. Herron (1837–1902), a native of Pennsylvania, moved to Dubuque, Iowa, in 1855 where he was involved in banking. In the Civil War he fought with Iowa troops, primarily in the Trans-Mississippi West, and rose from the rank of captain to that of major general. Herron resigned his post in the summer of 1865. Thereafter he settled in New Orleans for about ten years, working variously as a commission agent, lawyer, secretary of state (1871–73), and in several capacities with mortgages. At the time of King's telegram, Herron was under consideration for the much contested post of U.S. marshal for Louisiana, an appointment which he received. Conrad, *La. Biography*; Warner, *Blue*.

From Baltimore 8th Ward Conservative Organization[1]

Baltimore   March 18th 1867

At a large and enthusiastic meeting of the 8th ward Conservative Organization held on Thursday evening March 14 1867[2] The following Resolutions were unanimously adopted.

Whereas The late Congress of the United States, in their malignant efforts, to degrade the white inhabitants of the Southern States, and place them at the mercy of an inferior race, formerly their slaves, and have passed what is known as the Military Reconstruction Bill, and

Whereas Notwithstanding the able legal and Constitutional objections of the President to the same, they passed it over his veto, and in violation of the solemn resolution of Congress of July 1861, which declared that the war was, and should be carried on for no purpose of subjugation, but solely to enforce the Constitution and laws; and that when this was yielded by the parties in rebellion the contest should cease, with the Constitutional rights of the States and of individuals unimpared, therefore

Be it Resolved. That Andrew Johnson President of the United States, should have the unlimited support of all lovers of their country and the Constitution, irrespective of party politics.

Resolved That the Conservative voters of the 8th Ward of Baltimore city, in mass meeting assembled, pledge him their unanimous support in his efforts to stay the tide of fanaticism and madness, now threatening to engulf the liberties of our Country.

Resolved That we endorse the sentiment of Andrew Johnson that whenever administration fails or seems to fail in securing any of the great ends for which republican government is established the proper course seems to be to renew the original spirit and form of the Constitution itself.

Resolved That we sustain the President in his patriotic efforts, and would recommend him to offer to the present Congress as proper for them to study, consider and reflect, that which their predecessors appeared to be ignorant of *the Constitution of the United States*.

Resolved That we have unbiding faith in the patriotism and integrity of Andrew Johnson, and believe him to be the right man in the right place.

Resolved That the course as heretofore pursued, and the present path in which Andrew Johnson treads, has our undivided support, and we hope that he may be spared to demonstrate to the leaders of the present agitation of the countrys peace, that, *"Treason is a crime, and should be punished."*

Resolved That we recommend the President to steer the Ship of State, the Constitution—straight through the breakers, for after the storm will *surely* come the return of dawning reason in the minds of most of our deluded breathren of the North, and with him at the helm, we will soon see the rainbow of peace arching over our beloved Land proclaiming, "Peace on earth and good will to all."

F. H. Shallus,   President.

S. H Martin   Rec Secretary

LS, DLC-JP.

1. The letter is signed by Frank H. Shallus and Stephen H. Martin. Shallus (c1836–fl1901), a Maryland native, was a printer during the war. Afterwards he was a clerk and broker in Baltimore's customhouse (c1867–c1901). Martin (c1839–fl1891), a native of Pennsylvania, was a clerk in various establishments. Other members of the organization are unknown. 1870 Census, Md., Baltimore, Baltimore, 8th Ward, 292, 333; Baltimore directories (1864–1901).

2. No information has been found concerning this meeting.

From George W. Jones

Fayetteville Tennessee   March 18, 1867

Permit me to introduce to your favorable acquaintance, consideration and *confidence* Mrs K. L. Hodges[1] of New York City by whom this will be handed to you. Mrs Hodges is a lady of fine sense and intelligence. She presents herself to you not as an applicant or supplicant for favors for herself nor friends. She possesses information, which she desires to communicate to you in confidence which is important for you to know; and which relates to you personally and officially and is of importance as regards the public welfare. She will make known to you the information she possesses.[2] Again I commend her to your kind consideration and confidence.

G. W. Jones

ALS, DLC-JP.
   1. Not identified.
   2. It is unknown exactly what information Mrs. Hodges had, but William G. Moore subsequently noted that she told the President that, should the impeachment committee lack sufficient testimony to impeach him, they were going to manufacture it. St. George L. Sioussat, ed., "Notes of Colonel W. G. Moore, Private Secretary of President Johnson, 1866–68," *AHR*, 19 (1913): 107.

From Samuel J. Randall

Washington D.C.   Mar. 18, 1867

Mr. President

Knowing your desire to appoint meritorious officers & soldiers to position and being made aware of your indisposition to return Wm. Harbison[1] Esquire as Collector of the Port at Philada. I submit for your consideration the names of two brave and gallant soldiers.

Gen. Peter Lyle[2] &

Gen. Peter Fritz.[3]

either of whom would add great strength to your friends in Philada. The War Department records attest their services.

Gen Lyle recently ran in Philada for Clerk of District Court, and was 4000 votes ahead of his party associates. The Senate would hardly venture to reject him. He has already been confirmed as "General." He was in the war from the hour of the firing at Sumpter until Peace was said to have been made by Gens. Grant & Sherman.

You cannot go astray as to either gentlemen.

Sam J Randall

P.S. I will see Senator Buckalew & Ex Senator Cowan. I believe they will respond cordially to my suggestion.[4]

ALS, DLC-JP.

1. Harbeson was rejected by the Senate for the collectorship in March, but in April 1867 he was approved as surveyor of Philadelphia. See Charles Brown to Johnson, Jan. 28, 1867, *Johnson Papers*, 11: 632–34.

2. Lyle (1821–1879), a tobacco merchant and carriage maker, had served as colonel, 19th Pa. Inf. and 90th Pa. Inf., and been brevetted brigadier general in March 1865. On April 13 Johnson nominated Lyle as collector at Philadelphia, but the Senate rejected the nomination two days later. *Senate Ex. Proceedings*, Vol. 15, pt. 2: 700, 710; Hunt and Brown, *Brigadier Generals*.

3. Peter Fritz, Jr. (1838–1907), was an insurance agent and clerk who served as lieutenant colonel, 99th Pa. Inf. He was brevetted brigadier general in March 1865. On April 16, 1867, Johnson nominated Fritz as surveyor of customs for Philadelphia, but the Senate rejected the nomination the next day. Ibid.; *Senate Ex. Proceedings*, Vol. 15, pt. 2: 746, 750.

4. Charles R. Buckalew and Edgar Cowan. In August Randall thanked Johnson for Harbeson's appointment. See Randall to Johnson, Aug. 16, 1867, Johnson Papers, LC.

From Andrew J. Rogers

Washington, D.C.   March 18 1867

My dear President.

I deem it my duty to lay before you a true statement of the course & character of Martin Ryerson who in his letter[1] has so wickedly & shamefully abused me. First it is utterly false that your friends tried to prevent me from controlling patronage in my district, but it was your & my enemies, just such men as Mr Ryerson as all the party except a few dissatisfied politicians were strongly with me, as the proceedings of the convention which nominated me composed of the best men of the party, will show. In which, I received 105 out of 143 votes on the first ballot. I was nominated for Congress in 1862 on the first ballot, carrying every delegate from my own county where Mr Ryerson lives also. Mr Ryerson then abused me in speeches & in the papers charging me with being a drunkard, gambler, whoremaster and dishonest practitioner in my profession at law & that he would have me thrown over the bar. I was elected by 2000 majority. In 1864, I was nominated by acclimation & elected by 1800 majority. In 1865 my district was carried by the democratic candidate for governor by only 46 majority & in 1866 I was defeated by less than 200 votes with three candidates in the field. I made an extraordinary run & can be elected next time. I have been wanting to practice my profession in N York City for several years & would have done so had it not been for my being elected to Congress. I intend to practice there, but to keep my residence in the district to best such cowards in the next contest. Mr Kelsey who was post master at Newton was your warm friend & his paper was full of articles in your favor, except that he was for McClellan in 1864. He was not opposed to the war & gave his money & made speeches to assist in raising volunteers. Mr Conger who was nominated by you for post master is a gentleman and a republican & will be confirmed I feel sure. Mattison is one of Ryerson's pimps & a loud mouthed radical. Mr

Hill is a rabid radical & was elected as such. Ryerson says I am hanging around Washington, as a paid lobby. This is a wicked falsehood. I am acting from the highest motives of honor & for the best interest of my country. He says the 5th dist was lost because you removed Halsey from the assessorship. This is false as the facts will show. In 1865 that district was carried by the radicals by 2500 majority & in 1866 it was run down to less than 1000, in electing Halsey over a Johnson republican. Ryerson says I have boasted of my influence with you. That is false, as I have only said you were my friend. He says he has been informed that I said "that you was as big a whoremaster as himself." This is a wicked lie, and so are all the charges he makes of my saying any thing against you. I hope death may overtake me at once, if the whole thing is not a base falsehood. If you ever had a true friend, I am the one. God knows, I have stood by you in every emergency & shall, I be ruined in your estimation by such wicked and cowardly attacks. Now as to Ryerson's character politically, as his private one has been much below any thing I could write. With that, I have no concern. He is a bitter radical & abused you last fall in his speeches, calling you a drunkard, a loafer, a traitor & other vile names. He has persecuted & abused me since the Spring of 1858 & his abuse of me was the cause of my first nomination. I have never done him a wrong, except that I have been opposed to him politically. You have seen enough of me to know me & shall I be cast aside by you & the pimps of Mr Ryerson put in office over me. If so it will be ungrateful. Such abuse of me hurts my feelings to the bottom of my heart. If I am to be cast off, let me know it, & I will ask no appointments. The secret is, I come up from a poor barefooted boy & such aristocrats as Mr Ryerson cant bare to see me hold any position or have any influence.

A J Rogers.

ALS, DLC-JP.
1. See Martin Ryerson to Johnson, Mar. 15, 1867. Various persons mentioned in Rogers's letter were also referred to in the Ryerson letter.

From Ethan A. Allen

Mobile, Ala.   March 19th 1867.

Dear Sir,—

I made my respects to you from Augusta Georga on 13th. Inst.[1] & beg leave to continue such observations as I have made since that period. I have visited Atlanta, West-Point, & Montgomery since that time and must express my admiration of the universal desire of the people to see & Maintain order & yield obedience to the Federal Government. There is not the slightest desire on their part to impede its perfect & harmonious workings. I can assure you Mr President that I do not believe that a more loyal people *ever* existed than is now to be found in the Southern States. They universally accept the situation of affairs. They have made up their minds to this course & I pledge my reputation on the fact that they *can* be *fully trusted* by you in any position of responsability to which you may feel inclined to appoint them.

The question of Slavery is a dead issue with them long since, & the feeling by the former owner of the Negroes toward them is that of the tenderest consideration & kindness. The best friend to the Negro here is those "native to the Manor born." They willingly engage them to work & pay them faithfully. There have been *many* instances in this country in which *Northern* men have *hired* plantations attempted to raise crops, by doing every thing on credit, & *promising* the Negroes a *liberal* pay, but when the time came for payment the imployer was "non este." The Negroes poor devils get nothing, hence in cases of this kind they become doubtful in any *new* engagements. The old planters understand raising crops, hence succeed much better, & the Negroes would rather engage with *Native planters* than those Northern adventurers.

I have been travelling in the South for the last Six weeks & have heard of no outrage whatever on "Loyal Union Men." Should I hear of such inconsequence of riot or anything of the kind I shall at once proceed to the theatre of action & make a careful examination & report to you *all* the Circumstances in detail.

The cause of any trouble which exists is caused by such white men as had no status here prior to the War but think that in the unsettled state of the Country they may possibly come to the surface by playing into the hands of the *Radicals*. The *solid & respectable* portions of the inhabitants Mr President have no part or agency whatever in the disturbances which occasionally do occur & in themselves trivial but which by the time it reaches the Northern Press is magnified to great importance.

Again I assure you the people want only encouragement in order to recuperate their fallen fortunes, reestablish the prosperity of the Country, & heal up the terrible calamity which the War which by the course of fanatics forced upon our once prosperous & happy Country.

I still find the people much dispirited. They know not what the North may *force* upon them.

Now the great dread among them is the prospect of "confiscation" of their property.

The very men who could & would do most to reestablish the prosperity of the Country Sir are the very men who are by existing Laws *Proscribed*. Still the People indulge the hope the with the North reason may yet resume its sway in their councils & hope for ultimate rest from that *mean* persecution which now pursues them.

Ethan A. Allen

P.S. I shall be in New Orleans on 22d Inst.

E.A.A.

ALS, DLC-JP.

1. Allen is undoubtedly referring to his letter of March 11, not the 13th. See Allen to Johnson, Mar. 11, 1867, Johnson Papers, LC.

From Edward D. Holbrook and Henry C. Street[1]

Washington, D.C.   March 19th 1867.

Sir

We the undersigned would recommed Major William A West[2] for the position of Internal Revenue Collector for the District of Idaho In place of A Haas rejected.[3] The Majors has served his country for over four years during the late rebellion—resigned his position as Maj of the first Regiment of Veteran Reserve Corps—received a severe wound while in the Army of Potomac.[4] The office is at present filled by an irresponsible and disreputable character.[5]

The Major is evry way competent to perform the duties pertaining to said office. While we would greatly prefer to have an actual bona fide citizen of our Territory appointed if it were possible to have them confirmed but feeling it impossible we cordially recommend the Major for the position. Trusting that the appointment will be made . . . [6]

E D Holbrook   Del—Idaho T
H. C. Street, Commissioner from Idaho

ALS (Holbrook), DNA-RG56, Appts., Internal Revenue Service, Collector, Dist. of Idaho, William A. West.

1. Street, who is not further identified, was a member of the Idaho territorial council (1865–67) from Boise County and was named a special commissioner to go to Washington, D.C., in 1867 to find out what had happened to the $53,000 issued to Idaho's territorial secretaries. Bancroft, *Washington, Idaho, and Montana*, 466, 470; Merle W. Wells, "David W. Ballard, Governor of Idaho, 1866–1870," *OHQ*, 54 (1953): 11–12, 22.

2. West (c1816–fl1871), a native of Pennsylvania, served as U.S. marshal of Nebraska around 1859. He may be the same William A. West who enlisted as a captain in the 1st W. Va. Cav. with other Pennsylvanians in 1861 and was dismissed in April 1862. He is certainly the Major West who served with the 16th Pa. Cav. from late 1862 until the fall of 1863. In 1864–65 he was serving with the Veteran Reserve Corps in the Washington, D.C., area. Two years afterwards he was a special agent of the customs office in Philadelphia and in 1871 was apparently a Treasury Department clerk in Washington, D.C. *U.S. Off. Reg.* (1859, 1867); Washington, D.C., directories (1871); CSR, William A. West, RG94, NA.

3. Haas (or Hass), not further identified, who was county assessor for Ada County, Idaho Territory, was nominated on March 14, 1867, and rejected on March 18. *Senate Ex. Proceedings*, Vol. 15, pt. 2: 466; Holbrook to Johnson, Mar. 7, 1867, Appts., Internal Revenue Service, Collector, Idaho Terr., A. Hass, RG56, NA.

4. West fell from his horse on April 27, 1863, near Warrenton, Virginia, "while in the performance of his duty," receiving an injury which placed him on the sick list for most of the time until October 1863, when he was discharged due to his disability. CSR, William A. West, RG94, NA.

5. Joseph C. Geer (1825–1908), a native of Ohio who had engaged in logging in Oregon and gold mining in California, was nominated for the collectorship on July 24, 1866, and confirmed and commissioned three days later. Haas was the third unsuccessful potential replacement for Geer. 1870 Census, Idaho, Ada, Boise, 23; Ser. 6B, Vol. 4: 394, Johnson Papers, LC; Geer Family Association records, Phoenix, Arizona.

6. West was not appointed, but Johnson nominated three more candidates before apparently giving up after July 1868. Geer remained collector until at least the fall of 1871. Ser. 6B, Vol. 4: 394, 398, Johnson Papers, LC; *U.S. Off. Reg.* (1867–71).

From Nathaniel P. Sawyer

Pittsburgh, March 20th 1867

Respected Sir—

Enclosed please find Adam's Express Cos. receipt[1] for one box of good old whiskey, which is said to be equal to any in our State for age and quality. I directed it to Mr. Cushaw.[2] If it suits your taste be kind enough to let me know, as there is a little more left of the same sort. We appear to be gaining strength in this part of our State, and trust by another year that we will be able to have matters in Penna. entirely satisfactory. There is still some complaint in regard to the appointments of McClelland[3] to our Pittsburgh Post office, and Nevin[4] assessor of the 23d Dist., both bitter Radicals; the latter belongs to a family who have been very bitter against us, and if his commission could be witheld, it would prove beneficial to us. Capt Wm. Haslet, Col. Loyd[5] the former assessor's deputy, performs the business of the office at present, and is fully qualified for its duties. Pardon me for again calling your attention to And. Robinson,[6] Post Master of Allegheny City. He is your true and devoted friend. The gentlemen who are trying to succeed him, are bitter Radicals, and should not be allowed to triumph over your friends. Wishing you health happiness and success over all your enemies . . .

Nathl. P. Sawyer

ALS, DLC-JP.
1. Not found.
2. Edward L. Cushaw.
3. James H. McClelland. See Sawyer to Johnson, Mar. 4, 1867.
4. Daniel E. Nevin (c1813–fl1871) was a farmer and Presbyterian clergyman whom Johnson nominated in March 1867 to be assessor of the Twenty-third District, Pennsylvania. His nomination was approved by the Senate on March 14. 1870 Census, Pa., Allegheny, Leet Twp., 283; *Senate Ex. Proceedings*, Vol. 15, pt. 1: 412, 452; John W. Jordan, ed., *Genealogical and Personal History of the Allegheny Valley, Pennsylvania* (3 vols., New York, 1913), 3: 843; Pittsburgh directories (1865–71).
5. William Haslett and Alfred G. Loyd. Haslett (c1831–c1894) was a steamboat captain before he became assistant assessor. Later, he earned his support variously as contractor, bookkeeper, and clerk. 1860 Census, Pa., Allegheny, Allegheny, 2nd Ward, 58; Pittsburgh directories (1861–95).
6. Andrew L. Robinson.

From Laura C. Holloway

New York   March 21d 1867—

It is with extreme reluctance that I intrude myself upon your time and attention, but your uniform kindness to me in times past prompts my faltering pen. From a letter recieved from Maj. Gen'l Thomas,[1] I find you can appoint my Brother Wm. H. Carter,[2] from Tennessee, to a vacancy at West Point. He is a noble boy a hard student, and asks from you a place at West Point, that he may recieve a thourough education, which at present my Father[3] is not able to give him. Mr President I earnestly urge you, if possible to make this appointment. No Family in America would appreciate the bestowal more, and I can ask no greater boon than to see my ambitious Brother preparing to be an educated man. With this letter, accept the warmest assurances of goodwill a citizen can offer the President of our Country. Gen'l Thomas assures me Willie can be appointed from Tennessee, and in closing allow me to urge this matter.[4]

Laura Carter Holloway.
147. East 17th St

ALS, DNA-RG94, USMA, Corres. *re* Mil. Academy, 1867–1904, File C-30-1867.
1. George H. Thomas.
2. Carter (1851–1925), a Nashville native, did in fact receive a West Point appointment in the summer of 1867; he graduated in 1873. From that point until his final retirement in 1918, Carter was a professional soldier who had a wide variety of assignments and rose through the ranks to become brigadier general in 1902 and major general in 1909. *NCAB*, 21: 37; *West Point Register*, 269.
3. Samuel J. Carter.
4. Johnson dealt directly with the matter on April 22 when he referred the appointment request to the secretary of war "for special attention."

From Davidson M. Leatherman

St Nicholas Hotel   New York   Mch 21/67

May I, Sir, as your friend, suggest to you the importance of at once inaugurating an investigation of the affairs of the Treasury Department. Here is one of the mudsills of your advantage. The debt of the country is enormous,[1] and the question is presented to the minds of all thinking men whether it can, will, or ought to be paid. True you are not responsible for the acts of a single individual in this Department, yet the people may hold you, as the executive officer of the government, in some degree responsible, for the manner in which the important duties of this department have been discharged by the officers who have been placed at its head.

The debt of the country, large at the close of the war, has been greatly augmented by the iniquitous system adopted by the party who are now making war upon you.

The investigation which I have suggested will, I am satisfied, expose a state of things which will overwhelm and destroy the Radical party. Let their official conduct be thoroughly sifted, and you will find they will be condemned and ruined by the iniquity of their own acts.

Make a committee of such men as you know to be true to truth, to patriotism, and to yourself, to exemanine and scrutinize every act of the Treasury Department of the government, and the result will be, the complete destruction of the present temporary power which is making war upon you, and embarrassing your administration in every possible way. This will give you strength with the whole country; and if the chief of this committee be true to himself, to the country, and to you, the result will be none other, nor less than the overthrow of the Radical power; and to give you the most prominent place in the mind and heart of the whole people.

There is much more in this than I can express in a letter. Indeed, as was said in a communication to the "World" last week, "repudiation must be the result of the legislation of the past, and present Congress."[2] Now suppose repudiation shall be the result, and even revolution ensue, were it not better that this should be, than by a temporising course the prosperity of the country should be blasted, and the happiness of millions of the purest and best men an women of the country should be crushed, and you, who, with more than Roman firmness, have resisted the attacks upon the constitution by the Radical party and their usurpation of power, should fall a victim to their foul machinations.

I hope you will not feel it your duty to appoint a Navy Agent at this place[3] until I see you. I will be in Washington in a day or two.[4]

D. M Leatherman

ALS, DLC-JP.

1. Undeniably the national debt was "enormous" in 1867, but it had been steadily dropping since the summer of 1865. Nevertheless, by March 1, 1867, the debt stood at $2.5 billion. See figures in the *New York World*, Mar. 15, 1867.

2. Not found.

3. On March 27 Johnson nominated Henry W. Slocum for naval officer at New York, replacing the resigned John A. Dix. The Senate rejected Slocum the following day. There is no evidence that Leatherman influenced Johnson. *Senate Ex. Proceedings*, Vol. 15, pt. 2: 555, 572.

4. There is no record of Leatherman's being in Washington or visiting with the President.

From Edwin M. Stanton

War Department, Washington City,
March 21st 1867.

A Joint Resolution of Congress, approved July 26, 1866, authorized the President to set apart to the *Union Pacific Railway Co., Eastern Divn.*, a portion of the *Fort Riley Military Reservation*, provided, the location of such railroad or the diminution of such Reserve in any manner so as to impair its usefulness for military purposes, so long as it shall be required therefor, shall not be permitted.

Lieut. Genl. Sherman, to whom the Resolution was referred, has reported thereon as follows:—

Hd. Qrs. Mil. Div. of the Missouri,
St. Louis, Mo., Mch 12, 1867.

* * * * * * I have the honor to * * * report * * * that I am personally familiar with all the ground included within the Reservation of Ft. Riley Kansas; that the location of the Union Pacific Railroad through it has been judiciously made so as not to impair its usefulness for military purposes, and that the 20 acres chosen for a Depot and the fractional section one on the west side of said Reservation near Junction City can also be granted to the Company without impairing the usefulness for military purposes of the Reservation.

(Signed) W. T. Sherman, Lt. Genl. Comdg.

and the Quartermaster General as follows:—

* * * I have the honor to return herewith the papers connected with the application of the Union Pacific Railroad Co., for 2 small pieces of land in the Fort Riley Military Reservation, and to report:—

That the Chief Qr. Mr. of the Military Division of the Missouri[1] has investigated the matter and consulted with the Lt. Genl. Comdg. that Division on the subject and as to the result, reports his opinion that the land asked for can be granted for the purpose stated, viz:—the erection thereon of depots, shops and offices for the operation of the road without impairing the value of the Reservation for military purposes. The main portion of the land desired is in the South-west corner of the Reservation and is not needed for any military purpose whatever.

Thus advised, I respectfully recommend a favorable consideration of the application.

(Signed) D. H. Rucker   Actg. Qr. Mr. Genl.[2]
Bvt. Maj. Genl. U.S.A.

Having no information in conflict with the foregoing reports, they are approved by this Department and, in accordance therewith, I have the honor to report that, in the opinion of this Dept., the location of said railroad and the diminution of the military reserve, by the right of way to said Railroad Co. of 100 feet in width as the road and its connecting branches are located over & upon, and through said Reserve, and setting apart 20 acres in the bottom opposite Riley City for Depots and other purposes, and fractional section *One* on the west side of said Reservation, near Junction City, for the same purposes, will not impair the usefulness of said Military Reservation for military purposes.

Edwin M. Stanton,   Secy. of War.

LBcopy, DNA-RG107, Lets. Sent, Mil. Bks., Executive, 58-C.

1. James L. Donaldson held this post from 1866 to 1869. Brown, *Am. Biographies*, 2: 487.

2. Daniel H. Rucker (1812–1910) joined the U.S. Army as a second lieutenant in 1837 and twelve years later transferred to the Quartermaster Department in which he spent the rest of his long career, serving as assistant quartermaster general (1866–82). Warner, *Blue*.

From James Birney [1]

Bay City Mich   Mar 22 '67

Sir;

You were pleased to send my name to the Senate for confirmation as assessor of the 6th district of Michigan.[2]

The Representative of this district Mr Driggs[3] regards me as a competitor for his place, and seeks every mode to prevent my having any position. By a concession which the Senate make to representatives as to local offices, he has succeeded in preventing my confirmation.[4]

The act places the Senate in a most inconsistent position. It demands nominees from the Republican party and when they get them they reject them because they may not be favorites of the Representative.

It is a cruel outrage on the part of Mr Driggs, and I trust he will not be accommodated in having his choice.[5]

James Birney.

ALS, DNA-RG56, Appts., Internal Revenue Service, Assessor, Mich., 6th Dist., James Birney.

1. Birney (1817–1888), eldest son of abolitionist James G. Birney, practiced law in Cincinnati before moving to Bay City, Michigan, in 1857. He served in the state senate, was briefly lieutenant governor of the state, and then held the post of judge for the eighteenth judicial circuit. *DAB*.

2. Birney was nominated on March 13, 1867. Ser. 6B, Vol. 4: 276, Johnson Papers, LC.

3. John F. Driggs.

4. Birney had been rejected on March 18. Ser. 6B, Vol. 4: 276, Johnson Papers, LC.

5. Henry Raymond, nominated as assessor on March 25, was confirmed and commissioned on April 5, 1867. Ibid., 277.

From John A. Dix

Paris   22 March 1867.

My dear Sir:

Yesterday's mail brought me the news of my confirmation,[1] which in consequence of the long delay and my advices from home I had nearly given up as hopeless. It brought also accounts of a better feeling in Congress, & we all hope that they may be confirmed by further information.

My relations with the government here are very pleasant, and I know that the strongest desire exists to be on good terms with the United States. The Emperor always enquires after our affairs at home and in regard to you personally with much interest, and expresses the hope that we may have no further disturbance. Our unsettled condition has impaired confidence to some extent in the final adjustment of our difficulties, but there is a better feeling than there was two months ago & our Stocks have risen in price.

There is a very general feeling of uneasiness in Europe, and the principal states are strengthening their military preparations. France is likely, if the new law proposed by the government should be adopted, to be a good deal disturbed, and very seriously injured if it is continued in force long. It puts an immense force under arms, burdening the industry of the country with the support of a great body of non-producers & withdrawing from it the laborers it needs for its full development. The enemies of the government say that all this is the legitimate consequence of its failure to prevent by its interposition the inordinate extension of the power of Prussia and the corresponding diminution of that of Austria, thus allowing the balance among the German states to be disturbed. I have written an unofficial letter to Mr. Seward in regard to the great debate in the Corps Legislatif on this subject.

The Exposition[2] will be opened, but will not be ready, on the 1st of April, and from all appearance we shall be as much behind in our preparations as others. Our Commissioners are just beginning to arrive.

I avail myself of the earliest moment after being informed of my confirmation to renew the expression of my thanks for the confidence you have reposed in me.

Wishing you all happiness, and, what is first of all the most desirable, a vindication of the present by the verdict of the future on our public acts . . .

John A. Dix

ALS, DLC-JP.
1. Dix had been nominated as minister to France on December 12, 1866, but was not commissioned until March 2, 1867. Ser. 6B, Vol. 2: 58, Johnson Papers, LC.
2. The Universal Exposition (Paris).

From James B. Steedman

March 22, 1867

My Dear Mr President,

The action of the House to day on Smythe, the New York Collector, clearly indicates, in my judgement, the purpose of your enemies.[1] The intention is, unless you remove him, to make his case a precedent for their action towards yourself. They intend to impeach him and supend him during his trial. Of course, they care nothing about Smythe—whose conduct, in the opinion of your best friends, demands his removal—but it is the purpose of your enemies—the extremists—in pursuing him, to commit the moderate of their party to the suspension of the functions of a public officer, during his trial on articles of impeachment, so as to hold them to a suspension of yourself, should they be able to get articles of impeachment against you before the Senate. Many of your best friends believe this and feel that you ought to be apprised of their intentions.

I have frequently heard the whole subject discussed and there appears to be unanimity of opinion that Smythe ought to be removed on account of the testimony he gave before the Committee, *if no other reason.* I am satisfied from what I have heard that his prompt removal, would greatly strengthen you, not only in New York, but throughout the Country—for it is universally conceded that he has shown himself to be a weak man— totally unfit to deal with those who duped him into the ridiculous statements he made before the Committee.

You will, I trust, excuse me for making these suggestions—for I assure you I venture to do so only because I am so situated that I hear and see a great deal that never reaches you, and on account of my solicitude for your success.

I have an abiding confidence—a conviction that a triumph yet awaits you—but I some times feel, that perhaps, my zeal may make me appear officious to you. I hope, however, that you will attribute all I have ever said to you to my anxiety for your success. I sincerely feel that the condition of the New York Collectorship is unfortunate, whether Smyth is a good or a bad man. The nomination for the place of a man of high position and irreproachable character—like John T. Hoffman—would make you impregnable.

James B. Steedman.

P.S. I saw and talked with Senator Morgan[2] last night and he spoke freely of Smythe and expressed the hope that you would remove him. He deprecated the proceedings in the house—for, said he "the President is not easily frightened, as we all know," by which, I infered he meant that you might regard the House proceedings as an attempt to bully you into the removal of Smythe.

J.B.S.

ALS, DLC-JP.
1. Henry A. Smythe, collector of the port of New York, was the subject of congressional scrutiny as well as resolutions. Among the proposals voiced in the U.S. House were ones on March 22 calling for the removal and/or impeachment of Smythe. *National Intelligencer*, Mar. 23, 1867; *Washington Evening Star*, Mar. 23, 1867. See also Smythe to Johnson, Mar. 6, 28, 1867.
2. Edwin D. Morgan.

From Jeremiah S. Black

[Washington, March 23, 1867][1]

Mr. President:

I have drawn up a paper which I submit. It is transcribed by a perfectly confidential person—a member of my own family. I think a veto message ought to be confined as closely as possible to the very subject of the bill objected to. Therefore I have said nothing about your proposition for a new election. That requires time, consideration, the assent of friends and a careful framing of the agreement. Besides it needs some material to make it up which I do not possess.

I would have called on you to day but you are in Cabinet consultation. I must leave this evening for Phila. on an important professional engagement. I shall therefore not be able to see you for several days. For that reason I send the paper now and in this way.

There is another thing which you ought to know: Those low devils on the Judiciary Committee summoned me up and nothwithstanding my protest compelled me to testify concerning the last veto.[2] I mentioned to Mr. Stanberry what I felt obliged to reveal. I told him too beforehand what I would have to say and he agreed with me that there was no escape. You are well aware that not a word was ever uttered by you to me that the purest patriot would be ashamed of. So far as I know you seemed to me always anxious for the liberty and laws of your Country. I told them that conversations of this character had drawn me on to put the substance of them into written form and you had used some of them in that message.

J. S. Black

ALS, DLC-JP.
1. This date has been assigned by the Library of Congress. Internal evidence reveals Black was in Washington when he wrote the letter.
2. On March 14 the Judiciary Committee attempted to pin Black down on his part in the President's veto of the First Military Reconstruction Act—whether he corresponded with Johnson on the subject, wrote any of the veto message, or which parts of the message did not originate with Black in substance or form. See *House Reports*, 40 Cong., 1 Sess., No. 7, "Impeachment Investigation," pt. 2, pp. 271–73 (Ser. 1314).

Veto of the Second Military Reconstruction Act

WASHINGTON, *March 23, 1867.*

To the House of Representatives:

I have considered the bill entitled "An act supplementary to an act entitled 'An act to provide for the more efficient government of the rebel States,' passed March 2, 1867, and to facilitate restoration,"[1] and now return it to the House of Representatives with my objections.

This bill provides for elections in the ten States brought under the operation of the original act to which it is supplementary. Its details are principally directed to the elections for the formation of the State constitutions, but by the sixth section of the bill "all elections" in these States occurring while the original act remains in force are brought within its purview. Referring to these details, it will be found that, first of all, there is to be a registration of the voters. No one whose name has not been admitted on the list is to be allowed to vote at any of these elections. To ascertain who is entitled to registration, reference is made necessary, by the express language of the supplement, to the original act and to the pending bill. The fifth section of the original act provides, as to voters, that they shall be "male citizens of the State, 21 years old and upward, of whatever race, color, or previous condition, who have been residents of said State for one year." This is the general qualification, followed, however, by many exceptions. No one can be registered, according to the original act, "who may be disfranchised for participation in the rebellion"— a provision which left undetermined the question as to what amounted to disfranchisement, and whether without a judicial sentence the act itself produced that effect. This supplemental bill superadds an oath, to be taken by every person before his name can be admitted upon the registration, that he has "not been disfranchised for participation in any rebellion or civil war against the United States." It thus imposes upon every person the necessity and responsibility of deciding for himself, under the peril of punishment by a military commission if he makes a mistake, what works disfranchisement by participation in rebellion and what amounts to such participation. Almost every man—the negro as well as the white —above 21 years of age who was resident in these ten States during the rebellion, voluntarily or involuntarily, at some time and in some way did participate in resistance to the lawful authority of the General Government. The question with the citizen to whom this oath is to be proposed must be a fearful one, for while the bill does not declare that perjury may be assigned for such false swearing nor fix any penalty for the offense, we must not forget that martial law prevails; that every person is answerable to a military commission, without previous presentment by a grand jury, for any charge that may be made against him, and that the supreme authority of the military commander determines the question as to what is an offense and what is to be the measure of punishment.

The fourth section of the bill provides "that the commanding general of each district shall appoint as many boards of registration as may be necessary, consisting of three loyal officers or persons." The only qualification stated for these officers is that they must be "loyal." They may be persons in the military service or civilians, residents of the State or strangers. Yet these persons are to exercise most important duties and are vested with unlimited discretion. They are to decide what names shall be placed upon the register and from their decision there is to be no appeal. They are to superintend the elections and to decide all questions which may arise. They are to have the custody of the ballots and to make return of the persons elected. Whatever frauds or errors they may commit must pass without redress. All that is left for the commanding general is to receive the returns of the elections, open the same and ascertain who are chosen "according to the returns of the officers who conducted said elections." By such means and with this sort of agency are the conventions of delegates to be constituted.

As the delegates are to speak for the people, common justice would seem to require that they should have authority from the people themselves. No convention so constituted will in any sense represent the wishes of the inhabitants of these States, for under the all-embracing exceptions of these laws, by a construction which the uncertainty of the clause as to disfranchisement leaves open to the board of officers, the great body of the people may be excluded from the polls and from all opportunity of expressing their own wishes or voting for delegates who will faithfully reflect their sentiments.

I do not deem it necessary further to investigate the details of this bill. No consideration could induce me to give my approval to such an election law for any purpose, and especially for the great purpose of framing the constitution of a State. If ever the American citizen should be left to the free exercise of his own judgment it is when he is engaged in the work of forming the fundamental law under which he is to live. That work is his work, and it can not properly be taken out of his hands. All this legislation proceeds upon the contrary assumption that the people of each of these States shall have no constitution except such as may be arbitrarily dictated by Congress and formed under the restraint of military rule. A plain statement of facts makes this evident.

In all these States there are existing constitutions, framed in the accustomed way by the people. Congress, however, declares that these constitutions are not "loyal and republican," and requires the people to form them anew. What, then, in the opinion of Congress, is necessary to make the constitution of a State "loyal and republican"? The original act answers the question: It is universal negro suffrage—a question which the Federal Constitution leaves exclusively to the States themselves. All this legislative machinery of martial law, military coercion, and political disfranchisement is avowedly for that purpose and none other. The existing constitutions of the ten States conform to the acknowledged standards of loyalty and republicanism. Indeed, if there are degrees in republican forms of government, their constitutions are more republican now than when these States, four of which were members of the original thirteen, first became members of the Union.

Congress does not now demand that a single provision of their constitution be changed except such as confine suffrage to the white population. It is apparent, therefore, that these provisions do not conform to the standard of republicanism which Congress seeks to establish. That there may be no mistake, it is only necessary that reference should be made to the original act, which declares "such constitution shall provide that the elective franchise shall be enjoyed by all such persons as have the qualifications herein stated for electors of delegates." What class of persons is here meant clearly appears in the same section; that is to say, "the male citizens of said State 21 years old and upward, of whatever race, color, or previous condition, who have been resident in said State for one year previous to the day of such election."

Without these provisions no constitution which can be framed in any one of the ten States will be of any avail with Congress. This, then, is the test of what the constitution of a State of this Union must contain to make it republican. Measured by such a standard, how few of the States now composing the Union have republican constitutions! If in the exercise of the constitutional guaranty that Congress shall secure to every State a republican form of government universal suffrage for blacks as well as whites is a *sine qua non*, the work of reconstruction may as well begin in Ohio as in Virginia, in Pennsylvania as in North Carolina.

When I contemplate the millions of our fellow-citizens of the South with no alternative left but to impose upon themselves this fearful and untried experiment of complete negro enfranchisement—and white disfranchisement, it may be, almost as complete—or submit indefinitely to the rigor of martial law, without a single attribute of freemen, deprived of all the sacred guaranties of our Federal Constitution, and threatened with even worse wrongs, if any worse are possible, it seem to me their condition is the most deplorable to which any people can be reduced. It is true that they have been engaged in rebellion and that their object being a separation of the States and a dissolution of the Union there was an obligation resting upon every loyal citizen to treat them as enemies and to wage war against their cause.

Inflexibly opposed to any movement imperiling the integrity of the Government, I did not hesitate to urge the adoption of all measures necessary for the suppression of the insurrection. After a long and terrible struggle the efforts of the Government were triumphantly successful, and the people of the South, submitting to the stern arbitrament, yielded forever the issues of the contest. Hostilities terminated soon after it became my duty to assume the responsibilities of the chief executive officer of the Republic, and I at once endeavored to repress and control the passions which our civil strife had engendered, and, no longer regarding these erring millions as enemies, again acknowledged them as our friends and our countrymen. The war had accomplished its objects. The nation was saved and that seminal principle of mischief which from the birth of the Government had gradually but inevitably brought on the rebellion was totally eradicated. Then, it seemed to me, was the auspicious time to commence the work of reconciliation; then, when these people sought once more our friendship and protection, I considered it our duty generously to meet them in the spirit of charity and forgiveness and to conquer them even more effectually by the magnanimity of the nation than by the force of its arms. I yet believe that if the policy of reconciliation then inaugurated, and which contemplated an early restoration of these people to all their political rights, had received the support of Congress, every one of these ten States and all their people would at this moment be fast anchored in the Union and the great work which gave the war all its sanction and made it just and holy would have been accomplished. Then over all the vast and fruitful regions of the South peace and its blessings would have prevailed, while now millions are deprived of rights guaranteed by the Constitution to every citizen and after nearly two years of legislation find themselves placed under an absolute military despotism. "A military republic, a government founded on mock elections and supported only by the sword," was nearly a quarter of a century since pronounced by Daniel Webster, when speaking of the South American States, as "a movement, indeed, but a retrograde and disastrous movement, from the regular and old-fashioned monarchical systems;" and he added:

> If men would enjoy the blessings of republican government, they must govern themselves by reason, by mutual counsel and consultation, by a sense and feeling of general interest, and by the acquiescence of the minority in the will of the majority, properly expressed; and, above all, the military must be kept, according to the language of our bill of rights, in strict subordination to the civil authority. Wherever this lesson is not both learned and practiced there can be no political freedom. Absurd, preposterous is it, a scoff and a satire on free forms of constitutional liberty, for frames of government to be prescribed by military leaders and the right of suffrage to be exercised at the point of the sword.[2]

I confidently believe that a time will come when these States will again occupy their true positions in the Union. The barriers which now seem so obstinate must yield to the force of an enlightened and just public opinion, and sooner or later unconstitutional and oppressive legislation will be effaced from our statute books. When this shall have been consummated, I pray God that the errors of the past may be forgotten and that once more we shall be a happy, united, and prosperous people, and that at last, after the bitter and eventful experience through which the nation has passed, we shall all come to know that our only safety is in the preservation of our Federal Constitution and in according to every American citizen and to every State the rights which that Constitution secures.

ANDREW JOHNSON.

Richardson, *Messages*, 6: 531–35.
  1. *U.S. Statutes at Large*, 15: 14–16.
  2. Not found.

From Frank W. Anthony [1]

Jackson Mich.   March 25/67

Honored Sir

Permit me hereby to thank you for appointing me Post Master of this city.[2] This would have been done personally when in Washington last week had I not known that a personal interview if obtained would trespass upon your time.

Whatever of personal inconvenience or sacrifice the late acceptance of this appointment (unsolicited on my part) may have caused, is amply compensated for, by its placing me right upon the public record. Hitherto acting with the Republican party, I ceased to act with it because I could not forget what made a Republican;—loyalty to the Nation loyalty to human equality, loyalty to the Union and loyalty to the Constitution. The party has become disloyal to all and herein. This Nation rests and must rest, if it endures, upon human equality, which springs from mans creation in the divine image. The unlawful enfranchisement of a black aristocracy of ignorance by the real or practical disfranchisement of the intelligent white race of the South under any pretext or provocation violates this fundamental principle of the Nations life. Because I see and proclaim the impolicy and the injustice of this action I am called a renegade. The Republican party was successful in the late war because it was fought for the Union. Not the Republican party—but love for the Union, with or without regard to the Negro carried the Nation through it. Because I cannot turn my face from this truth and forget the glory & the strenght of the Union and consent to perpetuate disunion for the brief aggrandisement of party I am called a traitor. A traitor to what? My Country? No. My party? No. A traitor only to its ephemeral success. The War established the supremacy of the Constitution. Because I still maintain this supremacy, by a confinement of its powers to its written word (which is all there is to it) I am called a copperhead. It is not pleasant to be called renegade, traitor, Copperhead—but I console myself with the words of M. Emile Girardin,[3] "I have faith in the truth although it may for a season be called error or calumny. Every repressed truth is a gathering force which awaits a sure day of triumph. I should not be a politician if I did not know how to wait for it."

You Sir have set us an example of patriotic devotion. As President you had only to turn your back upon your past and the platform upon which you were elected, accept the usurpations of the party in power and glide quietly through your official term. Instead as in the Senate and during the War you resisted the open and violent secession and disunion of the South, so in the Presidential chair have you planted yourself like a rock against the more secret and assiduous secession and disunion of the North. As you triumphed over the first so is your triumph assured over the last. When it comes, as it must, you can say with Horace

> "Exegi monumentum aere perennius Regalique situ pyramidum Altius Quod non imber edax possit diruere Non Aquilo impotens, Aut innumerabilis annorum series et fuga temporum."[4]

With feelings of smpathy and cheerful hope shining beyond what clouds and darkness I know not . . .

F W Anthony   L.P.M.

ALS, DLC-JP.

1. Anthony (c1823–fl1880), a merchant who had retired by 1880, was a native of Rhode Island and married three times. 1860 Census, Mich., Jackson, Jackson, 3rd Ward, 114; (1870), 2nd Ward, 183; (1880), 4th Ward, 328.

2. Anthony apparently received a recess appointment to the Jackson post office and be-

gan his duties on October 16, 1866. He was nominated on March 2, 1867, and promptly rejected by the Senate on the same day. *U.S. Off. Reg.* (1867); Ser. 6B, Vol. 4: 275, Johnson Papers, LC.

3. Émile de Girardin (1805–1881), a French newspaper editor, novelist, and playwright, also served in the chamber of deputies. *The New Columbia Encyclopedia* (1975).

4. "I have completed a memorial more lasting than bronze and higher than the royal grave of the pyramids, that neither biting rain nor the north wind in its fury can destroy nor the unnumbered series of years and the flight of ages." Gordon Williams, ed. and trans., *The Third Book of Horace's* "Odes" (Oxford, England, 1969), 150.

From Lewis P. Clover, Jr. [1]

Lanesboro Berkshire Co Massachusetts   March 25/67

Dear Sir

You will perhaps bear in mind that I took the liberty some time since of writing to you in relation to the removal of my father Mr. Lewis P. Clover[2] from a subordinate position in the New York Custom-House by Mr. Collector Smythe the present incumbent.

My father though a Democrat all his life, received his appointment not on political grounds, but in consideration of services rendered his country in the war of 1812, he having been one of the unfortunate prisoners confined in Dartmoor Prison during the massacre.

Soon after I wrote you my father called upon the collector, and in the most respectful manner asked for his testimonials which are warmly endorsed by the late President Lincoln, James Gordon Bennett Esq and other distinguished gentlemen.

Mr. Smythe was much displeased that you had been written to upon the subject, and expressed himself in language so gross, insulting and profane as not to bear repeating—adding in conclusion that neither you nor all the powers in —— could secure his retention. My father shocked and surprised quietly withdrew.

Here the matter would have rested had I not read in a late issue of the U.S. Express a report of the evidence of Smythe before a committee of investigation appointed by Congress.

In his evidence, referring to the remarks made by him, he is reputed to have said that he only "weeded out incompetency, ignorance, intemperance and vice." A slander so gross and infamous may serve the purpose of one who I judge has little or no reputation at stake, but it will also I fear if not promptly rebuked by the removal of Smythe from office have the effect to estrange a very large number of persons in New York and elsewhere who now warmly espouse the policy of the present Executive.

Though as a clergyman of the Prot Episcopal church, I take no party in party politics, I shall in the future as I have in time past pray for the prosperity and success of him, whom I believe to be striving honestly and faithfully to restore peace and happiness to our distracted country and people.

My father who has been a resident of the city of New York upwards of sixty years and a reputable member of the presbyterian church more than thirty years is well known to most of the old residents of that city, and with many others deeply regrets the imposition that has been practiced upon the President by designing and unworthy men.

Lewis P Clover.

ALS, DLC-JP.
1. Clover (1819–1896), although an Episcopal priest and rector of a number of different parishes, was also well known as a painter. *Appleton's Cyclopaedia*; *NUC*.
2. Clover (1790–*fl*1869) had quite a career in the War of 1812, especially aboard ship in the Indian Ocean. In the late 1830s he received an appointment in the New York customhouse where he remained until the 1850s. By 1859 Clover was once again employed at the New York customs office, staying until 1867. "Memoir of Lewis P. Clover, A Prisoner of War," *The United States Magazine and Democratic Review*, 26 (1850): 260–65; Brooklyn directories (1867–69); *U.S. Off. Reg.* (1859–65).

From Samuel Johnson [1]

Greeneville, March 25 1867.

I have been appointed one of the Commissioner of the Freedmens Bureau, to raise money with which to purchase a suitable Lot on which to build a School House for the education of the Coloured children of Greeneville—and my object in troubling you upon, the subject is to ascertain if there would be any chance for me to purchase an acre Lot off of one of your Tracts that lies out West of Town close to the Reble Grave yard. If you will let us have the Lot and will send me word as to the price of it I will send you the money, and would like for you to send me a deed to it.[2] I am getting along as well as usual and have not changed any in Politics still being for you as much as ever. I would like to see you all very much.[3]

Sam. Johnson.

ALS, DLC-JP.
1. Evidently this is the same Samuel Johnson who earlier had been one of Andrew Johnson's slaves. See Charles Johnson to Johnson, Jan. 29, 1860, *Johnson Papers*, 3: 405.
2. According to county deed records, the President conveyed to Samuel Johnson et al. one acre of land for a church and schoolhouse; this took place in September 1867. Greene County, Tennessee, Deeds, Vol. 36, pp. 188–89. See also John P. Holtsinger to Johnson, Apr. 19, 1867; Johnson to Holtsinger, Apr. 27, 1867, Johnson Papers, LC.
3. On a separate page following Samuel Johnson's letter, Holtsinger attached a note indicating that Johnson had asked him to urge the President to grant the request of the freedmen. At the bottom of this note is a typed notation dated November 1, 1930, and signed by Johnson's grandson, Andrew J. Patterson, which states: "Andrew Johnson gave the lot in question, for the purpose requested in this letter."

From Thomas Shankland

Washington   Cor 17th & C Streets   March 25, 1867.

The President will remember that I urged his appointment of the present Collector of the Port of New York,[1] and I deem it proper and due to the President as well as myself to say that the Collector violated the pledges he made to me, prior to his appointment, so far as his pledged support of the President was concerned. In his Testimony he assails me by name and charges that I set on foot the gross charges against two Senators.[2] So far from that, I knew nothing, until told, as coming from the Collector himself by a Treasury Agent, that any Senator was apportioned any part or portion of the Genl. order business. Early in December when I heard a general talk of the Presidents Daughters being in New York shopping on this Genl. order account I contradicted it in the New York Times and wrote to Asst. Secy. Chandler why I had done so. I think all these rumours, come from Mr. Smythes indiscretions, and that the Senators should hold him responsible.

If afforded a personal interview the President has known me long enough to be satisfied, that he would get the whole truth.

Thos. Shankland

ALS, DLC-JP.
1. Henry A. Smythe.
2. Apparently this is a reference to Smythe's testimony before the House committee in December 1866. He told the committee that Thomas Shankland was responsible for the erroneous information that he had had conversations with Senators David T. Patterson and James R. Doolittle about how they might benefit financially from certain arrangements with the New York customhouse. On March 27 the Judiciary Committee exonerated Patterson and Doolittle of any involvement in the controversy. *House Reports*, 39 Cong., 2 Sess., No. 30, pp. 75–76 (Ser. 1305); *Congressional Globe*, 40 Cong., 1 Sess., p. 381.

From Robert B. Mitchell

Executive Office, Terr: of New Mexico
Santa Fé, March 26, 1867.

Sir:

I learn from the mail to day that the confirmation of General James H. Carleton as Brevet Major General in the Army was reconsidered on the last day of the last session of Congress and by omission or otherwise his name was not returned with others that were reconsidered and afterwards confirmed.[1]

The friends of General Carleton feel that this act on the part of the Senate was doing him a great injustice. A more faithful and efficient officer I have never met—and I will guarantee he has done more for this country and its people than all other commanding officers since the occupancy of this country by American troops. I ask for General Carleton a renomination as Brevet Major General—feeling that he deserves this mark of respect from a Government he has so faithfully served for the past twenty seven years.[2]

Robt B Mitchell   Gov Ter New Mexico

LS, DNA-RG94, ACP Branch, File C-5058-CB-1872, James H. Carleton.
    1. On December 14, 1866, Carleton's name was proposed, along with several others, to the Senate for a brevet major generalship. Over the next few months these nominations were considered several times and were finally confirmed on March 2, 1867. There is no indication why Carleton's name was omitted from those confirmed, but apparently it was. Senate Ex. Proceedings, Vol. 15, pt. 1: 34–35, 55–56, 238, 246, 268, 328, 337.
    2. On January 2, 1868, Robert Johnson, by order of the President, endorsed the letter, referring the request to interim secretary of war U. S. Grant, "who will please issue the Brevet as recommended." Grant duly proposed the brevet on January 10 which was then considered by the Senate in a rather lengthy process and finally confirmed on June 6, 1868. Ibid., Vol. 16: 132, 134, 190, 205, 235, 252.

From John Morrissey

[Washington, ca. March 26, 1867][1]

Sir

I venture to solicit the appointment of Assessor in the Fifth District of the City of New York, for my friend & constituent Elijah F. Purdy[2] a worthy son & namesake of the illustrious, Patriot,[3] who for thirty years, was styled "the War Horse of the Democratic Party" and whose memory is green in the hearts of thousands as a fearless, spotless and upright Citizen.

I feel that, in certain cases, it may seem invidious and be unjust to remove one man to make room for another. But the District I have the honor to represent is so overwhelmingly Democratic that it resembles treating it as a conquered rebel state, to put the controll of all the offices in the hands of my Political opponents.

Last November you encouraged me to hope that I might get Mr Hoxie[4] displaced from its collectorship to make way for my friend Mr Hayes,[5] who is a champion representative of its "bone & sinew." But Mr Hoxie has grown so old, so gray & so infirm from the continued emoluments of office, that an outcry might be raised should you anticipate the summonds which, in the course of nature, must soon remove him.

In favor of Mr Purdy, I can produce, when required, the most brilliant and satisfactory testimonials of his ability, industry and integrity and, I am happy in feeling able to add that, should your Excellency grant my prayer, he will be spared the humiliation of a rejection by the Senate.[6]

John Morrissey

LS, DNA-RG56, Appts., Internal Revenue Service, Assessor, N.Y., 5th Dist., Elijah F. Purdy.

1. Since Morrissey was serving in the U.S. House at this time, it is assumed that his letter was written from Washington. William G. Moore's endorsement on the letter's cover sheet gives the date March 26, 1867.

2. Purdy, Jr. (*fl*1872), was a clerk at Clinton Hall in New York City for a number of years. New York City directories (1860–72).

3. Purdy, Sr. (*c*1796–1866), was long involved in New York City politics, holding several different public offices and positions with Tammany Hall. *New York Times*, Jan. 9, 10, 1866.

4. Joseph Hoxie (b. 1795) was engaged in the clothing business in New York City for a number of years. He was appointed collector of internal revenue for the Fifth District during Lincoln's administration. *Appleton's Cyclopedia*.

5. James Hayes.

6. According to William G. Moore's note on the cover sheet of Morrissey's letter, Johnson asked the treasury secretary to make the appointment of Purdy as assessor. In fact, Johnson nominated Purdy to that post on March 26. But, on March 29, Johnson withdrew Purdy's nomination as assessor, having decided instead to nominate him as *collector* of the Fifth District (in place of Joseph Hoxie, who was to be removed). A few weeks later, however, the Senate tabled this nomination and Hoxie remained as collector. *Senate Ex. Proceedings*, Vol. 15, pt. 2: 555, 574, 586, 765; *U.S. Off. Reg.* (1867).

From Montgomery Blair

Ex Mansion   Mrch 27. 67

My dear Mr. President,

I have just learned that the Secy of the Treasury has asked you to send over Hurleys[1] commission for Assessor of the 4th Md. Dist. I hope you will see Mr. McCulloch before doing so. Hurley has been residing in Washington City & offering himself here for appointment as School Commissioner showing that he claimed his residence in the Dist. He is ineligible by law & is obnoxious to even the Radicals of the Dist.

I have this morning presented a recommendation for this office on [*sic*][2] from Col Maulsby[3] our candidate for Congress in the 4th Dist for Maj Van Lear[4] who is warmly commended to me by Genl Shiras[5] of Commissary Dept as a most efficient officer. I think the Secy of the Treasury will agree to this appt. on consultation with him.

M Blair

ALS, DNA-RG56, Appts., Internal Revenue Service, Assessor, Md., 4th Dist., B.F.M. Hurley.

1. Benjamin F.M. Hurley (*c*1834–1906), teacher and lawyer, served in a variety of civil and government offices in Washington, D.C., Maryland, and the Washington Territory, as well as consul to Holland. On March 27 Hurley's nomination was forwarded to the Senate but then withdrawn; two weeks earlier Hurley's nomination had met the same fate. In June Hurley was named register in bankruptcy for the Fourth District of Maryland. Thomas J.C. Williams, *A History of Washington County, Maryland* (2 vols., Baltimore, 1968 [1906]), 2: 1245; *New York Tribune*, June 10, 1867; Ser. 6B, Vol. 4: 107, Johnson Papers, LC.

2. Here Blair originally wrote "on behalf of." In changing the wording he crossed out "behalf of" but inadvertently left "on."

3. William P. Maulsby (1815–1894), a lawyer and former president of the Chesapeake and Ohio Canal Company, served as colonel of the 1st Potomac Home Brig., Md. Vols. Following the war he was appointed chief judge of the sixth circuit and was a member of the Maryland appeals court. In September 1867 he was incarcerated in an insane asylum.

T.J.C. Williams, *History of Frederick County, Maryland* (2 vols., Baltimore, 1967 [1910]), 2: 1329; *Washington Evening Star*, Sept. 20, 1867; Jacob M. Holdcraft, *Names in Stone* (2 vols., Baltimore, 1985), 2: 776.

4. John Van Lear (1832–1916), a bank teller before the war, served as captain of commissary subsistence with the volunteer forces. He was nominated for Fourth District assessor on April 15 and confirmed and commissioned three days later. He lived in Hagerstown until 1875, and afterwards lived in Washington, Cincinnati, and Baltimore before returning to Hagerstown. Ser. 6B, Vol. 4: 108, Johnson Papers, LC; Pension Files, John Van Lear, RG15, NA.

5. Alexander E. Shiras (1812–1875), a graduate of West Point and a career army officer, served in the Commissary Department. During the war he was brevetted brigadier general in 1864 and major general in 1865. A year before his death, Shiras achieved the rank of brigadier general. Hunt and Brown, *Brigadier Generals*; Powell, *Army List*, 585.

From John F. Coyle

Office of the National Intelligencer
Washington   Mar 27/67

Mr J. P. O'Sullivan[1] who will present this has been most earnestly recommended for a Diplomatic appointment and is the Gentleman I spoke of to you some time ago in terms of praise of his ability and experience.

The Austrian Mission being again vacant by the rejection of Genl. Blair[2] I take just pleasure in joining in the recommendation of the friends of the administration of Mr. O'Sullivan for that position as a Gentleman eminently fitted for so distinguished a Post.

John F Coyle

ALS, DNA-RG59, Lets. of Appl. and Recomm., 1861–69 (M650, Roll 36), John P. O'Sullivan.

1. O'Sullivan was evidently a career diplomat, having served in the mid-1850s as consul at Bayonne, France, and from 1858 through at least 1861 as consul at Singapore. He was a native of New York and a sometime resident of California. O'Sullivan to Seward, Mar. 15, 1861, Feb. 21, 1867, Lets. of Appl. and Recomm., 1861–1869 (M650, Roll 36), John P. O'Sullivan, RG59, NA; *U.S. Off. Reg.* (1861).

2. Johnson had extremely hard luck with the Austrian appointment, for Francis P. Blair, Jr., was only one of several persons whose nomination to the Austrian post was rejected by the Senate. There is no indication that O'Sullivan was ever nominated. Curiously, the Senate rejected Blair's nomination on March 28, although Coyle wrote about it on March 27. Perhaps Coyle misdated his letter. *Senate Ex. Proceedings*, Vol. 15, pt. 2: 504, 572; Ser. 6B, Vol. 2: 37, 46, 51, Johnson Papers, LC.

From William J.C. Duhamel

Private

[Washington]   Mch 27th 1867

Mr. President

Whilst on my visit to the Jail Miss Surrat requested me to prescribe for her; after which she informed me that Gen'l Butler and Mr. Ashley had *sent for her*, and *she* told them that it was the wish of her lawyer Mr.

Bradley[1] to see them only in his presence to which proposition Genl B. Butler and Mr. Ashley *declined seeing her*.

I spoke of the infamous attempt to implicate the President by the evidence of her brother John; Miss Surrat replied in a most earnest manner, that John her brother knew nothing in that case against the President and could say nothing and she knew John could not be induced to *swear away his own soul*.

I am inclined to believe that Mr. B. Wade Presdt U.S. Senate is most *anxious* to wield *more* power; as I am attending a patient next door to Mr. Ashley's rooms (No. 359 9th st) and Mr. Wade is seen there every day, and *very* often Mr. Summner[2] with him.

This is what I wanted to speak to you of last night.[3]

Believe me your devoted friend.

W.J.C. Duhamel   M.D.

ALS, DLC-JP.
    1. Anna E. Surratt, Benjamin F. Butler, James M. Ashley, and Joseph H. Bradley, Sr.
    2. Benjamin F. Wade and Charles Sumner.
    3. Duhamel had previously written to Johnson about the Surratts. See Duhamel to Johnson, Feb. 26, 1867.

From Wallace P. Ryon[1]

Pottsville, Schuylkill County   Pa.
March 27th 1867

My Dear Sir

Public attention has been called to a meeting, held in this place a few evenings since, advocating your immediate Impeachment, &c.[2]

Hon. Thadeous Stevens is the medium through whom the people are informed that the meeting in question was one of the largest ever held in this section of the State. I believe the above is about the substance of his remarks in Congress.[3] Mr. Stevens has been greatly misinformed upon the subject. This meeting was held in a small room, and there was not present more than fifty persons at any one time, a majority of whom were men of no character or standing in this City. If any considerable number of their own party had been in favor, or in sympathy with the object of this meeting, many more could have been gotten together for timely notice was given to *all* by large posters. I have thus taken the liberty of correcting any impression the remarks of Mr. Stevens may have made upon your mind, as to the importance of this meeting—it had no significance, whatever—taking into view the character and numbers present, and if any weight attaches to it at all, it is through Mr. Stevens remarks.

Your course with regard to the questions arising out of reconstruction, is highly approved by all good men, and the hope is earnestly expressed that you will continue firm in your views, as expressed in the very able state papers which have emenated from your pen.

W. P. Ryon

ALS, DLC-JP.
1. Ryon (1836–*fl*1897) was a Pottsville lawyer and cashier of the Pennsylvania National Bank. In 1879 he moved to Philadelphia where he engaged in the coal and iron business; a few years later he returned to the family's homestead at Lawrenceville and resumed the practice of law. *History of Tioga County, Pennsylvania* (n.p., 1897), 166, 1024–25.
2. Citizens of Pottsville held a meeting on March 11 and charged Johnson with impeding the execution of the First Military Reconstruction Act and interfering with the protection of civil rights. Resolutions called on Congress, in "the best interests of the nation," to begin impeachment proceedings immediately. *The Miner's Journal and Pottsville General Advertiser*, Mar. 16, 1867.
3. Stevens delivered the remarks on March 23. See *Congressional Globe*, 40 Cong., 1 Sess., p. 316.

From Henry A. Smythe

Custom House, New-York,
March 28 1867

Sir:

As I was leaving Washington last night I learned that a resolution had passed the House of Representatives declaring it as "the sense of the House that Henry A. Smythe should be immediately removed from the office of Collector of the Port of New York."[1]

I respectfully ask your attention to the following facts. On Monday of this present week a resolution passed Congress by a two-thirds vote that I might be permitted to be heard before the Committee on Public Expenditures by counsel and to introduce witnesses.[2] On the afternoon of the same day I received from Mr. Hulburd,[3] the Chairman of that Committee the following note:—

In House of Rep.
March 25 1867

Henry A. Smythe, Esq.
Sir:

The Committee on Pub. Expenditures will be in session at their room in the Capitol at 10 o'clock, A.M. to-morrow morning. If you desire you can then appear before the Committee, in person, *or by counsel.*

Yours &c
C.T. Hulburd Chm. of Comm. on Pub. Exp.

The next morning, which was the day before yesterday, I appeared before the Committee and stated to them that both my counsel and my witnesses were in New York, but that I would be ready on any day to proceed with the investigation in New York where the witnesses all were, or in Washington, if the Committee should prefer the latter place.

It was suggested by one of the members that perhaps a Sub-Committee would conduct the investigation in New York. I stated that before the investigation proceeded, I should like to make a statement of facts before the Committee, which proposition did not seem to be very favorably received.

I then went before the Judiciary Committee of the Senate to testify in relation to the charges made against Senators Patterson and Doolittle.[4] As I came out from that Committee-Room, in the afternoon, I was met by a messenger stating that Mr. Hulburd wished to see me in the House of Representatives. I immediately went to the House and was met in the Lobby by Mr. Hulburd and Mr. Broomall.[5] Mr. Hulburd addressing me in the most friendly manner, placing his hand upon my shoulder with an air of the greatest kindness, said that the Committee had concluded that I might make a statement before the Committee, if I wished, on the following morning. Accordingly, (yesterday) I went before the Committee at 10 o'clock in the morning, made a general statement and told the Committee that I was ready to proceed either in New York or Washington with the investigation, aided by my counsel and witnesses, whenever they would fix the time, and suggested on leaving that they should advise me when they were ready. I left the room with the clear understanding that the investigation was to proceed, and heard no suggestion or intimation to the contrary until just as I was leaving Washington last night I was informed of the resolution that had been so unexpectedly and so unfairly introduced by Mr. Hulburd, soon after leaving me with such friendly treatment and apparently cordial acquiesence in my proposition to have the investigation continued.

I herewith enclose a copy of the statement which I yesterday filed before the Committee. I protest against the gross injustice of the resolution and ask that no action may be taken by the Executive until I can have a fair investigation before the Committee, and have that same opportunity to defend myself by the aid of counsel and witnesses which I could have in any court of Justice in case I were charged with the simplest breach of duty, or common indebtedness. I appeal to the President to grant me this justice and to protect me in this plain right.[6]

Henry A. Smythe

LS, DLC-JP.

1. *Congressional Globe*, 40 Cong., 1 Sess., pp. 394–95.

2. Ibid., pp. 334–336; see also Smythe to Johnson, Mar. 6, 1867.

3. Calvin T. Hulburd (1809–1897) received his law degree from Yale and served several terms in the New York state assembly before being elected to Congress. A three-time representative (1863–69), Hulburd chaired the committee on public expenditures from the 38th through 40th congresses. *BDUSC*.

4. David T. Patterson and James R. Doolittle. While the committee charged Smythe with "contemplated distribution" of the general order business, the two senators were implicated by allegedly "having been contemplated" as recipients by Collector Smythe. *New York World*, Mar. 8, 1867.

5. John M. Broomall.

6. In early April Johnson, "with the advice and consent of most of the Senators," decided to "disregard the vote of the House requesting him to remove Collector Smythe." Smythe continued as collector of the port of New York until the end of Johnson's presidency. *New York World*, Apr. 3, 1867; Smythe to Ulysses S. Grant, Mar. 4, 1869, Appls., Customs Service, Collector, New York, Henry A. Smythe, RG56, NA.

From John S. Miller

Washington   Mar 29/67

Sir:

I see by the morning papers that Saml. J. Royer[1] has been nominate by you for Collector for the 17th Dist. of Penna. (Morrell M.C.[2]) vice, *Caldwell*[3] *rejected*.

Mr Royer was removed by you last fall during the recess of 39th Congress.

Mr Morrell has had two *worthy men "slaughtered"*[4] to make room for this man *Royer*, who is his *pet*, and favorite.

I therefore most respectfully earnestly *protest* against *Royers appointment.* I do so not only for myself but in name of over *four thousand conservative voters who supported me the administration candidate for the Legislature of Penna., who I assure you are to a man opposed to the reappoint of this man, at the dictation of Danl. J Morrell.*

Royer's reappointment will be hailed as a *radical triumph over you* and *your friends* in the district. I therefore hope it will not be consumated.[5]

It may be said that the Senate will not confirm democrats or conservatives. If so would it not be well to *let them take the responsibility* of leaving the *offices vacant.* They passed the "tenure of office bill" let them take the consequences.

Hoping that you will excuse me for thus trespassing on your valuable time. I will close by assuring you that your efforts in favor of civil liberty will enshrine your memory, in the hearts of all true lovers of the government founded by the "Patriots of 76." "Truth must & Justice will prevail."

John S. Miller
Huntingdon Pa.

ALS, DNA-RG56, Appts., Internal Revenue Service, Collector, Pa., 17th Dist., Samuel J. Royer.

1. Either the Royer (*c*1816–*fl*1870) who was a prosperous Martinsburg farmer, or Royer (b. *c*1811) who had been a clerk in 1850. He served as collector during 1862–66. Apparently Johnson nominated Royer on March 27, 1867, but the nomination was withheld. There is no evidence the Senate ever received this nomination. *U.S. Off. Reg.* (1865); Ser. 6B, Vol. 4: 88, Johnson Papers, LC; 1850 Census, Pa., Blair, Blair Twp., 202; (1870), Woodbury Twp., Martinsburg, 493; D. T. Caldwell et al. to Johnson [1867], Appts., Internal Revenue Service, Collector, Pa., 17th Dist., Samuel J. Royer, RG56, NA.

2. Daniel J. Morrell (1821–1885) was a businessman in Johnstown for a number of years before being elected to the U.S. House (1867–71). *BDUSC*.

3. Either the David Caldwell (c1810–fl1870), a well-to-do tanner and farmer, or the David Caldwell (c1831–1881), an iron worker and furnace keeper who served in the 191st Pa. Vols. during the war. Johnson nominated Caldwell for collector on March 14, but the Senate rejected the nomination five days later. 1850 Census, Pa., Blair, Gaysport, 154; (1870), 216; (1860), Huntingdon, Franklin Twp., 242; *Commemorative Biographical Encyclopedia . . . of . . . the Juniata Valley, comprising the Counties of Huntingdon, Mifflin, Juniata, and Perry, Pennsylvania . . .* (2 vols., Chambersburg, Pa., 1897), 2: 731; *Senate Ex. Proceedings*, Vol. 15, pt. 2: 455, 486.

4. The reference here is to Alexander C. Mullin and David Caldwell.

5. After withholding Royer's nomination, the President submitted two other names in April before finally succeeding with the appointment of W. J. Rose as collector. Ser. 6B, Vol. 4: 88–90, Johnson Papers, LC; *Senate Ex. Proceedings*, Vol. 15, pt. 2: 746, 751.

From Jonathan Worth

Executive Dept. of NC
Raleigh, Mar. 29 1867

Dear Sir

You are probably apprised that immediately after the publication of the act of the 2nd March inst., Govr. Holden & some of his friends got up the project of electing members to a State Convention by action of the people in primary meetings. After the passage of the supplemental bill which frustrated this purpose, the call for a meeting of delegates here from the whole State, including black, as well as white, was continued. The persons active in getting it up claimed to be the par excellence Union men of the State. They met on the 27th & adjourned yesterday evening, the 28th.[1] There was a large number in attendance, from most of the Counties of the State, I think, about half black & half white. They adopted the name of the Republican party. They avowed their purpose of cordial cooperation with the Republican party of the North. All or nearly all the whites, were followers of Mr. Holden & advocated last Summer the ratification of the constitutional amendment, popularly called the Howard amendment.[2] In their debates & proceedings they evinced the purpose of excelling the Northern Radicals in Radicalism, though a very large majority of the whites & nearly all the leaders among them, are disfranchised for participation in the rebellion under the late action of Congress. The hope of attaining political ascendency in the State and the fear of confiscation were probably the chief incentives which controlled their action. They took measures for thorough organization in every County in the State, in order to carry out their designs at the elections.—and they expect, as I understand, liberal supplies of money from the North to aid them in carrying out their purposes.

The great body of the people of the State would like to vote for the best men among us who can take the teste oath, and who indulge no malevolence towards their fellow citizens who participated in the late rebellion. I mean real Union men and not latter day saints—but this great body of the people can adopt no systematic plan of co-operation—have no money—are paralyzed by their accumulated calamities. The issue, under these circumstances, must be regarded as doubtful.

The negroes, so far, are apparently more conservative, than the white men now claiming to be their special friends. In this organization, of course, there was no kind word for you; but while you are doubtless mortified by the desertion of many sunshine friends, it may be some consolation to you to know, that the vast majority of the intelligent & patriotic people of this State admire the firmness with which you adhere to constitutional duty, and regard the record you have made as one of the most enviable which our history will record.

I mentioned to you when in Washington,[3] a subject about which I may have troubled you too often—but so firm are my convictions that I trust you will pardon me for once more calling your attention to it. It relates to the omission to pardon Govr. Graham, Jo. Turner jr, B. S. Gaither & Govr. Vance.[4] Every one of these men were as utterly opposed to secession as you were, and exerted themselves to their utmost power, to avert disunion & war until war was begun, and they were compelled to elect between the evils which beset them. After they did elect to go with the South, each of them was elected to the Confederate Congress & cooperated in good faith with the South. This is the extent of their sin. Are they more in fault than Dortch, Venable, Arrington, Lander, McLean, Bridgers and Davis,[5] who were ardent secessionists & were also members of the Confederate Congress? I do not disapprove of these latter pardons. I think the granting of them does credit to you as a statesman. All of them are now loyal:—not more loyal than the four unpardoned gentlemen named. Your friends in North Carolina universally complain of the discrimination. I am sure you would but do an act of magnanimous statesmanship in pardoning these men & that you would thereby warm the hearts of your friends.

There are two other gentlemen, Govr. Clark,—and Owen Keenan[6] whom I should be glad to see pardoned. They are most estimable men & their case no way distinguishable from that of the other four, save that they were secessionists, and favored the measures which led to the rebellion.

As I have heretofore said to you I favor universal amnesty & therefore would not with-hold my recommendation of any body:—but if you deem it prudent to withhold your pardon from a few, will not the officers educated at West Point & who joined in the Rebellion, Genl. Clingman,[7] who was a Senator in Congress at the breaking out of the war, and Judge Biggs,[8] a district judge of the U.S. who resigned for a like position under the Confederate States, be a sufficient number of victims to reserve?

Govr. Vance, you will remember, was for a time, held a prisoner in the old Capitol prison at Washington. By your indulgence he was liberated on his parole not to leave the State. If you should decline to pardon him I hope you will relieve him from his parole.

Jonathan Worth   Govr. of NC

ALS, DNA-RG94, Amnesty Papers (M1003, Roll 43), N.C., Jonathan Worth.

1. For a brief discussion and analysis of the Raleigh convention that became the North Carolina Republican party, see William C. Harris, *William Woods Holden: Firebrand of North Carolina Politics* (Baton Rouge, 1987), 219–23; Raper, *Holden*, 93–94.

2. The Fourteenth Amendment.

3. Evidently the only trip to Washington made by Worth was the one in the summer of 1865.

4. William A. Graham, Josiah Turner, Jr., Burgess S. Gaither, and Zebulon B. Vance. Worth seems confused about the status of pardons for these four men; for example, Graham had been pardoned by Johnson in December 1865 and Turner in February 1866. He probably did not know that Vance had just been pardoned in early March. Gaither would have to wait until July 1867 before the President offered him an individual pardon. Gaither (1807–1892) served in the North Carolina legislature before the war and then in the Confederate Congress. Wakelyn, *BDC*; Dorris, *Pardon and Amnesty*, 218–19; *House Ex. Docs.*, 40 Cong., 1 Sess., No. 40, p. 16 (Ser. 1311); Amnesty Papers (M1003, Rolls 39, 43), N.C., Burgess S. Gaither, William A. Graham, Josiah Turner, Jr., and Zebulon B. Vance, RG94, NA.

5. William T. Dortch, Abraham W. Venable, Archibald H. Arrington, William Lander, James R. McLean, Robert R. Bridgers, and George Davis. McLean (1823–1870) was a lawyer and state legislator before the war and an active secessionist. He served in the Confederate Congress and then saw limited military duty. Wakelyn, *BDC*; *House Ex. Docs.*, 39 Cong., 2 Sess., No. 31, pp. 17–18 (Ser. 1289); ibid., 40 Cong., 1 Sess., No. 32, pp. 3, 23 (Ser. 1311).

6. Henry T. Clark and Oren R. Kenan. Clark (1808–1874), a lawyer and planter, served in the state legislature and subsequently as governor (1861–63). Kenan (1804–1887), also a lawyer and planter, was elected to the Confederate Congress. Afterwards, he resumed the practice of law. Both Clark and Kenan were eventually pardoned in June 1867. Amnesty Papers (M1003, Roll 40), N.C., O. R. Kenan, RG94, NA; Wakelyn, *BDC*; Dorris, *Pardon and Amnesty*, 217–19.

7. Thomas L. Clingman. He was pardoned by Johnson in June 1867. Amnesty Papers (M1003, Roll 38), N.C., Thomas L. Clingman, RG94, NA.

8. Asa Biggs. No individual pardon date for Biggs has been located.

From Francis P. Blair, Jr.

Washington City   March 3[0], '67[1]

I had no opportunity in the interview I had with you to-day[2] to express my thanks for your great kindness in giving me the nomination as Minister to Austria. I assure you Mr. President that I am not less grateful for your kindness than I should have been if I had recieved the confirmation of the Senate. I feel very little concern about the rejection of my nomination by the Senate and have no wish to express in regard to the disposition to be made of the mission hereafter.[3]

Frank P. Blair

ALS, DLC-JP.

1. Based on internal evidence, Blair misdated the letter, for he was not nominated until March 25 and was rejected on the 28th. We have suggested March 30 as the probable date, reasoning that Blair inadvertently omitted the second numeral in the date. The 30th fell on a Saturday, a more likely day for conducting business than Sunday the 31st. Ser. 6B, Vol. 2: 37, Johnson Papers, LC; *Senate Ex. Proceedings*, Vol. 15, pt. 2: 504, 572.

2. The subject of the meeting has not been determined.

3. Both his father and brother had advised him not to accept the position, believing his

services were needed in the reorganization of the Democratic party. Smith, *Blair Family*, 2: 331.

From John W. Crisfield

Princess Anne Md.   March 30th 1867

Dear Sir:

Two nominations of Collector of Customs, for the Eastern District of Maryland, and have been made and rejected by the Senate.[1] We are not informed that any further nomination has been made. It is very important that the place should be filled at once. The business of the office is totally suspended, and very great inconvenience is felt in consequence. Both the gentlemen you nominated were fair and proper men, and either of them ought to have been accepted by the Senate. That body appears to intend to block the wheels of government, if its own prejudices or caprices, are not gratified; and situated as things are, it must be yielded to, or the functions of governent must be suspended in a great degree.

I there fore venture to press the nomination of Hance Lawson,[2] whom I have here to fore recommended conditionally, in letters to the Secretary of the Treasury and Mr. McCullough,[3] member of the House from this District. Whether his name has been brought to your notice or not, I do not know.

Mr. Lawson was a Union man from the start. He served two or three years in the Army during the war, and has always sustained the government. He is said to be a Republican; it may be so, but he uniformly sustains your policy in regard to the Southern States. He has friends among the republicans, and would be confirmed, if nominated. He is a good business man, and excellent private character. He would make a faithful and good officer. I hope you will nominate him. His appointment would be generally acceptable.

If however, from any cause, you think fit to pass him by, then I suggest the name of Isaac Smith Lankford,[4] who is a very deserving man, and would make a good officers. Though not the first choice of any party, he would not be offensive to any class; and probably would command the good will of both sides, more generally, than any one who could be named.

Pardon the liberty I take in making these suggestions. They are designed to provide for the public service, which is now suffering, and to relieve you from embarrassment. And let me add, no one of the people of this great country more than I more sincerely approves of the general policy of your administration for the restoration of National tranquility, or more deeply sympathises with you in the trials and difficulties which environ you. May a gracious Providence give you strength to maintain your position, and lead your Country to a haven of safety and repose.

J. W. Crisfield

ALS, DNA-RG56, Appts., Customs Service, Collector, Crisfield [Eastern Dist., Md.], Hance Lawson.

1. Wealthy farmers Nathaniel P. Dixon (b. *c*1821), nominated March 14 and rejected a week later, and Benjamin Lankford (b. *c*1798), nominated March 25 and rejected three days later. Ser. 6B, Vol. 4: 107, Johnson Papers, LC; 1870 Census, Md., Somerset, Brinkley's Dist., 296; (1870), Lawsons Dist., 400.

2. Lawson (*c*1825–1889), a farmer, served as a second lieutenant in the 1st Eastern Shore Rgt., Md. Inf. He was nominated by Johnson for collector on April 19 and confirmed and commissioned by the Senate the same day. He served until at least mid-1870. Ibid., 411; *Off. Army Reg.: Vols.*, 3: 1068; Ser. 6B, Vol. 4: 108, Johnson Papers, LC; Pension Files, Emeline Lawson, RG15, NA.

3. Hiram McCullough (1813–1885), a lawyer, served in both the state senate (1845–51) and house (1880–81), the U.S. House (1865–69), and was for many years counsel for the Philadelphia, Wilmington, and Baltimore Railroad. *BDUSC.*

4. Lankford (b. *c*1804), a native of Maryland, was a carpenter, farmer, and father of at least five children. 1850 Census, Md., Somerset, Brinkley's Dist., 1st Div., 365; (1870), 283.

From John Williams, Jr.

Knoxville, March 31st 1867

Dear Sir:—

The canvass in Tennessee this Summer, is to be the most bitter, & fierce conflict that has ever taken place in the State.[1] Your administration is to be assailed in the most violet & unprecedented manner. Your friends are determined as far as I am advised to meet this negro party on half way ground, & give them at least as good as they send.

The Conservative party of Tennessee, have too long been *spit upon* by our *bogus Governor*, and his immediate friends. We must make a bold & vigorous fight—a fight to win at any cost. Now, my object is to ask your permission to make public at the proper time, a fact which you stated to me last winter, that you had out of the goodness of your heart, contributed to Gov. Brownlow, when he first met you in Nashville, in 62, the sum of fifteen hundred dollars.[2] I am anxious to make known this fact that his base ingratitude may be seen & known. I do not think you are under the slightest obligation to keep concealed any thing you may know in regard to him.

I do not know that you ever see his paper. If you do, you know he charges you with every thing, except being an honest man, & gentleman. Your friends in Tennessee, have a different opinion of you, & think you the reverse of what he charges; & therefore, desire with your consent, to tell this among other things, to show his want of good faith towards you.

I think by proper management, & a good candidate, we will be able to beat Mr. Brownlow.[3]

An unprejudiced mind could come to no other conclusion, than that your last veto,[4] left the Rads without a single square inch of ground to stand upon. I trust you will go on with your good work. The people in whom you have always trusted, will in the end bring you out triumphant, and consign to eternal degradation your revilers.

John Williams.

ALS, DLC-JP.

1. Studies of the 1867 gubernatorial campaign in Tennessee seem to bear out the prediction made by Williams here. See, for example, Alexander, *Reconstruction*, Chapter 10; Patton, *Unionism and Reconstruction*, 175–79 passim.

2. Johnson's alleged gift to Brownlow evidently did not become a public issue during the 1867 campaign.

3. Thanks to black voters, Brownlow won handily in August. See Richard O. Curry, ed., *Radicalism, Racism, and Party Realignment: The Border States during Reconstruction* (Baltimore, 1969), 67.

4. A reference to Johnson's veto of the Second Military Reconstruction Act on March 23.

April 1867

From Hiram B. Swarr and John M. Cooper [1]

Lancaster, Pennsylvania,   April 1, 1867.

Sir:

In explanation of the telegram which we took the liberty of sending you on Saturday evening,[2] begging you not to nominate Dr. Henry Carpenter for Collector[3] and John B. Warfel for Assessor[4] of this (the 9th) district of Pennsylvania, we beg leave respectfully to state that it was reported and to some extent believed here that a very strong effort was being made (with the approbation of Hon. Thaddeus Stevens) to procure the nomination of the gentlemen named. We are anxious to prevent these nominations, should an effort be made to procure them, for the reason that, if made and confirmed, the Revenue Offices would be under the complete control of Mr. Stevens. We have reason to believe that Mr. Stevens' great anxiety to have these offices filled by reliable friends of his does not grow wholly out of his political feelings, but is in part owing to interests he is understood to have in revenue cases that remain to be decided. He is specially desirous of having an Assessor whom he can mould at will, and for this reason he is believed to have assented to the appointment of Dr. Carpenter for Collector, on condition that the Assessorship be given to Mr. Warfel, who now holds a Clerkship in some one of the Departments at Washington, which Mr. Stevens procured for him.

In our telegram we took the liberty of referring to Hon. J. S. Black, with whom we have the honor to be acquainted, and we now respectfully repeat that reference.

H. B. Swarr.
J. M. Cooper.

ALS(Cooper), DNA-RG56, Appts., Internal Revenue Service, Assessor, Pa., 9th Dist., John B. Warfel.

1. Swarr (1821–*fl*1874), a prominent lawyer, had been active for a number of years as chairman of the county Democratic party committee. Originally appointed in 1856 as postmaster of Lancaster, he held that job for several years. Swarr ran unsuccessfully for Congress in 1868. Cooper (*c*1823–*fl*1887), formerly a pardon clerk in the U.S. attorney general's office in Washington, subsequently served in the 1880s as clerk in the state's internal affairs department. *The Biographical Encyclopaedia of Pennsylvania of the Nineteenth Century* (Philadelphia, 1874), 479–80; 1860 Census, D.C., Washington, 2nd Ward, 124; J. M. Cooper to Edward Bates, Oct. 19, 1861, Lincoln Papers, LC; Harrisburg directories (1883–87).

2. See Swarr and Cooper to Johnson, Mar. 30, 1867, Johnson Papers, LC.

3. Carpenter (1819–*fl*1883), a native of Lancaster, began the practice of medicine in the 1840s. He was very active in public service and in a variety of business ventures. Carpenter was never nominated by Johnson for the collector's post in 1867. Ellis and Evans, *Lancaster County*, 250.

4. Warfel (1830–fl1903), originally a schoolteacher and farmer, held a variety of public offices from the late 1850s into the 1890s. He began practicing law after studying at Columbia College in Washington, from which he graduated in 1867. After several attempts to appoint other persons to the assessor's post, Johnson finally turned to Warfel in April and was successful. Afterwards, Warfel was longtime president of the Lancaster school board and served several terms in the state senate. *Biographical Annals of Lancaster County*, 136–37; Ser. 6B, Vol. 4: 84, 87–90, Johnson Papers, LC.

From Edward A. Pollard[1]

Private.

Washington City, Willard's Hotel. April 2, 1867.

Sir,

Not having yet obtained an opportunity for an interview with you, I beg, in writing, your attention for a brief space.

My design is to establish, some time in the coming autumn, in the City of Washington, a daily newspaper, and organ of public opinion of the first class. In most of the countries of Europe the most powerful presses are planted at the capital of the nation; for various but insignificant reasons it has not been so at Washington; and I propose now to make an exception to the former weak journalism of the capital, in a paper that, by its enterprize, and choice assemblies of intellect, North and South, shall compare with what is best known of the daily press in America. The enterprize is an ambitious one; it will be necessary to secure the best writers of the country, and to maintain a high literary standard; but I do not despair, when I estimate the value of my past experience, and am already assured of a corps of able and enthusiastic co-labourers.

The name of the paper will be "THE RECALL." I mention it as indicating its principles—the main political idea and inspiration of the paper being to recall the country to the Constitutional standards of government, to revive our traditions, and to re-assert the past, in opposition to the present tendency of the Radical party to manufacture out of the war a new civil polity, and to run after experiments in the political administration. It is a broad idea, but one replete with sources of popular inspiration, and having a range of application to all the leading questions of the times.

Maintaining this idea, the paper will coincide with the support of your Administration, and will rally to it whatever sentiment in the country attaches to our best established and cherished political traditions, in opposition to the errant school of the Radicals and their disposition for experiments. The issue and challenge I do not think could be better made than by such appeals to the popular affection for the past, enforced against the idea of a Constitutional revolution following upon the war. The support the paper would give you on this line of policy you may be sure would be steady and courageous.

Permit me to say, Sir, with profound respect and sincere regard, that as the head of a party, I do not think you yet have the weapon you most need. This weapon should be a strong, vigorous, combative paper at the capital, that should meet on the spot, and match with brave and ready intellect the assaults of your enemies. I believe such service would be acceptable to you, undertaken in the general cause of truth, and in the especial interest and inspiration of the Constitution you uphold; and the paper that would profess it should fear no consequences.

My name perhaps, may be unfavourably known to you as a Richmond editor *during the war*. But the past cannot embarrass me; the controversy in which I would engage is new and patriotic, and, re-commencing editorial service, I should tear away every scale of former sectional prejudice, and know in this matter only the Constitution and its defenders. I have secured the aid of writers in the North as well as in South; it is not necessary or desired that my own name should unpleasantly appear as head of the enterprise; my only ambition is to establish a journal of new and enlarged power at Washington, no matter who may attach their names to it, and assume its auspices.

I have written this much, Sir, and besought your attention so far, that you may understand my design, hoping that you will honour me with your approval of it.[2] I am anxious to get an expression of your approval, as an encouragement of the design; it, indeed, will go far to decide its execution, and determine me in my purpose; and I trust you will not find it inconsistent with public and official consideration to express such interest as you may conceive in an enterprise that really concerns the liberties of the country, and aims at the highest objects of the public good.

Edwd. A. Pollard.

ALS, DLC-JP.

1. Pollard (1831–1872), the author of numerous books, was editor of the *Richmond Examiner* from 1861 to 1867. He was captured in 1864 while blockade running and was imprisoned at several different locations before being exchanged in January 1865. Pollard founded two short-lived papers in Virginia after leaving the Richmond editorship; no Washington paper was set up. *DAB*.

2. On April 3 Pollard notified Johnson that he had tried unsuccessfully for two days to visit with the President at the White House. Afterwards, he had to return to Richmond, whence he entreated Johnson to grant approval to Pollard's publication plans. Pollard to Johnson, Apr. 3, 1867, Johnson Papers, LC.

From Joseph R. Flanigen

Philadelphia, April 3d 1867

My dear Mr President

I regret very much that after waiting five hours yesterday I was unable to see you. My purpose was two fold; first to confer with reference to the filling of vacant positions here, and second to consult with regard to political movements. I have sought several times within the last two or three months to see you in regard to the latter, but as I have been so unfortunate as to fail on each occasion, I adopt the only means of communication left to me.[1]

The public believes that I have earned the right to be heard on these subjects, but if you think diferently, and will so indicate to me, that I may not waste time in the effort to confer with you, I shall of course be content, but—I am not satisfied that the patronage and political power of your administration should be placed in the hands of a party who care nothing for you, and with which it is imposible for your true friends to affiliate, and which, when those who control it have gained their ends, will fling you from them and it, as they did Mr Tyler after he had submitted himself to their dictation.[2] Appearances would seem to indicate, and I am very sorry that most of your friends with whom I meet, feel compelled to believe, that the "Democrats" are controlling to a very large extent the distribution of your patronage. It is of course your right to determine on such a policy, and however much I in common with your freinds who do not belong to that party may regret such a determination, we shall of course, so soon as satisfied of the fact, acquiesce in it, so far as to induce us to refrain from further attempt to interfere in the premises. But I submit to you that it is a fearfull sacrifice.

Your *National Union* freinds—if I may use a simile,—left good and comfortable homes in the ranks of the Republican party, to join you in the maintainance of the Constitution and the support of an unimpaired Union. This step on their part has caused them to be tabooed, ostracised, and most ruthlessly persecuted, but they do not tire of the assertion of the principles which led them into this position. But they complain.

They complain that they are apparantly disregarded, that they seem to lack your sympathy or even recognition, and that when they are enabled to reach the scourse of Executive power—it is too frequently by haveing been first obliged to conciliate, so called, democratic influence. I desired to say these things to you personally, in the frankness of that freindship which I have allways felt for you, and you may readily immagine, how greatly preferable it would have been to communicate these thoughts oraly, rather than by such a medium as this.

You will say perhaps that I am offended. I am not, but to use an expresive term, I feel hurt. I have no personal greivance to convey to you, but as a journalist, and as the original organizer of the Conservative Opposition to radicalism in this City, there are weighty obligations resting upon me, and you know I think, that I am not a person to ignore such things. In the struggle which I have made for the promotion of the views of your administration, for its defense, and its support, I have simply beggared myself, after which if would seem I am obliged to present to myself the significant interogatory "Cui Bona."

You will remember that in our early conversations, in relation to the diferences existing between yourself and Congress, I was carefull to say to you, and to have you say, that the struggle should be made in the Union party and with such an understanding, and the repetation of it as coming from yourself, I drew together the people who formed the organizations that were established in this City and State for the purpose of sustaining your administration *against Congress.*

These people are now asking for explanations, and as delicately as may be, inquireing if I was not mistaken. I am sure that I was not, and you will therefore doubtless appreciate my solicitude on the subject.

Now my dear Mr President I object to the distribution of the patronage of your administration by democrats Wether they be senators or members of the House, and our freinds here protest with great earnestness against the combinations, through the operation of which you yeild to the parceling out of the positions at your disposal to Democrats and Radicals share and share alike. We entered this contest upon principle, and shall continue it from the same motive but the direction of the patronage of an Administration is to some extent the index to its principles, and must therefore necessarily claim the attention of parties in the contest.

Do not think my dear Sir that I am lecturing you. Those who have sought to be your freinds look to me very much for advice, for counsell, and at times for direction, and I confess to you that I am able to meet them on the many questions they present—with but poor apologys.

In conclusion I beg to repeat the assureance of my warm personal regards and to request, that you will either personaly or through your Secretary indicate wether an interview is desireable with the purpose to confer with reference to the views herein expressed.

J R. Flanigen

P.S. This letter was forwarded to the care of Governor Johnston[3] as per its date, but that gentleman having left Washington previous to its receipt it was returned to me. I now forward it through our fnd Col Moore.[4]

J R F

ALS, DLC-JP.
    1. See Flanigen to Johnson, Feb. 18, 1867.
    2. Very similar opinions were expressed by Flanigen in a November letter. See Flanigen to Johnson, Nov. 15, 1866, *Johnson Papers*, 11: 460–61.
    3. William F. Johnston.
    4. William G. Moore.

From Daniel G. Burr[1]

Paris Edgar Co Ills   April 4th 1867.

Dear Sir,

    I deem it my duty as a mason to inform you that certain persons of this place are imposing upon you for Office, to wit: A. K. Campbell, Henry

Byles, Jas Smith Dr Stephen J Young, N Link[2] & others. They are the *radical* of the *Radicalest*. These very men, were among the crowd that sought to insult you, when you passed through this place last Sept, the day you left St Louis.[3] You will recollect the place, by Mrs L. H. Ficklin,[4] who steped on the cars to see Mrs Patterson,[5] and you brought, her on to Paris and let her off. It is the wish of your friends, that none of the above persons should be appointed, if Wm. S. Cook[6] cannot continue Your friends will Sugest, a man that is your friend. I will have Mrs Ficklin write to you or Mrs Patterson as to who I am. I saw you a number of times just after the Philadelphia Convention. We will sugest one that the Senate we think will confirm. I must say that some men who claim to be your friends are recomending some of these men, when they know they are bitter against you. Should like to heare from you if convenient.

D. G. Burr, Assistant
Assessor 10 Div 7th Dist Ills

ALS, DNA-RG56, Appts., Internal Revenue Service, Assessor, Ill., 10th Dist., D. G. Burr.

1. Burr (c1821–fl1870), a farmer, had served as postmaster at Paris from 1855 to 1861. Johnson had nominated him for the same position in March 1867 but the Senate rejected him in April. *U.S. Off. Reg.* (1855–61); Ser. 6B, Vol. 4: 303–4, Johnson Papers, LC; 1860 Census, Ill., Edgar, Paris, 396; (1870), 175.

2. Andrew K. Campbell (b. c1828) was a merchant tailor in 1860; Byles [Beyls] (c1844–fl1870), a store clerk in 1870; Smith (c1836–fl1870), a bank clerk in 1870; Young (1829–fl1914) served as a surgeon with the Illinois volunteer infantry during the war and practiced medicine in both Paris, Illinois, and Terre Haute, Indiana, during his career; Nathaniah Link (c1820–fl1870) was with a furniture store in 1860 and a lumber dealer in 1870. 1860 Census, Ill., Edgar, Paris, 383, 385, 393; (1870), 163, 166, 175, 178; Atkinson, *Physicians and Surgeons*, 596–97; C. C. Oakley, *Greater Terre Haute and Vigo County* (2 vols., Chicago, 1908), 2: 830–37; *American Medical Directory* (1914), 507.

3. On September 10, 1866.

4. Not identified.

5. Martha Patterson, Johnson's daughter.

6. Cook (c1820–fl1870), a tanner, was appointed by Johnson postmaster at Paris on October 12, 1866. He served officially from November 25, 1866, to March 31, 1867; he was rejected in early March. Ser. 6B, Vol. 3: 593; Vol. 4: 302, Johnson Papers, LC; *U.S. Off. Reg.* (1867); 1870 Census, Ill., Edgar, Paris, 190.

From John M. Glover

Washington City   Room No. 248, F. St.
April 4th 1867

Mr President!

The Senate, yesterday rejected the *fifth man* for Collector[1] of 3d. Intl. Rev. Dist Mo.—Four of whom are *union Soldiers*,—two of whom are *"Radicals."*[2]

I now, according to the Suggestion of Genl. Blair,[3] in our interview on yesterday, & approved by you, respectfully & urgently request that my name be sent back to the Senate, together with the *announcement*, that it is the *last* that will be sent them in connection with said office. This done, there is no doubt *I shall be Confirmed*. If per chance the Senate does not confirm me, I ask, to be permitted to give other names to the end.[4]

J M Glover

ALS, DNA-RG56, Appts., Internal Revenue Service, Collector, Mo., 3rd Dist., J. M. Glover.

1. Augustus Shoppe (b. *c*1839), a native of Germany, was a clerk in 1860. He had been nominated April 2. Ser. 6B, Vol. 4: 317, Johnson Papers, LC; 1860 Census, Mo., Lewis, Lagrange, 285. For previous discussions of this collectorship, see Glover to Johnson, Mar. 5, 1867, and Smith S. Allen to Johnson, Mar. 14, 1867.

2. The other four rejected candidates were Glover himself (twice), John Williams, William P. Moore, and David Oyster. Glover had served in the Union army and was not a radical, but the experiences and opinions of the others have not been determined. Ser. 6B, Vol. 4: 315–17, Johnson Papers, LC; *BDUSC*.

3. Francis P. Blair, Jr. Blair and Missouri representative T. E. Noell affixed to Glover's letter their approval of Glover's nomination.

4. Johnson took Glover's advice and renominated him on April 5, but to no avail as the Senate rejected him on the same day. After William P. Moore was once again nominated and rejected, Johnson nominated John M. Cashman, who was approved by Glover and his allies. At last, the Senate confirmed his nomination on April 19, apparently as part of a deal also involving the position of pension agent. Ser. 6B, Vol. 4: 318, Johnson Papers, LC; T. E. Noell, J. M. Glover, and Allen P. Richardson to Johnson, Apr. 18, 1867; J. M. Glover to William Moore, Apr. 19, 1867, Johnson Papers, LC.

From Edmund Cooper

Shelbyville Tenn.   April 5 1867.

My Dear Mr President.

I enclose to your address by the mail of today—copy of the speech which I delivered at this place on Monday last[1]—and in which, I endeavoured to discuss evenly and without passion the great years before the country, as well, as to do justice to your character and course.

The audience was very large the largest we have had in the village since the termination of the war—and they gave close attention during its delivery.

I hope that it may do some good in rescuing the state from the control of the Extreme Radicals, but I fear the result.

The conferring of political suffrage upon the negroes—gives to them an immense power—and if the colored voters as a body cast their votes for Brownlow, the result is evident.[2]

It is true that the glorious triumph in Connecticutt,[3] has given new courage to the friends of the Administration, and many of us feel that the tide has turned, and that soon the true patriot will have reason to rejoice at the indications of a return to reason on the part of the people.

The people must retrace their steps. They must forgive one another. They must bury their animosities, and reunite with heart and mind in rebuilding the shattered temples of our Nationality.

I announce myself as a candidate for re-election to Congress. I believe that I can carry the district—and therefore propose making the race.[4] However, since the delivering of my speech, which I send you—the "politicians" are anxious for me to make the race for Governor. This I have as yet refused to consent to do. What are your wishes? Which would you prefer my doing?[5] My only object being the safety of the country, and the success of your administration.

Edmund Cooper

ALS, DLC-JP.

1. Although not found enclosed, Cooper's speech, presented on Monday, April 1, was conveniently reprinted in the *Nashville Union and Dispatch*, Apr. 4, 1867. Two days earlier the same Nashville paper lauded Cooper's speech as "one of the most powerful and effective speeches of his life." The paper subsequently criticized its rival, the *Press and Times*, for its attack upon Cooper as a man who upholds submission to law. See *Nashville Union and Dispatch*, Apr. 2, 6, 1867.

2. Most post-election analyses have attributed Brownlow's 1867 victory to the newly-franchised black voters. See Alexander, *Reconstruction*, 159–60; Patton, *Unionism and Reconstruction*, 139–40.

3. The spring elections in Connecticut yielded a Democratic victory for governor (James E. English) and in three of four U.S. congressional seats. As one of the Nashville papers expressed it: "This is the first check the Radical power has had in New England for several years." *Guide to U.S. Elections*, 371, 618; *Nashville Union and Dispatch*, Apr. 3, 1867.

4. Cooper in fact did run for the Fourth District seat, but he was overwhelmingly defeated in the August elections. *Guide to U.S. Elections*, 618. One historian attributes Cooper's defeat to the black vote which went to the Republican opponent. See Alexander, *Reconstruction*, 157–58.

5. No evidence of Johnson's advice to Cooper has been located.

From Abner A. Steele

Lewisburg, April 5th 1867

Dear Sir,

Allow me to return you my grateful thanks for the friendship & confidence you have shown for me in nominating me for assessor of this District.[1] I had succeeded in getting the district organized, and we were getting along successfully in assessing & collecting taxes, when the Senate through partisan motives rejected my nomination to gratify your enemies in Tennessee. When I think of the friendship & favors you extended to Fowler, Stokes, Maynard, Mercer & Brownlow[2] whilst Military Governor, and now see how ungrateful & malignant they are to you on account of your steady adherence to the union & constitution and your efforts to prevent such men from destroying both, I am astonished and feel indignant. These men & their allies have made here in Tennessee a despotism, that grows more lawless and reckless every day. They have the ballot sword & purse of the State in their hands & for their friends alone. Three fourths of the people of Tennessee are denied their constitutional rights by this oligharchy & I am afraid there is no help for it soon.

I have not yet heard who will be my successor, although I presume that by this time he is appointed. If no appointment is made of those gentlemen whose names were left with you by Mr. Cooper[3] and the Senate adjourns without confirming, then permit me to recommend Mr. John M. Benton[4] of this county. He is consistently loyal, is a promising worthy young man & will make a fine assessor. He is a relation of the Hon Thomas H. Benton.

Mr. Cooper will be re-elected to Congress; & he is about the only friend of ours, that I have any hopes now, of sending to the house of Representatives from Tennessee, under the franchise law & old Brownlow's militia.

Abner A. Steele

ALS, DNA-RG56, Appts., Internal Revenue Service, Assessor, Tenn., 4th Dist., John M. Benton.

1. For an earlier reference to Steele's appointment and rejection, see Steele to Johnson, July 19, 1866, *Johnson Papers*, 10: 706–7.

2. Joseph S. Fowler, William B. Stokes, Horace Maynard, Samuel C. Mercer, and William G. Brownlow.

3. Edmund Cooper. According to a subsequent Steele letter, Cooper had recommended James L. Reed, the assistant assessor, for possible appointment to the assessor's post. Steele to Johnson, Apr. 10, 1867, Appts., Internal Revenue Service, Assessor, Tenn., 4th Dist., James L. Reed, RG56, NA.

4. Benton (b. *c*1847), a schoolteacher in Marshall County, Tennessee, was the son of F. W. and Mary Benton of Marshall County. By April the President had made several attempts to fill the Fourth District assessorship but none successfully. William Little, Joseph H. Thompson, and William Tune had all been nominated at one time or another between late February and early April 1867. 1860 Census, Tenn., Marshall, 13th Dist., 11; (1870), 2; Ser. 6B, Vol. 4: 228, Johnson Papers, LC.

From William E. Robinson

Washington, April 6th 1867

Sir:

In my District there are vacant the offices of Collector & Assessor of Internal Revenue, and Postmaster of Brooklyn. The P.O. Delivery runs over Mr. Barnes'[1] District & my own. The Collector and Assessor are exclusively in my District. From present appearances some concessions must be made to the Senate. I am contented in any such concession, to have the naming of a proper man for Assessor, and do hereby name as such Thomas Welwood Esq.,[2] an old and well known resident of the District, for whom letters are on file in the Secretary's office from the Mayor, Judges, Corporation Counsel, &c of the city of Brooklyn.[3]

W. E. Robinson   M.C. 3rd Dist. N.Y.

ALS, DNA-RG56, Appts., Internal Revenue Service, Assessor, N.Y., 3rd Dist., Thos. Welwood.

1. Demas Barnes (1827–1888) was a New York businessman before traveling in the West. He served one term in the U.S. House (1867–69) and afterwards edited the *Brooklyn Argus* for a short time. *BDUSC*.

2. Welwood (*c*1818–*fl*1892) was long involved in real estate in Brooklyn. He was indeed nominated by the President for the assessorship of the Third District, first on April 10 and then again on April 15. The Senate approved the nomination five days later. 1870 Census, N.Y., Kings, Brooklyn, 7th Ward, 370; Brooklyn directories (1867–92); Ser. 6B, Vol. 4: 55, Johnson Papers, LC; *U.S. Off. Reg.* (1867).

3. Robinson sent two anxious messages to the President subsequent to his April 6 letter. Four days later, for example, the congressman begged Johnson not to nominate anyone, if Welwood were rejected, without consulting with him (Robinson). On the 14th Robinson wondered if someone was trying to interfere in his district. Robinson to Johnson, April 10, 1867, Johnson Papers, LC; Robinson to Johnson, Apr. 14, 1867, Appts., Internal Revenue Service, Assessor, N.Y., 3rd Dist., Thomas Welwood. For another view on appointments in the Third District, see Demas Barnes to Johnson, Apr. 11, 1867.

From Thomas Cottman

Grand Junction Tenn—April 7th 1867

Mr. President

As there no longer exists an occasion for your rendering me a service & I think the Government also; I can speak freely in relation to my being entitled to some consideration. In 1860, John Slidell Wm. Yancey & co deliberately formed a plan for the dismemberment of the united states. I with equal deliberation determined to sustain the Government. Their first overt act was at Charleston by seceding from the Convention leaving me the only Vice President from the Cotton States.[1] This divided the Democracy of Louisiana between Slidell & myself.[2] I being the only Democrat he could not defeat. We returned home from Charleston: he revived the Convention, defunct from having adjourned sine die after selecting delegates to the National Convention.[3] They approved the Secession. I called a new Convention freshly elected by the people to select delegates to the adjourned Convention at Baltimore[4]—considering the secession of the other delegates as a resignation of the trust imposed in them by the Democracy of the State. The Convention at Baltimore so regarded it admitting the new delegates Benn. F. Butler & Caleb Cushing his alter ego seceding with the Representatives of the Cotton States.[5] After these gentlemen had attained their object—the election of Lincoln—the work of segregating the states commenced. In the Cotton States no ticket was polled for the Union outside of Louisiana & none polled there except what was paid for out of my pocket, & upon which I was elected to the Secession Convention & opposed every motion or act tending to the destruction of the Government of the United States.[6] When the War broke out consequent upon the acts of these gentlemen, I became exceedingly obnoxious to the Confederates & when Genl. Butler came to New Orleans in command, I was equally obnoxious to him. So I have been obliged to leave my home in the Confederacy & recieve the cold shoulder from the other side from personal pique. My friends being Confederates set fire to & burnt up my dwelling & appurtinances, leaving my family during my absence, houseless & without apparel & without the means of living. I care not about entering into further details of what followed, in my disagreements with Genls Butler & Banks. I called upon you at Hooper's house F street Washington[7] in company with B Hill[8] of the firm of Browning, Ewing & Hill,[9] in the month of May, when there existed a very strong prejudice against you, to overcome which I called again in a few days with Reverdy Johnson. After which I went to Baltimore, called up John Garret Johns Hopkins, Wm. McKins,[10] &c & soliced their immediate action, by calling as a committee & tendering their support & confidence. I did the same thing in Philadelphia New York, Cincinnati, Chicago Columbus & Milwaukee—making it my business to elicit favorable expression of sentiment to you as head of the Government. Mr. Seward well knows what my course was during the War. I mention these things to you, having nothing better to do in a lonely place & of a sabbath even—for which you will excuse me. The probability is that I shall never see you again, but may the blessings of the Almighty, be bountifully bestowed upon you is the prayer of your obt. sevt.

Thos. Cottman

ALS, DLC-JP.
    1. Cottman was not listed among the delegates elected to that convention by the Democrats at Baton Rouge. Mary Lilla McLure, "The Election of 1860 in Louisiana," *LHQ*, 9 (1926): 647.
    2. Slidell's major opponent in Louisiana was Pierre Soulé, and Cottman was apparently one of Soulé's backers. Ibid., 658 and passim.
    3. This convention met at Baton Rouge on June 4, 1860, but some delegates did not attend because, due to various technicalities, they did not believe that the convention could be reassembled legally. Ibid., 654–55.
    4. The Democratic State-Right Central Club of New Orleans called for new delegates to be elected to a meeting to be held at Donaldsonville on June 8 where they would elect delegates to the convention at Baltimore. When the Louisiana delegates withdrew from the Baltimore convention, remaining delegates voted to have the Donaldsonville electors admitted in their place; Cottman was a delegate from the Second District. Ibid., 656–59; *New Orleans Times Picayune*, June 8, 26, 1860.
    5. Cushing had been the chairman of the Democratic convention but resigned and became chairman of the seceders at Baltimore. McLure, "The Election of 1860 in Louisiana," 651, 659–60.
    6. Cottman was among the seventeen Louisianans who futilely opposed secession at their state convention. Ibid., 697.
    7. Johnson stayed at the home of Congressman Samuel Hooper, which was actually located at 15th and H streets, while waiting for Mary Lincoln to vacate the White House in 1865. Trefousse, *Johnson*, 208.
    8. Britton A. Hill (1816–1888) moved to St. Louis in 1841 and practiced law there until he retired in the early 1880s. J. Thomas Scharf, *History of St. Louis City and County* (2 vols., Philadelphia, 1883), 2: 1502–3; William Hyde and Howard L. Conrad, eds., *Encyclopedia of the History of St. Louis* (4 vols., New York, 1899), 2: 1024.
    9. Orville H. Browning, Thomas Ewing, Sr., and Hill had a legal partnership in Washington (1863–65). Ibid.; Scharf, *St. Louis City and County*, 2: 1503.
    10. Hopkins (1795–1873), a Baltimore commission merchant, banker, and railroad stockholder, endowed the university and hospital which bear his name. William McKim

(1808–1879) was a Baltimore businessman and banker. *DAB*; J. Thomas Scharf, *History of Baltimore City and County* (Philadelphia, 1881), 476–77.

From Samuel J. Randall

Washington D C
April 7, 1867   Sunday.

Mr. President

On tomorrow you will be asked to nominate to the Senate—the names of two gentlemen—one for naval officer and the other for Surveyor at Philadelphia.[1] My wish is that you select for these positions two reliable friends, and not enemies.

You will be urged to send in the names of two "Cameron men" thus to push through the Senate in a "bargain and sale"—Mr Goodwin[2] as Collector of the Port of Philadelphia. I write to guard you against such transaction. The people in our City utterly scorn such a course of action.

The two offices are now under the control of your friends—altho' occupied by men not in strict inside political accord with me they are however much to be preferred to any radical in the land. Let matters run as now—and you will at least have men at these two posts—who by conviction approve your policy.

Should you by law be compelled to name—I would recommend Peter Fritz[3]—& Dr. McClintock[4] respectively—for the places. One a soldier with honorable record and the other a prominent connection with the Methodist Church. Let the Senate slay such.

Sam J. Randall

ALS, DLC-JP.

1. Later in April Johnson nominated William Harbeson as surveyor of customs at Philadelphia and he was approved by the Senate. See Randall to Johnson, Mar. 18, 1867.

2. Probably William Goodwin (1810–*fl*1876), a retired hatter-turned-gentleman, whose personal worth was estimated at $40,000. He had already been nominated by Johnson in March for the collector's post. Three days after Randall's letter, the Senate rejected Goodwin's nomination. Ser. 6B, Vol. 4: 87, Johnson Papers, LC; 1870 Census, Pa., Philadelphia, Philadelphia, Germantown, 73rd Dist., 233; Philadelphia directories (1868–78).

3. Randall had recommended Fritz in his March letter. See Randall to Johnson, Mar. 18, 1867.

4. James McClintock (1809–*fl*1878), a Philadelphia physician, was nominated for the surveyor's post on April 10 but rejected the following day by the Senate. *NUC*, 349: 217; Philadelphia directories (1867–78); Ser. 6B, Vol. 4: 88, Johnson Papers, LC.

From David W. Lothrop

West Medford, Mass.   Apr. 8, 1867

"Judge me not ungentle,
Of manners rude, and insolent of speech,

If when the public safety is in question,
My zeal flows warm and eager from my tongue."
Rowe's Jane Shore.[1]
"Greatly unfortunate, he fights the cause
Of honor, virtue, liberty and Rome:
His sword ne'er fell but on the guilty head:
Oppression, tyranny, and *power usurped*,
Draw all the vengeance of his arms upon them."
Addison's Cato.[2]

Honored Sir,—

Allow a friend to apply the above lines to you. Your endeavors to check a party in Congress whose will is not only law but the *Constitution* also, deserves the hearty praise of every wellwisher of his country. But a *progressive party fanaticism* rules the hour; yet as it is rapidly working its own cure, I firmly believe that before many years—perhaps months— your name will be as exalted above the *popular* patriots as it is now debased in their estimation. I do not so much envy you as President, as for the noble stand you have taken and adhered to, for the welfare of the *whole* country. The Radicals at the north wish to rule the South *now*, and to exert an indirect influence over it *forever*! Hereafter they will invidiously seek to rule by *negro proxy*. Already we see Northern adventurers in the field, patronizing their noble brothers, and

"Wooing poor craftsmen with the craft of smiles."[3]

Well, Enough has been said; the country has talked out; reason has become impotent. Let the rank experiment be tried and the responsibility put in its proper place. No history and not one attribute of common sense supports the political amalgamation of the two races; but it finds succor only in that patriotism most frequently known as the *Core of power* instead of country; or the necessity of a new lease of the *negro hobby*. And if it is true that the late masters of this new political entity show a disposition to ride also, for their own security, both parties may find that it has

"Horsed them on its back to show 'em
Only a jadish trick and throw 'em."[4]

For it is presumed that the negro loves his own race sufficiently well to honor it with his vote; and when he does so the struggle of the races will have commenced, if not already. In this contest the blacks will be either driven abroad, scattered to the North and West, or exterminated. At any rate they will have little or no permanent power among the whites. In this I think all parties and religious sects are united *at heart*, whatever the present manifestation may be. They will not associate with the colored race, nor allow them to take the power out of their hands in any section of the country.

Mr. Sumner, the head and front of the Radicals,

—"at once the bellows
And tinder-box of all his fellows,"[5]

knows this very well; but he only smiles and says they must be made equal before the laws, and God will take care of the consequences. I trust that he will, and hope he may not be *impeached* for it! Congress *proposes*, the President *opposes*, and God *disposes*. The bow of Mr. Sumner is bent to its utmost. That *ignis fatuus*, the "unknown good" of the black man, he is still pursuing, and perchance it may lead him into pools and ditches, and ultimately, in his mad and purblind progress, fasten him in the mud. For each concession he makes a new demand. First, he pressed the Emancipation proclamation; the "irreversible guarantees" against slavery in the Constitution, as an ultimatum; then Negro Suffrage; then the Impeachment of the President; then Rebel Confiscation and *contraband* rewards. So that thus stands the *sum* of the Radicals: The Emancipation Proclamation × the Constitutional Guarantee × Negro Suffrage × the Impeachment Conspiracy × Rebel Confiscation and Negro Rewards = *Party Power*!

I am glad to see one New England state showing sounder reason on the subject of national politics. May Connecticut be an example.[6] Had a third party been formed in the Northern States last autumn, into which the conservative Republicans could have gone, the result would have been far different.

Trusting that this letter may not be considered intrusive, allow me to quote the finest lines Armstrong ever wrote. They will bear a poltical application.

"Virtue (for mere good nature is a fool),
Is sense and spirit with humanity:
'Tis sometimes angry, and its frown confounds;
tis even vindictive, but in vengeance just.
Knaves fain would laugh at it; some great ones dare;
But at his heart the most undaunted son
of fortune dreads its name and awful charms.[7]

D. W. Lothrop, (Beechcroft)

ALS, DLC-JP.
  1. Nicholas Rowe, *Jane Shore*, act 3, sc. 1, lines 226–29.
  2. Joseph Addison, *Cato*, act 1, sc. 1, lines 31–35.
  3. King Richard in Shakespeare's *Richard II*, act 1, sc. 4, line 28.
  4. Not found.
  5. Not found.
  6. An apparent reference to the Democratic victories in Connecticut.
  7. John Armstrong, *The Art of Preserving Health*, bk. 4, lines 267–73.

From Ethan A. Allen

St. Charles Hotel New Orleans—La
April 9—1867

Dear Sir.

I have been here for several days & mixed much with the people—& find the most perfect good will & feeling existing toward the Federal Government. There is not the slightest desire on their part to oppose the power of your Administration. The only turbulent spirits to be found here are *Northern men* who really appear to be in the interest of the radical element in the *Eastern States*—their whole aim & ambition is to ferment trouble & they are ready at any time to get up any excitement which may be damaging to the harmonious working of the Government—& make some political Capital for that party in the North to the injury of the South. You will doubtless Mr President agree with me in the conclusion that the existence of such an element in this Country is a great misfortune to say the least.

The removal from office[1] of Mayor Monroe here & substitution of Heath by General Sheridan of Lynch for Atty Genl. in place of Herron & Howe for Judge of the Criminal Court in place of Abel[2] is truly unfortunate. Judge Abel has *ever* been a *strong & uncompromising* union man—his devotion to the Union has never faultered—he stood up manfully throughout the War for the Union & nothing but the Union at the risk of his life during the fearful struggle through which our Country has so recently passed. He is a man of fine character & much respected & liked by the people. His removal is certainly a *poor recompense* for his unfaultering love of Country.[3] Heath was one of Butlers[4] *dirty* spies when that General commanded here.

In fact Mr President not a single one of the three appointments made by General Sheridan are at all Creditable. They are men of *no* status in this Community—they are not or have they *ever* Commanded the least respect. They are *strangers* whose feelings are not all identified wih the interests of this City,[5] or the concilliation of the people. There are many, many—good & true, respectable, & responsible men in New Orleans who could have been appointed by Genl S. who would have been perfectly satisfactory to Citizens. Then why irritate & insult New Orleans by giving such appointments to *Imported* Yankees. Sheridan is becoming more & more unpopular with the people here every day—still do, & still will they submit to the Government.

The Negroes are peacable. They see that they must work & they begin to find out that their best and most reliable friend in this Country is their former masters. Many hundreds yes thousands of the Negroes are returning to their former owners.

I leave here tomorrow for the interior of Mississippi & shall visit several large plantations & see & talk with Planters & Negroes. My old acquaintance among the planters will enable me to go & see how they feel—and act. I shall go from here to Columbus, Miss. & So back through Augusta Georgia to New-York via Washington City which place I expect to reach within four or five weeks.

The unsettled state of our Political affairs is certainly very damaging to the prosperity of our Country. Capital is withheld from investments & people anxiously wait to see the results of the *wise* legislation of our wise rulers (in Congress). The most *desirable* thing which could be done for the Southern States is you may *depend* on it Mr President the issuing by you of a general pardon. When this is done, will you see our *whole* Country at a bound leap into life. Prosperity will crown the labors of the Capitalist, the husbandman & the Artisan. The horrors of our War will in a measure soon be forgotten & the onward march of our Country with the North & South hand in hand as Brothers, will soon recover from the horrors through which we have passed & stand before the world a proud emblem of a Republican Government. Our internal dissentions will be healed up & we bid defiance to the world in arms against us.

Ethan A. Allen

ALS, DLC-JP.
1. The gentlemen mentioned were removed by Sheridan's General Orders No. 5 of March 27, 1867. General Orders, No. 5, in Edward McPherson, *The Political History of the United States of America During the Period of Reconstruction* (Washington, 1880), 206–7.
2. John T. Monroe, Edward Heath, Phillip H. Sheridan, Bartholomew L. Lynch, Andrew S. Herron, William W. Howe, and Edmund Abell. Heath (1819–1892), a native of Maine, had worked in the customhouse and served on the board of Straight University. He was mayor from March 1867 until after the 1868 elections. Attorney Lynch (b. c1830), an Irish native, had been attorney general, having been elected in February 1864 during Lincoln's reconstruction of Louisiana's government. Howe (1833–1909), a lawyer from New York, settled in New Orleans after his Civil War service. He was a justice of the Louisiana Supreme Court (1868–72), U.S. district attorney for the eastern district (1900–1907), a noted authority on civil law, and much involved with New Orleans charitable and cultural activities. Holli and Jones, *American Mayors*, 157; New Orleans directories (1867–69); 1860 Census, La., Jefferson, Jefferson City, 534; Taylor, *La. Reconstructed*, 30; *DAB.*
3. For Abell's own protest against his removal, see Abell to Johnson, June 3, 1867.
4. Benjamin F. Butler.
5. While it appears that Howe was a recent arrival, Lynch had been in New Orleans since 1851 and Heath since 1842. Taylor, *La. Reconstructed*, 30; Holli and Jones, *American Mayors*, 157.

From Thomas W. Dewell [1]

New York, April 9, 1867

Sir,

I beg leave to submit to your Excellency the following statement bearing upon the administration of Henry S Smythe, Collector of the Customs of the Port of New York. On the first day of August 1866, I was assigned a position, that of night Watchman, in the Custom House, by

Mr Smythe. I performed my duties faithfully and promptly, until the first day of March 1867, when I was removed. Before, and during my official duties and since, I have uniformly, consistently and vigorously supported the measures and acts of your Excellency. I have contributed pecuniarily and voluntarily to the support of the Philadelphia Convention; believing then as I do now, that the principles and measures then and there enunciated are the best means of carrying out the successful working of this Government. While in the employ of the administration I had ample opportunity of observing the various phases of political opinion among my immediate associates by frequent animated and vehement discussions in which the policy, acts, &c of your Excellency were freely commented upon. That the Presidents policy, messages and acts were grossly denounced by men holding position under Mr Smythe, I can truthfully testify. That His Excellency was shamefully maligned and traduced by those who were then and are now holding these same positions, and that they hoped and wished he would be impeached, together with language unfit for repetition, I can truly bear witness. Believing as I do, that "to the victor belong the spoils" that patronage should be bestowed upon those who uphold the Executive's acts, &c, I do most emphatically protest against the serpent like attitude of Henry A. Smythe, and the men in his employ, who are by deeds and words doing all in their power to deride and bring into comtempt the acts policies, messages &c of His Excellency.

I herewith give you the names of those who so fiercely and without warrant, maliciously and unsparingly maligned and traduced every act of the President within the past six months

John Glastaeter, night watchman Public Store 56 Bway
Abraham Becute, "   "   "   "   56 Broadway
Jacob Bohem   "   "   "   "   "   "

The persons[2] herein named have been in office six years and are reputed to be worth from $70,000 to $25,000 each. They have a lucrative business outside of their official duties.

In view of my displacement from the Custom House, not on account of unworthiness or of laxity in performance of duties, but of perhaps a necessity of Mr Smythe to give place to others who I fear are as wilful and malignant towards the President as those I have mentioned, and as I bear no malice toward the above mentioned persons, I deem it my duty to earnestly and sincerely protest against these persons occupying the above positions and would beg you to give the same your earliest attention.

I will readily and cheerfully give affidavits to the facts I have herein stated.

Thos W. Dewell
85 Broad St

ALS, DNA-RG56, Appts., Customs Service, Collector, N.Y., T. W. Dewell.

1. Not identified.
2. Possibly John Glastaeter, a mason and clerk living in New York. Becute may have been Abraham G. Becude, a Brooklyn fruitseller and restaurant operator. Bohem could have been Jacob H. Cohen, a New York clerk who had worked in the customhouse since at least 1865. They are otherwise not identified. New York City directories (1860, 1862–64, 1867); Brooklyn directories (1864–68); *U.S. Off. Reg.* (1865–67).

From James B. Eads [1]

St. Louis   April 9th 1867

I have just learned today that arrangements have been effected by which the nomination of *Bernard Poepping* [2] as surveyor of this port will be confirmed by the Senate if his name is sent in by you. I presume from this that there is some probability of his being nominated.

Acting upon this supposition and being possessed of certain facts that you can scarcely be expected to know, I have this moment telegraphed you the following.

"Make no nomination for Surveyor of this port until after receiving my letter of today. Treachery will be thereby defeated."[3]

I KNOW that Mr. Pepping is in league with your enemies here. His confirmation by the Senate will be purchased only at the cost of his future treachery to you. I *know positively* that he intends treachery to you, and this information I dont think you can get through any other channel unless some of his radical coadjutors turned states evidence.

I have to request that you will consider this letter strictly confidential. Mr P.s relations and my own are friendly, although not intimate; it is, however chiefly because the knowledge by others that this information reached you through me, might be the means of being traced to others whom it would injure, that I ask that this letter be kept strictly private. I know, absolutely, that what I have communicated to you is true.[4]

Jas B. Eads

ALS, DLC-JP.
1. Eads (1820–1887), a noted civil engineer, developed a fleet of armor-clad gunboats which patrolled western rivers for the Union forces during the Civil War. By 1874 he had constructed a bridge across the Mississippi River at St. Louis. *DAB*.
2. Poepping (c1835–fl1875) was a Carondelet City and St. Louis lawyer and eventually a music teacher. St. Louis directories (1870–75); 1870 Census, Mo., St. Louis, Carondelet City, 594.
3. See Eads to Johnson, Apr. 9, 1867, Johnson Papers, LC.
4. By the time Eads wrote to Johnson six candidates had already been nominated and rejected for the post of surveyor of customs, one of them twice. Poepping was never nominated. After one further rejection, a candidate supported by Eads, Samuel M. Breckenridge, was nominated, confirmed, and commissioned on April 13, 1867. Ser. 6B, Vol. 4: 315–18; Eads to Johnson, Apr. 10, 1867, Johnson Papers, LC.

From Charles K. Graham

Washington   April 9th 1867

Mr. President,

I, accidentally, met Mr. Thurlow Weed, this morning, & he volunteers the information that he had just had an interview with you, in the course of which he had suggested my name in connection with the Collectorship of the 6th (Mr. Morrissey's) District, and that he had no doubt it would be favorably entertained by you, provided Mr. Morrissey's consent could be obtained, which he expected to procure by tomorrow.

To Mr. Weed, I made no response, merely treating him with the deference due from a man in the prime of life, to one of his advanced years. I consider the communication, however, a remarkable one, as Mr. Thos. C. Stewart,[1] Mr. Weed's mouth piece & his associates Mssrs Ketchum, Robertson & Laflin[2] have been protesting to you against my appointment in the Eighth (Mr. Brooks)[3] District, on the ground that I was not a resident of it—(a statement at variance with the fact,)—although these very same gentlemen, in order to get me out of the way of their Candidate, Mr. Thomas E. Smith, had previously offered through Mr. Ketchum, to recommend me to you for a similar position in the City of Brooklyn,—where I had never resided.

I make this statement because I desire it to be distinctly understood that no person has been authorized by me, to use my name in connection with any other District than the Eighth, and that I shall make no compromise with any parties, who profess to be able to manage matters of this kind, but shall remain untrammelled, entertaining the firmest conviction of your desire to do me equal and exact justice.

Charles K. Graham

ALS, DLC-JP.

1. Thomas E. Stewart (1824–1904), a New York City lawyer, served in the state legislature prior to his election to the U.S. House (1867–69). *BDUSC*.

2. Hiram Ketchum, Jr., William E. Robinson, and Addison H. Laflin. Laflin (1823–1878) served in the New York legislature in the 1850s. He was a member of the U.S. House for three terms (1865–71). Laflin became naval officer of the port of New York during the Grant administration. *BDUSC*.

3. James Brooks. For the struggle over the Eighth District appointment, see William E. Robinson to Johnson, Feb. 18, 1867; Charles G. Halpine to Johnson, Feb. 25, Mar. 13, 1867; Daniel E. Sickles to Johnson, Mar. 5, 1867.

From Oliver O. Howard

April 9th [1867][1]

Sir:

I recommend that the case of Mr. Wylly Woodbridge,[2] a truly loyal man of Savannah Ga. be taken under special consideration. His cotton was his property and should have been secured to him, if it could lawfully be secured to any owner under like circumstances in the United States.

I believe on careful investigation his claims will constitute an exceptional case.[3]

O. O. Howard

ALS, MeB-Correspondence of O. O. Howard.

1. The year is derived from other documents pertaining to the Woodbridge case, especially the April 13, 1867, endorsement of U.S. Grant, Simon, *Grant Papers*, 17: 427–28.

2. Woodbridge (1814–1878), a well-to-do merchant, had been given a recess appointment as collector of customs but resigned in early 1866. At the time of his death he was superintendent of a rice mill. 1860 Census, Ga., Chatham, Savannah, 302; *Savannah Morning News*, Sept. 23, 30, 1878; Ser. 6B, Vol. 2: 125; Vol. 5, Johnson Papers, LC.

3. Woodbridge was attempting to recover the proceeds, $48,294.30, for 117 bales of cotton seized from him by treasury agents in March 1865. Although on April 22, 1867, Johnson referred this case to the secretary of the treasury with the hope that relief could be extended, settlement was ultimately sought in the court of claims, where, by 1877, he was "entitled to recover" $22,941. *Senate Reports*, 40 Cong., 2 Sess., No. 70, p. 1 (Ser. 1320); McCulloch to Johnson, Apr. 30, 1867, Simon, *Grant Papers*, 17: 428; Woodbridge to Johnson, May 8, 1867, Office of Atty. Gen., Lets. Recd., President, RG60, NA; Gen. Jurisdiction Case File 2639, RG123, NA.

From Allen P. Richardson [1]

Private

Washington City, D.C.   April 9th 1867

As I am unable like Senators and members of congress to call at pleasure and interchange views with you, I am driven to communicate by note.

By the adroit management of the Radicals of Missouri through their doubly viled tongued Senator Henderson[2] they have already secured by deception & false representation more than two thirds of the Federal offices in our state; and they now present a list[3] from the office of the Secretary of the Treasury by which if successful, they will obtain the ballance of the important offices left vacant.

They wisely and knowingly hold in reserve their favorits, and rejected your *representative* friends one after another in the 3d. & 5th Collection Districts Missouri,[4] ignoring all arrangement except an unconditional surrender of the patronage of the Government and the constitutional power confered upon the President to nominate his own political friends in place of his relentless enemies.

This list they have secured & presented in the person of Mr Clemens for collector 3d & Mr Sampson[5] 5th Collection district, both intended to overide the claims of your *representative friends* of those districts, and place power and patronage into the hands of the Ashlies[6] of House & the Senate of the U.S.

Let me as an humble citizens fore warn you of pretended friends and open foes, with whome you are surrounded within and without, many of whome seak to strangle your administration as did Mr Chase that of President Lincolns, and the latter movement is in the interest of a *Chase* for the Presidency in 1868.

Allow me to repeat again, that if My Name or that of Mr Glover[7] is embarrassing to you in filling the offices of collector for the 3d & 5 District we are ready to give place to other representative men of your own party true & tried advocates of your policy. But we feel that to surrender to our enemies is to be untrue to ourselves and false to our friends.[8]

Allen P. Richardson   Mo

No 431 12 st. Washington city

ALS, DLC-JP.

1. Richardson (*c*1822–1892) was a substantial Cole County, Missouri, farmer. An outspoken opponent of slavery and supporter of Lincoln and Republican principles, he served in the Mo. Home Guard on several occasions during the Civil War. He was appointed postmaster of Jefferson City, an office he held from May 3, 1861, until early 1867 apparently. At the time he wrote he was actively seeking either to be restored to his postmastership or to become collector of internal revenue for the Fifth District of Missouri, but had been rejected for both by the Senate in March. 1860 Census, Mo., Cole, Jefferson Twp., 11; Ser. 6B, Vol. 4: 317, Johnson Papers, LC; *U.S. Off. Reg.* (1861–67); Richardson to the Honorable Senators of the United States, Apr. 15, 1867, Johnson Papers, LC; Pension File, Frances A. Richardson, RG15, NA.

2. John B. Henderson.

3. Such a list, signed by Henderson and addressed to Johnson, is found in the Johnson Papers, LC. Although not dated by Henderson, it contained the names of people who were under consideration at that time.

4. Discussions of the problem of finding a collector for the Third District can be found in John M. Glover to Johnson, Mar. 5, 1867, Smith S. Allen to Johnson, Mar. 14, 1867, and Glover to Johnson, Apr. 4, 1867. A similar difficulty had occurred in the Fifth District where four men, including Richardson, had already been nominated and rejected (one twice). Ser. 6B, Vol. 4: 315–17, Johnson Papers, LC.

5. John T. Clements and Archibald J. Sampson. Sampson (1839–1921) rose from the rank of private to captain during the Civil War. Admitted to the bar in 1865, he practiced law in Sedalia, Missouri, until 1873 when he moved to Denver, Colorado, where he was state attorney general (1876–79). He subsequently held several diplomatic posts. *Who Was Who in America* (5 vols., Chicago, 1943–73), 1: 1075.

6. Rep. James M. Ashley.

7. John M. Glover.

8. Although Johnson renominated Richardson for collector of the Fifth District on April 15, the Senate rejected him the same day. Sampson was never nominated and the collectorship remained a problem, as Johnson had to nominate five more candidates before William J. Chandler was confirmed in December 1867. Ser. 6B, Vol. 4: 318, Johnson Papers, LC.

From Lewis D. Campbell

Confidential.

New Orleans, April 10, 1867.

Dear Sir:

I presume the time when a minister will have to go to Mexico is drawing near. This fact is my excuse for adding to your many troubles this
unofficial letter which I regard due to myself as well as to the public service.[1]

Last October when I was required to proceed with Gen. Sherman to
Mexico, on a few days notice, I had no Secretary and no time to canvass
the merits of applicants. Under these circumstances I wrote to you and to
Mr. Seward recommending E. L. Plumb and you promptly appointed
him. I had but a slight personal acquaintance with him and acted solely
on the recommendations which men in the City of New York had sent me
whom I then supposed to be disinterested.

Experience soon satisfied me that I had been led into a very great mistake. I discovered before I left New York in November that *the persons on
whose recommendations I acted were concerned in schemes of speculation in
Mexico and that Mr Plumb was jointly interested with them*. And further
experience has convinced me that the advancement of these schemes has
far more influence on the mind of Mr. Plumb than the public interest. In
this connection I will state a circumstance that occurred when we were at
Brownsville and Matamoras. Becoming satisfied that we could not reach
President Juarez on that line, I stated to Mr. Plumb my purpose to return to New Orleans for instructions from the Department. He opposed
it with much warmth of feeling and became dictatorial and offensive. He
at first refused to come with me, saying with much feeling that he "*had
large individual interests in Mexico that needed his attention*." Finally, dis-
covering that my judgment was not influenced by such arguments and
that I meant to come *without him*, with a surly reluctance he accompanied
me. During his sojourn in this City I learn he has spoken of his large
mining interests, his coffee plantations &c. &c. in Mexico.

Soon after our arrival in New Orleans he became even more dictatorial
imperious and offensive—So much so as to call from me a rebuke which
produced the effect of *terminating our friendly relations*. Since that time
(about the 1st of January) I have performed all the clerical duties myself—
preparing and copying despatches papers &c. &c, without the slightest
aid from him.

Again: Wherever we go he affiliates with newspaper editors correspondents and reporters, which is objectionable to me and disqualifies
him, in my judgment, for the confidential position he holds in the Legation. The day before we left New York, as I am reliable informed, he

called at the "Herald" office and had an interview with its editors. In a day or two after we left articles appeared in that paper disparaging to Gen. Sherman and myself, declaring us unfit for the mission &c &c. and lauding Mr. Plumb as highly qualified &c.[2] When we arrived at Brownsville in December he immediately made the acquaintance of the newspaper men. He called on and spent some time with the editor of the "Courier" who is also the correspondent on the Rio Grande of the "N.Y. Herald."[3] The next morning an editorial appeared in the "Courier" highly derogatory of Gen. Sherman and myself, and adding: "*but Mr. Plumb furnishes the brains for the commission.*" And since our arrival here he has been affiliating with the same class of men; but how far he has succeeded in further disparaging me or gratifying his own inordinate vanity I do not know. I have withheld from him the power to disclose any of the secrets of the Legation.

In addition to these, to me objectionable acts, I am convinced that, because I have not yielded to his arrogance and dictation, he has craftily and unscrupulously attempted to injure if not to degrade me.

I could detail other objectionable matters, but I forbear for the present. He has not been of the least practical service to me since the 1st of January. I do not see how he can be of any hereafter. *I have lost all confidence in him.* I should much prefer to perform all the clerical labor hereafter myself, as I have done for the last three months, without his aid, than to be connected with him. Should he be relieved I shall expect to get along without any Secretary until some qualified gentleman can be found who is not mixed up in Mexican schemes of speculation, and in whom confidence may be reposed.[4]

It is with profound regret that I feel myself called upon to make these statements; but I regard it my duty. I know the public interest requires that there should be *harmony and good feeling in the Legation.* As it is now constituted that is impossible.

Lewis D. Campbell

P.S. I mark this "confidential" but do so with the expectation that you will show it to Mr. Seward.

L.D.C.

ALS, DLC-JP.

1. This letter was accompanied by a cover letter of the same date in which Campbell stated that Edward L. Plumb had turned out to be a radical opponent of the administration and he believed Plumb to be corresponding with someone in the State Department who had an interest in his personal schemes.

2. See the *New York Herald*, Nov. 14, 15, 17, 20, 1866.

3. Not identified.

4. Johnson sent this letter to Seward for him to read and return. Plumb was eventually recalled. However, he went on to serve as interim chargé d'affaires in Mexico from August 1867 to December 1868, replacing Marcus Otterbourg, who replaced Plumb as legation secretary. Plumb remained in Mexico until 1876 representing the International Railway

Company of Texas that sought various railroad concessions. Endorsement, Campbell to Johnson, Apr. 10, 1867, Johnson Papers, LC; Ser. 6B, Vol. 2: 243, ibid.; *Records of the Department of State* (Washington, D.C., 1872), 64; James M. Callahan, *American Foreign Policy in Mexican Relations* (New York, 1932), 278, 476, 480–82.

From John W. Leftwich

Memphis Tenn   Apr 10th 1867

Sir

We are just to day informed of the rejection by the Senate of Mr Jones as Marshall of West Tenn whose appointment was confirmed on the 19th ult. but it seems was reconsidered.[1]

This is sad news to every conservative in West Tenn and especial to the Federal Court and Bar who esteem him one of the best if not the best marshall that can be found.

Mr Mitchell[2] the Clerk of the Court—himself a radical but with sense and liberal views—has just returned from Washington and while there urged Mr Fowler[3] to consent to his confirmation as a necessity to the Court the business of which is rapidly increasing; but for the most insignificant reasons—his failure for instance to advertise in the "Post"—he refused to do it and said in substance that *no* Conservative should be confirmed for this district.

If consistent with duty it will be greatly to the interests of all Plaintiffs and especially the Govt to make no other appointment for the present; but if an appointment must be made I beg to suggest the name of Geo C Holmes[4] who is an intelligent industrious and popular farmer and whose rejection will damage the rejecting party and such are the only names I will send you from this district.[5]

Jno W Leftwich

P.S. The failure of the "Commercial" through financial mismanagement during Mr Keatings[6] absence in Washington leaves us I am ashamed to say without a genuine Administration & Conservative paper in Memphis. This will be corrected in a short time and an able and earnest one put on foot.

Jno W Leftwich

ALS, DNA-RG60, Appt. Files for Judicial Dists., Tenn., George C. Holmes.

1. In October 1866 Samuel H. Jones (1824–1879), a farmer, justice of the peace, and former sheriff of Maury County, was given a recess appointment as marshal by President Johnson. Once Congress convened, Jones was nominated for the marshal's office. The Senate first approved the nomination in mid-March 1867 but then reversed itself on April 5. In a telegram Leftwich urged that Johnson make no appointment until after receiving his letter. Ser. 6B, Vol. 3: 425; Vol. 4: 227–28, Johnson Papers, LC; Leftwich to Johnson, Apr. 10, 1867, Johnson Papers, LC; *BDTA*, 2: 478.

2. Abram S. Mitchell.

3. Joseph S. Fowler.

4. Holmes (*c*1833–1884), a Memphis businessman and collector, did not receive nom-

ination or appointment to the marshal's post. 1870 Census, Tenn., Shelby, 6th Dist., 4; Memphis directories (1865–85).

5. Leftwich followed up with recommendations of W. W. Coleman or James B. Driskell, if George Holmes were not to be considered, but neither of these two men was nominated by Johnson. In that letter, Leftwich also noted that he had heard that James B. Bingham had been mentioned for the marshalship. As a matter of fact, Bingham had been nominated by the President on April 6 but rejected by the Senate ten days later. A few days afterwards James M. Tomeny received the marshalship. Ser. 6B, Vol. 4: 228; Leftwich to Johnson, Apr. 13, 1867, Appt. Files for Judicial Dists., George C. Holmes, RG60, NA.

6. John M. Keating (1830–1906) emigrated to America from Ireland and, before the Civil War, had a career in printing and publishing in Louisiana and Tennessee. During the war years Keating was one of the editors of the *Memphis Argus*. After establishing the *Memphis Commercial* in 1865, he united it with the *Argus* the following year. He spent part of 1867–68 in Washington as one of President Johnson's advisers. After his failure to receive the Memphis postmastership in 1868, Keating returned to Memphis to edit the *Memphis Appeal* for the next twenty-one years. *DAB*.

From Demas Barnes

Washington   Apl 11th 1867

President Johnson

Referring to the 3d Dist N Y—I am *informed & believe* that Mr Wellwood[1] nominated for Assessor is Radical. I am *informed and believe* that Mr Brewster[2] for Collector—has given *written* pledges of fidelity to *our* party and *also to the Radical party*. We want no such men.

I respectfully ask that *both* these names be withdrawn from the Senate.[3] We are entitled to, and can get the patronage of two offices out of three—(Collector Assessor and P Master) in this way *and in no other way*. To effect this the three names should be sent in at *one* time on a previous agreement of confirmation. I have just conversed with Gov Morgan. Names now in will *not be rejected*. They are satisfactory to Senators unless three can do better.

I am informed & believe that an arrangement exists between my Colleague and Senators—which if effected sells us out. I am compelled to protest.

In no other way than as above indicated can the Administration preserve an organization in our county.

I am not straining for names—but desire to be consulted & can only defend myself upon those now in the Prest. hands, unless changed by subsequent consultation.

Demas Barnes

ALS, DLC-JP.
1. For a recommendation for Thomas Welwood, see William E. Robinson to Johnson, Apr. 6, 1867.
2. William R. Brewster had been recommended for appointment by Daniel E. Sickles. See Sickles to Johnson, Mar. 5, 1867.
3. Brewster's name was not withdrawn, and he was rejected by the Senate on April 20, 1867. Johnson did withdraw Welwood's nomination on April 11, but resubmitted it on

April 15; the Senate confirmed him on April 20, 1867. *Senate Ex. Proceedings*, Vol. 15, pt. 2: 693, 714, 779–80.

From Joseph R. Flanigen and Thomas C. MacDowell

Philadelphia   April 11th 1867.

Sir.

In accordance with instructions We have the honor to certify to you the extract from the proceedings of the Executive Committee at its meeting held on Monday the 8th inst.

J. R. Flanigen   Chairman

Thos C. MacDowell   Secretary

HEAD-QUARTERS OF THE

National Union Johnson Club,

136 S. Third St., (2d Story.)

The "Executive Committee" of the National Union State Central Committee of Pennsylvania regarding with deep Solicitude the present aspect of affairs at the National Capital, and lamenting what appears to be an undue influence of the Democratic Party, with the administration hereby, Resolve;

That any effort to transfer the Conservative element represented by this Committee, to the Democratic party, or to induce it to act or affiliate, with that party as a political organization will deserve and meet the universal condemnation of the true friends of the President of the United States.

Resolved. That this Committee on behalf of the National Union men of Pennsylvania hereby most respectfully but earnestly, protest against the distribution of offices, by the present administration, at the dictation of Democratic Senators and members of the House of Representatives, and that the combinations which are made by Democrats and Radicals, acting together for the purpose of securing place for members of one or other of these parties are disreputable, demoralizing and subversive of every sentiment of political honor.

Resolved. That it is the sense of this Committee that the patronage of the existing administration ought to be distributed by the advice and concurrence of National Union men only, and that the huckstering now being practised by Democrats and Radicals who affiliate for the purpose of securing the "Spoils of Office" is a reproach on the political organizations of the country and should therefore be discountenanced and condemned.

Resolved. That this committee, appeals to the President of the United States to protect the political sentiments of the country, from such debasement, and that it suggests and urges upon him, that if the Senate will persist in refusing its assent to the appointment of honest and capable Conservative men to office, the responsibility for any detriment that occurs to the public service thereby, ought to rest with that body.

Resolved, That the National Union organization in Pennsylvania, was based on the declaration of the President, that the contest forced upon him by Congress should be fought in the Union party, and that its patronage should be bestowed upon such persons only as had supported the candidates and platform of the Baltimore Convention, and that such a distribution of patronage is essential because of the fact that the principles of an administration can be neither illustrated or upheld by any other course of conduct.

Resolved, That the Chairman & Secretary of the Committee are hereby directed to forward official copies of these procedings to the President of the United States and the members of his Cabinet, and that their publication is hereby authorized whenever in the judgment of the chairman, the cause of the National Union party will be promoted thereby.

LS and D, DLC-JP.

From Frederick Koones

Washington   April 11 1867.

Sir

It was my wish to have seen you in person relative to my nomination for the Assessorship of this District, but after having made a number of ineffectual attempts to do so I have concluded to address you a letter upon the subject. In August last my relative, the Hon: Henry Stanbery, *nominated me to you for the position of Registrar of Wills but Col: OBierne[1] received the appointment. Subsequently he again recommended me for the Registrar of Deeds. A Mr. Eddy,[2] at that time a clerk in the Navy Department and recommended by Senator Fessenden,[3]* received the preference. Again I was endorsed by yourself and Mr. Stanbery (see copy of letter herein) for a Special Agency of the Treasury; there being no vacancy I was advised by the Department to apply for this assessorship, the present incumbent being considered inefficient. My application received your favorable consideration you nominated me to the Senate, but thro' the *false* and *malicious* statements made to the Committee, by John R. Elvans,[4] Sayles J. Bowen and Z. C. Robbins prominent *Republicans*, and *your bitterest enemies*, my name was at first rejected. These persons were exultant at my supposed defeat and triumphantly boasted of their exploit about the streets. So soon however as an opportunity was given to defend myself, the Committee were speedily convinced of the falsity of the charges, the matter was reconsidered and recommitted on Sunday night March 3d at 10 P.M. and was not taken up again for want of time. My friends in the

Senate are much mortified, for it was a misapprehension on the part of the Committee, and say that the matter now rests entirely with you. They assure me that I will be confirmed if my name be again sent in. It may not be improper for me to state that Mr. Stanbery's recommendation is *not a mere matter of form*. He takes much interest in the matter, and is anxious that I should get the place, but knowing how you are annoyed with applicants he forbears to say anything more to you about it. He informed me yesterday however, that he believed you would send my name up again, and as the adjournment of the Senate is rapidly approaching I would most repectfully beg that you will give the matter your immediate attention.

In addition to the personal intercession of Mr. Stanbery, I have the endorsement of Judge M. Blair, Senators Hendricks and Cowan,[5] and also am recommended by the members of National Union Ex: Committee, and 180 of our best and most influential Merchants and Business men of the City, nearly all of whom know me personally.

Under the foregoing circumstances, and as it appears to be customary to renominate persons when their confirmations have been passed over by the Senate I would most repctfully request that your Excellency would extend the same favor to me.[6]

Fredk. Koones

ALS, DNA-RG56, Appts., Internal Revenue Service, Assessor, D.C., 1st Dist., Fred. Koones.

1. James R. O'Beirne.
2. Edward C. Eddie (c1830–1868), a native of New York, moved to Washington in 1853. From 1863 to 1867, he was a Navy Department clerk and then became register of deeds for the District of Columbia sometime following March 2, 1867. *U.S. Off. Reg.* (1863–65); Washington, D.C., directories (1866–68); *Washington Evening Star*, Feb. 26, 1868; *National Intelligencer*, Mar. 2, 1867.
3. William P. Fessenden.
4. Elvans (c1832–fl1871) was a hardware dealer and Washington native. 1870 Census, D.C., Washington, 3rd Ward, 211; Washington, D.C., directories (1866–71).
5. Montgomery Blair, Thomas A. Hendricks, and Edgar Cowan.
6. We have found no evidence to indicate that Koones received an appointment.

From Frederick G. Edwards [1]

Atlanta Georgia   April 12 1867

Mr. President.

You must be aware that the existance of the Abolition Party and its growth and increase and final success was brought about by detailing mainly from the Pulpits of the North—how cruelly the negroes were treated by the Southern people—as to the truth of these details you can form your own estimate.

The amount of cruelty practiced towards the Slaves was mainly caused by the secretly intermeddling of the fanatics of the North.

These fanatics for a period of over 50 years have endeavored to stir up the negroes against the White race secretly before the war and now that the Negroes are turned loose they do it openly.

Negro Bureaus, School Marms civil right Bills and lastly Shermans Military bill are the means resorted to stir up the negroes against the white race of this southern country.

If you desire to save this country from the Abomination of desolation you will at once send out impartial observers in all sections to watch the doings of these Bureaus, civil rights and Military bills &c. Genl. Sheridan will stir up the niggers if human means can effect it. I single out Sheridan because he is decidedly more fanatical than either of the four other Genls.

The Southern people are desirous of treating the Niggers with considerations and kindness as they have always done, and are perfectly willing to let time work out the finally destiny of the Nigger without molestation and will do all they can to advance them.

But as long as the Radicals pursue the course they are now pursuing there will be no *hope* for the white or black races.

I make the suggestion that you have the Bureaus and school marms and Military Governors watched and I repeat that these machines were intended to *Stir up the Niggers against* us and for nothing else.

We are doomed to utter Ruin if these Radical machines are not controled in their operations in some manner.

Sheridan requires more watching because he is deeper dyed. I again say we are lost forever if this thing of stirring up the Niggers against us is not put a stop to.

F G Edwards

ALS, DLC-JP.
    1. Edwards (c1805–fl1870), a merchant and farmer, lived in Louisville, Kentucky, before the war, where in the early 1850s he served as postmaster. 1850 Census, Ky., Jefferson, Louisville, 7th Ward, 681; (1860), 2nd Dist., 117; 1870 Census, Ga., Fulton, Atlanta, 5th Ward, 21; *U.S. Off. Reg.* (1851–53).

From Hunter Brooke

Cincinnati   April 13th 1867

Dear Sir
    I feel it my duty to thank you for your nomination for the Post Office of this City and to say a word in explanation of the action of the Senate. I am aware that you were lead to beleive that this nomination would be confirmed and I regret the annoyance and trouble my rejection may have occasioned.[1] If the House had been in session I would have been able to bring a very strong influence to bear upon the Senate from the personal assurances of members. But their absence—the ignorance of their where-

abouts and especially the absence of Senator Sherman and the member
from the 2d dist. Mr. Hayes[2]—has deprived me of that influence. The
Chairman of the Postal Committee Mr. Ramsey[3]—has written to me assuring me of his favor, but states that rule of the Senate leaving all such
approvals to the decision of the State Senators has been most rigidly adhered to, and that Ohio's only representative Mr. Wade[4] who has no voice
upon the floor declined to support me or any other of democratic proclivities. He is undoubtedly and I am told avowedly controlled by Mr.
Eggleston[5] of the 1st dist. and Mr. E. is determined to consummate his
plans of removing Capt. Sebastian[6] from the path of his (E's) brother in
law Mr Sands[7] for the County Treasurership next fall—by forcing you to
appoint Sebastian to the P.O. I was—greatly surprised to learn on yesterday that a large number of the prominent Republicans of this City, who
were excellent friends of mine and would gladly have favored me,—were
solemnly pledged to this place of forcing Sebastian upon you,[8] and some
of them regretted these obligations. A number of dispatches were sent
yesterday—to the Senate—recommending my confirmation "if Capt S.
could not be nominated." In this state of things, there could be no chance
for any one of Democratic proclivities, and I could not beleive that such a
gross attempt to *compel* the President to favor Republicanism, would
have been persisted in.

I hope you will pardon this intrusion as I deemed it due to explain any
representation of my own as to the probability of my confirmation. Again
I thank you sir, and assure that the action of the Senate has secured you at
least one *unyielding* and *earnest* adherent.

Hunter Brooke

ALS, DLC-JP.

1. Brooke was nominated on April 11 but rejected the next day. Ser. 6B, Vol. 4: 261,
Johnson Papers, LC.

2. John Sherman and Rutherford B. Hayes.

3. Alexander Ramsey.

4. Benjamin F. Wade.

5. Benjamin Eggleston.

6. John Sebastian (*c*1828–*fl*1870), a native of Kentucky and ship's captain, served as
Hamilton County, Ohio, treasurer in 1869–70. Cincinnati directories (1861–70); 1860
Census, Ohio, Hamilton, Cincinnati, 15th Ward, 369; *History of Cincinnati and Hamilton
County, Ohio* (Cincinnati, 1894), 246.

7. Alexander C. Sands. He did not become county treasurer; instead, Miles Greenwood
was chosen. Ibid.

8. Several telegrams recommending the appointment of Sebastian are found in Tels.
Recd., President, Vol. 5 (1866–67), RG107, NA.

From Samuel J. Tilden

New York   Ap 13th '67

My Dear Sir,

Your friends here are astonished by a rumor that Mr. Anthony J. Bleecker,[1] Assessor of the 8th District, has been removed, and another name sent in to the Senate in his place.[2]

Mr. B. is a gentleman of high character, in respect to whose official character and conduct there is not a shadow of question; who was, in former years a democrat, became a republican in 1855 and has adhered to your policy & administration.

He is of one of our oldest families—having the general esteem of the community and particularly of our business men.

It seems nearly impossible to get any true friends of yours confirmed, when they are appointed; but the few already appointed and confirmed, who happen to adhere to the administration,—why it should remove them utterly passess the comprehension of its friends.

It is assumed that there must have been some error in the matter.

S. J. Tilden

ALS, DNA-RG56, Appts., Internal Revenue Service, Assessor, N.Y., 8th Dist., Anthony J. Bleecker.

1. Bleecker (1799–1884) was an auctioneer and real estate agent in New York City. He was one of the founders of the Republican party in that city. Lincoln appointed him as assessor for the Eighth District. *New York Times*, Jan. 18, 1884.

2. There was truth in the rumors, for on April 10 the Senate received Johnson's nomination of John Foley to replace Bleeker as assessor. Efforts to remove Bleeker, however, failed for quite some time because the Senate could not reach agreement until the summer of 1868 upon a replacement for him. *Senate Ex. Proceedings*, Vol. 15, pt. 2: 676, 765; Ser. 6B, Vol. 4: 55–57, Johnson Papers, LC; *U.S. Off. Reg.* (1865–67).

From Francis J. Herron

Washington, April 14, 1867

To the President

I have read the letter of Col Hovey[1] regarding myself and have only to say, that his statements are utterly false.

I have no interest pecuniary or otherwise in the paper mentioned, or any other paper, and have never talked with Gov Hahn as stated.[2] All I know of the "Republican," is what I have seen stated in other papers, not even knowing who are the owners or editors. The statement that I visited the Senate chamber with Gov Hahn is true,[3] the object being to ask Mr Trumbull not to oppose the confirmation of Col Tisdale appointed by you a Collector of Revenue in La,[4] the visit being made at the urgent request of Col Tisdale. I have made no promises to any one in regard to the Marshalship, nor have I talked with any of these persons about it. This Col. Hovey who writes the letter to you was dismissed from the U.S. Army for cowardice, or swindling,[5] I have forgotten which, and is engaged at present in the business of blackmailing persons seeking office. His support was offered me *for money*, and my refusal brings the letter to you.

I should be pleased to see you this evening.

F. J. Herron

ALS, DLC-JP.

1. Charles E. Hovey.

2. Hovey stated that he was "led to believe" that Herron "is one of the Proprietors of the New Orleans 'Republican' a radical paper just started there by Gov. [Michael] Hahn to support Congress." Hovey was therefore sure that Herron would provide the radical paper with patronage if appointed to the post. Hovey to Johnson, Apr. 13, 1867, Johnson Papers, LC.

3. Hovey cited as evidence of "an understanding & intimacy" between Herron and Hahn that on Thursday or Friday of the preceding week they went to the Capitol together believing that Herron's name had been sent to the Senate. Hovey saw Hahn call out to Sen. Lyman Trumbull and introduce Herron to him. The three then engaged in "a somewhat protracted & confidential talk." Ibid.

4. Eugene Tisdale (1834–1886) served as captain, 13th Conn. Vols. and later as lieutenant colonel of the 1st New Orleans Rgt. He was nominated, confirmed, and commissioned as collector of internal revenue for the Third District of Louisiana on April 13, 1867, and apparently remained in the post until the end of Johnson's term. Rosa D. Tisdale, *Meet the Tisdales: Descendants of John Tisdal of Taunton, Mass., 1834–1980* (Baltimore, 1981), 503–4; 1870 Census, La., Ouachita, Monroe, 3rd Ward, 36; *Off. Army Reg.: Vols.*, 1: 280; 4: 1159; Ser. 6B, Vol. 4: 203, Johnson Papers, LC; Pension Files, Maggie E. Tisdale, RG15, NA.

5. Hovey's departure from the service occurred sometime in 1863, but the reasons remain obscure. Warner, *Blue*.

From William B. Ranken[1]

Washington DC   April 15, 1867

Respected Sir

Permit me to State to you; the alarming fact, that Thad Stephens has in his possession a declaration from Col. Alexander; M White;[2] of Pennsylvania that Edgar Cowan; late United States Senator from Pensylvania offerd to Said White to use his influence in aiding the nomination of a Collector of the Port of Philadelphia for the Sum of Ten Thousand Dollars. Leaveing no doubt that the report prevalant that Cowan is useing his influence at the Executive Chamber, for money.

Wm. B. Ranken
Metropolitan Hotel   Room 182

ALS, DLC-JP.

1. Probably Ranken (c1822–fl1893), a Pennsylvania-born attorney who practiced law in New Jersey into the 1880s. 1870 Census, N.J., Hudson, Jersey City, 1st Ward, 140;

Jersey City and Hoboken directories (1870–71, 1878, 1880); William B. Ranken to Grover Cleveland, May 15, 1893, Cleveland Papers, LC.

2. Possibly Alexander Moss White (1815–1906), a banker and businessman who became one of the leading financiers in New York. At the time White was also under investigation for allegedly defrauding the War Department. 1870 Census, N.Y., Kings, Brooklyn, 1st Ward, 83; *New York Times*, Nov. 1, 1906; Simon, *Grant Papers*, 17:573–74.

From Lewis V. Bogy

Metropolitan Hotel
New York   Apl 16 1867.

Sir.

I hope you will pardon me for the liberty I now take of writing to you about a matter which I deem to be of very great importance. The treaty for the acquisition of the Russian Territory on this continent having been ratified by us—as it will no doubt be by the Russian government— nothing is left to make it final, but the appropriation of the necessary amount by the next Congress.[1] It has seemed to me that this would be greatly facilitated, if the President could place before that body at its next meeting a full and accurate report on this country, giving a full account of its rivers, harbors, & bays—soil & minerals—its fisheries, fur trade, and commercial advantages. I deem this acquisition of the greatest importance to the country in a material point of view, and as another step towards the fulfillment of our destiny on this continent. The flag of the Republic can be carried no farther in that direction, as we have literally got to the end of the earth at that point.

I think a commission of three men, one military—one civil, & the other a scientific geologist & mineralogist, should be sent to that country to make the report here indicated and as this report should be laid before congress at the earliest period, this commission should leave here and rendezvous at San Francisco by the time the Russian government has ratified the treaty on its part. This I understand from the papers to be the last of June. If the commission was ready then to leave San Francisco it would have time (and no more) to visit this country, and be here by the meeting of the next Congress. The cost of the expedition would be very little indeed, as a government vessel no doubt could be furnished on the Pacific to make the voyage.

I not only can see no objection for the President to appoint such a commission, during the recess of the Senate, but it seems to me under the circumstances, it is an imperative duty imposed on him by the action of the Senate approving the treaty.

If such a commission should be appointed by you, I hope you will excuse me for saying that I would be very much gratified to be one of the commissioners. I am neither a military or scientific man—but I feel that I could creditably & usefully fill the position of civilian.[2]

Thomas Nast's cartoon commenting on the April treaty
with Russia for the purchase of Alaska.
Harper's Weekly, April 20, 1867

I shall be here perhaps one week longer—finishing the work placed in my hands by Secretary Browning—& I will then return to Washington City, when I will do myself the honor to call on you.

Lewis V. Bogy

This matter better not be mentioned till after the adjournment of the Senate.

ALS, DNA-RG48, Patents and Misc. Div., Lets. Recd.

1. The Senate ratified the treaty on April 9, 1867; by May 15, 1867, Russia had also ratified. However, it was not until July 27, 1868, that the U.S. Congress appropriated the $7,200,000 required by the treaty. *Senate Ex. Proceedings*, Vol. 15, pt. 2: 675–76; *Washington Evening Star*, May 16, 1867; *U.S. Statutes at Large*, 15: 198. See also William W. Warden to Johnson, May 15, 1867; Johnson to the Senate and House of Representatives, July 6, 1867.

2. Seward, through McCulloch, had the Smithsonian Institution conduct a survey of the Russian territory to present to Congress. Conducted during the summer of 1867 by Capt. W. A. Howard and others from the Coast Survey and revenue service, the Alaskan survey report was put before the House in February 1868 in reply to a resolution requesting correspondence and information concerning Russian America. There is no indication Bogy was considered for the expedition. Van Deusen, *Seward*, 545; *House Ex. Docs.*, 40 Cong., 2 Sess., No. 177, pp. 1, 189–361 (Ser. 1339).

From Samuel J. Holley [1]

Willard Hotel   Washington   April 17, 1867

Herewith please find letters from his Hon The Mayor of Buffalo[2] & from many of the most respectable citizens irrespective of political parties, of that City addressed to your Excellency recommending the writer for the office of Collector of the Port of Buffalo made vacant by the recent death of Chas. D. Norton Esqr. Since I came to Washington yesterday, I have been informed that you would nominate no man for such position who was not recommended to your Excellency for such nomination by Hon James M. Humphrey who now represents the 30th Congressional District in the present Congress from New York. There is no personal ill feeling existing between Mr Humphrey & the writer but as an old Democrat I cannot consistently ask a favor of your Excellency through him. I never in my life voted a Republican Ticket untill 1861 & in the year previous voted the Democratic Ticket favoring Mr Douglas against Mr Lincoln. In 1864 whilst Hon James M. Humphrey was denouncing & vilifying your Excellency to the People of his district I was praising & eulogising you from every cross roads in the same locality, & have ever acknowledged your noble & patriotic services in standing by & sustaining the union & government in the darkest hour of their peril. The difficulty of getting a personal interview with you is why I address your Excellency in this way. I am too poor to spend much time or money in Seeking for office & hence shall leave for home Buffalo, tomorrow evening. Should your Excellency be pleased to nominate me for the office for

which I am so strongly recommended the favor will at all times be gratefully acknowledged & the duties of the office honestly & faithfully discharged.

Sam J. Holley

P.S. I am personally & I think favorably known by His Hon Secy Mc-
Culloch. Since writing the above I learn your Excellency has sent the
name of my friend J. K. Tyler[3] to the Senate for the office for which I am
an applicant. Mr Tyler is a good man for the position & no influence of
mine shall prevent his confirmation.

ALS, DNA-RG56, Appts., Customs Service, Collector, Buffalo, Samuel J. Holley.
    1. Holley (fl1870) had been a Buffalo merchant for a number of years. His desire to be
named collector was deferred until 1869, when the Grant administration appointed him to
that post. Buffalo directories (1861–70); New York Tribune, Apr. 9, 1869; U.S. Off. Reg.
(1869).
    2. Chandler J. Wells (1814–1887) was a prosperous building contractor and then
branched into a variety of businesses in Buffalo. Before the war he served as alderman; afterwards he was elected Buffalo's mayor in 1866 and served one term. Holli and Jones, American Mayors.
    3. Joseph K. Tyler (fl1873) was at one time city treasurer of Buffalo and for a number of
years superintendent of the Omnibus Company there. Johnson nominated him as collector
on April 17 and the Senate approved him two days later. Buffalo directories (1861–73);
Senate Ex. Proceedings, Vol. 15, pt. 2: 747, 766.

From Hugh McCulloch

Treasury Department.   Apl 17 1867

My Dear Sir

I think it important that all the nominations for the Treasury Department should go in today. It is apparent to me that some of your bitterest
enemies desire that important offices should remain unfilled in order
that there may be an alleged necessity for the meeting of Congress in
July.[1] You have nothing to fear from an intermediate session, but the
Country has.

I am clearly of the opinion that Mr Buckalew[2] is one of your most sincere and judicious friends and that his recommendations are entitled to
great consideration. It is also my opinion that Bingham[3] should be
obliged in the matter of Collector 5th Dis. I send you names for a number
of offices this morning. The sickness of Mr Chandler[4] keeps me closely at
my desk, but I shall be at your service when required.

H McCulloch

ALS, DLC-JP.
    1. Congress did meet in an adjourned session, July 3–20.
    2. Charles R. Buckalew.
    3. John A. Bingham.
    4. Assistant secretary of the treasury William E. Chandler.

From Edmund Cooper

Shelbyville Ten   April 18 1867

My Dear Sir:

The resignation of Horace H. Harrison, District Attorney of the Middle District of Tennessee,[1] has been forwarded—and I have no doubt received.

May I once more call your attention to the claims of my friend Joseph H. Thompson, of Shelbyville,[2] for this place.

He deserves for his energy, and faithfulness, this slight token of favor at the hands of the Administration. He is well qualified for the performance of its duties.

If consistent, it would afford me great pleasure, to be instrumental in procuring this appointment for a true friend.[3]

Edmund Cooper

ALS, DNA-RG60, Appt. Files for Judicial Dists., Tenn., Joseph H. Thompson.

1. It was announced in the newspapers as early as April 3 that Harrison had just been appointed chancellor by Governor Brownlow. Five days later Cooper asked the President to appoint Joseph H. Thompson to replace Harrison; Johnson responded that Harrison's resignation had not yet been received. In fact, Harrison indicated that he had resigned on April 11, effective May 6. Harrison recommended his assistant Roswell Cary to be his successor. *Nashville Union and Dispatch*, Apr. 3, 1867; Cooper to Johnson, Apr. 8, 1867; Harrison to Johnson, Apr. 12, May 7, 1867, Appt. Files for Judicial Dists., Tenn., RG60, NA; Johnson to Cooper, Apr. 10, 1867, Tels. Sent, President, Vol. 3 (1865–68), RG107, NA.

2. Ironically, Thompson, at Cooper's request, had already been nominated for the position of assessor of the Fourth District; the nomination was withdrawn, also at Cooper's request. This time, however, the President did not heed Cooper's desires, instead nominating Edward H. East for the district attorney's post. East resigned the appointment shortly after receiving it, thereby throwing the whole situation into confusion. Throughout 1867 the position remained vacant, despite the President's efforts to fill it. In August Thompson himself resubmitted his claims for the appointment but to no avail. Cooper to William G. Moore, Apr. 12, 1867, Tels. Recd., President, Vol. 5 (1866–67), RG107, NA; Ser. 6B, Vol. 4: 228–29, Johnson Papers, LC; *U.S. Off. Reg.* (1867); Thompson to Johnson, Aug. 2, 1867, Appt. Files for Judicial Dists., Tenn., RG60, NA.

3. For further developments regarding the district attorney appointment, see Edwin R. Glascock to Johnson, July 15, 1867.

From James R. Doolittle

Private

Washington   Apl 19 1867

Dear Sir;

In the case of the Naval Officer of the city of New York.

I am inclined to think that Franklin will be laid over and not acted on.[1] This will leave a vacancy. It is the opinion of many that as this office became vacant before the passage of the Tenure of Office bill that the Executive has the power to fill the vacancy. You will doubtless take the opinion of the Attorney Genl. upon the point.

It is very desirable that it should be filled and in the hands of a real friend.

Among the names presented, the name of Col Ludlow[2] has stood prominent for a long time and what makes him entitled to the highest consideration his appointment was specially desired and recommended by Dean Richmond, Tilden[3] and others who represented and still represent the great mass of those who sustain your administration and upon whom we must rely to overcome that wild and crazy radicalism at the North which in its tendencies is so dangerous to constitutional liberty.

J. R. Doolittle

ALS, DNA-RG56, Appts., Customs Service, Naval Officer, N.Y., William H. Ludlow.

1. Cornell S. Franklin did not receive the appointment of naval officer at New York City. See Deen to Johnson, Mar. 7, 1867.

2. William H. Ludlow was not nominated for the naval officer position by Johnson. See Dix to Johnson, June 19, 1866, *Johnson Papers*, 10: 597.

3. Samuel J. Tilden.

From John P. Holtsinger

Greenville   April 19, 1867

Sir.

With your indulgence, I will trouble you again, tuching the lot of land, which Sam. Johnson, Colored, asked you to donate the Colored people of Greenville.[1] The facts are these. The Freedsman's Bureau, has proffered to the colored people of Greenville if they will procure a good title to a lot of ground and rear the frame of a house upon it, that they would advance the means to finish it. Sam. handed me the letter, over the signature of Col. R. Johnson,[2] which contained your kind offer to the Freedmen. Sam. showed it to those who understood the matter. And it was decided that without a title to the lot, the Bureau would give no aid. Sam was very much discouraged. I told him I would write to you, again, and state facts to you. The lot of land selected is situated *thus*. The Reble graveyard is located imediately in the corner, where Mrs. William's[3] woodlot and the Lasley[4] field bound your land North, and West. It is small not more than 1/8 of an acre. Sam. wants his lot just joining between it and town. *The Radicals* have not met the expectations of the Freedmen, and they are loosing confidence in them. I Send in letter a rough plot, of the situation. It will not disfigure your plot of land a great deal. And if you can donate from one half, to one acre to the colored people of our town, please do so.[5] If not please let me know the most reasonable terms upon which it can be purched. Pardon me for this intrusion.

President we all want you to come and see us. We want a visit from you,

after the old *fashioned sort*. I want yout to come to Greenville the 12 day
of next June, the Sixth anaversary of your departure. Come if posible.
May Heaven grant you the prvlige, of visiting your home, and large circle
of friends in Old Greene once more.

John P. Holtsinger

ALS, DLC-JP.
  1. See Samuel Johnson to Johnson, Mar. 25, 1867.
  2. President Johnson's son Robert.
  3. Probably Catharine D. (b. *c*1802), widow of Alexander Williams. 1850 Census,
Tenn., Greene, Greeneville, 284; (1860), 10th Dist., 91; Goldene F. Burgner, comp.,
Greene County, Tennessee Wills, 1783–1890 (Easley, S.C., 1981), 109.
  4. Most likely Alexander Lasslie (1793–1869), a farmer. Buford F. Reynolds, comp.,
Greene County, Tennessee Cemeteries (n.p., 1971), 246; 1850 Census, Tenn., Greene, 10th
Subdiv., 595.
  5. Johnson responded to Holtsinger's letter by instructing him to "select the lot wanted
have it surveyed, plat made, and a deed drawn up . . . and send the instrument to me. I will
convey the land to them without charge." Johnson to Holtsinger, Apr. 27, 1867, Johnson
Papers, LC.

From John W. Leftwich [1]

Memphis Tenn   Apr 21st 1867

Sir

The "Memphis Post" the organ of Radical Brownlowism in West Tenn
is daily threatening us with what the "Militia" are going to do and many
property owners in the Country are being intimidated into seeming affil-
iation with the Radical Party.

May I say "the *National* Army and regular Army officers will protect
the People against this partizan organisation?" I know the condition of
Tennessee gives you much anxiety and I do not wish to add to it. This
will save us and the State. Nothing else will.

Begging an early answer . . . [2]

[John W. Leftwich]

L, DLC-JP.
  1. Although the signature is missing from this extant copy, the letter is definitely in
Leftwich's handwriting. Moreover, a clerk noted on the cover sheet that the letter was from
Leftwich.
  2. No reply from Johnson has been uncovered.

From Edwin R. Glascock

[Nashville, Tenn.] [1]   April 22nd, 1867.

Dear Sir—

With your permission I would respectfully withdraw my resignation
as Marshal for the Middle District of Tennessee, [2] though I beleive it was
understood between us, while in Washington last winter, that it was

withdrawn. I so took it. Under the provisions of the Bankrupt Law, I will be able to make a living out of the office.[3]

Politically speaking the people of Tennessee, are in a bad fix, from the efforts of bad men in high places, though of this you are well aware, and how long this state of things is to continue, the future will have to develope.

There is to be a Convention here next Saturday of the Radicals to nominate a Candidate for Congress for this District.[4] The Candidates are the *Hon*. John Trimble, of whom you know, the Hon. Judge Lawrence of the Freedmens' Beaureau,[5] and Judge Palmer,[6] late of the Army. Both of the latter gentlemen are *sweet nuts* in cracking time, and if you are to be cursed with them in Congress next winter, I can but feel sorry for you and the country. They are endeavoring to foist themselves upon the people here and take them altogether we shall never see their like again. It does seem that we are to be cursed with such *trash*, to the end of time, but I hope for the best.

All eyes are tuned to you for succor, and confidently beleive you will ultimately triumph over all opposition, and that you will be able to right the Ship of State, and when the Bone & Sinew of the country have a voice in the matter, they will come to your rescue;—they have an abiding faith and confidence in your honor and integrity.

The *Hon*. Horace Maynard is here, looking as wise as ever, and the *Hon*. Wm. B. Stokes is croaking over his District, and edified a small crowd at the Capitol a few nights since.[7] How happy the dear people should feel to have such *great* leaders. The Lord deliver us, I say.

The appointment of Mr. Embry as Post Master here,[8] has created some consternation, and disappointment among a few. All right. Should any thing transpire here worthy of note, I will advise you. My respects to your household. Accept for yourself my warmest friendship and esteem.

E. R. Glascock

ALS, DLC-JP.

1. Internal evidence indicates that Nashville was the place of origin of Glascock's letter.

2. Glascock, who had held the marshalship of the Middle District since 1865, continued to serve in this post through 1869. *U.S. Off. Reg.* (1865–69).

3. The new bankruptcy law provided that marshals would serve as "messengers" in bankruptcy proceedings. Not only were certain duties prescribed in the law for messengers but also fees and other expenses. Obviously Glascock calculated that he would reap these fees and compensations in addition to his marshal's salary. See *Congressional Globe*, 39 Cong., 2 Sess., Appendix, pp. 230, 236.

4. Glascock was mistaken about the convention scheduled for Saturday, April 27. It was not for the purpose of choosing a congressional nominee (this would be done at the mid-May convention); instead, it was to select delegates from Davidson County to attend the forthcoming congressional district convention. The April 27 convention chose a delegation "made up of many of the most active, intelligent and influential white and colored Republicans." *Nashville Press and Times*, Apr. 22, 29, 1867. Concerning the May congressional convention, see Edward H. East to Johnson, May 15, 1867.

5. John Lawrence (1824–1889), a native of Ohio, was a United Brethren clergyman who moved to Nashville to serve as a judge in the freedmen's court and as an official in the

Freedmen's Bureau. In August 1867 Lawrence was appointed by Gen. W. P. Carlin as a special agent to assist black laborers who had lost their jobs. Afterwards, he became a Nashville attorney. William Coyle, ed., *Ohio Authors and Their Books* (Cleveland, 1962), 375; Everly and Pacheli, *Records of Field Offices*, pt. 3: 447; Nashville directories (1877–89); *Nashville Republican Banner*, Aug. 6, 1867.

6. John M. Palmer (1814–1876) studied and practiced law in Ohio before the war and was judge of the court of common pleas. During the war he was a captain, 65th Ohio Inf. By early 1867 he was operating a large sawmill at Johnsonville on the Tennessee River. The mill was burned by incendiaries in February of that year. Palmer was under contract with the federal government to manufacture and provide coffins for the reinterment of deceased Union soldiers. In 1868 before a congressional committee he sought special payment for his services. J. A. Kimmell, *Twentieth Century History of Findlay and Hancock County, Ohio* (Chicago, 1910), 122; *Cincinnati Commercial*, Feb. 21, 23, 1867; *Senate Reports*, 40 Cong., 2 Sess., No. 89, pp. 1–7 (Ser. 1320); *Off. Army Reg.: Vols.*, 5: 154; Powell, *Army List*, 811.

7. Glascock's reference here is to the speech which Stokes gave at the state capitol building on April 18. The next day's newspaper carried an account of the "grand mass meeting at the State House" and a lengthy version of Stokes's speech. See *Nashville Press and Times*, Apr. 18, 19, 1867.

8. Bowling Embry served two years as Nashville's postmaster (1867–69). *U.S. Off. Reg.* (1867–69).

From Andrew J. Steinman [1]

Lancaster Pa   April 22 1867

Sir—

We understand that the Senate last week confirmed, as Collector of Internal Revenue of this District, Mr. Wiley,[2] a Republican, pressed by Senator Cameron, and for Assessor, Mr. Warfel,[3] also a Republican who was urged by Thaddeus Stevens.

A party of Democrats here, had combined with Mr. Wiley to procure his nomination for Collector, on condition that he through Mr. Cameron, would obtain the confirmation of their candidate for Assessor.

Another party had combined with Thaddeus Stevens to procure Warfel's appointment as Assessor and that of a Democrat as Collector.

The Democratic party of the County was not consulted in regard to this trading, but if they had been I am sure, they would have discountenanced it.

On Thursday last Mr. Wiley was confirmed as Collector, and the Democrat nominated at the same time for Assessor,[4] was rejected. Mr. Cameron being thus satisfied, through some means, Mr Warfel, Stevens friend, was on Saturday nominated to the Senate for the Assessorship and was confirmed.

We have thus in this District a Radical Collector, and a Radical Collector [assessor]; and our Post Master at Lancaster,[5] also being a radical, we have here no friend of the administration in office.

While the Democratic party of this County, does not sympathize with those of its members who have been cheated in their bargains with the opposition, it is a matter of deep regret, that the administration party here must suffer so severely, from its total deprivation of the patronage of the Government. The loss of the Assessors office will be particularly felt, as it will involve the removal of many of our friends in subordinate positions.

I am led to believe that you have consented to nominate for these offices, two of your political enemies through some gross misrepresentation of facts, made to you; and I feel it to be my duty to make this statement of the case to you for your information and in justice to the party of which I am the official head in this County.

Trusting that, if you have been *deceived* into making these nominations, you may feel empowered to *withhold Commissions* from the appointees, or *in some other way*, may be able to *foil this cunningly executed scheme of your enemies*, and begging to refer you to the Hon. J. S. Black or the Hon. S. J. Randall for any desired information as to myself.

A. J. Steinman
Chairman Dem. Co. Committee of Lancaster County.

ALS, DNA-RG56, Appts., Internal Revenue Service, Assessor, Pa., 9th Dist., A. J. Steinman.

1. Steinman (1836–1917) was a prominent Democrat, lawyer, and also editor and publisher of the *Lancaster Intelligencer*. He became involved with ownership of the Penn Iron Works as well. *Biographical Annals of Lancaster County*, 46–48; *NUC*.

2. William M. Wiley, a Lancaster contractor and iron founder, was nominated as collector on April 15 and approved by the Senate four days later. Lancaster directories (1859–63); Ser. 6B, Vol. 4: 89, Johnson Papers, LC; *U.S. Off. Reg.* (1867).

3. John B. Warfel.

4. Perhaps a reference to Robert B. Patterson (1824–1901), who was nominated as assessor on April 15 but rejected by the Senate three days later. Ser. 6B, Vol. 4: 89, Johnson Papers, LC; *Biographical Annals of Lancaster County*, 326.

5. John J. Cochran (1816–1879) served as Lancaster's postmaster for a number of years until 1868. He was in the newspaper business before the war and in the late 1870s he resumed his journalistic career. Ellis and Evans, *Lancaster County*, 510.

From John Sherman

Cork Ireland   April 23rd 1867
Sir

I came to Europe at this period mainly to acquire information as to the Revenue systems of France & Great Britain and especially to promote uniformity in Coinage weights and measures.[1] I expected at the time that Mr. Kasson[2] of Iowa would be engaged to promote postal arrangements for the P.O. Dept. and I expected much assistance from him upon the matter of Coinage with which he is very familiar. I now understand his appointment as Post office agent with authority to negotiate Postal Treaties has not been made. I sincerely trust that for the public service he will be at once appointed. No more useful duty can be rendered than to facilitate and cheapen the passage of letters from our Country to Europe.

Every letter is an emigrant agent, & we want now all the surplus labor of Europe.

I came away so very rapidly that I did not call to express my obligations in the appointment of Col Sherman as Judge of the Northern District of Ohio.[3] Though I was not in a position to ask it and therefore did not mention it to you yet I was much gratified at the appointment and am glad to know that it was so kindly received. I have no doubt this appointment will prove a good one and that you will never regret it.

John Sherman

ALS, DLC-JP.

1. Sherman was accompanied by John A. Kasson and Col. Henry A. Howard. He returned by mid-July 1867 and resumed his Senate seat. Henry A. Howard to Johnson, Apr. 24, 1867, Johnson Papers, LC; *Washington Evening Star*, July 15, 1867.

2. John A. Kasson was eventually appointed a special commissioner and negotiated a postal agreement with the United Kingdom on June 18, 1867. For the postal treaty's text, see the *Washington Evening Star*, July 24, 1867.

3. Charles T. Sherman was nominated and confirmed on March 2, 1867, as district court judge of Ohio's northern district. *Senate Ex. Proceedings*, Vol. 15, pt. 1: 281, 329.

From Michael A. Zabriskie[1]

(Copy)

Rio de Janeiro, April 25/67.

Sir:

I am the associate and partner of Major Perry McDonough Collins[2] of the Russian overland Telegraph—Am a citizen of the United States, but for the last four years have been most of the time in South America negotiating with the Imperial Government of Brazil for the purpose of connecting that Empire by telegraph with the United States.

In the prosecution of this enterprise the Honorable Secretary of State, Mr. Seward, under date of August 13, 1864, issued to our diplomatic representatives in South America a circular letter invoking their aid in this matter to the utmost extent consistent with their official character.

The conduct of Genl. Webb.[3] during his mission here has been of such a nature as to prevent the consummation of the business so far as Brazil is concerned, for the reason that his demands were so exorbitant they could not be complied with. It is due certainly to the few Americans who endeavor to accomplish something which shall add to the interest of their fellow-citizens at home, the support of the representative to whom they are accredited abroad.

In a word Genl. Webb has prostituted the Legation of the United States of America into a broker's office. The ears of all the Americans in the Empire are made to tingle with the recital of his degradation. Charges have been made to Mr. Seward again and again, but of course that would amount to nothing—except perhaps to a reprimand.

The Minister is very infirm and for the preservation of his health it is becoming urgent that he should return, which I learn will be in the course of two or three months. The General desires to make an arrangement by which a friend of his who acted as Chargé during his absence last year, a Mr. Lidgerwood,[4] shall perform the duties of Minister and divide the salary. Mr. Lidgerwood is a very worthy person individually, but he is in business here as a machinist, and the balance of his fellow-tradesmen think as Brazil is a second class mission they are entitled to a proper representative.

I earnestly hope that the President will, for the sake of justice, for the dignity of the Government and above all for the relief of the American residents in the Empire send us at least a gentleman, to remove the stigma that now rests on us from the disgraceful conduct of Genl. Webb.[5]

M.A. Zabriskie.

Copy, CtY-J. Watson Webb Papers.
1. Not identified.
2. Collins (c1814–1900) explored and planned for the establishment of a worldwide telegraph system. NUC; Van Deusen, Seward, 513.
3. J. Watson Webb.
4. William V.V. Lidgerwood (c1832–1910) served as chargé d'affaires from 1865 to 1869. Lidgerwood and his brother were in charge of the Speedwell iron works in New Jersey before its machinery was moved to Scotland. At the time of his death he was the London representative for the Lidgerwood Manufacturing Company. Register of the Department of State (Washington, D.C., 1872), 52; New York Tribune, July 28, 1910.
5. At Johnson's direction, Seward forwarded a copy of Zabriskie's letter to Webb on May 30. Webb replied that "Z. is a drunken Vagabond; and his charges all, triumphantly refuted." Seward to Webb and Webb to Seward, May 30, 1867, J. Watson Webb Papers, CtY.

From J.F.G. Mittag[1]

Lancaster C. H. S.C.   Apr the 27/67.

Dear Sir

Gen. D. E. Sickles the Commander of this Military District, under the late acts of Congress, has issued a lengthy document, that he styles "General Orders No 10,"[2] which among many other extraordinary provisions, contains the following desperate military edicts, Viz:

II   Judgements or decrees for the payment of money, on causes of action arising between the 19th of December 1860, and the 15th of May 1865, shall not be enforced by execution against the property or the person of the Defendant. Proceedings in such causes of action, now pending, shall be stayed; and no suit or process shall be hereafter instituted or commenced for such causes of action.

V. All proceedings for the recovery of money under contracts, whether under seal or by parole, the consideration for which was the purchase of negroes, are suspended. Judgments or decrees entered or enrolled for such causes of action, shall not be enforced.

I am at a loss to know whether his extraordinary Order was influenced by local pressure, proceeding from the broken-down aristocracy and bankrupt politicians of this state, or whether it promulgates the settled policy of the Government of the United States. And my purpose in communicating with you is to ascertain, if practicable, the fact.

The order, if it is intended to be permanent, and enforced by the Government, will ruin me pecuniarly, as it will a great number of others, who are guiltless, and who had no hand in causing and carrying on the late "wicked rebellion." We (have been kept) in a state of terrible suspense (for two long years), without any certain admonition as to what will be the end of all this military rule. The great mass of the patriotic class here now covet nothing so much as certainty—they seem to desire to see doubt and uncertainty removed, let come what will, so that they may have some certain, descriptive and permanent status. I would be very glad if you could give me the probable policy of the Government, in regard to the subject matter of Gen Sickles Order as above quoted, so that I may govern myself accordingly. The order in the points alluded to is very unjust, unequal and oppressive to many loyal people here; and its enforcement will entail upon me and my family, in my advanced age, poverty and hardships too intolerable to be borne, even by that equinimity of mind which becomes a sage and philosopher. But I desire to know the end, whether adverse or favorable, if adverse, that I may summon forth all my fortitude and direction to guide me as becomes a man amid such trying circumstances, and if favorable, that no imaginary ill or anticipated misfortune may disturb my tranquility in declining age. Your early attention to this matter will confer a favor that will not soon be forgotten by your friend.[3]

J.F.G. Mittag

ALS, DNA-RG60, Office of Atty. Gen., Lets. Recd., President.

1. Mittag (c1804–fl1870) was listed as a phrenologist before the war and a lawyer afterwards. 1860 Census, S.C., Lancaster, Lancasterville, 149; (1870), Gills Creek Twp., 12.

2. General Orders No. 10, issued April 11, 1867, with its seventeen parts, may be seen in the *New York Times* edition of four days later.

3. On May 10, 1867, Mittag's letter was referred to the attorney general. Ser. 4A, Vol. 4: 522, Johnson Papers, LC.

From Gordon Granger

New York   April 30th 1867.

Mr President,

During the late war and since its close, I have given considerable thought and investigation to our Militia System, with a view of mobilizing & perfecting the same so as to make it at all times efficient and uniform throughout the United States and Territories.

The laws of Congress, as well as those of the several States are so general in their character upon this subject, that no fixed or uniform organization can be said to exist.

Perhaps no subject connected with our National defence and public welfare more imperatively demands the early attention of the National Authorities, and probably no period since the formation of the Government could be more favorable than the present for the accomplishment of this universally admitted desirable object.

Since the Crimean War and especially since the breaking out of our civil War, Europe has been wide awake to the importance of this Subject and, has made and is still making valuable improvements in its Militia Volunteer and Conscript Systems.

The advantages claimed are apparent, such as Economy, readiness at all times to resist invation, quell insurrection, riots &C, and a prompt enforcement of the laws.

With a view of gathering all possible information bearing upon these subjects, I have thought it proper to suggest that a Commission of one or more experienced and competent Officers be ordered to Europe to examine into and report upon the various systems of European Countries as may be applicable throughout the United States.[1]

This information could be collected and, put in convenient form, in time to be laid before the War Department and the Military Committees of Congress during its next Session.

In other branches of Military Art and science, valuable information could be obtained at the same time, such as the modern improvements in Fortifications, Heavy and Field Artillery projectiles & small Arms.[2]

Gordon Granger   Bvt Maj Genl USA

ALS, DNA-RG94, Lets. Recd. (Main Ser.), File G-369-1867 (M619, Roll 552).

1. Granger's letter stirred strong reactions. General Grant, for example, emphatically opposed the notion that Granger should be appointed to the commission proposed by him. President Johnson, on the other hand, held the view that Granger had not actually applied for an appointment. Johnson took some offense at Grant's response. In late May General Townsend ordered Granger to report immediately to his regiment, but this was followed by the granting of a delay. In fact, Granger was on leave until September 1, when he took command of the District of Memphis. Grant to Stanton, May 7, 1867; Johnson to Stanton, May 15, 1867, endorsements attached to Granger's April 30 letter. See also Simon, *Grant Papers*, 17: 140–41.

2. In mid-May two correspondents, Thomas Ewing and James Dixon, urged Johnson to appoint Granger to a European investigative commission. A week later Granger himself wrote to the President to ask again for an assignment to Europe. Ewing to Johnson, May 13, 1867, Lets. Recd. (Main Ser.), File G-369-1867 (M619, Roll 552), RG94, NA; Dixon to Johnson, May 13, 1867, Johnson Papers, LC; Granger to Johnson, May 21, 1867, Lets. of Appl. and Recomm., 1861–69 (M650, Roll 20), Gordon Granger, RG59, NA.

From William H. Huestis

[Washington, D.C., ca. May 1867][1]

Sir:

Allow me to trespass upon your time for a few moments on a matter which is considerable importance to me but may not be worthy of much consideration on your part but I take the liberty of submitting the same to your excellency.

I have been informed that the present Warden of the Jail for this District,[2] has sent certain papers to you[3] which are calculated if believed, to be true to prejudice you against me and lead you to believe that I have been and am now your political enemy. I can only say that I have used my influence with my friends in the Senate to have your appointees confirmed, and to verify this I can safely refer to Col. OBeirne Register of this District, Generals Cuminger and Steadman.[4] I have taken no interest in procureing Registration of Colored people, have Registered my own name attend to my own affairs and let others do as they prefer. Since my nomination by your Excellency,[5] to supercede Mr Brown the present Warden, I find all the other applicants for the position with Mr. Brown have united against me and are exerting them selves strenuously to create a prejudice against me without Just cause.

I have now said all I desire to say concerning myself, but there is a matter which I desire to bring to your notice in my conclusion which I think is intended to operate against you and would seem highly improper. It is this, Mr. Brown the present Warden of the Jail, permits Mr. Ashley[6] and others to have access to Conover[7] lately convicted and sentenced to the Penatentiary for Perjury, in order to obtain testimony to implicate you in the assasination of the late President Abraham Lincoln, and in order to effect your impeachment, and that said Conover is boasting that he will say any thing to keep out of the Penatentiary, and that he is being retained here after sentence for the purpose of enabling the parties interested to get his testimony.[8] Robert Walters[9] one of the Guards at the Jail will prove what I state about this matter if put to the test. I have brought the forgoing facts to your notice for your consideration and respectfully submit the same.

William H. Huestis

ALS, DLC-JP.
1. Internal evidence suggests that this letter was written fairly soon after Huestis's first nomination on April 20, 1867. *Senate Ex. Proceedings*, Vol. 15, pt. 2: 776, 778, 780. See also Huestis to Johnson, Apr. 23, 1867, Johnson Papers, LC.
2. Thomas B. Brown.

3. Not found.

4. James R. O'Beirne, Henry S. Commager, and James B. Steedman.

5. The Senate decided to table Huestis's first nomination on April 20. In June he wrote Johnson a frantic letter lamenting his debts caused in large part by his work on the extension of the capitol building. He pleaded with Johnson to give him the warden's post. Nominated again on July 19, he was speedily confirmed on July 20. *Senate Ex. Proceedings*, Vol. 15, pt. 2: 776, 778, 780, 848, 854, 856, 857; Huestis to Johnson, June 8, 1867, Appts. Div., Misc. Lets. Recd., RG48, NA.

6. Congressman James M. Ashley.

7. Sanford Conover was an alias of Charles A. Dunham (*fl*1869), who also used the alias James Watson Wallace. He was a New York lawyer before the war. Apparently in the South at the war's outbreak, Dunham allegedly was conscripted into the Confederate army, serving there until wounded, after which he was assigned to the War Department as a clerk. After his escape from the Confederacy, he wrote anonymous articles for the *New York Tribune* and possibly other papers. As Sanford Conover, he was an important witness for the prosecution in the Lincoln conspiracy trials. Hanchett, *Lincoln Murder Conspiracies*, 26–29, 72; Dunham to William G. Moore, Nov. 8, 1868, Pardon Case File B-567, Charles A. Dunham, RG204, NA; Sanford Conover pardon, Feb. 11, 1869, Pardons and Remissions, Vol. 9 (T967, Roll 4), RG59, NA.

8. For more on the perjury conviction and the attempt to get testimony from Dunham, see Dunham to Johnson, July 26, 1867. See also Dunham to Johnson, July 29, 1867, Johnson Papers, LC.

9. Waters (*c*1803–*c*1885), a native of Pennsylvania and a former shoemaker, worked at the jail at least during 1858–69. 1860 Census, D.C., 4th Ward, Washington, 51; (1870), 2nd Ward, 113; Washington, D.C., directories (1858–86).

From Zeno Secor & Co. and Alexander Swift & Co.[1]

Washington   May 1867

Sir

The undersigned desire to represent to your Excellency that Zeno Secor & Co. did on the 1st day of September 1862 enter into contract with the Navy Department for the construction of three monitors, the Mahopac, Manhatten and Mahongo, at a fixed price; that during the construction of these vessels, various important and expensive alterations were made by order of the Department thereby delaying their completion and adding greatly to the cost of construction,—occasioning heavy losses to the contractors.

Also that Alexander Swift & Co. did on the 1st Sept. 1862 enter into a similar contract, to construct the Catawba and Oneota, vessels of the same class and at the same price. That during the construction of these vessels the same alterations were ordered by the Department, as were made upon the first named vessels, and with the same results as to time of completion and cost of construction.

We desire to represent that in view of the heavy losses sustained by us in consequence of the alterations ordered by the Department, we have petitioned Congress for this extra cost, occasioned by the advanced price of materials and labor during the delays, but thus far have received no compensation.[2]

We are suffering greatly from the heavy losses sustained in building these vessels and having exerted our best efforts to fulfil our engagements in an honorable and satisfactory manner, and with the hope of being thereby enabled to extricate ourselves from our present pressing difficulties, we respectfully petition your Excellency for the privilege of purchasing these vessels from the Government at the price paid to us by the Government for them, and also that we may have the refusal of the purchase on the above terms, for the term of twelve month.[3]

Zeno Secor & Co. New York
Alex Swift & Co. Cincinnati

LS, DNA-RG45, Lets. Recd. from President and Executive Agencies (M517, Roll 29).
1. Secor (1808–1875) was the son of Francis Secor, who, with Robert Fulton, had built the first steamboat. Zeno Secor was a naval designer and engineer whose firm built several naval shipyards and nearly a quarter of the ironclads used by the Union in the Civil War. He later became president of the Toledo, Warsaw, and Peoria Railroad, but retired after a stroke in 1871. Swift (1819–*fl*1881), an iron merchant from Connecticut, moved to Cincinnati where he founded Swift's Iron and Steel Works, which also built ironclads for the Union. *New York Tribune*, Nov. 2, 1875; 1860 Census, Ohio, Hamilton, Cincinnati, 99; Cincinnati directories (1873, 1876, 1881).
2. Several naval boards examined the firms' claims and by December 1869 awarded them $614,312 for modifications completed after the original contract. *House Reports*, 45 Cong., 2 Sess., No. 270, p. 2 (Ser. 1823).
3. In April 1868 the Navy Department sold the ironclads *Catawba* and *Oneoto* to Alexander Swift and Co. for $755,000. The next month, however, the State Department attempted to halt the sale, arguing the firm intended to resell the ships to Peru for use in its war against Spain. The sale went as planned, and at least the *Oneoto* saw service with the Peruvian navy as the *Manco Capac*. *House Reports*, 40 Cong., 2 Sess., No. 64, p. 17 (Ser. 1358); *House Ex. Docs.*, 40 Cong., 2 Sess., No. 294, pp. 1–2 (Ser. 1343); James L. Mooney, ed., *Dictionary of American Naval Fighting Ships* (8 vols., Washington, D.C., 1959–81).

From Edward D. Holbrook

Washington   May 1st 1867[1]

Sir:

For the following reasons I ask that D. W. Ballard, Governor of Idaho Territory be suspended from said office.[2]

1st   Misconduct in Office: In this as will appear by the following official letter from the Indian department, bearing date January 30th 1867, May 21st 1867—[3]attached to this application, and marked exhibit A, & B—He, the said Governor failed and neglected for the period of nearly one year, as Superintendent of Indian Affairs, to visit the only Indian Reservation and Agency in the Territory (the Nez Perces) giving, as will appear by exhibit referred to, as an excuse, that he did not have time (See ans. to Ques. 1st).[4]

I allege that his answer to the Indian department is a gross misrepresentation, as Gov. Ballard could have visited the Agency by regular stage line then running in four days: that instead of doing so he absented himself from the Territory and visited his people in Oregon, where he remained for a long period.[5]

2d   Gross misconduct in failing to inform the Indian department that an Indian war was existing in Southern Idaho, where almost daily some of our citizens were the victims of Indian brutality and hundreds of thousands of dollars worth of property was being and still is, being stolen and destroyed by the savages. (See ans. Qus 7 in exhibit above referred to)[6]

3d   That said D W Ballard is notoriously incapable of performing the duties of the office: that by the inefficiency of his administration he has lost the confidence and respect of the people of the Territory who urgently desire his immediate removal from the Office.[7]

In conclusion I will state that much depends upon the conduct of the Superintendent to prevent outbreaks among the Indians who are at peace with the white settlers (as was the case with the Nez Perces) who have been daily threatening to commence hostilities,[8] and who have in common with our people justly lost all confidence in the present Governor. Our citizens have been murdered within the past three months within a few miles of the Capital of the Territory and their bodies mutilated in the most barbarous manner by the Shoshones, who are now and have been for months engaged in active hostilities against the whites. Large portions of the Territory have been abandoned during the past year by the whites by reason of these depredations from a tribe whose rule is to take no prisoners but to kill by dreadful tortures their captives. In short, Gov. Ballard has no influence whatever with any of the Indian tribes of Idaho Territory, and has no control whatever over their movements.[9]

E D Holbrook   Del—Idaho

ALS, DNA-RG59, Territorial Papers, Idaho (M445, Roll 1).
    1. Although this letter was obviously begun on May 1, additions within the letter and an added note at the end indicate that it was not sent until at least May 27.
    2. For an earlier attempt by Holbrook to have Ballard removed and replaced by John M. Murphy, see Holbrook to Johnson, Nov. 26, 1866, *Johnson Papers*, 11: 487–89.
    3. Lewis V. Bogy to Holbrook, Jan. 30, 1867, and N. G. Taylor to Holbrook, May 21, 1867, Territorial Papers, Idaho (M445, Roll 1), RG59, NA. At the end of this letter Holbrook adds a note to Seward, dated May 27, 1867, in which he says that he is submitting the May 21 letter which he has received "since writing the above letter."
    4. On December 5, 1866, Ballard had written to Bogy that because the legislature convened on December 3, as well as "Owing to the great distance from the Capital (350 Miles), and the pressure of other official duties, I have not as yet been able to visit them." Bogy thought Ballard should have visited the Indians but admitted that Ballard's failure was "not an exception." Bogy to Holbrook, Jan. 30, 1867, ibid.
    5. Apparently Ballard, a physician by profession, had gone to Oregon because of the illness of a family member. Wells, "David W. Ballard," *OHQ*, 54 (1953): 17.
    6. This was the so-called "Snake War." As Bogy described the situation, he had heard "from other sources that the difficulties with bands of Indians, long existing in that region, still continue." Ibid., 6, 18–19; Bogy to Holbrook, Jan. 30, 1867, Territorial Papers, Idaho (M445, Roll 1), RG59, NA.

7. In fact, in the fall of 1867 Ballard's friends in Idaho, learning that he had been removed, inundated the State Department with petitions in his behalf. W. Turrentine Jackson, "Indian Affairs and Politics in Idaho Territory, 1863–1870," *PHR*, 14 (1945): 323.

8. The unrest among the Nez Percé was primarily the result of the federal government's failure for four years to ratify the Nez Percé treaty or pay them their promised annuities. Wells, "David W. Ballard," 18–19.

9. Holbrook switched from complaining about the Nez Percé in northern Idaho to the Shoshone in the southern part of the state who did not at this time have a reservation there. Holbrook was more concerned with removing Ballard than with presenting an accurate picture of Idaho Indian affairs. Howard R. Lamar, ed., *The Reader's Encyclopedia of the American West* (New York, 1977), 1107–8. For Holbrook's continued attack on Ballard, see Holbrook to Johnson, July 22, 1867.

From Hezekiah L. Hosmer

Virginia City Montana   May 2nd 1867

Our Territory is invaded by hostile Indians. We have telegraphed Grant and War Department, get no reply.[1] Can we have authority to raise eight hundred men? Gen Meagher has gone to frontier.[2]

H. L. Hosmer   Chief Justice Montana

Tel, DNA-RG107, Tels. Recd., President, Vol. 6 (1867–68).

1. Apparently during the winter Montanans heard rumors that Red Cloud and his Sioux warriors would attack the Gallatin Valley in the spring. The precipitating cause of the alleged crisis reported by Hosmer was the death of one man and wounding of another who had been traveling together with no other companions. As a result of this incident, acting governor Thomas F. Meagher generated a territorial Indian panic by telegraphing Grant on April 9 requesting permission to raise 1,000 volunteers to be paid by the federal government. Meagher to Grant, Apr. 9, 1867, Tels. Recd. by Grant (M473, Roll 47), RG107, NA; Robert G. Athearn, *William Tecumseh Sherman and the Settlement of the West* (Norman, Okla., 1956), 134, 136.

2. Apparently both Hosmer and Meagher telegraphed the War Department on April 28 but these telegrams have not been found. On May 3 Johnson telegraphed Hosmer that his telegram had been referred to the secretary of war. The next day Edward D. Townsend, assistant adjutant general, sent telegrams to Hosmer and Meagher informing them that General Sherman had authority to summon such a militia force in Montana as he deemed necessary for protection against hostile Indians. In a letter to Stanton, Sherman expressed his conviction that governors could not be trusted to call out militia because most would take advantage of every opportunity to call for volunteers, at great expense to the government. Fearing that regular troops might not reach Montana in time, Sherman authorized Meagher to summon volunteers if Indians should *enter* the Gallatin Valley. Meagher took liberties with these instructions, however, and eventually secured about 250 volunteers (fifty of them officers), resulting in bills to the government of more than one million dollars. Ibid., 139–43, 148; Johnson to Hosmer, May 3, 1867, Tels. Sent, President, Vol. 3 (1865–68), RG107, NA; Townsend to Hosmer and Townsend to Meagher, May 4, 1867, Tels. Sent, Sec. of War (M473, Roll 91), RG107, NA; Sherman to Stanton, May 4, 1867, Lets. Recd. (Main Ser.), File W-286-1867 (M619, Roll 601), RG94, NA.

From William H.C. King
IMPORTANT
Confidential

New Orleans, May 2 1867

I write hastily on a matter of *great importance.*

The day for registration here expires on 15th inst.[1]

By reason of the arbitrary course of the registrars, giving their own absurd interpretations of the law—disqualifying whom they saw fit— our people, disgusted, have not gone forward to register.[2]

The *Negroes* crowd the registry office, and the result is, as you can suppose, a great, very great preponderance of Negro registration.[3]

Can you not order Gen. Sheridan *to extend the time for registration one month*—say to the 15th of June.

Then, if by the law, you have not the power, can you not *bring influences* to bear to accomplish that result.

If you do this we will carry city and State.

If not I am afraid we will be defeated.

For Heaven's sake, *give this your* IMMEDIATE *attention.*

A word in private from the Attorney General on this subject would give great confidence to your friends here.

I write, also, to Attorney General Stansberry.[4]

There are a thousand strong reasons for the urgency of this matter, which I doubt not, you will readily perceive.

I write in haste *and at the request of your most strenuous supporters, who are at home, looking to the best interests of the country, and not annoying you for office at the capital.*[5]

Wm. H.C. King

ALS, DLC-JP.

1. Registration began in New Orleans on April 16 and in the rest of Louisiana on May 1. It was to run through May 15 in the city and June 30 in the rest of the state. However, there were extensions of these deadlines. *New Orleans Picayune,* Apr. 16 (morning), Apr. 21 (morning), 1867; Simon, *Grant Papers,* 17: 125.

2. Sheridan stringently interpreted the "unspecified 'executive and judicial' officers" of the Confederacy whom the reconstruction acts did not permit to vote and thus included even those who had held such posts as school board member, policeman, city councilman, or public auctioneer. Apparently most officeholders and former Confederate soldiers did not try to register at first. Dawson, *Army Generals and Reconstruction,* 49.

3. When the extended registration period finally closed on the first of August, 127,639 Louisianans had registered, of whom 82,907 were black. Ibid., 55.

4. The letter to Henry Stanbery has not been located.

5. On May 7 Johnson's secretary, William G. Moore, telegraphed King, "Your letter has been received. All will be set right." On the same day Secretary Stanton wrote to Grant, "In General Sheridans order relating to the registering of voters in the Parish of New Orleans, he directs that the registry must be completed by the 15th of this month. The President is of opinion that the time allowed by General Sheridans order, as above mentioned, is too short for a full and fair registry and that so much of said order as limits the registry to

the 15th of May should be rescinded. You will please communicate this to Major General Sheridan." Grant telegraphed Sheridan to this effect on May 9. The next day Sheridan replied that he "had already extended the time in the city until the thirty first (31st) of May." Although Louisiana had begun voter registration earlier than the other military districts, by late June Johnson had asked that Sheridan keep registration open until August 1, the date on which the other districts would close their books. Sheridan was reluctant to do so, having already extended the deadline again to July 15, but eventually Grant persuaded him to do as Johnson had requested. Ibid., 54–55; Moore to King, May 7, 1867, Tels. Sent, President, Vol. 3 (1865–68), RG107, NA; *House Ex. Docs.*, 40 Cong., 1 Sess., No. 20, pp. 68–69 (Ser. 1311); *Senate Ex. Docs.*, 40 Cong., 1 Sess., No. 14, pp. 235–39, 252 (Ser. 1308); Simon, *Grant Papers*, 17: 125.

From John W. Leftwich

Memphis Tenn   May 2d 1867

Sir

Col Saml. Tate starts to Washington to-night, and hopes to have an interview with you.

Your ungenerous disregard of my opinions, relative to the appointment of U.S. Marshall for West-Tenn, determined me never again to volunteer my advice even in matters of local interest;[1] but the crisis is so grave that *I beg* you to hear Col Tate attentively.

His knowledge of our wants is *practical*, and his opinions cannot be disregarded, if you feel the interest I believe you do in, the welfare of Tennessee.

We hope you will be able to embrace Memphis in your visit to North Carolina.[2]

Jno W Leftwich

ALS, DLC-JP.
1. See Leftwich to Johnson, Apr. 10, 1867. By the time of the May 2 letter from Leftwich the marshal's post had been filled by James M. Tomeny.
2. The President visited North Carolina in early June but did not travel to Memphis or any other Tennessee location.

From Benjamin H. Hill

Athens Ga.   May 3rd 1867.

Sir:

In July 1865 you were so kind as to say that if any attempt should be made to disturb my property, you would send me a pardon.[1]

Under a late Act of Congress any non-resident party to a suit involving over 500$ can transfer the case at any time before final trial from the State to the U.S. Courts.

Some of the most important causes in which I am engaged have been so transferred, and Judge Erskine[2] holds I can not follow them, nor practice at all in his court, without a pardon.

I need scarcely say my *chief* property is my profession, and this state of things does seriously depreciate it. Knowing how you are pressed on this subject, I have been very reluctant to trouble you, and would not have done so but from this necessity which no act of mine has brought about.

May I now expect it?

Pardon me for adding that I have watched with intense interest the progress of your contest with that bane of all banes to the peace and stability of the Republic—Northern Radicalism. Surely, Surely, the Northern people can not require many more lessons to teach them the plainest of all facts—that their extreme men *hate* the Constitution!

If you succeed, unnumbered Millions for all generations will bless you; and if you fail, liberty is lost forever to all the Continent.

May God grant you wisdom, and strength and victory.

Benj. H. Hill

ALS, DNA-RG94, Amnesty Papers (M1003, Roll 19), Ga., Benjamin H. Hill.
1. For references to earlier exchanges between Johnson and Hill, see Hill to Johnson, Nov. 1, 1865, *Johnson Papers*, 9: 317–18. The President pardoned Hill on May 10, 1867.
2. John Erskine.

Interview with Japanese Commissioners [1]

[Washington, D.C., May 3, 1867]

I bid you a cordial welcome to the seat of Government of the United States. You will please make know to his Majesty the Tycoon[2] my thanks for the good wishes which, in his behalf, you have expressed to me for my health, and for the happiness and prosperity of my countrymen.

I believe, without any distrust, that the desire of your Government for friendly and intimate relations between the United States and Japan is sincere. I believe this, because I am sure it is a sound principle of human nature that trust begets trust, and that jealousy is always born of envy and suspicion. Why should not the United States and Japan be friends? They are so widely separate that neither have any reason to covet what the other possesses, and that, without unnecessary provocation, neither can find cause to do the other an injury.

I am glad to see the representatives of Japan here, that I may say to them personally, and with a full knowledge that what I am saying may go abroad throughout the world, that from the first hour in which the United States were admitted to look in upon Japan, we have sought to obtain from her people no advantage which was not reciprocally beneficial to themselves; and, on the other hand, that while my own country has been tried in the furnace of civil war, as Japan now is, every word that has been uttered to us by the Tycoon of Japan has been frank and sincere, just and honorable; and that whatever difficulties have at any time arisen between some of his people and citizens of the United States, your sovereign has always done all that was in his power to avert and heal them. We are advancing our frontiers near to Japan, while we are, at the same time, connecting our ports with hers by a new, regular, and frequent steamship line.

It shall not be my fault if the two countries do not come to esteem each other the more by reason of greater commercial and social intimacy.

You will make your business known to the Secretary of State at your own convenience, and it will receive the attention and respect which is always bestowed by this government upon the wishes of a friendly nation. If beyond this it shall be in the power of this Government to aid you with disinterested advice, counsel, and assistance, they will be cheerfully afforded.[3]

National Intelligencer, May 4, 1867.
1. Ono Tomogoro and Matsumoto Indayu. Ono (d. 1882) was a mathematician who also studied navigation. The chief navigator on the voyage of Japan's first western-style warship to America (1860), he later served at the shogunate's Western Literature Research Institute. Matsumoto has not been identified. *The Japan Biographical Encyclopedia and Who's Who*, 3rd ed. (2 vols., Tokyo, 1964–65), 2: 1202.
2. Tokugawa Yoshinobu (1827–1913) became the fifteenth Tokugawa shogun in January 1867. In November 1867 he resigned his position as shogun and returned government power to the throne. The new government was known as the Meiji Restoration. *Biographical Dictionary of Japanese History* (New York, 1978), 264–65; *American Annual Cyclopaedia* (1866), 414; (1867), 416–18.
3. The commissioners arrived in Washington on May 1, accompanied by George S. Fisher, late U.S. consul in Japan, who had requested this assignment, for the purpose of purchasing ships, preferably monitors, studying naval architecture, and resolving a price dispute concerning the *Fusiyama*. They eventually bought the Confederate ram *Stonewall* for $400,000 and received a $500,000 refund on the *Fusiyama*. Beale, *Welles Diary*, 3: 87, 89, 91–92, 99; Van Deusen, *Seward*, 521; George S. Fisher to Johnson, May 3, 1867, Lets. of Appls. and Recomm., 1861–69 (M650, Roll 17), RG59, NA; *New York World*, Apr. 23, 27, 1867.

From Hugh McCulloch

Private.

Treasury Department. May 6th 1867.

My Dear Sir:—

I have read the article you enclose to me entitled "the President and the Treasury."[1] It contains some truth and a good deal of "*bosh*." Not a dollar was lost by the Boston transaction referred to,[2] and if there are honest men in the country they are at the head of the office of Internal Revenue. Great demoralization pervades the country, and great frauds are being unquestionably committed upon our revenues, particularly in smuggling and the illicit distilling of liquor, but I assure you that earnest efforts are being made to prevent them, and I hope not altogether without success. It would, however, afford me great pleasure to receive any suggestions and aid from the President for the purpose of exposing fraud and punishing scoundrels.

In exchange for the article from the "New Orleans Times," I enclose an article from the "New York Herald"[3] which may have perhaps, escaped your attention. There is no paper in the United States so mischievous in its influence as the "New York Herald."

H McCulloch

ALS, DLC-JP.
    1. Not found enclosed. See the *New Orleans Times*, May 2, 1867.
    2. Apparently a federal official in Boston had loaned several hundred thousand dollars' worth of gold certificates. Ibid.
    3. Not found enclosed. See the *New York Herald*, Apr. 29, 1867, for the article, also on recent problems in Boston's customhouse.

From Robert Morrow

Knoxville Tenn   May 6th 1867

My dear Mr President

I arrived here safely on Thursday. Have yet been able to learn but little of interest. The first thing that strikes me is the extreme activity of the Radicals and the complete want of energy and co-operation among the Conservatives. Gov. Brownlow is here and he has his officers throughout the country mustering in his Militia. They (the Radicals) have gone into the country and brought the negroes (as one of them said to me "like conscripts") into town and sworn them into their "Loyal League," which will secure their solid vote for the Radical ticket, unless something is done. The only thing that will divide this vote is public speaking to the blacks alone, and the presentation of the other side of the question. They have had but *one*. Well-informed persons say that the Radicals are losing in the white vote, and I believe this to be true especially in the mountain counties of this district. Nothing can be told certainly until Etheridge[1] speaks thro' East Tennessee. He is looked for with interest.

I trust your health is now good,[2] and your labors lighter. I will write again in a few days.

R Morrow

ALS, DLC-JP.
    1. Emerson Etheridge, Conservative gubernatorial candidate.
    2. Perhaps a reference to Johnson's bout with illness in early April. *Washington Evening Star*, Apr. 10, 11, 15, 26, 1867.

From Adolph Pintkert[1]

New Holstein, Calumet Co. Wisconsin
the 8. day of May Ad. 1867.

The sincere conviction, that Your Excellency's benevolence, extending over the whole of the people of the United States, is not therefore disregarding the individual citizen of this vast Empire, emboldens me to address these lines to You, though well aware that Your valuable time is almost entirely engrossed by the cares of Your high and responsible office.

A member of the Church, which I preside as Pastor[2] has requested me to direct his humble petition to Your Excellency, the granting of which would fill his heart with unalterable joy and everlasting gratitude.

Jürgen Theede,[3] a German, a respectable citizen and farmer of the Town of New Holstein is so blessed by an Almighty Providence, that in a most happy union with his wife Emilie, nee Born,[4] seven hearty boys were born to them in uninterrupted succession, as follows:

1. Johann Wilhelm Theede, born Oct. 24, 1859 christened Dec. 17. 1859
2. Michael Friedrich Theede. " January 3, 1861 " " April 1. 1861.
3. Hermann Gustav Theede " March 29, 1862 " " June 14. 1862
4. Heinrich Edward Theede born May 14, 1863 christened June 7, 1863
5. Jürgen Carl Theede " Sept. 17, 1864 " " Octob. 23. 1864
6. Gustav Theede " January 10. 1866 " " Febr. 14, 1866
7. ___ ___ Theede " March 25 1867[5]

As now in the old country, from which he emigrated to the United States, it is a time-honored custom, that the sovereign Ruler of the Country allows his name to be entered on the baptismal register as sponsor to the seventh boy born in uninterrupted succession in the same family, Mr Theede, in his love and confidence to the President of his new fatherland, makes bold to petition Your Excellency to kindly take upon you this christian duty and allow your name to be entered upon said register as one of the Sponsors of the newly born baby.

I consequently supplicate Your Excellency to kindly grant this petition, to name the day when the baptism is to take place, and allow your name to be registered as Sponsor to the said infant.[6]

For myself I have to ask pardon for requesting a few lines in answer to our humble petition, signing my name with the deepest reverence as . . .

Adolph Pintkert,
Paster of the evangelical Church at New Holstein, Wis.

ALS, DLC-JP.

1. Pintkert (c1826–fl1871) apparently served churches in Pennsylvania and New York before moving his family to New Holstein about 1864. 1870 Census, Wisc., Calumet, New Holstein, 257; Diamond Jubilee pamphlet for St. John's Evangelical and Reformed Church, New Holstein, Wisconsin (1940) [New Holstein Public Library], p. 3.

2. The New Holstein Evangelical Protestant Congregation was organized in February 1865 and Pintkert became its first pastor. In addition to his ministerial duties he also served as organist, janitor, and church secretary. Ibid., pp. 3–7.

3. Thede (c1828–fl1880), a native of Holstein, Prussia, had emigrated to New Holstein, Wisconsin, by about 1858. In 1870 he had $2,500 worth of real estate and personal property worth $720. He was one of the original members of Pintkert's church. Ibid., p. 4; 1870 Census, Wisc., Calumet, New Holstein, 246; (1880), 107.

4. Emilie (c1838–fl1880), also a native of Prussia, kept house for her growing family. 1870 Census, Wisc., Calumet, New Holstein, 246; (1880), 107.

5. The seventh son, Wilhelm (1867–fl1880), was attending school in 1880. 1870 Census, Wisc., Calumet, New Holstein, 246; (1880), 107.

6. Johnson agreed to be listed as a sponsor for the Thede baby although he did not specify any date for the baptism. Johnson to Pintkert, May 22, 1867, Johnson Papers, LC.

From James R. Doolittle

Private

Washington   May 9 1867

Dear Sir

No language can express my regret that under the influence of such men in the House as Kasson & Schenck[1] the Bill introduced by the Special Committee on Indian Affairs[2] and which passed the [Senate] failed in the House.[3]

I have no more doubt than I have of my existence that had it passed and the Boards been organized the present Indian War[4] might have been entirely avoided.

My soul was deeply wounded at what I regarded the greatest of mistakes when that measure was lost.

The present war will cost us $50,000,000, I fear and more.

The whole expense of such boards including escorts would not exceed $500,000.

And peace once established, these Boards could maintain it with little military aid.

If now such a man as Mr Dole or Mr Bogy with Bishop Whipple of Minnesota,[5] and some general, Hancock perhaps,[6] could form a commission[7] to see them it might still hasten an end to the troubles. Old father Schmidt[8] of the Catholic Church who knows every chief of the Sioux would be worth more than 5000 cavalry men to make peace.

If this war continues it must be one of extermination and will rage from the Assinniboin[9] in British America to Mexico.

J R Doolittle

ALS, DLC-JP.

1. John A. Kasson and Robert C. Schenck.

2. Also known as the "Doolittle Committee" after its chairman, the committee, made up of members of both houses of Congress, was appointed in March 1865. The committee was supposed to investigate the condition of the Indians and the treatment they received from civilians and the military. The committee's report was published in January 1867. Donald Chaput, "Generals, Indian Agents, Politicians: The Doolittle Survey of 1865," *WHQ*, 3 (1972): 269, 271, 273.

3. The bill (S. 204) divided the western states and territories into five districts, each to be served by a three-member board with both civilian and military members who were to perform annual inspection visits to each tribe in their district. After passing the Senate, the bill was introduced in the House on January 29, 1867. There, Schenck attached an amendment which actually changed the entire bill to a proposal for a transfer of the Indian Bureau

from the Interior to the War Department. This amended bill passed the House but was rejected by the Senate. Led by Kasson, the House voted not to give up its version, but to set up a conference committee. Such action, however, came too late in the session of Congress. Ibid., 281; *Congressional Globe*, 39 Cong., 2 Sess., pp. 843–44, 898–99, 1662.

4. In the spring of 1867 multitudes of rumors about Indian attacks and atrocities, given credence by unconfirmed newspaper reports, alarmed the country. Early in May there was an Indian panic in the Montana Territory. Athearn, *Sherman*, 116–25. See also Hezekiah L. Hosmer to Johnson, May 2, 1867.

5. Former commissioners of Indian affairs William P. Dole and Lewis V. Bogy. Henry B. Whipple (1822–1901) became the first Episcopal bishop of Minnesota in 1859. He was tremendously concerned about the Chippewa and Sioux Indians in his state and worked diligently on their behalf. He gave the federal government advice on Indian matters and served on several commissions. *DAB.*

6. Winfield S. Hancock. If Doolittle had known about Hancock's April 19 order to burn a Cheyenne and Sioux village, he probably would not have recommended Hancock for a peacemaker post. *Washington Evening Star*, May 2, 1867; Robert M. Utley, *Frontier Regulars: The United States Army and the Indian, 1866–1891* (New York, 1973), 116, 118.

7. A commission headed by Gen. Alfred Sully had already been sent to the Northern Plains to meet with the Sioux. An act of July 20, 1867, appointed yet another seven-member peace commission, this one including Commissioner of Indian Affairs Nathaniel G. Taylor and Gen. William T. Sherman. Ibid., 113, 131–33.

8. Pierre Jean DeSmet (1801–1873) was a Belgian Jesuit who in the 1840s was involved in missions to the Indians in Iowa, Montana, Oregon, and elsewhere in the upper Midwest. The U.S. government frequently called on him to assist in negotiations. Apparently DeSmet did go to meet with the Sioux in 1867 but soon had to return to St. Louis because of illness. John J. Delany, *Dictionary of American Catholic Biography* (New York, 1984).

9. The Assiniboin were Plains Indians of Montana and Canada. They were often middlemen in the white-Indian trade and generally friendly to whites. Lamar, *Reader's Encyclopedia.*

From Garland B. Lipscomb et al. [1]

Marshall Texas   May 9th 1867.

Sir:

We the undersigned practising attorneys in the sixth judicial District of the state of Texas, feel it our duty to call your attention to the enclosed public order No. 13[2] issued by Gen. Griffin[3] on the 27th April last the practical effect of which has been to close the civil courts of this District, and we understand, throughout the state. It will be perceived by your Excellency, that the oath required of jurors, by this order, is the same, if not more stringent, than was required of officers under the act of Congress of July 1862, known as the test oath.[4] When the late war broke out our people were as unanimous for it, as they are now for peace and good order; all these aided or simpathised with the south; all now are for a restoration of the Union on the principles of the Constitution. Hence it is believed that no county in the state can furnish the requisite number of jurors possessing the qualifications required by Gen. Griffin's order, unless we resort to the colored population, and that we are not willing to do in consequence of their want of intelligence. We are prosecuting many suits in the civil courts in favor of citizens of the Northern states, and other portions of the Union, and we are not willing to risk the causes of our clients in the hands of such jurors. Our jails are full of criminals white and black, and they will have to continue in confinement at enormous expense to the public, unless this order of Gen Griffin can be modified so as to give the courts the benefit of intelligent jurors. The only qualification required of a juror in this state, is that he shall be twenty one years of age, and shall be an elector of the most numerous branch of the Legislature. All men in the state will be such under the provisions of the military Bill and supplement, who are not within some of the exceptions to amnesty contained in your Excellency's Proclamation of the 29th of May 1865 and who have not taken an oath to support the constitution of the United States, and afterwards joined in the rebellion. This order of Gen Griffins imposes hardships upon the people of Texas not contemplated by the Bill under which he received his appointment, for under it no citizen is disfranchised, with the exceptions before stated, but under this order the disfranchisement is almost universal except as to the colored population. Heretofore in this state every voter was a juror, and it is believed that the true construction of the military bill referred to contemplates the same thing, and if such be the fact, Gen. Griffin is imposing onerous and unwarranted burdens upon the people of this state. We therefore respectfully call your Excellency's attention to the subject, that these burdens may be removed, if in your Excellency's opinion sound policy would dictate such a course. Jury trials have ceased in this District and can not be renewed unless the order referred to can be rescinded or modified.

LS, DLC-JP.
    1. Lipscomb (c1834–c1877) was a native of Tennessee. Fourteen other lawyers signed the letter with him. 1860 Census, Tex., Harrison, Beat No. 5, Marshall P.O., 103; Dorothy Garr Helmer, comp., *Lipscomb 300 Years in America, 1679–1979* (Indianapolis, 1979), 313.
    2. Circular No. 13, Apr. 27, 1867, attached to J. W. Throckmorton to Johnson, May 2, 1867, Office of Atty. Genl., Lets. Recd., President, RG60, NA.
    3. Charles Griffin (1825–1867), a West Point graduate, saw extensive action in the Mexican and Civil wars. By 1865 he had attained the rank of major general of volunteers and colonel in the regular army. In 1866 he was given command of the District of Texas; he refused to leave his post at Galveston during a yellow fever epidemic and died of the disease in September 1867. Warner, *Blue*.
    4. The prospective juror had to swear that he had never voluntarily borne arms against the U.S.; never given voluntary aid, encouragement or support whatsoever to Confederates; nor sought, held, or exercised any Confederate office. He also had to swear future loyalty. Circular No. 13, Apr. 27, 1867, attached to J. W. Throckmorton to Johnson, May 2, 1867, Office of Atty. Genl., Lets. Recd., President, RG60, NA.

From John T. Monroe

Washington, May 9th, 1867.

Sir:

I have been informed that certain charges are now pending against me alleged as reasons for my removal from the office of Mayor of the City of New Orleans.[1]

These charges, as I am informed, are made alone by Major General Sheridan, and from the accompanying document[2] which I have received as a copy of the charges, I am somewhat astonished to see that the reasons alleged for my deposition are those connected with the riot which occurred in New Orleans the 30th. July last.[3]

In reply, I have the honor to say that my sole object, desire and determination was on that occasion to preserve the peace and public order; that if I in my official capacity as Mayor of New Orleans did violate any law of the United States, or of the State of Louisiana, it was by no means intentional.

I am now, as I have been, since the cessation of hostilities between the United States and Confederate States, a Union man, and in the difficulties which occurred in New Orleans last Summer, I tried, to the utmost of my ability to conform my official, as well as my personal course, to the laws of the United States and of the State of Louisiana.

Since that time, if it possibly could be, I have been more devoted to the same cause, and now although I do not like the present Law of Congress usually termed the Military Reconstruction Bill, yet I pledge my word and honor that I have never violated its provisions; on the contrary when it became the law of the land, I felt it my duty as a law-abiding citizen to carry out the provisions of the same.

So far as the specific charges made against me are concerned; in the accompanying document, I beg leave to emphatically deny the allegations therein contained. And, instead of being guided by the Attorney General of Louisiana, or advised by the Judge of the Criminal Court of New Orleans, (as is therein erroniously charged) I acted solely in my own capacity as Mayor and as an old citizen of the City and State, believing that the well-being of the people of each could be best secured, in the then political condition, by the preservation of order.

So far as relates to the latter charge, I emphatically affirm that Gen. Sheridan has never had good cause to say nor has he said in the accompanying document, that in the discharge of my official duties I have ever violated the word or spirit of the Constitution and laws of the United States or of the State of Louisiana.

In conclusion, I beg to say that I am now, as I have been, not only willing but determined to assist as far as is in my power, to carry out the laws of Congress.

John T. Monroe
Mayor   New Orleans

ALS, DLC-JP.
1. Monroe had been removed on March 27, 1867, along with Judge Edmund Abell and Attorney General Andrew S. Herron. Dawson, *Army Generals and Reconstruction*, 47.
2. Not found enclosed.
3. Sheridan blamed Monroe for inciting the city police to violence or at least for failure to control their violence during the riot. Ibid.; Taylor, *La. Reconstructed*, 139.

To Edwin M. Stanton

Washington, D.C.   May 9 1867

The Secretary of War will furnish the Pres with copies of all orders issued or instructions given to Genl Sheridan relating to the discharge of his duties since his assignment to the command of the fifth district created by an act entitled "An act to provide for the more efficient Govment of the Rebel States" passed on the 2d day of March 1867.[1]

AL, DLC-JP.
1. A list, probably prepared to accompany the copies of these documents, indicates twenty relevant missives dated March 9 to May 9, 1867. Ten were from Grant to Sheridan, six from Sheridan to Grant, and four from the adjutant general's office to one or the other of the generals. List attached to Grant to Sheridan (first letter), Mar. 9, 1867, Johnson Papers, LC.

From Hugh McCulloch

Treasury Department. May 10th 1867

Sir:

I have the honor to enclose herewith a letter from the Acting Secretary of the Interior,[1] covering a copy of an Act of the Chickasaw Legislature, asking for one hundred thousand dollars ($100,000#) from the Chickasaw National Fund, held in trust for these Indians by me (ex officio).[2] I also enclose a printed copy of the Memorial of the Chickasaw Commissioners[3] in relation to the same subject.

If upon examination it is found competent and proper that this request be complied with, I would respectfully ask that you give me authority in writing to sell such portion of the U.S. Stocks held in trust for these Indians, and maturing January 1st 1868, (These being the securities which can be sold to the best advantage at the present time.) as may be required to make as nearly as possible the amount asked for.

In this connection I would call your attention to the fact that in the case of all other Indian Trust Funds the Secretary of the Interior is ex officio

Trustee, and suggest that if no insuperable objection be found, you will issue an order directing that these Chickasaw Trust Funds be turned over to him, to be kept in like manner with other Indian Trust Funds.[4] It is my opinion that the best interests of both the Indians and the Government will be conserved by this change. The Secretary of the Treasury was designated to Invest and keep these funds by a special order from the President of the United States, as provided by Section 3 of Act of April 20th 1836. Nothing in this act prohibits the Secretary of the Interior from being designated in the same manner.[5] I transmit all the papers in relation to this case now, and will make it the subject of a personal interview at an early day.[6]

H McCulloch   Secretary of the Treasury.

ALS, DLC-JP.
    1. William T. Otto to Hugh McCulloch, May 4, 1867, Johnson Papers, LC.
    2. Resolutions of the Chickasaw Legislature, Nov. 14, 1866, ibid.
    3. No printed material was found enclosed.
    4. As of December 16, 1867, the secretary of the interior held Indian securities for $2,983,000 and the secretary of the treasury held $1,308,808.20, all of it, as McCulloch wrote, for the Chickasaws. *House Ex. Docs.*, 40 Cong., 2 Sess., No. 59, pp. 2, 19 (Ser. 1332).
    5. Certainly no change had been made by December 1867. At that time, however, the attorney general, as ordered by Congress, was determining which Indian investments were not paying any interest and recommending steps to solve this problem for the benefit of the Indian funds. Ibid., pp. 1–19.
    6. A letter from the Chickasaw commissioners suggests that a negative decision was made on their request for funds. Holmes Colbert and G. D. James to Johnson, June 14, 1867, Johnson Papers, LC.

From Joseph R. Cobb

Private

Washington D.C.   11 May 1867

President Johnson

I called upon Hon James Ashley at his room at Metropolitan Hotel. After I had charged you with ingratitude, & a want of magnaminity toward our interests, I requested to be called before the investigating Committee (as a mutual protection). When he had concluded a sharp examination he said they did not want us in fact would not allow us to appear.[1] I see in the New York evening express that "Jonathan Wild" alias detective Baker and his boasted evidence upon pardons before the Committee fell through, in fact came to grief—Evening Express 9th ult.[2]

Jos. R. Cobb

N.B. I wonder if Sec'y Seward or McColloch would give me employment or an asylum in some far removed territory amidst the Russian American (*Seals*).[3]

ALS, DLC-JP.

1. The Judiciary Committee's impeachment investigation was looking into the pardon brokerage business and particularly Mrs. Lucy Cobb's role and her business with the President. Lafayette C. Baker, who had been indicted for falsely imprisoning Mrs. Cobb in November 1865, testified extensively on Mrs. Cobb's character and business. Despite Cobb's statement here that Ashley and others refused to allow him to testify, he did so on May 29 "for the purpose of making explanations relative to the charges against [his] wife." *House Reports*, 40 Cong., 1 Sess., No. 7, "Impeachment Investigation," pt. 2, pp. 2–15, 449–71, 664–71 (Ser. 1314); Baker to Johnson, Nov. 11, 1865, *Johnson Papers*, 9: 370–72.

2. Despite all of Baker's testimony, no charge concerning abuse of the President's power to grant pardons or amnesty was included in the final indictment. The New York paper reported that Baker's testimony had not been confirmed. Indeed, one claim agent, alleged to have sent a thousand pardons to the South with the expectation of at least $100 each, actually had not sent any during the specific time period. Dorris, *Pardon and Amnesty*, 351; *New York Evening Express*, May 9, 1867.

3. In the *Washington Evening Star* of June 19, 1867, it was reported that the Cobbs were moving to Colorado. Mrs. Cobb had been absent from Washington "for some months" according to the paper.

From E.D. [1]

Personal to Mr Johnson—private—he had better not read.
Strictly private

[May 11, 1867][2]

Sir,

However unaccountable the enclosed may appear, if you wish the most conclusive proof of its being genuine—even to the point of compelling the confession of the guilty party—only give me the assurance that Genl Grant will protect me, will hold me harmless on condition that I clearly convict the Senator.[3] Either drop me a line directed to E.D. New Orleans, La.[4] or perhaps it would be better just to put a line in the N. Y. Herald stating that E. D. is assured of the protection of Gen'l G & A. J. in proving the truth of certain charges against a Senator of the U.S. Genl S. was not Mr S—n's first choice.[5] The mystery of the Charleston Postmark can be very readily cleared up. If you need any preliminary confirmation of this have some one ask Mr S. how he would like having his Southern correspondence published *and watch his face*.[6]

E. D.

L, DLC-JP.

1. Not identified.

2. The date is based on a notation on the document indicating that it was enclosed with William G. Moore's letter of May 11, 1867.

3. Nothing was found enclosed, so the nature of E.D.'s information remains a mystery.

4. Moore sent the requested note: "'E.D.s' communication is at hand. The letter is important, if genuine, and its contents should be made known to the country. The protection asked will be accorded." William G. Moore to E.D., May 11, 1867, Johnson Papers, LC.

5. Probably General Sheridan and Mr. Stanton.

6. Clearly Johnson and his staff were curious about E.D. and his information, since Moore also wrote to Gen. James B. Steedman in New Orleans, instructing him to place someone in the post office to determine the name of the person who picked up the letter. Steedman did as directed and reported that five days after the letter's arrival no one had yet

collected it. He suspected, however, that "one Dr. [William M.] Daily, a Special Agent of
the Post Office Department," would have gotten the letter, "but I think he 'smells a rat.'"
Moore to Steedman, May 11, 1867; Steedman to Moore, May 23, 1867, Johnson Papers, LC.

From John C. Gaut

Nashville Tennessee   May 13th 1867.

Dr Sir.

Hoping that it will interest you to know the true condition of public
affairs in Tennessee, I take the liberty of making the following statement.

First. There has never been an instant of time in the history of the
State, either while in a territorial condition or since her admission into
the Union as a state in 1796, up to the present, when the people were as
submissive and as much disposed to be peacible, loyal and law abiding, as
they now are. Nothing, but the lack of wise and humane rulers and laws,
prevents Tennessee and her people from being contented, prosperous
and happy.

Second. There can be no question, that the people in the state of Tennessee, are nearer pressed, and have less of the liberties and privileges
common to white men, than in any state in the Union. The condition of
the people today is far worse, than that of the people of any one of the ten
Southern States now subject to military dictation. What those ten southern states may yet be subject to is yet to seen. The State government of
Tennessee, so called, administered and ruled by Gov. Brownlow and his
faction, is a burlesque upon constitutional liberty and republican government. It is far more than a burlesque, it is a despicable tryanny, usurped,
in violation of the constitution and laws, and exercised to perpetuate the
power of Brownlow & faction, at the sacrifice of liberty and freedom.
They seem to be powerless for good, but all powerful for evil and ruin.
They seem determined to crush out all independance, and integrity, of
the Judiciary, and make them subservient and willing instruments, in
their hands, in robing the people of their rights, liberties and privileges.
Gov. Brownlow is a candidate for reelection, under the third franchise
law passed since he was inaugurated Governor. He has the appointment
and removal of all the Registers of voters. He has the power by proclamation to set aside the registration of voters in any county. He has set them
aside already in many of the counties, and I believe will set them aside in
evry county, in the state, before August next, where he apprehends a majority will vote against him. Brownlows Register appoints the Judges to
hold the elections in each county. That is taken away from the County
Court. Brownlow is organizing his militia & arming them & stationing
them at different points, and will organize and arm the whole force as fast
as he can. Nearly all of the white men in the state are disfranchised. It is
difficult for conservative men to get certificates to vote though they have

been union loyal men all the time. In short Brownlow and faction intend to carry the August elections, by force, and intimidation. The people are tied hand & foot so to speak. They have no means of redress. To attempt to vote without a certificate, would be revolutionary, and in violation of the *so called* franchise law. Their votes would, & could, not be counted. Brownlow in effect will decide who shall & who shall not vote. He is the candidate and holds the game in his own hands. The people are discouraged and intimidated. Brownlow would be gratified if he could bring about a collision and bloodshed. It would do for northern consumption. He intends, as much as he can, by the aid of his military to stifle free discussion, and to intimidate the voters from going to the polls. I refer you to Brownlows Knoxville Whig May 8th 1867, which but faintly discloses his purposes.[1] If it is possible for some Federal officer, of sense and discretion, to be sent to Tennessee with some force at his command to take charge of Brownlows malitia it would be a blessing to the people of Tennessee. It is a great misfortune, that arms have been sent to Brownlow. If they could be put in charge of·some discreet Federal officer it would be a good thing. Brownlow is not to be trusted in times like these. He now has, as he always has had, a sovereign contempt for constitutions & laws if they stand in the way of his purposes. He is playing a bold game now, as I think to please the taste of the Radicals North, hoping thereby to be nominated a candidate on the Radical Ticket for Vice President.

It is impossible for the people of Tennessee ever to be happy and prosperous under such despotic rule as now dominions the people of the state—under such partial, unequal and unjust and unconstitutional laws as have been enacted by the radical majority of the legislature at the dictation of Governor Brownlow. The impeachment trial of Hon. Thomas N. Frazier[2] judge of the criminal court of Davidson & Rutherford counties for having honestly and faithfully performed his duty to the constitution and laws, last summer in the Habeas Corpus cases; by discharging the members of the legislature imprisoned by the radicals. They impeach Frazier to put him out of office & disgrace him, but mainly to intimidate the other Judges and keep them from deciding their laws unconstitutional. And I am sorry to believe, that I see evident signs, that they will be successful in intimidating many of the Judges now in office in this state.

                                                                    John C. Gaut

ALS, DLC-JP.

   1. This is probably a reference to Brownlow's extended essay, "To the Voters of Tennessee," which occupied several columns on the front page of the May 8, 1867, issue of the *Knoxville Whig*. Gaut may be referring specifically to the paragraph near the end of Brownlow's essay wherein the governor declared: "I deem it my duty to station troops, and shall do so, let the consequences be what they may. . . . I do not conceive it to be the duty of the State Guards to stand quietly by and hear any man excite the mob spirit by denouncing the Federal and State Governments—resistance to the courts—and the setting aside of their decisions by force of mob violence."

2. For an earlier reference to Judge Frazier's actions in 1866, see John S. Brien and John C. Gaut to Johnson, July 19, 1866, *Johnson Papers*, 10: 705–6. The impeachment trial of Frazier actually began on March 11 but was adjourned until May 6. It continued from that latter date until completion on June 4. Gaut was one of Frazier's lawyers. Frazier was convicted by vote of the state senate and removed from office. See *Proceedings of the High Court of Impeachment in the Case of the People of the State of Tennesse, vs. Thomas N. Frazier, Judge, etc.* (Nashville, 1867), 3, 20, 123–24, passim; Patton, *Unionism and Reconstruction*, 222–23. See also Edward H. East to Johnson, May 15, 1867.

From Robert Morrow

Knoxville Tenn   May 13th 1867.

My dear Mr President,

On Saturday the 11th instant a Radical Convention met at Athens to nominate a Candidate for Congress.[1] Gen. Jos. Cooper had been led to believe that his chances were as good as Maynard's for the nomination, and was thus persuaded to go into the Convention. He was doomed to disappointment, as Maynard received the nomination and is now the Candidate of the Brownlow party in this District. Cooper cannot now with good grace run independently. The negro delegates in the Athens Convention were for Maynard. I think that there is no doubt of the fact that Col. John Williams[2] will be the Conservative Candidate against Maynard, and he and his friends are most hopeful and confident. God grant that their hopes may be well founded, and fully realized, for the prosperity and well-being of our State depends upon their success. I did not, until I reached home this time, fully appreciate the enormity of the iniquities of Brownlowism, and its blighting effect upon all of the material interests of the State. I think that as the August election approaches, the people will rid themselves entirely of the apathy that now seems to possess them, and that the election itself will be interesting and closely contested.

Etheridge, I see, has opened the Canvass. I regret that he did not commence it in East Tennessee, for the Radicals are working harder and expecting more in this Section than in Middle or West Tennessee.

I trust that your health is good, and that you now have some relaxation from business.

R. Morrow

ALS, DLC-JP.
1. Although the *Knoxville Whig* carried announcements of the forthcoming Athens meeting, it did not publish an account of that nominating convention. Instead, it simply reported that the Athens meeting had been well attended and harmonious and had successfully nominated Horace Maynard as the congressional candidate. *Knoxville Whig*, May 1, 8, 15, 1867.
2. John Williams, Jr., was indeed the Conservative congressional candidate. Maynard soundly defeated him in the August elections. Alexander, *Reconstruction*, 157.

From Daniel W. Voorhees

Terre Haute Inda.   May 13" 1867

Mr President.

This note will be handed to you by Miss Vinnie Ream,[1] the eminent and accomplished sculptor, of Washington City.

I am informed that it is her purpose to go abroad soon in order to execute in Rome the great work with which she was recently entrusted by Congress—the statue of Abraham Lincoln. It is her earnest wish that her father[2] should accompany her.

My object in addressing you is to ask you to assist him to do so by appointing him to a Consulship in southern Europe. I know him well and when I assure you that he will do credit to your administration in such a position I but feebly state his merits. He is an excellent French and German Scholar, a ripe and intelligent observer of the world, an accomplished gentleman and a man of the purest integrity.

High however as are his own merits I make this request still more strongly in the interest of the noblest art in the world and in the interest of one who by her exquisite genious and indefatigable labor is rapidly enhancing the claims of that art to the admiration of her country men.

The success of this application is a matter of great moment to Miss Ream; and I will join my gratitude with hers, as if you had done for me the *highest personal* favor you could bestow—for such I will regard his appointment.

While you are doing so much for your country and laying so many claims to the grateful remembrance of posterity by your political labors I am sure you will be pleased to aid struggling genious in its aspirations, and establish your right to be regarded as a patron of Art.

D W Voorhees

ALS, DNA-RG59, Lets. of Appl. and Recomm., 1861–69 (M650, Roll 41).

1. Ream (1847–1914) worked as a clerk in the Post Office Department during the early years of the war. In 1863 she began sculpting, and by late 1864 her work garnered the attention of congressional friends who commissioned a bust of Lincoln. In the summer of 1866 Congress commissioned Ream to do a full-size marble statue of Lincoln for the Capitol rotunda, the first woman so honored. She traveled to Europe in 1869, accompanied by her parents, to work on the Lincoln statue. In January 1871 the statue was unveiled in the Capitol. Edward T. James et al., eds., *Notable American Women, 1607–1950: A Biographical Dictionary* (3 vols., Cambridge, 1971).

2. Robert Lee Ream (c1806–c1885), a native of Pennsylvania, was a government surveyor and recorder of deeds in Missouri and Arkansas prior to the war. During the war he held a government position, though partially incapacitated by rheumatism. Despite several letters of recommendation, including one signed by various members of Congress, there is no evidence that Ream received an appointment in southern Europe. By 1880 he was a clerk in the Interior Department. Ibid.; 1870 Census, D.C., Washington, 5th Ward, 38; (1880), 73rd Enum. Dist., 45; Washington, D.C., directories (1878–89); *U.S. Off. Reg.* (1883); Lets. of Appl. and Recomm., 1861–69 (M650, Roll 41), Robert L. Ream, RG59, NA.

From Fernando Wood

New York   May 13 1867

Dear Sir

Please consider me as withdrawing my recomendations in favor of the appointment of Genl. Egan to some responsible position. I do not wish to be held in any way responsible for the appointment if it shall be made.[1]

Fernando Wood

ALS, DLC-JP.
1. For earlier documents that deal with Thomas W. Egan's appointment, see Daniel E. Sickles to Johnson, Mar. 5, 13, 1867.

From Charles G. Halpine

32 Beekman Street, N.Y.
May 14th 1867

My dear Sir:

First let me congratulate you on the partial riddance of your White Elephant, Jefferson Davis[1]—a thing that will do more to reconstruct the South then all the schemes of Congress;—and secondly, let me thank you for your kind, but unavailing nomination of John Foley to be Assessor in Anthony J. Bleecker's place.[2] Had Mr. Foley been nominated for the vacant Collectorship in that District, he would have been confirmed; but I suppose your action was controlled otherwise than by your own wishes. I feel confident that, if I had had time, I could have had Foley confirmed in Bleecker's place; and shall hope to have this done at the next Executive Session of the U.S. Senate. With kindest regards to Col Robert Johnson, and hoping soon to have the honor of returning you my thanks in person . . .

Chas. G. Halpine

ALS, DLC-J.
1. On Saturday, May 11, Davis left Fortress Monroe to go to Richmond to appear in federal court on May 13, at which time the judge released him on $100,000 bail. Hudson Strode, *Jefferson Davis* (3 vols., New York, 1955–64), 3: 306–9. See also L. H. Chandler to Stanton, May 4, 1867; Edward D. Townsend to H. S. Burton, May 8, 1867; Stanton to Johnson, May 18, 1867, Johnson Papers, LC.
2. For an earlier reference to this matter, see Samuel J. Tilden to Johnson, Apr. 13, 1867.

From Edwin M. Stanton

Washington City, May 14th 1867

Sir:

I have the honor to submit herewith a copy of the entries contained in the memorandum book found on the person of J. Wilkes Booth at the time of his capture, certified by General Holt, Judge Advocate General, (who has possession of the book,) together with his report in relation thereto.[1]

The memorandum book was first seen by me about the 26th day of April 1865, shortly after Booth's capture and a few hours before his remains reached Washington. It was brought to my house by Provost Marshal Baker and another person, who was, I think, Lieutenant-Colonel Conger.[2]

The book was then examined by me, in presence of General Eckert,[3] Assistant Secretary of War, and was found to contain only the entries certified by General Holt, also some photographs of females. Immediately preceding the entries some pages appeared to have been cut out, but there was nothing indicating what had been written thereon or whether anything had been written, nor when or by whom they had been cut out.[4]

Immediately after careful examination of the book and its contents, it was placed in the hands of General Eckert, in the same condition as when I first saw it, to be delivered to the Judge Advocate General, in whose possession, after its delivery to him by General Eckert, I am informed and believe it has continued until the present time.

The last time I saw the book was some time last winter. It was then before the Judiciary Committee of the House of Representatives, and was, in all respects, in exactly the same condition as when I saw it first, without any change or alteration, so far as I could discover, in its contents.

General Eckert reported to me that, upon receiving the memorandum book from me, he sealed it up, and locked it up in his safe, and it continued in his possession until he delivered it to the Judge Advocate General, and that it was then in the same condition as when it was brought to my house by Baker.

Edwin M Stanton   Sec of War

LS, DLC-JP.

1. Stanton was replying to a request from Johnson for "a certified copy of the 'Diary' found upon the body of J. Wilkes Booth, together with a succinct statement of all the facts connected with the capture, and its possession by the War Department." The text of Booth's diary and Holt's report were published in various papers. Johnson to Stanton, May 9, 1867, E. M. Stanton Papers, LC. See the *Washington Evening Star*, May 21, 1867.

2. Lafayette C. Baker and Everton J. Conger. Conger (1831–1918) served during the Civil War with Ohio, West Virginia, and District of Columbia units. The last was under the command of Col. Lafayette C. Baker and engaged in the pursuit and capture of Booth. A legal resident of Montana, Conger died in Honolulu, Hawaii. Pension File, Everton J. Conger, RG15, NA.

3. Thomas T. Eckert.

4. Earlier in 1867 the House Judiciary Committee, investigating Johnson's conduct, had heard from Baker about Booth's diary and the disappearance of pages from it during its two years in the custody of the Executive Department. Many believed the pages implicated Johnson in Lincoln's assassination. However, evidence to the contrary, especially that of Baker's cousin, L. B. Baker, who had removed the diary from Booth's body, verified that the pages had been missing when the diary was taken from Booth. Hanchett, *Lincoln Murder Conspiracies*, 83–86. For the testimony on this issue taken in the Judiciary Committee's impeachment investigation, see *House Reports*, 40 Cong., 1 Sess., No. 7, "Impeachment Investigation," pt. 2, pp. 32–33, 323–33, 479–90, 450–52, 457–59 (Ser. 1314).

From Edward H. East

Nashville   May 15/67

Dear Govenor,

A few days since I found myself the recipient from you, of an unexpected honor, for which I am constrained to express to you, my thanks. I am sorry that I am so situated that I cannot except the Commission,[1] and regret my inability to express to, as I really feel, my gratitude for your kind offer, and well wishes.

The trial of Judge Frazier commenced on the 6- inst.[2] All last week, and until yesterday of this week, was spent, in skirmishing—over the organization of the court, on collateral questions. On yesterday the Prosecution introduced as a witness, Maj Gen Thomas. You will see his evidence in the papers (Union and Dispatch is the best report),[3] and will learn that the Prosecution, goes upon the idea that the opposition to the radicals—is a conspiracy against the Government, and that Judge Frazier aided in the conspiracy, by releasing on habeas corpus—a member that the radicals had arrested. Trimble Maynard, Patterson[4] of East Tennessee and a fellow named Noah (*a Jew*),[5] are the attorneys for the Prosecution. The court is dead set against us, and sustain every motion made by the prosecution. You will see from the examination of Gen'l Thomas that Trimble made an effort to involve you. I suppose he thought that this would strengthen the Prosecution, before the Senate.

Trimble and Laurence (the Bureau man)[6] are having a mixed race for Congress—each going for the negro vote alone,—and will doubtless corrupt the poor devils. I heard several speeches to-day at a Laurence-meeting of Colored citizens—made by white & black men,[7] the first I have heard—and am satisfied, that in less than two years there will be a *collision* of the races—hatred is being daily engendered, and the passions appealed to—which will find vent in a riot. I learned my first lesson to-day—in the management—and organization of that bloody picture of French Revolution,—we are as capable of its reenactment as any people in the world. Great God! the wickedness and misery—that will enter into such a scene, and result from it.

Franchise in this state is fettered with registration, with power in the Govenor to revoke at any time, at will, the Legislation of any County, and an organized and armed malitia to enforce it, upon which is also conferred the power to arrest any speaker, who in their opinion transcends the bounds of loyalty to the state Government. I need not say to you, that if Brownlow and the entire radical ticket is not elected it will be difficult to explain why. The regime they have laid out by legislative enactment— paves the way—with certainty of success.

Thanking you again for your kindness . . .

Edward H East

ALS, DLC-JP.

1. Presumably East is referring here to Johnson's appointment of him as U.S. attorney for the Middle District of Tennessee. East was nominated, approved, and commissioned all on April 20. However, the President nominated J. D. Maker on July 13, 1867, to replace East, who had resigned. Ser. 6B, Vol. 4: 228, Johnson Papers, LC. See also Edmund Cooper to Johnson, Apr. 18, 1867.

2. See John C. Gaut to Johnson, May 13, 1867. East served as one of the attorneys for Judge Frazier.

3. A somewhat abbreviated version of Gen. George Thomas's testimony is found in the *Nashville Union and Dispatch*, May 15, 1867.

4. John Trimble, Horace Maynard, and N. A. Patterson.

5. Jacob J. Noah (*c*1831–*fl*1897) had served in the 2nd Minn. Inf. during the war. In July 1868 Noah was nominated by Johnson for the position of U.S. attorney for the Middle District of Tennessee but the Senate rejected this nomination. Later supervisor of the internal revenue for Tennessee, he resigned in 1869 in order to participate in the statewide elections of that year. In 1880 Noah had become the private secretary to the secretary of war. *Off. Army Reg.: Vols.*, 7: 314; *Washington Evening Star*, June 28, 1869; 1880 Census, D.C., Washington, 18th Enum. Dist., 34; Washington, D.C., directories (1882–98); Ser. 6B, Vol. 4: 229, Johnson Papers, LC.

6. See Edwin R. Glascock to Johnson, Apr. 22, 1867. On May 16 the Radicals held a congressional nominating convention at the state capitol. The rival claims of John Trimble and John Lawrence divided the convention; after many of the Lawrence supporters bolted from the convention, Trimble received the nomination. Eventually, he ran successfully against the Conservative nominee Balie Peyton. *Nashville Union and Dispatch*, May 17, 1867; Alexander, *Reconstruction*, 158.

7. On May 15 a gathering of Lawrence Radicals—some two hundred black men and a few whites—assembled at the courthouse in Nashville for the purpose of choosing Davidson County delegates to the next day's congressional convention. A number of speeches were made by whites and blacks. The formal convention to choose Davidson County delegates had been held on April 29. *Nashville Union and Dispatch*, May 15, 16, 1867.

From Joseph H. Geiger
Private

Mobile Ala.   May 15th 1867

Dr. Sir

I write you from this branch of the "Lords vineyard" to give you the *plain truth* as to the riot of last night at this City.[1]

While Judge Kelly was speaking a policeman was having a verbal altercation with a drunken fellow who was misbehaving and siezed him for arrest. The crowd immediately around was excited but not noisy or violent. At this particular time the horses attached to the ambulance of Col Shepherds[2] 15th Infantry were frightened and started to run through the crowd. Of course every person tried to get out of the way and rushing furiously in every direction pressed against others, and some person believing it to be a riot fired a pistol, whereupon there was a general firing, some toward the speakers stand and some from it. Lights were blown out, Kelly got under the table and then got away to the Hotel—no one attempting to molest him. There was *no person* on the stand hurt. The only persons wounded & killed were opposed to the Radicals except one negro who was found dead some distance from the scene. The whole affair sprang up in a moment. There was no preparation for it. The party mostly armed were the negroes. There is not a respectable man here who does not greatly regret the occurrence. Many of them, of course do not like Kellys radicalism but there was no disposition to prevent his speaking or break up his meeting by any leading man here. I was at the meeting awhile and all then seemed attentive and were quiet.

Judge Kelly came very hastily to the "Battle House" and a guard of soldiers were thrown about the house to guard him. He was taken to his meal by military, and seemed afraid to leave here for Montgomery in the regular Steamer, having a special boat to carry him from this Wharf. He was in no more danger than I am, and could walk the streets with just as much safety. He did not need military protection any more than I do, but he called on the military for effect. It sounded more martyr-like to need protection. It would create more sensation North. It was a trump card. The whole affair will give Kelly more notoriety than all his other acts combined. I regret that the affair took place, because of the lives that were lost, because of the interruption of free speech (which the Radicals practiced on you) and because it does gross injustice to the people of Mobile.

Kelly will make a strong move to turn out Col. Mann[3] the Assessor of this District who he blames for publishing a paper which is not radical and which supports you. He is a first rate Assessor and let me urge you earnestly not to consent to his removal. There is I understand an attempt made by Mr. Flanders,[4] of New Orleans, one of Mr. Chases pets to turn out F. W. Kellogg, Collector Intl. Rev. here and get in a radical. Kellogg is a good officer, popular with every body and is your friend. Please make no changes here. I will be in Washington I hope within two weeks. Excuse length, but I have not said half I might state in regard to the difficulty.

Jos. H. Geiger

P.S. I enclose from the "Times" of this City owned by Assessor Mann.

An exaggerated depiction of Judge Kelly's reception
during his speech at Mobile.
Harper's Weekly, June 1, 1867

ALS, DLC-JP.

1. A public meeting addressed by Philadelphia congressman William D. Kelley was broken up "by a small party of ruffians" in an affair which left two persons (one white, one black) mortally wounded. *American Annual Cyclopaedia* (1867), 22.

2. Oliver L. Shepherd (1815–1894), a West Point graduate and career army officer, commanded the post of Mobile. Hunt and Brown, *Brigadier Generals*; *American Annual Cyclopaedia* (1867), 23.

3. William D. Mann (1839–1920) served in three Michigan cavalry regiments and ended the war as colonel. Settling in Mobile, he manufactured cottonseed oil, became the proprietor of the *Register*, and was appointed U.S. assessor in July 1866. In later years he patented various railroad car inventions and moved to New York City. *NCAB*, 11: 444; *Who Was Who in America*, 1: 773.

4. Benjamin F. Flanders.

From Hugh McCulloch

Treasury Department.   May 15th 1867.

My Dear Sir:—

Your reference of Mr. Smith's note[1] under date of the 13th inst. is received.

The case to which Mr. Smith refers is one of great difficulty, and one which I do not feel at liberty to act upon decidedly, without the advice of the Attorney General. The question submitted to him is whether it is a case which the government ought to prosecute; and not as to the rights of the informer. We have never paid to an informer or to a person employed as Mr. Smith anything beyond the actual expenses incurred until we were satisfied of the right of the government to the property seized and of its ability to hold it.

I have already advised you that suits are pending in New York for the Dennistown cotton[2] or its proceeds, and that in order to keep possession of it it was necessary for the government to secure the signers of the replevin bond by a deposit of five hundred thousand dollars with a Trust Company in New York, which is very much more than the cotton sold for, and which has never been returned to the Treasury, and will not be until the plaintiffs are beaten in the Courts or the case is compromised.

I have said to Mr. Smith that we are doing in this case everything that can be done both to protect the interests of the government and the interests of the informer. We have already paid him $15,000 on account of expenses &c. &c. and he must wait patiently for any further sum he may be entitled to.

H McCulloch   Secretary.

LS, DLC-JP.

1. Frank Smith. The note has not been found.

2. For information regarding the "Dennistown Cotton Cases," see Johnson to McCulloch, Dec. 8, 1865, *Johnson Papers*, 9: 497–98, and Frank Smith to Johnson, June 17, 1867.

From William W. Warden[1]

[Washington, D.C.][2]
Wednesday morning, May 15, 1867.

Mr. President.

I have made an examination with regard to the paragraphs you mentioned last night, referring to the *visit* of *Mayor Monroe*,[3] and the *"secret mission* of Senator Doolittle."

In the Washington column of the *Times, Tribune*, and *Herald*, and in the Boston papers, etc there appeared in Thursday's and Friday's[4] papers dispatches of the character you pointed out in *Monday's Tribune*.[5] I read two of those paragraph's to you, and you explained how Monroe came to see you. Thereupon I sent the following paragraph to the papers I represent:

> Paragraphs telegraphed from this city announce that ex-Mayor Monroe called on the President on Thursday last, and had a confidential talk about Sheridan's conduct, and this was published in Friday morning's papers. The fact is, Monroe did not call until twelve hours after the announcement was made, and then he was conducted to the White House and introduced to the President by R. King Cutler, a Southern Radical who was present at the interview, which lasted about two minutes, during which no allusion was made to political subjects. The call was made by Monroe simply to pay his respects as he was passing through the city en route to New York.

Notwithstanding this, the article you called my attention to appeared afterwards in the *Tribune*.[6] I called the attention of the writer of that paragraph to these facts.

He says, in brief, he did not consider that he was in anywise affecting you directly, because he does not say you did anything but give Monroe an audience.

As to the *"secret mission"* affair, something was said of it by most of the papers, and the following appeared in the *World*:

SENATOR DOOLITTLE GOING TO RUSSIA

> Senator Doolittle had an interview with the President to-day preparatory to his departure for St. Petersburg *on a secret service mission* to the Russian government. The inference is that it relates in some way to the recently ratified Russian Cession treaty.[7]

And the following in the *Tribune*:

> The expenses attending Secretary Seward's Walrussian treaty are not yet at an end. Seven millions two hundred and fifty thousand dollars in gold will not begin to cover all expenses of the job. A confidential mission has been fixed up by Mr. Seward and Mr. Johnson to the Czar of Russia. Senator Doolittle is to be the bearer of dispatches on said mission, which concerns our recent purchase of the Russian American Territory around the North Pole. Mr. Doolittle will leave here immediately. His expenses will be paid from the contingent fund of the State De-

partment. Senator Doolittle left here to-night for New-York, whence he sails on Saturday for Europe.[8]

I had nothing to do with any of these, but did send a mention of Mr. Doolittle's departure, which you will see at the bottom of the enclosed telegram to *Philadelphia* Ledger, and another to *Cin. Enquirer*.[9]

Wm. W. Warden.

P.S. I send also copy of my last paragraph on Booth Diary.[10] I have thus published substance of the testimony, having despaired of getting copy of Diary.

ALS, DLC-JP.
    1. Warden (1827–1890), a lawyer and journalist, lived in Cincinnati until the mid-1860s. At various times he was the Washington correspondent for the *New York Times*, the *New York Tribune*, and the *Boston Post*. *NUC*; Cincinnati directories (1850–68); Washington, D.C., directories (1872–90); *Washington Evening Star*, Apr. 25, 1867.
    2. Internal evidence, particularly the assertion that Warden had had a conversation with the President the previous evening, indicates that he was in Washington, D.C.
    3. Former New Orleans mayor John T. Monroe arrived in Washington on May 1 or 2. *Washington Evening Star*, May 2, 1867. See John W. Overall to Johnson, Sept. 5, 1867, Johnson Papers, LC.
    4. The *New York Times*, on Thursday, May 9, 1867, reported that Monroe and his private secretary "had a lengthy interview with the President" on May 8 in which they discussed the extension of the deadline for voter registration in New Orleans. No similar article was found in the *New York Tribune* or *New York Herald* on either May 9 or 10. A notice of Doolittle's trip, printed in the *New York Tribune* on May 10, is quoted later in this letter. See note 8.
    5. "Ex-Mayor Monroe of New-Orleans and R. King Cutler of Louisiana had an interview with the President on Saturday, and urged him to countermand the orders of Gen. Sheridan and restrict his actions under the Reconstruction bill. Monroe and Cutler have been fast friends lately, and it is given out by the judicious Johnson men that Cutler is anxious for the removal of Gov. Wells of Louisiana, that the place be given to him." *New York Tribune*, May 13, 1867.
    6. Ibid.
    7. *New York World*, May 10, 1867.
    8. *New York Tribune*, May 10, 1867.
    9. In both the *Cincinnati Enquirer* and *Philadelphia Public Ledger* of May 11, 1867, it was reported from Washington that Doolittle was traveling on behalf of railroad interests and that Seward had empowered him to negotiate with Denmark over the island of St. Thomas.
    10. Enclosed was a clipping from the *Baltimore Sun* of a special dispatch from Washington, dated May 13, 1867, concerning publication of John Wilkes Booth's diary. For more on the diary, see Stanton to Johnson, May 14, 1867.

From John Bigler

Sacramento   May 16 1867

Dr. Sir

I write you because your friend and anxious for the triumph of your policy which I regard as correct and as indicating on your part great devotion to best interests of the country.

I am frank in the expressions of my views, and I heartily despise tricksters and hypocrites.

I enclose a speech delivered by Senator *Conness* a few days after his arrival in San Francisco.[1] As he has found not fault with his speech as reported I presume no unjustice has been done him. You will see that he assails you as "recreant" to the views & principles of his party; he regards you as desiring to favor the restoration of the slave power.[2] I also enclose a letter of mine[3] called forth by a malignant attack made by *Conness* upon me a short time after my rejection by the U.S. Senate.[4] You will see by reference to my letter that I know the man well, and that I predicted what his course would be toward you in case necessary to the advancement of his own interests. Of one thing rest assured *he will not* be re-elected to the United States Senate.[5] His own party are at least free to rise against him, and there is no man in our state so universally despised by the Democracy as John Conness.

John Bigler

ALS, DLC-JP.

1. Although the speech was not found enclosed, a synopsis of the speech, delivered by Conness from the balcony of the Occidental Hotel to a crowd of serenaders on May 4, was printed in the *San Francisco Alta California*, May 5, 1867.

2. Conness referred to the "faithlessness" of Johnson, criticized his reconstruction policy, and claimed that the policy "could have no other result than the reestablishment of the power of the slaveholders who had made war on the country." Ibid.

3. Bigler's letter has not been found.

4. Bigler's nomination for assessor of internal revenue of the Fourth District of California was rejected by the Senate on January 22, 1867. Ser. 6B, Vol. 4: 347, Johnson Papers, LC. See also Bigler to Johnson, Dec. 1, 1866, *Johnson Papers*, 11: 501–2.

5. Conness, in fact, was not reelected in 1868 and apparently was not even a major contender. Hubert H. Bancroft, *History of California, 1860–1890* (7 vols., San Francisco, 1890), 7: 327–28.

From Thomas Cottman

Washington D.C   May 16th 1867

Mr. President

The enclosed telegram from New Orleans,[1] will give you an inkling of the reasons for extraordinary exertions for obtaining nominations & confirmations for U.S. Marshal of Louisiana. The investigations into the affairs of the SubTreasury & the First National Bank[2] will disclose operations not very creditable to certain parties claiming exclusive privileges to consideration from the Chief Executive of the United States. Personally I have nothing to say upon the subject as it is impossible that human discerment should be able to discriminate between *interested statements* and actualities & the appointing power should not be held responsible for mistakes made upon improper representations.

Business detains me in the United States until Wednesday 22nd instant when I leave Boston on the Cunard steamer China for Liverpool; on my way to Paris, St. Petersburg & Madrid. I had not the honor to recieve from either you or the Secretary of State, the official recognition which I had anticipated if you should not have changed your views upon the subject. Any communication addressed—No. 24 India Wharf Boston prior to May 22nd will reach me, for which you will allow me in anticipation to express my grateful consideration.[3]

Thos. Cottman

ALS, DLC-JP.
1. No telegram was found enclosed.
2. Thomas P. May, former assistant treasurer of the U.S. at New Orleans and president of the First National Bank at New Orleans, and his successor as assistant treasurer, William R. Whitaker, were accused of defalcations amounting to about a million dollars when the government suddenly closed the sub-treasury and the national bank several days before this letter was written. *New York Tribune*, May 15, 1867; *New Orleans Picayune*, May 16, 1867; *New York Times*, June 9, 1867. For more information about this financial difficulty, see William H.C. King to Johnson, May 21, 1867.
3. No indication of a response to Cottman's request has been found.

From Robert Morrow

Knoxville Tenn   May 16th 1867

My dear Mr. President

I have received at the hands of Col. Johnson notification of my appointment by you as Pay Master.[1] I said to you in parting that I wished you to dispose of this matter as you deemed *best for me*, and that I would be *better satisfied* with *your* opinion upon this point, than I would be with my own. I meant this. Lest you may have given me this appointment more because you thought I desired it than because you considered it the best for me, I will not accept or decline it until I reach Washington on the 26th instant, and see you, and learn from you your opinion in the matter. In any event the honor of your confidence shown in the appointment is sufficient gratification to me, and, if anything had been, though nothing was, needed to increase my gratitude and devotion to *you*, this would have sent the mercury in that thermometer up to the maximum. You have been to me more than a father, and if a son's affection and devotion will be of any gratification, you have it from the bottom, and with all the intensity of my heart.

I will finish my business, and leave here on the 24th.

With best wishes for your health.

R. Morrow

ALS, DLC-JP.
1. Evidently Robert Johnson notified Morrow that the President had decided to appoint Morrow as major and paymaster on May 9, 1867. After having made this appointment, the President submitted Morrow's nomination to the Senate on July 19; on that same day the Senate rejected the nomination. On the following day, however, the Senate decided to reconsider its rejection of Morrow, but then agreed to postpone the matter until December. Ser. 6B, Vol. 2: 217, Johnson Papers, LC; *Senate Ex. Proceedings*, Vol. 15, pt. 2: 847, 853, 855, 857.

From Ethan A. Allen

Columbus, Miss., May 17, 1867

Dr Sir.

Again I beg leave to make my respects to you.

I am much pleased to observe the good feeling of the people & their entire desire for a full & final settlement of all unfriendly relations between the Southern & Northern States. They are sick & weary of this continual misrepresentations of their feelings & objects. The universal desire on their part is to see the Union of the States accomplished & to be allowed to act as freemen of this great Republic. They are anxious nay their unceasing prayer is that the occurrences which have taken place resulting in the frightful loss of life & property may as far as possible be forgotten & now that one universal feeling of friendship may take the place of the estrangement which for so many years have divided our common country. Were it not for the unwarrantable conduct of many men who curse this country by their presence (Northern men too) there would be no riots, & no occurrences to mar the universal hopes of this people. The recent riots in New-Orleans & Mobile were produced by vagabonds. I send you today the "Southern Sentinel" of this place & beg you to read the account of Judge Kelley a member of Congress from Pennsylvania.[1]

The people are already bowed down to the dust by the course pursued in Congress, & such conduct by men from the North cannot fail to irritate, & I think you will agree with me in concluding that there is just grounds in the citizens of the South being goaded to madness.

It would be well if the commanding Generals of the various Departments of the South should positively prohibit *political meetings* while the Southern States are under a military Despotism. Such course would prevent the evil disposed in planning & inciting riots, for the purpose of manufacturing "Republican polital capital."

The military stationed here under Col. Gay[2] command the respect of the citizens by their peaceable Conduct—& this officer is much esteemed.

The Negroes are doing very well, & were they left alone & not at all interfered with by the "Freedmans Bureau" there would be no cause of complaint whatever, but the effect of that institution produces a *demoralizing effect* on them. The planters employ & pay them most willingly, & the negroes are satisfied with the remuneration which they receive, their pay being ample.

The dread that the approaching Congress may *confiscate* their property haunts the people like a midnight dream. Should that event *not* take place & Congress should resolve to ignore such a policy, then would confidence be in a measure restored and capital find investment, which it can *never* do in the present unsettled condition of the country.

While Genl. Sheridan commands at New Orleans just so long will you hear of riots. His course promotes such a state of things.

At a meeting of Negroes & low whites in New Orleans[3] a few evenings since Governor Wells presided & had a *negro* wench seated on his right & left hand & the meeting was opened by prayer from a Negro. Now Mr President was it not disgraceful in the Executive officer of Louisa. thus to act—should Genl Sheridan who professes to desire that good feeling should exist in his Department & who has the *Military* right to depose this fellow Wells—tolerate such conduct. I certainly believe that a Gentleman of your purity of character, & high tone will answer in the Negative. Certain it is that no kind feeling can exist where such conduct is tolerated.

A little discretion on the part of Department commanders will do much good, while neglect will produce trouble.

Citizens wish repose. The very men who pray for quietude are those who for four long years, carried the Confederate States flag triumphantly to the very gates of Washington & sought to establish the Confederacy. That struggle with all its horrors—which filled every house in these states with mourning is over & now those very men are the most *loyal* to the Federal Government who can be found in *all* our country.

Ethan A. Allen

ALS, DLC-JP.
  1. For another discussion of Kelley and the Mobile riot, see Joseph H. Geiger to Johnson, May 15, 1867.
  2. West Point graduate Ebenezer Gay (c1833–1871) served on the frontier in Kansas, Utah, and New Mexico. Remaining in the regular army throughout the war, he was often on staff duty and was breveted lieutenant colonel. During the spring of 1867, while he commanded at Columbus, Mississippi, his actual rank was captain, 34th U.S. Inf., but later that year he was promoted major of another regiment. The next year he became the commandant of the post of Austin, Texas. ACP Branch, File G-87-CB-1867, Ebenezer Gay, RG94, NA; *West Point Register*, 248.
  3. No additional reference to this meeting has been uncovered.

From George Bancroft

New York, 18 May 1867.

Dear Mr. President,

I was very much obliged to you & Mrs. Patterson for the kind reception you gave to Mrs. Bancroft. She returned greatly delighted with her visit.[1]

Yesterday I received a fresh instance of your thought for me in the commission to Berlin.[2] It is the only office in your gift, which I could accept with satisfaction; & in doing so, I hope to be able to promote the interest

& honor of the government. The German language is almost as familiar to me as the English; my studies have made me familiar with Prussian history; and the present tendency of Germany to unity interests me exceedingly. I feel sure of a kind reception, and though the climate is very severe, I shall hope we may find our residence agreeable, & I shall do all that is in my power to make it useful to the country, & satisfactory to your administration.

Geo. Bancroft

ALS, DLC-JP.
   1. No information concerning the visit has been found.
   2. Johnson nominated Bancroft for minister at Berlin on July 13, 1867, and he was confirmed two days later. Bancroft remained as minister until 1874. *Senate Ex. Proceedings*, Vol. 15, pt. 2: 788, 794; *U.S. Off. Reg.* (1867–73).

From Kate Coyle

Paris   May 18th [1867][1]

My dear President
   I know you desire to ask pardon for seeming forgetfulness of my last letter, written so long ago, I scarce remember what it contained. I therefore accept your explanation in advance, freely forgiving you. Through the letters of my husband[2] and by the paper articles I have read, I am well informed of the vexations and trials you have endured during the past six months, and know full well you have had no time to devote to absent friends.
   It is unnecessary for me to renew my assurances of continued devotion to you, and your measures—as well as of my thorough disgust with the mean, bitter, and vindictive spirit, evinced by that horrid radical Senate. Many a time and oft, have I wished for a rope about their consolidated necks, that I might pull it with an avenging power. "Whom the Gods would destroy, they first make Mad"[3] said some wise Philosopher. That destruction will inevitably follow the madness of your opposition—is to my mind a foregone conclusion. You believe in the doctrine of "Compensation" so do I. That for all your present endurance of abuse and persecution there will come a day when justice will accompany compensation to you, I most firmly hope, pray for and believe.
   I have just returned to Paris from a charming tour of Italy and a portion of Switzerland—occupying about nine weeks made in company with Mr & Mrs McGinnis.[4] Had you time to read a discription of what I saw, most gladly would I convey some of my enthusiastic impressions thereof—but I see now, not less than one hundred persons waiting in the anti-chamber for an audience with "His Excellency" and will not detain you with that which I can better relate to you when the audience is mine, and you have plenty of time and patience to hear.

This morning I learned of the death of Mr Wright—our Minister at Berlin and cannot resist the impulse in my heart to ask his place for my friend Mr McGinnis. With my experience in Europe, I know full well what is required of a Minister representing our Government at a foreign Court! know what qualifications a man should possess to fill such position acceptably and well and with my intimate acquaintance with Mr McGinnis formed during our journeyings in Europe together, I can vouch for his fitness—and most sincerely hope you will name him, as the successor of Mr Wright at Berlin. He was rejected by the Senate at a time when a spirit of vengeance ruled and governed that body. Since that time I learn that even those who opposed him most bitterly, have been conciliated by his friends—and would now make amends for their unjust action, were you to offer them an opportunity.[5] I have a deep personal feeling in this matter, & if you wish to gratify me, in a manner *most* acceptable to my heart, do not allow anything to prevent your speedy & favorable action in this matter. I hope my dear President you have not forgotten *your promise*, to send my husband *to Paris* FOR ME. I am anxious to return home and *you must send him for me*.[6]

My best love to Mrs Johnson, Mrs Patterson and Mrs Stover.

K. Coyle

Care of Norton & Co[7]   Rue Auben 14   *Paris*

ALS, DLC-JP.

1. The year has been supplied by the Library of Congress and is supported by internal evidence.

2. John F. Coyle.

3. From Longfellow's *The Mask of Pandora*, VI.

4. John (c1831–fl1900), a banker, and Lydia (c1838–fl1875) McGinnis, natives of New Jersey and Illinois, respectively, resided in Chicago before moving to New York City in late 1866. 1870 Census, N.Y., New York, New York, 2nd Enum., 19th Ward, 29th Enum. Dist., 557; Chicago directories (1864–65); New York City directories (1868–1900); Randall, *Browning Diary*, 2: 421; Lydia McGinnis to Johnson, Oct. 4, 1866, Johnson Papers, LC.

5. McGinnis was nominated as minister resident to Stockholm in December 1866 but was rejected by the Senate a month later. There is no evidence of his applying or being considered for the late Joseph Wright's post in Berlin. Ser. 6B, Vol. 2: 206, Johnson Papers, LC.

6. Mrs. Coyle made a similar reference in a letter to Johnson on July 30, 1866. She claimed Johnson had promised to appoint her husband as one of the U.S. commissioners at the Paris Exposition. Kate Coyle to Johnson, July 30, 1866, Johnson Papers, LC

7. Coyle was staying with Charles B. Norton (1825–1891), U.S. commissioner to the Paris Exposition of 1867. A lifelong publisher and bookseller, Norton had also served in the Civil War, attaining the rank of brevet brigadier general of volunteers. Norton's activities with regards to international fairs are notable as well; he was a commissioner to the London World's Fair in 1851, proposed the Centennial Exhibition of 1876, and was in Chicago organizing the World's Fair there when he died. Brown, *Am. Biographies*, 6: 29–30; *National Intelligencer*, June 10, 1867; *New York Tribune*, Jan. 30, 1891.

From Richard Oulahan

663 Penna. Avenue
Washington D.C.   May 18th 1867.

Sir:

Respectfully referring to the interview, which the committee of Irish-American citizens[1] had the honor to have with your Excellency, on Monday evening May 13th inst., I beg to ask if any action has been taken by our Government, towards the liberation, or *legal trial* of the American citizens of Irish birth, or blood,—as well those who have been already condemned, as those on trial, or *awaiting* conviction,—now illegally suffering in the crowded dungeons of England and Ireland?

The great majority of those prisoners, Mr. President, have served as Officers in the Union Armies, during the late rebellion;—in "Meagher's Irish Brigade,"—"Corcoran's Irish Legion,"—"Irish Rifles," or 37th New York,—"Tammy," or 42nd N.Y.V., and in several other brigades and regiments, distinctly recognized as Irish commands,—and that citizenship to which they were entitled by the laws of their adopted country, was again won by those gallant soldiers, on many a red field of battle.

Since Your Excellency received the committee on Monday evenig last, a cable telegram announces that the bug-bear sentence of Col. Thomas Burke[2] has been commuted to imprisonment, *with hard labor*, for life! Col. Burke had anticipated, and denounced this cold-blooded, brutal, hyprocrisy,—called "clemency," or "mercy,"—as he knows, but too well, what it means. Thus does the red savage spare his captive, that he may *have the fiendish* pleasure of torturing him to death by a slow process.

We would not do anything, Mr. President, to embarrass the Government of our Adopted Country; but the intense anxiety which pervades our whole people, on this question of citizenship;—and the position in which so many of our late brothers-in-arms are placed,—will, the committee respectfully hope, be their excuse for asking what, if anything, has been done in the premises.

Such an Answer as Your Excellency may be pleased to communicate, will be thankfully appreciated by . . .

Richard Oulahan.   Chairman of Comm.

ALS, DLC-JP.
    1. James R. O'Beirne, William M. Garrsham, James D. Power, and Richard Oulahan. Garrsham has not been identified. Power (c1846–fl1870) was a clerk in the Treasury Department in 1870. James R. O'Beirne et al. to Johnson, May 11, 1867, Misc. Lets., 1789–1906 (M179, Roll 258), RG59, NA; 1870 Census, D.C., Washington, 1st Ward, 32.
    2. Possibly the Burke (b. c1828) who was an Irish-born clerk and a three-year veteran of the 155th N.Y. Inf., where he rose to the rank of first lieutenant. On May 1, 1867, Burke had been found guilty of treason and sentenced to be hanged, drawn, and quartered on the 29th. But sometime between May 1 and 18 it appears that his sentence was commuted to life imprisonment. However, information published in the *New York Tribune* on May 27

contained the statement of Earl Derby that Burke would surely hang, despite his commuta-tion. As late as the 27th Oulahan pressured Johnson to avert Burke's execution. On May 26 Lord Stanley informed Charles Adams that all capital sentences were commuted to life sen-tences; American newspapers carried this report on the 28th. Burke and others, however, did not serve their full sentences, for he and at least eight others were released in 1871 and exiled to the United States. *New York Tribune*, May 7, 14, 27, 28, 1867, Jan. 28, 1871; Oulahan to Johnson, May 27, 1867, Misc. Lets., 1789–1906 (M179, Roll 258), RG59, NA; Brian Jenkins, *Fenians and Anglo-American Relations during Reconstruction* (Ithaca, 1969), 234–36; CSR, Thomas Burke, RG94, NA.

From F. Marion Shields [1]

Macon Noxubee Co. Miss   May 18th 1867.

My *dear Sir*

To-day (Sunday) I heard one man swear by all that is good—that he would take your life as soon as you left the *Presidential Chair*—or sooner if he got the opportunity. The man once lived in Tennessee. At the begin-ing of the War—one of his sons[2] was captured by the *Federals* & lodged in jail. He said—that his wife[3] & other ladies begged & implored of you to release him (son) or give him a fair trial—& said you refused them. The man now lives in Okolana Miss. I can establish his threats and I ver-ily believe he will try to take your life. I learn that he is a dangerous and wreckless man. He is about 55 years old. I have forgotten his *name*—but will not be content until I learn it again. He will be here in a short-time again. I could not go to sleep to night I am so pestered. It is now 12 o-clock. Hoping you a long and prosperous life—believe and accept with assurance my highest Esteem.

F. Marion Shields
Macon Miss

Confidential

May 20

The gentleman I Speak of is named——*Mosely*.[4] Lives in Okolona Miss.

F. M. Shields

ALS, DLC-JP.

1. Shields (b. *c*1836), a native of South Carolina, was a farmer in Noxubee and also the inventor of a turkey decoy which he advertised in 1867 in various newspapers. 1860 Census, Miss., Noxubee, 4th Dist., 4; *Rome Weekly Courier*, May 10, 1867.

2. Possibly a reference to Jordan C. Mosley who was executed in 1864. See Mosley to Johnson, Sept. 1, 1864, *Johnson Papers*, 7: 130–31.

3. Margaret Moseley (b. 1822) of Tennessee was the mother of at least seven children. 1860 Census, Tenn., Bedford, Western Div., 19th Dist., 66.

4. Probably Ben Moseley [*sic*] (b. *c*1817), Jordan's father, who was a Tennessee farmer in 1860. Ibid.

From Albert B. Sloanaker

Philadelphia, May 18th 1867

My dear Sir.

On the 1st inst Chas. Abel[1] Esq. the newly appointed & confirmed Collector of Internal Revenue of our District, entered upon his Official duties; and my direct & indirect control of said office ceased from that date; therefore I embrace the first convenient opportunity to address you this my valedictory letter; inasmuch as I was deprived in all my recent visits to the Capital, of the pleasure of a personal interview.

Permit me at the onset to return to you my sincere & heartfelt acknowledgements for the very many kind offices that you have extended me in your personal and executive capacity; for I beg to assure you, that so long as memory performs its functions & my morality obeys the teachings of my inmost soul, so long will I remain true, steadfast & endearing to you & your interests; for I have weighed you in the scales of political experience, and have never—thank God!—found you wanting; & I freely confess to you, that to me personally your services have been incalculable; for, from a meagre existence in my struggles in life, you have placed me on my feet; independent of giving me a social & political status in society. In return for these tokens of your kindness, I can but offer you at present—which is unhesitatingly, presented—an unimpeachable, intelligent & truly just administration of my office of Collector; which fact I challenge in truth, the Treasury Dep't, Internal Revenue Bureau, or the Public to gainsay; & to these tribunals do I leave this attestment, only adding that the short careers of Messrs Kelly & Buckby[2] the Acting Collectors who were under my direct control, can stand the same test and may justly be placed in the same category.

My political course and career as an humble member of your administration, stands out in like relief to my character as a public officer, & I need but add, that the principles enunciated by our Baltimore Convention of which you in part, as one of our glorious standard bearers led us on to victory, are the honest expressions of my political faith, only necessarily changed by the conditions made necessary on the return of peace; & I pray God, that before the dawn of your administration, the historian may be able to record, our Union fully restored; by the people respecting its laws, maintaining & upholding alike common interests & brotherly charity, in mutual reverence of each other in all the sections of the Country; and above all revering our institutions as near in their purity, as bequeathed to us by the early fathers of the Republic.

But one duty remains & I am done; namely, a passing notice of what is popularly called my "coup d'etat" on my offical retirement on the 4th of last March; which I beg to assure you was superinduced entirely by the actions of Congressman Randall, towards me in my efforts to preserve the interests of the Johnson Republicans of the District. It was for this alone that I permitted Acting Collector Kelly, to assume the duties of the Collectorship; and he maintained his faith in every respect towards our friends, for the twenty one days of his official existence; & I may add that Acting Collector Buckby, until succeeded by Collector Abel, did preserve alike your & our friends interests. Therefore nothing was lost by my stroke of policy put forth to maintain the rights of your true & original supporters in opposition to the machinations of Congressman Randall. But I do not desire to impose upon you by any further reference to Randalls & my estrangement, other than to say that "sufficient for the day is the evil thereof." In closing, allow me to indulge in the thought, that the motives that actuate me in thus writing you, will be duly appreciated & I beg to extend towards you & yours, a grateful prayer for your future prosperity & happiness—in all & every particular in this life, only trusting that your career may be alike blessed by God & man.

A B Sloanaker

LS, DLC-JP.

1. Abel (fl1881) was a longtime painter in Philadelphia who was confirmed as collector in late April 1867. Philadelphia directories (1858–81); Ser. 6B, Vol. 4: 90, Johnson Papers, LC.

2. George Kelly, a district court prothonotary, and Wilson Buckby, a Philadelphia clerk. Each man in succession served three to four weeks as acting collector, March-April 1867. They are not otherwise identified. *House Ex. Docs.*, 40 Cong., 2 Sess., No. 78, p. 4 (Ser. 1332); Philadelphia directories (1865–66, 1868–69).

From Thomas J. Henley[1]

Washington D.C.   May 20th 1867.

Sir,

Referring to the conversation I had with you some days ago, in reference to the importance of appointing as Commissioners on the Union Pacific Rail Road,[2] persons who are friendly to the principles and policy of your administration, I beg leave especially to recommend as one of said Commissioners Frank Denver[3] Esq. of Nevada. Mr Denver who resides in Nevada, which is properly entitled to representation on that board, is a gentleman well qualified for the position, and is also a mechanic, being an Architect and builder, which renders his appointment peculiarly proper, there being now no practical mechanic on the board. I should be much gratified with his appointment.[4]

Thos. J. Henley,

ALS, DNA-RG48, Appts. Div., Misc. Lets. Recd.

1. Although *BDUSC* gives Henley's dates as 1810–1865 (dates which we also reported in our Volume 3), he was actually born in 1807 and did not die until 1875. See Brown, *Am. Biographies*, 4: 10–11.

2. As part of the acts authorizing the construction of the transcontinental railroad, the federal government was to appoint several representatives to the governing boards of the Union Pacific Railroad. John Hoyt Williams, *A Great and Shining Road: The Epic Story of the Transcontinental Railroad* (New York, 1988), 45, 78–79.

3. Denver (c1828–fl1873), a native of Virginia, served as lieutenant governor of Nevada in the early 1870s and as warden for the state prison about 1873. Bancroft, *Nevada, Colorado, and Wyoming*, 189–90, 314; 1870 Census, Nev., Elko, Elko, 37.

4. Several months later Johnson did appoint Denver as a railroad commissioner. William G. Moore to Henley, Sept. 5, 1867, Tels. Sent, President, Vol. 3 (1865–68), RG107, NA.

From William F. Johnston

No. 424 Walnut St.
Philadelphia   May 20, 1867

My dear Sir

Pardon this intrusion upon your time & patience.

I have understood, that my esteemed frind, Henry M. Watts[1] Esq. of this city, will be named by other frinds for the position of Minister at Berlin or Vienna.

I have known Mr. Watts for thirty years & from that fact, I am prepared and enabled to speak of him, in terms of the warmest commendation.

No *man* in the country is more fitly qualified to represent our country abroad, than Mr. Watts. Amiable in social life, [upright?] & high toned in all relations of life a lawyer of eminent ability, a pure & truthful gentleman, a profound scholar & faithful Christian man. I know & feel that his selection, would do credit to the administration at home & our country abroad.

Mr. Watts has spent four years in Europe, residing in Paris, Dresden & Fribough and seeks the position for its *honors*, and not its rewards.

No Senate, however malignant dare refuse a confirmation. Gov Swann of Maryland[2] I am told favors this nomination. If I have the liberty of requesting an answer, whether other testimonials are necessary, I would be glad to furnish such recommendations of this application, as such are satisfactory.

Wm. F Johnston

ALS, DNA-RG59, Lets. of Appl. and Recomm., 1861–69 (M650, Roll 51), Henry M. Watts.

1. Watts (1805–1890), a lawyer and member of the prewar Pennsylvania legislature, also served as U.S. attorney for the eastern district (1841). A frequent traveller to Europe, he was nominated and confirmed in July 1868 as minister to Austria, a post he held for one year. Following more European travels, he returned to Pennsylvania to engage in coal and iron interests. *NCAB*, 4: 305; Ser. 6B, Vol. 2: 371, Johnson Papers, LC.

2. Thomas Swann.

From William H.C. King

New Orleans   May 21st 1867

There is no doubt in the minds of the people that Knox[1] has been bought by the Swindlers of first Natl Bank & Sub Treasury.[2] Have immediately power taken from Knox & vested in Meline[3] the other Commissioner. You know I warned you of these frauds for a year past. Now do what I say & all will be right. Make this change immediately & I will be responsible for this dispatch. Answer please.[4]

W.H.C. King

Tel, DNA-RG107, Tels. Recd., President, Vol. 6 (1867–68).

1. John J. Knox (1828–1892) held a variety of banking posts in New York and Minnesota, until he was appointed a clerk in the Treasury Department in 1862. In October 1867, after his investigation in New Orleans, he became deputy comptroller of the currency. He served as comptroller (1872–84), and then as president of the National Bank of the Republic of New York City until his death. *DAB.*

2. See Thomas Cottman to Johnson, May 16, 1867.

3. James F. Meline, Jr. (1841–1908), served in the Union army, with the exception of three months, from April 1861 to March 1866. He advanced to the rank of captain and was brevetted major. He became a clerk in the Treasury Department and eventually assistant treasurer of the U.S. (1893–1907). *Who Was Who in America,* 1:828.

4. No answer to this telegram has been found. The telegram was, however, discussed by the Washington correspondent of the *New York Times*, who accused King of sending the telegram after Knox refused a bribe to render the accounts more favorable. This King hotly denied in his own newspaper. In any case, Knox continued as acting assistant treasurer until the arrival of the new official, John S. Walton, and was able to secure $600,000 toward making up the defalcation. *New York Times*, June 9, 1867; *New Orleans Times*, June 13, 22, 1867; *Mobile Advertiser and Register*, July 11, 1867.

To William D. Haywood[1]

[Washington, D.C.]   May 22d, 1867.

Dear Sir:

I have received your letter of the 15th instant,[2] and thank you for the cordial terms in which, as the Representative of the citizens of Raleigh, you ask me to visit that place.

I accept the invitation of my native city to be her guest, and, deeply grateful for the respect in which they hold my father's memory, will endeavor to be present with your citizens on the 4th day of June next, the day set apart for the erection of a monument to commemorate his worth.[3]

A.J.

Copy, DLC-JP.

1. Haywood (c1810–*fl*1870), a farmer, was mayor (formerly called intendant of police) of Raleigh for many years before the war and again in 1867. Later, he was clerk in the local land office. 1860 Census, N.C., Wake, Raleigh, 72; (1870), Raleigh Twp., 213; Elizabeth R. Murray, *Wake: Capital County of North Carolina* (Raleigh, 1983), 545, Appendix D.

2. On that date Mayor Haywood officially invited the President to be present in Raleigh at the dedication of a monument erected to the memory of his father, Jacob Johnson. The same day, David L. Swain and Gov. Jonathan Worth reiterated this invitation and also asked the Executive to attend the state university's commencement. Haywood to Johnson, Swain to Johnson, Worth to Johnson, May 15, 1867, Johnson Papers, LC.

3. Johnson, his secretary William G. Moore, cabinet members William H. Seward and Alexander W. Randall, and others left Washington on June 1. After a stopover in Richmond, on the third they reached Raleigh, where they were given a ceremonious welcome. The next day they attended the dedication of the ten foot high monument to Johnson's father, and on the sixth they witnessed a portion of the university's graduation exercises at Chapel Hill. Leaving Raleigh on the seventh, they again spent the night in Richmond and returned to the nation's capital during the afternoon of the eighth. *National Intelligencer*, June 3, 4, 6, 7, 8, 1867; *Washington Evening Star*, June 8, 1867. See Speech at Raleigh, June 3, 1867.

From Oliver G. Carter[1]

New York   May 24. 1867

Sir.

Unless your memory serves you well, and you can recall to mind a letter which I had the honor of sending you upon the announcement of your policy, and in support of it, or my formal call to pay my respects to you in November last, this will appear as the first time I have addressed you.

I again come to you, but now in behalf of a fellow citizen.

The facts are these. In 1865 a convention of prominent men was desired to formally bring South Carolina back into the Union. This was called and by its action remodelled the State Constitution, abolishing slavery and submitting to the issues of the war. Among its members, and not the least influential among them was *Mr F. W. Pickens*.

The Provisional Governor[2] of the State at that time urged Mr Pickens to go into that Convention because of his great influence, holding out as an inducement for him to do so that he would *assuredly be pardoned* if he would.

Mr Pickens did enter that Convention—the result is known.

Every *other* member of that Convention, upon assembling received his pardon—Mr Pickens did *not*, and *has not since*.

Will your Excellency take this case into consideration and if possible (and consistent with your high station, which under the circumstances I think it is) send Mr Pickens his pardon also.

Nothing I can add in pleading can alter the state of this case—it must stand upon its own merits,—and I must not trespass upon your valuable time. I appeal to your sense of justice and beg most respectfully that you will give Mr Picken's case the attention which would seem to be entitled to.[3]

O. G. Carter   29 Pine St.

ALS, DNA-RG60, Appt. Files for Judicial Dists., S.C., F. W. Pickens.

1. Carter (*c*1830–*fl*1871) was variously a clerk, bookkeeper, and an insurance official

in Brooklyn. Brooklyn directories (1859–71); 1860 Census, N.Y., Kings, Brooklyn, 11th Ward, 3rd Dist., 532.
  2. Benjamin F. Perry.
  3. Johnson did not grant a special pardon to Pickens. For a much earlier plea on Pickens's behalf, see Benjamin F. Perry to Johnson, Aug. 20, 1865, *Johnson Papers*, 8: 626–27.

From Thomas Ewing, Sr.

Capitol Hill   May 24/67

Dear Sir

Do not I pray you go to Boston.[1] The occasion is not a propitious one—there are yet anti Masons as well as Masons, and your visit will be a disturbing element in the coming elections which now promise fair. Besides there will be fifty lying scamps dogging at your heels who will circulate more fresh slander, than can be corrected in six months. Your proposed trip to Raleigh is well—the occasion more than warrants it— but scoundrels will intrude upon you there & on the way, and falsify and pervert all that you may say. I hope you will meddle not at all with politics even in private conversation but let all who honestly or dishonestly en- quire as to your opinions and purposes find them in your official papers. Foolish friends and crafty enemies will publish their version of what you say, alike to your injury. Condemnation of gross wrong and expressions of anger or impatience of insult and injustice will, as perverted and given to the world, do evil and not good. Hotspur might exclaim,

> "O I am whipped with rods
> Nettled and stung by pissmires"[2]

but he who is President must in his intercourse with the public forget that he is a man.

T. Ewing

ALS, DLC-JP.
  1. On the very day of Ewing's letter newspapers carried the statement that the Presi- dent would not be going to Boston in June to participate in Masonic ceremonies. That decision was subsequently changed, however, for in late June he traveled to Boston. *New York Times*, May 24, 1867; S. P. Hanscom to Johnson, May 17, 1867, Johnson Papers, LC; Trefousse, *Johnson*, 286. See also Johnson to Otis Norcross, June 11, 1867.
  2. A slightly inaccurate rendering of the lines from Shakespeare's *Henry IV*. Ewing had the second line correct, but the first line was actually: "Scourged with rods."

From Henry Stanbery

May 24, 1867, Washington, D.C.; Benjamin F. Hall et al., eds., *Official Opinions of the Attorneys General of the United States* (43 vols. to date, Washington, D.C., 1852–).

In this formal opinion submitted to the President, Stanbery responds to the two Military Reconstruction acts passed by Congress in March 1867. He wrestles with the questions presented by these laws concerning the right to vote in the ten ex-Confederate states. Inasmuch as the matter of voter registration determined whether a person could vote, Stanbery examines registration questions. He is mildly perturbed that the residence requirement was tied to the date of *election*, whereas the age requirement was linked to the date of *registration*.

When scrutinizing disfranchisement, Stanbery takes exception to the stipulation that one could be denied suffrage on the basis of having committed a felony.

The attorney general focuses next upon the offices or officers encompassed in the disfranchising clause of the Reconstruction acts. Readily conceding the obvious ones, such as state legislators and members of Congress, he does not believe that state militia officers, municipal officials, and subordinate legislative officers are included in the disqualifying provisions. Officials who had largely local functions should be reviewed further, promises Stanbery. He proceeds to enumerate various state officials who definitely should not be excluded from the franchise—mainly members of various institutional boards. Concerning U.S. officers, Stanbery applies the exclusionary provisions to military and civil officials who had taken the oath to support the Constitution. Any state officer who violated that oath must have been an executive or judicial officer in order to fall under the restrictions of the Reconstruction acts.

What acts make one guilty of insurrection or rebellion against the U.S. government or giving aid and comfort to the enemies? To Stanbery the new Reconstruction laws encompass not only the Civil War but also any foreign war waged by the U.S. To engage in insurrection or rebellion implies active conduct rather than passive, argues the attorney general. A conscript or a slave forced into military service should not be included; and officers in Rebel states who discharged "duties not incident to war" should not be construed as having engaged in rebellion.

Turning to the matter of *individual* participation in the war, Stanbery notes that there were large numbers of people in the Confederacy "more or less opposed to the rebellious movement, and who were yet more or less necessarily involved in its support." He would not interpret them as being guilty of insurrection. Moreover, maintains Stanbery, merely sentiment or expression in support of the Rebel cause is not sufficient; there must have been a direct overt act to further the rebellion. He furthermore declares that "the person applying for registration is not required to clear himself from the taint of disloyalty."

Stanbery concludes by looking briefly at the registration boards and the process of registration. A person seeking voter registration is required to swear that he has met the qualifications set by the new Reconstruction acts; according to the attorney general, that is the only oath that should be stipulated. Any other oaths would be extra-judicial and without authority.

From John M. Schofield

Richmond Va.   May 26. 1867

Dear Mr President

Seeing from the papers that you contemplate visiting Raleigh soon,[1] and presuming that you will stop in Richmond on your way, I hasten to request that you will do me the honor to be my guest during your stay in the City.

My family being absent I am living in bachelor quarters and taking my meals at the Exchange Hotel. But you can have your meals served in the house if you wish to be so quiet as that. Or you can take your meals at the

Reverse of the commemorative medal struck in honor
of Johnson in 1867. The First Constitutional Club
of Pennsylvania presented a gold version to President Johnson
in January 1868.
Photograph courtesy Special Collections,
University of Tennessee Library

Hotel and have a parlor there for the reception of your many friends, while using my quarters as a quiet retreat where you can escape from the crowd. It will afford me great pleasure to arrange it in whatever way will best suit your convenience and comfort, if you will let one of your secretaries inform me of your wishes and at what time you will be in Richmond.[2]

J. M. Schofield   Maj Genl

ALS, DLC-JP.
1. See Johnson to William D. Haywood, May 22, 1867.
2. Johnson telegraphed his thanks to Schofield but announced he would be staying at a hotel. Arrangements had been made for Johnson to stay in the Spottswood Hotel's best rooms. Johnson to Schofield, May 28, 1867, Tels. Sent, President, Vol. 3 (1865–68), RG107, NA; *New York Tribune*, June 3, 1867.

From William S. Huntington

Washn.   May 29/67 8:30 P.M.

Dear Mr Johnson,

I have seen Mrs. P.[1] She says she will leave "for parts unknown" *early* tomorrow morning & *not* appear before any "questioners" if she can be assured that while S. remains Collector[2] she can have $150 per month, as agreed.

I said, "I know nothing about it & do not propose to interfere in the matter" & then left.

I have only say that if you desire it—or think best—to have *anything* done, I will do it *as your friend*.

No one knows or ever will know of this, or that I have even spoken to you about it. Only signify your wishes in the *most general* or most *specific* way, & I will act & *no* one shall be aware of it. I will await your answer anytime tonight, or until *8 tomorrow morning*.[3]

Wm. S H

ALI, DLC-JP.
1. Jennie A. Perry.
2. Henry Smythe, collector of the port of New York.
3. See Smythe to Johnson, Mar. 6, 1867, for details on this situation. No reply from Johnson has been found.

From Stephen F. Cameron[1]

Elkton, Cecil Co. Md.   May 30th 1867

Sir.

I have the honor to enclose the card of a gentleman[2] in Paris who had kindly promised to interpose in my behalf at some future time on his return, and who has also given me a line to Col. J. D. Perryman and the Hon. John W. Leftwich.

So soon as I had recd. the intimation by past events that *civil* law was re-established in the land, I have not hesitated to place myself within the jurisdiction of the United States, secure of protection under the laws and Constitution I desire faithfully to observe and uphold, and dreading no investigation from the exercise of *legitimate* authority.

I renewed my allegiance to the United States before Col. John Hay in Paris last fall, and I now ask of the hands of your Excellency the formal restoration of the high privilege of American Citizenship.

Praying earnestly that Your Excellency may deem this moment of solemn duty in sacred visitation to a Father's tomb a favorable opportunity to offer the same privelege to one who desires to gaze upon and abide near the *graves of those lost in absence*, I am, sir, with fervent wishes for the health and prosperity of your Excellency . . . [3]

S. F. Cameron.

ALS, DLC-JP.

1. Cameron (b. *c*1835), a native of Maryland and an Episcopal minister, was with the Confederate secret service and worked in the U.S., Great Britain, and Canada. 1860 Census, Md., Cecil, 3rd Dist., Elkton P.O., 91; James D. Horan, *Confederate Agent* (New York, 1954), 249; William A. Tidwell with James O. Hall and David W. Gaddy, *Come Retribution: The Confederate Secret Service and the Assassination of Abraham Lincoln* (Jackson, Miss., 1988), 177, 178, 306.

2. A name card with D. M. Leatherman written on it was enclosed. Leatherman of Memphis was in Paris as a commissioner to the Universal Exposition there. See Johnson to Leatherman, Nov. 26, 1866, *Johnson Papers*, 11: 491.

3. On May 30, Cameron had written Joseph H. Bradley, counsel for John H. Surratt, and asked him to forward to Johnson this letter requesting pardon. Bradley did so the same day and added his support for Cameron's pardon. Cameron received a pardon on June 14, 1867. However, an inquiry was made by the House and its judiciary committee into Cameron's pardon, as Cameron was a witness for the defense in Surratt's trial. S. F. Cameron to Joseph H. Bradley, may 30, 1867; Bradley to Johnson, May 30, 1867, Johnson Papers, LC; *Washington Evening Star*, July 17, 1867. For more on this issue, see Joseph H. Bradley to Johnson, July 20, 1867.

From John T. Tanner

Athens, Ala., May 30 1867

Sir.

D H Bingham is here availing of the military bill to oppress, and gratify his old grudges against, the good people of North Alabama. He openly denounces yourself and Secretary McCullock and does not stop to assail the inmates of the White House, saying that it is composed of "Harlots & thieves." This I can substantiate by Gen Houston[1] Hon Luke Pryor & others of equal respectability.

It is reported that he is one of the Receivers in Bankruptcy for this State. A sad misfortune for the Government and a great calamity to have this people harrassed by such a man—and if you can prevent it you will be serving the best interest of the Govt. and will confer a lasting favor on our whole community.

He and his wife[2] are grossly violating the franking priviledge by using the frank of Congressmen & other officials on all of their private Correspondence. The Post Master[3] here has retained a batch of his letters and written to the Dept for instructions.

On Monday night some young boys took him from his Hotel and blacked his face, and nothing more, for the manner he had spoken of the President & family and for his bad treatment to our people. His wife went to Huntsville and from statements she made to the Commander of the Post[4] he sent a squad of soldiers here and arrested three *innocent* young men—one of them Jas. E Russell Late Depty Collector[5]—much embarassing my settlement with the Govt. as Mr Russell is now under arrest in Huntsville and my successor Dr. Johnson[6] pressing me to turn over the office to him, which I cannot possibly do in the absence of Mr Russell. These arrests are made at the instance of this man Bingham by U.S troops who would two years ago have hung Bingham had he used the same language toward Mr. Lincoln that he seems to be permited to heap upon you almost daily.

The whole of our troubles here with Bingham are not of a political character—they are personal—no one objecting to his enjoying his political sentiments in any manner most acceptable to himself, and it is hoped the military will not undertake to sustain him in the oppression of our people—but protect him and the people alike. Everything was peace and quiet until he came here and nothing but disorder has ruled ever since.[7]

Jno. T. Tanner

ALS, DNA-RG94, Lets. Recd. (Main Ser.), File R-265-1867 (M619, Roll 578).

1. George S. Houston.

2. Sarah C. Moyers (b. *c*1817), an Alabama native, married Daniel H. Bingham in 1858. 1860 Census, Ala., Limestone, Div. No. 1, Athens, 81; Faye A. Axford, *Limestone County After Appomattox, 1865–1870* (Athens, Ala., 1985), 18.

3. Probably William P. Tanner (1831–1888), brother of the writer, who served ten years as mayor of Athens before moving to Montgomery in the mid-1870s. Eulalia Y. Wellden, abs., *Death Notices from Limestone County, Alabama Newspapers, 1828–1891* (n.p., 1891), 134; *U.S. Off. Reg.* (1867).

4. William B. Occleston (*c*1835–1867), who originally enlisted as a cavalry private in 1857, early in the war won a lieutenant's commission and transferred to the infantry. Promoted to captain and breveted major, he died suddenly in Providence, Rhode Island, in August 1867. *Mobile Advertiser and Register*, June 8, 1867; *Providence Journal*, Aug. 26, 1867; Powell, *Army List*, 510; Simon, *Grant Papers*, 17: 531.

5. Russell, George William Tanner, and William R. McWilliams. Russell (1843–1870), a clerk and son of a saddler, died in Helena, Arkansas. Tanner (1846–1888) became a dry goods clerk and died in Matagordo County, Texas. McWilliams (1847–1912), a veteran of the 11th Ala. Cav., CSA, for a while was a drugstore clerk and ultimately became a dentist. *Nashville Union and Dispatch*, June 7, 1867; 1860 Census, Ala., Limestone, 1st Div., Athens, 82; (1870), Twp. 3, Range 4 (Athens), 4, 11; Axford, *Limestone County after Appomattox*, 58; Chris Edwards and Faye A. Axford, *The Lure and Love of*

Limestone County (Tuscaloosa, 1978), Addenda 20, 42; *Limestone County, Alabama Cemeteries* (3 vols., Athens, Ala., 1977–79), 3: 3, 75.

6. Robert Johnston (*c*1825–*fl*1870), a native Pennsylvania physician, had been confirmed as collector February 21, 1867. 1870 Census, Ala., Madison, Huntsville, 3rd Ward, 6; Ser. 6B, Vol. 4: 180, Johnson Papers, LC.

7. Endorsements attached to this letter indicate that on June 3 Tanner's letter was referred to the secretary of war and subsequently down the chain of command to Gen. Wager Swayne, commander of the District of Alabama. Swayne noted that "within a day or two after the arrest of the parties" Bingham "made a personal request, based on a desire to show that his feeling towards the people of his county were not such to have been attributed to him, that all . . . implicated in the assault might be released, which request was immediately complied with."

June 1867

From Edmund Abell

New Orleans   June 3d 1867.

The unwavering attachment of myself and the people of the State of Louisiana to you, and the broad national principles so wisely conceived, and firmly persued by you, I trust will be sufficient appology for the earnest manner I press the correction of what appears to me an error involving individual injustice, humility to the State and a violation of the Laws of the Country.

On the 26th of May, I forwarded to you a memorial[1] in which it is made to appear that General Sheridan's action on my attempted removal was illegal, unjust and unnecessary. If I only were affected by General order No. 5 which purports to remove me from a high judicial office by a subaltern military officer,[2] it appears to me that the Commander in Chief will not withold Summary redress. Assuming as the order does the power to remove Judges and other State officers without cause, it leaves two great States[3] at the mercy of a single person and virtually deprives me of my ordinary redress in the Courts of the State, as it strikes down the independence of the judiciary.

I am a plain old man and will venture to say that if the laws are permitted to be trampled upon all the offices under one pretext or another will fall into the hands of extreme men, they will want no new Constitution, the people will have power to make none, or if permitted it will be rejected, the object of the Act of Congress defeated and the people tantalized.

Unconstitutional, unjust, and oppressive as we believe the Law[4] to be, it is forced on us and we all accept and forward it, that we may have some sort of State Government, and representation in Congress, and feel that we are entitled to have the law executed according to its words and intendment.

So far from impeding the action of the Commander I am firmly of the mind that if the State officers and people were left free to act, they would present a Constitution of the State, in accordance with the Act of Congress, no less than four months from this date.

Of Andrew S. Herron the Attorney General of the State who is made by Law the principle officer of the 1st District Court, allow me to say, that although he has been in the Confederate service, he is a man of great merit, and dearly beloved by the people, and has been to my knowledge with myself, zealously engaged in forwarding the Act of Congress of the 2d March 1867.

As a Union man and faithful public servant the record must speak for

me. All my public acts are of record in the debates of the Convention of
'64 and in the 1st District Court. All my decisions and charges to the
Grand Jury were read from manuscript and cannot be garbled, and are
now on file.

If any thing appears illegal or improper it could easily be shown.

With the exception of Genl. Sheridan and a few of the Conventionists,
I do not hesitate to say that all my official acts are fully approved by the
people of the State of all parties.

I have not had the pleasure of seeing General Sheridan and have never
conflicted with military jurisdiction. I have no prejudice to indulge, but
respectfully contend that he has no right to use the power of government
to remove and oppress any one without clear law and no necessity could
Justify it in times of peace.

Since writing the above Governor Wells has been removed and Mr.
Thomas J. Durant appointed in his stead.[5] The Governor appears to be a
man in whom no party has confidence, but if the object be only to get rid
of a bad man as stated by General Sheridan why not let his Constitutional
successor Hon. A. Voorhies[6] Lieutenant Governor against whom nothing can be said, proceed with the discharge of the functions of Governor
of the State. I fear these things will end in an overthrow of republican
institutions. I pray the President to retain the state governments in tact
until allured, modified or superceded by the United States as provided in
the 6th Section of the Act of Congress of the 2d March 1867.

I forward with this suppliment a duplicate of my memorial to the Attorney General of the United States, which you can inspect in case the
original has failed to reach you.

In renewing my prayer contained in my original memorial, for restoration to my judicial functions, I remain . . .

Edmund Abell.

ALS, DLC-JP.
1. Edmund Abell to Johnson, May 25, 1867, Johnson Papers, LC. See also *New York Tribune*, June 14, 1867.
2. Sheridan's General Orders No. 5, promulgated March 27, 1867, removed Louisiana state attorney general Andrew S. Herron and New Orleans mayor John T. Monroe, in addition to removing Abell from the office of judge of the first district court, New Orleans. McPherson, *Political History*, 206–7.
3. Louisiana and Texas.
4. The First Military Reconstruction Act. Abell mentions it by date later in the document.
5. J. Madison Wells was removed on June 3 but refused to vacate the office until forced out on June 7. Thomas J. Durant declined the governorship, so Sheridan appointed Benjamin F. Flanders. Dawson, *Army Generals and Reconstruction*, 53, 54.
6. Albert Voorhies.

From Colorado Territorial Officials[1]

Denver Col.   June 3rd, 1867

We are menaced by hostile Indians[2] Our line of communication cut off, the US Mails captured, Coaches and stations destroyed The occupants murdered. Private trains are plundered burned & the men murdered & scalped.[3] The arts of peace suspended & the people suffering from a feeling of insecurity which paralyses every branch of industry & all from the foe the lives of the whole of which are & should be considered by the Authorities as worthless compared with that of one American Citizen. This we have suffered more or less for some time & yet no adequate protection or relief has been afforded us. In the name of God & Humanity we make this appeal to you & ask that the too long continued temporizing policy towards these merciless Devils shall cease and that you will at once direct that prompt & decisive measures be taken for protection of the Country.[4]

Tel, DNA-RG94, Lets. Recd. (Main Ser.), File W-286-1867 (M619, Roll 601).

1. The telegram was signed by territorial governor A. C. Hunt, eleven other federal appointees, and one man without an official title.

2. Rumors of impending Indian attack were prevalent in Colorado in the spring of 1867, as they were elsewhere in the West. Hunt had already telegraphed to the secretary of war on May 27 complaining that "Depredations from Indians on our Eastern and Western borders are of daily occurrence. . . . I would most respectfully ask as in Montana authority to organize mounted volunteers for a campaign against the savages." Stanton answered Hunt by referring him to Sherman. Athearn, *Sherman*, 116; A. C. Hunt to Edwin M. Stanton, May 27, 1867; Stanton to Hunt, May 29, 1867, Tels. Sent, Sec. of War (M473, Roll 91), RG107, NA. For an account of the Indian panic in Montana, see Hezekiah L. Hosmer to Johnson, May 2, 1867.

3. During 1867 Indian raiding parties attacked Ben Holladay's stage lines rather extensively, stealing 350 head of livestock, burning twelve stage stations, destroying three coaches, killing more than twelve employees, and wounding some passengers. Sherman himself went to the Colorado Territory in June and reported that small bands of Indians "are very widely scattered and are engaged mostly in stealing horses." Williams, *A Great and Shining Road*, 149–50; Simon, *Grant Papers*, 17: 173.

4. Since Johnson was on his trip to North Carolina, his secretary Robert Morrow referred the letter to the secretary of war, who sent it to Grant. Based on Grant's response, Stanton informed Hunt "that all the military force which can possibly be given to protect the frontier has been put under the orders of Lieutenant General Sherman." Sherman authorized Hunt to raise 300 men in four mounted companies, but Hunt was unable to recruit these volunteers in the time allotted. Sherman thus insisted that Hunt would have to rely on the regular troops. Stanton to Hunt, June 10, 1867, Lets. Sent *re* Military Affairs (M6, Roll 59), RG107, NA; Simon, *Grant Papers*, 17: 173.

From Joseph S. Payne[1]

Winchester   Franklin Co. Tenn   June the 3d 1867.

Please pardon the liberty taken by an humble citizen of thus addressing the President, and I can assure you that I would dare not venture this intrusion, if I did not think the peace and happiness of our country demand it. And with this connection, and for the love of my People the prosperity and future glory of my country, "Like *Queen Esther* of old, I would go in unto the King, which although might not be in accordance to law, and if my petition perish, it can but perish,"[2] and as She prevailed with the King, and her People were saved, you are the only person, to whom we can look for protection and redress.

I most cheerfully subscribe to the Petition addressed to your Excellency by the citizens of Franklin County, Tennessee this day,[3] and I more cheerfully and readily address you in view of the character an confidence which I sustained to the Government during the late *war*, and would respectfully if necessary, refer you to Generals Thomas, Rosseau, and Milroy,[4] for my character. Evry command or requisition by the Government or Military, from the time of the occupancy of the Federal Army under the command of Gen. Rozencrans,[5] in reference to the people I subscribed to it, and tried with all the influence that I could command to get my People to adopt, and every Election from the one which placed your Excellency in the position, which you now occupy, up to the present I have humbly subscribed my vote in favor of the Government, and its supremacy and all the while a citizen of this once Rebel County. I think I can with safety say, we need no *army* to protect *Union men*, or to enforce the laws, and I believe there are numbers of those who fought in the rebellion would fly to the rescue or assistance of our Sheriff,[6] to quell a mob, or to enforce the laws as the most Loyal man in the country, and more especially do we not need the *State Guards*, ordered by the Governor. Union men from the northern states who have but recently settled in our county, (and who are not aferd) said to me that they feel more safe here than in the North, as far as Robbery and molestation are concern, and not until the present excitement produced by the conduct of the State Guard, have they expressed any uneasiness, and if their course is not checked, that northern immigration will stop, and the enterprises of the county suffer, and as it regards those, who were connected with, the Guarilla Band, during the Ware, so far as my acquaintance goes, many of them I would be willing if necessary to subscribe to any sort of a bond, as to their conduct.[7]

J. [L or S]. Payne
Decherd Depot   Franklin Co   Tenn

ALS, DNA-RG94, Lets. Recd. (Main Ser.), File C-635-1867 (M619, Roll 544).

1. Payne (c1813–*fl*1873), a farmer in Rutherford County in 1850, moved to Coffee County and opened a shoemaker's shop. It is likely he served as justice of the peace in 1870. 1850 Census, Tenn., Rutherford, Mechanicsville Dist., 389; (1860), Coffee, Tullahoma, 130; (1870), 13th Civil Dist., 3; Betty A. Bridgewater, comp., "Coffee County in Early Business Directories," *Coffee County Historical Society Quarterly*, 7 (1976): 11.

2. This is a slightly garbled quotation from the Old Testament story of Esther: "and so will I go in unto the King, which *is* not according to the law: and if I perish, I perish." See Esther 4: 16 (KJV).

3. On June 3 a meeting was held in Winchester at which time an extensive petition to President Johnson was devised. It protested against the actions of the state guard, particularly the murder of James R. Brown, and entreated Johnson to send federal troops to the county and thereby remove the state militia. According to one account, a thousand citizens signed the Franklin County petition. *Nashville Republican Banner*, June 5, 1867; *Fayetteville Observer*, June 6, 1867. A handwritten copy of the June 3 Franklin County petition, signed by committee members, is A. S. Marks et al. to Johnson, undated, Lets. Recd. (Main Ser.), File T-197-1867 (M619, Roll 597), RG94, NA.

4. George H. Thomas, Lovell H. Rousseau, and Robert H. Milroy.

5. William S. Rosecrans.

6. Not identified.

7. Franklin County citizens had assembled earlier on May 29, 1867, to voice their protest against the activities of the state guard. On that occasion a committee drew up a report outlining the atrocities of the militia and urging that the citizens "combine and protect themselves." *Nashville Republican Banner*, May 31, 1867; *Nashville Union and American*, May 31, 1867.

Speech at Raleigh, North Carolina[1]

June 3, 1867

Sir:

Permit me, through you,[2] to tender to those here present, and to the people of the State of North Carolina, my sincere thanks for the welcome tendered me on the occasion of my return to my native town. I confess that under the circumstances, and in view of the demonstrations which have been made since I reached Raleigh, as well as on the way, I am inspired with emotions which language is wholly inadequate to express here. In the language of another, it is not worth while to attempt to improve upon it. Here, in the City of Raleigh, is where my infant eyes first saw the light of heaven; here are the scenes of my childhood; here is everything to bind man to his fellow, and to associate him with surrounding objects; here is where the tendrils of the heart have taken a firm hold upon everything to which it is attracted. In making my entrance into this city to-day my mind involuntarily wandered back to the time when I left its streets a penniless and inexperienced boy, to make my way in the world. ⟨Applause.⟩ When looking back forty years ago, and returning here to-day, I begin to inquire where are those I left behind? In the language of poetry itself, "The friends of my childhood, where are they?" Echo answers, where? Some have emigrated and gone to other lands. Some have complied with the inexorable and irresistible call, and have passed to that undiscovered country from whose bourne no traveler returns. I again ask, friends of my childhood, where are they? Where are the Haywoods, Hunters, and Lanes? Where are the Pearces, the Roysters and Smiths and Jones? Where is the long list of men who lived at that day, and who commanded respect for constancy to principle? ⟨Applause.⟩ Under these circumstances, could I feel indifferent? I would be false to my nature if I forgot you, and not to indulge in self adulation, I can say I feel proud of the demonstrations in my honor by the citizens of my native land.

UNIVERSITY OF NORTH CAROLINA.

ORDER OF PROCESSION

THURSDAY, JUNE 6TH., 1867.

MUSIC.

FRESHMAN CLASS.
SOPHOMORE "
JUNIOR "
CITIZENS.
ALUMNI.
VISITORS.
FACULTY OF THE UNIVERSITY.
GRADUATING CLASS,
TRUSTEES OF THE UNIVERSITY.
GUEST'S.
GOVERNOR OF NORTH CAROLINA.
PRESIDENT OF THE UNIVERSITY.
PRESIDENT OF THE UNITED STATES.

The procession will form in front of South Building at 9 1-2 **A. M.**

No Seats for Gentlemen in the Chapel until the Procession enters it.

J. S. BARLOW.   Chief Marshal.
J. S. BATTLE.
G. G. LATTA.   } Ass't. Marshals.
W. S. PEARSON.

Program indicating Johnson's participation at the university's commencement.
Courtesy North Corlina Collection,
University of North Carolina Library at Chapel Hill

Breathes there a man with soul so dead,
Who never to himself has said,
This is my own, my native land.[3]
⟨Applause.⟩

This is not the time or occasion to discuss the political issues which disturb the public mind; but as allusion has been made to my first going out from among you, I may say that ever since I formed an opinion as to the fundamental principles of the Government, I have adhered to them, and to the Constitution, the Union, and the flag of my country. ⟨Applause.⟩ When I went out from among you, and from the time I became connected with politics, I laid down as my rule a conscientious performance of duty, and adopted the Constitution of my country as my guide— ⟨applause⟩—and by these, whether in prosperity or adversity, I have always been guided and controlled, and come weal or woe, in high places or low places, with the Constitution as my guide, with my hand laid on the altar of my country, I will leave these great principles for those who are to follow. ⟨Applause.⟩ One of my leading tenets has been the prosperity of the great mass of the people, holding that all persons, without regard to condition or color, should be esteemed according to the intrinsic merit or worth, leaving each to rise on his own merit, courage and energy. Let this be the standard, so that to every one may be assigned his true position. I trust and hope, instead of discussing party issues, creating factions between North, South, East or West, that all will exert themselves to the restoration of the Union of these States, so that the flag may float over a contented and prosperous people. ⟨Applause.⟩ Let us, my friends, repair the breeches made by the war, and restore the Union. This being accomplised, we may then make such issues as the public prosperity and safety may demand. Let us efface from our minds the memory of the past; let us pour oil on the troubled waters, and restore peace to the States. This has been my constant object, but let this pass. I simply come to this place in compliance with your invitation to participate in another ceremony to confer an honor upon the memory of one who was a few years ago in your midst. This has not emanated, as I understand, from any particular quarter or family.

One word to you, young men. There is much said as to educational advantages, &c., but if any of you wish to succeed, or, in common phrase, make yourselves men, you will have to do so through your own exertions. I know some of you are familiar with the hardships and fiery trials through which I have passed during the time that has elapsed since I left you. It is not for me to say whether I have succeeded or not. Let that be as it may, my race is nearly run. I am no aspirant for anything. The way is open for all; all places of emolument and distinctions are before you. There are here a few of those in whose hands the administration of the Government is placed. We are passing away; the next wave will bring you young men and women in our places, and our work will fall into other hands. Therefore the greater should be your efforts to prepare yourself for the responsibilities that must in turn devolve upon you.

In conclusion, permit me to tender you my thanks for this cordial welcome, extended through your distinguished representative, the Governor of the State. Though she sent me out penniless and friendless, and did not afford me those advantages which you now enjoy, and though on returning I cannot do so in the language of my *Alma Mater*, I can say, with pride and satisfaction, she is my mother, and whatever may have been her delinquencies, I love her still. Then, ladies and gentlemen, let me again express my heartfelt thanks for this warm and sincere welcome, on returning to this, my native city.

New York Times, June 4, 1867.

1. Johnson delivered this speech on his arrival at the Yarborough House where he was residing. The following day he was to attend the dedication of the monument to his father who had died in 1812 from health complications resulting from his rescue of two men who were drowning. *National Intelligencer*, June 6, 1867.

2. Gov. Jonathan Worth, who had just introduced Johnson.

3. From Sir Walter Scott's *Lay of the Last Minstrel*, canto 6, stanza 1.

From Francis J. Herron

New Orleans, June 4, 1867

Mr President

When in Washington a few weeks since[1] you asked me regarding sundry matters here, and beleiving you would like the opinions of various persons on the condition of affairs, I take the liberty of sending forward mine. The Military Bill passed during my absence from here,[2] and it was put into operation in this District by General Sheridan with unnecessary haste, I thought, yet I beleived he would use the great power given him, with caution, and do the community full justice. I find upon my return, and after carefully looking into the matter, that the people are not getting justice. The great subject of complaint, and it is well founded, is the management of Registration,[3] which if carried out on the present plan, will give the entire control of this State to the colored population and the few whites operating with them. No attention is paid to the opinion of Mr Stanbery[4] but the Registars are permitted to decide according to thier own feelings, and are rejecting large numbers for the most trivial reasons, who are properly and legally entitled to vote. The fault of course is with Genl Sheridan, who, although he proclaims himself not a politician, is nevertheless one, and a very ambitious one too, of the most extreme views. Not having had much experience, he has unfortunately selected for his advisors Dr Newman,[5] a Methodist preacher, and two or three other utterly impracticable men. With an ungovernable temper of his own, and bad advisors, you can readily see how he makes such errors, and manages to keep his District in commotion. Another serious objection is his refusal to mix with the people and see and hear for himself. At present everything he hears of and from the citizens, comes to him through detectives or some hanger-on and is conveyed in a way to suit the circumstances. It is utterly impossible for anyone to properly command one of these Districts without mingling with the citizens, and seeing for himself. I can assure you the Generals course has caused great regret to many Northern persons here, who really have the good of the country at heart, and desire that justice at least be done the community. After the late undignified quarrel between the General and Gov Wells,[6] I do not hesitate to express the opinion that Sheridan ought to be removed. His standing in the District is gone, and with the feeling of a large majority of the people as it now is, he can do no good here. It would only be an act of justice to replace him with some officer of more experience and broader views, and if possible one who is not too ambitious. A suggestion from me is out of place I know, but I cant help adding that I should like to see such a man as Rousseau here. Genl Canby[7] would fill the place well, if he did not keep himself so completely wrapped up in his shell. I trust at least you will give some releif in the matter of Registration by having the time extended, and compelling the Registrars to act in accordance with Mr Stanberys opinion. If you have no objection I will from time to time write you about our matters, and may give some information that you would like to have.

F. J. Herron

ALS, DLC-JP.

1. Herron was in Washington as late as April 14 as he wrote to Johnson from there on that date.

2. The First Military Reconstruction Act was passed on March 2. Foner, *Reconstruction*, 276.

3. William H.C. King also complained to Johnson about voter registration in his missive of May 2, 1867.

4. See Stanbery's opinion of May 24, 1867, calendared in this volume and printed in its entirety in Benjamin F. Hall et al., eds., *Official Opinions of the Attorneys General of the United States* (43 vols. to date, Washington, D.C., 1852–), 12: 141–68.

5. John Philip Newman (1826–1899), who had previously served several large Methodist congregations in New York City, was sent to New Orleans to reestablish the Northern Methodist denomination in the South (1864–69). He founded several schools and a newspaper in addition to his pastoral duties. Newman was closely associated with Ulysses S. Grant, serving as his pastor while he was president. In 1888 Newman was elected a Methodist bishop. *DAB.*

6. For more information on this quarrel, see J. Madison Wells to Johnson, June 4, 1867, and Eugene H. Angamar to Johnson, July 3, 1867.

7. Lovell H. Rousseau and Edward R.S. Canby.

From Russell R. Lowell[1]

Millford Ohio   June 4, 1867

Dear Sir

I am solicited by your friends to take this liberty of addressing you and to say, That that part of the article in the Tribune relating to L C Bakers going to Richmond is false,[2] and that the same letters upon which Baker got his position from the secty of War[3] were all written by a man in Washington and never written nor signed by the parties whose names purported to be attached to them.[4]

It is quite necessary he should be tried on the Indictments now agt him in N Jersey. He once undertook to Injure Mr Chase while he was secty Treasury but failed.[5]

He now attacts you. With your permission I would wish to show him up and see that Justice was done him, and take the responsibilities myself only.

Hon N Sargent[6] can inform you where I am at all times. S P Chase can also If the secty of the Treasury[7] will allow me a leave of Absence for thirty days.

I will see that the *Tribune* gives a different version of Mr Bakers experience for the last Six years.[8]

R R Lowell

ALS, DLC-JP.
    1. Lowell (*c*1821–*fl*1869) lived for a time in Syracuse, New York, where he was a deputy sheriff, ran a restaurant and ticket office, and was a deputy marshal. In 1869, while with the U.S. Secret Detective Service, Lowell was indicted in Canandaigua, New York, for "conspiracy and collusion with counterfeiters" during the past two years. 1860 Census, N.Y., Onondaga, Syracuse, 7th Ward, 911; *OR*, Ser. 2, Vol. 2: 552; Ser. 3, Vol. 3: 578–79; *Washington Evening Star*, June 23, 1869.
    2. On May 21, 1867, the *New York Tribune* printed extracts from Lafayette C. Baker's recently published history of the secret service.
    3. Lowell is mistaken, for Baker was allegedly sent to Richmond by Gen. Winfield Scott, not Secretary Stanton.
    4. Baker was supposedly introduced to Scott by Hiram Walbridge and M. D. Kelley. It is unknown what other person Lowell was referring to here. *New York Tribune*, May 21, 1867.
    5. In early 1864 treasury secretary Salmon P. Chase hired Baker from the War Department to investigate rumors of fraudulent operations and flagrant improprieties. Baker's investigation brought to light not only dishonest practices but also immoral relations between treasury officials and female clerks. The congressional investigation's majority report, however, charged Baker with conspiracy against the treasury officials named by him. Margaret Leech, *Reveille in Washington, 1860–1865* (New York, 1941), 317.
    6. Nathaniel K. Sargent.
    7. Hugh McCulloch.
    8. No evidence has been found that Lowell or the *Tribune* provided any version other than Baker's.

From Edwin M. Stanton

War Dept 2 30 P M
Washington D C   June 4" 1867

Pursuant to your directions Gen Sheridan was directed to Suspend proceedings in relation to the Board of Levee Commissioners at New Orleans.[1] The accompanying telegram has just been received from him[2] which seems to be of sufficient importance to communicate to you without delay together with the reasons for his action assigned in another telegram received this morning,[3] and extract from which is also transmitted herewith.[4] All well.

Edwin M Stanton   Secty of War

Tel, DLC-JP.

1. Stanton to Sheridan, June 3, 1867, Johnson Papers, LC. This order was the result of protests by Governor Wells and others to have Sheridan's levee commissioner orders revoked. For a discussion of the problem, see Eugene H. Angamar to Johnson, July 3, 1867.

2. Probably Sheridan to Stanton, June 4, 1867, Tels. Sent, Sec. of War (M473, Roll 91), RG107, NA. A notation on the telegram indicates it was received at 2:20 p.m. Sheridan, in obedience to orders, had "suspended the operation of the Levee Commissioners" but urged that "Now is the time to commence work on the Levees and it will be a great misfortune to the state to let the funds appropriated be controlled by unscrupulous politicians."

3. Sheridan to Stanton, June 3, 1867, Johnson Papers, LC.

4. See also Johnson to Stanton, June 12, 1867.

From J. Madison Wells

New Orleans, June 4th 1867

Sir

The enclosed order from Gen'l Sheridan removing me from office,[1] is respectfully submitted for your consideration, as to the question of his power to do so. As to the reasons assigned by him for taking this step viz, that I have impeded him in the execution of the law of Congress, I enter a respectful but emphatic denial to the accusation. I am prepared to establish the truth of this assertion. It is evidently a mere pretext on the part of the General to give the color of cause for an act which originated in personal malice towards me because I dared to defend myself from his personal attacks.[2] Had the General stated that I was an "impediment" in the way to the gratification of his inordinate ambition to make himself a great man, he would have come much nearer the truth than he did. His abuse of me personally, I do not condescend to notice. His eminent skill in that line is well known to this community. That he should so far degrade the office he holds, as to make his official orders the vehicle of his malice, may surprise you but not me, who know his reckless habits.

It is not my purpose however in this communication to make your Excellency a party to the personal quarrel of General Sheridan and myself. It is foreign to the question at issue, *which is simply* if military commanders under the law of congress have the right to remove civil officers under the provisional governments of the States established thereby, or in other words, if they possess any power beyond those delegated, in said act and definitely expressed.

Knowing that the question, touching the general powers of the military commanders thereunder, particularly growing out of the frequent exercise of the removing power by General Sheridan, is now under consideration by the attorney General, I respectfully submit the case of my removal in connection therewith as another instance of the illegal exercise of power by General Sheridan, beleiving the importance of the questions involved, will call forth an early decision.[3]

J Madison Wells
Governor of the State of Louisiana.

ALS, DLC-JP.

1. Special Orders No. 59 of June 3, 1867.

2. In a telegram to Stanton, Sheridan made it clear that his removal of Wells was precipitated by the levee board controversy. He also called Wells "a political trickster, and a dishonest man." Sheridan to Stanton, June 3, 1867, Johnson Papers, LC. For a full account of the levee board difficulties, see Eugene H. Angamar to Johnson, July 3, 1867.

3. In his opinion Stanbery did mention Wells's case. See Stanbery to Johnson, June 12, 1867.

From Thomas C. Cain et al.[1]

Knoxville Tennessee   June 9th 1867

The undersigned beg leave to call your attention to the following facts. We attended a public meeting yesterday at Morristown in Grainger County Tennessee.[2] The people had assembled to hear The Hon. Emerson Etheridge speak, he being a candidate for Governor, and having made the appointment several days before, and published the same in the newspapers.

A large church was generously thrown open for the accommodation of the public. It was full to overflowing, many ladies being in the building.

After Mr. Etheridge had spoken about twenty minutes, one Bill Sizemore,[3] who was two years in the rebel army (but now a Tennessee Radical, engaged in insulting and persecuting Union men), came into the church and demanded a division of time for some other speaker, known to be one Howk.[4] The demand was made to Hon. John Netherland while Mr. Etheridge was speaking. Upon being told by Mr. Netherland that he had nothing to do with the matter, said Sizemore announced that all the Radicals were directed to leave the church. They did so, yelling and howling in the church as they withdrew, and by their general conduct, alarmed the ladies present. After their withdrawal the church building was immediately filled by those who had before been unable to obtain seats. The speaking was resumed and after about thirty minutes, the noise and disturbance was so great that the speaking was again suspended. A Company of Brownlow's Militia, armed with muskets, and commanded by one Evans,[5] was present participating in the disorder. They (the Militia) were ordered to "fix bayonets," and did so, having first formed in line, immediately in front of the church building, and within twenty feet thereof, for the purpose of intimidating and dispersing the audience. Full details of the proceedings of these armed persons, called State Troops or "Brownlow's Militia," who have been organized under what purports to be an act of the Tennesee Legislature, during the day, would make this paper too long. We therefore content ourselves with the foregoing, and with the further statement that similar bodies of armed men were at Jonesboro and Bristol, on Wednesday and Friday last when Mr. Etheridge addressed the people on political subjects. These armed bodies of Militia, so called, are engaged in overawing, insulting, and oppressing the people. They keep them in constant alarm, frighten them away from public meetings, and in the opinion of the undersigned they will prevent free discussion, and free elections, unless their organizations are broken up, or counteracted by opposing military Power. We make this statement of facts and leave the matter to your Excellency. In view of that provision of the Federal Constitution which declares that no State shall keep "troops &c &c in time of peace," and that the Federal Authority is bound to guarantee us a republican government, we ask that the people of Tennessee may be relieved of the presence of these lawless bands of armed men, or protected by a counteracting force, so that free speech, and free elections may be secured to the qualified voters of the state.

	Thomas C. Cain
John Baxter	John J. Wolfe, Late 1st Lt. 1st T. Cavy
John Williams	Jno. M. Fleming
A. A. Kyle	W. C. Kyle

ALS (Cain), DLC-JP.

1. Cain (1842–1915) became a hotel manager and proprietor in Morristown. He served one term in the state legislature (1879–81) and afterwards as superintendent of the state prison. Wolfe (1842–1922), of Rogersville, had served in the 1st Tenn. Cav. during the war and subsequently was clerk of the Hawkins County circuit court (1870–78). *BDTA*, 2: 127; *Cemeteries of Hawkins County Tennessee* (4 vols., Rogersville, 1985–91), 2: 112; Goodspeed's *History of East Tennessee*, 880.

2. For a brief account of the Morristown meeting which agrees in broad outline with the version reported by Cain et al., see the *Nashville Union and Dispatch*, June 16, 1867.

3. William O. Sizemore (c1834–1867), a shoemaker who briefly served in a Confederate Tennessee cavalry regiment and was an infamous postwar troublemaker. In October

1867, while a jury was being chosen to try him for murder, he was shot in the head and killed by an irate citizen. 1860 Census, Tenn., Hawkins, 8th Dist., 49; CSR, William O. Sizemore, RG109, NA; Hawkins County Circuit Court Minutes, Oct. 1866-Oct. 1867, p. 191; Jan. 1868-Jan. 1871, pp. 17, 27, 48, 151; *Brownlow's Knoxville Whig*, Oct. 16, 1867.

4. Probably Leonidas C. Houk.

5. James R. Evans (1847–1921) was one of the captains of the militia regiments commissioned in 1867. He had served in the 4th U.S. Cav. as private and later sergeant (1864–65). By the time of the 1870 census, he was listed as a clerk and master in Claiborne County. CSR, James R. Evans, RG109, NA; *Nashville Republican Banner*, June 9, 1867; *Nashville Union and Dispatch*, June 9, 1867; 1860 Census, Tenn., Claiborne, 179; (1870), 7; Pension Records, James R. Evans, RG15, NA.

From John Jacobs [1]

Memphis   June 9th 67

President Johnson

Permit me in God's name to adjure you to hear the truth; nineteen twentieths of the people of the southern states, are very desirous for you to be their next President; & if you will give them the protection and Priviledge of voting according to the opinion of your Attorney General,[2] which is all they ask for you will be the next President as certain as two & two make four. Now my dear friend take the advice of a poor old man into consideration; and by Proclimation Grant Universal Pardon & order Elections in all the southern states according to the opinion of the Attorney General. It will be noting but just & Right and will make you more popular both north & south. The people of Tennessee are begining to believe that you are holding your protection from them in reveng because they mistook your motives & spoke much against you while Govenor under Lincoln. For they all believe you have the power to stop Brownlow in his mad, wild & furious carier. General Thomas[3] is a Radical with Brownlow but not so bad. He will never carry out your wishes, unless you say what he shall & what he shall not do. Give us a chance to vote. It is all we ask, and we would not ask this if we did not believe it to be in your power to give us this privilege under the laws of Congress. Sir our lives are not safe. Our property we care not for: but out lives and the lives of our wives & dear Chidren, does need your Protection. I have just left East & Middle Tenn and there is not a day passes but Brownlow men murder one two or three persons; and they are doing worse than murder; they have Ravished both married and single woman, and sir in some neighborhoods the people are horrow stricken with fear to tell how bad they are doing for several have been killed for reporting to Brownlow which report he paid no attention to. He has secretly turned loose many in Pententiary to vote for him & unless you come to our Protection he will be the next Governor by a large majority of the vots cast.

John Jacobs

ALS, DLC-JP.
    1. Possibly either John Jacobs (b. c1818) or John Jacobs (b. c1820), both of whom
were laborers in Memphis. 1870 Census, Tenn., Shelby, Memphis, 7th Ward, 253;
(1870), 8th Ward, 119.
    2. Among other things, Stanbery declared that district military commanders could
not deny the right to vote to anyone who had taken the oath of eligibility. See Stanbery to
Johnson, May 24, 1867; Albert Castel, *The Presidency of Andrew Johnson* (Lawrence,
Kans., 1979), 126; Trefousse, *Johnson*, 288–89.
    3. George H. Thomas.

From John Williams, Jr.

                                        Knoxville   June 9, 1867
Dear Sir:
    A petition will be forwarded to you to-morrow asking your protection
against Brownlows Militia.[1] It is useless for me to repeat in detain the
disgraceful conduct of this militia at Morristown on yesterday. I have witnessed many scenes of disorder, but never in my life have I seen any that
would compare with this. I expected every moment after the line of battle
was formed, to see a charge of bayonets into the Church, where Mr.
Etheridge was speaking. The Conservatives however, were firm & reso-
lute, which had the effect to stay for the time being, the infamous conduct
of these infuriated outlaws. Mr. Etheridge manifested a courageous spirit
& thereby stimulated his hearers. If this Militia is not disbanded, or sent
out there will be actual war in East Tennessee before the election as I
believe. If they are permitted to remain in our midst, we will be compelled to fight them, or surrender our liberties to the negroes, & a few
white scavengers. This condition of affairs is much to be deplored. We
cannot much longer submit to Brownlowism. He is pretending to be in
such ill health, that he confines himself to his house, & issues his orders to
his pimps, & they execute them by following Mr. Etheridge through the
Country, and creating disturbances wherever he proposes to address the
people.
    Read the statement, & you will understand the case. For *Gods sake* come
to our relief, & spare an effusion of blood, which must, & will certainly take
place unless the Government at Washington interposes in our behalf.
    Since this statment referred to above was written, I have heard of an-
other outrage this Militia committed on their way from Claibourne
County, to Morristown. It was this. In crossing the mountain they came
upon some men working the road. They ordered the men to shout for
Brownlow. The men, being friends of your Administration, refused to
comply with their demand. Whereupon, they arrested these men, took
them from their work to the foot of the mountain before discharging
them, & offered them many indignities, shuch as should not be tolerated
in any civilized Government.
    Mr. Etheridge leaves here to-morrow for Athens & Cleveland. He has

made a fine impression in East Tennessee, & every thing would be in good working order, if we could only get rid of this abominable Militia.

John Williams.

ALS, DLC-JP.
    1. Probably Thomas C. Cain et al. to Johnson, June 9, 1867.

From Dan Rice

Columbus O.   June 10th 1867

Your Excellency,

During my present tour, and especially in this great Radical stronghold, the State of Ohio, I have taken unusual pains, both before audiences and in confidential conversations, to ascertain the public temper with reference to the policy of the Government, and I cannot be mistaken in the conclusion that there is a marked, though gradual and quiet, reaction, progressing in the minds of the masses, particularly that portion embracing the rural population. The extremists are slowly and surely losing the confidence of the rank and file of their supporters—the floating vote, so potent in determining results, and tending with the natural instinct for spoil to the supposed successful party is irresolute, and will, in my opinion, turn towards conservation if encouraged to do so by wisdom and moderation on the part of your friends. I have improvised an original test, in which one of my Masks, is made to impersonate the character of your friend, impeachment Ashley,[1] shroud in a ridiculous costume, typical of the character of the attempt. The audiences go wild over it, and one universal shout of "How are you Ashley," greets the impersonation. So much for Buckingham,[2] let him writhe on the cross of ridicule where I have nailed him.

But to drop serious matters of State, permit me to remind you of your promise to honor me with your photograph and autograph. It is a trivial matter to you, and one which you cannot but lose sight of in the mighty cares oppressing you, but to me it is of an interest which will I trust be a sufficient excuse for its introduction here.

While in Marietta O. recently, my attention was called to a case in which an honest and warm friend of yours has both suffered and been most unjustly treated, because of his sterling fidelity to your principles. Mr. T. G. Fields,[3] a gentleman of education, position and popularity, enlisted at the outbreak of the rebellion as a private, and fought the good fight out, receiving his discharge at the close of the war, as Lieutenant. He then commenced the publication of the News, and prospered, until the inauguration of the radical war upon you, when from the highest toned principle he stood manfully by you, and as a result has been utterly ruined. He applied for the position of Post Master, and his papers, signed by L. D. Campbell, Minister to Mexico, Genl W. P. Richardson[4] Revenue Collector, and others, are now on file at Washington. The present Post Master, W. C. Buck,[5] was confirmed in August last, but has never qualified. He filed one bond for $1000, but the other he has failed to file, probably because of a strong protest addressed to Post Master General Randall, by the business men of Marietta. He is your bitter enemy, and a bad man and worse official.

Mr. Field's appointment would be hailed with satisfaction by his community, you would secure an honest, able and energetic supporter and his appointment I am sanguine would be confirmed. This is a case in which I have no personal interest whatever beyond a desire to advance your interest and secure justice for a brave soldier, desiring your Excellency's consideration. On these grounds your attention to the matter, at your convenience is respectfully urged. In referring to Mr. Buck it should be understood that he is not acting as Post Master, the one appointed by Mr. Lincoln—Mr. Bosworth[6]—still performing the duties of the office.

Please address me at Girard, on this subject when convenient and oblige.

Dan Rice

ALS, DLC-JP.
1. James M. Ashley.
2. Probably an allusion to Henry Stafford (c1454–1483), duke of Buckingham, who played a central role in bringing Richard III to the throne of England. He soon rebelled against Richard, however, and was leading his army against the king when he was betrayed. He was quickly captured and beheaded. *The New Columbia Encyclopedia* (1975).
3. Theodore G. Field (c1834–1894) served with the 1st Va. Lt. Arty. (USA) from 1862 to 1865. After the war he was an editor and correspondent in Ohio, Pennsylvania, and Kentucky. No evidence has been found that Field was considered for the postmaster position. Pension Records, Henriette L. Field, RG15, NA.
4. William P. Richardson (1824–1886), a lawyer, was a Mexican War veteran and served during the Civil War with the 25th Ohio Inf. and as commander of Ohio's Camp Chase Military Prison. In December of 1864 he was brevetted brigadier general. In late 1865 he commanded a subdistrict and later the District of East South Carolina. Upon leaving the army he was commissioned collector for Ohio's Fifteenth District, a post he held from 1866 to 1869, after which he resumed his law practice. Hunt and Brown, *Brigadier Generals*; *The Biographical Encyclopaedia of Ohio of the Nineteenth Century* (Cincinnati, 1876), 139–40.
5. William C. Buck (c1828–1887) of Marietta served as captain in the 39th Ohio Vol. Inf. from 1861 to 1865, and as postmaster from July 1866 to July 1867. Pension Files, William C. Buck, RG15, NA; Martin R. Andrews, *History of Marietta and Washington County, Ohio and Representative Citizens* (Chicago, 1902), 662, 802; Ser. 6B, Vol. 4: 257, Johnson Papers, LC.
6. Salah Bosworth (1805–1890), a portrait painter, held the offices of county auditor and postmaster at Marietta during the Lincoln administration. He was again appointed postmaster, replacing Buck, in July 1867. Andrews, *Marietta and Washington County*, 211; *U.S. Off. Reg.* (1861–69); Ser. 6B, Vol. 4: 261, Johnson Papers, LC.

From J. S. Shangle [1]

Bristol   Sullivan County Tennessee
June the 10th 1867

Whereas a portion of the Radical party of said County by lawlessness and misguided temper have thretned to assault Moultiest [molest] & assinate the Conseritives of Sullivan County

And whereas we have been stoped from speaking & have been informed by this rag-tag-&-bob-tail-malitia, that all discussion & criticism of the past Legislature would be considered treason against the state, we would therfor respectfully Call your attention to the fact, that unless something is done by the strong arm of federal Power we believe that there will be, serious difficulties in Tennssee before the August Elections.

Good & true men who have ever been Loyal to the government of the united states are dayly thretned because they dare act & speak for the Constitution & Laws. Your petitioners is a Justice of the peace & a candidate for the Legislature and has allways been a Loyal and true man to the govment of the united states. The undersigned bear witness to the above facts and pray that your Excellency may take the matter into speedy Consideration. [2]

All of which we respectfully submit to his Excellency Andrew Johnson President of the united States.

J S. Shangle   Bristol Tennssee

ALS, DLC-JP.
1. Shangle (b. c1825) was a hotel keeper in Sullivan County prior to the outbreak of the war. He was not successful in his bid for a legislative seat in 1867. 1860 Census, Tenn., Sullivan, 17th Dist., 61.
2. Appended to Shangle's letter were endorsements from J. S. Goforth and Joseph R. Anderson, who testified to the veracity and loyalty of Shangle.

From Daniel E. Sickles

Charleston, 10th June '67

My dear Mr President.

I trust your return to Washington was attended with every circumstance to make your journey agreeable. [1] As soon as I can dispose of business accumulated in my absence I shall avail myself of your permission to address you directly upon matters of public interest, by forwarding (during the present week) a few suggestions and reflections upon the powers and duties of District Commanders according to my interpretation of the Acts of Congress; and also as to the best mode of making the action of District Commanders conform to the wishes and requirements of the

Commander-in-Chief.[2] I regard these States as having been placed under your control as Commander in chief, by Congress which assumed that the United States had paramount & exclusive jurisdiction. Your control as Commander in Chief is exercised through District Commanders appointed by yourself. These Commanders are subject to your orders. You may revoke or suspend any order they give. You may control their action by general or particular instructions. You may relieve them and supersede them.

Allow me to suggest that it will be better to *control the execution* of the Reconstruction Acts according to your judgment as to the means employed & measures addressed, than by *Construction* of the true & intent and meaning of the Acts to raise new issues with Congress involving perhaps a contradiction of the views expressed in your Veto Message in relation to those Acts and possibly giving supposed occasion for further legislation. In other words I would recommend you to review the action of Commanding officers in cases as they arise—preferably referring complaints made to the responsible officer for a report before your final action;—that is to say *I hope you will follow in these matters the usual course of Military Administration*, persuaded as I am that in this way you will best carry out the purposes of the Acts of Congress, correct the errors of those you have appointed to command, and secure as the basis of your actions reliable reports and suggestions from all who exercise command or authority subordinate to yourself as Commander in Chief.

I pray you, dear Sir, to excuse the freedom of these views frankly expressed in harmony with the spirit of your request when I had the honor to take leave of your Excellency at Raleigh.[3]

D Sickles

ALS, DLC-JP.

1. This is a reference to Johnson's return from his North Carolina trip.

2. Four days later Johnson thanked Sickles for his suggestions and solicited "further expressions" of his views. The same day Sickles replied, noting he had been so busy he had "not had time to devote to the subject," and instead enclosed copies of an eighteen-page letter he had earlier written to Henry J. Raymond of the *New York Times* and a telegram he had just sent (on the 14th) to E. D. Townsend, the adjutant general, which covered some aspects of the topic, as it pertained to the Carolinas. Sickles to Raymond, June 10, 1867; Johnson to Sickles, Sickles to Johnson, Sickles to Townsend, all June 14, 1867, Johnson Papers, LC.

3. See Sickles's earlier request for information about Johnson's travel plans; he wanted to meet the President and escort him to Raleigh. Sickles to Robert Johnson, May 2, 1867, Johnson Papers, LC.

To George H. Thomas

Washington, D.C., June 10th 1867

The people of Winchester Franklin County, Tennessee, are represented to me as in great terror[1]—produced by outrages committed by

Rickman[2] and his men. I see it stated that Genl Whipple has been sent to investigate it.[3] Have you any information in regard to this matter?[4]

Andrew Johnson,   Prest

Tel., DNA-RG107, Tels. Sent, President, Vol. 3 (1865–68).

1. Undoubtedly Johnson's statement here was in direct response to Arthur S. Colyar's telegram of June 8 which declared: "People still in terror." The frame of reference is, of course, to the activities of the state guard in Franklin County. Colyar to Johnson, June 8, 1867, Johnson Papers, LC. See also J. S. Payne to Johnson, June 3, 1867.

2. William O. Rickman (1833–1868) served as a captain in the 5th Tenn. Cav. (USA) during the war. In 1867 Brownlow appointed Rickman to serve as captain of Co. "H," 1st Rgt., of the state guard. The murder of James Brown by Rickman's outfit was the principal atrocity that stirred the wrath of Franklin County citizens. CSR, William O. Rickman, RG94, NA; Off. Army Reg.: Vols., 4: 1179; Directory Williamson County, Tennessee Burials (2 vols., Williamson County, 1973–75), 1: 355. For the adjutant general's account of these events, see Samuel Hunt to Brownlow, June 3, 1867, Brownlow Papers, Special Collections, TU.

3. See William D. Whipple's report, dated June 7, 1867, in Lets. Recd. (Main Ser.), File C-524-1867 (M619, Roll 544), RG94, NA.

4. See Thomas to Johnson, June 11, 1867.

To Otis Norcross [1]

Washington, D.C.   June 11th 1867

Sir:

I have the honor to acknowledge the receipt of your letter of the 7th instant[2] tendering to me in accordance with a vote of the Council, the hospitalities of the city of Boston during my contemplated visit. I intend being present at the dedication of the new Masonic Temple in your city on the 24th instant, and during my short stay in Boston I will feel honored to accept the hospitalities of your city, receiving them with a reciprocation of the friendship and courtesy which prompted the Council in their offer.[3]

Andrew Johnson

LS, MHi.

1. Norcross (1811–1882), Boston mayor in 1867, had been a successful businessman, state legislator, and Boston alderman. Holli and Jones, American Mayors, 269.

2. See Norcross to Johnson, June 7, 1867, Johnson Papers, LC.

3. Once word went out of Johnson's intended trip to Boston, invitations to visit other New England towns arrived at the White House. See, for example, William B. Lawrence to Johnson, June 12, 1867; Peter Lawson to Johnson, June 12, 1867; Charles R. Chapman to Johnson, June 13, 1867, Johnson Papers, LC.

From Nathaniel G. Taylor

June 11, 1867, Washington, D.C.; ALS, DNA-RG48, Indian Div., Lets. Recd.

Taylor, the commissioner of Indian affairs, requested Johnson to mediate Taylor's differences with Acting Secretary of the Interior William T. Otto over whether or not to send a special agent to the Navajo reservation, the Bosque Redondo near Fort Sumner, New Mexico. The 7,000 Navajos there had been under the control of the War Department, at the cost of about $1,500,000 each year, since 1864, but as of July 1, 1867, they were being transferred to Taylor's charge and Congress had appropriated only $200,000 for their care. Taylor had written to Otto on May 25 making suggestions about the "management and subsistence" of the Navajos and asking permission to purchase supplies for them on the open market. Although Otto approved these suggestions, he did not approve Taylor's request of June 1 for a special agent. Taylor argued that because the agency superintendent, A. Baldwin Norton, was absent sick in Ohio, there would be too much work for the agent, Theodore H. Dodd, to do alone because, in addition to his regular duties, he would have to arrange subsistence for the 7,000 Indians, as well as appraise and receive the reservation property being transferred from the War Department. Taylor did not know why Otto refused to send a special agent when other agents had been appointed recently "in cases far less urgent, and at *large Salaries*." On June 12 Johnson referred the letter to the secretary of the interior "for examination and early report."

From George H. Thomas

Louisville Ky   June 11th 67

The terror among the people of Franklin County Tennessee in consequence of the organization of Militia under Rickman is very much magnified for political purposes.[1] The murder reported to have been committed by the Militia was committed but there is no danger whatever of a repetition of a similar offence.

The officer Comdg the Company has been ordered into arrest by Governor Brownlow for trial.[2]

Geo H Thomas Maj Gen

Tel, DLC-JP.
    1. Thomas's telegram was in direct response to Johnson's of the previous day. General Whipple had reported that the difficulties in the area were due to the political contest going on in Tennessee. See the report of William D. Whipple, June 7, 1867, Lets. Recd. (Main Ser.), File C-524-1867 (M619, Roll 544), RG94, NA.
    2. There were several reports that Governor Brownlow had ordered the arrest of Captain Rickman and others implicated in the Franklin County problems. Yet, there were subsequent indications that Rickman was not arrested and in fact was seen in Nashville "quite unchained and roaming at will." Brownlow's secretary suggested that the governor could contend that he had not yet seen the adjutant general's report when he decided to have Rickman arrested. *Nashville Union and American*, June 12, 14, 16, 1867; H. H. Thomas to Brownlow, June 7, 1867, Brownlow Papers, Special Collections, TU.

From Jacob Ziegler

Harrisburg   June 11th 1867

Dear President

Sharswood[1] will be nominated for Judge. The matter looks to me as settled. Wallace[2] will be continued as Chairman of State Central Committee. This conclusion is arrived at this morning in order to harmonize all interests and to enable us to go into the contest with the prestige of success from the beginning. There is a full convention or nearly so, and all speak hopeful of the future. I do hope that matters will take a turn so that we will have peace and quiet in the land and these vexatious questions of public policy established and settled upon an enduring basis. Taxation is beginning to be severely felt by all classes of the community and if they will not awaken to a just sense of their condition all is lost. You I know trust the people. I hope they may rise up and shake off the incubus that is weighing them down.

As usual they wish me to do all the running. I am willing to do any thing for my country.

I trust your trip[3] promoted your health, and increased your faith in the people.

J. Ziegler

ALS, DLC-JP.
1. George Sharswood (1810–1883), formerly a member of the Pennsylvania legislature and district court judge, was chosen state supreme court judge in October 1867. *Biographical Encyclopaedia of Pa.*, 75–76; *DAB*.
2. William A. Wallace (1827–1896), a lawyer in Clearfield for many years, served in the state senate (1863–75). Afterwards, he was in the U.S. Senate for one term (1875–81). *BDUSC*.
3. Ziegler is referring to Johnson's trip to North Carolina.

From James E. English

Hartford, June 12 1867

My dear Sir

By the news papers of yesterday I notice you propose to leave Washington for Boston—on the 21st inst. I avail myself of the occasion not only on my own account, but in behalf of your very many friends in this State, to request that you do not fail to pass through Connecticut, either in going to or returning from Boston. You are doubtless aware that the Cities of New Haven and Hartford, are on the direct line of travel between New York and Boston, between which cities several trains of cars pass daily, thus affording you an opportunity of remaining for a longer or shorter time as circumstances may require. I assure you our friends here will feel greatly disappointed should you not come and if you should not remain but a short time in each place. Please let me hear from you on this subject giving particulars as to wether you propose to come and if so wether going or returning from Boston . . . [1]

James E. English

P.S. Come, I assure you a free cordial and hearty reception. Connecticut is a small state but her citizens are true to the Constitution and Union.

ALS, DLC-JP.

1. Governor English followed this letter with two communications to Johnson on June 18; one a telegram notifying the President that the Connecticut legislature had authorized an official invitation and the other a letter which enclosed the resolution passed by the legislature. Also on the 18th, apparently before receiving the communications from English, Johnson wrote to him, thanking the governor for the June 12 letter and specifying some of his travel itinerary. The President promised to spend some time in Connecticut. All these letters are in the Johnson Papers, LC. An account of some of Johnson's sojourn in Connecticut may be found in the *New York World*, June 27, 1867.

From Benjamin B. French

Washington   June 12, 1867

My Dear Sir,

The heating apparatus of the White House is, as you are aware, very old & dilapidated. Last winter I got Mr. George W. Goodall,[1] who understands it better than any other Plumber in Washington, to examine it thoroughly and make an estimate of the cost of renewing it. He did so. I laid the estimate before the Committee and obtained the appropriation, and, had I remained in office, I should have employed Mr. Goodall to do the work.

There is no man in Washington more capable of doing the work than Mr. G. He is your warm personal friend and is mine. He is anxious to do the work, and I am anxious to have him do it. I have not a doubt that if you will make the request of Gen. Michler,[2] that Mr. Goodall may be employed, that he will be.

It is very important to you that the work should be commenced soon, otherwise it cannot be completed and you will all suffer inconvenience from the cold, should it not be in order when winter sets in.

I most respectfully ask, in behalf of my friend Goodall, that you will grant this request.

B. B. French   Late C.P.B.

ALS, DNA-RG42, Lets. of Appl., Box 4, George W. Goodall.

1. Goodall (*c*1825–*fl*1901), a plumber and gas fitter, was a native of Washington, D.C. 1860 Census, D.C., Washington, 7th Ward, 143; Washington, D.C., directories (1866–1901).

2. Nathaniel Michler (1827–1881), a career army officer, served as chief topographical engineer for various army groups during the Civil War and was brevetted brigadier general on April 2, 1865. After the office of commissioner of public buildings was abolished Michler was appointed to perform the duties associated with that office. Hunt and Brown, *Brigadier Generals*; Cole and McDonough, *Benjamin Brown French*, 533–34.

From Henry Stanbery

ATTORNEY GENERAL'S OFFICE,   *June* 12, 1867.

Sir:

On the 24th ultimo, I had the honor to transmit for your consideration my opinion[1] upon some of the questions arising under the reconstruction acts[2] therein referred to. I now proceed to give my opinion on the remaining questions, upon which the military commanders require instructions.

First, as to the powers and duties of these commanders.

The original act recites in its preamble that "no legal State governments or adequate protection for life or property exist" in those ten States, and that "it is necessary that peace and good order should be enforced" in those States "until loyal and republican State governments can be legally established."

The first and second sections divide these States into five military districts, subject to the military authority of the United States as thereinafter prescribed, and make it the duty of the President to assign from the officers of the army, a general officer to the command of each district, and to furnish him with a military force to perform his duties and enforce his authority within his district.

The third section declares "That it shall be the duty of each officer assigned as aforesaid to protect all persons in their rights of person and property, to suppress insurrection, disorder, and violence, and to punish, or cause to be punished, all disturbers of the public peace and criminals, and to this end, he may allow local civil tribunals to take jurisdiction of and try offenders, or, when in his judgment it may be necessary for the trial of offenders, he shall have power to organize military commissions or tribunals for that purpose; and all interference under color of State authority with the exercise of military authority under this act shall be null and void."

The fourth section provides "That all persons put under military arrest by virtue of this act shall be tried without unnecessary delay, and no cruel or unusual punishment shall be inflicted; and no sentence of any military commission or tribunal hereby authorized, affecting the life or liberty of any person, shall be executed until it is approved by the officer in command of the district, and the laws and regulations for the government of the army shall not be affected by this act, except in so far as they conflict with its provisions: *Provided*, That no sentence of death under the provisions of this act shall be carried into effect without the approval of the President."

The fifth section declares the qualification of voters in all elections, as well to frame the new Constitution for each State as in the elections to be held under the provisional government until the new State Constitution is ratified by Congress, and also fixes the qualifications of the delegates to frame the new Constitution.

The sixth section provides "That until the people of said rebel States shall be by law admitted to representation in the Congress of the United States, any civil governments which may exist therein shall be deemed provisional only, and in all respects subject to the paramount authority of the United States at any time to abolish, modify, control or supersede the same; and in all elections to any office under such provisional governments, all persons shall be entitled to vote, and none others, who are entitled to vote under the provisions of the fifth section of this act: and no person shall be eligible to any office under any such provisional governments who would be disqualified from holding office under the provisions of the third article of said constitutional amendment."

The duties devolved upon the commanding general by the supplementary act relate altogether to the registration of voters and the elections to be held under the provisions of that act. And as to these duties they are plainly enough expressed in the act, and it is not understood that any question not heretofore considered in the opinion referred to, has arisen or is likely to arise in respect to them. My attention, therefore, is directed to the powers and duties of the military commanders under the original act.

We see clearly enough that this act contemplates two distinct governments in each of these ten States, the one military, the other civil. The civil government is recognized as existing at the date of the act. The military government is created by the act. Both are provisional, and both are to continue until the new State constitution is framed and the State is admitted to representation in Congress. When that event takes place, both these provisional governments are to cease. In contemplation of this act, this military authority and this civil authority are to be carried on together. The people in these States are made subject to both, and must obey both, in their respective jurisdictions.

There is, then, an imperative necessity to define as clearly as possible the line which separates the two jurisdictions, and the exact scope of the authority of each.

Now as to the civil authority, recognized by the act as the provisional civil government, it covered every department of civil jurisdiction in each of these States. It had all the characteristics and powers of a State government, legislative, judicial, and executive, and was in the full and lawful exercise of all these powers, except only that it was not entitled to representation as a State of the Union. This existing government is not set aside; it is recognized more than once by the act. It is not in any one of its departments, or as to any one of its functions, repealed or modified by this act, save only in the qualifications of voters, the qualifications of persons eligible to office, the manner of holding elections, and the mode of framing the constitution of the State. The act does not in any other respect change the provisional government, nor does the act authorize the military authority to change it. The power of further changing it is reserved, not granted, and it is reserved to Congress, not delegated to the military commander.

Congress was not satisfied with the organic law, or constitution, under which this civil government was established. *That* constitution was to be changed in only one particular to make it acceptable to Congress, and that was in the matter of the elective franchise. The purpose, the sole object of this act is to effect that change, and to effect it by the agency of the people of the State, or such of them as are made voters, by means of elections provided for in the act, and in the meantime to preserve order and to punish offenders, if found necessary, by military commissions.

We are, therefore, not at a loss to know what powers were possessed by the existing civil authority. The only question is upon the powers conferred on the military authority. Whatever power is not given to the military, remains with the civil government.

We see, first of all, that each of these States is "made subject to the military authority of the United States"—not to the military authority altogether, but with this express limitation, "as hereinafter prescribed."

We must, then, examine what is thereinafter provided, to find the extent and nature of the power granted.

This, then, is what is granted to the mililtary [*sic*] commander: the power or duty "to protect all persons in their rights of person and property, to suppress insurrection, disorder, and violence, and to punish, or cause to be punished, all disturbers of the public peace and criminals," and he may do this by the agency of the criminal courts of the State, or, if necessary, he may have resort to military tribunals.

This comprises all the powers given to the military commander.

Here is a general clause making it the duty of the military commander to give protection to all persons in their rights of person and property. Considered by itself, and without reference to the context and to other provisions of the act, it is liable, from its generality, to be misunderstood.

What sort of protection is here meant? What violations of the rights of persons, or of property, are here intended? In what manner is this protection to be given? These questions arise at once.

It appears that some of the military commanders have understood this grant of power as all-comprehensive, conferring on them the power to remove the executive and judicial officers of the State, and to appoint other officers in their places, to suspend the legislative power of the State, to take under their control, by officers appointed by themselves, the collection and disbursement of the revenues of the State, to prohibit the execution of the laws of the State by the agency of its appointed officers and agents, to change the existing laws in matters affecting purely civil and private rights, to suspend or enjoin the execution of the judgments and decrees of the established State courts, to interfere in the ordinary administration of justice in the State courts, by prescribing new qualifications for jurors, and to change, upon the ground of expediency, the existing relations of the parties to contracts, giving protection to one party by violating the rights of the other party.

I feel confident that these military officers, in all they have done, have supposed that they had full warrant for their action. Their education and training have not been of the kind to fit them for the delicate and difficult task of giving construction to such a statute as that now under consideration. They require instruction, and nearly all of them have asked for instruction, to solve their own doubts, and to furnish to them a safe ground for the performance of their duties.

There can be no doubt as to the rule of construction according to which we must interpret this grant of power. It is a grant of power to military authority, over civil rights and citizens, in time of peace. It is a new jurisdiction, never granted before, by which, in certain particulars and for certain purposes, the established principle that the military shall be subordinate to the civil authority, is reversed. The rule of construction to be applied to such a grant of power is thus stated in *Dwarris on Statutes*, page 652: "A statute creating a new jurisdiction ought to be construed strictly."[3]

Guided by this rule, and in the light of other rules of construction familiar to every lawyer, especially of those which teach us that, in giving construction to single clauses, we must look to the context and to the whole law, that general clauses are to be controlled by particular clauses, and that such construction is to be put on a special clause as to make it harmonize with the other parts of the statute, so as to avoid repugnancy. I proceed to the construction of this part of the act.

To consider, then, in the first place, the terms of the grant. It is of a power to protect all persons in their rights of person and property. It is not a power to create new rights, but only to protect those which exist and are established by the laws under which these people live. It is a power to preserve, not to abrogate; to sustain the existing frame of social order and civil rule, and not a power to introduce military rule in its place. In effect, it is a police power, and the protection, here intended, is protection of persons and property against violence, unlawful force, and criminal infraction. It is given to meet the contingency recited in the preamble, of a want of "adequate protection for life and property;" and the necessity also recited, "that peace and good order should be enforced."

This construction is made more apparent when we look at the immediate context, and see in what mode, and by what agency, this protection is to be secured. This duty, or power, of protection is to be performed by the suppression of insurrection, disorder, and violence, and by the punishment, either by the agency of the State courts, or by military commissioners, when necessary, of all disturbers of the public peace and criminals; and it is declared that all interference, under color of State authority, with the exercise of this military authority, shall be null and void.

The next succeeding clause provides for a speedy trial of the offender, forbids the infliction of cruel and unusual punishment, and requires that sentences of these military courts, which involve the liberty or life of the accused, shall have the approval of the commanding general, and, as to a sentence of death, the approval of the President, before execution.

All these special provisions have reference to the preservation of order, and protection against violence and crime. They touch no other department or function of the civil administration, save only its criminal jurisdiction, and even as to that the clear meaning of this act is, that it is not to be interfered with by the military authority, unless when a necessity for such interference may happen to arise.

I see no authority, nor any shadow of authority, for interference with any other courts or any other jurisdiction, than criminal courts in the exercise of criminal jurisdiction. The existing civil authority in all its other departments, legislative, executive, and judicial, is left untouched. There is no provision, even under the plea of necessity, to establish, by military authority, courts or tribunals for the trial of civil cases, or for the protection of such civil rights of person or property as come within the cognizance of civil courts as contradistinguished from criminal courts. In point of fact there was no foundation for such a grant of power, for the Civil Rights act, and the Freedman's Bureau act, neither of which is superseded by this act, made ample provision for the protection of all merely civil rights where the laws or courts of these States might fail to give full, impartial protection.

I find no authority anywhere in this act for the removal by the military commander, of the proper officers of a State, either executive or judicial, or the appointment of persons to their places. Nothing short of an express grant of power, would justify the removal or the appointment of such an officer. There is no such grant expressed or even implied. On the contrary the act clearly enough forbids it. The regular State officials, duly elected and qualified, are entitled to hold their offices. They, too, have rights which the military commander is bound to protect, not authorized to destroy.

We find in the concluding clause of the sixth section of the act that these officials are recognized, and express provision is made to perpetuate them. It is enacted that "in all elections to any office under such provisional governments, all persons shall be entitled to vote, and none others, who are entitled to vote under the provisions of the fifth section of this act; and no person shall be eligible to any office under such provisional governments, who would be disqualified from holding office under the provisions of this act."

This provision not only recognizes all the officers of the provisional governments, but, in case of vacancies, very clearly points out how they are to be filled; and that happens to be in the usual way, by the people, and not by any other agency or any other power, either State or federal, civil or military.

I find it impossible under the provisions of this act to comprehend such an official as a governor of one of these States appointed to office by one of these military commanders. Certainly he is not the governor recognized by the laws of the State, elected by the people of the State, and clothed as such with the chief executive power. Nor is he appointed as a military governor for a State which has no lawful governor, under the pressure of an existing necessity, to exercise powers at large. The intention, no doubt, was to appoint him to fill a vacancy occasioned by a military order, and to put him in the place of the removed governor, to execute the functions of the office as provided by law. The law takes no cognizance of such an official, and he is clothed with no authority or color of authority.

What is true as to the governor is equally true as to all the other legislative, executive, and judicial officers of the State. If the military commander can oust one from his office, he can oust them all. If he can fill one vacancy he can fill all vacancies, and thus usurp all civil jurisdiction into his own hands, or the hands of those who hold their appointments from him and subject to his power of removal, and thus frustrate the very right secured to the people by this act. Certainly this act is rigorous enough in the power which it gives. With all its severity, the right of electing their own officers is still left with the people, and it must be preserved.

I must not be understood as fixing limits to the power of the military commander in case of an actual insurrection or riot. It may happen that an insurrection in one of these States may be so general and formidable as to require the temporary suspension of all civil government, and the establishment of martial law in its place. And the same thing may be true as to local disorder or riot in reference to the civil government of the city or place where it breaks out. Whatever power is necessary to meet such emergencies, the military commander may properly exercise. I confine myself to the proper authority of the military commander where peace and order prevail. When peace and order do prevail, it is not allowable to displace the civil officers and appoint others in their places under any idea that the military commander can better perform his duties and carry out the general purposes of the act by the agency of civil officers of his own choice rather than by the lawful incumbents. The act gives him no right to resort to such agency, but does give him the right to have "a sufficient military force" to enable him "to perform his duties and enforce his authority within the district to which he is assigned."

In the suppression of insurrection and riot, the military commander is wholly independent of the civil authority. So, too, in the trial and punishment of criminals and offenders, he may supersede the civil jurisdiction. His power is to be exercised in these special emergencies, and the means are put into his hands by which it is to be exercised, that is to say, "a sufficient military force to enable such officer to perform his duties and enforce his authority," and military tribunals of his own appointment to try and punish offenders. These are strictly military powers, to be executed by military authority, not by the civil authority or by civil officers appointed by him to perform ordinary civil duties.

If these emergencies do not happen, if civil order is preserved, and criminals are duly prosecuted by the regular criminal courts, the military power though present must remain passive. Its proper function is to preserve the peace, to act promptly when the peace is broken, and restore order. When that is done and the civil authority may again safely resume its functions, the military power becomes again passive, but on guard and watchful.

This, in my judgment, is the whole scope of the military power conferred by this act, and in arriving at this construction of the act, I have not found it necessary to resort to the strict construction which is allowable.

What has been said indicates my opinion as to any supposed power of the military commander to change or modify the laws in force. The military commander is made a conservator of the peace, not a legislator. His duties are military duties, executive duties, not legislative duties. He has no authority to enact or declare a new code of laws for the people within his district under any idea that he can make a better code than the people have made for themselves. The public policy is not committed to his discretion. The Congress, which passed this act undertook in certain grave particulars to change these laws, and these changes being made, the Congress saw no further necessity of change, but were content to leave all the other laws in full force, but subject to this emphatic declaration, that as to these laws and such future changes as might be expedient, the question of expediency and the power to alter, amend or abolish, was reserved for "the paramount authority of the United States at any time to abolish, modify, control, or supersede the same." Where, then, does a military commander find *his* authority "to abolish, modify, control, or supersede" any one of these laws?

The enumeration of the extraordinary powers exercised by the military commanders in some of the districts would extend this opinion to an unreasonable length. A few instances must suffice.

In one of these districts the governor of a State has been deposed under a threat of military force, and another person, called a governor, has been appointed by the military commander to fill his place.[4] Thus presenting the strange spectacle of an official entrusted with the chief power to execute the laws of the State whose authority is not recognized by the laws he is called upon to execute.

In the same district the judge of one of the criminal courts of the State has been summarily dealt with. The act of Congress does give authority to the military commander, in cases of necessity, to transfer the jurisdiction of a criminal court to a military tribunal. That being the specific authority over the criminal courts given by the act, no other authority over them can be lawfully exercised by the military commander. But in this instance the judge has, by military order, been ejected from his office, and a private citizen has been appointed judge in his place,[5] by military authority, and is now in the exercise of criminal jurisdiction "over all crimes, misdemeanors, and offences," committed within the territorial jurisdiction of the court. This military appointee is certainly not authorized to try any one for any offence as a member of a military tribunal, and he has just as little authority to try and punish any offender as judge of a criminal court of the State.

It happens that this private citizen, thus placed on the bench, is to sit as the sole judge in a criminal court whose jurisdiction extends to cases involving the life of the accused. If he has any judicial power in any case, he has the same power to take cognizance of capital cases, and to sentence the accused to death, and order his execution. A strange spectacle! where the judge and the criminal may very well "change places;" for if the criminal has unlawfully taken life, so too does the judge. This is the inevitable result, for the only tribunal, the only judges, if they can be called judges, which a military commander can constitute and appoint under this act, to inflict the death penalty, is a military court composed of a board, and called in the act a "military commission."

I see no relief for the condemned against the sentence of this agent of the military commander. It is not the sort of court whose sentence of death must be first approved by the commander and finally by the president; for that is allowed only where the sentence is pronounced by a "military commission." Nor is it a sentence pronounced by the rightful court of the State, but by a court, and by a judge, not clothed with authority under the laws of the State, but constituted by a military authority. As the representative of this military authority, this act forbids interference "under color of State authority" with the exercise of his functions.

In another one of these districts a military order commands the governor of the State to forbid the reassembling of the legislature, and thus suspends the proper legislative power of the State. In the same district an order has been issued "to relieve the treasurer of the State from the duties, bonds, books, papers, &c., appertaining to his office," and to put an "assistant quartermaster of United States volunteers" in place of the removed treasurer;[6] the duties of which quartermaster-treasurer are thus summed up: He is to make to the headquarters of the district "the same reports and returns required from the treasurer, and a monthly statement of receipts and expenditures; he will pay all warrants for salaries which may be, or become, due, and legitimate expenditures for the support of the penitentiary, State asylum, and the support of the provisional State government; but no scrip or warrants for outstanding debts of other kind than those specified will be paid without special authority from these headquarters. He will deposit funds in the same manner as though they were those of the United States."

In another of these districts[7] a body of military edicts, issued in general and special orders regularly numbered, and in occasional circulars, have been promulgated, which already begin to assume the dimensions of a code. These military orders modify the existing law in the remedies for the collection of debts, the enforcement of judgments and decrees for the payment of money, staying proceedings instituted, prohibiting, in certain cases, the right to bring suit, enjoining proceedings on execution for the term of twelve months, giving new liens in certain cases, establishing homestead exemptions, declaring what shall be a legal tender, abolishing in certain cases the remedy by foreign attachment, abolishing bail "as heretofore authorized" in cases *ex contractu*, but not in "other cases, known as actions *ex delicto*," and changing, in several particulars, the existing laws as to the punishment of crimes, and directing that the crimes referred to "shall be punished by imprisonment at hard labor for a term not exceeding ten years nor less than two years, in the discretion of the court having jurisdiction thereof." One of these general orders, being number ten of the series, contains no less than seventeen sections embodying the various changes and modifications which have been recited.

The question at once arises in the mind of every lawyer, what power or discretion belongs to the court having jurisdiction of any of these offences, to sentence a criminal to any other or different punishment than that provided by the law which vests him with jurisdiction. The concluding paragraph of this order, No. 10, is in these words: "Any law or ordinance heretofore in force in North Carolina or South Carolina, inconsistent with the provisions of this general order, are hereby suspended and declared inoperative." Thus announcing, not only a power to suspend the law, but to declare them generally inoperative, and assuming full powers of legislation by the military authority.

The ground upon which these extraordinary powers are based is thus set forth in military order No. 1, issued in this district: "The civil government now existing in North Carolina and South Carolina, is provisional only, and in all respects subject to the paramount authority of the United States at any time to abolish, modify, control, or supersede the same." Thus far the provisions of the act of Congress are well recited. What follows is in these words: "Local laws and municipal regulations not inconsistent with the Constitution and laws of the United States, or the proclamations of the President, or with such regulations as are or may be prescribed in the orders of the commanding general, are hereby declared to be in force, and in conformity therewith, civil officers are hereby authorized to continue the exercise of their proper functions, and will be respected and obeyed by the inhabitants."

This construction of his powers under the act of Congress places the military commander on the same footing as the Congress of the United

States. It assumes that "the paramount authority of the United States at any time to abolish, modify, control, or supersede," is vested in him as fully as it is reserved to Congress. He deems himself a representative of that paramount authority. He puts himself upon an equality with the law-making power of the Union, the only paramount authority in our government, so far, at least, as the enactment of laws is concerned. He places himself on higher ground than the President, who is simply an executive officer. He assumes, directly or indirectly, all the authority of the State, legislative, executive, and judicial, and in effect declares "I am the State."

I regret that I find it necessary to speak so plainly of this assumption of authority. I repeat what I have heretofore said, that I do not doubt that all these orders have been issued under an honest belief that they were necessary or expedient, and fully warranted by the act of Congress. There may be evils and mischiefs in the laws which these people have made for themselves through their own legislative bodies, which require change; but none of these can be so intolerable as the evils and mischiefs which must ensue from the sort of remedy applied. One can plainly see what will be the inevitable confusion and disorder which such disturbances of the whole civil policy of the State must produce. If these military edicts are allowed to remain even during the brief time in which this provisional military government may be in power, the seeds will be sown for such a future harvest of litigation as has never been inflicted upon any other people.

There is, in my opinion, an executive duty to be performed here, which cannot safely be avoided or delayed. For notwithstanding the paramount authority assumed by these commanders, they are not, even as to their proper executive duties, in any sense, clothed with a paramount authority. They are, at last, subordinate executive officers. They are responsible to the President for the proper execution of their duties, and upon him rests the final responsibility. They are his selected agents. His duty is not all performed by selecting such agents as he deems competent; but the duty remains with him to see to it that they execute their duties faithfully and according to law.

It is true that this act of Congress only refers to the President in the matter of selecting and appointing these commanders, and in the matter of their powers and duties under the law, the act speaks in terms directly to them; but this does not relieve them from their responsibility to the President, nor does it relieve him from the constitutional obligation imposed upon him to see that all "the laws be faithfully executed."

It can scarcely be necessary to cite authority for so plain a proposition as this. Nevertheless, as we have a recent decision completely in point, I may as well refer to it.

Upon the motion made by the State of Mississippi before the Supreme Court of the United States at its late term, for leave to file a bill against the president of the United States, to enjoin him against executing the very acts of Congress now under consideration, the opinion of the court upon dismissing that motion, and it seems to have been unanimous, was delivered by the Chief Justice. I make the following quotation from the opinion: "Very different is the duty of the President in the exercise of the power to see that the laws are faithfully executed, and among those laws the acts named in the bill. By the first of these acts he is required to assign generals to command in the several military districts, and to detail sufficient military force to enable such officers to discharge their duties under the law. By the supplementary act, other duties are imposed on the several commanding generals, and their duties must necessarily be performed under the supervision of the President as Commander-in-Chief. The duty thus imposed on the President is in no just sense ministerial. It is purely executive and political."[8]

Certain questions have been propounded from one of these military districts touching the construction of the power of the military commander to constitute military tribunals for the trial of offenders, which I will next consider.

Whilst the act does not in terms displace the regular criminal courts of the State, it does give the power to the military commander, when in his judgment a necessity arises, to take the administration of the criminal law into his own hands, and to try and punish offenders by means of military commissions.

In giving construction to this power, we must not forget the recent and authoritative exposition given by the Supreme Court of the United States as to the power of Congress to provide for military tribunals for the trial of citizens in time of peace, and to the emphatic declaration as to which there was no dissent or difference of opinion among the judges, that such a power is not warranted by the Constitution. A single extract from the opinion of the minority as delivered by the Chief Justice will suffice. "We by no means assert that Congress can establish and apply the laws of war where no war has been declared or exists. Where peace exists the laws of peace must prevail. What we do maintain is, that when the nation is involved in war, and some portions of the country are invaded, and all are exposed to invasion, it is within the power of Congress to determine in what States or districts such great and imminent public danger exists as justifies the authorization of military tribunals for the trial of crimes and offences against the discipline or security of the army or against the public safety."[9]

Limiting myself here simply to the construction of this act of Congress and to the question in what way it should be executed, I have no hesitation in saying that nothing short of an absolute or controlling necessity would give any color of authority for arraigning a citizen before a military commission. A person charged with crime in any of these military districts has rights to be protected, rights the most sacred and inviolable, and among these the right of trial by jury according to laws of the land.

When a citizen is arraigned before a military commission on a criminal charge, he is no longer under the protection of law, nor surrounded with those safe-guards which are provided in the Constitution.

This act, passed in a time of peace, when all the courts, State and federal, are in the undisturbed exercise of their jurisdiction, authorizes, at the discretion of a military officer, the seizure, trial, and condemnation of the citizen. The accused may be sentenced to death, and the sentence may be executed, without an indictment, without counsel, without a jury, and without a judge. A sentence which forfeits all the property of the accused, requires no approval. If it affects the liberty of the accused, it requires the approval of the commanding general; and if it affects his life, it requires the approval of the general and of the President. Military and executive authority rule throughout, in the trial, the sentence, and the execution. No *habeas corpus* from any State court can be invoked; for this law declares that "all interference, under color of State authority, with the exercise of military authority under this act shall be null and void."

Questions have arisen whether, under this power, these military commissioners can take cognizance of offences committed before the passage of the act, and whether they can try and punish for acts not made crimes or offences by federal or State law.

I am clearly of opinion that they have no jurisdiction as to either. They can take cognizance of no offence that has not happened after the law took effect. Inasmuch as the tribunal to punish, and the measure or degree of punishment, are established by this act, we must construe it to be prospective, and not retroactive. Otherwise it would take the character of an *ex post facto* law. Therefore, in the absence of any language which gives the act a retrospect, I do not hesitate to say it cannot apply to past offences.

There is no legislative power given under this military bill to establish a new criminal code. The authority given is to try and punish criminals and offenders, and this proceeds upon the idea that crimes and offences have been committed; but no person can be called a criminal or an offender for doing an act which, when done, was not prohibited by law.

But as to the measure of punishment, I regret to be obliged to say that it is left altogether to the military authorities, with only this limitation, that the punishment to be inflicted shall not be cruel or unusual. The military commission may try the accused, fix the measure of punishment, even to the penalty of death, and direct the execution of the sentence. It is only when the sentence affects the "life or liberty" of the person that it need be approved by the commanding general, and only in cases where it affects the life of the accused that it needs also the approval of the President.

As to crimes or offences against the laws of the United States, the military authority can take no cognizance of them, nor in any way interfere with the regular administration of justice by the appropriate federal courts.

In the opinion heretofore given upon other questions arising under these laws, I gave at large for your consideration the grounds upon which my conclusions were arrived at, intending thereafter to state these conclusions in a concise and clear summary. I now proceed to execute that purpose, which is made especially necessary from the confusion and doubts which have arisen upon that opinion in the public mind, caused in part by the errors of the telegraph and the press in its publication, and in part by the inaptitude of the general reader to follow carefully the successive and dependent steps of a protracted legal opinion.

PD, DNA-RG94, Lets. Recd. (Main Ser.), File W-572-1867 (M619, Roll 602).

1. See Stanbery to Johnson, May 24, 1867.

2. The First and Second Military Reconstruction acts.

3. Sir Fortunatus Dwarris, Knt., *A General Treatise on Statutes: Their Rules of Construction, and the Proper Boundaries of Legislation and of Judicial Interpretation* (Albany, 1878 [1871]), 259. It is unknown what version Stanbery was quoting.

4. On June 4, 1867, Gen. Philip H. Sheridan of the Fifth Military District removed J. Madison Wells from his post as governor of Louisiana and replaced him with Benjamin F. Flanders. For more on this removal, see Wells to Johnson, June 4, 1867.

5. Sheridan removed Louisiana judge Edmund Abell on March 27, 1867, and replaced him with William W. Howe. See Ethan A. Allen to Johnson, April 9, 1867, and Edmund Abell to Johnson, June 3, 1867.

6. In Arkansas the Fourth Military District commander, Major General Ord, issued the order on April 15, 1867, dissolving the state legislature and later he removed the state treasurer as he deemed him ineligible and untrustworthy. *American Annual Cyclopaedia* (1867), 49.

7. The Second Military District, commanded by Maj. Gen. Daniel E. Sickles and comprised of North and South Carolina.

8. *The State of Mississippi, Compt.* v. *Andrew Johnson, President of the United States, and E.O.C. Ord*, 4 Wall. 475–602 (1866).

9. *Ex parte Milligan*, 4 Wall. 2–142 (1866).

To Edwin M. Stanton

Washington, D.C.   June 12th 1867

Will the Secretary of War please furnish me with a copy of his telegram to Genl. Sheridan of the third instant, directing him to suspend proceedings in relation to the Board of Levee Commissioners of Louisiana?[1]

Also, a copy of General Sheridan's reply,[2] an extract from which was sent to me at Raleigh; and, in addition,

A copy of the order of General Sheridan removing J. Madison Wells from the office of Governor of the State of Louisiana.[3]

Andrew Johnson

LS, DLC-Stanton Papers.

1. Stanton to Sheridan, June 3, 1867, Johnson Papers, LC.

2. Sheridan to Stanton, June 3, 1867, ibid.

3. Special Orders No. 59, Fifth Military District, June 3, 1867. The requested materials were enclosed with Stanton to Johnson, June 12, 1867, ibid. See also Stanton to Johnson, June 4, 1867.

From Edmund Abell

New Orleans   June 13th 1867.

Nothing could astonish me more than to find the extraordinary statements contained in a telegram from General Sheridan to General Grant dated the 6th Inst. So far as it relates to me nothing could be more at variance with the record and facts of the case. It seems to me that they are not only made in error but are most incredible.

The telegram reads:

Headquarters Fifth Military Dct.
New Orleans   June 6th 1867.

To General U. S. Grant Commanding Armies of the United States:
General:—

On the 20th of March last I removed from office Judge Abell of the Criminal Court of New Orleans, Andrew S. Herron, Attorney General of the State of Louisiana, and John T. Monroe, Mayor of the City of New Orleans. These removals were made under the power granted me in what is usually termed the Military Bill passed March 27th 1867, by the Congress of the United States.

I did not deem it necessary to give any reason for the removal of these men, especially after the investigation made by the Military board on the Massacre of July 30th, and the report of the Congressional Committee on the same massacre, but as some inquiry has been made for the cause of these removals I would respectfully state as follows:

The Criminal Court over which Judge Abell presided is the only Criminal Court of the City of New Orleans: for a period of at least nine months previous to July 30th he had been educating a large portion of the Community to the perpetration of this outrage, by almost promising them no prosecution in his Court against the offenders, in case such an event occured. The records of this Court will show that he fulfilled his promise as not one of the guilty ones has been prosecuted. In reference to Andrew S. Herron I considered it his duty to indict these men before the Criminal Court.

This he failed to do, but went so far as to attempt to impose on the good sense of the whole nation by indicting the victims of the riot instead of the riotors. In other words making the innocent guilty, and the guilty innocent.

He was therefore an abettor and coadjutator with Judge Abell in bringing on the massacre of July 30th. Mayor Monroe controlled the element engaged in this riot and when backed by an Attorney General who would not prosecute the guilty, and a Judge who advised the Grand Jury to find the innocent guilty and let the murderers go free, felt secure in engaging his police force in the Riot and massacre. With these three men exercising a large influence on the worst elements of this, giving to these elements an immunity for riot and bloodshed, the General in Chief will see how insecure I felt in letting them occupy their positions in the troubles which might occur in registration and voting in the reorganization.

I am, General, very Respectfully your obedient Servant
P. H. Sheridan   Major General U.S.A.

Respect for the officers of my government forbids my characterizing this telegram in the language that it certainly appears to deserve, or such as General Sheridan sees fit to use towards officers of rank and merit. I shall content myself with a candid and earnest refutation of the numerous groundless assertions made in it.

In the 3d paragraph of the telegram General Sheridan says: "The court over which Judge Abell presided is the only Criminal Court of the City of New Orleans: for a period of at least nine months previous to the 30th of July he had been educating a large portion of the Community to the perpetration of this outrage, by almost promising them no prosecution in his Court against the offenders in case such an event occured."

This statement is extraordinary without foundation and utterly impossible. I never thought of such a thing. It is utterly impossible that I could have known nine months previous to the 30th of July that such a meeting would take place. The Conventionists and their friends held nearly every office in the State and appeared well pleased with the Constitution. Its author Gen. Banks pronounced it "the best ever made." President Lincoln said "it was a most excellent Constitution." The Conventionists continued to hold nearly all the offices under it until they were displaced by the newly elected Democrats which occured only about three months before the Riot.

How could I know nine months before that these men would assemble to alter so good a Constitution?

Unless the General ranks me with,

> Chalcas the wise, the grecian priest and guide,
> That sacred seer, whose comprehensive view
> The past, the present, and the future knew.[1]

If the General be satisfied with his assertions I shall not complain. He proceeds "The records of this Court will show that he fulfilled his promise as not one of the guilty ones has been prosecuted."

This assertion is plainly contradicted by the record refered to. It shows that the Grand Jury of the parish indicted about 25 of those whom they believed to be the guilty parties, and in doing so they concurred with General Sheridan who telegraphed to the president that the meeting of the Convention was the immediate cause of the riot, and the law only punishes those who are the immediate cause of breaches of the Law.

Gen Sheridan proceeds "In reference to Andrew S. Herron I considered it his duty to indict these men before the Criminal Court. This he failed to do but went so far as to attempt to impose on the good sense of the whole nation by indicting the victims of the riot instead of the riotors. In other words making the innocent guilty and the guilty innocent. He was therefore an abettor of and coadjutator with Judge Abell in bringing on the massacre of the 30th of July."

Fortunately for the Country what amounts to unlawful assemblies riots etc are questions of Law and not mere opinions of our Generals.

I did every thing in my power by legal means to prevent that meeting and I have always believed that had the military Commanders of this department done half as much as I did to prevent the meeting, there would have been no Assembly, no riot and consequently no bloodshed, and I so stated to General Sheridan in a letter I had the honour of addressing him on the 29th of August last.[2] The Conventionists claimed up to the very day of their assembling that they had promise of military assistance and if their assertion has been denied I have never seen it.

Finally General Sheridan says "Mayor Monroe controlled the element engaged in this riot and when backed by an Attorney General who would not prosecute the guilty and a Judge who advised the Grand Jury to find the innocent guilty, and let the murderers go free, felt secure in engaging his police force in the riot and massacre. With these three men exercising a large influence on the worst elements of this City, giving to these elements an immunity to riot and bloodshed the General in Chief will see how insecure I felt in letting them occupy their positions in the troubles which might occur in registration and voting in the reorganization."

So far as I am concerned the statement here made has no foundation on facts: it is too unreasonable to give credence among an intelligent people.

My charges to the Grand Jury which are on file in the 1st District Court will show exactly the contrary. I am prepared to prove by the whole pannel of the Grand Jury, most of whom are men of equal intelligence and worth with General Sheridan or myself that I never gave them such advice as here stated. I never spoke to them upon that or any other subject before them, except through my charges, which are on file, read from manuscript and cannot be garbled.

As to controle the elements of which General Sheridan speaks with the exception of the occurence of the 30th of July, no City in the United States had order better preserved. That that occurence was forced on the people by irresponsible men admits of no doubt.

I have endeavoured to show to the Chief Executive officer of the United States, to Generals Grant & Sheridan that the telegram of the 6th Inst. from General Sheridan to Gen. Grant is unsustained by facts, and unjust in its application. I respectfully ask, that it be overruled as insufficient and that myself and the officers of the State of Louisiana and corporation of New Orleans be restored to the functions of their offices until superseded by officers elected under a new Constitution, as intended by Congress, as clearly appears by the 6th Section of the Act of March last which declares:

"That until the people of the said Rebel States shall be by Law admitted to representation in the Congress of the United States any Civil government which may exist there in shall be deemed provisional only and in all respects subject to the paramount authority of the United States at any time to abolish, modify, control, or supersede the same etc."

If the foresight of Congress in the preservation of state governments until new Constitutions are formed as contained in the 6th Section, be disregarded and five independent governments erected in their stead with fully organized armies, and an Auxilliary Bureau, and one million and a half of efficient registered men with powerful allies in the North I venture to predict that the Legislative & Executive would be over-shadowed. Through the light of history I speak in sorrow and apprehension for the future of my unhappy country, and not through prejudice towards General Sheridan as might be supposed from the tenor of his telegram.

My duty to myself as a Citizen to repel a libel, or correct an error committed by a government official and to demand at the hand of my government redress for injuries done me, by one them is my appology for addressing those, in whom the government has entrusted the duty to protect the citizen and maintain the honour of the Government.[3]

Edmund Abell

ALS, DLC-JP.
1. The quote has not been found, but it obviously refers to Calchas, who, according to mythology, was a Greek seer who accompanied the Greeks to Troy. Abraham H. Lass, David Kiremidjian, Ruth M. Goldstein, *The Facts on File Dictionary of Classical, Biblical and Literary Allusions* (New York, 1987).
2. Abell to Sheridan, Aug. 29, 1866, *New York Tribune*, June 14, 1867.
3. For Abell's previous protest against his removal, see Abell to Johnson, June 3, 1867.

From John B. Rogers [1]

Virden Ill   June 13—1867

D Sir:

A certain worthy official—Assessor of the 10th District Illinois—whose initials are—J.F.[2] formerly Treasurer's clerk at Washington, D.C.—is blowing around here—about politics. I consider he received the nomination of Assessor by the President, Who is a friend of mine. And he shall not blow his horn without being reported.

I am Late P.M. at Virden Ill—refused to be confirmed by the Senate—when the salary of this office, Should be less than $1000.00. I could have been confirmed—as it was—but I refused to sell my vote—for the next Presidenttial election—for the sake of this P.O. and I also refused a base proposition to conceal all Democratic circulars &c.—during the political contests. These propositions were put to me—with the fact in view—of my confirmation by the Senate—but I refused as I always will—any base proposals from any party whatever. I told them to telegraph whatever they please. I am an A Johnson man—office or no office. I voted for you. I will do it again. I do not ask for any office. I can—and will live—but I will live honorably.

This J.F. Assessor of the 10th District Ill—thinks he has his office now and is safe. He says—you are "played out." I say "spot him." Any man—who will hold an office as he does—and malign his benefactor—

as he did yesterday in Virden—ought to be "tarred & Feathered." Why can't he hold his tongue.

No Sir: No bribe—no persecution—no molestation will drive me from supporting—my views—as to the future of our Country.

My Successor,[3] may—or may not—have acquired his confirmation, by promises. I know not. But one thing I know. That if the parties—who are my neighbors—will propose to me these ignoble propositions—they will to others.

This I wish to be confidential—as all the parties are my neighbors—and I suppose are no worse—than others of their like.

May God bless you—in your efforts, in laboring—for the social, industrial and political interests of our common country—by espousing the cause of Liberty and God!!

John B. Rogers

ALS, DNA-RG56, Appts., Internal Revenue Service, Collector, Ill., 10th Dist., James Fishback.

1. Rogers (b. c1834), a native of Pennsylvania, was a lawyer. He had been nominated postmaster at Virden on March 27, 1867, but was rejected three days later. 1860 Census, Ill., Macoupin, Virden, 130; Ser. 6B, Vol. 4: 303, Johnson Papers, LC.

2. James Fishback.

3. John J. Beattie (c1806–fl1869), a merchant and Pennsylvania native, was nominated for postmaster on April 5, 1867, and commissioned the next day. He served for two years at Virden. Ibid.; 1860 Census, Ill., Macoupin, Virden, 134; U.S. Off. Reg. (1869).

From J. Warren Bell

Brownsville, Texas, June 14 1867

My dear friend

I am not able yet to give you all the information I will be after awhile. I have been in this country but a short time. I came through Tenn. Miss. La &c. I stopped at Greenville Ten. Jackson—Canton & Brandon Miss and at N.O. I am a pretty quick reader of passing events. I *guess* pretty well. Matters are very uncertain. The people will perhaps submit to the Mil Bill, and accept because compelled to, but certain, Johnson, there is a day of awful retribution coming some time. The policy you suggested would have done better, and if therewith *absolute amnesty*, my opinion is, all would be right even now. When the Mil. Bill has filled its mission then will come the strife. *Remember this*. Honor Johnson I dont want to write of these matters now. After I learn more I will write you more advisedly, yet I read the "handwriting on the wall."

I want to write you of myself. I am Treasury Agent at $8. pr day. I wanted $5000. pr year & expenses paid.[1] Mr. Chandler desired this. Mr Hartly also I understood, but Mr McCulloch feard to as it.[2]

Now you know I have three children to support[3] & I'l *do it*, for I love them. But I have to pay $3.00 pr day for *eating* here, in *specie*. I go one days ride & pay $25.00. Next day I rode 27 miles & paid 12$. I find all things thus. It is simply impossible to get along in this Country this way, without getting behind. Now if you will say to Mr McCulloch that I should have more it will be done. I have heavy work to do & I am doing it. I wont neglect it. There is no comparison, this place with any other. Expenses here excel any place. I want *you* to send for Mr McCulloch and just tell him to raise my wages to $5000. pr year & travelling expenses, and I can show him what can be done, by energy and perseverance. I have a large field and heavy work to perform. I will prove myself worthy. I only want to live and support my children.

If you will do this for me I will say "thank you" and show you that I earn it all *well and truly*.

Without an energetic Agent here smuggling can be carried on at will. Millions are made by smuggling.

If you dont want to do this just let it pass and tell me so. You know I would be pleased to hear from you. My address is Custom House Galveston Texas.[4]

One thing, certain, the people almost to a man approve of your course.

J. Warren Bell

ALS, DLC-JP.

1. According to the 1867 *U.S. Official Register*, no special treasury agent was earning more than six dollars per day, plus limited traveling expenses.

2. William E. Chandler, Hugh McCulloch, and possibly special agent Edward Hartley.

3. In 1850 Bell was listed with six children who, by 1867, would have ranged in age from 17 to 29. We are not sure which three children he was supporting at the time this letter was written. Byron and Barbara Sistler, trs., *1850 Census, Tennessee* (8 vols., Evanston, Ill., 1974–76), 1: 113.

4. There is no known response from Johnson. The 1869 *U.S. Official Register* showed Bell stationed at New Orleans and earning eight dollars per day, plus ten cents per mile.

From Lewis E. Parsons

Montgomery Ala.   June 15th 1867

I leave for Washington in the morning. Have important information for you relative to General Pope's removals in this State[1] and beg your Excellency to take no action until it is laid before you.[2]

Lewis E. Parsons

Tel, DNA-RG107, Tels. Recd., President, Vol. 6 (1867–68).

1. Although General Pope, as commander of the new Third Military District, had earlier removed a few officeholders, this telegram no doubt refers to the dismissal of the mayor, Jones M. Withers, and all the city officers of Mobile, following the May 14, 1867, "riot." *American Annual Cyclopaedia* (1867), 20, 22, 23, 24.

2. Parsons reportedly was "probably" going to "take with him the spontaneous expressions of the best public men" in Alabama "against the restoration of any of the persons removed." John Pope to Grant, June 17, 1867, Johnson Papers, LC.

From Edwin M. Stanton

Washington City, June 15 1867

Sir:

I have the honor herewith to return the papers relating to the appeal of Mess. McCorkle and Chenery,[1] members of the Board of Visitors to the Military Academy at West Point, referred to this Department for report.

The claim of Mess. Chenery and McCorkle is for constructive mileage and compensation which, in the opinion of the Secretary of War, is not authorized by law.

The Act of Congress[2] provides that "no compensation shall be made to members of the Board beyond the payment of their expenses for board and lodging while at the Military Academy, and an *allowance* not to exceed eight cents per mile, for traveling, by the shortest mail route, from their respective homes to the Academy and back to their homes."

It will be observed that the Act of Congress regards the appointment of Visitors as complimentary and contemplates only the reimbursement of actual expenses, and *that* within a certain maximum limit, where they have travelled from their homes to the Academy, beyond which the allowance shall in no case extend; to wit: "not to exceed eight cents per mile."

In the present instance the applicants, being at Washington, on their own business, personally solicited and received their appointment at Washington. Their claim would give them about five hundred dollars each for a constructive journey not made, under the appointment, to and from their homes.

It has grown to be the custom of late years to appoint in some cases persons temporarily in Washington, to represent the states to which they belong when such states are entitled to representation, and Mess. McCorkle and Chenery, being in Washington, were so appointed. They did not travel from their homes to the Academy nor will they of necessity travel from the Academy to their homes, because when appointed on the Board of Visitors they were already away from their homes. The only distance they travel under their appointment is from Washington to West Point. Whether they return to Washington from West Point is optional with themselves: they will be paid their mileage for the journey back to Washington whether they make it or not.

The section of the Act of Congress appears on the face of their appointments and they cannot properly claim more than its benefits. Even if they had travelled from their homes under the appointment they would not necessarily have a right to the mileage but only to *an allowance* to cover actual travelling expenses, not to exceed mileage at the specified rate. The order of the Department of the 25th of May[3] is an instruction to the proper officer in making the allowance and does not conflict with the law.

The Secretary of War does not therefore feel justified in allowing more than the travelling expenses to and from Washington and West Point.

Edwin M Stanton   Secretary of War.

LS, DNA-RG107, Lets. Recd., Executive (M494, Roll 96).
    1. Joseph W. McCorkle and Richard Chenery. Chenery (c1817–fl1879), a native of Massachusetts, went to California in 1849. He was an agent for a steamer line, U.S. naval agent in San Francisco, a wholesale merchant of wines and liquors, and was involved with mining. McCorkle and Chenery had written to Johnson trying to collect mileage from their homes in Virginia City, Nevada, and San Francisco, California, respectively. McCorkle and Chenery to Johnson, June 11, 1867, Lets. Recd., Executive (M494, Roll 96), RG107, NA.
    2. Passed August 8, 1846, the act authorized the appointment of the board of visitors and determined payment. *Congressional Globe*, 29 Cong., 1 Sess., p. 1213.
    3. This order stated "That when appointments as Visitors to the Military Academy are given to persons residing in, or temporarily at, the City of Washington, the mileage will be computed from Washington to West Point and back." Receipt of this order provoked McCorkle and Chenery's letter to Johnson in which they asked whether the secretary of war's order negated the congressional law. Order by the Secretary of War, May 25, 1867, Lets. Recd., Executive (M494, Roll 96), RG107, NA.

From Nathaniel G. Taylor

June 15, 1867, Washington, D.C.; ALS, DNA-RG48, Indian Div., Lets. Recd.

Taylor, the commissioner of Indian affairs, feels compelled to address Johnson "upon the grave differences existing between the Secretary of the Interior and myself as to our respective rights, duties and responsibilities in the management of Indian Affairs." He cites various acts and regulations such as those of July 9, 1832, creating the bureau; June 30, 1834; November 8, 1836; November 11, 1836; June 1, 1837; and March 3, 1849, creating the Department of the Interior. In all these pronouncements the commissioner of Indian affairs was to have full responsibility for all matters relating to the Indians, under the President and the secretary of war, prior to the 1849 act. When the secretary of the interior was given the supervisory role in 1849, he was not given any additional control over the Indians. Nevertheless, over the past fifteen or twenty years he has assumed powers "which properly and rightfully belonged to the Commissioner of Indian Affairs." These "encroachments" may not have been resisted by past commissioners for fear they would be removed. Andrew Jackson, when issuing regulations, had clearly given the commissioner control of Indian affairs, "directing that . . . he is not merely to be the register of the will and wishes of the Secretary, having no controlling voice in any thing, as has been the case with few exceptions since I have had charge of this Bureau." Taylor claims that, according to the regulations, the Indian commissioner has more authority in his area than the pension, patent, and general land offices do in theirs. But Taylor's requests for appointments and suggestions for Indian management have been "*persistently denied.*" He asks Johnson to "prescribe specific regulations as to my power and duties so that I can exercise and discharge them without hinderance or delay." [Johnson ordered the letter referred to the secretary of the interior "for early consideration and remark."]

From Lewis D. Campbell

New Orleans La.   June 16th, 1867

In pursuance of telegrams of yesterday I now formally resign my position as Envoy etc: etc:—of the United States to the Republic of Mexico.[1]

I should do injustic to my own feelings not to avail myself of the occasion to say that my appointment and confirmation excited my grateful sensibilities and that the compliment was more highly appreciated because when the nomination was made you knew I did not desire it. It is gratifying to me also to know that during the entire career of this moving & somewhat anomilous legation *your instructions* were *always obeyed and that all my official acts have been approved and some of them highly commended by the Department of State*, and permit me to add that it is not fully understood why, upon such a record, the Government has recently declined to furnish me the slightest facility for going under its own glorious flag directly to the shores of the struggling sister Republic and has required me to furnish my own conveyance to Havana, now sorely afflicted by a scourging epidemic, and thence proceed on my mission to Vera Cruz, a point of doubtful access under the protection of the ensign of England or France, both enemies of Republicanism & responsible to some extent for the misfortunes of Mexico and neither friend of the United States during our late terrible struggle for National existence. The primary object of this requirement would seem to be the safety of a fallen Emperor whose unhallowed ambition led him to bid defiance to a principle long cherished in the hearts of the American people. If the Government to which my whole Soul is attached is content with its record I must be with mine. If you its highest officers are willing to receive a resignation forced on me by want of transportation I am far more happy in returning the commission, of which I have been proud, than when I received it.[2]

Lewis D. Campbell

Tel, DLC-JP.

1. The previous day Campbell had telegraphed William H. Seward informing him that he was ill and could not at that time go to Mexico, and "if government considers it important to send minister immediately, I will tender my resignation, if desired." Seward replied by telegraph: "It is important that the minister to Mexico should proceed at once. Your resignation will, therefore, be accepted, with thanks for your service, and regret for your retirement." Campbell then sent another message saying "Your telegram of this day received. I send formal resignation by mail and start for Ohio Tuesday." *House Ex. Docs.*, 40 Cong., 1 Sess., No. 30, pp. 74–75 (Ser. 1311). See also Martin H. Hall, "The Campbell-Sherman Diplomatic Mission to Mexico," *Bulletin of the Historical and Philosophical Society of Ohio*, 13 (1955): 268–70.

2. Upon Campbell's resignation, Marcus Otterbourg, then consul at Mexico City, was appointed to the post. *House Ex. Docs.*, 40 Cong., 1 Sess., No. 30, p. 76 (Ser. 1311).

From Alfred P. Aldrich [1]

Barnwell C. H   So. Ca.   17 June 1867.

The President,

I am informed, that Pardons have been granted to all the Judges of the Superior Courts of this State, myself excepted. As I believe there is no reason for placing me on a different footing from my Associates, and suppose I have been overlooked, or my name has not been brought to the attention of Your Excellency, I Respectfully petition The President to extend to me the same grace that has been granted to my Brethren. [2]

Before I was elected, I served in the Army of the Confederate States, Rank of Major, was disabled by an accident and retired. My Real Estate was valued at over Twenty Thousand Dollars before the war. I beg leave to submit, a copy of the Oath of Amnesty taken by me 27 June '65. Also a letter from His Excellency Governor Orr. [3]

A. P. Aldrich   Law Judge, State of S. Carolina

ALS, DNA-RG94, Amnesty Papers (M1003, Roll 44), S.C., A. P. Aldrich.

1. Aldrich (1814–1897) was a planter and lawyer from Barnwell who served in the state legislature before and during the war and was in fact its speaker (1862–65). He resigned his judgeship in 1867 under pressure from General Canby. In the late 1870s Aldrich once more became a state judge. Stephen Meats and Edwin T. Arnold, eds., *The Writings of Benjamin F. Perry* (3 vols., Spartanburg, 1980), 1: 509; John S. Reynolds, *Reconstruction in South Carolina* (Columbia, S.C., 1905), 70.

2. According to information written on the file cover sheet, Aldrich was pardoned on June 22, 1867.

3. The amnesty oath is enclosed in Aldrich's file but the letter from Governor Orr is not.

From Daniel A. Carpenter

(This letter is Private)

Knoxville, June 17th 1867

My dear Sir

I will venture to lay a few facts before you for the purpose of telling you something of the condition of affairs in your native *East Tennessee*.

We are now having considerable excitement politically in this country.

The radical party are almost killing themselves running over the country making stump speeches at every time they can get five men together and holding negro legues every night.

They call them loyal leagues but I deny their loyalty because they have in their legues some of the meanest rebels that ever were in Tennessee. Then we have Brownlows Militia and they are the verry trash of the earth.

One company stationed at this place—another company stationed at Clinton. The radicals say this Militia is organized for the purpose of keeping the rebels in subjection.

Well I have no doubt but you will remember that Anderson County was one of the loyalest counties in East Tennessee put more men into the federal army than she had voters and now Sir we are disloyal and have to be governed by military force and why and how are we disloyal.

Sir because we have endorsed your administration and do endorse your policy and plans of restoration. Such men as Lee Houk James Doughty[1] and others of the same character are setting themselves up as leading politicans in our country. That class of men who were dishonrable dismissed [from] the service of the united [States] and others who resigned their positions in the army because they were too cowardly to face the music are now to be our leaders—are now going through the country making speeches calling men who served out their three years and have honorable discharges rebels and backed by the militia at the expense of broken up State. Now there is plenty of loyal men in East Tennessee who will not be able to vote from the fact that they cannot get a certificate. And why can they not get a certificate because they are not going to vote for Brownlow but let a beardless negro of eighteen summers step up and he receives his certificate and is asked no further questions than *are you* going to vote for Brownlow.

Now President we the loyal men we the men who served our three years in the federal army we the men who left our homes and crossed the Cumberland Mountains we who went into the federal army when the dark clouds of Bull run and manasses were gathering over this land of ours are not going to submit to such outrages. There is plenty of Enfield rifles scattered through this country.

If you cant help us we will help our selves.

D. A. Carpenter

ALS, DLC-JP.
1. Leonidas C. Houk and James A. Doughty. There appears to be at least a germ of truth to Carpenter's assertions about the resignations from military service of Houk and Doughty. See *Johnson Papers*, 5: 42n; 6: 542n.

From Thomas W. Humes

Knoxville, Tenn   June 17, 1867.

I respectfully represent that about two years since an application was made to your Excellency, by W.Y.C. Humes of Memphis,[1] for pardon of his offence against the United States Govt., by his participation in the late rebellion, and that his request is still unanswered. The facts of the case, I believe to be, that at the beginning of the work of secession and during his residence at Knoxville, he was a warm friend of the Union; but having removed to Memphis, such was the overwhelming nature of adverse surroundings and the force of numerous influences against the Union in that city, that after the war began, he was induced to enter the

Southern army. From a very sub-ordinate position, he was gradually promoted, until elevated to the rank of a Brigadier General of the Confederacy. Holding this position at the close of the war, he was consequently
excluded from the Amnesty offered by your Excellency, to participants in
the rebellion. I beg leave respectfully and urgently to request that you
will grant him a pardon. For nearly two years, he has been diligently pursuing the duties of his profession of the law, with a steadfast purpose of
obedience to the Government of the country, abstaining from all interference with the politics of the State and Nation, and leading a quiet and
peaceable life. Considering all the facts of the case, I sincerely trust that
your Excellency will deem him now a fit subject of Executive clemency,
and will release him from the civil disability and penalty, under which he
has labored for two years past, by granting him a full & free pardon.[2]

                                                        Thos. W. Humes.

ALS, DNA-RG94, Amnesty Papers (M1003, Roll 49), Tenn., William Y.C. Humes.
    1. William Y.C. Humes (1830–1882), nephew of Thomas W., reached the rank of brig-
adier general in the Confederate army late in 1863. He served primarily with Gen. Joseph
Wheeler's forces. He practiced law in Memphis before and after the war years. Humes, in
fact, did apply to Johnson for pardon in June 1865 and took the oath of allegiance on June
26 in Nashville. A number of Memphis citizens endorsed Humes's request for presidential
pardon. No explanation is provided in Humes's amnesty file for Johnson's two-year delay in
granting a pardon to him. See Amnesty Papers (M1003, Roll 49), Tenn., William Y.C.
Humes, RG94, NA; Ezra J. Warner, *Generals in Gray* (Baton Rouge, 1959); William S.
Speer, ed., *Sketches of Prominent Tennesseans* (Nashville, 1888), 497–98.
    2. Ironically, by the time Thomas Humes wrote this letter, the President had already
decided to pardon William Humes. The pardon was issued on June 10, apparently in direct
response to Sam Milligan's June 3 letter in behalf of Humes. Amnesty Papers (M1003,
Roll 49), Tenn., William Y.C. Humes, RG94, NA.

From Frank Smith

                        No. 48 Pine Street   New York   June 17/67
My Dear Sir
    Your esteemed favor of 15th inst[1] I recived this morning. I was happy
to learn that you had refered my statement and papers in the "Dennistown Cotton Case" to the Attorney Genl.[2] I must thank you for this kind
consideration of my interests and hope it may be my good fortune to be of
some service to you in the future. I shall be pleased to see Mr Cushing[3]
and learn from him anything in regard to a settlement of my matter.
    It would afford both Mrs Smith[4] & myself great pleasure to entertain
you or any of your family when you visit this city. Can you not make it
convienant to stop a few days on your trip to Boston? Everything very
dull here. It seems as if the people have lost all interest in politics and
think of nothing but the almighty dollar.

                                                        Frank Smith

ALS, DLC-JP.
    1. Not found.

2. Henry Stanbery. The firm of Dennistown & Co. had filed an action of replevin to gain redress for 2,000 bales of cotton confiscated by agents of the Treasury Department. Dennistown & Co. eventually received a settlement of $53,000. *Sen. Ex. Docs.*, 40 Cong., 2 Sess., No. 32, pp. 1–18 (Ser. 1316). See also Johnson to McCulloch, Dec. 8, 1865, *Johnson Papers*, 9: 497–98.

3. Caleb Cushing served as counsel to the Treasury Department for the cotton cases. *Sen. Ex. Docs.*, 40 Cong., 2 Sess., No. 32, p. 3 (Ser. 1316).

4. Not identified.

From Benjamin B. French

[Washington, D.C.]   June 18th. 1867.

My Dear Sir & Brother.

The Supreme Council of the Ancient & Accepted Scottish Rite of the Southern Jurisdiction of the U.S. have been long desirous of placing you on their roll of Chiefs of that Order. They cannot do it however unless you are a 32d of that Rite, and only then by election at a regular meeting of that Body.

It is our wish now that you should possess the 32d Degree before going to Boston,[1] and Brother A.T.C. Pierson[2] being now in this City, if it should be your pleasure to become a 32d we can make you one in a short time, occupying not over one hour.

It can be done so privately too, that no one need know when you received the degrees, but it will only be known, after it, that you are a 32d.

Brother Pierson has been with me this morning, and proposes to call on you tomorrow morning to ascertain your wishes as to this matter, and I write this note that you may give the matter some thought before we see you.[3]

B. B. French 33d
Sov∴ G∴ Ins∴ Gen∴ for
the Dist. of Columbia

ALS, DLC-JP.

1. Johnson was scheduled to be in Boston for the dedication of the new Masonic temple on June 24.

2. After working with various Indian tribes, Azariah T.C. Pierson (1815–1889) became chief draftsman in the surveyor-general's office in St. Paul. Pierson served the Masons of Minnesota for thirty-six years in various capacities, such as grand master (1856–64). *NUC*; Edward Neill, *History of Ramsey County and the City of St. Paul* (Minneapolis, 1881), 587; Robert F. Gould et al., *The History of Freemasonry: Its Antiquities, Symbols, Constitutions, Customs, etc. Derived from Official Sources throughout the World* (4 vols., New York, 1885–89), 4: 518.

3. On June 20 Pierson and French met with Johnson at the White House, had lunch, and then conferred upon him the fourth through thirty-second degrees. William L. Boyden, "The First Scottish Rite President of the United States," *New Age Magazine*, 22 (1915): 199–200; Trefousse, *Johnson*, 286.

From George W. Frazier[1]

Columbus Ohio   June 19th 1867

Sir

I beg leave to make the following proposition to the U.S. Government: There are in and through Colorado and Dakotah Territories vast amounts of Government property in the hands of persons not in the service and who are not in any way connected with it. Many who go out as traders hold property which should be in the hands of the Quarter Masters, and from which the U.S. now receives no benefit.

I propose to look after and hunt up such property, and turn it over to the nearest Q. M. post and let the commander of the Post or the Q. M. put a valuation on it. I will perform this service for 10 per cent of the amount recovered for the Government, or for a salary of $150—per month and transportation.

I have been engaged in this business for some time—in June & July 1866 I turned over some $35,000—worth of Govt property at Forts Sedgwick & Laramie.[2] I have been all through that country and am thoroughly acquainted with it.

Letters of Capt Niel,[3] commandant of the Post at Fort Sedgwick, with those of other officers of the Post are on file in the War Department,[4] strongly recommending me as a proper person for that business and for that place.

I hope your Excellency will favorably consider this application. I am sure it will be of great advantage to the Government—as all such property is now entirely lost to it.

I was relieved from that post by a Q. M. because I was about to turn in some property that *he had smuggled*. He has since been dismissed from the service.[5]

The sooner this is attended to the greater will be the advantage to the Government—as large amounts of property are being stolen every day.[6]

George W Frazier

ALS, DNA-RG59, Lets. of Appl. and Recomm., 1861–69 (M650, Roll 18), George W. Frazier.

    1. Nothing further is known about Frazier except that at least some military officials regarded him as unscrupulous and believed that he had attempted blackmail. "Case of George W. Frazier," Lets. of Appl. and Recomm., 1861–69 (M650, Roll 6), George W. Frazier, RG59, NA.

    2. Frazier was hired by Bvt. Brig. Gen. George B. Dandy, with whom he went to Fort Laramie. There, according to Dandy, Frazier did "good service . . . in finding stolen animals & other public property," until, on June 23, 1866, the quartermaster general ordered Dandy to discharge Frazier. Ibid.

    3. James P.W. Neill (*c*1825–1899), a druggist before the war, served as a first lieutenant and captain in the 18th Inf. Although wounded at Chickamauga, he was able to return to duty and after the war served in the 36th and 7th Inf., mostly at forts in the west. He was

mustered out January 1, 1871, and became a clerk in Philadelphia. Pension File, James P.W. Neill, RG15, NA; *New York Tribune*, Nov. 2, 1899.

4. The letters have not been found.

5. Probably Col. Raymond Burr (b. *c*1821), the chief quartermaster at Columbus, Ohio, until he was mustered out in November 1866. Some of his negative comments about Frazier appear in "Case of George W. Frazier," Lets. of Appl. and Recomm., 1861–69 (M650, Roll 6), George W. Frazier, RG59, NA; ACP Branch, File CB-1864-B-1534, Raymond Burr, RG94, NA.

6. Johnson referred Frazier's letter to the secretary of war, from whom it then moved down the chain of command. On September 18, 1867, J. L. Donaldson, chief quartermaster of the District of the Missouri, wrote, "It is a bad practice to entrust agents with authority . . . of seizing property . . . as it gives them a power which properly belongs only to the Law, and which they could prostitute at any time for unworthy purposes." Lets. of Appl. and Recomm., 1861–69 (M650, Roll 6), George W. Frazier, RG59, NA.

From Lewis J. Speed[1]

Newburg, Ky.   June 19th 1867.

Dr. Sir

At the time of Gen. Buel's retrograde march from Tenn. through Ky. in Sept./62, I was living at Toll-Gate No. 3 on Salt River Turnpike leading from Louisville to Nashville. Gen. Rousseau's Division camped near me and his men took my hay, corn, bacon, vegitables, and poultry, and wood also, all of which I was promised vouchers for, but the army having received orders to march before day I was prevented getting them while they were there. My wife was sick at the time and I could not follow after them. Shortly after my wife died leaving me with three little orphans to watch over and protect.[2] Having much to distress me I made no inquiry as to recovering my loss for some time. I have been unable to obtain the names and whereabouts of the Q. M. & Commissary of this division,[3] whom I have been told were the proper ones to have given me vouchers.

Having heard that cases similar to mine have been made known to your Honor and have met with due and proper notice and consideration by you, I also have been induced to make a similar appeal to your Honor and Justice. All proof necessary as to my loss, etc. can be obtained from good and loyal citizens. I hope you will give my case due consideration, as am much in need.[4]

Lewis J. Speed   Newburg, Ky.

ALS, DNA-RG92, General Records 1792–1929, Consolidated Corres. Files, L. J. Speed.

1. Speed (*c*1811–*fl*1870), a native Kentuckian, was a farmer and later a horse doctor in Jefferson County. 1850 Census, Ky., Jefferson, 2nd Dist., 491; (1870), Louisville, 5th Ward, 248.

2. Speed's wife was Rachel (b. *c*1822), also of Kentucky. Their three children were John F. (b. *c*1855); Mandeville (b. *c*1858), who died sometime between 1862 and 1870; and James L. (b. *c*1863). Ibid.; 1860 Census, Ky., Jefferson, 1st Dist., Grassy Pond P.O., 6.

3. Not identified.

4. The letter was referred to the War Department, which in turn referred it to the quartermaster general's office, and then to General Swords, who sent it to Bvt. Brig. Gen. Sidney Burbank, assistant commissioner of the Freedmen's Bureau in Kentucky. Subassistant commissioner Capt. J. S. Catlin at Louisville investigated Speed's case and on September 13, 1867, he reported it as justified. No settlement was forthcoming, however, because the following spring Deputy Quartermaster General James A. Ekin noted that it could not be considered for it had been improperly submitted. It is not known whether Speed resubmitted his claim. General Records, 1792–1929, Consolidated Corres. Files, L.J. Speed, RG92, NA.

From James B. Steedman

New Orleans La.　June 19th 1867　9. P.M.

Louis D. Campbell leaves New Orleans for home this evening.[1] Want of respect for Governor Wells personally alone represses the expression of indignation felt by all honest and sensible men at the unwarranted usurpation of General Sheridan in removing the Civil Officers of Louisiana.[2] It is believed here that you will reinstate Wells. He is a bad man and has no influence. I believe General Sheridan made the removals to embarrass you believing the feeling at the North would sustain him. My conviction is that on account of the bad character of Wells and Monroe[3] you ought not to reinstate any who have been removed because you cannot reinstate any without reinstating all, but you ought to prohibit the exercise of this power in the future.

James B. Steedman

Tel, DNA-RG107, Tels. Recd., President, Vol. 6 (1867–68).

1. Campbell had just resigned as U.S. minister to Mexico. See Campbell to Johnson, June 16, 1867.

2. Steedman was responding to a telegram from Johnson enquiring, "Has Lewis D. Campbell left New Orleans? I would like to have your opinion as to the removal of Governor Wells, &c." Johnson to Steedman, June 19, 1867, Tels. Sent, President, Vol. 3 (1865–66), RG107, NA.

3. John T. Monroe.

From R. King Cutler

Washington, D.C.　June 20th, 1867.

Respected Sir.

Permit me to say that I have just been informed of a wicked, vindictive, malicious, unjust and false defense made by W. P. Kellogg[1] Collector of Customs at the Port of New Orleans.

Such is the outrageous conduct of Kellogg, that in my opinion, and in the opinion of many of your best friends, here and in Louisiana, he should be immediately suspended.

As to the vile, low and contemptible defense to the fair and indisputable charges made against him,[2] I shall within a few days make such a

reply thereto as will not only drive him to shame but to everlasting disgrace and ignominy.

I am aware that you leave tomorrow for Boston, therefore I beg of you
to grant me the high privilege and permission to see you at some hour
this day in company with your friend Mr. Crawford.[3]

We have something to say to you, which we believe to be important.[4]

R. King Cutler of New Orleans La.

ALS, DLC-JP.
    1. Illinois lawyer William P. Kellogg (1831–1918) served as colonel of the 7th Ill. Vol.
Cav. until he resigned due to illness. On April 13, 1865, Lincoln appointed Kellogg collector of the port of New Orleans. Kellogg served in the U.S. Senate from Louisiana (1868–
72, 1877–83), resigning when elected governor (1873–77). Then he served in the U.S.
House of Representatives (1883–85). *BDUSC*; Conrad, *La. Biography*.
    2. On May 24, 1867, Cutler and five other men filed charges against Kellogg in the
U.S. Treasury Department in Washington, D.C. The alleged activities included seizure of
goods without cause, illegal detention of vessels and employment of stevedores, employment of rebels, and speculating in shares of insurance companies. Of the thirty citizens cited
as witnesses, twenty-three declared they knew nothing about the charges. Kellogg and a
number of officers in the customhouse also sent affidavits claiming Kellogg's innocence.
The defense which probably was the main cause of Cutler's outrage was an affidavit from
one John B. Hicks, circuit court clerk at Massac, Illinois, dated January 1, 1861, giving the
history of the indictment of Rufus King Cutler and Wyatt C. Cutler for counterfeiting in
1849. *New Orleans Picayune*, June 15, 1867, (morning).
    3. Crawford remains unidentified. It is not known whether Cutler and Crawford visited
the President.
    4. For the next letter in Cutler's series, see Cutler to Johnson, July 6, 1867.

From Simeon M. Johnson

Washington   June 20th 1867

Sir.

The Commissioner of Indian Affairs[1] has in charge and is about to report, I understand, upon the award by Rice & Jackson,[2] in the matter
of claims against the Chocktaw & Chickasaw Nations, under the 49th
Article of the Treaty between the U.S. & said Indians, of July of last
year.[3]

By the provisions of the Treaty referred to, it is made the duty of the
Secretary of the Interior[4] to affirm or reject the said award. The indians
effected by the proceeding, inform me, that the amount declared to be
due by the award is considerably more than five times the amount of real
indebtedness in the premises; and I am fully convinced that great injustice would be done by the approval of the report of Mess Rice and
Jackson.

The Secretary of the Interior is absent from his post, and it occurs to
me that any action of the Commissioner of Indian Affairs for or against
the report of Rice and Jackson, would not be advisable, till the return of
the Secretary.

I beg leave, therefore, on behalf the two Nations, to request that you will bring this matter to the notice of the Commissioner of Indian Affairs and suggest the fitness of the course of proceeding I have thought it my duty lay before you.[5]

S. M. Johnson
of Counsel for Chocktaw & Chicasaw Nations

As this matter relates exclusively to the execution of a Treaty, I have thought it my duty to make this request of you.

S.M.J.

LS, DLC-JP.

1. Nathaniel G. Taylor.

2. Elliott W. Rice and Allan H. Jackson. Rice (1835–1887) practiced law in Iowa before the war and then served in the 7th Iowa. He saw quite a bit of military action and was promoted to brigadier and brevetted major general. From 1865 to 1885 Rice practiced law in Washington, D.C. Jackson (c1835–1911), a native of New York, began his military career with the 91st N.Y. Inf. Rgt. He mustered out in the summer of 1865 but the following year joined the regular army. He finally retired from active duty in 1898. Warner, *Blue*; Powell, *Army List*, 395; *New York Tribune*, Aug. 23, 1911.

3. Rice and Jackson were appointed by President Johnson to examine claims made against the Choctaws by Joseph G. Heald and Reuben Wright, both licensed traders from Massachusetts. In their report of January 1867 Rice and Jackson accepted the claims of Heald for amounts in excess of $70,000 and of Wright for a sum in excess of $20,000. *House Ex. Docs.*, 40 Cong., 2 Sess., No. 204, p. 26 (Ser. 1341).

4. Orville H. Browning.

5. In August 1867 Browning accepted the claims of both Heald and Wright but indicated that they slightly exceeded the maximum authorized to be paid under terms of the treaty. Therefore, acting commissioner Charles E. Mix proposed that the awards be reduced by several hundred dollars. Ibid., p. 27.

To Samuel A. Parker[1]

Washington, D.C., June 21st 1867

Have received the resolution of the Common Council of Newport, which invited me to visit that city. I expect to be in Newport on the evening of Wednesday the 26th.[2] If any change in the plan, will communicate it to you.

Present to the Council my thanks for the honor of their invitation.[3]

Andrew Johnson.

Tel, DNA-RG107, Tels. Sent, President, Vol. 3 (1865–68).

1. Parker (c1810–1872) served as mayor of Newport, state treasurer, and was an auctioneer by trade. 1860 Census, R.I., Newport, Newport, 263; Newport directories (1856–58); *New York Times*, Feb. 6, 1872.

2. See Newport, R.I., Common Council to Johnson, June 12, 1867, Johnson Papers, LC.

3. The presidential party did not, however, pass through Newport as it made its way from Washington to Boston. *New York Tribune*, June 23, 24, 26, 1867.

From Lucy E.W. Polk

Warrenton [N.C.]   June 22d 1867.

Sir

Pardon my trespassing again on your valued time, but having written about two months ago[1] requesting you would give me a letter endorsing my faithful adherance to the Government of the United States throughout the Rebellion, this endorsement I wish to reserve for future use or when the Government becomes honorable enough to pay its just debts. As to the right of property in slaves, that has been so often, and so ably discussed, that I will not venture a remark, further than to assert.as such, it was recognized by the Government & now having forfeited my right to its protection I feel I am entitled to compensation. My Negro property valued at $90,000 was almost my entire Estate, the passing of the Military bill, rendering our lands entirely valueless & without capital I cant have mine cultivated at all. This Mr President is a repetition of what I have told you before, & you will doubtless think why trouble you with such things when you cant relieve them. Perhaps not—but we cant divest our minds of the idea that the President is the Father of the Country & as such we must all pour into his ear our wants & cares.[2]

I regretted much not seeing you as you passed the Warrenton Depot,[3] had my Bonnet on to go out to pay my respects, but was disappointed in getting a carriage. There was quite a delegation from this town to Chapel Hill who returned much pleased with the President's appearance but not the pleasure of an introduction.

With my compliments to the Ladies of the "White house."[4]

Mrs. W. H. Polk

ALS, DLC-JP.

1. See her letter of March 4, 1867.

2. On July 27 Johnson granted Mrs. Polk's request for a letter. He acknowledged her wartime adherence to the Union, stated that she was "entitled to respect and confidence," and that she should receive the protection of the government. Johnson to Lucy E.W. Polk, July 27, 1867, Johnson Papers, LC.

3. Warrenton Depot was on the Raleigh and Gaston Railroad, which route Johnson's presidential party apparently used both to and from Raleigh on June 3 and 7, 1867. *Washington Evening Star*, June 1, 3, 4, 7, 8, 1867.

4. On August 3 Polk wrote Johnson to thank him for the letter, and added: "Should such an endorsement prove of no avail I shall have the proud consciousness of having done my duty & in my leisure hours abuse the ingratitude of Republics." Polk to Johnson, Aug. 3, 1867, Johnson Papers, LC.

From John C. Vaughn

Thomasville Geo   June 22" 1867

Dear Sir:

Permit me to address you. I take the liberty bacause I know you was one of my best freinds before the late war. And from my boyhood days to the present time I have never ceased to respect you. We differd during the last war or Rebellion. But during the time or from the last time you was at my house in Sweetwater, Tenn at the Barbacue untill the close of the war I never would have done you a wrong, If you had fallen into my hands while I was a commander in the Rebble Army. Brownlow tried to make the impression in his paper that I wanted to do so or have some of my command to do so. Let me ashure you that it is not so. And I want you to know so from me, as we may never meet this side of the Judgement bar. You may not have saw in his paper what he said. But believe me that he charge things that were not true. I am still that true freind (even more so If I could be). I am an exile from Tennessee as yet, did not wish to return while Brownlow had controll. I filed my petition for a Pardon in Sept/65, through Gov. Johnson of this state but have never heard from it.[1] Pardon me for beeing So free with you. Nothing would give me so much pleasure on this earth as to know that you had forgiven any wrong that you thought I had done *you*, my state & Goverment.[2]

Permit me to say that the people of the South only desire to know what plan you wish them to Suport, and they would do so cherfully & freely.

John. C. Vaughn

ALS, DNA-RG94, Amnesty Papers (M1003, Roll 24), Ga., John C. Vaughn.

1. Vaughn had written to President Johnson from Augusta, Georgia, in June 1865, but it may have been September before he was able to forward the letter to the Georgia governor, James Johnson. Judging from one of the file cover sheets, his request for pardon likely did not succeed initially because Governor Johnson refused to recommend Vaughn's pardon. See Vaughn to Johnson, June 16, 1865, Amnesty Papers (M1003, Roll 24), Ga., John C. Vaughn, RG94, NA.

2. One of the President's private secretaries endorsed this June 1867 letter in late August with the notation that the request by Vaughn was to be referred to the attorney general "who will please let pardon issue in this case." On August 30, 1867, this was done.

From Jennie A. Perry

New York   June the 24th [1867]

President Johnson

Will yoo listen to me and think well of what I have to say to yoo. Let all the past be forgoten and done away with and loock wonce more on me as a friend for such I will be if yoo will be reasonable to me. It is this—I have a Dear friend[1] that has been sentance to prisen for 2 or 3 years. He has gone for that witch thousands would if they were found out. He is not so guilty as some of his friends that have had all the benifit then they forsaken him when he most needed friends. He did not do no more than Thousands have don and are still doing. Now Johnson I want yoo to Pardon him. I do not ask yoo to do so Just now but within 2 or 3 months from now but I want your promise now wether yoo will do so or not. If yoo will do so I will forever abanden the ideia of ever exposing the matter of the general ordar buisness or show to the Public the claims that I have on yoo and Smyth.[2] Yoo can Pardon this Gentleman without anny wone knowing who soliceted it from yoo. That will be keep a secreet from the Public. Now if yoo will do this I will see *Col* Moore at anny time that yoo say or any place yoo may say and tell him all about the matter. It can be done through him. Yoo need not see me at all—unless yoo *wish* to—yoo must let me know at wonce what yoo will do. Yoo must say yes or no within 3 days from this Just so soon as a letter will *reach me* for Johnson Just as sure as I live and were I to know that I should die the moment that yoo Receive this that I am a telling yoo the truth. There is something afoot that will come out soon that yoo will regret as long as yoo live—and now yoo have it in yoar Power to avert it and listen to me. I have delayed the matter for a few days untill I can hear from yoo—*yes or no* it will be all the same. But if you think well of this the matter can be settled through *Col* Moore satisfactory. I will bind myself any way that yoo chose. It will be best for all parties conserned that you should think well of *this*. This favor I ask of yoo as antonement of the wrong yoo have done me and it will serve a friend languishing in prison. Johnson I beg an intreat of yoo to comply with my request—do not distroy this untill yoo read it.

If yoo answer this do so at wonce.

My Box in 1398.

Mrs. Jennie A. Perry   New York City

ALS, DLC-JP.

1. Unidentified.

2. Perry had made this threat eight days earlier in a letter to Johnson concerning the fulfillment of agreements she believed Johnson and Henry A. Smythe had made with her. Perry to Johnson, June 16, 1867, Johnson Papers, LC. See also Smythe to Johnson, Mar. 6, 1867.

From F. H. George[1]

Lewiston   June 25/66 [1867][2]

To A. Johnson

Hearing that the trial of John A. Surratt has commenced, I his friend and confederate feel it my duty to write you this letter of warning. I solemnly swear that if any harm befall John A. Surratt you will curse the day that you were born. The wrath of Achilles will be nothing to the terrible vengeance which will be visited upon your head. Look at your past life and see if there is nothing there which will implicate you with some of the most fiendish plots on record. Free Surratt or leave the country. "The mills of the gods grind slowly," and I knowing that which will hurl you from your high position, will spend my last farthing and lose the last drop of my hearts blood but that my very design shall be accomplished. Hang Surratt indeed, one who is comparatively innocent of every crime with which he is charged when there are so many others whose hands are red with blood and whose hearts are black with guilt. Foul traitor that thou art, again I say free Surratt or leave the country. Do not regard my words as mere empty ravings, and cast them aside unheeded or you will suffer one of the most shamefull deaths. *Beware.*

F. H. George   Lewiston N Y

ALS, DLC-JP.
   1. Unidentified.
   2. Although George clearly wrote "66" as the year of this letter, references to John Surratt's trial make it obvious that the letter has to be 1867. The trial began in the courts of the District of Columbia on June 10, 1867.

From Samuel S. Marshall[1]

Washington, D.C.   June 26 1867.

Mr. President.

I some days ago wrote from Philadelphia[2] in favor of the appointment of Gen John A. McClernand, of Illinois as Minister to Mexico. Since returning to the city I have received the inclosed reccommendation made by prominent citzens of Illinois.[3] They have said nothing in favor of the Generel that is not strictly true. With his ability your excellency must be satisfied, as it is everywhere acknowledged, and he has at all times proven himself a decided and active friend of your administration. I am satisfied that no better selection could be made for that position.[4]

S. S. Marshall

ALS, DNA-RG59, Lets. of Appl. and Recomm., 1861–69 (M650, Roll 30), John A. McClernand.
   1. Marshall (1821–1890), a lawyer and native of Illinois, served in Illinois in the state house, as attorney in the third judicial district, circuit court judge, and in the U.S. House (1855–59, 1865–75). *BDUSC.*
   2. Marshall to Johnson, June 18, 1867, Lets. of Appl. and Recomm., 1861–69 (M650, Roll 30), John A. McClernand, RG59, NA.
   3. Enclosed was a Springfield petition, dated June 21, 1867, signed by more than two dozen men, many federal officeholders.
   4. McClernand was nominated on July 20, 1867, and again on July 20, 1868. Both times he was rejected. Ser. 6B, Vol. 2: 217, 221, Johnson Papers, LC.

From James A. Abrahams[1]

Livingston Sumter Co.   Alabama   June 27th 1867.

The undersigned J. A. Abrahams, acting under an appointment by Maj. Gen. John Pope, as Probate Judge of said County, respectfully begs leave to submit the following statement of facts. Geo. B. Saunders[2] was elected, on the 1st Monday of May 1866, Probate Judge of the County & entered upon the duties of the office. The Probate Judge, besides his jurisdiction over estates of decedents & minors, has jurisdiction of all criminal offences not amounting to felony & is recorder of deeds, & collector of that part of state & county revenue which arises from licenses & he is the presiding officer at the session of the road Commissioners.

Geo. B. Saunders, after he had been in the office two weeks, fell back into his old habits of drunkenness & from that time to my appointment he hardly drew a sober breath. He did not enter on the records one thirtieth part of his judicial acts. He became defaulter to amount of $2700.00 in state & County revenue money. At the last spring term of the Circuit Court three different true bills were found against him by the Grand Jury for Misfeasance & Malfeasance in office—and in addition the Grand Jury reported that his official bond was insufficient & the Circuit Court ordered him to give a new bond, within ten days. Within the first five or six days he made strenuous efforts to give a new bond & failed. He then stated to C. S. McConnico,[3] who once filled the office & was a candidate for it in case of Saunder's removal, that he, Saunders, could not give bond, & that he McConnico had better apply for the office. McConnico thereupon left for Montgomery & on the tenth of the ten days allowed Saunders for giving the bond, he, Saunders, telegraphed McConnico that the bond had been given.

In the meanwhile I thought I saw, as every one did, there would be a vacancy in the office. I believed I was competent to fill it. I never took any steps whatever in the way of exposing to the authorities, what I knew to be Judge Saunders' derelictions of duty. But I knew that I had been reduced by the war from affluence to poverty that I had suffered great opprobrium because in a population almost universally in favor of Secession, I a southern man born & raised & a large slave-holder, had from the beginning to the end, been uncompromisingly in favor of the Union. I knew that when during the war I undertook to save some of my losses by buying cotton to hold till the war had ended, I was warned that if I dared to buy any more, it as well as my buildings would be burned. I believed my claims to the office were, at least as good, as those of any one else. I applied for it to Gov. Patton & Gen. Swayne.[4] Gov. Patton had, prior to my interview, been informed of Saunders' derelictions & promised to assist me. Some days afterwards Communications came from Gen. Pope at Atlanta, removing Saunders & appointing me, & on the 6th day of May last, I took charge of the office.

Last winter, our Legislature passed an act allowing decrees of probate Judges which had not been entered on the record at the proper times, to be entered subsequently by decrees nunc pro tunc. This act was passed at the instance of a leading lawyer in this County, who had his eye upon the condition of things in our Probate Court. After I took charge of the office, parties at once, commenced moving for decrees, nunc pro tunc under above act & I have been harder worked in getting upon the records the unrecorded official acts of my predecessor than in keeping up the regular business which has come into the office since my appointment. At this time, I have in my employment six clerks hard at work.

This condition of things, has involved the paying out by me of considerable sums in the way of expenses and the receiving in of considerable sums as fees. Under the interpretation of the Military bill by your Excellency and the Cabinet as published, the questions come up.

Are my acts as Probate Judge void? Are the records of Deeds, the receipts of County Revenue, the sentences passed upon criminals, the issuance of letters of administration, the recording of the unrecorded official acts of Judge Saunders &c done & made since I went into the office, void?

As regards the above statement of facts, I will, the moment it shall be intimated, that it will be proper for me to do so, authenticate them by forwarding certified copies of the indictments, and affidavits by gentleman of the first respectablity as to the other facts.

I have believed that your excellency would consider it right that I should make this communciation all of which is most respectfully submitted by . . .

James A. Abrahams

ALS, DNA-RG60, Office of Atty. Gen., Lets. Recd., President.

1. Abrahams (1804–1881) was a longtime Livingston merchant. Pauline J. Gandrud, comp., *Alabama Records* (245 vols., Easley, S.C., 1981), 70: 25; 1860 Census, Ala., Sumter, Southern Div., 72.

2. Saunders (c1816–1872) had served a considerable time as register in chancery. Ibid., 94; Pauline J. Gandrud, comp., *Marriage, Death and Legal Notices from Early Alabama Newspapers, 1819–1893* (Easley, S.C., 1981), 108.

3. Christopher S. McConnico (1820–1868) was a lawyer. Gandrud, *Alabama Records*, 19: 88; 70: 19; 1860 Census, Ala., Sumter, Southern Div., 80.

4. Robert M. Patton and Wager T. Swayne.

From Pierce Burton [1]

(Personal)

Demopolis Ala   June 27th 1867

Sir.

I have the honor to enclose herewith an article[2] cut from a news paper from which you may learn that General Swayne has ordered my discharge from the position of a clerk in the Freedmans Bureau because I took the liberty to criticise the action of Congress on the "cotton tax" in a letter published in a northern newspaper. Said letter is again republished and a copy enclosed herewith.

I am compelled to "accept the situation" although it leaves me out of employment in a "far Country," but I desire to call your attention to the political action of the commanding General[3] of the District of Alabama, who by virtue of the influence of his position controlled the "Republican Union State convention"[4] which lately met in Montgomery, and who is using such influence for the purpose of securing his election to the *United States Senate* by the next legislature which shall meet in Alabama.

I would respectfully suggest that the preservation of Republican institutions demands that the military power of the Government should not be used for the political aggrandizement of military Leaders and that the only sure way for the *commander in chief* to be relieved from the responsibillity of such use of a military position, is to *assign military political aspirants to duty in other states than those they now command.*

Hoping that your convictions will lead you to take the action indicated above.

Pierce Burton

ALS, DLC-JP.
1. Burton (1834–1916), a New Englander who had worked in Ohio, Massachusetts, and Indiana, went to Alabama after the war. In late September 1867 he was again hired as clerk in the Freedmen's Bureau, afterwards attending the state constitutional convention and serving as a legislator. Later he edited a Republican newspaper (1869–71) at Demopolis and in 1870 lost a bid for the lieutenant governorship. Removing to Aurora, Illinois, he continued to be a newspaper editor. *Commemorative Biographical and Historical Record of Kane County, Illinois* (Chicago, 1888), 444–48; *NUC*; F. D. Sewall to Wager T. Swayne, Records of the Commr., Lets. Sent (M742, Roll 1), RG105, NA.
2. Not found, but according to the file cover sheet the article was from the *Demopolis New Era* which evidently had reprinted Burton's critical article originally published in the *Springfield (Mass.) Republican* of April 13, 1867.
3. Wager T. Swayne.
4. This convention met June 4–5, 1867, and issued a set of nine resolutions. *American Annual Cyclopaedia* (1867), 25–26.

From Edmund Cooper

At Home [Shelbyville]   June 27 1867

Dear Mr President.

The Governor of the state in the exercise of unlimited power conferred upon him, by the Legislature, has doomed me to political defeat—and that too in the very face of the written law—and in violation of the vested rights of the voter.

By the "franchise law" of the state, all persons who voted in the November election 1864, in the February election 1865, and in the March election 1865, are entitled to vote at the August election.[1]

In the counties of Lincoln, Franklin, & Coffee, four thousand votes were cast in those elections, and therefore four thousand qualified voters reside in those counties—and were when I announced myself as a candidate for re-election, registered voters. Under a law enacted by the Legislature, the Governor is clothed with the power of declaring the registrations void in any counties in the state, by proclamation.

This he has done in the three counties I have mentioned—and new Registrations abound.

And the new Registers, in violation of the written law, in direct opposition to the legal opinion of the Attorney General of the State,[2] and the Secretary of the State,[3] openly and boldly refuse to register the qualified voters—and to day—in the county of Franklin, where there are not less than Thirteen hundred qualified white voters, the Register[4] has registered only about 120—and closed his books—and in Lincoln county where there are not less than 1800—qualified voters, the Register[5] has registered less than one hundred.

Now with every desire to restore our beloved state to lasting and permanent peace, and to do all that I can possibly do, to induce the people to stand by the Land marks of constitutional liberty; to oppose the notion of military despotism; to atain the trial by jury and the binding force of written law—yet, I can see no advantage that will result to the people of the fourth congressional district by my continuing the struggle any longer—and the mortification of a defeat by my competitor is too great for me to bear.

Now I write to you for advice as to what I should do? Is there no plan, that you can devise, by which I can escape the humiliation of such a defeat, and at the same time enable me to retire from the canvass without the public concluding that I was driven from it?

Have you no temporary mission that you could send me upon that would give me a reasonable excuse?

Think about it! I have no desire for office, as you know—and only now, ask for some excuse to retire from a hopeless struggle—when my defeat is certain because the Governor and his party have determined that it shall be so.[6]

By this action the voting population of the District is made up of seven thousand negroes and four thousand whites—under the law it would have been eight thousand whites to seven thousand negroes—and my election would have been safe.

Besides, the Governor has placed two companies of his militia in my District—and unhesitatingly says to his friends that he will spare no means to defeat me.

With this mocking of an election going on around me, why should I sacrifice myself? Write to me! Tell me what to do! I have canvassed more than half the District—and made friends—but how can I contest five thousand ignorant negroes—sustained as they are by reckless and vicious white men and state bayonets?

I do not believe that I can do it!

Remember me kindly to the family.

Edmund Cooper

ALS, DLC-JP.
1. See Alexander, *Reconstruction*, 159.

2. Thomas H. Coldwell.

3. Andrew J. Fletcher.

4. Evidently the register of voters in Franklin County was Daniel E. Davenport (*fl*1869), later a receiver of the Winchester and Alabama Railroad and a candidate for the state senate. *Nashville Press and Times*, Apr. 18, 1867; Davenport to William G. Brownlow, Jan. 13, 1868, Brownlow Papers; J.W.C. Bryant to John Eaton, Jr., July 13, 1869, Eaton Papers, Special Collections, TU.

5. John Carey (1821–1886), a farmer, was justice of the peace and county tax assessor before serving in the Tennessee state legislature (1867–69). *Nashville Press and Times*, Apr. 18, 1867; Robert M. McBride and Dan Robison, *Biographical Directory of the Tennessee General Assembly* (2 vols., Nashville, 1975–), 2: 131.

6. Despite his pleas, Cooper remained in the congressional race but was defeated overwhelmingly by his Republican opponent, James Mullins. Ben: Perley Poore, comp., *The Political Register and Congressional Directory* (Boston, 1878), 547.

From Charles T. Daniel [1]

Cynthiana   June 27th 1867

Sir

During the fall of last year my brother-in-law Mr. Tucker[2] presented for your consideration an application for a pardon for myself[3] signed by Gov. Bramlette[4] & other leading union men of this State. You however declined acting on the same because I was then without the limits of the United States but gave Mr. Tucker a verbal assurance that if I returned I should not be molested. I was not included in any of the classes excepted from your amnesty proclamation except that I had been sentenced by the Military commission at Cincinnati O. to be shot for having attempted to release my fellow confederate prisoners from Camp Douglas Chicago whence I had formerly escaped.[5] I had also escaped from Cincinnati & my sentence was found on the alleged ground that by escaping I had acknowleged myself guilty.[6] Under these circumstances I went & remained abroad until the public mind had been somewhat quieted and the Supreme Court of the United States in the Milligan case had decided the tribunal which tried me to be entirely illegal & unconstitutional & all its acts void when I returned to my avocation as a lawyer in this place where since the 1st of last February I have been conducting myself as I hope always to do as a good citizen. Considering myself included in the proclamation of general amnesty & relying on your verbal promise as well as the decision of the highest tribunal of the land I have prosecuted my profession without fear of molestation but in the interim have won the affections of a noble woman whose father[7] fears to trust her to my keeping without some written document from yourself as a protection against further molestation.[8]

The contents of this letter show why I have marked it "confidential" & do not wish it by any means to be filed as a public document.

Though *I* feel no uneasiness whatever on the subject you can relieve the anxious fears of a parent & others & win a warm friend in.

Chas. T. Daniel   Cynthiana Ky

ALS, DNA-RG153, Court-Martial Records, NN-3409.

1. Daniel (*fl*1867), alias Charles Travis, a lawyer, served with the 14th Ky. Cav. (CSA) and was captured at least twice before escaping to Canada. Endorsements, Daniel to Johnson, June 27, 1867, Court-Martial Records, NN-3409, RG153, NA; *House Ex. Docs.*, 39 Cong., 2 Sess., No. 50, p. 14 (Ser. 1290).

2. Not identified.

3. Not found.

4. Thomas E. Bramlette.

5. In the first week of November 1864, Daniel and others unsuccessfully attempted to release the Confederate prisoners at Camp Douglas. Ibid.

6. While on trial in Cincinnati in early 1865 for the attempted prison break in Chicago, Daniel escaped and fled to Canada. The judge advocate declared, and the military commission agreed, that "he has, by his escape, said in effect that he has no witnesses to produce and no defence to make." Daniel was, therefore, sentenced to death. Ibid., pp. 274, 276.

7. Unidentified.

8. In July both Stanton and Holt recommended that Daniel not be pardoned and that the original sentence be carried out or commuted to a specific jail term. Johnson chose to take no action; Daniel was notified of this August 1. There is no evidence that Daniel was ever pardoned or served prison time. Endorsements, Daniel to Johnson, June 27, 1867, Court-Martial Records, NN-3409, RG153, NA.

From John A. McClernand

Springfield Ill   June 27th 1867

I beg to recommend Hon. Ira O. Wilkinson,[1] of Rock Island, Illinois, late Judge of the sixth circuit in this state, for district Judge in Nebraska.[2]

Judge Wilkinson enjoys an enviable reputation, both, as a scholar and a Judge. His application is strongly supported by leading officials within and without this state.

It would be very gratifying to many of your friends, including myself, that he should receive the appointment.[3]

John A. McClernand.

ALS, NNPM.

1. Wilkinson (1820–1894) practiced law at several places and with various partners in Illinois. He served two terms as judge of the circuit court, the second being during 1861–67. John M. Palmer, ed., *The Bench and Bar of Illinois* (2 vols., Chicago, 1899), 1: 563–64.

2. Nebraska had just become a state in March and therefore, no longer being served by territorial justices, needed a federal district judge.

3. Wilkinson was nominated to the post on July 20, 1867, but apparently no action was taken by the Senate. Eventually, former territorial justice Elmer S. Dundy received the post but not until April 1868. Ser. 6B, Vol. 4: 363, Johnson Papers, LC.

Remarks at Reception at Baltimore[1]

June 28, 1867

Sir:

Permit me to return to you and to the Mayor,[2] on this occasion, my sincere thanks for this kind welcome given to me by the city of Baltimore on my return from the visit just made to the North.[3] Words are inadequate to express the feelings of my heart for the manifestations on this occasion. My business has not been, on the tour, to make speeches or addresses, but simply to participate in and extend civilities that are due among citizens of a common country. The other day, in connection with my distinguished associates, I visited the State that gave me birth,[4] and a few days after my return to Washington, I, in company with the same associates, set out on a visit to one of the cities in the far East; and permit me to say that my reception both North and South, has been of that character which indicates to me an era of good feeling and reconciliation between the two sections of the Union. (Applause, an a bouquet was presented to him.) Thank God it is so. (Renewed applause.) In the very dawn of the difficulties, when one portion of the Union threatened the other, I took my position which is known to the people I now address. But, my friends, there are two kinds of courage, one which will enable a man to meet his foe in the field, this is physical courage; but the other is moral courage, which strengthens a man to stand upon the face of menace and threats, and denounce those who are conspiring to overthrow the government; which enables a man to plant himself firmly on the principles of the government, and bid defiance to all fury whencesoever it may come. It is easy to apply the word "traitor" to me, as some have done, but I defy any man to put his finger on any great principle of the Constitution, or of liberty, that I have abandoned. I have held to the Constitution as the palladium of our civil and religious liberty, as the chief ark our safety. (Applause) Let me say to the people of Baltimore, to-day, if you expect, and are determined to preserve the Constitution, and liberty, let me here appeal to you, in the language of the shipwrecked mariner, to cling to the Constitution as the last plank of liberty, while the night and the tempest may close around you. I have, my fellow-citizens, tried to discharge my duty. I may have committed errors, but they have not been of the heart. Now that the era of good will has commenced let us forgive one another, in the spirit of charity, and in order to a closer fellowship.

New York World, June 29, 1867.

1. Johnson was introduced on the balcony of his hotel by ex-Governor Augustus W. Bradford to speak to the crowd that had gathered in front of the hotel.

2. John L. Chapman.

3. On June 21 Johnson left Washington to visit New York City, Springfield, Boston, Philadelphia, Hartford, New Haven, Baltimore, and Annapolis before returning to Washington on June 29.

4. Johnson had made a trip to North Carolina in early June.

From George Mountfort[1]
Private.

Boston, 29th June, 1867.

Sir

Several years since when on a brief visit to the *Island of Malta*, my personal friend & brother Free Mason *William Winthrop*, Esqr.[2] U.S. Consul at that place, presented *to me an old oil* painting, *representing a Naval engagement*, in May 1728 in the neighborhood of that island between the "*Knights of Malta & the Algerines*["] which painting was owned by, & for very many years suspended in the hall of the residence of the "*Grand Commander*" of aforesaid "*Knights of Malta.*"

Although as a "*Work of Art*," this painting has no especial merit, yet still as it represents one of the gallant conflicts of that period in defence of the Christian faith, & the noble devotion of the "*Knights*" of that Era, & also probably, as this painting, is the only relic in this country of that renouned band of Christian soldiers, the *association* connected with it, cannot but render it of much value to every reflecting mind, and of especial interest to every true *Free Mason*, with which consideration, I am prompted respectfuly to address you & enquire if I may be permitted to present & forward it to you for your private cabinet.[3]

I avail myself of this occasion to enquire if the honey *prescription for the Gravel*, which, during my several years residence in Candia, I was aware was used by the Turkish physicians for that malady, & which, on 11th April last, through the Hon W. H. Seward, I recommended to you, was of service? In fact, on several very aggravated cases, I have recommended this *Turkish pine honey* remedy to my friends in this city, all of whom, it immediately releived, & I am of opinion *permanently cured*.

I sincerely trust that your late visit to this, my native city, was agreable to you, at all events, it cannot but greatly soften the severity of the prejudices of your political opponents & more firmly attach your many strong & reliable political & personal friends in this region.[4]

George Mountfort
formerly U.S. Consul for the Island of Candia

P S. This *old painting, is in its original old frame.*

ALS, DLC-JP.
    1. Mountfort (c1803–fl1881) had been consul at Candia for several years, beginning in 1850. Also, he had for some time engaged in international business dealings. 1850 Census, Mass., Suffolk, Boston, 1st Ward, 8; Boston directories (1867–81); *U.S. Off. Reg.* (1851–55); Mountfort to Daniel Webster, Aug. 23, 1850, Lets. of Appl. and Recomm., 1845–53 (M873, Roll 62), George Mountfort, RG59, NA.
    2. Winthrop (c1808–1869) held the post at Malta for over thirty years; he was a native of Boston. *New York Tribune*, July 14, 27, 1869; *Proceedings of the Massachusetts Historical Society* (1869–70), 146–47.

3. About a week later Mountfort sent a receipt to Johnson from the Adams Express Company for the delivery of the painting. See Mountfort to Johnson, July 6, 1867, Johnson Papers, LC.

4. In September Mountfort indicated to the President that he would like to be considered for a diplomatic appointment. He assured Johnson that he, Mountfort, had a number of influential conservative friends. This letter is one of several in the applications files. See Mountfort to Johnson, Sept. 5, 1867, Lets. of Appl. and Recomm., 1861–69 (M650, Roll 34), George Mountfort, RG59, NA.

Speech at Annapolis [1]

June 29, 1867

SIR:

In being presented here to-day under these peculiar circumstances, and on a spot which, at an early period of our history, was consecrated to freedom, I confess to you that a reception so kind and so cordial and so gratifying, incapacitates me from making suitable acknowledgment; but I cannot refrain from saying that my visit to this capital affords me much pleasure—among other reasons, because events have recently transpired which were not the result of any preconceived arrangement or design, but which, it seems to me, were brought about by Providence itself. But a few days since without any agency on my part, I was called to my native State to participate in a ceremony of great interest to me personally. After my return to Washington I was invited to visit the opposite extreme of the country. When I consider these two events connected with my visit here today, it looks to me as the result of a kind and overruling Providence. But the other day it would have been impossible for the Chief Magistrate to travel as far South as I did, and we know, from the prejudice existing it would have been unpleasant for my honored friend (Mr. Seward) to have gone so far in that direction. But when I look at the pleasant incidents connected with our visit to North Carolina, it seems to me, and I trust I am not mistaken in saying, that an era of good will is about to be inaugurated. ⟨Applause.⟩ If I know myself, from the beginning of our late unhappy civil strife, I had but a single object in view, and that was to preserve the harmony, peace, and Union of these States. ⟨Applause.⟩ It would have been at any time the highest object of my ambition to tie up the bleeding arteries which caused so much blood and the expenditure of so much money. Now, however, there is a new era, and I trust we shall have peace on earth and good will toward men. ⟨Applause.⟩ I trust the time has come when man is no longer to be set on man, and, in the name of God to lift his hand against the throat of his fellow, and that the land that gave a brother birth will be spared from being again drenched with a brother's blood.

To be invited to visit the State of Maryland by a convention which has a reputation for talent, to be welcomed by the chairman of your committee, by the Governor of your State, and by your president, irrespective of party, is peculiarily gratifying to me. The history of Maryland, and especially of Annapolis, is more familiar to you than to me, and, therefore, it is not necessary for me to indulge in a narration of facts whch will last as long as history itself.

If my memory serves me, after we had passed through the revolutionary struggle for independence, and it was found that the articles of confederation were not of sufficient strength to secure the Government, the first proposal to remodel the Government under which we now live emanated from this place, and this is the Constitution I have been taught to believe sacred in principle, and for the preservation of which I have perilled my all. I now rely on the principle upon which I have always relied, namely: first be convinced that you are right, and thoroughly understand the principle, and then you can rely on it that in pursuit of correct principle you never can reach a wrong conclusion. Satisfied that the principles of the Constitution would preserve the Union, I never hesitated or debated the question; and when we reflect on the patriotism of those who formed that sacred instrument, and when we know that Washington, the Father of his Country, who, in the language of his eulogist, was "first in war, first in peace, and first in the hearts of his countrymen," was the president of the convention which formed the Constitution which we are sworn to support, we cannot but feel for it additional veneration. You, gentlemen of the Convention now in session at Annapolis, are engaged in a work similar to that which occupied the attention of our forefathers— the task of amending the constitution. Theirs was undertaken at a time when this nation was comparatively a handful of people, and our boundaries comprised within narrow limits. Our resources were but a miniature of what they now are. That wise man asserted that government was instituted for the convenience of man, and to be accommodated to every emergency, this was to be secured by a Constitution founded on the great principle of civil and religious liberty, not to be overrun and borne down by the majority, in a storm of fury and passion. ⟨Applause⟩

When the requirements and securities of the Constitution are set at naught by a tyrannical majority, and their will made law, liberty is gone, and despotism takes its place. ⟨Applause⟩

Amendments to the Constitution are to be made in the mode designated by the instrument itself. Washington, having assisted in making that Constitution, says in his farewell address, that the people should submit to the Constitution as it is, and if there is any objection its amendments should be made in the mode which the instrument itself provides. Now, if this safeguard is not respected, where is free government? None of it is left. In politics, as in religion, when my facts give out and reason fails, my conviction is strong that truth is mighty and will ultimately triumph. ⟨Applause.⟩ Though I may go down and perish, my proud consolation at the last moment will be that I have done my duty, and this for me will be a sufficient reward. In support of the Constitution there are other things to which I must allude. Washington helped to make the Constitution, and handed it down as it is. I am proud, I am gratified that I have it in my power today to stand beneath the roof where that great man spoke the Government into existence and laid down the basis of government. Here, on this consecrated ground, by resigning his commission, he set the great example of love of freedom and of constitutional government by lifting the crown from his head and laying it at the feet of the people. ⟨Applause.⟩ This is the spot where the great act was performed.

It was here that George Washington tendered his resignation as Commander-in-chief in the colonies as they then existed, and passed from the soldier to the citizen. He taught an admiring world that to be truly great a man must be truly good. This spot claims that honor; would to God that we had an example of such wisdom and virtue in modern times. It was left for him to set the example. He performed the great act that stands out alone and lifts itself above any other act of any other man who ever lived. Hence I am proud to stand here to-day and refer to subjects so familiar to you all. For the kind, for the sympathetic, and, I think I may add, for the sincere and cordial respect manifested here today, you have my thanks, the thanks of a heart which will never cease to be grateful as long as the life current animates it. The remembrance of this kindness will ever be green in my memory. ⟨Applause.⟩ I repeat, I do hope and believe an era of good feeling has commenced. Let us all endeavor to feel better and kinder toward one another. ⟨Applause.⟩ I am satisfied if the North and the South were brought into a closer intimacy there would be a better feeling, for the friction would round the sharp corners and remove the asperity which now exists. Let us try to be one people and go on and fulfil our noble destiny, and I trust through the difficulties which we have just passed, a beneficent Providence will insure for us a more permanent existence. I will not admit that this nation has completed its mission. We are extending our possessions and power, and though some may be opposed to the extension of our jurisdiction, yet, in my honest conviction, the great principle of government, instead of being too weak, as some contend, to cover a greater area, would, if properly carried out, be strong enough to embrace within its sphere and influence the whole civilized world. ⟨Great applause⟩ We have tried too much to make the public mind assume the direction of invention and discovery. We have been making too much law. If we cease to direct and invent the mind to discovery, and ascertaining what the law is, conform our action to it, the world, I am sure, would move in more harmonious motion. The North and the South can work in harmony with the Federal Government. The parts are essential to the whole, and the whole is essential to the several parts. Without law the machinery will not work smoothly and accomplish the great ends which is was designed to attain.

Pardon me, my friends, for trespassing so long on your patience, and permit me to conclude by repeating that you and the Governor of the

State, the members of this Convention, their committee and all that you represent, have my sincere thanks and gratitude for the welcome which has been extended to me on the occasion of my visit to the capital of Maryland.

National Intelligencer, July 1, 1867.

1. Johnson had been invited to address a session of Maryland's constitutional convention which met in Annapolis from May to October 1867. The President and William H. Seward were escorted to the meeting by a committee of the convention and Gov. Thomas Swann, who introduced Johnson to the convention. Swann to Johnson, June 26, 1867, Johnson Papers, LC; Jean H. Baker, *The Politics of Continuity: Maryland Political Parties from 1858 to 1870* (Baltimore, 1973), 179; *National Intelligencer,* July 1, 1867.

July 1867

From George Bancroft

Private. (*not* to be printed on any account.)

Paris   1 July 1867.

Dear Mr. President.

My instructions bringing me through Paris,[1] I seized the opportunity of a short rest after the voyage to visit my old friends in this city. I met with the most cordial welcome on all sides. The first word of Mr. Thiers[2] was an inquiry after you, and an emphatic statement that your clemency towards Jefferson Davis had won for you the esteem of all Europe, and had made many converts to republicanism. I said I shall write that to the President—and he repeated his words: that your treatment of Jefferson Davis had given you a very high place in the esteem of the best men in all Europe, & had made many republicans, *made many republicans*, repeating his words, so as to fix my attention. Such a remark from Thiers is very significant.

In another quarter a person of celebrity, though not equal in reputation to Thiers, and who during the war was strongly on our side, assured me, that our suppression of the rebellion had established republicanism in European opinion; and that the fact of our success having been followed by forbearance towards the rebels individually, but by inexorable severity towards the system which caused the rebellion, had endeared our institutions more than ever to the friends of Europe, & more than ever commanded the respect & admiration of all moderate men.

I have seen enough here to convince me that the dread of democratic institutions has very much worn off in the minds of the prudent statesmen of this country; & that thoughtful men now look to a republic if not altogether with favor yet with less apprehension than heretofore.

L, DLC-JP.

1. Bancroft, urged by Seward to stop at several European cities, was en route to Berlin to take up his duties as minister there. Lilian Handlin, *George Bancroft: The Intellectual as Democrat* (New York, 1984), 292–93.

2. Adolphe Thiers (1797–1877), statesman, journalist, and historian, served the French government in many capacities, including premier and president (1871–73). *The New Columbia Encyclopedia* (4th ed.).

Interview with Cincinnati Commercial *Correspondent*[1]

[Washington, D.C., July 2, 1867][2]

I called on the President last evening, having been previously informed that he would be pleased to have me do so. I had scarcely been seated, when Mr. JOHNSON, alluding to one of my letters from Georgia,[3] said he was very glad I had published the fact that he had advised against the election of ALEXANDER H. STEPHENS to the United States Senate in 1865. He couldn't imagine, he said, where I had got the information, as he didn't think anybody knew the facts of the case except himself and one or two others with whom he had corresponded on the subject by telegraph. I told him my informant was an ex-army officer,[4] who, in the Spring of 1865, was chief of staff to Gen. STEEDMAN, then commanding the District of Georgia; that he had informed me of a dispatch[5] sent by Gen. STEEDMAN to the President, inquiring if it would be advisable to elect STEPHENS, and of the President's prompt reply,[6] that it would be very unwise to think of doing so—that Mr. STEPHENS was a prisoner of war, and ought not to enter political life while such was the case. "I couldn't make out where you got the facts, but you got them right," said the President. "I told them not to think of electing Mr. STEPHENS, or any man who had been engaged in the rebellion as he had, and yet I was denounced all over the country for trying to get rebels into office, and appointing rebels to office. I never did anything of the kind. It was wrong to elect such men then, and it would be wrong to elect them now."

I told Mr. JOHNSON what, in my judgment, were the views of leading Southern men on the subject of reconstruction under the Military Act; that the mode which was being adopted by a certain class of worthless and irresponsible men to secure negro votes would engender strife between the negroes and whites in the South, and lead to endless trouble, if not war and bloodshed; that my own observations led me to believe that the negroes were being taught by these low-lived fellows to look upon the whites as their natural enemies, and that I did not see how, with that idea once prevalent among the negroes, the two races could live together in the South. "They can't do it," said Mr. JOHNSON. "A war of races is inevitable if such a state of affairs goes on. People may laugh at the idea of a war of races, but it will be brought about by such doctrines as these." He then remarked that negro suffrage would have been brought about by State action—that it was inevitable, and would not have been resisted by the Southern States if left to themselves. It might not have come as soon as it has been forced upon them by Congress but, said he, "it would have come quite as soon as it ought to have come, and quite as soon as the negroes were fit for it."

In reply to a question, I told the President that I had seen very few men in the South who were in any true sense of the word rebels, and that these few were men who had not been in the rebel army; that I thought most of what was called "disloyalty" was the effect of the unjust and ungenerous treatment of the South by Congressional legislation since the close of the war. He replied that he did not believe that there were many rebels in the South, and that especially the men who had fought against the Union were not rebels now, and had no desire or intention to rebel again.

He seemed to be very deeply interested in the affairs of Tennessee, and listened attentively to what I told him of my travels through that State. I was surprised to find him so well posted even as to the names of men who are candidates for office there. In regard to the Brownlow militia, he said he had received a hundred petitions from the best people of Tennessee, asking him to send United States troops there to protect them against the outrages now being commited by this "State Guard." I asked him if he could, under the Constitution, send troops into Tennessee without the request of the Governor or Legislature. He replied that that was a difficult question which he had not yet determined. He certainly could send troops there on recruiting service, and station them at Knoxville, Nashville, Chattanooga and such points, and if any disturbance occurred while these troops were there it would be the duty of the commanding officer to use them in suppressing it. He feared very much that BROWNLOW's militia would provoke riot and bloodshed. I told him that was what they were organized for, and the only question was, whe[t]her when they got ready for fight, they should have armed soldiers or unarmed citizens to shoot at. I thought the best way would be to regard the militia as an insurrection, and send soldiers to suppress it and clean it out. He didn't know, he said, what was best to be done; he wanted to see the peace of the State preserved, but didn't know exactly how best to preserve it. He regarded the State Government of Tennessee as the worst despotism he had ever heard of—a military despotism in its worst form—and about the meanest despot he ever heard of at the head of it. Some men make even a despotism a respectable sort of government, said he, but BROWNLOW can't get up a decent despotism. He believed the people of Tennessee would live quietly and obey the laws and Constitution, if let alone, and that they did not need any militia there at all, and that half the trouble in that State was brought about by Northern men going down there to stir up strife and make capital out of it.

The conversation then turned upon Gen. SHERIDAN and the conduct of affairs in Louisiana. The President spoke with great warmth and earnestness when he referred to this subject. At times his voice rose high enough for an audience of five hundred, though I was the only person in the room, and was sitting within two feet of him. "Now," said he, "Gen. SHERIDAN says he had to remove Gov. WELLS because he was an impediment in the way of reconstruction. He doesn't say *how* he was an impediment; he doesn't say in what way he had obstructed him in the official duties, but merely says he is an impediment, and removes him. Well, how much better has he got along since he removed him? Has that helped him any? I can't see that it has. And, again, suppose I should replace WELLS, how would that obstruct the execution of this law? These are questions which no one has attempted to answer."

A little later he said:

"They have talked about my putting impediments in the way of the execution of this law. I have done nothing of the kind, and don't intend to—never thought of doing it. They have spoken of the Attorney-General's opinion as an obstruction. That's all nonsense. It's no such thing. The removal of civil officers doesn't assist the execution of this bill at all. It has nothing to do with it."

I then told him that Mr. WILSON had prepared a bill to offer in the Senate, giving the military commanders the power to remove all civil officers, or rather vacating all civil offices, and authorizing the military commanders to fill them by appointment, reappointment or election.[7]

"Well," said he, "that won't help reconstruction at all. The few officers that are there don't affect the execution of the law one way or the other, and it would be a good deal better to let men serve out their term of office, and, when they run out, order an election to fill them."

I spoke of Gen. SHERIDAN's orders and dispatches as insubordinate, and such as the people of the North ought not to applaud; that the same state of affairs, during the war, might have led to incalculable evil in the army, and that it was just as if Gen. MEADE should have telegraphed to Mr. LINCOLN that if Grant's policy was carried out the Army of the Potomac would soon be surrendered to Gen. LEE. "That's just about it," said the President, "and the people ought to see that encouraging such things is bringing the office of President into disrespect, no matter what they may think of me." He said nothing whatever against SHERIDAN, unless what I have just related be viewed in that light, but I could easily see from his manner that he felt very keenly the attempts of that military chieftain to bring him and his office into contempt. Just here, perhaps, I may as well state that I have very good authority for setting at rest all anxiety on the subject of SHERIDAN's removal. Nothing of the kind will be attempted; and if any of the "Generals-Commanding" in the South want political promotion they must seek it in some other way than by trying to get the President to tread on their coat tails. He won't do it.

Referring to the subject of impeachment, which I had introduced in some remarks as to what Congress would attempt at the present session, the President asked me if the Judiciary Committee had had another meeting, or had made up its report yet. I told him I thought it held its last meeting to-day, (Tuesday,) and that it was understood that its members were divided—four for impeachment, three for censure and two for acquittal. He smiled at the idea of a "censure" from political opponents, and thought that it might be kept as a standing report for all Administrations opposed to Congress. I asked him if he had read GREELEY's testimony, published that day in the *Tribune*.[8] No, he said, he had not, and asked me what it was about. I told him that it related entirely to the bailing of JEFF. DAVIS, and entirely exonerated him from any hand in the matter. "O pshaw," said he, "what had I to do with bailing JEFF. DAVIS?" and he smiled again. I told him I was glad GREELEY had run off with the manuscript of his testimony and furnished it to the public; that it would do good in showing to the country the style of testimony they have been taking. He laughed again and said, "I wish they had published it all as they took it down. Of course I don't know what they have against me, but I know what the facts are, and I'm not afraid of them." I asked him if he knew the character of some of the witnesses they had brought against him, such as BAKER's[9] detectives. He said he did not, and I inferred from the way he said it that he didn't care much who they were. I told him a few incidents in the career of his "great prosecutor," Mr. ASHLEY[10]— various historic and biographic matters connected with the Toledo member. He laughed very heartily and said, "That man seems to be very strangely infatuated about some things; I can't understand him at all"— and then laughed again, and added—"but perhaps he means well enough." Mr. JOHNSON had heard that afternoon that STANLEY MATTHEWS, of Cincinnati, had been summoned before the Judiciary Committee, and asked me if I knew what the object was. I told him I did not; that I had seen Col. MATTHEWS in Washington, but hadn't learned his mission here. I asked him what Col. MATTHEWS could possibly have known about him. He said he didn't know, unless the Judiciary Committee wanted to go back to the time when he (JOHNSON) was Provisional Governor of Tennessee. MATTHEWS was then Provost-Marshal of Nashville. I replied to this that all I knew about it was that ASHLEY asked Mr. BINGHAM,[11] during the last session of the Thirty-ninth Congress, if a President could be impeached for what he had done before he became President, and that BINGHAM very promptly replied by calling ASHLEY a fool. "That was a pretty sharp answer," said the President, with another big laugh.

My own impressions as the result of the interview are these: That the President, whatever may be his opinions of the constitutionality or the propriety of Military Law, never had any other purpose with reference to it than that of enforcing it justly and properly; that if he feels a little vexed when he finds Major-Generals who never read a law-book, running a tilt with such a lawyer as Attorney-General STANBERY, on the interpretation of a statute, he is not much to blame; that he will not and ought not to allow BROWNLOW's militia to create bloodshed in Tennessee; and that he is very little concerned about the impeachment which he evidently regards as a big joke.

MACK.

New York Times, July 10, 1867.

1. Joseph B. McCullagh (1842–1896), a native of Ireland, moved to the U.S. around 1853 and worked for various newspapers in New York, St. Louis, and Cincinnati. In 1861 he entered the Union army as a lieutenant and served as war correspondent for the *Cincinnati Gazette* and later the *Cincinnati Commercial.* In 1863 he left the army to become the *Commercial*'s Washington correspondent and Senate reporter for the New York Associated Press. He became the managing editor of the *Cincinnati Enquirer* in 1868 but soon left for the *Chicago Republican* (1868–71) and later the *St. Louis Democrat.* He edited the latter until his death. *DAB.*

2. Though the report of the interview to the paper is dated July 3, internal evidence makes it clear the interview took place on July 2.

3. Not found.

4. Seth B. Moe (1831–1917) enlisted in April 1861 with the 14th Ohio Vol. Inf. By the time of his discharge in September 1866, he had attained the rank of colonel and assistant adjutant general. Following the war he resided in Toledo, Ohio; briefly in Washington, D.C.; and finally in Chattanooga, Tennessee. Pension Files, Seth B. Moe, RG15, NA; James B. Steedman et al. to Johnson, Aug. 17, 1866, Appt. Files for Judicial Dists., Ohio, Seth B. Moe, RG60, NA.

5. Steedman to Johnson, Nov. 25, 1865, Johnson Papers, LC.

6. Johnson to Steedman, Nov. 26, 1865, *Johnson Papers,* 9: 434.

7. On July 3 Henry Wilson introduced in the Senate what came to be the Third Military Reconstruction bill, of which Section 2 would give military commanders removal and appointive power over civil offices. Passed by Congress on July 19, Johnson vetoed it and Congress overrode his veto that same day. *Congressional Globe,* 40 Cong., 1 Sess., p. 466; Appendix, pp. 43–44.

8. *New York Tribune,* July 2, 1867.

9. Lafayette C. Baker.

10. James M. Ashley.

11. John A. Bingham.

From James W. Scully

Vicksburg Miss   July 2, 1867

An Officer named Folsom[1] made charge against me. I demanded Court Martial am now being tried.[2] In mean time Folsom went to stores bribed clerks for my private bills for family purchases. Has maliciously reported me to Qr. Mr. Genl.,[3] was this morning ordered to turn over my retained papers to officer whom I believe to be personal enemy. Knowing my official affairs will be straight would feel thankful if you set private character right before Quarter Master General and so order it that I have a chance to defend myself on my trial without being badgered to death by interested parties.[4]

J. W. Schully[*sic*]

Tel, DLC-JP.

1. Charles W. Folsom (b. *c*1826), regimental quartermaster and first lieutenant, 20th Mass. Vols., was honorably discharged in April 1865 and transferred to the regular army and promoted to captain. Folsom mustered out of military service in August 1868. Powell, *Army List,* 789; CSR, Charles W. Folsom, RG94, NA.

2. Scully's court-martial trial began at Vicksburg in late June 1867. He was charged with malfeasance in office (regarding the purchase of coffins from Julius J. Casparo, from which purchase Scully reaped a share of the profits in the amount of some $1,850) and with conduct to prejudice of good order and military discipline (regarding Scully's permitting Casparo to establish a sutler's store at the U.S. cemetery and the questionable financial

transactions that flowed therefrom). Gen. Court-Martial Order No. 48, June 28, 1867, RG94, NA.

    3. Montgomery C. Meigs, quartermaster general.

    4. See Scully to Johnson, Aug. 29, 1867.

From William B. Tipton[1]

Dyersburg Tenn   July 2nd 1867

I had a Conversation with the Sherriff of our County[2] Last night. He is a strong Radical. He tells me he expects one hundred & Twenty Malitia soldiers to be at this place on the day of election firs thursday in August intimating they intend to elect their Radical Ticket. There is getting considerable excitment here and daily Threatning is common but few Certificates as yet isued. The Blacks has not got any yet.

W B Tipton Post Master   Dyersburg Tenn

ALS, DLC-JP.

    1. Tipton (1801–1880), in addition to being postmaster in the late 1860s, was also a farmer in Dyer County. Married to Ruth B. Tipton, they had four children. 1860 Census, Tenn., Dyer, 4th Civil Dist., 63; W. Hord Tipton, Sr., *The Tipton Family History* (Mt. Sterling, Ky., 1948), No. 571.

    2. James W. Tarkington was elected sheriff of Dyer County in March 1865 and was still in office three years later. Arahwana H. Ridens, *Dyer County and Newbern, Tennessee* (Easley, S.C., 1979), 25, 26; J. W. Tarkington to [Daniel T.] Boynton, Feb. 6, 1868, William G. Brownlow Papers, Special Collections, TU.

From Eugene H. Angamar[1]

Washington, D.C.   July 3d 1867.

Your petitioner, E. H. Angamar, special Levee Commissioner and agent of the State of Louisiana, duly appointed and commissioned, begs leave, in the name of said State, respectfully to submit the following.

The people of Louisiana appreciating how wrong has been their attempt at Secession, into which they were dragged against their better judgment by ambitious and unscrupulous leaders, are willing, nay anxious, to submit fairly, fully and unequivocally to the terms of the acts of Reconstruction passed by the Congress of the United States.

But, however anxious they are to be reinstated in the Union by the process provided by the acts of Reconstruction, still the Laws of nature and self-protection compel them to attend at once to the necessities of life and to the imperious demands of Hunger!! . . .

And, starving and helpless, the people of Louisiana now come to you, begging that you extend over them the hand of Kindness and Justice, and save them from the sufferings and starvation which will be the result of certain acts of General Sheridan, who, however trust-worthy and well-meaning, has certainly made a serious mistake in his action concerning the Levee Board of Commissioners of Louisiana.[2]

The paramount interests are in the flooding of about 16,000,000-acres of most fertile lands, formerly yelding crops to the value of over one Hundred million Dollars per annum, thus directly supporting more than 700,000 American Citizens, three-fifths of whom are now Freedmen, and which product would net to the United States Treasury an annual tax of about ten million Dollars.

The above figures are certainly large enough to commend themselves to the earnest consideration of the National Government, and to obtain the redress prayed for, especially if proper notice is taken that the questions involved are of a purely civil and financial nature, which can in no wise interfere with the Reconstruction Laws of Congress.

The facts are as follows.

More than one half of the cultivable soil of Louisiana is of alluvial formation and has been reclaimed from the Swamps of the Mississippi River by means of earthen embankments, called Levees, erected at a cost of upwards of Sixty million Dollars.

During the late Civil War those Levees were neglected, and at *times cut away by both Federal* and Confederate Armies.

At the return of peace Louisiana went to work to repair them; but her Treasury, then, as now, in a very poor and low condition, could not endure the drain of such expensive works, and therefore, the Levees being but slightly repaired, but little crops were produced in 1866.[3]

The same unsufficiency of repairs brought like results in 1867.

In order to ensure the raising of a crop in 1868, and thereby save her people from starvation, Louisiana has provided for the very large issue of four millions of Levee Bonds and had been endeavouring to negotiate them, with fair prospects of success, when the action taken by Genl. Sheridan, by his appointment of a Board of Levee Commissioners, in place of the *legal* one by him dismissed, and the removal of Governor Wells from his office as Chief Executive of the State, has defeated such negociations and blasted all prospects of success for the present; and to-day Louisiana finds herself without money or credit, and destitute of all means to repair her Levees, except by the sale of her Bonds.

Now, in order to sell them (Capital is so timid and cautious), they must be placed on the market with and surrounded by all the care and technicalities of the Civil Law under which they have been authorized, so that there be not even a doubt raised as to their validity and legality.

It is in the surroundings of such circumstances that the action of Genl. Sheridan above mentioned, preventing, for the present, the sale of said Bonds, will also prevent the repairs of the Levees for this year (unless timely relief is afforded); the result of which would be, to the general wealth of the Country for 1868, a loss of over One hundred million Dollars, and for the Treasury of the United States, for the same year, a loss of over ten million Dollars, and finally inflict upon a population of over seven hundred thousand souls the horrors and sufferings of starvation.

The business of repairing the Levees in Louisiana had, by the Legislature, been confided to a Board styled "the Board of Levee Commissioners," whose term of office expired in April last by Express provision of Law. (The majority of that Board could not legally hold office under the Reconstruction Acts of Congress.)

In April last, Governor Wells being satisifed that the Board of Levee Commissioners had ceased to exist by the very terms of the Act by which they were created, and seeing that there was no Board to take charge of the Levees and attend to the negociation of the Bonds authorized to be issued by the Legislature, appointed a new Board of Levee Commissioners, taking good care to select none but undoubted loyal men who could hold office under the Reconstruction Acts of Congress, and even went so far as to appoint one colored Citizen a member of the Board.[4]

The Board whose term of office had expired, as above stated, refused to vacate and applied to Genl. Sheridan to support them in their resistance.[5]

As a matter of self-defense, the new Board appointed by Govr. Wells also applied to Genl. Sheridan to assist them to obtain possession of their office.

Thus applied to by both parties, Genl. Sheridan, Soldier-like, cut the difficulty with his sword, by vacating or abolishing both Boards, and thereupon, without warrant of Law, appointed one of his own selection.

Your petitioner respectfully suggests, that

What Genl. Sheridan might and should have done was to refer the contending Boards for adjudication of their claims, to the civil courts, which are now and have at all times for years past been open and ready to hear and determine controversies involving legal questions between the citizens of Louisiana.

Unfortunately for the welfare of Louisiana, Genl. Sheridan thought proper to adopt a different course and he appointed a Board of his own: and, as ill luck would have it his appointees or a *majority of them are prohibited from holding office* by the Constitution of Louisiana or *under the Congressional acts of Reconstruction* of 1867.

Thus it will be seen that by some unaccountable accident or mishap, a *District Commander of well known loyalty, who has been entrusted to execute* and *carry out the laws of Reconstruction passed by Congress, has unwittingly but nevertheless unquestionably violated said Reconstruction Law* in one of its most essential and prominent features, and *has turned out of office a Board composed of Loyal White and Colored Citizens*, and *appointed in their stead, a Board composed* of *a majority* of *aliens* and REBELS!!!

Now, let it be remembered that the money wherewith to repair the Levees has to be raised upon the sale of the Bonds and that it cannot be obtained unless the Board negociating them be, beyond any possible doubt, legally established according to the mandates of the Civil Law of Louisiana and of the Reconstruction Laws of the United States.

These points had been well taken care of in the selection of the Board appointed by Govr. Wells and consisted of Messrs. W. J. Blackburn, Robert Stille and others, all Union men of undoubted antecedents, one of whom is a colored Citizen.[6]

The Board appointed by Genl. Sheridan is composed of Messrs J. Burnside, an unnaturalized foreigner, who abetted and assisted the Rebellion: Effingham Laurence, a *member* of *the Rebel Convention that passed* the *Ordinance* of *Secession,* and *who did sign it*; and three others, one of whom has been court-martialed for being a blockade runner, and aiding and abetting the Enemy. As to the antecedents of the other two members of the Board, we are not sufficiently informed to say anything.[7]

The effect of the action of Genl. Sheridan has been such that the negociation of the said Bonds, which was progressing favorably, has come to a dead stop, and the Capitalists who had promised to advance money, now refuse it to do it.

Under such circumstances, your Petitioner did some time ago apply to the President of the United States for relief, and thereupon, on the first of June last, the following order was issued: "Executive Mansion, June 1st 1867.—Referred to the Secretary of War for early consideration and action. All further proceedings should be suspended until further information (Signed. Andrew Johnson)."[8]

That order was transmitted to Genl. Sheridan on the third of June, P.M. and *on the same day,* he, for reasons unknown to your Petitioner, thought fit to remove Governor Wells from the office of Executive of the State of Louisiana.[9]

Of Governor Wells, all we have to say is, it is conceded even by his bitterest enemies that he is and always has been a strictly unflinching loyal, Union man, opposed to Secession, and *openly in favor of the Reconstruction* Laws of Congress.

As affecting the rebuilding of the Levees of Louisiana, the removal of Governor Wells from office assumes a grave importance, deeply touching the material interests of the people, because the *Legislature* of that state *had ordered that the Levee Bonds shall be signed by the Governor* of the State.

Now, the only Governor who can legally sign them, so as to render them obligatory upon the people, so as to bind and pledge the faith of the State for their redemption, is the chosen agent of the people, the Governor elected by the people, and *not* a military Governor, appointed by a District Commander, in the selection of whom the people to be bound thereby had neither voice nor choice.

Several Capitalists who have been consulted upon this matter have expressed the opinion that the above mentioned Bonds could not be negociated, if signed by B. F. Flanders, as Governor of the State of Louisiana, *even if his appointment* as Governor by General Sheridan *were to receive* the *sanction* of a *solemn act of Congress*: and futhermore, that said Bonds could not be negociated if they were signed by Genl. Sheridan himself, in his official capacity, by and with the authority of an Act of Congress, unless their payment be guaranteed by the Government of the United States.

Now then, if those Bonds cannot be made available unless signed by Governor Wells, it follows that General Sheridan, by removing Governor Wells, has, in fact, destroyed said Bonds, as far as their availability is concerned, and it is a very remarkable fact that while General Sheridan is thus, for the time being, preventing and rendering impossible the repairs of the Levees of Louisiana, the Congress of the United States is, on the contrary, manifesting a disposition to assist that suffering people in the erection of those very same works, as fully appears from the Bill and Report which were presented in the United States Senate, on the 27th of March last, by Hon. Senator J. B. Henderson, on behalf of the Committee of Finance of that Body.[10]

From the foregoing we are forcibly brought to the conclusion that Governor Wells and his Board of Levee Commissioners should be reinstated, *at least for a short time*, so that the said Levee Bonds may be legally signed, issued and negociated, in order that the repairs of the Levees may be speedily commenced and speedily completed, thereby saving those people from the danger of starvation, and giving a new impetus to the growth of the great Southern staples, Cotton and Sugar,—a matter of very deep concern, not only to the people of Louisiana, but also to the people of the United States at large: for, the crops to be raised on the lands now inundated and unproductive will give rise to a great interchange of produce and manufactures of all kinds with the North, the East and the West, and therefore advance the prosperity, trade and Commerce of the entire Commonwealth of the United States.

To this end your Petitioner respectfully prays for the interposition of your authority.

E. H. Angamar.
Special Levee Commissioner of Louisiana.

ALS, DLC-JP.
1. Angamar (*c*1821–*fl*1879), a native of France, was a civil engineer. 1870 Census, La., Orleans, New Orleans, 1st Ward, 157; New Orleans directories (1872–81).
2. Angamar discusses this in great detail later in the letter.
3. Gov. J. Madison Wells addressed this issue in a letter to Johnson on May 26, 1866, *Johnson Papers*, 10: 540–41.
4. Wells's order of April 23 dissolving the old levee board and appointing a new one can be found in the *New Orleans Picayune*, April 26, 1867 (morning).
5. The old board had some justification for refusing to give up their posts since an act passed by the state legislature on March 15, 1867, provided that all officers elected by the people or the legislature under the 1864 constitution should retain their offices after their terms had expired until their successors were properly elected and qualified. Ibid.
6. William Jasper Blackburn (1820–1899) moved to Louisiana in 1848 and edited several vehemently Unionist newspapers before the Civil War. He was a member of the state constitutional convention (1867), the U.S. House (1868–69), and the state senate

(1872–76). He was also a parish judge before he moved to Arkansas and returned to journalism in 1880. Stille (b. c1805) was a merchant in Sabine Parish before the war. The other members of the board were A. W. Walker, J. J. Guiterrez, J. V. Duralde (a member of the old board), Elbert Gantt, and W. M. Wilson. It was not possible to determine which was the "colored citizen." Conrad, *La. Biography*; 1860 Census, La., Sabine, Many, 301; *New Orleans Picayune*, Apr. 26, 1867 (morning).

7. John Burnside (1800–1881), a merchant and sugar planter, came to the U.S. from his native Ireland in the 1820s and moved to New Orleans by 1837. Henry Effingham Lawrence (1810–1875) was a coffee merchant, railroad promoter, and planter. The other members of the committee were Joseph H. Oglesby, W. D. Smith, and W. L. McMillen. The blockade runner has not been determined. Conrad, *La. Biography*; *New Orleans Picayune*, May 4, 1867 (morning); New Orleans directories (1861–89).

8. Johnson thus endorsed Angamar's undated letter of late May. Lets. Recd. (Main Ser.), File M-692–1867 (M619, Roll 563), RG94, NA.

9. See, for example, J. Madison Wells to Johnson, June 4, 1867.

10. John B. Henderson of Missouri.

From Francis P. Blair, Sr.

Silver Spring [Md.]   3 July '67

My dear Mr. President.

Gen Capron[1] whom you nominated for Commissioner of Agriculture, tells me that he is charged with *Radicalism* by those who would have him forfeit your confidence & supplant him. He has given evidence that his ultraism consists as yours did in a willingness to sacrifice himself & all his family to the cause of the Union. His three sons[2]—one killed & rest crippled & made incapable, gives earnest of his patriotism. Trust me, if you support him in the position you have placed him in, neither you nor the country will ever have reason to regret it.[3]

F. P. Blair.

Private note for the President.

F. P. Blair

Copy, DLC-Papers of Horace Capron.

1. Horace Capron.

2. Horace, Jr. (c1840–1864), who farmed with his father before the war, served as lieutenant with the 14th Ill. Cav. and died of wounds received at Deep Creek, North Carolina. Albert (1841–1901), also a farmer before the war, served in the same unit as his brother and was a brevetted major. He resided at Chicago after the war and was a commission merchant. Osmond T. (c1846–*fl*1870) worked for a short time in the Agricultural Department. 1860 Census, Ill., Peoria, Jubilee Twp., 841; Merritt Starr, "General Horace Capron, 1804–1885," *Journal of the Illinois State Historical Society*, 18 (1925): 274, 290; *Off. Army Reg.: Vols.*, 6: 202; Washington, D.C., directories (1869–70); *Chicago Inter Ocean*, May 10, 1901.

3. Johnson nominated Capron on April 9, 1867, but on April 16 the Senate voted to postpone its decision until December. However, Johnson renominated Capron on July 19, 1867, and the Senate finally confirmed him on November 29. *Senate Ex. Proceedings*, Vol. 15, pt. 2: 663, 739, 851, 860.

From the Senate

In the Senate of the United States
July 3d 1867

Resolved, That the President be respectfully requested to communicate to the Senate copies of all orders, instructions circular letters or letters of advice issued to the respective military officers assigned to the command of the several military districts, under the act passed March 2d 1867, entitled "An Act to provide for the more efficient government of the rebel states" and the act supplementary thereto passed March 23d 1867; also copies of all opinions given to him by the Attorney General of the United States touching the construction and interpretation of said acts, and of all correspondence relating to the operation, construction or execution of said acts, that may have taken place between himself and any of said commanders, or between him and the General of the Army, or between the latter and any of the said commanders touching the same subjects; also copies of all orders issued by any of said commanders in carrying out the provisions of said acts or either of them; also that he inform the Senate what progress has been made in the matter of registration under said acts and whether the sum of money heretofore appropriated for carrying them out is probably sufficient.[1]

Attest   J W. Forney   Secretary
by W. J. McDonald.[2]   Chief Clerk.

D, DNA-RG60, Office of Atty. Gen., Lets. Recd., President.
   1. Johnson replied on July 15 with reports from the secretary of war and attorney general. Johnson to the Senate, July 15, 1867.
   2. William J. McDonald (c1815–fl1881), a native of the District of Columbia, was the Senate's chief clerk until the late 1870s. 1870 Census, D.C., Washington, 5th Ward, 39; NUC; Washington, D.C., directories (1869–77).

From Israel C. Woodruff[1]

Washington   July 3, 1867

Sir:

I have the honor to solicit your attention to the following facts.

In February last my Son Thomas M. Woodruff[2] was appointed a Cadet in service of the United States on the nomination of the Delegate from the Territory of Nebraska.[3]

He has reported for duty at the military academy, passed both mental and physical examinations, taken the prescribed oath of allegiance and is now fairly started in his duties as Cadet.

The new Representative from the State of Nebraska[4] objects to this appointment on the grounds of non-residence[5] and notwithstanding the fact that an army officer can neither gain nor lose a residence, the appointment has been cancelled and orders are now on their way to West Point dismissing in effect Cadet Woodruff from the Academy.

In view of these facts and of the blighting effect of such a dismissal where other prospects looked so bright and promising, I would respectfully request that my son be allowed to remain at West Point in place of one of his classmates appointed at large, who failed at the preliminary examination, and I trust that the granting of this request will not prove detrimental to the public interest.[6]

I. C. Woodruff   Lieut. Col. of Engineers,
Bvt. Brig. Gen. U.S.A.

ALS, DNA-RG94, USMA, Correspondence *re* Military Academy, File H-2-1867.
1. Woodruff (1815–1878) graduated from West Point in 1836 and made his career in the army, serving with the topographical engineers and eventually reaching the rank of colonel. He was breveted brigadier general in 1865. Hunt and Brown, *Brigadier Generals*.
2. The younger Woodruff (c1848–1899) also made his career in the army, serving as lieutenant and finally captain in the 5th Inf. During the Spanish-American War he was a major and inspector general of volunteers and was stationed in Santiago, Cuba, where he died of yellow fever. *West Point Register*, 267; Powell, *Army List*, 688; *New York Tribune*, July 13, 1899.
3. Phineas W. Hitchcock.
4. John Taffe (1827–1884), lawyer and Indiana native, moved to Nebraska in 1856. A member of the territorial house of representatives and council, he served as major with the 2nd Nebr. Vol. Cav. during the Civil War. A Republican, he served three terms in Congress (1867–73). *BDUSC*.
5. According to young Woodruff, he had resided in Washington, D.C., for about ten years. T. G. Pitcher to L. H. Pelouze, June 25, 1867, USMA, Correspondence *re* Military Academy, File H-2-1867, RG94, NA.
6. Johnson endorsed the senior Woodruff's letter on July 3, "The special and early attention of the Secretary of War is called to this communication." Thomas Woodruff was appointed either at large or from Washington, D.C., on August 31, 1867. Thomas M. Woodruff to Secretary of War, Aug. 31, 1867, ibid.; Powell, *Army List*, 688; *New York Tribune*, July 13, 1899.

From J.A.H. Cleveland[1]

Galveston, Texas, July 4th 1867.

Sir:

As a citizen of the U. States, and believing myself unjustly deprived of a right I hold most dear of all others, I make my last appeal to you. The enclosed communication was made to Genl. Griffin,[2] and the officer to whom he referred me, refused to make any endorsement or give any reasons for refusing me the right to register, upon the paper, stating however, that the holding the appointment as Dep. marshal, admitting I took no oath, was sufficient to disfranchise me.

I was Depy Marshal[3] for Ben McCulloch, managed and conducted the business, as he was absent from his District nearly all the time—took only the oath, of which the enclosed is a copy, and the Records in the several Departments at Washington show the fact, that it is the only instance in which the marshal's accounts have ever been settled at the Treasy Department from this District—all the rest were defaulters, and sued in the courts. But for the fact of my having been such officer—never having held any other—I am refused and denied the right to prepare to assist in raising, and trying to get our Government to rights once more.

J A H Cleveland

ALS, DNA-RG94, Lets. Recd. (Main Ser.), File C-1124-1867 (M619, Roll 546).

1. Cleveland (c1803–1876), a Texas resident since about 1830, was a Galveston insurance agent in his later years. *Galveston News*, Feb. 27, Mar. 5, 1876; Galveston directories (1867–77); Cleveland to Charles Griffin, July 3, 1867, Lets. Recd. (Main Ser.), File C-1124-1867 (M619, Roll 546), RG94, NA.

2. Ibid.

3. Cleveland became deputy marshal for the eastern district of Texas in 1853. Ibid.

From Gazaway B. Lamar, Sr.

Washington City, July 4th 1867

The Memorial of G. B. Lamar Senr, respectfully showeth; That himself and his Nephew, G. B. Lamar Jr. were arrested in December 1865 & tried by a Military Commission, in the City of Savannah in January 1866—that they were citizens of the State of Georgia, and had never been in the Military or Naval service of the United States, and therefore, by a decision of the Supreme Court were not subject to be tried by any Military Tribunal. And moreover, that the Charges & specifications, were all of them unfounded & untrue, made up from papers, taken from them after their arrests & imprisonment—all of which was done by & at the instance of a Treasury Agent called A. G. Browne Jr,[1] in order that he might with the greater facility rob your Memorialist, of about 548 Bales Cotton, which he did accordingly in December 1865, during the imprisonment of himself & his nephew—though your Memorialist, had previously, on the 2d October 1865, proven his loyalty, & his property to the Cotton before Maj Genl. Steedman, then the Military Commander of the State of Georgia—and had his order to receive & ship it which order, & all his other papers were taken from his Nephew, at the time of his arrest.

Your Memorialist is in his old age, & has through life, mantained, an unspotted reputation which is dear to him. His Nephew is a young man, just entering on business, & having no fortune, is in a great measure dependant upon his fair character, for success in life—and your memorialist confidently relies on Andrew Johnson President to interpose his just authority, and to remove at once, and forever, all & every stigma & stain attempted upon either—by the actings & doings of the said A. G. Brown Jr, who is a robber of property & a defamer of character, & by the findings, whatever they were of the said illegal & unauthorized Courts—

acting under Military orders—by declaring the same & every part of the findings of both said Courts, to be utterly & entirely null & void, as they ought to be.

And your Memorialist further prays, that the President will order the proceeds of the 548 Bales Cotton, taken by the said A. G. Browne Jr. as aforesaid, & ever since held apart by the Secretary of the Treasury for investigation, to be promptly restored to him, that he may perform the first duty of every honest man, by paying the same to his just creditors.

Your memorialist relies the more confidently on President Johnson, to cause reparation to be made to him, for these outrages—because they have been perpetrated upon him, under and during his own Administration, and contrary to law—& the good faith guaranteed to him by Act of Congress—& under the proclamation of his lamented Predecessor—all of which he is prepared to prove to the full satisfaction of any impartial Referee, to be chosen by the President.[2]

G. B. Lamar Senr.

ALS, DNA-RG153, Court-Martial Records, MM 3469.

1. Albert G. Browne (1835–1891), lawyer, journalist, and author, during the war had been military secretary to John A. Andrew, the governor of Massachusetts. Resuming his law practice in Boston in 1867, he eventually moved to New York City where he edited several newspapers. *NCAB*, 19: 316.

2. Lamar had previously written Johnson on August 6, 1866, concerning this situation which was resolved somewhat successfully by Lamar and his descendants. See Gazaway B. Lamar, Sr., to Johnson, *Johnson Papers*, 11: 32–33.

From James Johnson

United States Internal Rev.   Assessors office
1st Dist Texas   Galveston   July 5th 1867

Dr. Sir:

I have been shown an agreement in writing entered into between Marshall W. Brewster[1] & Genl Milton Stapp[2] Collector of Int Rev. of this Dist., in which the said Stapp agrees to resign the collectorship in behalf of said Brewster & to secure the appointment & confirmation of said Brewster; and in consideration of which the said M. W. Brewster agrees to give said Stapp a nominal situation in the office at the rate of $2000.00 per annum for two years, and also to give to the son of said Stapp[3] the position of Dept'y Collector at Galveston or Houston at a like salary of $2000.00 pr annum for two years![4] Genl. Stapp has always been to me courteous, and our intercourse has been of the most agreeable nature, and I believe him to be honest upright & of full capacity for the position he holds, but I do not think the same of Mr Brewster, whom he proposes to take his place. The fact of Mr Brewster entering into a contract to pay the Genl & his son the salarys as stated, is prove to me that he does not expect to conduct the office in strict conformity to Law & with honesty to the Government.

I have no complaint to make against Genl Milton Stapp, and expressed myself to him before he left here, wishing that he might retain the office & signed a letter in his behalf to the Department, but if he should resign I wish to call your attention to the claims of Genl James J. Byrne[5] the present United States Marshall at this place. He is in my judgement of more capacity and more of a Gentleman of honor & integrity than M. W. Brewster & I know both very well. Besides Mr Brewster is a southern *Radical* & Genl Byrne & Ex officer of U.S. Army & an staunch friend of yours—and advocate of your course as President.

Should a vacancy occur in the Collectorship of Int. Revenue for this Dist, I hope you will give Genl Byrne's claims your consideration.[6]

J Johnson   Assessor

ALS, DNA-RG56, Appts., Internal Revenue Service, Collector, Tex., 1st Dist., Milton Stapp.
    1. Brewster (c1832–fl1870) had been deputy collector of internal revenue for almost two years. By 1870 he was county judge in Houston. 1870 Census, Tex., Harris, Houston, 4th Ward, 12; Stapp to Hugh McCulloch, July 18, 1867, Appts., Internal Revenue Service, Collector, Tex., 1st Dist., Milton Stapp, NA.
    2. Stapp (c1812–fl1868), a lawyer, had opposed secession so vigorously that he had to leave Texas in 1862 and flee to Indiana. He was nominated for the post of collector of internal revenue for the First District of Texas on July 19, 1866, and confirmed and commissioned on July 27. 1860 Census, Tex., Goliad, Goliad P.O., 114; Stapp to Johnson, June 27, 1865, Appts., Customs Service, Collector, Galveston, Milton Stapp, RG56, NA; T. H. McMahan to Andrew Johnson, Feb. 28, 1868, Appts., Internal Revenue Service, Collector, Tex., 1st Dist., Milton Stapp, RG56, NA; Ser. 6B, Vol. 4: 211, Johnson Papers, LC.
    3. According to the 1860 census Stapp had at least four sons. Robert B. Stapp (c1837–fl1876) was a deputy collector in 1868 and still in that post in 1870. Peyton G. Stapp (c1846–fl1881) was a revenue clerk. Howard Stapp (fl1880), who may also have been a son, was a deputy collector in 1868 but a clerk in 1870. 1860 Census, Tex., Goliad, Goliad P.O., 114; Galveston directories (1868–81).
    4. Several weeks later Stapp did write to the secretary of the treasury proposing to trade places with Brewster (to make Brewster collector and Stapp his deputy) because it seemed that Stapp found the "great responsibility of the collection office" annoying. However, if the arrangement did not suit Johnson and McCulloch, Stapp preferred to retain the office. Nothing about financial arrangements or the employment of Stapp's son was mentioned in this letter. Stapp to McCulloch, July 18, 1867, Appts., Internal Revenue Service, Collector, Tex., 1st Dist., Milton Stapp, RG56, NA.
    5. Byrne (1841–1880), who served in several New York regiments, rising to the rank of colonel, was brevetted brigadier and major general for gallant conduct in several battles in Louisiana. He was nominated to be U.S. marshal for the eastern district of Texas on February 6, 1867. His nomination was confirmed and his commission was issued on February 23. Eventually he became a land speculator. Hunt and Brown, *Brigadier Generals*; Ser. 6B, Vol. 4: 211, Johnson Papers, LC.
    6. Johnson endorsed the document, "The special attention of the sec of the Treasury is called to this letter." While some attempt was made to have Stapp removed in February 1868, he seems to have remained as collector until after Johnson left the presidency. T. H. McMahan to Johnson, Feb. 28, 1868, Appts., Internal Revenue Service, Collector, Tex., 1st Dist., Milton Stapp, RG56, NA; Ser. 6B, Vol. 4: 211, Johnson Papers, LC.

From R. King Cutler

"Private"

Washington D.C.   July 6th, 1867.

Respected Sir.

Enclosed you will find a New Orleans Journal,[1] containing a correspondence from this city in regard to myself. About the middle of last month, I addressed a letter to the Honorable Secretary of the Treasury,[2] in which I stated the principal facts set forth in this correspondence. That letter was marked "Confidential," and not intended for publication. Notwithstanding the discourtesy of the Secretary, I am neither afraid nor ashamed of its contents, in fact, am rather pleased at its being heralded to the people of this nation.

The sentiments contained in that letter are mine. I believe that Conservative Republicanism (now sometimes called Democracy) will ere long be the ruling power of this Nation.

Extreme measures are of but momentary existence. I feel convinced that my political position is not misunderstood, and as a man of nerve, and determination, I will soon demonstrate the fact, but your sanction is necessary in order to decided political success in my State.

I am sorry to be compelled to say that the Secretary of the Treasury manifests a disposition to adhere to W. P. Kellogg, although the evidence is overwhelming and conclusive that said Collector Kellogg is a traitor and a scoundrel, and has robbed the Treasury of this Government.

I hope that you will pardon me for asking your early and decisive action in the premises; and in common with many others of your friends, most respectfully request you to immediately suspend the said W. P. Kellogg, from the Office of Collector of Customs at the Port of New Orleans.[3]

R. King Cutler
27 Indiana Avenue   Washington

ALS, DLC-JP.
1. Not found.
2. Not found.
3. Johnson did not remove Kellogg. For Cutler's next request for him to do so, see Cutler to Johnson, July 15, 1867.

To the Senate and House of Representatives

Washington   July 6th 1867

I transmit to Congress a copy of a treaty between The United States and His Majesty The Emperor of all the Russias the ratifications of which were exchanged in this City on the 20th ultimo.[1]

This instrument provides for a cession of territory to the United States, in consideration of the payment of seven million, two hundred thousand dollars in gold.

The attention of Congress is invited to the subject of an appropriation for this payment, and also to that of proper legislation for the occupation and government of the Territory as a part of the dominion of the United States.[2]

Andrew Johnson

LBcopy, DNA-RG59, Misc. Corres., Reports to President and Congress.
1. The treaty between the U.S. and Czar Alexander II can be found in *U.S. Statutes at Large*, 15: 539–44.
2. The Fortieth and Forty-first congresses passed only two acts concerning Alaska— one on customs and the other granting a concession on the seal fisheries. The funds were not appropriated until July 27, 1868. No civil government was established by Congress until 1884. Ibid., 15: 198, 240–42; 17: 530; Ernest Gruening, *The State of Alaska* (New York, 1968 [1954]), 33–35, 43.

From Thomas M. Cook

At Willard's Hotel   Monday Morning [July 8, 1867][1]

Mr. President—

Another dispatch received last evening,[2] after I left you, from Gen. Sickles advises me that he has sent me a copy of his revised communication to Senator Trumbull[3] and authorizes its use for publication at the discretion of Senator Trumbull. I shall probably receive this copy tomorrow.

In the mean time permit me to renew my suggestion that Sickles be ordered here for consultation, and to aid in impressing the ideas of universal amnesty he espouses upon Congress.

In case it is determined to call him here, may I ask to be advised of the fact, confidentially if so desired.

T. M. Cook

ALS, DLC-JP.
1. This date has been assigned by the Library of Congress as Monday would have been July 8. However, based on the communications mentioned, which are dated July 6, reference to receipt "last evening," and other supporting documents, a date of July 7 might be more accurate.
2. D. E. Sickles to T. M. Cook, July 6, 1867, Johnson Papers, LC.
3. The first letter to Lyman Trumbull on the various plans for Reconstruction was written on July 1, with a copy being sent to Cook on July 2; the revised communication to Trumbull, dated July 5, appeared in the *New York Times* of July 10. Sickles to Trumbull, July 1, 1867, Johnson Papers, LC.

From Hugh McCulloch

Treasury Department   July 8. 1867.

Sir:

Since my interview with you yesterday, I have received a petition in favor of the appointment of *Theodore Denike* [1] as Collector of Customs at Wilmington N.C. and after a conversation with *Mr Cook*, [2] Internal Revenue Agent for N.C. I am of the opinion the appointment would be the better one. He is highly recommended by prominent business men of Wilmington, Members of the Chamber of Commerce, and strongly endorsed by *Hon John T. Hoffman*, Mayor of N.Y. [3] as an intelligent active energetic and reliable business man. I therefore transmit his nomination for your consideration in place of that of *Denard Rumby* [4] transmitted on the 6th inst.

H. McCulloch   Secty of the Treasury

LBcopy, DNA-RG56, Lets. Sent *re* Customs Service Employees (QC Series), Vol. 7.

1. Denike (b. *c*1825), formerly of New York, was a wholesale commission merchant in Wilmington. 1870 Census, N.C., New Hanover, Wilmington, 218.

2. Thomas M. Cook.

3. For an example of Hoffman's support of Denike, see Hoffman to Johnson, July 1, 1867, Appts., Customs Service, Collector, Wilmington, Theodore Denike, RG56, NA.

4. Rumby (b. *c*1844) was nominated by the President on July 19 and confirmed by the Senate the following day. He held the post of collector from 1867 into the Grant administration. *U.S. Off. Reg.* (1867–71); 1870 Census, N.C., New Hanover, Wilmington, 196; Ser. 6B, Vol. 4: 141, Johnson Papers, LC; *Richmond Dispatch*, July 22, 1867.

From Joshua W. Sharp [1]

Lexington Va.   July 8th 1867

Sir

I have the honor to request an appointment in the Regular Army. [2] My friend Governor Letcher [3] will explain to you the circumstances under which I find myself placed. For my adherence to the great Constitutional Principles on which our government was founded, by which alone it can be preserved, and for which you are now so staunchly contending, I expect to be ignominiously mustered out of the army "Services no longer needed."

You, and you alone, have power to retain me by giving me a place in the regular army. I believe that both Generals Schofield and Brown [4] are well disposed towards me, but my personal and political enemies either have already gone or intend to go higher than these officers. They propose to have me removed through the Radical members of Congress and Genl Howard Commissioner Freedmans Bureau. My more immediate antagonists Col Carse and Mr Johnston are on the most intimate terms with Judge Underwood Hunneycutt [5] "Et omne hoc genus."

You may think I have shown duplicity in my relations with these men. I answer that they have certain good and estimable qualities—especially Carse—which I liked, and, besides, it was necessary for me to find out their intentions. Of late I have ceased to have any intercourse with them.

Their plan is to exasperate the Freedmen against me as a "Copperhead," and to arouse the hatred and jealousy of the Radicals on the same ground.

By an admirable piece of diplomacy I have learned that Johnston proposes representing me to Genl Howard as an intemperate man because I have sometimes, according to the custom of Virginia, treated my friends in my own private room to a glass of wine. The Governor can tell you what my morals are in this respect.

In August 1862 I left my venerable and most unwilling mother, my property, and my books and other pleasures behind me and entered the army. Excuse my boldness when I say I did good service at Fredericksburg and Chancellorsville. The original papers in my case deposited in the War Department on my entering the old Veteran Reserve Corps in April 1864—if now there—will show this. In those papers are recommendations from, the then, Lieut. General Grant—Maj Genl French my Division Commander—Brig Genl Wm. Hays Comdg my brigade (2nd—3rd Division 2nd Army Corps) Col Levi Maish[6] and other officers of my regiment—the 130th Penna. of 1862 & 1863—and several distinguished civilians.

When Lee invaded Pennsylvania in 1863 I rose from a sick bed—the result of overexertion and exposure at Chancellorsville—and raised a company[7] with which—sick as I was—I marched to Harrisburg to resist the invader, when most of the male citizens of the border counties of the State were flying away in terror with their horses and other stock. Mr Stevens letter[8] certifies to what I then did.

In the winter of /65 and /66 I thought of applying for a position in the regular army—and then placed in the hands of Genl Grant's brother-in-law Genl Dent[9] certain papers in company with my application. Among these were testimonials from Col Ingraham Provost Marshal Defenses North of the Potomac—Col Woodward of the 22nd Regt. V.R. Corps under whom I had served—Maj Johnson 14th Regt. V.R.C. ditto—Hon Edgar Cowan—Hon Thaddeus Stevens—Hon Joseph Casey[10]—Court of Claims &c &c. Genl Dent promised to place these with my original papers in the War Department, and perhaps the whole together were placed in the hand of Genls Rawlings and Comstock[11] of Grants staff last Autumn. I have not heard from them since I forwarded them to Genl Dent.

I had since concluded not to remain in the army until I saw that the posture of affairs in Lexington required my doing so for some time to come until the public relations of the country become more settled.

I but once had the honor of meeting you. It was in your apartment in the Treasury Building soon after the assassination of Mr Lincoln. I was the officer who took Ex. Gov. Joseph Brown of Georgia to see you there. The same afternoon I took him to your lodging place which was, I believe, the residence of the Hon Mr Hooper.[12] There you introduced the Governor to Senator Sherman, and had some conversation with me as to his accommodations at the Old Capitol. You will perhaps recollect the incident. I was then on Genl Augurs[13] Staff—in the office of Col Ingraham Provost Marshal Defenses North of the Potomac.

J. W. Sharp   Capt. Veteran Reserve Corps
Ass't. Sub. Asst. Com Freedmans Bureau &
Military Commissioner   Rockbridge—Bath—& Alleghany Cos. Va.

ALS, DNA-RG94, ACP Branch, File S-77-CB-1868, J. W. Sharp.

1. Sharp (fl1868), in August 1862, enlisted with the 130th Pa. Inf. and then served with the 14th, 9th, and 22nd Rgt., VRC. After the war he was assigned to the Freedmen's Bureau in Lexington, Virginia (December 1866-January 1868), to succeed George B. Carse. *Off. Army Reg.: Vols.*, 8: 43, 53, 66; Everly and Pacheli, *Records of Field Offices*, pt. 3: 502; *History of Cumberland and Adams Counties, Pennsylvania* (Chicago, 1886), pt. 2: 116.

2. Despite Johnson's endorsement, Sharp was informed in December 1867 that there were no vacancies in the VRC regiments. Endorsements, ACP Branch, File S-77-CB-1868, J. W. Sharp.

3. John Letcher.

4. John M. Schofield and Orlando Brown.

5. George B. Carse, James Johnston, John C. Underwood, and James W. Hunnicutt. Carse (d. 1883), a prominent New Jersey Republican, served with the 40th N.Y. Vols. and later the VRC before being mustered out in June 1867. He then served as a captain in the regular army and Freedmen's Bureau in Virginia and Florida before retiring in December 1870. Johnston (fl1868) served with the 14th Rgt., VRC, from 1863 to 1868, when he was discharged with the regular army rank of major and brevet lieutenant colonel. Powell, *Army List*, 235; *New York Times*, Nov. 30, 1883; George R. Bentley, *A History of the Freedmen's Bureau* (Philadelphia, 1955), 191; Everly and Pacheli, *Records of Field Offices*, pt. 3: 502; *Off. Army Reg.: Vols.*, 8: 53, 322.

6. William H. French (1815–1881) graduated from West Point in 1837 and served in the Creek-Seminole wars, Mexican War, and Civil War. He attained the rank of major general of volunteers and command of the Third Corps. He mustered out of volunteer service in May 1864; upon his death he held the rank of colonel. Hayes (1819–1875), an 1840 West Point graduate, served in the Mexican War and with the Second Corps as a brigadier general of volunteers. Between November 1863 and February 1865 he was provost marshal of New York's southern district; the last few months of the war saw him back with the Second Corps. His regular army rank following the war was major. Maish (1837–1899) served with the 130th Pa. Inf. and mustered out in 1863 as a colonel. He then became an attorney in 1864, served in the Pennsylvania state house (1867–68), and U.S. House (1875–79, 1887–91). Warner, *Blue*; *BDUSC*.

7. Not known.

8. Not found.

9. Frederick T. Dent (1820–1892), an 1843 graduate of West Point, served in the Mexican War and was a captain at the outbreak of the Civil War. During the war he served on military commissions, as Grant's aide-de-camp, and as military governor of Richmond, attaining the rank of brevet brigadier general. Following the war he served as military secretary to President Grant, retiring from active service in December 1883 as a colonel. Warner, *Blue*.

10. Timothy Ingraham and George A. Woodward. Woodward (1835–1916), a native of Pennsylvania, practiced law until 1861, when he organized a company of Pennsylvania reserves. After the war he joined the volunteers and in July 1866 was made a lieutenant

colonel in the regular army. He retired in 1879 as a colonel, but by act of Congress in April 1904 he became a brigadier general. Casey (1814–1879) was admitted to the Pennsylvania bar in 1838. During his career he served in the U.S. House (1848–51), as a court reporter, judge of the U.S. Court of Claims (1861–70; chief justice, 1863–70), and professor at the National University in Washington (1870–79). *NCAB*, 10: 518; *Who Was Who in America* (5 vols., Chicago, 1943–73), 1: 1379; *DAB*.

11. John A. Rawlings and Cyrus B. Comstock.
12. Samuel Hooper.
13. Christopher C. Auger.

From Augustus H. Garland

Little Rock, Arks.   July 9/67

Mr. President:

I beg leave, very respectfully to call your attention to the within slip of paper containing matters relative to our state legislature.[1]

It did occur to me, that after the att'y Genl. gave his opinion,[2] there would be no difficulty at all in the legislature's meeting. But such, it seems, is not true.

This is a matter I deem of such importance, as to be laid before you; and on behalf of our state I do hope you will take such steps as may be necessary to place this affair in its true & proper shape.[3]

A. H. Garland

ALS, DLC-JP.
1. The enclosure was probably a communication from the state legislature with copies of a letter from five members to Brevet Brigadier General C. H. Smith, Smith's reply to that letter, and the further protest of the five legislators, all dated July 8, 1867. The legislature, which convened in November 1866, had mostly Confederate antecedents and proceeded to pass a number of "rebel" bills, including one rejecting the Fourteenth Amendment. In addition, the legislature planned to impeach two unionist circuit judges. It adjourned on March 23, 1867, with plans to reassemble July 8. Gen. E.O.C. Ord, commander of the Fourth Military District, provoked by the threat of this trial, issued an order on April 15 directing Gov. Isaac Murphy to inform the legislature that they would not be permitted to assemble in July, because to do so would be inconsistent with the Reconstruction Act. The legislators had written to Smith, commander of the sub-district of Arkansas, asking if Ord's prohibitory order would be enforced. Smith assured them that it would, so the legislature did not assemble. Correspondence from Arkansas Legislators, July 8, Johnson Papers, LC; *American Annual Cyclopaedia* (1867), 49, 51; Paige E. Mulhollan, "Arkansas General Assembly of 1866 and Its Effect on Reconstruction," *ArHQ*, 20 (1961): 331, 333–34, 338–42.
2. Henry Stanbery to Johnson, June 12, 1867.
3. Johnson apparently took no action. The only notation on the document reads, "File under Arkansas."

From Edwin M. Stanton

Washington City, July 9 1867[1]

Mr. President

I have the honor to inform you that Gee[2] who is under sentence of death in South Carolina (and concerning whom I spoke to you yesterday requesting a suspension of execution until further order or long enough to procure evidence to show his innocence) was tried and convicted by a State Court in South Carolina.

I would respectfully reccommend that Governor Orr be requested to suspend execution and that General Sickles be notified thereof and directed to interfere and postpone the execution in case Governor Orr declines to do so.[3]

Edwin M Stanton

ALS, DNA-RG94, Lets. Recd. (Main Ser.), File 569-W-1867 (M619, Roll 591).

1. While the date of the letter appears to be July 4, internal evidence, related documents, and comparison with other samples of Stanton's handwriting suggest the 9th as the accurate date.

2. Jeff Gee, a freedman, had been sentenced to death for shooting Darius Ganby, a Marion District overseer, in 1865. It was believed by some that the murder was actually done by two escaping Union soldiers whom Gee was guiding. Robert K. Scott to Oliver O. Howard, July 9, 1867, Johnson Papers, LC; Charleston Mercury, July 11, 1867; Charleston Courier, July 13, 1867.

3. A flurry of telegrams between Washington and the Second Military District resulted in Governor Orr's suspension of Gee's execution until the second Friday in August. Orr acted on July 8, but the Federal authorities did not learn of the suspension until the 11th. In the meanwhile Stanton, under Johnson's authority, was prepared to have the military authorities suspend Gee's sentence for thirty days in case Orr could not be located. Our research has not ascertained Gee's ultimate fate. Stanton to R. K. Scott, July 10, 1867, Stanton to D. E. Sickles, July 10, 1867; Stanton to Orr, July 10, 1867; D. E. Sickles to E. D. Townsend, July 11, 1867, Johnson Papers, LC.

From Joseph W. McCorkle

New York City   July 11th 1867

Sir.—

Hon. John Nugent[1] will be recommended to you, as a proper, suitable, and in all repects well qualified gentleman to represent the United States at the Republic of Mexico. I have known Mr Nugent, on the Pacific Coast, for the last eighteen years, and take great pleasure in urging him upon your consideration. His accurate knowledge of the Spanish language, and his intermarriage with one of the oldest and most influential families of Mexico, render him personally the man for the place. In knowledge of the condition of Mexican politics & public affairs and her leading men, he has no superior on the Atlantic or Pacific Coast, and his appointment to that position, would give the fullest satisfaction to the business men of San Francisco, that this interest would be fully protected. In political matters, Mr Nugents position is one that no man can mistake. He is for the Constitution, & is your warm supporter in all your efforts to maintain and support it. He was for a year the Chairman of the National State Conservative Committee for Nevada, and used his position to sustain your administration.

I am satisfied that in all respects, as regards the policy of your Adminis-

tration at home, and your policy in regard to Mexico, you will find Mr
Nugent your friend and supporter.

The appointment of Mr Nugent to this position, would be especially
satisfactory to the people of the Pacific Coast, who have more material
intrests to be protected and fostered in Mexico, than all the ballance of
the Country.

Jos. W. McCorkle

ALS, DNA-RG59, Lets. of Appl. and Recomm., 1861–69 (M650, Roll 35), John
Nugent.
    1. Nugent (c1824–fl1874) arrived in California in 1849, taking up residence in San
Francisco and working as a policeman. Eventually he became a lawyer and for a time owned
and edited the *San Francisco Herald*. At one point he also maintained a law practice in Virginia City, Nevada. He was not nominated for the Mexican ministry. San Francisco directories (1867–74); 1860 Census, Calif., San Francisco, 8th Dist., 1295; Frank Soulé, John
H. Gihon, and James Nesbet, *The Annals of San Francisco* (New York, 1966 [1854]), 5,
823; Dorothy H. Huggins, comp., *Continuation of the Annals of San Francisco* (San Francisco, 1966 [1939]), 17–47 passim.

From Edwin M. Stanton

War Department, Washington City, July 11th 1867.

Sir,

I have the honor to submit herewith an estimate by the Paymaster
General and Adjutant General[1] of the amount of appropriation required
to cover *expenses of the Reconstruction* Acts of Congress.

This estimate is compiled from the separate estimates made out by, or
under the direction and approval of the several District Commanders,
and amount in the aggregate to the sum of $1,648,277. and may be in-
creased largely by an extension of the time during which the Registry
Boards continue under pay. I would respectfully recommend that application be made to Congress for an adequate appropriation, and submit
the accompanying estimate of the officers named as the nearest approx-
imation of the required sum that is attainable.

Edwin M. Stanton, Secy. of War.

LBcopy, DNA-RG107, Lets. Sent, Mil. Bks., Executive, 58-C.
    1. Benjamin W. Brice and Lorenzo Thomas, respectively.

From Edwin M. Stanton

War Department, Washington City,
July 11" 1867

Sir,

In partial answer to the Senate Resolution of inquiry, dated July 8"
1867, addressed to this Dept.,[1] I have the honor to submit a copy of the

latest communication received by this Dept. from *Lt. Genl. Sherman*,[2] to whose command the military *operations in the Indian territory* have been committed. Other correspondence and report, containing full details on the subject of inquiry are being prepared with all possible diligence to be submitted. One report is herewith transmitted.[3]

Approving the recommendation made by the Lt. Genl., I would respectfully recommend an application to Congress for authority to enlist organize and mount 4 regts. of Cavy. under the general provisions of enlistment; to be disbanded when their services are no longer required, and that a specific appropriation of two millions of dollars be made for repressing Indian hostilities in the Western Territories.[4]

Edwin M. Stanton, Secy of War.

LBcopy, DNA-RG107, Lets. Sent, Mil. Bks., Executive, 58-C.

1. *Congressional Globe*, 40 Cong., 1 Sess., p. 507.

2. William T. Sherman requested that Stanton ask Congress for the right to call out four new regiments of cavalry and for appropriations to keep them in service for six months. Sherman to Stanton, July 2, 1867, Lets. Recd., Executive (M494, Roll 102), RG107, NA.

3. The nature of this report has not been determined. It seems probable that the other materials being gathered were never submitted to Congress.

4. Although two Senate bills providing "for the calling out of volunteers to suppress Indian hostilities" were proposed in the fall, both were indefinitely postponed. There was no increase in cavalry until after George A. Custer's disaster at the Little Big Horn in 1876. *Congressional Globe*, 40 Cong., 1 Sess., p. 767; Utley, *Frontier Regulars*, 67.

From Lewis V. Bogy

St. Louis, July 12th 1867.

Sir:

I hope you will pardon me for the liberty I take in sending you a slip from one of our city papers,[1] expressing my views of the organization of the present session of Congress. I firmly believe that the present session is not Constitutional—for the reasons given in the slip I now send you. If it be true that it organized with only 34 members—I think it clear beyond doubt that it is illegally organized.

The radical party has itself on repeated occasions decided that the Southern States—were states. The Supreme Court has also made the same decision. Their 20 Senators therefore must be counted as a part of the representative body—whether the members be admitted or not. I am of opinion that if this question was plainly and squarely put to the people, when the first law passed by it is presented for your approval—that you would be sustained. The usurpations and constant aggressions of Congress as well as the bold avowal by Senators—of a determination to crush out all State rights—so that Congress may be the only power in existence—are beginning to be seen and understood. And I repeat if the question was fairly placed before the people—I think the decision would be favorable.

For a long time we drifted to Centralization—but now we are going it at rail road speed. The honest mind of the Country is against this tendency—& if a proper and bold appeal was made to it—the response would be favorable.

Again hoping you will excuse me.

Lewis V. Bogy

LS, DLC-JP.
  1. Not found.

From David P. Hurley[1]

Lumpkin, Ga.   July 12/67.

Dr Sir:

When you read my signature, you will probably remember me as the former Editor of the "Knoxville Statesman,"—your personal friend, and the admirer & supporter of your political principles, not only during your candidacy, & official career in Tennessee, but in your able, manly, fearless, and statesmanlike,—and I will add,—patriotic vindication of the Constitution of our common, but unfortunately distracted country. You doubtless remember my late lamented brother, Dr. W. R. Hurley,—Editor of the "Nashville Democrat," the uncompromising opposer of Secession.

I frankly confess, that in all my life, I have never been involved in such perplexing doubts as to the course I should take in regard to the great political questions now agitating the public mind of Georgia & the South. I need hardly remind you of what you doubtless already well know:—That the great mass of our people,—with rare exceptions,—endorse the principles, which you have so frequently enunciated in the recent past, and to which, in your official action, you have adhered with such fearless and patriotic firmness. I will add, that they are still ready to follow your lead. There is perhaps not a living official, whose political dictation they would follow with such implicit and unquestioning promptitude. They confide in your discretion as well as your integrity.

You stand in the midst, and at the head, of the elements of national politics and power. You comprehend the status of the South and of the Country.

Please state to me, whether you would advise us to "reconstruct" under, and in pursuance of the "*Sherman Military Bill.*" Do you think, as a measure of *policy*, it would be wise in the people of Georgia to vote for a convention and organize a new State Government in pursuance of that Bill?

This inquiry is made primarily for my own individual benefit, and your answer will of course be held as private & confidential unless you indicate otherwise, by submitting to my discretion what use I shall make of it.

The premises disclose considerations, which I trust will be accepted as sufficient apology for obtruding upon your attention the inquiry above submitted.

Hoping at your earliest convenience to receive a satisfactory response,[2]— and with best wishes for you personally and for your success in your sublime struggle for the maintenance and perpetuation of constitutional liberty.

D. P. Hurley

ALS, DLC-JP.
1. Hurley (b. c1825) had been a lawyer and an alderman in Monroe County, Tennessee, in the 1850s before moving to Lumpkin, where he continued the practice of law. 1850 Census, Tenn., Monroe, 10th Civil Dist., 15; (1870), Ga., Stewart, Lumpkin, 53; Reba B. Boyer, comp., *Monroe County, Tennessee Records, 1820–1870* (2 vols., n.p., 1969–70), 1: 146, 153.
2. No reply from the President has been located.

From John M. Keating

Memphis, Tenn.   July 13, 1867.

Sir

I venture to recall myself to your remembrance in this letter, having reference to the present deplorable condition of affairs in our State, hoping that my statement, made without party bias or in any other than the true spirit of an upright citizen, will have the effect of inducing you to take steps additional to those already taken by the military authorities for our safety & the peace & dignity of the State you served so long and so faithfully.

In their determination after supremacy in the State the Radicals in every part of Tennessee have organized Loyal Leagues, the membership of which is chiefly composed of negroes, who at the regular weekly meetings are drilled in the "school of the soldier" & "manual of arms" and afterwards are lectured upon the maintenance of their rights under any and all circumstances, but especially on occasion of the coming election in August, when they are told they will be confronted by a portion of the Conservative element sworn to prevent the free exercise by them of the privileges of the franchise. This they are educated to believe will be their time to avenge the deaths of May 1866.[1] To accomplish this revenge, they have been armed with every species of firearms, to learn the use of which, they are also taught, should be one of the first duties of freemen. They are being constantly reminded of their former servile condition & exasperated by the recital of tales—imaginary & real—of suffering endured by their fellows while occupying this condition, & of contemplated persecutions that have never been thought of save by the cunning &

scheming scoundrals who are thus seeking to make use of this element of our population for their own benefit. An excitable people, these poor negroes are easily worked upon. They firmly believe as a result of all this teaching that Gov has measured them as part & parcel of the economy wherewith he is to accomplish great moral changes & reversals of the results of human authority & law. They are constantly being told that you are a monster of all the iniquities, surrounded by renegades from the cause of the black, that as combating your influences & those of the Tennesseeans supporting you, our irreverant Governor is the forerunner of the Messiah's second coming & that a part of his duty is through their agency to scourge Tennessee & sweep away by riot & bloodshed, if not by a sumptuary law, all opponents of his will & their desire. Bible revelation is aptly quoted to suggest to these poor ignorant people that all the chief men of the nation occupy their places, foreordained of God, for the fulfillment of prophesies which foretell the future complete assimilation and social equality of all the people of the earth. They are firmly persuaded the day of jubilee is at hand when they are to reign where the white man once was master. They are puffed up with promises of division of lands by the Legislature & a general proscription of the wealthy & industrious of our people who at any time & in any way sympathised with the rebellion. They say they will not be put off with political equality. They must have their share of the legislative, judicial & executive offices of the State & be received by all upon the most complete social equality. Those who shall resist these sweeping & violent changes, they have been educated to believe are rebels and as rebels should be marked & "put out of the way" on the first convenient occasion. The highest of the reserved rights of the citizen—the selection of his friends or companions—is to be denied to a population with whom rests the virtue, the intelligence, the industry & the integrity of the State. All men opposing Radicalism are marked as traitors the definition of which word has been extended so as to include those who served the Union as those who opposed it. Entirely in the hands of the Radical leaders (comprising much of the worst element of the northern & western States) whom they regard as the authors of their freedom, there does not seem to be any way of steming this tide unless through the agency of U.S. troops, which unless ordered here for our protection by you we have no hope of seeing through the authority of the Governor, who unfortunately for the peace & dignity of the State is the most violent & proscriptive of his party. Here just now we have but three companies of infantry, a mere handful in presence of as many thousand infuriated blacks. The parties most prominent among the negroes have been expostulated with, but to no good end. Arming for self-protection suggests itself, but as any public effort of that kind would be construed by the dominant party into rebellion, the white men are constrained in the interests of law & of order to be silent. There is no resort short of that limit to human endurance when patience shall cease to be a virtue, save in the national army. If the strong arm of military authority is not interposed before the election it is believed by many that this condition of things must culminate in bloodshed, in perhaps a riot that shall prove the signal of a war of extermination. The fathers of these white people contended successfully with an Indian element more troublesome as cruel & more brave than the negro. Removal & extermination resulted. It will prove so in this case, too, unless this tubulent spirit of self-assertion is quelled in its incipiency, & the negroes is content to take his chance in the battle of life, laboring in his own way for his own good contributing not only to the general physical prosperity but the general security by his observance of law & respect for property rights. If the negroes ever "rise," as the phrase goes, I firmly believe extermination will follow. It will be white vs. black. Only two sides to a war that may be begun and ended in twenty-four hours & long before its commencment could be published to the people of the Republic. The whole army, if stationed here would not serve to stop this tide if once permitted to set in. It may be prevented by a strong force of regulars here in August. This we hope for as the means of prevention of evils before which many are now fleeing who before never crossed the borders of the State.

J. M. Keating

ALS, DLC-JP.
1. Doubtless a reference to the Memphis riots of May 1866.

From Neal Brown[1]

Raleigh   July 15, 1867

It affords me a Great pleasure to write to one who in our Boysh days spent so many happy moments in our Boyish plays. Many a hour have we spent at cat and Bass Ball and Bandy whitch was my choyest Game. But them days is past and Gone. While on your visit to Raleigh I had a Great Desire to have seen you that we might have had a social chat. But there was such a desire of all to see you that I could not Rush up.[2] I concluded that after you Got Back from Boston[3] I would write you a letter to Inform you of the Great troubles I have had to incounter with. In 1857 I moved in the country 2 miles west of Raleigh went to makeing hats for a liveing. I continued there untill Genrals Sherman army come on. The army encampd all around me and they Distroyd Every thing that I had made. They did not leave me a second shirt on my Back. They did not leave me a Rail on the fence. They Distroyd my Hatting tools took my all of my stock & all of my hats. I was left without one muthful of any thing to Eat.[4] All around where I lived fared as I did. I and my old woman[5] is verry much afflicted. I am nearly Blind. My Children is married and living to them selves. One of them Married a shoemake and lives in chapel Hill.

They have 5 Children. His name is Jas. E. Howell.[6] He lost all He Had
By the war. My son william Brown[7] is a printer By trade. His wife is the
daughter of Henry J. Brown[8] son of Joel Brown.[9] His wife has 8 children. His House was pulled down after Johnson Surrender.[10] He lost all
he had. So you see President we have seen Hard times and I am a fraid
that in our old age we will suffer gratly. I do hope that we may all Be
disappointed that Every thing may settled agreeable. In conclusion I
wish you a long life and a hapy one and when you come to change worlds
I pray that you may Be receivd up in to Glory where the wiced cease to
trouble and the weary are at rest. Fare well.

Neal Brown

ALS, DLC-JP.
1. Brown (c1800–fl1870) was a hatter, jobber and watchman at various times in
Raleigh. 1850 Census, N.C., Wake, Raleigh, 548; (1860), Southern Div., Morisville, 134;
(1870), Raleigh, 196.
2. An obvious reference to Johnson's June trip to North Carolina. A year later Brown
claimed that he actually shook hands with Johnson during his Raleigh visit. See Brown to
Johnson, June 20, 1868, Johnson Papers, LC.
3. The President went to Boston in late June to participate in Masonic activities there.
4. Brown repeated much of this same story in his letter of a year later. See Brown to
Johnson, June 20, 1868, Johnson Papers, LC.
5. Neal Brown's wife's name was reported differently by the census takers: as Lucy in
1850, as Basheba in 1860, and as Lowisa in 1870. The ages of these individuals at any
given point seem to indicate that, despite the varying names, there really was only one wife,
born approximately 1805. 1850 Census, N.C., Wake, Raleigh, 548; (1860), Southern
Div., Morisville, 134; (1870), Raleigh, 196.
6. Howel (b. c1823) lived with his in-laws at the time of the 1850 census, but ten years
later he was well established at Chapel Hill as a mail contractor and shoemaker. 1850
Census, N.C., Wake, Raleigh, 548; (1860), Orange, Chapel Hill, 19.
7. Brown (b. c1825) married sometime between the 1850 and 1860 censuses; by the
latter date he and his wife Frances (b. c1835) had five children. Between 1860 and the
1870 census, they had four more children. 1850 Census, N.C., Wake, Raleigh, 548;
(1860), Southern Div., Morisville, 76; (1870), Raleigh, 196.
8. Brown (b. c1811) was a cabinet and coffin maker in Raleigh. 1850 Census, N.C.,
Wake, Raleigh, 544; Murray, *Wake*, 269, 285, 562.
9. Joel Brown (c1760s–fl1846) moved his cabinet-making business to Raleigh from
Petersburg, Virginia, in 1816. Ibid., 212, 568; 1830 Census, N.C., Wake, 487.
10. A reference to Gen. Joseph E. Johnston's surrender to Gen. William T. Sherman in
North Carolina on April 18, 1865.

From R. King Cutler

"Private"

Washington, D.C.   July 15th, 1867.

Respected Sir—
Not being able to have an interview with you, for several days past; and
believing that I have something of importance to communicate, beg leave
most respectfully to make the following statement, to wit:
The letter published in all the New Orleans news papers,[1] a copy of
which, I, a few days since, sent to you,[2] must unquestionably convince

you of my political status, and my determination to act for the cause therein stated, and as I have frequently stated to you.

You will please allow me to candidly and knowingly say, that the states of Louisiana & Texas will go radically radical by an overwhelming majority, unless Commander Sheridan is relieved from duty, & some honest Conservative Union man placed in his stead. The number of votes in Louisiana are no greater than I stated in that letter. The reason why the negro registered vote as published, appears to be so large, is that a great many negroes registered twice and some of them six or eight times. I am extremely happy to know that the present extraordinary military bill just passed by Congress,[3] does not deprive you of your high Constitutional prerogative of relieving those Commanders in the South, and appointing others in their stead; and I am extremely happy to know that the power of saving this Nation, and the power of largely increasing the great Conservative vote of this Nation, is yet in your hands, and by Congress adjourning in a day or two, the hearts of the Conservative people of this Nation, will leap with joy, particularly so, when Sheridan and Sickles are relieved.

The additional affidavits this day filed against W. P. Kellogg, are of a very strong & conclusive character;—again! W. P. Kellogg has recently written to members of the U.S. Senate, that he is a confirmed radical, as he has ever been, & begging them not to allow his suspension from office, and again—he has recently written to Secretary McCulloch (which letters the Secretary now has)[4] that he is a devoted friend to the Administration, & a particular friend to the policy of the President of the United States.

Now, respected Sir, these solemn facts together with the facts which have already come to your notice, justifies me in again begging of you to suspend from office this treacherous man, Kellogg, knowing full well, as I do, that the evidence fully justifies the same, and that all of your friends in Louisiana, would heartily rejoice at the act.

I am compelled to leave for my home in Louisiana, in a few days, and in order to a successful carrying out of the programme so often stated, myself and your numerous friends in Louisiana, beg of you to immediately relieve Genl Sheridan, suspend W. P. Kellogg Collector at New Orleans, and F. J. Herron, U.S. Marshal.

Without so doing, all is lost. By so doing all is success, and Louisiana & Texas will roll up overwhelming majorities for your people for your cause, and for yourself.

I hope, Mr. President, that my earnestness & sincerity, coupled with a desire to immediately act, and knowing full well that unless you assist us, all is lost, will be considered by you a sufficient apology for this intrusion.[5]

                                                R. King Cutler

ALS, DLC-JP.
1. Not found.
2. Probably in Cutler's letter to Johnson of July 6, 1867.
3. Probably the Third Military Reconstruction Act.
4. The only relatively recent letter found from Kellogg to McCulloch is dated June 25, 1867. In that letter Kellogg thanked McCulloch for sending him a copy of a letter sent by Cutler to McCulloch. Kellogg wrote that "the statements and assertions of this man [Cutler] are unworthy of serious notice and . . . would be regarded here [New Orleans] as the gibberish of a man of besotted or unsound mind." Lets. Recd. from Customs Collectors at Large Ports (I Ser.), Vol. 3, RG56, NA.
5. For Cutler's next plea in the Kellogg case, see Cutler to Johnson, July 19, 1867.

From William W. Duffield

Belmont Bullitt County Kentucky
July 15", 1867

My Dear Sir

I wrote you last from Woodside Penna. but have since then purchased an interest and been elected Prest of the Belmont & Nelson Iron Compy located at this point.

As you probably know I have "no axe to grind"—have never been a candidate for any office and never will be—but as a plain honest soldier—the son and grandson of soldiers when the country needs my help she can have it—provided that when the war is over I can hang my old sabre on the wall and retire once more to private life and civil pursuits. As a soldier I give you frankly my own opinion as seen from my own stand point. If from your more elevated position such opinion is erroneous you need not give it a moments thought. I recognize you as an earnest well wisher of the country and am anxious therefore to aid you by every means in my power.

You probably are aware that there is a fixed determination in Congress to impeach and remove you. The committee lacked but one vote of adopting a report to that effect and were restrained from so doing not from any love for you but from the fear, of the commercial and financial disasters likely to result from such a movement. That a more successful attempt will be made in the fall I have no doubt,[1] and the surest mode of preventing it is to adopt a foreign policy which carry the people with you. Such an opportunity now is offered you in the Mexican question. The radicals have committed themselves to this cardinal doctrine of their bloody creed.

"To hang Jeff Davis on a sour apple tree"

and cannot therefore do other wise than approve of the execution of Maximilian. Not so with the people irrespective of party. By them his execution is regarded as a cruel and cold blooded murder. Any movement towards the occupation of Mexico by our Government would meet with a hearty & cordial approval not only from the American people, but from every European Government also. The administration which acquires Mexico will be the most popular one which has ever controlled the destinies of the nation, and there would be no more certain and surer road to political ruin than opposition to such a measure. This the radicals cannot fail to do. The logic of events will compel them to such a course, and their leaders already designate the sympathy shown for Maximilian as a "childish sentimentalism for the greatest criminal that ever lived." Moreover they would from necessity be compelled to oppose any measure which you would advocate, and particularly one which would in less than three months deprive them of their present power.

This movement would be exceedingly popular, because the American people are greedy of territory. Any movement which enlarges our boundaries is certain to be a popular one. The American farmer is always anxious to buy more land and this nation of acquisitive farmers is always willing to buy, more territory. A war for the permanent occupation of Mexico would be the most popular of all wars, and the men or party who opposed it would be ruined forver.

It would be moreover the most politic move that could be made, for many reasons.

It would become the great topic of the day, and the reconstruction question would soon shrink into insignificance. It would enable the nation to occupy and possess the very richest and best portion of the American continent and thus increase the wealth and resources of the people.

But above all it would rub out the sectional lines between North and South and restore the nation once more to a happy and united people. Nothing endears men to each other so soon or so strongly as the mutual sharing of hardship and danger, and if under the same old flag perhaps in the same brigade—the regiments from the North and West march shoulder to shoulder with their old antagonists of the South—and above all if the southern regiments when hotly pressed are relieved or sustained by their former enemy the men from the North and West, it will not be long before the old sectional lines of North and South will be effaced forever.

Napoleons favorite maxim was "il faut battre le fer quand il est chaud."[2] The death of Maximilian has heated public opinion to such a fervent heat that it is now as plastic as clay. But remember that it is also unstable as water. Act promptly and before it cools. Strike while the iron is hot, and strike boldly.

W. W. Duffield

ALS, DLC-JP.
1. It appears Duffield was correct in his prediction. On November 20 the Judiciary Committee voted 5–4 to recommend to the House the impeachment of Johnson. The reports and testimony were ordered printed on the 25th, with consideration postponed until December 4. *House Reports*, 40 Cong., 1 Sess., "Impeachment Investigation," pt. 1, pp. 1, 59 (Ser. 1314).
2. Strike while the iron is hot.

From Edwin R. Glascock

Nashville, Tenn., July 15th 1867.

Dear Sir:—

I hope you will pardon me for this intrusion, but the necessity of the case demands prompt action, and I feel at liberty to speak to you plainly on the subject, and I am satisfied in so doing, you will give the subject that consideration, which it demands, and I feel assured from your knowledge of me personally, that I would not suggest or recommend an appointment to office of any man, that would in a great degree be objectionable to the community, or to yourself. I feel too great an interest in you *personally* & officially to do so.

Mr. R. Carey[1] is an applicant for the office of District Atteny, for Middle Tennessee. Mr. Carey, it is true is a Northern man, and is classed with the Radicals, but in justice to him I will say that he is moderate in his views and opinions, and respects the rights and opinions of his opponents. I have had repeated conversations, with him in regard to the questions of the day, and personally of yourself, previous to, and since his application, and he has invariably spoken in respectful terms of you as President &c.

He is a man of fine legal attainments and would fill the office, with dignity, and without prejudice or partiality. He is not vindictive or malignant in his feelings or expressions. Since his residence here he has gained the esteem and confidence of his immediate associates, and I feel free to say that his appointment would give satisfaction.

There is none of our old citizens belonging to the legal profession, who are competent, that would accept, from the fact that it does not pay, and those that would, I am satisfied you would not appoint, so the matter stands.

If it were possible for me to have an interview with you, I am confident you would bestow the appointment upon him, and I would respectfully urge it. It should be made as soon as possible, as the interst of the Govement is suffering from the office being vacant. I feel a great interest in the appointment, officially, and I trust you will take the matter in hand, and give it a careful examination.[2]

I have not the heart or disposition to speak of matters in Tennessee. They are terrible, beyond expression, what is to become of, God only knows. I presume you are well posted. I hope for a brighter day, and trust yet, that you may be able to trample under your feet, your enemies and persecutors. I will not dwell on this subject. It is too sickening.

E. R. Glascock

ALS, DNA-RG60, Appt. Files for Judicial Dists., Tenn., Roswell Carey.

1. Roswell Carey, an attorney in Nashville, had accumulated quite a bit of experience in the district attorney's office by the summer months for, prior to Horace H. Harrison's

resignation in April, Carey had served as his assistant for eighteen months. In addition to Harrison himself, several other prominent figures recommended Carey's appointment. The President, however, did not heed those early recommendations. See the letters found in Appt. Files for Judicial Dists., Tenn., Roswell Carey, RG60 NA. See also Edmund Cooper to Johnson, Apr. 18, 1867.

2. There seemed to be a jinx on the U.S. district attorney's slot, for it remained vacant throughout 1867 despite the efforts of the President to fill the position. In November there was another spate of letters in support of Carey's nomination and appointment. Apparently, he continued to run the office, albeit in a temporary capacity. Among those renewing support for Carey were Glascock himself (letter to Johnson of November 25), Harrison (letter of November 26), and Edward H. East (letter of November 29); all are in the file cited above.

From George P. Ihrie [1]

Denver Col   July 15, 1867

Shameful treachery to obtain endorsements of Colorado Radicals to secure confirmation. Governor Hunt has in writing repudiated you and policy before Radical caucus admitting he deceived you to secure Gubernatorial appointment.[2] Radicals replied Having betrayed President would betray them & refused endorsement. Radicals forwarded written proofs of Hunts duplicity to Senator Yates.[3] We recommend Gen Patrick Edward Conner[4] of Utah for Governor of Colorado.[5]

Geo P Ihrie, B. Brig. Gen USA

Tel, DLC-JP.

1. Ihrie (1827–1903), who had attended the U.S. Military Academy but did not graduate, served in the prewar years as a lieutenant in the 3rd Arty. and subsequently joined the 3rd Calif. Inf. as lieutenant colonel during the Civil War. In 1866 he was appointed a paymaster with the rank of major, a post he held until he resigned in 1873. As a civilian he was a merchant and mine operator. Hunt and Brown, *Brigadier Generals*; *West Point Register*, 242.

2. In a letter the next day Ihrie elaborated that in the presence of five witnesses Alexander C. Hunt had explained that he "had practiced a ruse upon the President" because "when he [Hunt] reached for anything, he used every means within his grasp to get it." Ihrie to Robert Johnson, July 16, 1867, Johnson Papers, LC.

3. Richard Yates of Illinois.

4. Conner (1820–1891) served in the U.S. Army and the Texas volunteers during the 1840s and then went to California, where he was involved in mining. In 1861 he became colonel of the 3rd Calif. Inf. and commander of the District of Utah (including Nevada). He was commissioned brigadier general in 1863, brevetted major general in 1865, and mustered out in 1866. He became a newspaperman and mining promoter in Salt Lake City. Warner, *Blue*.

5. Hunt remained governor until removed by President Grant in the spring of 1869. Pomeroy, *The Territories*, 124; Bancroft, *Nevada, Colorado, and Wyoming*, 436.

To the Senate

WASHINGTON, D.C., *July 15, 1867.*

To the Senate of the United States:

I transmit herewith reports from the Secretary of War and the Attorney-General, containing the information called for by the resolution of the Senate of the 3d instant,[1] requesting the President "to communicate to the Senate copies of all orders, instructions, circular letters, or letters of advice issued to the respective military officers assigned to the command of the several military districts under the act passed March 2, 1867, entitled 'An act to provide for the more efficient government of the rebel States,' and the act supplementary thereto, passed March 23, 1867; also copies of all opinions given to him by the Attorney-General of the United States touching the construction and interpretation of said acts, and of all correspondence relating to the operation, construction, or execution of said acts that may have taken place between himself and any of said commanders, or between him and the General of the Army, or between the latter and any of said commanders, touching the same subjects; also copies of all orders issued by any of said commanders in carrying out the provisions of said acts or either of them; also that he inform the Senate what progress has been made in the matter of registration under said acts, and whether the sum of money heretofore appropriated for carrying them out is probably sufficient."

In answer to that portion of the resolution which inquires whether the sum of money heretofore appropriated for carrying these acts into effect is probably sufficient, reference is made to the accompanying report of the Secretary of War. It will be seen from that report that the appropriation of $500,000 made in the act approved March 30, 1867, for the purpose of carrying into effect the "Act to provide for the more efficient government of the rebel States," passed March 2, 1867, and the act supplementary thereto, passed March 23, 1867, has already been expended by the commanders of the several military districts, and that, in addition, the sum of $1,648,277 is required for present purposes.

It is exceedingly difficult at the present time to estimate the probable expense of carrying into full effect the two acts of March last and the bill which passed the two Houses of Congress on the 13th instant. If the existing governments of ten States of the Union are to be deposed and their entire machinery is to be placed under the exclusive control and authority of the respective district commanders, all the expenditures incident to the administration of such governments must necessarily be incurred by the Federal Government. It is believed that, in addition to the $2,100,000 already expended or estimated for, the sum which would be required for this purpose would not be less than $14,000,000—the aggregate amount expended prior to the rebellion in the administration of their respective governments by the ten States embraced in the provisions of these acts. This sum would no doubt be considerably augmented if the machinery of these States is to be operated by the Federal Government, and would be largely increased if the United States, by abolishing the existing State governments, should become responsible for liabilities incurred by them before the rebellion in laudable efforts to develop their resources, and in no wise created for insurrectionary or revolutionary purposes. The debts of these States, thus legitimately incurred, when accurately ascertained will, it is believed, approximate $100,000,000; and they are held not only by our own citizens, among whom are residents of portions of the country which have ever remained loyal to the Union, but by persons who are the subjects of foreign governments. It is worthy the consideration of Congress and the country whether, if the Federal Government by its action were to assume such obligations, so large an addition to our public expenditures would not seriously impair the credit of the nation, or, on the other hand, whether the refusal of Congress to guarantee the payment of the debts of these States, after having displaced or abolished their State governments, would not be viewed as a violation of good faith and a repudiation by the national legislature of liabilities which these States had justly and legally incurred.

ANDREW JOHNSON.

Richardson, *Messages*, 6: 525–27.
  1. See Senate to Johnson, July 3, 1867.

From William H. Seat[1]

Washington D.C.   July 16th 1867.

Mr President.—

I go to Europe not only for the purpose of securing aid in building up two grand central Institutions in Texas[2] but also with the view (as an adjunctive design) of obtaining information and fixing channels of communication that may be of service to our Institutions generally in Texas and elsewhere in the South.

I expect to spend sometime (a year or two it may be) abroad and to apply to all classes including the royalty and the nobility of Europe for information and material aid.

In order to the successful accomplishment, I go with the cheerful and hearty endorsement of the highest authorities of this continent in the domain of Science and Literature as Prof's Agassiz Henry Longfellow Whipple Holmes[3] and others and in the realm of commerce of such firms as H. B. Claflin & co. Spofford Tileston & co. New York.[4]

I also earnestly desire a general letter from your Excellency sealed with the great Seal of the United States[5] which as Hon Reverdy Johnson remarked yesterday would be a sufficient basis for whatever letters from the United States Ministers abroad I might need in the prosecution of my work.

I should be exceedingly glad too to have your name in my subscription book I doubt not will contain many of the most honorable names in Europe and America before the list shall have been completed. I expect to have the book handsomely rebound and lodged in the Archives of the University.

Without undertaking to dictate or to insist permit me respectfully to propose that if your Excellency will head a proposition to be called "The Presidents Proposition," to contribute one in the number of one thousand donations of one hundred dollars each I will make up the whole number or else never call on you for your Subscription.

Permit me to say in conclusion that if I did not feel the importance of obtaining the highest possible moral support in my important mission to Europe I should not have the audacity to apply to the president of the United States for a subscription to a University enterprise. But as I felt on obtaining the subscription of Prof Agassiz that I could then go much further in obtaining supplies for our Institution so I shall feel if it should be your excellency's pleasure to comply with my request that my success is assured as to the securing of financial aid.

I have taken the liberty of making out the form of a proposition which may if your excellency please be adopted or changed and either signed on a separate slip and pasted in my book or transfered to the book itself.[6]

Wm. H. Seat

P.S. You will observe the fact that two institutions are named. I am Agent for both though the agency has main reference to the University. The design is to greatly enlarge and fully develope both as grand central Institutions though donations may be given to one or both at the option of the donor.

W.H.S.

P.S. Mr President. Finding this to be Cabinet day I leave the within for your inspection at your leisure. I will be here to morrow morning at 10 oclock—or if not then Thursday morning at 10 oclock. I leave the matter to be disposed of as your excellency may think best.

W.H S

ALS, DLC-JP.

1. Seat (c1825–fl1867), a native of Tennessee, was a Methodist minister who had served in various cities in Texas. 1860 Census, Tex., Travis, Austin, 124; *Minutes of the Annual Conferences of the Methodist Episcopal Church, South* (Nashville, 1845–1923) (1858), 78; (1859), 175; (1860), 277; (1861), 351; (1862), 415; (1865), 587.

2. It is unknown exactly which institutions he refers to.

3. Jean Louis Rodolphe Agassiz, probably Joseph Henry, Henry Wadsworth Longfellow, probably Rev. George Whipple, and Oliver Wendell Holmes. Agassiz (1807–1873) was an eminent natural scientist who had studied, taught, and published in Switzerland, Germany, France, and the United States. Henry (1797–1878) had served professorships in mathematics and natural philosophy and had done extensive research in physics before he became the first secretary and director of the Smithsonian Institution (1846–78). Longfellow (1807–1882), world-renowned poet, was an intimate friend of Agassiz's. Holmes (1809–1894), professor of anatomy at Dartmouth and Harvard Medical School, where he became dean, was best known for his medical, poetic, and prose writings and as an engaging teacher. *DAB*.

4. H. B. Claflin & Co., a wholesale dry goods business, headed by Horace B. Claflin. Spofford, Tileston & Co., shipping merchants in New York City, was led by Paul Spofford (1781–1869). Thomas Tileston (1793–1864) was the original partner of Spofford, beginning in 1818. Following his death, his son Thomas was involved with the company. New

York City directories (1865–1900); *New York Times*, Mar. 6, 1864, Oct. 29, 1869, Nov. 15, 1885, Dec. 9, 1906.

5. The next day, the 17th, Johnson wrote Seat a short letter of commendation to U.S. representatives abroad. Johnson Papers, LC.

6. Not found.

From William M. Daily

New Orleans, La.   July 17th 1867

Mr. President:

I am determined to keep my name before you, as an applicant for some *lucrative place*, or *position*, from your Excellency. I have been *pleading, hoping*, and *waiting* for nearly, or quite, *Two Years*. Your term is fast passing away, and if it dont come while you are in power—my hopes will perish—as I have placed *all my hopes on you* !!!

Why not make me *Minister* to *Mexico*—in place of Mr. Campbell,[1] resigned? I am ready to go any place, or to accept any position that will pay—as my *poverty* is pressing me sore. I desire to hold what I have, until the better place offers, which I flatter myself, now will be very soon. Now dont forget the *best*, the most *ardent* and *devoted friend* you ever had.

Give me the Mission to Mexico or something that will pay.[2]

Wm. M Daily   New Orleans Louisiana

ALS, DNA-RG59, Lets. of Appl. and Recomm., 1861–69 (M650, Roll 6), William M. Daily.

1. Lewis D. Campbell.

2. Daily did not receive the requested appointment and continued to write Johnson asking for some position. See, for example, Daily to Johnson, Nov. 23, 1867, Johnson Papers, LC.

From Henry N. Frisbie [1]

"Private"

Washington, D.C.   July 17th 1867

Respected Sir.

The speedy adjournment of Congress will give you leisure probably to consider the propriety of acting upon the application, I had the honor of verbally bringing to your consideration.[2] The great length of time that has intervened has given my enemies ample opportunity to place before you, all the objections that might be urged to my being sustained by you and appointed to an honorable and responsible position in the affairs of the Government, which you have been called to administer.

That there may be no misunderstanding, I have thought proper to briefly recapitulate in writing, my former suggestions, observations and requests, as well as my obligations therefor.

At the commencement of the War I offered my services, and in the 37th Illinois Volunteer Infantry, served in the Battles of Pea Ridge, Prairie Grove and the siege of Vicksburg, commanding the Regiment much of the time, as Captain, Major and Lieutenant Colonel, showing how I stood with my comrades in arms, as I was promoted each time to the first vacancy. After this famous siege, I suggested the propriety, and solicited the privilege to commence the organization of a Regiment of Volunteers in the City of New Orleans, (afterwards so useful), but as no authority for this had been granted, I solicited and obtained permission to recruit and organize a regiment of colored men, and received the order therefor on the 2nd September, 186[3], and on the 30th of the same month, I had mustered into the service a regiment, completely officered, clothed, armed, equipped and ready to take the field.[3] And that during 1863, "64, "65, and "66, until mustered out of service, I commanded a regiment a Brigade and a Division in the "Corps D'Afrique," taking part in all the operations of the Army, in the Department of the Gulf, including the Red River Campaign; and all the battles incidental thereto, and the building of the Red River dam. I was President of the Board of Education that established colored schools in the State of Louisiana; also President of the Board to determine the names of battles, regiments might bear upon their colors.

This brief military history is mentioned, not that I claim any merit for it, but to show that in her hour of need, the country found me at the post of duty. In the manner of conducting business, I have had large experience and believe myself a thorough business man. When the war terminated, I everywhere saw the doubt and demoralization existing among good men, as to the results of Free labor, so as I had had long acquaintance with it, I determined to organize the labor in my own regiment, as an example to the doubting planters, and encourage the reorganization of the nearly ruined industries of the State; and to this end, I gathered the families of my soldiers together, and placed them upon plantations, fed and clothed them, worked and paid them, and successfully made large crops of Cotton, Sugar and Corn, upon five of the largest plantations in the State of Louisiana; and for this I claim some credit. Now, I have organized the colored people as soldiers, fought with them, assisted in their education, taught them and their former masters free labor, often addressed large assemblies of them, on their *rights* and *duties*, and am today, better known among those of Louisiana than any other northern man except Abraham Lincoln.

And now, Mr. President, these men are voters, and are consequently a political power. It is useless to stop and enquire how they became so, or whether you or I would have it so, yet it is nevertheless a fixed fact, and they will wield their great power for good or evil. I would try and control it for good. Next week, I certainly go to take part in the reconstruction of the State of Louisiana. I believe these new elements should be so directed as to conserve the best material interests of the State and Union, and to this end, I intend to labor, and will assist in returning to Congress such persons as are for the country above party, and those that will not be objectionable to you.

In fact, I expect to work, act and vote in the political field with the Hon. R King Cutler, and to this end, I ask your assistance as heretofore, and herein indicated; and in this connection, I beg to remind your Excellency of the endorsements in regard to my character, military career, capacity, business qualifications, social standing &c. delivered to you personally, and ordered by you to be placed on file, and preserved for your future consideration.[4]

1st.   Because while the great contest was still doubtful and your Excellency not at the head of affairs, you made that celebrated promise[5] that gave great encouragement to the officers and soldiers of colored troops; and whose moral effect materially assisted in your elevation; but to be justly so considered you should now recognize those who took a prominent part, for and in behalf of the colored people, for as yet, to my knowledge, not any of them has been appointed to any office, thereby securing their recognition by the Government. By this, I represent and mean that the great body of the officers of the old Corps d'Afrique, are eminently Conservative, no matter how radical they were when they joined this branch of the service. They soon became Conservative, and left the organization, finally feeling that the most important duty to, and want of, the colored people, was attention to their physical condition; and that a proper organization, so as to procure them bread, clothing and homes, thereby restoring the industries of the State, and reviving Commerce, was more needful than placing them in political conditions, which they did not understand, nor were competent to fill. And that these officers are now more by the force of circumstances gathered in the political fold, to which they are aliens at heart, and marshaled to the support of principles they disallow and disapprove, than by willingness and free choice. 1st. because the Government not in theory, but practically ignored them as a class, affirming *that* distinction of officers of white and colored troops made during the war by prejudice fashion and power. 2ndly.—because they feel bitter sour and disagreeable discontented, and are made to believe they have few or no friends. The Government as a convenience only used them; and discarded and disregarded them as soon as the exigency had passed. Thus this famous declaration of your Excellency becomes to them of great consideration, and now may be made to fulfil a double purpose,—that of doing justice to a body of brave and honest officers as ever fought for the integrity of any country, and securing to your Excellency, a historical renown that cannot but be pleasing, and desirable to anyone, no matter how high in position; and you may add to the great title "Leader and Lawgiver,"—that of Protector.

2nd.—I believe I am a representative man, among those who served in the (at that time) doubly dangerous service of the "Corps d'Afrique," and over two hundred officers of that old corps, are now in the City of New Orleans, and will, I sincerely believe, assist me in sustaining the views and principles herein presented.

3rd.—The elements of political power as well as the means to develope them are in the great offices of Louisiana, and most of the present incumbents are unfriendly to you.

4th. All who accept office under the President should do so, expecting to "obey orders" or resign.

5th. Because I work with the party sustaining you.

6th. In consideration of the above, and hope for the future, I most respectfully ask the President to appoint me Collector of Customs at the Port of New Orleans.[6]

H. N. Frisbie.

LS, DNA-RG56, Appts., Customs Service, Collector, La., New Orleans, H. N. Frisbie.
   1. Frisbie (1829–1897), a New York native, was a manufacturer of hay pressers before the Civil War and a lawyer afterwards. Hunt and Brown, *Brigadier Generals*.
   2. Frisbie was applying to be collector of customs at New Orleans.
   3. The 92nd USCT. Hunt and Brown, *Brigadier Generals*.
   4. Lovell H. Rousseau was among those who at some time recommended Frisbie. Rousseau to Johnson, Aug. 31, 1867, Appts., Customs Service, Collector, New Orleans, Henry N. Frisbie, RG56, NA.
   5. Frisbie probably refers to Johnson's "The Moses of the Colored Men" speech of October 24, 1864. *Johnson Papers*, 7: 251–53.
   6. Frisbie apparently was not nominated. Ser. 6B, Vol. 4: 204, Johnson Papers, LC.

To Sam Milligan

Washington, D.C.   July 17th 1867

Will you accept office of Solicitor of Treasury, salary four thousand dollars?[1] Or would you prefer Consulship to Cuba, salary six thousand, or appointment as Minister to Bolivia South America salary seven thousand five hundred? Both of the latter have to go before the Senate. Answer immediately.

Andrew Johnson

Tel, DNA-RG107, Tels. Sent, President, Vol. 3 (1865–68).
   1. See McCulloch to Johnson, Jan. 21, 1867, *Johnson Papers*, 11: 621; and McCulloch to Milligan, Jan. 21, 1867, Johnson Papers, LC.
   2. Immediately upon receipt of the President's telegram, Milligan notified Johnson that he could not "accept either of the foreign places." Milligan to Johnson, July 18, 1867, Johnson Papers, LC.

From Thomas R. Jennings and W. Matt Brown

Nashville Tenn   July 18, 1867

Sir

We have the honor herewith to transmit to you, through General Duncan Commandant of this military post,[1] a printed coppy of certain resolutions[2] recently adopted by a verry numerous assemblage of our fellow citizens of this vicinage, in which you are verry distinctly, and, at the same time, most respectfully and gratefully referred to, in your official character, though for reasons Sufficiently obvious it was deemed most delicate and proper, in drawing up, to refrain from any formal mention of your name. Had these resolutions originated in a mere political or party meeting, or been in the least degree, marked with a partizan or controversional spirit, we should have been verry far indeed from calling your special attention to them in the manner we now presume to do; feeling the fullest assurance, that in the exercise of the verry delicate and important powers entrusted to you as the Chief Military Commandant of this District, you have no objects or desires incompatible with the welfare and happiness of evry class of your fellow citizens who have been committed to your protecting care, and that you are annimated with an inflexible determination to maintain justice, support law and order, and suppress all movements calculated to generate needless strife, and rekindle the flames of civil contention and violence in our midst. That there are a few excited and imprudent persons to be found in various parts of the State of Tennessee, who, in the absence of the restraining influence which it is in your power, to bring into action, might more or less put the public peace in danger, we are not at all disposed to deny; but, that a verry large majority of our citizens, of all classes and conditions, are at this moment intensely solicitous of contributing, as far as they may be able, to the maintenance of civil repose and to the avoidance of all discord and collisions, we do not entertain the smallest doubt. Some verry disagreable occurrences, which have taken place in this neighborhood a few days since,[3] togather with the excitement naturally incident to the political elections which is now nearly approaching, have induced us, and those whom we represent on this occasion, to feel excedingly desirous that you should, so far as you may deem it wise and proper to do so, strengthen the military force of the Federal Government in different parts of our state, for the purpose of guarding against mischief which it is to be seriously feared might otherwise ensue. We are excedeingly anxious to aid to the extent of our ability in the prevention of evils to which we cannot but believe that our community is to some extent now liable, and feel assured that you will pardon the liberty that we take of asking at your hands such present interposition in behalf of law-abiding and order-respecting citizens, as your own high sense of propriety shall prompt you to supply.

Thomas R. Jennings Chairman
W Matt Brown President

ALS (Jennings), DLC-JP.
1. Thomas Duncan (1819–1887) was a career soldier who saw action in the Mexican War before serving as a major in the 3rd U.S. Cav. in the Civil War. He was brevetted brigadier general in March 1865. After the war he commanded the Nashville district until September 1868. Hunt and Brown, *Brigadier Generals*; *Appleton's Cyclopaedia*.
2. A handwritten copy of the resolutions was affixed to the Jennings-Brown letter. Evidence that General Duncan permitted a printed copy to be forwarded to the President has not been uncovered. At a meeting at the Market House in Nashville on July 10, speeches were made and resolutions adopted. The assembled crowd agreed that it desired to work for peace in the state, that it would submit to constituted authorities, and gave thanks for General Duncan; finally it resolved that a committee of fifteen persons should draw up a memorial setting forth grievances and asking for relief. *Nashville Republican Banner*, July 11, 1867.
3. It is not clear if Jennings and Brown are referring here to particular incidents or to the more general pattern of disturbances. Issues of the *Nashville Republican Banner* for mid-July do not indicate specific problems in Nashville.

From R. King Cutler

"Confidential"

Washington, D.C: July 19th 1867

Respected Sir.

I have considered it necessary to give you information which perhaps would not otherwise reach you concerning W. P. Kellogg, and others.

A few days ago, an affidavit voluntarily made by Charles S. Randall[1] of Louisiana, was sent to the Secretary of the Treasury.[2] This affidavit with an accompanying affidavit of two others conclusively establishes a *Forgery*, on the part of Kellogg, or some of his accomplices.

Yesterday, the Secretary was put in possession of a number of documents[3] clearly proving another *Forgery*, of the name of C. B. White,[4] and showing the falsity of Kellogg's affidavits, in so far as Governor Wells and F. J. Herron are concerned. These documents prove that F. J. Herron and J. Madison Wells Ex-Governor, have in the most positive manner, contradicted themselves.

Then upon the whole the latter evidence herein alluded to, added to the evidence against Kellogg, which you have had the occasion to see, fastens conclusively upon him, Kellogg, the guilt of every charge made in the pamphlet entitled—New Orleans Custom House Frauds.[5]

Mr. Sullivan,[6] Naval officer at New Orleans is now here, absent without leave, and I would be glad if you could converse with him. He reports and does not hesitate to say, that F. J Herron, W. P. Kellogg, C. A. Weed, James McKee (the two latter being now here) A. S. Mansfield,[7] J. Madison Wells, B. F. Flanders, Secretary McCulloch and some others are all concerned in the great Louisiana Cotton Frauds; and that in an interview between McCulloch and himself yesterday, McCulloch told Sullivan he intended to protect every one of them, and that Kellogg should not be removed. Mr. Sullivan has also said that Kellogg and others there have declared that they will spend a million of dollars to keep Kellogg and others in office.

Mr. President, another strange thing is that Secretary McCulloch has within the last ten or fifteen days, received not less than three letters from Kellogg, and those letters are now in his possession, in which he states that he is now as ever, heart and soul with the Administration, and your policy, while at the same time he has written letters to several radical senators, stating that he is as ever in thorough accord with them; and unchangably radical; and requesting those Senators to see that he is not removed from the office; that he wants to hold it as long as he can by humbugging you.

On page 10, of the pamphlet, the testimony of Alfred Reid,[8] refers to a person who was employed in the Custom House, and paid without rendering services. That gentleman is now ascertained to be a prominent radical politician of Northern Illinois, who says he went down there to make money, but that Kellogg was so shy and greedy, that he wanted to do the most of it himself. This gentleman's name, I am ready to give. Further, Sullivan, the naval officer, who made two affidavits against the above Mr. Reid now declares that Mr. Reid is not the man he supposed him to be, on signing these affidavits. Sullivan also says that when he signed these affidavits, he did not read them, and did not know what they were, except simply that they were something for Mr. Kellogg, that they were brought to his office by J. Morris Day,[9] a notary, and he, Sullivan, simply signed them, not being under oath. These facts, Mr. President certainly establish all the allegations and charges in the above mentioned pamphlet.

I have deemed it my duty to make known to you these facts in this manner. The documents alluded to, you can easily see by requisition on your Secretary of the Treasury; and the letters to the radical Senators can be ascertained by reference to those who have seen them, whose names I can give.

Hoping this will not trespass on your time, and it may be of interest to you in the investigation now going on.

R. King Cutler

ALS, DLC-JP.
    1. A Charles Randall (b. c1846), a New York native, was a New Orleans clerk in 1870. He may also be the Charles S. Randall who was a New Orleans lottery agent in 1874–75. New Orleans directories (1874–76); 1870 Census, La., Orleans, New Orleans, 3rd Ward, 673.
    2. Hugh McCulloch.
    3. These documents have not been found.

4. Charles B. White (1826–1882), for many years a New Orleans physician, served as an assistant surgeon and surgeon with U.S. troops during the Civil War and afterwards was medical director on the staff of Maj. Gen. Gordon Granger (1863–66). New Orleans directories (1859–82); Francis B. Heitman, *Historical Register and Dictionary of the United States Army, from its Organization, September 29, 1789, to March 2, 1903* (2 vols., Washington, D.C., 1903), 1: 1027; *New Orleans Picayune*, Apr. 18, 1882.

5. The pamphlet has not been found. But the New Orleans correspondent of the *Chicago Republican* described it as the work of Cutler and five others who used this pamphlet to publicize their numerous serious charges but apparently without the proof to back up their accusations. Undated clipping attached to Cutler to Johnson, July 15, 1867, Johnson Papers, LC.

6. James B. Sullivan (b. *c*1799), apparently a doctor and planter residing in Rapides Parish for more than twenty-five years, was rewarded for his wartime Unionism with the post of naval officer for New Orleans in 1866. J. M. Wells to Johnson, Sept. [22?], 1865, Lets. Sent *re* Customs Service Employees (QC Ser.), Vol. 34, James B. Sullivan, RG56, NA; 1860 Census, La., Rapides, Alexandria, 222; *Senate Ex. Proceedings*, Vol. 14, pt. 2: 1163, 1174.

7. McKee has not been identified. Asahel S. Mansfield (*fl*1872) of Boston was in New Orleans during the Civil War, allegedly purchasing cotton behind Confederate lines for shipment north. After the war he remained in the city for a few years as a merchant and steamboat owner. New Orleans directories (1867–70); Boston directories (1861–72); Henry Clay Warmoth, *War, Politics, and Reconstruction* (New York, 1930), 157–58.

8. Virginia-born Reid (b. *c*1823), a New Orleans bookkeeper and accountant, was a U.S. treasury agent in 1866. New Orleans directories (1861–66); 1860 Census, La., Orleans, New Orleans, 2nd Ward, 11th Dist., 491.

9. Day (*fl*1870) was a bookkeeper and then principal clerk in the New Orleans customs office and a notary public in 1870. New Orleans directories (1867–70); *U.S. Off. Reg.* (1865).

From Sam Milligan

Greeneville Tenn.   July 19, 1867

Dear Sir:

Your telegram yesterday took me by surprise, and I assure you it was very gratifying to me under the circumstances.[1] Not that I felt in the slightest degree that I had claims upon you for any position. No, certainly not. The obligations are all the other way. They bind me; not you: and my regret is I have not been more able to discharge them. But since the decision in the Franchise case,[2] it is manifest, there has been a settled effort, through the news papers, and bad men, not only to place me in a false political position, but to sever our life long friendship. To this end I have been grossly misrepresented, and you, I know, equally slandered. But neither the one or the other has in the slightest degree, affected my political opinions, or diminished my respect & confidence in you.

I am glad therefore your telegram has given me an opportunity to say this much, which will be sufficient until I see you.

I want to say one thing more, and that is, I have not felt disappointed, that a position has not been heretofore formally offered to me.[3] You did all you could to meet my wishes, at the beginning of your administration; and I have felt ever since, they would be gratified, whenever they were expressed, if you could do so consistently with your sense of duty. What more could I ask, or desire. Surely nothing. And I have felt or desired at no time nothing more.

It is true, I have not taken an active or clamorous part in politics, since I have been on the bench. I have felt it improper to do so, with the degrading example of some of the inferior Judges before me. My great object has been to administer the law faithfully, and equally to all, without knowing either men or parties; and thus aid in restoring the country to peace, and the people to confidence in the faithful administration of the law. How far I have succeeded is not for me to say. I take some consolation in the fact, that I have not pleased all parties, & certainly not all men.

Now, as to the subject of your telegram. You know enough of the situation of my family to see at once, I could not without ruin to myself accept either the Mission to Bolivia, or the Consulship to Cuba; and as to the Solicitor of the Treasury, I know nothing of its duties. Whether I could discharge them satisfactorily or not I can only conjecture. I have therefore thought best to say, I will in a few days come to Washington, as I desire to see you a very short time on another matter.[4]

The place I have of itself, altho very laborious, would be pleasant enough if my associates were all that I could desire. But they are not, or at least one of them. But I will talk to you on this subject when we meet.

But let me say, if it is at all important, you should make the appointment before I reach Washington by all means do not delay it on my account, as I do assure you, I will not have the slightest reflection on you for it. As I said I want to talk with you a little about affairs in this State.

Since I began this letter I have been painfully afflicted with something like Pleurisy. I am not yet well but better. This is the reason I have not written sooner.

                                                                    Sam Milligan

ALS, DLC-JP.
1. Milligan obviously refers to the President's telegram of July 17.
2. The reference here is to the *Ridley* v. *Sherbrook* case. Bromfield L. Ridley sought a certificate of registration from Freeman Sherbrook, commissioner of registration for Rutherford County. Denied such a certificate under provisions of the May 1866 franchise law, Ridley brought suit in the lower courts. The circuit court, arguing that the franchise law was unconstitutional, required that Sherbrook issue a certificate to Ridley. The case then went to the state supreme court (where Milligan sat along with two other judges) on appeal. That court ruled in January 1867 that the lower court's findings were untenable, upheld the constitutionality of the franchise law, and maintained that the franchise was a political privilege, not an inalienable right. Thus, Ridley was denied his claim for a certificate of registration. Patton, *Unionism and Reconstruction*, 120–23.
3. Milligan's statement is puzzling in light of the January 1867 offer to him of appointment as solicitor of internal revenue. See McCulloch to Milligan, Jan. 21, 1867, Johnson Papers, LC.
4. Continuing problems with personal illness prevented Milligan from traveling to Washington to visit with Johnson. See Milligan to Johnson, Aug. 7, 1867.

Veto of the Third Military Reconstruction Act

WASHINGTON, D.C., *July 19, 1867.*

To the House of Representatives of the United States:

I return herewith the bill entitled "An act supplementary to an act entitled 'An act to provide for the more efficient government of the rebel States,' passed on the 2d day of March, 1867, and the act supplementary thereto, passed on the 23d day of March, 1867," and will state as briefly as possible some of the reasons which prevent me from giving it my approval.

This is one of a series of measures passed by Congress during the last four months on the subject of reconstruction. The message returning the act of the 2d of March[1] last states at length my objections to the passage of that measure. They apply equally well to the bill now before me, and I am content merely to refer to them and to reiterate my conviction that they are sound and unanswerable.

There are some points peculiar to this bill, which I will proceed at once to consider.

The first section purports to declare "the true intent and meaning," in some particulars, of the two prior acts upon this subject.

It is declared that the intent of those acts was, first, that the existing governments in the ten "rebel States" "were not legal State governments," and, second, "that thereafter said governments, if continued, were to be continued subject in all respects to the military commanders of the respective districts and to the paramount authority of Congress."

Congress may by a declaratory act fix upon a prior act a construction altogether at variance with its apparent meaning, and from the time, at least, when such a construction is fixed the original act will be construed to mean exactly what it is stated to mean by the declaratory statute. There will be, then, from the time this bill may become a law no doubt, no question, as to the relation in which the "existing governments" in those States, called in the original act "the provisional governments," stand toward the military authority. As those relations stood before the declaratory act, these "governments," it is true, were made subject to absolute military authority in many important respects, but not in all, the language of the act being "subject to the military authority of the United States, as hereinafter prescribed." By the sixth section of the original act these governments were made "in all respects subject to the paramount authority of the United States."

Now by this declaratory act it appears that Congress did not by the original act intend to limit the military authority to any particulars of subjects therein "prescribed," but meant to make it universal. Thus over all of these ten States this military government is now declared to have unlimited authority. It is no longer confined to the preservation of the public peace, the administration of criminal law, the registration of voters, and the superintendence of elections, but "in all respects" is asserted to be paramount to the existing civil governments.

It is impossible to conceive any state of society more intolerable than this; and yet it is to this condition that 12,000,000 American citizens are reduced by the Congress of the United States. Over every foot of the immense territory occupied by these American citizens the Constitution of the United States is theoretically in full operation. It binds all the people there and should protect them; yet they are denied every one of its sacred guaranties.

Of what avail will it be to any one of these Southern people when seized by a file of soldiers to ask for the cause of arrest or for the production of the warrant? Of what avail to ask for the privilege of bail when in military custody, which knows no such thing as bail? Of what avail to demand a trial by jury, process for witnesses, a copy of the indictment, the privilege of counsel, or that greater privilege, the writ of *habeas corpus?*

The veto of the original bill of the 2d of March was based on two distinct grounds—the interference of Congress in matters strictly appertaining to the reserved powers of the States and the establishment of military tribunals for the trial of citizens in time of peace. The impartial reader of that message will understand that all that it contains with respect to military despotism and martial law has reference especially to the fearful power conferred on the district commanders to displace the criminal courts and assume jurisdiction to try and to punish by military boards; that, potentially, the suspension of the *habeas corpus* was martial law and military despotism. The act now before me not only declares that the intent was to confer such military authority, but also to confer unlimited military authority over all the other courts of the State and over all the officers of the State—legislative, executive, and judicial. Not content with the general grant of power, Congress, in the second section of this bill, specifically gives to each military commander the power "to suspend or remove from office, or from the performance of official duties and the exercise of official powers, any officer or person holding or exercising, or professing to hold or exercise, any civil or military office or duty in such district under any power, election, appointment, or authority derived from, or granted by, or claimed under any so-called State, or the government thereof, or any municipal or other division thereof."

A power that hitherto all the departments of the Federal Government, acting in concert or separately, have not dared to exercise is here attempted to be conferred on a subordinate military officer. To him, as a military officer of the Federal Government, is given the power, supported by "a sufficient military force," to remove every civil officer of the State. What next? The district commander, who has thus displaced the civil officer, is authorized to fill the vacancy by the detail of an officer or soldier of the Army, or by the appointment of "some other person."

This military appointee, whether an officer, a soldier, or "some other person," is to perform "the duties of such officer or person so suspended or removed." In other words, an officer or soldier of the Army is thus transformed into a civil officer. He may be made a governor, a legislator, or a judge. However unfit he may deem himself for such civil duties, he must obey the order. The officer of the Army must, if "detailed," go upon the supreme bench of the State with the same prompt obedience as if he were detailed to go upon a court-martial. The soldier, if detailed to act as a justice of the peace, must obey as quickly as if he were detailed for picket duty.

What is the character of such a military civil officer? This bill declares that he shall perform the duties of the civil office to which he is detailed. It is clear, however, that he does not lose his position in the military service. He is still an officer or soldier of the Army; he is still subject to the rules and regulations which govern it, and must yield due deference, respect, and obedience toward his superiors.

The clear intent of this section is that the officer or soldier detailed to fill a civil office must execute its duties according to the laws of the State. If he is appointed a governor of a State, he is to execute the duties as provided by the laws of that State, and for the time being his military character is to be suspended in his new civil capacity. If he is appointed a State treasurer, he must at once assume the custody and disbursement of the funds of the State, and must perform those duties precisely according to the laws of the State, for he is intrusted with no other official duty or other official power. Holding the office of treasurer and intrusted with funds, it happens that he is required by the State laws to enter into bond with security and to take an oath of office; yet from the beginning of the bill to the end there is no provision for any bond or oath of office, or for any single qualification required under the State law, such as residence, citizenship, or anything else. The only oath is that provided for in the ninth section, by the terms of which everyone detailed or appointed to any civil office in the State is required "to take and to subscribe the oath of office prescribed by law for officers of the United States." Thus an officer of the Army of the United States detailed to fill a civil office in one of these States gives no official bond and takes no official oath for the performance of his new duties, but as a civil officer of the State only takes the same oath which he had already taken as a military officer of the United States. He is, at last, a military officer performing civil duties, and the authority under which he acts is Federal authority only; and the inevitable result is that the Federal Government, by the agency of its own sworn officers, in effect assumes the civil government of the State.

A singular contradiction is apparent here. Congress declares these local State governments to be illegal governments, and then provides that these illegal governments shall be carried on by Federal officers, who are to perform the very duties imposed on its own officers by this illegal State authority. It certainly would be a novel spectacle if Congress should attempt to carry on a *legal* State government by the agency of its own officers. It is yet more strange that Congress attempts to sustain and carry on an *illegal* State government by the same Federal agency.

In this connection I must call attention to the tenth and eleventh sections of the bill, which provide that none of the officers or appointees of these military commanders "shall be bound in his action by any opinion of any civil officer of the United States," and that all the provisions of the act "shall be construed liberally, to the end that all the intents thereof may be fully and perfectly carried out."

It seems Congress supposed that this bill might require construction, and they fix, therefore, the rule to be applied. But where is the construction to come from? Certainly no one can be more in want of instruction than a soldier or an officer of the Army detailed for a civil service, perhaps the most important in a State, with the duties of which he is altogether unfamiliar. This bill says he shall not be bound in his action by the opinion of any civil officer of the United States. The duties of the officer are altogether civil, but when he asks for an opinion he can only ask the opinion of another military officer, who, perhaps, understands as little of his duties as he does himself; and as to his "action," he is answerable to the military authority, and to the military authority alone. Strictly, no opinion of any civil officer other than a judge has a binding force.

But these military appointees would not be bound even by a judicial opinion. They might very well say, even when their action is in conflict with the Supreme Court of the United States, "That court is composed of civil officers of the United States, and we are not bound to conform our action to any opinion of any such authority."

This bill and the acts to which it is supplementary are all founded upon the assumption that these ten communities are not States and that their existing governments are not legal. Throughout the legislation upon this subject they are called "rebel States," and in this particular bill they are denominated "so-called States," and the vice of illegality is declared to pervade all of them. The obligations of consistency bind a legislative body as well as the individuals who compose it. It is now too late to say that these ten political communities are not States of this Union. Declarations to the contrary made in these three acts are contradicted again and again by repeated acts of legislation enacted by Congress from the year 1861 to the year 1867.

During that period, while these States were in actual rebellion, and after that rebellion was brought to a close, they have been again and again recognized as States of the Union. Representation has been apportioned to them as States. They have been divided into judicial districts for the

holding of district and circuit courts of the United States as States of the
Union only can be districted. The last act on this subject was passed July
23, 1866, by which every one of these ten States was arranged into districts and circuits.

They have been called upon by Congress to act through their legislatures upon at least two amendments to the Constitution of the United
States. As States they have ratified one amendment, which required the
vote of twenty-seven States of the thirty-six then composing the Union.
When the requisite twenty-seven votes were given in favor of that amendment—seven of which votes were given by seven of these ten States—it
was proclaimed to be a part of the Constitution of the United States, and
slavery was declared no longer to exist within the United States or any
place subject to their jurisdiction. If these seven States were not legal
States of the Union, it follows as an inevitable consequence that in some
of the States slavery yet exists. It does not exist in these seven States, for
they have abolished it also in their State constitutions; but Kentucky not
having done so, it would still remain in that State. But, in truth, if this
assumption that these States have no legal State government be true,
then the abolition of slavery by these illegal governments binds no one,
for Congress now denies to these States the power to abolish slavery by
denying to them the power to elect a legal State legislature, or to frame a
constitution for any purpose, even for such a purpose as the abolition of
slavery.

As to the other constitutional amendment, having reference to suffrage, it happens that these States have not accepted it. The consequence
is that it has never been proclaimed or understood, even by Congress, to
be a part of the Constitution of the United States. The Senate of the
United States has repeatedly given its sanction to the appointment of
judges, district attorneys, and marshals for every one of these States; yet,
if they are not legal States, not one of these judges is authorized to hold a
court. So, too, both Houses of Congress have passed appropriation bills
to pay all these judges, attorneys, and officers of the United States for
exercising their functions in these States. Again, in the machinery of the
internal-revenue laws all these States are districted, not as "Territories,"
but as "States."

So much for continuous legislative recognition. The instances cited,
however, fall far short of all that might be enumerated. Executive recognition, as is well known, has been frequent and unwavering. The same
may be said as to judicial recognition through the Supreme Court of the
United States. That august tribunal, from first to last, in the administration of its duties *in banc* and upon the circuit, has never failed to recognize
these ten communities as legal States of the Union. The cases depending
in that court upon appeal and writ of error from these States when the
rebellion began have not been dismissed upon any idea of the cessation of
jurisdiction. They were carefully continued from term to term until the

rebellion was entirely subdued and peace reestablished, and then they were called for argument and consideration as if no insurrection had intervened. New cases, occurring since the rebellion, have come from these States before that court by writ of error and appeal, and even by original suit, where only "a State" can bring such a suit. These cases are entertained by that tribunal in the exercise of its acknowledged jurisdiction, which could not attach to them if they had come from any political body other than a State of the Union. Finally, in the allotment of their circuits made by the judges at the December term, 1865, every one of these States is put on the same footing of legality with all the other States of the Union. Virginia and North Carolina, being a part of the fourth circuit, are allotted to the Chief Justice. South Carolina, Georgia, Alabama, Mississippi, and Florida constitute the fifth circuit, and are allotted to the late Mr. Justice Wayne.[2] Louisiana, Arkansas, and Texas are allotted to the sixth judicial circuit, as to which there is a vacancy in the bench.

The Chief Justice, in the exercise of his circuit duties, has recently held a circuit court in the State of North Carolina. If North Carolina is not a State of this Union, the Chief Justice had no authority to hold a court there, and every order, judgment, and decree rendered by him in that court were *coram non judice*[3] and void.

Another ground on which these reconstruction acts are attempted to be sustained is this: That these ten States are conquered territory; that the constitutional relation in which they stood as States toward the Federal Government prior to the rebellion has given place to a new relation; that their territory is a conquered country and their citizens a conquered people, and that in this new relation Congress can govern them by military power.

A title by conquest stands on clear ground; it is a new title acquired by war; it applies only to territory; for goods or movable things regularly captured in war are called "booty," or, if taken by individual soldiers, "plunder."

There is not a foot of the land in any one of these ten State which the United States holds by conquest, save only such land as did not belong to either of these States or to any individual owner. I mean such lands as did belong to the pretended government called the Confederate States. These lands we may claim to hold by conquest. As to all other land or territory, whether belonging to the States or to individuals, the Federal Government has now no more title or right to it than it had before the rebellion. Our own forts, arsenals, navy-yards, custom-houses, and other Federal property situate in those States we now hold, not by the title of conquest, but by our old title, acquired by purchase or condemnation for public use, with compensation to former owners. We have not conquered these places, but have simply "repossessed" them.

If we require more sites for forts, custom-houses, or other public use, we must acquire the title to them by purchase or appropriation in the regular mode. At this moment the United States, in the acquisition of sites for national cemeteries in these States, acquires title in the same way. The Federal courts sit in court-houses owned or leased by the United States, not in the court-houses of the States. The United States pays each of these States for the use of its jails. Finally, the United States levies its direct taxes and its internal revenue upon the property in these States, including the productions of the lands within their territorial limits, not by way of levy and contribution in the character of a conqueror, but in the regular way of taxation, under the same laws which apply to all the other States of the Union.

From first to last, during the rebellion and since, the title of each of these States to the lands and public buildings owned by them has never been disturbed, and not a foot of it has ever been acquired by the United States, even under a title by confiscation, and not a foot of it has ever been taxed under Federal law.

In conclusion I must respectfully ask the attention of Congress to the consideration of one more question arising under this bill. It vests in the military commander, subject only to the approval of the General of the Army of the United States, an unlimited power to remove from office any civil or military officer in each of these ten States, and the further power, subject to the same approval, to detail or appoint any military officer or soldier of the United States to perform the duties of the officer so removed, and to fill all vacancies occurring in those States by death, resignation, or otherwise.

The military appointee thus required to perform the duties of a civil office according to the laws of the State, and, as such, required to take an oath, is for the time being a civil officer. What is his character? Is he a civil officer of the State or a civil officer of the United States? If he is a civil officer of the State, where is the Federal power under our Constitution which authorizes his appointment by any Federal officer? If, however, he is to be considered a civil officer of the United States, as his appointment and oath would seem to indicate, where is the authority for his appointment vested by the Constitution? The power of appointment of all officers of the United States, civil or military, where not provided for in the Constitution, is vested in the President, by and with the advice and consent of the Senate, with this exception, that Congress "may by law vest the appointment of such inferior officers as they think proper in the President alone, in the courts of law, or in the heads of Departments." But this bill, if these are to be considered inferior officers within the meaning of the Constitution, does not provide for their appointment by the President alone, or by the courts of law, or by the heads of Departments, but vests the appointment in one subordinate executive officer, subject to the approval of another subordinate executive officer. So that, if we put this question and fix the character of this military appointee either way, this provision of the bill is equally opposed to the Constitution.

Take the case of a soldier or officer appointed to perform the office of judge in one of these States, and, as such, to administer the proper laws of the State. Where is the authority to be found in the Constitution for vesting in a military or an executive officer strict judicial functions to be exercised under State law? It has been again and again decided by the Supreme Court of the United States that acts of Congress which have attempted to vest *executive* powers in the *judicial* courts or judges of the United States are not warranted by the Constitution. If Congress can not clothe *a judge* with merely *executive* duties, how can they clothe *an officer* or *soldier* of the Army with *judicial* duties over citizens of the United States who are not in the military or naval service? So, too, it has been repeatedly decided that Congress can not require a State officer, executive or judicial, to perform any duty enjoined upon him by a law of the United States. How, then, can Congress confer power upon an executive officer of the United States to perform such duties in a State? If Congress could not vest in a judge of one of these States any judicial authority under the United States by direct enactment, how can it accomplish the same thing indirectly, by removing the State judge and putting an officer of the United States in his place?

To me these considerations are conclusive of the unconstitutionality of this part of the bill now before me, and I earnestly commend their consideration to the deliberate judgment of Congress.

Within a period less than a year the legislation of Congress has attempted to strip the executive department of the government of some of its essential powers. The Constitution and the oath provided in it devolve upon the President the power and duty to see that the laws are faithfully executed. The Constitution, in order to carry out this power, gives him the choice of the agents, and makes them subject to his control and supervision. But in the execution of these laws the constitutional obligation upon the President remains, but the power to exercise that constitutional duty is effectually taken away. The military commander is as to the power of appointment made to take the place of the President, and the General of the Army the place of the Senate; and any attempt on the part of the President to assert his own constitutional power may, under pretense of law, be met by official insubordination. It is to be feared that these military officers, looking to the authority given by these laws rather than to the letter of the Constitution, will recognize no authority but the commander of the district and the General of the Army.

If there were no other objection than this to this proposed legislation, it would be sufficient. Whilst I hold the chief executive authority of the United States, whilst the obligation rests upon me to see that all the laws are faithfully executed, I can never willingly surrender that trust or the powers given for its execution. I can never give my assent to be made responsible for the faithful execution of laws, and at the same time surrender that trust and the powers which accompany it to any other executive officer, high or low, or to any number of executive officers. If this executive trust, vested by the Constitution in the President, is to be taken from him and vested in a subordinate officer, the responsibility will be with Congress in clothing the subordinate with unconstitutional power and with the officer who assumes its exercise.

This interference with the constitutional authority of the executive department is an evil that will inevitably sap the foundations of our federal system; but it is not the worst evil of this legislation. It is a great public wrong to take from the President powers conferred on him alone by the Constitution, but the wrong is more flagrant and more dangerous when the powers so taken from the President are conferred upon subordinate executive officers, and especially upon military officers. Over nearly one-third of the States of the Union military power, regulated by no fixed law, rules supreme. Each one of the five district commanders, though not chosen by the people or responsible to them, exercises at this hour more executive power, military and civil, than the people have ever been willing to confer upon the head of the executive department, though chosen by and responsible to themselves. The remedy must come from the people themselves. They know what it is and how it is to be applied. At the present time they can not, according to the forms of the Constitution, repeal these laws; they can not remove or control this military despotism. The remedy is, nevertheless, in their hands; it is to be found in the ballot, and is a sure one if not controlled by fraud, overawed by arbitrary power, or, from apathy on their part, too long delayed. With abiding confidence in their patriotism, wisdom, and integrity, I am still hopeful of the future, and that in the end the rod of despotism will be broken, the armed heel of power lifted from the necks of the people, and the principles of a violated Constitution preserved.

ANDREW JOHNSON.

Richardson, *Messages*, 6: 530–45.
 1. See Veto of the First Military Reconstruction Act, Mar. 2, 1867.
 2. James M. Wayne.
 3. Before one who is not a proper judge.

From Joseph H. Bradley

Washington   20 July 1867

Sir.

Sometime since I addressed a letter to you in behalf of Stephen J. Cameron,[1] and asking a pardon for him.

I have been called before the Judiciary Committee of the Ho. of Reps. to testify[2] as to the contents of that letter, which to a great degree had passed out of my mind. My impression is very decided that in that letter I spoke of my having applied for a safe conduct for him to the Secretary of

State, & had been unsuccessful, and that I said he was a material witness for the defence in Surrats case & that I asked for his pardon among other reasons, that he might be able to testify fully and freely & without being under any apprehension of trouble for his connection with the rebellion. Yet I am unable to recollect the precise terms or even subject matter of the letter. My testimony is not closed, and I find it absolutely necessary to have that letter to enable me to speak with confidence of the contents. If compelled to answer without it I shall be obliged to say, as I now believe, that it did contain a reference to my application for a safe conduct, & also stated that Cameron was a material witness for Surrat.[3]

Will you do me the favor to let me have the original or a copy by Monday next & greatly oblige me.

I omitted to state that I at first replied to the committee that it did not refer to Cameron as a witness and was not intended to qualify or give credit to him: but subsequent reflection has recalled more fully the contents of the letter, & I am now inclined to think I was wrong in my first statements.[4]

Jos. H. Bradley

ALS, DLC-JP.

1. Bradley wrote to Johnson on May 30 endorsing Cameron's pardon and enclosing a letter from Cameron to Johnson, as Cameron had requested. Joseph H. Bradley to Johnson, May 30, 1867, Johnson Papers, LC. See Stephen F. Cameron to Johnson, May 30, 1867.

2. No published testimony for Bradley has been found nor any taken by the House Judiciary Committee in response to an official House resolution of inquiry. *Congressional Globe*, 40 Cong., 1 Sess., pp. 697–98.

3. Bradley's impression concerning the letter's content was erroneous.

4. As far as the letter of May 30 is concerned, Bradley's first impression was more accurate. While Cameron did testify for the defense in Surratt's trial, Johnson denied any knowledge of a connection between the issuance of a pardon and Cameron's participation in the trial. Cameron testified in late July to the Judiciary Committee that he sought the pardon solely at the suggestion of Confederate friends. It was also known that the pardon was unnecessary for him to testify as other unpardoned men such as Robert E. Lee had previously given testimony. *National Intelligencer*, July 20, 1867; *New York Tribune*, July 17, 24, 1867.

To the House of Representatives

Washington D.C.   July 20th 1867.

I have received a resolution adopted by the House of Representatives on the 8th instant,[1] inquiring whether a publication which appeared in the "National Intelligencer" and other public prints on the 21st day of June last,[2] and which contained a statement of the proceedings of the President and the Cabinet in respect to an interpretation of the acts of Congress commonly known as the Reconstruction Acts, was made by the authority of the President, "or with his knowledge or assent, and whether the full and complete record or minute of all the proceedings, conclusions, and determinations of the President and Cabinet relating to said acts of Congress and their interpretation, is embraced or given in said publication," and also requesting that "a true copy of the full and complete record or minute of such proceedings, conclusions, and determinations in regard to the interpretation of the said reconstruction acts," be furnished to the House.

In compliance with the request of the House of Representatives, I have to state that the publication to which the resolution refers was made by proper authority, and that it comprises the proceedings in Cabinet relating to the Acts of Congress mentioned in the inquiry, upon which, after taking the opinion of the Heads of the several Executive Departments of the Government, I had announced my own conclusions.

Other questions arising from those acts have been under consideration, upon which, however, no final conclusion has been reached. No publication, in reference to them has therefore been authorized by me, but should it at any time be deemed proper and advantageous to the interests of the country to make public those or any other proceedings of the Cabinet, authority for their promulgation will be given by the President.

A correct copy of the record of the proceedings published in the "National Intelligencer" and other newspapers in the 21st ultimo is herewith transmitted, together with a copy of the instructions based upon the conclusions of the President and Cabinet, and sent to the commanders of the several military districts created by the Act of Congress of March 2nd 1867.[3]

Andrew Johnson

LS, DNA-RG233, Fortieth Cong., Originals of Printed House Docs. (40A-G1), No. 34.
   1. *Congressional Globe*, 40 Cong., 1 Sess., p. 515.
   2. *National Intelligencer*, June 21, 1867.
   3. *House Ex. Docs.*, 40 Cong., 1 Sess., No. 34, pp. 2–8 (Ser. 1311).

From S. Snyder Leidy[1]

Philada.   July 20, 1867

Honored Sir.—

I have just concluded the reading of your last veto.[2] Like its predecessors it contains all that may justly be said to check a species of legislation, decided on in Caucus, reported in the high-chambers of the Nation and passed on by the familiar call of an Oath-bound cabal, The "Previous Question."

No debate,—No discussion, No reason—No argument is made—No attempt even at controversion,—but a stolid fixed indifference, amounting to an untamed feeling of contempt for the President of the U.S. the Constitution of the Country—Peace—Commerce—Unity—or aught else, until they shall have established and organized a power more despotic and tyrannical than any other Nation has done. At least we shall so feel it, after the liberty we have so long enjoyed.

Now my dear Mr. President what is next to be done. Your last Veto certainly occasions some alarm. I am not at all disappointed at the condition of things. I fully anticipated that these Oath-bound Conspirators would trench on your rights in a manner that would cause you from a sense of self respect as the Executive of the nation to protect your rights under the Constitution. I am glad of it. I am rejoiced to find that I was in no wise mistaken as to your determined purpose to stand by that great instrument. And I am free to say that I am prepared with many others here to move at a moments notice to protect the Constitution of the Country and its rightful laws.

God bless you.

S Snyder Leidy

ALS, DLC-JP.

1. Leidy (c1814–1875) was at one time the deputy collector at Philadelphia but lost his post in 1867. Subsequently, he was identified as a writer. *Philadelphia Evening Bulletin*, Jan. 13, 1875; *New York Times*, Mar. 5, 1867; Philadelphia directories (1867–74).

2. A reference to the July 19 veto of the Third Military Reconstruction Act.

From James Smith [1]

Private

Washington D.C.   July 20th 1867.

Sir

As various efforts have been made by W. P. Kellogg, and his associates, to deny the charges of corruption made against him, and to injure the characters of his accusers, I desire to say that my position for obtaining a knowledge of his transactions is such as to enable me to affirm that very little has yet been stated.

After the disbandment of my command, in 1864, I settled in New Orleans, and commenced the practice of law; soon after which I was retained by Mr Secretary McCulloch as Counsel for the Treasury Department at New Orleans, and in my official capacity, was brought in frequent contact with Collector Kellogg, as well as with all the principal Civil and Military officials at New Orleans. It was not long before I suspected Mr Kellogg of dishonest practices, but, believing that other prominent officials were implicated with him, and believing that any attempt to expose his rascality, would prove useless, I made no effort to that end.

Politically, Mr Kellogg has no influence, beyond that which his office gives, in the State of Louisiana.

Personally, being insolent and tyrannical to those under him, and obsequious and truculent to those above him, he has very few friends.

He is now continually writing to leading men of the opposition here, assuring them of his sympathys, coöperation and friendship.

Being a lawyer, and Counsel of the Treasury Department, my intercourse with the leading merchants, and other Citizens of New Orleans, enables me to know their wishes and they have long been desirous that W. P. Kellogg should be removed. I heard more complaints from this class of Citizens against him, than against any other public officer in Louisiana. Their grievances have been so incessant, and long continued, that I am satisfied they will never cease while he remains in office; and that the appointment to that office, instead of Kellogg, of General H. N Frisbie would be very acceptable to the mercantile community, as well as to the general public.

I take the liberty of asserting that the majority of the people of Louisiana are conservative in their views, and that, if the political offices were in the hands of your friends, there would be no difficulty in bringing together, at the State convention, the best and ablest men to frame a constitution conformable to the true principles, spirit and traditions of our government; in returning Conservative Senators and Representatives to Congress, in restoring peace and contentment to the people, and thereby putting an end to the fanaticism which it has been attempted to force upon us.

I went to Louisiana in 1862, as Lieutenant-Colonel of the 128th N.Y. Vols., and served in that capacity, and as Colonel of the same regiment, under General Banks.

A large number of the officers and soldiers of that Army settled in Louisiana, and most of them are far more friendly to conservative principles, than you, Mr President, can be aware of. Only give them a neuclus around which to rally and they will immediately come forward and show their strength.

I shall return, in all probability, within a month, and shall be identified with the party represented by yourself and Mr Cutler. Congratulating you, upon the improved condition of public affairs, and trusting that your future success may be equal to your acknowledged merit.

James Smith.

ALS, DLC-JP.
1. Smith (1838–1869) served as captain of the 20th N.Y. State Militia and the 80th N.Y. Inf. before becoming colonel of the 128th N.Y. Inf. He was brevetted brigadier general in 1864. Hunt and Brown, *Brigadier Generals*.

From Jeremiah S. Black

Washington, July 22d, 1867

Mr President:

I enclose you a brief from which you will learn without difficulty the facts of the claim made by Messrs Patterson and Merguendo,[1] of Baltimore, for restitution of the Island of Alta Vela.[2] My only request is, that you read it and then do what, in your judgment, is fit and proper.

The injury these parties complain of was committed more than seven years ago. They demanded the intervention of their own government immediately afterwards. They however consented not to press the subject at the time, lest it might aggravate the troubles of the country. But this was with the distinct understanding that the delay should not be charged upon them, or allowed to affect their rights. Since the war, the Department of State has exhibited so strong an inclination to do nothing, that the sufferers are compelled at last, to think of looking elsewhere for a remedy.

The wrong suffered by these men is so greivous—the illegality of it is so palpable—and the faith of the United States is so solemnly pledged to restore their property, that their *final* success in the pursuit of justice can hardly be doubted. The State Department has given no reason for its inactivity. We can only wonder what it means.

Patterson and Merguendo embarked their all in this enterprise. It was an enterprise not only lawful but laudable. They went into it under a solemn promise of protection. They were shamelessly robbed by men who had no coler of right, and who acted without the show of excuse. They were utterly ruined, and their business totally broken up.

But if the wrongs of two individual Americans were not sufficient to call for redress, the public and general aspect of the case ought to be considered. When a citizen of the United States discovers a guano deposit on an unoccupied island, not within the jurisdiction of any other government, and the discoverer takes the proper steps under the Act of 1856, such island becomes annexed to the Union and part of the country. To expel the American occupant under such circumstances, is like any other invasion of our territory; to submit, is to acknowledge either our inability or our unwillingness to protect our own people. The insult to our flag is as gross as if it had been forcibly hauled down from the mast of an American ship, and the injury as plain as if the ship had been forcibly appropriated by a band of pirates.

You will see, I think, that all the conditions required by law to create the American title have been met in this case. It is a guano island. The deposit was discovered by American mariners; it was wholly unoccupied; it was not within the lawful jurisdiction of any foreign government, being situated out on the high sea; it was open to the first taker; it was, in fact, taken by these claimants. The claimants gave the proper notice at the State Department, and fulfilled whatever else was required by law. They continued with the full sanction of their government, and with the tacit consent of all others, in full possession for seven months and after all this they were forcibly and without even a pretence of lawful authority detruded. This expulsion was an outrage in itself, but the papers show that it was accompanied with circumstances of great aggravation. The agents, workmen and employees of the claimants were carried to the island of St Domingo and kept in prison for twenty one days.

What is now asked, is that you send a vessel to Alta Vela and put Messrs Patterson and Merguendo into possession. This is the short and simple way of dealing with the business. Negotiation will be out of place until the parties are *in statu quo*. Repossession under such circumstances is not only required by public law and in general principle as the first step to be taken, but it is made the duty of the government in this case by an express statute. The Act of 1856 requires the Naval force of the United States to be used to maintain the American citizen in his possession. The right or the duty to repel force directed against a possession always includes the right to retake it after it has been unlawfully seized.

J. S. Black
Counsel for Patterson & Merguendo

ALS, DNA-RG59, Records *re* Guano Islands (M974, Roll 1), Alta Vela.

1. Abraham D. Patterson and Prudencio de Murguiondo were general commission merchants and importers of guano. Patterson (*c*1821–*fl*1893) was later a stock and real estate broker and, for several years, judge of the appeal tax court. Murguiondo (*c*1831–1910) was born in Buenos Aires and later served as consul general from Uruguay. 1860 Census, Md., Baltimore, Baltimore, 18th Ward, 867; Baltimore directories (1859–94); *New York Tribune*, Mar. 17, 1910.

2. Alta Vela, an island some twenty miles southwest of Santo Domingo (the Dominican Republic), was the site of a sizeable guano deposit. Since 1844 Santo Domingo had claimed Alta Vela as a dependency. However, in 1860 the island's ownership came into question, as competing parties from Baltimore laid claim under the U.S. Guano Act of 1856. Patterson and Murguiondo actually occupied Alta Vela from March to October 1860 and were recognized by the State Department in December 1860. But by the latter date the Dominicans had already forced the Americans off the island. Despite repeated pleas to the State Department over the next nine years from Patterson and Murguiondo and later their counsel Jeremiah Black, the U.S. government refused to take any action and Alta Vela remained under Dominican control. Ford Messamore, *Alta Vela: A Forgotten Isle of the Caribbean* (Williamsport, Pa., 1943), passim. See also *Senate Ex. Docs.*, 40 Cong., 2 Sess., No. 38, pp. 1–78 (Ser. 1316).

From Leonard T. Doyal[1]

Griffin, Ga., July 22nd 1867.

I was a member of the Whig party until the beginning of the late war, and was elected a member of the Georgia convention in 1850 as a *union* man. In 1860, I was nominated as one of the Bell & Everett elections & canvassed this state in *opposition to Secession*. When the war commenced, I was chosen captain of a volunteer company, went into the confederate service, and remained in the army eighteen months, during which time I was promoted to the colonalcy of a Regiment & took part in the seven days fight around Richmond; & in october theirafter resigned my commission in the army, & returned home. In 1865, I was elected a member of the convention, & voted to emancipate the slaves. This is briefly my record & yet, I am disfranchised, because I held the office of Judge of the

Inferior court, & clerk of the house of Representatives, & assistant secretary of the senate in 1849–50. Having summed up briefly, the positions I have heretofore occupied, I ask your Excellency to grant me a pardon. I am personally acquainted with Hon H. M. Watterson, & refer you to him. I have not thought proper to procure endorsement from gentlemen residing in this State, believing that Mr Watterson can give you all the desired information. Allow me however in conclusion to remark, that I am uncompromisingly opposed to the Sherman Bill.[2] I can never consent to voluntary enslavement, & if the provisions of that Bill must be fastened upon the people of this state for the benifit of the radicals, I will not be a party to the act. If the questions made in that measure should be adopted voluntarily by the people, the government of the state must, inevitably, pass into the hands of the negros and a few misguided, & untrust worthy white men who before the war, were not recognized as gentlemen. But, I will not discuss the merits of the bill, as you have done that to the entire satisfaction of nearly the *whole white population* of the south; but I hope you will pardon me for adding, that although there are about four newspapers in this state backed by Ex Gov. Brown,[3] & a *few others*, found advocating the adoption of the Sherman bill, yet nine tenths of the *white men* of Georgia, will vote *against* acquiesence. Finally, the people of the south, owe you a debt of gratitude for your devotion to the constitution, & human liberty, which they will never be able to discharge. We feel that you have stood like a tower of strength between us, & the resistless tide of fanaticism that has swept over the Republic, prostrating the hopes of freemen & destroying confidence in the stability and justice of the government. Posterity will do you justice, & the time will come, when the american people will honor the man who labored to save the liberties of the people.

L. T. Doyal

ALS, DNA-RG94, Amnesty Papers (M1003, Roll 18), Ga., L. T. Doyal.

1. Doyal (c1818–fl1871) was a lawyer in Griffin, in addition to the political/judicial and military offices mentioned in his letter. On July 26 Johnson referred the case to the attorney general for review; the outcome is not known. 1860 Census, Ga., Spaulding, 1001st Dist., Griffin, 179; *NUC*; Amnesty Papers (M1003, Roll 18), Ga., L. T. Doyal, RG94, NA.

2. Perhaps a reference to the First Military Reconstruction Act with which Sen. John Sherman was significantly involved. See Castel, *Presidency of Johnson*, 108.

3. Joseph E. Brown.

From Edward D. Holbrook

Washington, D.C.   July 22d 1867.

Since the filing of the papers relative to the official misconduct of Govr. Ballard[1] I have received letters from citizens of Idaho[2] of unquestioned veracity informing me that at the recent Council of the Nez Perces Indians called by himself to tell them what the "Great Father" had to say through his Agent the Supt. in relation to the treaty stipulations, instead of meeting them as he told them he would, and using his influence to appease the known hostile feeling of the Indians, and exerting the power his position afforded to quiet them—he did not go nearer than twelve miles, the place designated by himself and immediately but indignantly and against the earnest protest of the citizens of Idaho left the Territory— leaving a most imprudent address to be read to the Indians after he was out of harms way.[3]

The effect of this misconduct and gross neglect of duty and entire disregard for the interest of all, has resulted as was anticipated and feared. Many of our citizens have been masacred, and depredations occur daily—and instead of any interference from Govr. Ballard to prevent these cruelties he absented himself from the Territory.

The people of Idaho have reason to complain and do complain of Gov Ballard. His known inefficiency—his entire disregard of duty—want of influence or control over the Indians,[4] render him so unfit and his retention in office so improper that I ask in the name of the whole people of Idaho—their interests, growth and prosperity that Gov Ballard be suspended and a suitable man appointed in his place.[5]

E. D. Holbrook

ALS, DNA-RG59, Territorial Papers, Idaho (M445, Roll 1).

1. See Holbrook to Johnson, May 1, 1867.

2. See, for example, Charles F. Parnell to Holbrook, July 8, 1867, Territorial Papers, Idaho (M445, Roll 1), RG59, NA. Holbrook also sent excerpts of other letters in Holbrook to Johnson, Aug. 14, 1867, ibid.

3. Ballard had arranged for a council with the Nez Percé on June 19. Naturally, having no funds for treaty payments, Ballard could hardly have had a very successful meeting. Wells, "David W. Ballard," *OHQ*, 54 (1953): 18–19.

4. Holbrook and his supporters continued to ignore the fact that Ballard did actually achieve some positive things in Indian affairs. On June 14, 1867, for example, he arranged the establishment of Indian reservations at Fort Hall and Coeur d'Alene. Also, in August he successfully mediated a problem with a group of Bannock Indians. Ibid., 18.

5. Johnson made several unsuccessful attempts to remove Ballard, but the latter remained at his post until his term expired in 1870. Ibid., 19–25.

From James P. Boyce [1]

Private Business

Greenville S.C   July 23d 1867

Honoured and Dear Sir

I beg to call your attention to this circular and the printed one which accompanies it.[2] I have sent this one to you and not the one I am sending to our Southern people not because we do not regard you as one of the South but because our Southern circular appeals for aid to support professors and this for aid in supporting students. We are anxious to elevate the ministry by thorough education—and also to give such an impetus to religion and morality as shall bless our country. I have thought that you would feel especial interest in advancing the intelligence of our ministry. We are working at great disadvantages with unpaid salaries only hoping to do this work. One of our professors last year was offered a salary of six thousand dollars to leave us & take the Presidency of a college. He received here only one thousand & remains. The others have had some more brilliant and others equally or nearly as brilliant offers. I mention this to show that we are anxious to do this work at sacrifices. The institution was established by Baptists for their own ministry, but others are admitted without charge. We will have an Episcopal student next session.

You may chance to remember me as one of Gov Perry's[3] especial friends and political associates to whom you granted a pardon[4] at his request that I might be a member of the Convention of 1866. I have been strongly urged to leave my post and run for Congress from this District but my heart is in this work and nothing can make me leave it unless absolutely necessary for the country and no one else could be obtained which I do not think will be the case.

                                                        James P. Boyce.

ALS, DLC-JP.
    1. Boyce (1827–1888), a Baptist minister, was instrumental in the establishment of the Southern Baptist Seminary in 1859 at Greenville. After service as a chaplain during the Civil War, he returned to promote the work and progress of the seminary which ultimately moved to Louisville, Kentucky. Boyce served as president of the Southern Baptist Convention for several years. *DAB*.
    2. Enclosed were two documents: one was a handwritten appeal for financial support of Boyce's seminary; the other was a printed outline of the course of instruction offered by the professors at the seminary.
    3. Provisional governor Benjamin F. Perry.
    4. According to Boyce's amnesty files, the President pardoned him on July 24, 1865, partly in response to Boyce's letter of July 21. Amnesty Papers (M1003, Roll 44), S.C., James P. Boyce, RG94, NA.

From Joseph R. Flanigen

                                                Philadelphia, July 23d 1867
My dr Mr President
    At the meeting of the "National Union State Committee" held to day,[1] a Sub Committee consisting of seven members, was appointed to proceed to Washington and confer and consult with you in reference to the political situation of affairs.

    At the meeting to day the subject of the Presidency was an important element of discussion, and I may say to you, that it is in reference to that subject that a consultation with you was esteemed desireable, but the committee will not visit Washington *except by appointment*.

Will you be good enough to name a day and hour when it will be con-
veniant for you to see the sub committee? Tuesday next was named, but it
probably did not occur to the members, as it does to me now, that your
cabinet usualy meets on that day.[2] Have the kindness to let me hear from
you on the subject at your earliest convenience so that I may communicate with the members, several of whom reside in the interior.

J. R. Flanigen   Chmn.

ALS, DLC-JP.

   1. In addition to establishing a special subcommittee, the meeting adopted resolutions
lauding the President's work and policy and calling upon citizens of various counties to
choose representatives to a convention to put forth candidates to carry out views of the National Union State Committee. See a handwritten copy of the resolutions attached to
Flanigen to Johnson, July 24, 1867, Johnson Papers, LC. An account of the meeting and a
copy of the resolutions are found in the *Philadelphia Daily News*, July 24, 1867.

   2. Evidently a group of Pennsylvania citizens, including Flanigen, did meet with the
President on Wednesday, July 31. See Beale, *Welles Diary*, 3: 147.

From Edwin M. Stanton

War Department, Washington City, July 24th 1867.

Sir,

   I have the honor to acknowledge the receipt of your reference to the
claim of *Reece Hughes* [1] of Jefferson, Texas, with the following endorsement thereon—

   "Referred to the Honbl. the Secy. of War. This case is represented to
me as one of great hardship and oppression to the claimant. It is therefore
hoped that it will be taken up, in order that any relief may be afforded that
may arise from its early consideration."

July 22 1867   (Signed) Andrew Johnson

   In reply, I would respectfully represent, that this case has no merit beyond that of a very large class of other claimants, and it will be investigated and decided with all possible dispatch. But the faith of the Dept.
and of the Government, as well as equal and exact justice, requires that
cases should be heard and decided in their order as presented, and to direct the disposition of this case out of its order and before its turn, would
not only be unjust to other claimants, but would seriously disturb and
prejudice the proper administration of business in this Department.[2]

Edwin M. Stanton,   Secy. of War.

LBcopy, DNA-RG107, Lets. Sent, Mil. Bks., Executive, 58-C.

   1. Hughes (b. *c*1812), a native of Tennessee, moved to Texas about 1838 where he ac-
cumulated a large estate with holdings valued at more than $230,000 in 1860. During the
Civil War he refused to assist the Confederacy beyond paying the taxes he was forced to pay,
for which he was "bitterly denounced and his life and property continually endangered."
He was pardoned on December 8, 1865. 1860 Census, Tex., Cass, Beat No. 2, Hickory
Hill, 45; Amnesty Papers (M1003, Roll 53), Tex., Reece Hughes, RG94, NA.

2. Reece Hughes was not found in any of the court of claims lists of claims settled or dropped. The specifics of his claim have not been determined.

From Joseph H. Geiger

Private

Columbus O   July 25, 1867

Dr. Sir

Allow me to thank you for your last veto message. All the conservative men here consider it conclusive. I have had a *confidential* talk to Gov Cox[1] and he regards it as unanswerable and considers the conduct of Congress indefensible. If the *Democrats* (as they call themselves) had nominated anything but a mean Copper head ticket, Ohio would have been carried this fall, but with nearly all the Candidates opponents of the War it is lost.[2] Negro suffrage will be beaten to death in Ohio.[3] In my judgment the Legislature is not certain for the Republicans on the issues presented.

Jos. H. Geiger

ALS, DLC-JP.
1. Jacob D. Cox.
2. In the October 1867 elections in Ohio the Democrats gained control of both houses of the state legislature and came within 2,983 votes of capturing the governorship as well. Robert D. Sawrey, *Dubious Victory: The Reconstruction Debate in Ohio* (Lexington, 1992), 115.
3. An amendment to the state constitution had been proposed to allow for black suffrage. In the elections in October the amendment was defeated by some 50,000 votes. Ibid.; *American Annual Cyclopaedia* (1867), 605.

From John P. Holtsinger

Greenville Tenn.   July 25, 1867

Dear Sir,

After my regard, and best wishes, for your success, and prosperity, boath political and personal I will just say, that if it is consisent with your views, and executive orders To sation for the time a company of Federal Soldiers, at the town of Rogersville. There is a portion of our citizens, that have become so exasperated at Gov. Brownlows course, that they are liable at any moment to commit violence. *The Radicals* insult conserative men upon every occasion. And encourage the negroes to do so. As was the case last Tuesday. When a bloody affray took place.[1] A Negro fired the first shot so some of our citizens, who were present state. But the fire was returned by the Conservative Boys. I am very anxious for our people to live in peace with each other. But the pesence of Brownlows militia tends more to disorder, than otherwise. The above is submited to your consideration.[2]

John P. Holtsinger

ALS, DLC-JP.

1. For an account of the Rogersville disturbance of July 23, see the *Nashville Republican Banner*, July 27, 1867.

2. The exchange of dispatches between the War Department, General Thomas, and Governor Brownlow relative to the sending of federal troops and ammunition to Tennessee in advance of election day, may be conveniently followed in Simon, *Grant Papers*, 17: 236–38. General Grant informed Secretary Stanton that he had received Thomas's dispatches and that he had therefore requested Thomas to send all troops from Kentucky that he could spare "to such parts of Tennessee as in his judgement most require their presence to preserve peace during the election." Grant to Stanton, July 26, 1867, Johnson Papers, LC. Thomas was reluctant to remove many of his troops from Kentucky to Tennessee; he indicated to Grant: "I believe we shall be able to prevent riots in Memphis and Nashville and the other larger towns in Tennessee." Simon, *Grant Papers*, 17: 238.

From Lovell H. Rousseau

New Orleans La.   July 25/67.

My dear Mr President.

I got your dispatch of the 22d on yesterday, and answered it.[1] But such is the *espionage* here, that I feared to say what I felt you ought to know.

I cannot give you an adequate idea of the feeling here towards Genl. Sheridan. It is very intensely bitter, and I believe *almost universal.* All classes, and every body so far as I can learn, would heartily *rejoice* at his removal. The expectation has been very general, that he would be removed for what was considered the most insolent & uncalled for insubordination; it is firmly believed & *not doubted* here, that all he has done & desired to do, was in view of the Presidency, & hence all is attributed to selfish motives. It is certain his staff bend all their energies to this end, and openly too. One of them named Foresythe (called Toney Foresythe)[2] at the 4th of July dinner here, refused to allow Mr Blanchard[3] to offer as a sentiment "Andrew Johnson, President, &c." Blanchard insisted, and was told he must either refrain or leave. He *left* in disgust. But this feeling, which of course it has been tried to impart to every body, is not by any means universal among *Republicans*, very few favor it. It is certain the more sensible are becoming alarmed at the prospect. Alarmed to see their laws & liberties quietly passing into the hands of ignorant negroes & a few of the worst class of white man. I am glad to see the Army officers of this section, taking the same correct view of the matter, after seeing, and being with the negroes. I saw a major Parry[4] from Baton Rouge, yesterday, who said it never would or could be submitted to, when people came to understand it—that is, universal suffrage. He expressed great surprise at the abject ignorance of the negroes here. He is a northern man.

I have talked freely with Genl. Steedman, & to no one else, about coming here.[5] All others look upon my destination to Oregon as fixed. I took pains to make this impression through the newspaper and other wise, (to save you & my self too) any embarrassment in the premises. Steedman . . .[6]

L (incomplete), DLC-JP.

1. Johnson informed Rousseau that he had received Rousseau's two dispatches and asked about conditions in Louisiana. Rousseau replied, "Matters here gloomy. People generally greatly depressed. Any change that may be made will be received with universal satisfaction." Johnson to Rousseau, July 22, 1867, Tels. Sent, President, Vol. 3 (1865–68), RG107, NA; Rousseau to Johnson, July 24, 1867, Johnson Papers, LC.

2. One of two unrelated Forsythes on Sheridan's staff, James W. Forsyth (c1834–1906) graduated from West Point in 1856. After prewar service in the Washington Territory, Forsyth served in a number of staff positions, especially as chief of staff for Sheridan in 1864–65, and earned five brevets of various grades. He apparently remained on Sheridan's staff until 1878. In December 1890 he was the commanding officer at the battle of Wounded Knee, and retired from the service in 1897 with the rank of major general. *Providence Journal* (Rhode Island), Oct. 28, 1867; Warner, *Blue*; Heitman, *Register*, 1: 430; Utley, *Frontier Regulars*, 406–8; *West Point Register*, 250.

3. Perhaps Albert G. Blanchard (1810–1891), 1829 graduate of West Point who served in the army until 1840, taught school in New Orleans, fought in the Mexican War, and became a civil engineer. A Confederate brigadier general during the Civil War, Blanchard returned to engineering and surveying after the conflict. Conrad, *La. Biography*.

4. Capt. and Bvt. Maj. Edward R. Parry (c1833–1874) of Minnesota was appointed to the 11th U.S. Inf. on May 14, 1861, and served with those troops as first lieutenant and captain until transferred to the 20th Inf. in September 1866. He was discharged at his own request on August 1, 1870. Powell, *Army List*, 520; ACP Branch, File P-174-CB-1870, Edward R. Parry, RG94, NA; Pension Files, Frances D. Parry, RG15, NA.

5. James B. Steedman. Rousseau had been sent to Louisiana by Johnson to watch Sheridan but this purpose was not publicly announced. Roy Morris, Jr., *Sheridan: The Life and Wars of General Phil Sheridan* (New York, 1992), 292.

6. The rest of the letter is missing.

From Charles A. Dunham

Copy

Washington, July 26, 1867.

The petition of Charles A. Dunham respectfully shows that in the month of January last he was tried, convicted, and sentenced to the Penitentiary,[1] for perjury alleged to have been committed before the Judiciary Committee of the House of Representatives, during the investigation of said committee of charges against Jefferson Davis of complicity, in the conspiracy to assassinate President Lincoln.

That the perjury assigned in the indictment against your Petitioner was in having falsely testified that he had no reason to doubt, and did not doubt, the truthfulness of certain depositions made by two persons, called Campbell and Snevel,[2] at the time said depositions were given by them in the Bureau of Military Justice, and in testifying that he had first seen said Campbell in Canada in June 1865, and said Snevel in Wilmington, N.C. in August 1865.

That on the trial of your petitioner said Campbell and Snevel declared that their real names were Hoare and Roberts,[3] and that the depositions they had made and sworn to in the Bureau of Military were absolutely false from beginning to end, and were known to be so by your petitioner; and that they were not at—said Campbell in Canada in June 1865 or said Snevel in Wilmington in August 1865—the places at which your Petitioner claimed to have first seen them.[4]

That it was entirely upon this testimony, of said self-confessed perjurers, that your Petitioner was convicted; and that without the said testimony of said persons the Jury before whom your petitioner was tried could not possibly have found a verdict of "guilty."

Your Petitioner further says that he was tried and convicted by a jury not qualified to try him. That the jurors before whom he was so tried and condemned were illegally selected and drawn, as decided by the Court in the case of John H. Surratt—the manner and form of selecting and drawing the jurors in the case of Surratt and your Petitioner being identical. That in the discussion on the opening of the trial of Surratt as to the legal qualification of the jurors who had been summoned and empannelled to try him, it was contended by the prosecution, and decided by the Court, that said jurors were informally and irregularly selected and drawn, and that any verdict they might render upon any trial would be absolutely void.[5]

Your Petitioner further says that under the rules and practice of the Supreme Court of this District, the above informality in the selection and drawing of a jury, does not, *after sentence under a verdict found by such a jury*, constitute a ground for a new trial, or other relief by the Court; and that the only remedy for such an illegal conviction lies in an application to the Executive for pardon.[6]

(Signed)   Chas. A. Dunham

Copy, DLC-JP.

1. Dunham (Sanford Conover) actually remained in jail in Washington, D.C., from his arrest in the fall of 1866 until July 30, 1867, when he was incarcerated in the penitentiary at Albany, New York. Hanchett, *Lincoln Murder Conspiracies*, 81; Amos Pilsbury to Johnson, Nov. 4, 1868, Pardon Case File B-576, Charles A. Dunham, RG204, NA; Dunham to Johnson, July 29, 1867, Johnson Papers, LC.

2. William Campbell and Joseph Snevel.

3. Joseph A. Hoare (Campbell), a native of New York, was a "gas-fixer," while William H. Roberts (Snevel) was a former railroad ticket agent and tavern keeper. Neither had ever been to the South. Hoare first confessed to the perjury and implicated Dunham. *OR*, Ser. 2, Vol. 8: 921–23.

4. Although Hoare and Roberts were the only ones who confessed, Dunham had actually recruited eight persons using assumed names, including his wife, to testify to the complicity of Jefferson Davis in the Lincoln assassination. Dunham admitted his actions. Ibid., 921–23, 973–74.

5. Apparently the jurors originally assigned to the Surratt case had been chosen without regard to the specific case on which they would serve. The prosecutors felt that they should be drawn for the particular case. After Judge George P. Fisher dismissed the first jury, it was more difficult to select the second because many prospects were challenged or else disqualified themselves, having already formed an opinion about the case. Turner, *Beware the People Weeping*, 229–30.

6. In addition to applying to Johnson, Dunham seems to have attempted to procure his pardon by revealing documents which alleged that Congressman Ashley and his allies had tried to use him to provide perjured documents demonstrating Johnson's involvement in the Lincoln assassination conspiracy in order to help bring about the President's impeachment. In return for Dunham's services, Ashley was supposed to help him get his pardon.

This revelation resulted in much discussion in cabinet meetings over the following several weeks. It did not, however, result in a pardon for Dunham at this time. Johnson finally granted the desired pardon on February 11, 1869. Dunham to Johnson, July 29, 1867, Johnson Papers, LC; Randall, *Browning Diary*, 2: 152–54, 156–57; Beale, *Welles Diary*, 3: 144–46, 149, 152, 157, 161, 165, 168; Sanford Conover Pardon, Feb. 11, 1869, Pardons and Remissions, Vol. 9 (T967, Roll 4), RG59, NA.

From Frank Clark[1]

Steilacoom Wash. Tery.   July 27th 1867

My Dear Sir:

It is with some reluctance that I intrude this note upon your notice, knowing as I do, that your time is fully occupied with important National affairs.

I hope however, that you will find time to consider the following:—

I made the race for Congress at the late June Election for the Democratic Party in this Territory upon a strong administration Platform agt. Alvan Flanders,[2] Radical candidate who was elected according to the election returns by 96 majority upon a platform that denounced the administration and supported Congress. The present office holders made the platform for him and to them he is indebted for his election.

Was Congress governed more by facts than partisan considerations I would contest his seat, and undoubtedly would be successful in the contest. Notwithstanding Flanders gets the Secretary's[3] Certificate, I have but little doubt of being able to prove that I was elected by 100 to 200 majority of the legal votes cast at the late election.

The present Government officials contributed largely from their Salaries to a fund that was used to defray the expenses of 300 to 400 from Oregon, Idaho and British Columbia to our Territory to carry our election for us.

These Government Officials have the promise of Flanders I am told, to have them continued in their respective positions. Now I do not want these men thus rewarded for their reprehensible conduct. Washington Territory is Administration by a handsome majority if she is left to do her voting without improper influences being brought to bear. I have respectfully to request in behalf of that party that no Radical Resident be appointed, nor any present incumbent be reappointed to any official position in the Territory.[4]

If this request be complied with there is no doubt of our ability to route the enemy in the next election Foot, Horse and Dragoon.

Wishing you health, strength and life to realize and receive the public gratitude that is due, and that some day will be accorded to you for your Patriotic efforts to save the country and preserve to the people their constitutional rights and liberties.

Frank Clark

ALS, DLC-JP.

1. Clark (1834–1883), a lawyer, settled in the Washington Territory in 1852 and served in the territorial legislature. Bancroft, *Washington, Idaho, and Montana*, 266.

2. Flanders (1825–1884) moved to California in 1851 where he was involved in a lumber business and a newspaper ownership. He was also a member of the state legislature and an officer of the San Francisco branch mint before he moved to the Washington Territory in 1863. There he was postmaster of Wallula, territorial delegate to the U.S. House (1867–69), and finally territorial governor (1869–70), after which he returned to San Francisco. *BDUSC*.

3. The new secretary, Ezra L. Smith (1837–*fl*1889), who had been active in Illinois Republican politics, moved to California in 1861 where he served in the state legislature. Nominated and commissioned in April 1867, he arrived in the territory on June 27 and also assumed the duties of acting governor. He remained secretary until the spring of 1869, after which he settled in the Hood River area and engaged in a mercantile business and ranching. He also served in the state legislature. Bancroft, *Washington, Idaho, and Montana*, 266–67; Pomeroy, *The Territories*, 120; *History of the Pacific Northwest: Oregon and Washington* (2 vols., Portland, 1889), 2: 565–66; 1860 Census, Ill., Knox, Galesburg, 983.

4. The posts of territorial governor and secretary had undergone upheaval in the spring of 1867 and had been filled in April. There is no indication that other territorial officials, such as judges, were experiencing a similar turnover. Ser. 6B, Vol. 4: 389, Johnson Papers, LC; Pomeroy, *The Territories*, 119–22.

From Richard S.F. Peete[1]

Warren Plains P.O.   Warren Co. N.C.

July 29th 1867

Dear Sir

If it were possible & practicable, I, with many whom I represent, would be very glad to know your views of the best plan for us to adopt, under existing circumstances, touching the calling of a Convention in this State. If the policy of reconstruction instituted by yourself could have been carried on to completion, not a southern man would have hesitated how to vote. One qualification should be made in this statement—there are a few poloticians who opposed your views but all plain farmers like ourselves saw the reasonableness & justice, especially to us (Southerners) of your policy. But your good efforts in behalf of the whole U.S. & of the South, have not been concurred in by Congress. The Military Bill wh. you vetoed,[2] not only passed, but suppliments have been made in the Extra Session of Congress,[3] to this bill (which the South was ready to ratify by its call for State Conventions) and the new features of Suppliment 2nd and the enlargement of the powers of the District Commanders, exercised without control or power of removal by yourself, have made us hesitate whether we are not better off under military rule than we will be under a Constitution adopted by such members as must necessarily compose the Convention in N.C. The great question is, does Prest. Johnson consider the reconstruction of the South so shorn of its valuable features by bad legislation, as to require loyal men to oppose it? or does Prest. Johnson advise that we heartily cooperate in reconstruction as mapped out by Congress?

You are seldom addressed by a plain farmer and in thoughts of so little merit. This may never come to your eye, and even if it do, you may not have time to reply or think it prudent to write under such circumstances. I am not asking these questions for publicity, but for our own quiet of mind & regard to duty.

Permit me in conclusion to send you the regards of my special friend Mrs. Thomas Carroll,[4] with whom you met at Ridgeway Depot.

R.S.F. Peete

ALS, DLC-JP.

1. A physician, Peete (c1829–fl1890) had served during the war as surgeon of the 12th N.C. Inf. 1870 Census, N.C., Warren, Warren Plains, 13; Manly Wade Wellman, *The County of Warren, North Carolina, 1586–1917* (Chapel Hill, 1959), 141, 195.

2. A reference to the First Military Reconstruction Act which Johnson vetoed on March 2.

3. A reference to the Second and Third Military Reconstruction acts which Johnson vetoed on March 23 and July 19, respectively.

4. Mary Carroll (b. c1825), the wife of Thomas Carroll, a farmer, was a native of Virginia. They had several children. 1860 Census, N.C., Warren, Ridgway, 85; (1870), Nutbush Twp., Morrison, 47.

From A. Toomer Porter

Charleston   July 29 1867

Your Excellency—

I deem it due to you to let you see that we have been diligent in prosecuting the work for which you donated $1000.[1] Doubtless you will not have time to read the paper, but I feel it a mark of respect which I wish to pay in sending it. We have now one thousand children under our charge & more clamorous to enter. If they were only let alone—this Country would harmonize & soon restore peace & prosperity—but the perplexity which gathers round your devoted head, permeates this whole land & enters into every house hold of a miserable people. God defend & sustain you Sir. When passion has subsided & the party of the hour is dead, your name will be held up to unborn generations for admiration & your principles for imitation.

It is but little we can do to cheer or sustain you, but blessings are invoked upon you from many hearts that have almost ceased to hope.

A Toomer Porter

ALS, DLC-JP.

1. Johnson had subscribed that amount to help purchase the Charleston, South Carolina, Marine Hospital for use as a freedmen's school. See Porter to Johnson, July 28, 1866, *Johnson Papers*, 10: 745; and William E. Chandler to Johnson, Oct. 31, 1866, ibid., 11: 408–9.

From William H. Seward

Auburn N Y   July 29th, 1867

Have sent to Mr Hunter[1] directions concerning such business as has reached me here. We are renewing our health and strength and if not wanted at Washington will remain a few days longer.

If wanted please telegraph, and we come immediately.[2]

Wm. H Seward

Tel, DLC-JP.

1. William Hunter, second assistant secretary of state.

2. Johnson responded immediately indicating his gratification to learn that Seward's health "is improving." He assured the secretary that he would telegraph if Seward was needed in Washington. Johnson to Seward, July 29, 1867, Tels. Sent, President, Vol. 3 (1865–68), RG107, NA.

From Edward G.W. Butler[1]

Dunboyne, La., near Bayou Goula P. office,
July 30, 1867.

My dear Sir:

I have read your Veto Message, of the amended Reconstruction Bill,[2] with a feeling of both interest and gratitude; and, as one of the disfranchised and disinherited subjects of the Military Satrap of the 5th District,[3] I return you many and sincere thanks for your noble and manly efforts in defence of the Constitution, and of the rights of states and of individuals.

You are right, my dear Sir, in the declaration that it is impossible to conceive any state of society more intolerable than this; and the attempt to degrade the Executive, by transferring his duties to subordinate military Commanders, must open the eyes of the people to the intolerable usurpations of a factious and fanatical Congress, or the government of our Fathers is dissolved, and those who would be free must seek protection in other climes, and under other Governments.

I inclose to you a tabular Statement of the voters registered in this State, with Editorial remarks of the *Times*;[4] from which you will perceive that the negroes (thro' the management and manipulations of the Registrars and Military authorities) are greatly in the ascendant, and that Radical emisaries, thro' the *free negro* element, will manifestly, control the votes of the former and have entire control of our State Government.

In view of this state of affairs; of the impoverished condition of our people; and of the refusal of Congress to afford us any assistance or aid in reclaiming and protecting our inundated country;[5] you cannot be surprised to learn that many of our people have given themselves up to despondency, and appear indifferent to consequences.

Your suggestion, of the probable consequences of the abolishment of our State Governments, seems to have ignited the Radical magazine; and Mr. Reverdy Johnson's characteristic attempt to relieve them therefrom reminds me of the refrain in the childrens' Book:

> "There was a man of Islington,
> And he was wondrous wise,
> He jumped into a quickset hedge,
> And scratched out both his eyes;
> But, when he saw his eyes were out,
> It gave him wondrous pain;
> So, he jumped into another hedge,
> And scratched them in again."[6]

The concluding passages of your message remind me forcibly of my venerated, lamented and glorious old friend of the "Hermitage";[7] and I feel assured that "the sober, second thoughts of the people" will bring them to your support; as in his case, when a factious and unprincipled Congressional majority were compelled to erase from their records the stigma which they had dared to record against the reputation of as brave a soldier and pure a patriot as ever went down the tide of time.[8]

With an abiding sense of gratitude for your manly defence of the Constitution; the rights of the states; and of the rights and liberties of a proud, chivalrous and independent people; and, with constant good wishes for your success, welfare and happiness . . .

E.G.W. Butler

ALS, DLC-JP.

1. West Point graduate Butler (1800–1888) resigned from the army in 1831 and settled on a plantation in Iberville Parish, Louisiana, until he left to fight in the Mexican War. Afterwards he resumed plantation life in Louisiana before moving to Mississippi in 1868. Conrad, *La. Biography*.

2. Johnson vetoed the Third Military Reconstruction Act on July 19.

3. Philip H. Sheridan.

4. Not found.

5. For previous discussions of flood problems and levee disrepair, see J. Madison Wells to Johnson, May 26, 1866, *Johnson Papers*, 10: 540–41. See also E. H. Angamar to Johnson, July 3, 1867.

6. Not identified.

7. Butler's father died when he was six, and he became the ward of Andrew Jackson. Conrad, *La. Biography*.

8. In 1834 the Senate passed a resolution proposed by Henry Clay censuring Jackson for his actions in removing federal deposits from the national bank. Led by Thomas Hart Benton, the Senate expunged the censure in January 1837. Robert V. Remini, *Andrew Jackson* (3 vols., New York, 1977–84), 3: 148–51, 376–81.

From Thomas W. Conway

742 Broadway　New York　July 30th. 1867

Sir:

I beg leave most respectfully to say that Louisiana is now in nearly as good and orderly a condition as New York or Massachusetts and that the removal of Gen'l. Sheridan (which is reported as about to take place) will be the greatest of all misfortunes to that state at this time. Let the General alone—he is doing well. Add not another to the long list of misfortunes which the country has had to suffer by your will.

Thomas W Conway

LS, DNA-RG94, Lets. Recd. (Main Ser.), File C-1125-1867 (M619, Roll 546).

From R. King Cutler

"Private"

Washington D.C.　July 30th 1867.

Respected Sir.

This is the ninth explanatory letter I have written to you, since February last.[1]

Recently, in the brief interviews, I have had with you, and in fact considering my nature, I did not, and could not so readily explain to you, verbally, as I can, and have in writing.

I almost tremble at the idea of again explaining what I deem facts of importance to you, for the reason among others, that you are too remote from my State, to immediately appreciate the will of even your friends in that State.

In the State of Louisiana, I have for twenty three years, last past, had the good fortune of always being successful politically; and, according to the written expressed wishes of a majority of the actual voters of that State, I must immediately return to them. I *will* mould that State to your will and wishes, provided, you will give me the necessary encouragement. Yea, only that encouragement, I have heretofore indicated.

I am fully aware of the men who surround you, and I know their power. Men of Louisiana, some who stand high in society there, such as the Hon. Charles M. Conrad, and perhaps W.H.C. King, are men whom I know, and men who cannot under the most favorable circumstances, control fifty votes each in the State of Louisiana.

In all my struggles for position and power in that State, those men particularly W.H.C. King, have been my most bitter opponents, and yet I have had no difficulty in beating their efforts with overwhelming and rejoicing majorities.

I know the good things that the Hon C. M Conrad, and W.H.C. King, have done in your behalf, but the passage of the Reconstruction bills by Congress, presents a new issue, and by the Heavens, I hold the power among the men, and shall wield it.

It is all at your command. It has been and is, at your will. I have been and am sincere.

Your order, which may be issued, relieving Genl. Sheridan, a man whom all men know to be an enemy to you, and the placing in his stead, a man of honor, integrity and conservative principles, will not only be a God-send to the good people of Louisiana and Texas, but to all honest men of this Republic.

But Mr. President, to be plain, with sincerity, Louisiana, the great rebel state, and Texas, cannot and will not vote a Conservative majority, without further removals or suspensions,—to wit: Collector of the Port, Mayor Heath, Governor Flanders.[2]

In New Orleans, the majority of the negro population have registered in the four districts, eight times. Some of them have registered for every voting precinct, say twenty three times. With such conduct, the angels of God himself could not succeed: hence, where Justice prevails, it is entirely destitute of such enormities and acts of injustice.

I desired to call your attention to this enormity, yesterday, but you did not have time to hear me. Mr. President, the remedy is plain, perfect and conclusive.

My figures, in a letter to you recently, in regard to the numbers of voters is correct.[3]

The remedy therefore, in my judgment is this. Stop this unjust registration, by relieving Sheridan,—then, suspend his aiders and abettors, Kellogg, Flanders, Mayor Heath and Marshal Herron.[4] This done, the State of Louisiana will give 20,000, majority for the Conservative ticket; and it will be like lightening, combined with all the forces of electricity to the other rebel States, as well as having a corresponding effect upon the other States of this Union.

Mr. President, this is my last letter to you, prior to my departure for Louisiana.[5]

I hope you have read all my letters to Secretary McCulloch.

Justice should be done but will not be done until the men above referred to, particularly Sheridan and Kellogg are removed from office.

Mr. President, I again beg pardon for this intrusion. My anxiety and earnestness, is again my apology.

R. King Cutler

As this is Cabinet day I have concluded not to call upon you to day, knowing that you must be tired, but will call upon you to-morrow morning at about 10. A.M.

R. King Cutler

ALS, DLC-JP.

1. Four of Cutler's previous letters to Johnson, dated June 20, July 6, July 15, and July 19, are printed in this volume. A note of July 10 and letters of July 22 and July 26 can be found in Johnson Papers, LC. One letter seems to be missing.

2. William P. Kellogg, Edward Heath, and Benjamin F. Flanders.

3. No Cutler letter pertaining to voting figures has been found.

4. Francis J. Herron.

5. Cutler's next letter to Johnson, August 5, 1867, was again written from Washington.

From Hugh McCulloch

Treasury Department. July 30, 1867

Sir:

I notice in some Pennsylvania paper a statement that the Secretary and Commissioner testified before the Judiciary Committee[1] that appointments of revenue officers had been made against their remonstrances. As far as I myself am concerned, it is hardly necessary for me to say that the statement is without the slightest foundation.

In justice to the Commissioner, I deem it my duty to inform you, that I was present when the larger portion of his testimony was given in, and that the statement is equally untrue as far as he is concerned.

H McCulloch

ALS, DLC-JP.

1. Commissioner of Internal Revenue Edward A. Rollins gave testimony before the congressional committee on July 20. See *House Reports*, 40 Cong., 1 Sess., No. 7, "Impeachment Investigation," pt. 2, pp. 878–84 (Ser. 1314).

To Lovell H. Rousseau

Washington, D.C.   July 31 1867

Your despatch this date received.[1] Do not leave until you receive a despatch from me after this one.[2]

Andrew Johnson

Tel, DNA-RG107, Tels. Sent, President, Vol. 3 (1865–68).

1. The President was obviously responding to Rousseau's telegram of the same date which indicated that the State Department had summoned the general from New Orleans to Washington. Rousseau asked Johnson for advice. Rousseau to Johnson, July 31, 1867, Tels. Recd., President, Vol. 6 (1867–68), RG107, NA.

2. Johnson notified Rousseau that Seward and the Russian commissioner would be in Washington on the next Tuesday, August 6, and asked the general to arrive in town to confer with them. Rousseau responded that he would leave New Orleans immediately for Washington. Johnson to Rousseau, Aug. 1, 1867, Tels. Sent, President, Vol. 3 (1865–68), RG107, NA; Rousseau to Johnson, Aug. 3, 1867, Tels. Recd., President, Vol. 6 (1867–68), RG107, NA. For further developments, see Johnson to Rousseau, Aug. 7, 1867.

August 1867

From Ulysses S. Grant

Private

Head Quarters Armies of the United States,
Washington, D.C.   Aug. 1st 1867.

Sir;

I take the liberty of addressing you privately on the subject of the conversation we had this morning[1] feeling as I do the great danger to the welfare of the country should you carry out the designs then expressed.

First: on the subject of the displacement of the Sec. of War. His removal can not be effected against his will without the consent of the Senate. It is but a short time since the United States Senate was in session and why not then have asked for his removal if it was desired? It certainly was the intention of the Legislative branch of the Govt. to place Cabinet Ministers beyond the power of Executive removal and it is pretty well understood that, so far as Cabinet ministers are effected by the "Tenure of office Bill" it was intended specially to protect the Sec. of War who the country felt great confidence in. The meaning of the law may be explained away by an astute lawyer but common sense, and the mass of loyal people, will give to it the effect intended by its framers.

On the subject of the removal of the very able commander of the 5th Military District[2] let me ask you to consider the effect it would have upon the public. He is universally, and deservedly, beloved by the people who sustained this government through its trials; and feared by them who would still be enemies of the Government. It fell to the lot of but few men to do as much against an armed enemy as General Sheridan did, during the rebellion, and it is within the scope of the ability of but few in this or other country to do what he has. His civil administration has given equal satisfaction. He has had difficulties to contend with which no other District Commander has encountered. Almost, if not quite, from the day he was appointed District Commander to the present time the press has given out that he was to be removed, that the Administration was dissatisfied with him &c, &c. This has emboldened the opponents to the laws of Congress, within his command, to oppose him in every way in their power, and has rendered necessary measures which otherwise may never have become necessary.

In conclusion allow me to say as a friend desiring peace & quiet, the welfare of the whole country, North and South, that it is my opinion more than the loyal people of this country, (I mean those who supported the Government during the great rebellion) will quietly submit to see the very men of all others who they have expressed confidence in, removed. I would not have taken the liberty of addressing the Executive of the United States thus but for the conversation on the subject alluded to in this letter, and from a sense of duty feeling that I know I am right in this matter.

U. S. Grant   General.

ALS, DLC-JP.
1. Johnson told Grant that he planned to remove Edwin M. Stanton and wished Grant to replace the latter as acting secretary of war. Moore Diary, Aug. 1, 1867, Johnson Papers, LC.
2. Philip H. Sheridan.

From William Thorpe
Private

Washington, Aug. 1, '67.

Dear Sir:

The Hon. R. King Cutler leaves for Louisiana, I understand, within a day or two. I sincerely trust you will give him the appointments he asks,[1] in order that the conservative people there, and throughout the South, may have the evidence that you are willing to aid them in deed as in word.

Mr. President, the history of past civil wars, and all experience, prove that the principles laid down by you in your recent messages and speeches are the true ones to bring back a nation to the speediest and safest peace. Will you not aid the men struggling for the maintenance of those principles?—especially the men of a State whose example will greatly influence the other nine.

It is a well-known fact that Mr. Kellogg, Collector at New Orleans, is using the power delegated by you to him against the cause you and all good men espouse. So is Gen. Herron,[2] *who*, I am now satisfied, *never was anything but a Radical*, and is now employing his patronage in the interest of one of your Cabinet who seeks the Radical nomination for the next Presidency. These facts above ought to induce their removal; but now comes in the Tenure-of-Office Bill, which makes it your duty to suspend any officer guilty of "*malfeasance* or *misconduct* in office" which offences, on the part of thse individuals, are so notorious that all the world must be convinced by this time.

I hope you will see the matter in this light, which I believe to be the correct one, but deferring to your superior information and judgment . . . [3]

Wm. Thorpe.

ALS, DLC-JP.
1. As evidenced in Cutler's numerous letters to Johnson, his major concerns were the removal of William P. Kellogg, the collector of customs at New Orleans, and Philip H. Sheridan, the commander of the Fifth Military District. See, for example, Cutler to Johnson, July 30, 1867.

2. Francis J. Herron, the new marshal for Louisiana.

3. Another Louisianian then in Washington, William L. Randall, also wrote to Johnson on August 1 strongly supporting Cutler's requests. Johnson Papers, LC.

From Thomas A.R. Nelson

Knoxville Tenn.   2 August 1867.

Sir.

On the 8th Jan'y 1866, Hon. Walter Preston[1] of Abingdon Va. addressed a letter to me in which he stated that, in August 1865, he had forwarded, to your Excellency, a Petition for Pardon, and desired me to aid him in procuring it. I was very busily engaged at the time in the Federal Court and, unfortunately, postponed any attention to the matter until "a more convenient season." On my way home, from the Philadelphia Convention, last August,[2] I saw Mr. Preston and promised him to write to you, but, so soon as I reached home, a pressure of business banished the subject from my mind and I have not heard from him since. I have often thought of writing to you in his behalf but it has generally been under such circumstances that it was inconvenient for me to do so. I need not say that I feel heartily ashamed of such gross negligence, especially when I remember that Mr. Preston treated me with politeness when the Rebels held me a prisoner at Richmond and was, as I understood, opposed to my arrest or, rather, in favor of my discharge.

I suppose the reason why Mr. Preston's petition was not granted was because, at that early day, no Pardons had been granted to persons who had been members of the Rebel Congress; but as such clemency has since been extended in other cases, I presume the reasons for their exclusion has ceased.

Mr. Preston was, in politics, a Whig, and opposed the secession of Virginia up to the 6th of April 1861, when he surrendered his convictions of right to what he regarded as an inevitable necessity. He was a member of the Confederate Congress until the 22 Feb. 1864, since which time he has been a private citizen. Like all other citizens of the South, he suffered greatly, in a pecuniary point of view, by the War. Since its close, he has conducted himself—so far as I have any knowledge on the subject—as a peacable and law abiding citizen; and I sincerely hope, and urgently request, that your Excellency will immediately grant his Petition.[3]

Believing, as I have since the war, that one of the best means of restoring real peace to a distracted land would be to grant a universal, or almost universal, amnesty—your Excellency will not be surprised when I also respectfully request you to grant a Pardon to Hon. John C. Breckenridge.[4] I never was intimately acquainted with him and have had no communication with him since the War. I do not even know where he now is. But, in the Fall of 1864, my son Thomas[5]—then in his seventeenth year, and belonging to the eighth Tennessee regiment—was captured, together with some others of Gen. Gillem's command, at Morristown, and Gen. Breckenridge, voluntarily and without any solicitation on my part, treated him with much kindness and sent him to Knoxville on his own parole, to be exchanged. This he did, as he said, from motives of respect and kindness to me, altho' he knew I had left home and was then within the lines of the Federal Army at this place. The exchange could not be effected because communication with the North was then interrupted and I endeavored to get our military authorities to send my son back into the Rebel lines so as to save his honor, but this they refused and effected a different exchange, as I understood.

A sense of gratitude prompts me, unsolicited, to write in behalf of Gen. Breckenridge; but, as I think it would shock the moral sense of the world to try men and hang them for treason at this late day, and as I believe the South has suffered, and is suffering, more than enough to atone for its great crime, you will perceive that what I regard as a private duty does not interfere with my views of public policy.

It may be proper for me, as a lawyer, to add that, in thus addressing your Excellency, I am acting without fee or hope of reward.

Thos. A.R. Nelson.

ALS, DNA-RG94, Amnesty Papers (M1003, Roll 67), Va., Walter Preston.

1. Preston (1819–1867) was a lawyer and a planter in Virginia, though for a time he lived in Arkansas. After his service in the Confederate Congress, Preston retired to private life in Abingdon. He died in November. Wakelyn, *BDC*.

2. Nelson refers here to the pro-Johnson National Union Convention held in mid-August 1866.

3. Nelson's plea was both timely and effective, for the President granted a pardon to Preston on August 10, 1867—three months before Preston's death. Amnesty Papers (M1003, Roll 67), Va., Walter Preston, RG94, NA.

4. Perhaps Nelson did not know that Breckinridge never sought a special presidential pardon and was in fact in Europe at the time of Nelson's letter. Breckinridge did not finally return to the United States until March 1869; he was covered by Johnson's universal amnesty proclamation. Dorris, *Pardon and Amnesty*, 274–76; William C. Davis, *Breckinridge: Statesman, Soldier, Symbol* (Baton Rouge, 1974), 559–82 passim.

5. Thomas A.R. Nelson, Jr. (1847–1934), studied law after the war and became a practicing attorney in Knoxville. Subsequently, he served as district attorney and as a judge of the criminal court of Knox County. Mary U. Rothrock, ed., *The French Broad-Holston Country* (Knoxville, 1946), 463, 640–41; John W. Green, *Bench and Bar of Knox County, Tennessee* (Knoxville, 1947), 136–38.

From John Warren [1]

Kilmrainham Prison, Dublin, Ireland, Augt. 2d 1867

Dear Sir:

I respectfully call you Excellencies' attention to my case. By birth an Irishman, by adoption an American Citizen; here as a member of the press, collecting notes for the American press, coupled with a desire to revisit the old scenes of my boyhood and see near and dear relatives. I was arrested on the First of June, and have been since closely confined. No charge has been advanced aginst me. I have violated no law. I have demanded my release or immediate trial, and now as an American Citizen and freeman, ask your Excellencies' interposition in my behalf to obtain a right (my freedom) which England has no power to take, and which claims your Excellencies' protection. My friends will lay my case more fully before your Excellency.[2]

John Warren.

ALS, DNA-RG59, Misc. Lets., 1789–1906 (M179, Roll 263).
    1. Warren (c1837–1895) enlisted in August 1861 and served with the 63rd N.Y. Vol. Inf. as captain until cashiered in September 1862. In May 1867 he was on board the *Mackmel* (*Erin's Hope*), which attempted to land arms and men at Sligo, Ireland, and was arrested and detained without trial, for the habeas corpus had been suspended in Ireland. Pension Files, Bridget Warren, RG15, NA; Jenkins, *Fenians and Anglo-American Relations*, 237; Leon Ó Broin, *Fenian Fever: An Anglo-American Dilemma* (New York, 1971), 184.
    2. Some argued that Warren and the others had been arrested without having committed the slightest overt hostile act within Britain's jurisdiction. On October 30, 1867, Warren was placed on trial for treason felony. Complicating the issue were questions of Warren's nationality. Though sentenced to fifteen years, Warren was released from prison in 1869 and returned to the U.S. Jenkins, *Fenians and Anglo-American Relations*, 237, 284, 295; *House Ex. Docs.*, 40 Cong., 2 Sess., No. 157, pp. 61–197 (Ser. 1339).

From Hugh McCulloch

Private

Treasury Department. Aug 3d 1867

Dear Mr President

I am so much engaged at the Department that I may not be able to call upon you in person. Permit me to say, therefore, in this manner that after sleeping upon the question discussed yesterday,[1] I have in no wise changed my opinion.[2] I am satisfied that your own best interests, and the best interests of the Country will be promoted by non-interference on your part—letting the responsibility for impending evils, rest where it properly belongs. I may be wrong, but I think I am right, and so thinking, I cannot as a sincere friend of yourself, and a friend of the Country withhold this expression of my opinion.[3]

Hugh McCulloch.

ALS, DLC-JP.
    1. After the cabinet meeting on August 2, Johnson had asked his advisers (except for Stanton) for their opinions on the possible removal of Sheridan as commander of the Fifth Military District, leading to quite a vigorous discussion. Beale, *Welles Diary*, 3: 149–52.
    2. McCulloch was very much opposed to the removal of Sheridan, because it "would strengthen the extreme Radicals" while discouraging the conservatives. If Sheridan were left alone, the Radicals would divide among themselves over other issues. But if Sheridan were removed, it would cause more trouble for the administration because Sheridan was "exceedingly popular." Ibid.
    3. McCulloch not only wrote to Johnson on August 3 but also called on Gideon Welles,

asking Welles to see the President and urge him not to take any hasty action. Even though Welles did not agree with McCulloch, he nevertheless visited Johnson to discuss the Sheridan question. Ibid., 152–54.

From Samuel J. Randall

Cape Island New Jersey   August 4, 1867

My dear Mr. President

A Revenue Board has been established in Philadelphia similar to the one existing in New York. Four gentlemen holding Government positions under you have been selected as members of that Board. Politically they stand two and two in sentiment. It is asked by your friends in Philadelphia—that a fifth man be chosen—so as to preponderate in your favor. The Secretary of the Treasury proposes to send one of his employees from the Revenue Department in Washington as the fifth. (There are very few there but radicals.) This we dissent from respectfully but urgently for reasons which are of great weight.

We do not appeal for any particular person—Altho' Mr. Wm. Harbeson has been named and I beleive would be the best man to appoint. Many however urge the Appraiser—Mr. Chas. M. Hurley[1] a sterling gentleman and a man of great energy. Either would be satisfactory. In fact any unflinching known and avowed friend of yours in our city would suit.

The political power of this Board if weilded—against your friends will be over whelming. If constituted to aid your friends—the result in our State can hardly be doubted. Why then should our wish—your interests and welfare of the Country be overlooked or cast aside when no material interest of the Revenue Department is to suffer thereby? I cannot too strongly urge upon you to take the bit in your own mouth as to this appointment. Mr. Rollins[2] has talked Mr. McCulloch into his present view. I have written to the Secretary fully—on this subject and have asked him to read to you my letter—which oblige me by listening to. Something has—I learn, been said about this being urged from sordid motives. This is unjust—and is a most ungenerous mode of assailing the request which is made by your friends. I cannot portray to you the political importance of the action we seek and if not done—I think—I shall have just cause—to attach some of the blame—if defeat comes to us in October—to Mr. McCulloch in refusing to listen to those who I consider fully understand the situation in Philadelphia.

I thank you for your kindness towards Major Field.[3] It is now over and I can without any feeling—say that more outrageous—mean and unofficerlike conduct towards a fellow officer—never passed under my notice. Thanks to you however. I wish you and your family were here to enjoy the bathing. If you agree to go to Long Branch I shall certainly go there to see you as a friend.

Sam J. Randall

ALS, DLC-JP.
   1. Hurley (*fl*1884) later worked as a solicitor and freight agent in Philadelphia. He was nominated by Johnson in late February 1867 to be appraiser at Philadelphia and was approved by the Senate on March 2. He evidently held that post into 1869. Philadelphia directories (1868–84); *U.S. Off. Reg.* (1867); *Senate Ex. Proceedings*, Vol. 15, pt. 1: 247, 331.
   2. Edward A. Rollins.
   3. Major Field has not been identified.

From Gideon Welles

[ca. August 4, 1867][1]

Dear Sir

   I have thought much and seriously on the subject which we discussed on Friday, and which, with other matters entered into our conversation yesterday.[2] Mr McCulloch thinks I expressed my mind too frankly, and is apprehensive that my opinions may induce you to take steps which may lead to serious trouble to yourself and others.[3] I am free to confess that I see no relief from trouble in any quarter.

   Unfortunately, the administration has no policy but one of concession and forbearance under constant assaults and aggressions. The cabinet is not, and never has been a unit. Most of the members have views and opinions corresponding with yours, but it is not to be controverted or concealed that your views and theirs have been steadily and persistently tharted and defeated. A majority of congress is arrayed against the Exeutive, and has defeated and overthrown the policy with which you commenced your administration for re-establishing the broken relations of the Union, and for restoring order and constitutional goverments to the States which were in rebellion. That majority has had earnest and sympathysing friends among your confidential advisers. Some of these have very properly withdrawn from your councils, from a conviction that there was not, and could not be harmony in this & your political action, and they felt the indelicacy and impropriety of embarrasing you in your means of administrature, by continuing to associate with you in those intimate relations which ought ever to exist betwen the Prsident and his constitutional advisers. This, however was not the course pursued by all.

   There has been no personal dissension in the cabinet, yet there has been wanting that cordiality, confidence and concurrence of views, that are essential to a sucessful administration in stormy and eventful times like these. If you desired, or permitted this, it was not for any of your subordinates to take exceptions; but the result was foreseen. Your opponents as a consequence have been steadily acquiring strength—many who were with you at the begining have been gradually alienated, until nearly every man in the two houses of congress, who at first supported you is compacted in opposition, and to a great extent the popular sentiment which two years ago was with the administration, has become estranged and demoralized.

The policy, tone and character of the goverment are shaped, formed and directed by congress, and not by the administration. By usurpation and by disregarding the constitution, states are denied their rights—their organic laws are trampled under foot—military despotism is established over them—intelligent white men are proscribed and negroes are exalted above them. Coincident with these aggresive acts, and a part of them, the Executive Department of the government is invaded, its power circumscribed, and its authority destroyed.

You have, as measures were from time to time presented, interposed your veto and stated your objections. In these you have had the approval and support of most of your cabinet, but not of all. A portion of your advisers were in harmony with your enemies, and sanctioned their proceedings.

As a consequence, the usurping majority of congress, and that portion of your cabinet which is opposed to you have broken down your administration, and crippled and defeated the Executive. The President is almost powerless.

On or after the passage of the bill placing the government of the ten states in the hands of five Generals of the army, my opinion was not asked, nor do I know that the opinions of any of your staunch supporters in the cabinet was asked in regard to the officers who were to be selected. I regretted the choice of Sheridan, for though a brave and gallant officer, who has rendered great and distinguished service in the field, I have always considered him wanting in administrative ability. This I freely stated long before his selection in cabinet meeting and elsewhere. But after he was detailed for what is called the fifth Military district, I took no exceptions, but acquiesed in what was, I supposed a measure of policy that some of us were not permitted to understand. When, however, he proceded to remove the Govenor of Louisiana, the Attorney General and the Judge and to substitute others[4] I did not hesitate to say that he ought to be detached. When his insolent, insulting, insubordinate and defiant letter appeared,[5] I objected to his longer continuance, and insisted on his being immediately rebuked and removed. But he had a friend in the cabinet, and he has continued to be retained.

He has now removed the Governor of Texas[6] who was elected by the people of that state, and appointed in his place the defeated competitor[7] whom the people would not elect, and has displaced the municipal goverment of New Orleans and appointed others of his own selection.[8]

When asked whether this man ought to be removed, I have but one answer to give. He is wholly unfit to administer the bad law which he has been selected to execute. I know of no additional reason for removing him now, than has existed for some time past. It would be more impolitic to remove him now than when he assumed the power of displacing the Governor of Louisiana, or than when he wrote & published his inexcusably insulting letter. Had I been in a position to act, I should have preferred to have detached and rebuked him before, or during the session of congress than at this time, for although he has done some acts since, they are only repetitions of what he had previously done, without reproof or censure. I think there are those who would have justified his removal then, who would not think it expedient now.

Should you decide to remove him, you will be prepared to receive the most violent and tempestuous assaults that have yet been made upon you. The house of representatives, in the same spirit in which his insulting letter was written, passed a resolution approving of Sheridan's conduct.[9] He has committed no new offence since, except to repeat what he had already done, and what a majority of the representatives approved.

As a measure of right, or wrong he ought not to be retained in the position he occupies—as a question of expediency—of repose or turbulance—of peace or strife—you can best determine the course to be adopted. At this day, I cannot suppose it would operate as a check upon others, or that it would calm party animosity. You must consider it, as only the begining of a war of bitterness, the termination of which no one can tell. It will be well to remember, however that the President has not now the strength and power for such a contest that he had, until one or two years since. A usurping congress has encroached upon the Executive prerogative until it is almost entirely divested of its strength constitutional power and authority.

It cannot be expected that you would stop proceedings with the removal of Sheridan. That would be but the commencement of hostilities. And yet, what officer in the civil service are you permitted to remove? Encroachment after encroachment has been made, until little power is left with the President. You can detach the other generals it is true, but the policy of the government having been transferred from the Executive to Congress, almost the whole of the Military officers have, under the manipulations of the War department been persuaded that the administration is in congress—that the Executive is of little account.

The letter of Genl. Grant,[10] shows his bias and feelings, and he is a good index of the military. The army has been seduced and misled by designing men. A passive course on the part of the administration has led to its destruction. Your opponents have been continued in power, until they have deprived you of strength to resist. Is not Genl. G. with them?

I make no war upon any of my colleagus in the cabint. So long as you choose to retain them I shall acquiese; but it is imposible to look at this question of Sheridan's removal and fully consider it, without looking beyond. To remove him—a subordinate—and retain his superiors who direct and control him and others, can be attended with no good. They are more in fault than he. Had you been favored with an earnest friend and supporter of your measures and policy in the War Department, neither

Sheridan nor others would have give you trouble. But you cannot now remove the Secretary of War if you are disposed, and I know not that you are disposed to remove him. Of what benefit can it be, however, to remove Sheridan while a greater than Sheridan is here directing his movements, and the movements of your opponts military and civil? I would not enter upon these matters but for our conversation yesterday and the discussion on Friday. While I think it would be a matter of right to remove Sheridan, I see no object calling for it, that has not existed for some time—no object to be gained for the Administration without other and more important changes leading to the establishment of an administration policy and a political revolution—one that shall relieve the administration of them who oppose its measures and its principles.

Draft, CSmH-Gideon Welles Collection.

1. Internal evidence, such as meetings with Johnson discussing this subject, reference to Sheridan's removal of Governor Throckmorton, and indications that the process of removing Stanton had not yet begun, suggests this approximate date.

2. The removal of Sheridan was discussed after the cabinet meeting on August 2 and by Johnson and Welles on August 3. Beale, *Welles Diary*, 3: 149–56.

3. McCulloch visited Welles to discuss the issue on Saturday, August 3, before Welles went to see Johnson. Ibid., 152–54.

4. J. Madison Wells, Andrew S. Herron, and Edmund Abell, respectively, were replaced by Benjamin F. Flanders, B. L. Lynch, and W. W. Howe. Wells was actually removed several months after Herron and Abell. General Orders No. 5, Mar. 27, 1867, in McPherson, *Political History*, 206–7. See also Edmund Abell to Johnson, June 3, 1867.

5. Philip H. Sheridan to U. S. Grant, June 22, 1867, Simon, *Grant Papers*, 17: 198.

6. James W. Throckmorton was removed on July 30. Morris, *Sheridan*, 292.

7. Elisha Pease. Ibid.

8. On August 1 Sheridan removed twenty-two members of the New Orleans city council for alleged financial mismanagement, naming some blacks among their successors. Dawson, *Army Generals and Reconstruction*, 56.

9. The joint resolution passed in the House on July 5, 1867, tendered Congress's thanks to Sheridan "for his able and faithful performance of his duties as commander of the military district of Texas and Louisiana." *Congressional Globe*, 40 Cong., 1 Sess., p. 500.

10. Probably Grant to Johnson, Aug. 1, 1867.

From R. King Cutler

Washington City, August 5th, 1867.

Respected Sir—

In my ninth letter to you[1] I promised it should be the last, prior to my departure for New Orleans; but, finding the annexed article in the *Washington Chronicle* of yesterday,[2]—and learning this morning, to my great regret, that it is incorrect,—I felt that another occasion was afforded for again intruding myself upon your notice.

I desire to say that the article in question was not prompted by myself or my friends.

It must have been prompted by somebody.

It has been assumed by many that your apparent intentions have been given, in advance, to the press, in order to ascertain whether, and how, such acts would be sustained by public opinion. The result of the publication of this article must certainly be satisfactory to you, no matter how it originated. The tone of this article in the *Chronicle*—the most bitter and malignant of all the American press towards you—is that of respectful commendation. It acquits you of any partisan motive, by alleging that your action in this case was prompted by charges of Malfeasance in Office; and is satisfied that the charges are well founded and sufficient, because they were preferred "by prominent Louisianians."

If it is not a fact, originating in yourself, it must have been prompted by Secretary McCulloch, who could have had only two motives in so doing: *First*, he might have desired to rouse all the opposition of the radicals, and others, in the hope of deterring you from acting adverse to Kellogg. In this he has signally failed, because the most bitterly-hostile newspaper of the Opposition—the organ of the Congressional Committee, which gives the signal to the rest—can find no cause to assail you; but, on the contrary, speaks of your action in terms unmistakeable, and approves of your alleged order to McCulloch, turning out a dishonest official; *Second*, The only other reason the Secretary of the Treasury could have had is that it has become an impossibility for him to sustain Kellogg any longer, and he desires to learn the views of the Radical party, and at the same time to prepare them—should your action be sustained by that party—for a change of tactics. I know it to be a common practice for Secretary McCulloch to make every possible use of the public press, and to be guided by it frequently. Therefore I am the more inclined to think that this article originated with him.

Mr. President, the evidence before you is conclusive. Now is the time for you to so act as to hand down your name to future generations. But, sir, Washington himself only succeeded by virtue of his sustaining his friends. Let me ask you to look, for instance, to Tennessee: Had you appointed all the officers in that State, whom you had the power and the right to appoint, from among your friends, their influence and power would have produced a very different result.

But, Mr. President, it is not yet too late. There are ten States unrepresented in the councils of the nation, and there are nearly two millions of voters in the Northern, Eastern and Western States who are ready and willing to carry out a programme conservative in its character, fully confident of the issue. But, sir, there must be assurances from *you* before *they* will act. When you do act rest assured they will respond. In the ten rebel States (so-called)—by the example of the State of Louisiana, through the medium of your assistance, in your legitimate capacity, and in the full exercise of your Constitutional prerogative—the prospect is still more promising. There can be no doubt but that Louisiana will be the great exemplar, and as she goes so will the other nine rebel States go. Not only so, Mr. President, but, as the ten States go, in sanction of your policy, so will a large majority of the people of the States now represented in the Congress of the United States. But, sir, none of those States, yea, none of those people, will sanction or be controlled by your policy, or even sanction you, unless you, as the controlling power of the nation, grant to them those high privileges which it is within your power, by one stroke of the pen, to give. For instance, you but give to the people of this nation whom you know to be your friends the offices, what else remains? The power and patronage of the offices give the controlling influence over the people, and it matters not whether black or white, your friends in power control the destiny of the nation.

Mr. President, not only do you thus control the destiny of the nation, but you immortalize yourself; and your name goes down to posterity with all that glory, or even more, which attaches to the name of Washington.

Mr. President, why not, then, give the great power you wield into the hands of your friends instead of your enemies? Let me ask, again, why not appoint to the offices under your immediate control, in every State, rebel or otherwise, men whom you know to be true advocates of genuine conservative principles?—men whom you know to be true and devoted friends. How can a man serve God and Mammon, at the same time? How can you expect immortalization without giving your friends the power? Look, for instance, to the Treasury Department, under the auspices of Secretary McCulloch. Who are the men in his employ? Who are your friends there? Why, sir, your name is a bye-word and a reproach. This applies not only to the heads of the bureaus, but to the principal officers under him in New York, New Orleans, Chicago and other principal cities. Has he not appointed men to places conditional upon their abandoning you? As bearer of a message from you did he not treat me with insolence, and your orders with contempt? And are not these facts generally understood, not only by your friends but by your enemies? Look at the Department of War: Who is in power there? None, unfortunately none, but Radicals of deepest dye. Then, how can you expect that your desires—your boyhood, manhood, heartfelt desires—should be realized, with such men under your own control in power.

Mr. President, God only knows what may be the result of the action of the Administration and the Congress of this nation; but, sir, permit me to say that *now is the time*—and no longer should there be delay—for you to immortalize yourself. The facts are before you. All of Heaven's lights divine the same programme. In God's name—in justice to yourself—in justice to the great people of this nation let me urge that *it is now* YOUR DUTY to immediately place in power, throughout every State of this Union, those who are your friends; and to remove from position those who are your enemies. May God inspire you to an *immediate* and *proper* sense of your duty, and may I be pardoned for making even a suggestion to you!

Again, allow me to say that the present Secretaries of the Treasury and of War are your deadly political enemies. I say this, Mr. President, knowing the consequences of what I say.

The newspapers whose interests are against you have been *ridiculing* the idea of your yielding to those who have sworn to facts against disreputable men who rob this Government. But, sir, I beg of you to examine entirely the record now in the possession of Secretary McCulloch as against W. P. Kellogg; and, God knows, I need not ask you again to look into the most damnable character of the age—Sheridan; acts perpetrated by him most revolting.

Yet, Mr. President, I am still here, pleading, as it were, at your very feet for justice in behalf of the great people whom I represent, and, notwithstanding my devoted pleadings, my earnest purpose of soul, and my untiring efforts in behalf of the great and good conservative people of Louisiana, I find no cordial response. May God in his wisdom grant immediate action, not only in behalf of Louisiana conservatives but in behalf of the great conservative people of this Union, all of whom look to you, and to you alone, as their grand leader and the supreme power from whence all their aid must come.

With these remarks, Mr. President, permit me to bid you adieu! Louisiana is my home. To my friends I must go, and go I will[3]—go with a down-stricken heart, with a crest-fallen disposition, and in a most awfully melancholy mood. The power, I know, is here, but, unfortunately for me and my friends, I have not received it.

Ever thankful for your kindness;—ever devoted to you, and determined as I am to stand by you, come what will, allow me to say to you, finally, Adieu!

R. King Cutler   No 27 Indiana Ave.

LS, DLC-JP.

1. See R. King Cutler to Johnson, July 30, 1867.

2. The short notice announced that Johnson had decided to remove William P. Kellogg from his post as collector at the port of New Orleans based on the charges of malfeasance in office filed by Cutler and others. Given that Cutler had been continually pushing for the removal of Kellogg since May, he was understandably disappointed to learn that the paper's report had been incorrect. *Washington Chronicle*, Aug. 4, 1867.

3. Despite repeated statements that he was leaving, Cutler was still in Washington on August 27. Cutler to Johnson, Aug. 27, 1867, Johnson Papers, LC.

From Reverdy Johnson

Baltimore   Aug 5th 1866 [1867][1]

The rumor is so general that you contemplate issuing a proclamation of amnesty that I hope you will not consider it intrusive in my expressing to you a strong hope that the rumor is well founded. At the termination of the war, I thought and have ever since continued to think, that a measure of that kind would, tend more than anything else to the peace and prosperity of the whole country. Notwithstanding the repeal of the section of the act of '62,[2] which professed to give the President such a power, it is perfectly clear that it is vested in him by the Constitution itself. It was under this last authority that Washington during his administration issued alike proclamation, at the close of what was known as The Whisky insurrection in Pensylvania. In that instance the measure met with universal approval, and I have no doubt that such a measure now, would be sanctioned by the patriotic intelligence of the country.[3]

Reverdy Johnson

N.B.

By this mail I forward you a copy of a speech of mine on the pardoning power [illegible].[4]

R J

LS, DLC-JP.
    1. The year should be 1867, rather than 1866, based on internal evidence concerning an imminent amnesty proclamation and the repeal of Section 13.
    2. The bill to repeal Section 13 of the Confiscation Act of 1862 was introduced in the House on December 3, 1866; Congress approved it on January 21, 1867. *Congressional Globe*, 39 Cong., 2 Sess., p. 4; *U.S. Statutes at Large*, 14: 377.
    3. Johnson issued his second amnesty proclamation on September 7, 1867. Richardson, *Messages*, 6: 547–49.
    4. Not found.

From Kansas Residents[1]

State of Kansas   County of Wilson
This August 5th 1867

To be refered to Congress or the department of the Interior, Wasn. D.C.

We the undersigned, Your petitioners, whoo are a portion of the settlers on this Trust land, treated for, from the Osage Indians,[2] would Respectfully ask, with the feelings of the whole people; at the same time, Protest, aganst this land, being soald to a railroad, or any other Companey; wherby the settlers on this land, might be disturbed. Otherwise that by an aditional act of Congress, the settler might have the right, guarenteed to him, to by 160 achors, at $1.25 per achor, up to this presant time; from this fact that one half of the settlements have been made since the date of the treaty. Emigrants, from Iowa, Ill. & many Eastern states, have come in, to procure homes, & have made settlements, since the ratification of said Treaty.[3]

If Congress takes no action on this matter we would ask the Department of the Inter[ior] to give us, further time (so as to soot the poor) and when sold, grant the sail of said land to be at (Coyville, Wilson Co. Kans.) and at Public sail.[4]

This we ask in confidence, believeing &c.

Pet, DNA-RG75, Gen. Records, Lets. Recd. (M234, Roll 534).

1. Some 117 settlers signed the document.

2. In September 1865 the Osage ceded a thirty-mile strip from the eastern end and a twenty-mile wide strip on the northern edge of their reservation. This area, called the Osage Trust Lands, was to be sold to settlers in lots no greater than 160 acres and at not less than $1.25 per acre, with proceeds going to the Osage. This land, surveyed by the government in the spring of 1866, included about three-quarters of Wilson County. The treaty took effect January 21, 1867. L. Wallace Duncan, *History of Neosho and Wilson Counties, Kansas* (Fort Scott, Kans., 1902), 838–39.

3. The settlers seem to be protesting negotiations for another treaty, the Drum Creek or Sturgis Treaty, which was concluded on May 27, 1868. This treaty pertained to the Diminished Reserve, or the remaining thirty-mile wide strip of the Osage reservation. The entire area of 8,003,000 acres was to be sold to the Leavenworth, Lawrence and Galveston Railway for $1,600,000. Ibid., 840.

4. After a fight led by Kansas congressman Sidney Clarke, U. S. Grant, shortly after he became President in 1869, withdrew the treaty from consideration by the Senate. In 1870 a section of the Indian appropriations bill opened the Diminished Reserve, including about 82,000 acres which became a part of Wilson County, to settlers, with provisions similar to the previous treaty creating the Trust. Ibid.

To Edwin M. Stanton

Washington, D.C.   Aug. 5th 1867.

Sir:

Public considerations of a high character constrain me to Say, that your resignation as Secretary of War will be accepted.[1]

Andrew Johnson

CopyS, DLC-JP.

1. For details of Stanton's removal and the relationship between Stanton, Johnson, and the cabinet, see Benjamin P. Thomas and Harold M. Hyman, *Stanton: The Life and Times of Lincoln's Secretary of War* (New York, 1962), 533–52; Beale, *Welles Diary*, Vol. 3.

From Edwin M. Stanton

Washington City, Aug 5 1867

Sir

Your note of this date has been received stating that public considerations of a high character constrain you to say that my resignation as Secretary of War will be accepted.

In reply I have the honor to say that public considerations of a high character, which alone have induced me to continue at the head of this Department, constrain me not to resign the office of Secretary of War before the next meeting of Congress.

Edwin M Stanton

ALS, DLC-JP.

From J. Richard Barret[1]

New Haven Hotel   New Haven   Augst. 6th 67

Allow a few words from a *friend*.

Do not remove *P. H. Sheridan*. His removal will be the *making of him. He is seeking removal*.

Let the question of removal remain in *abeyance*. In his Anxiety to be removed, & to be made a big man, he will *go farther, than any other, in bringing* the *"Military Satrap Bill"* into dishonour, & disodour.

For God sake, let him remain in his present position, & still, under the impression, that he, *may provoke a removal*.

It would be well to *taunt*, if possible, that *mean Dog, Stanton*, into resignation. But I doubt whether such a thing could possibly be accomplished. Excuse the liberty Mr. President, which a friend in all sincerity takes, to express, his views. Being an outsider, he may be able to see, & hear & learn *some valuable things*.

Do not consider it, presumption, therefore for him, thus to address you for he feels for you the most respectful & distinguished consideration.

J. Richd. Barret

68 Broadway N. York is my address.

ALS, DLC-JP.
1. Barret (1825–1903), formerly a Missouri congressman (1859–61), moved to New York City afterwards and held a variety of jobs. *BDUSC*.

From William J.C. Duhamel

Washington D.C.   Augst 6 1867.

Mr. President,

Your record as Congressman, Governor, Senator, and President in denouncing and exposing fraud and corruption wherever found by you, will indicate with what designs *you* will view these papers—for your name is proverbial for honesty of purpose. I have been requested by Capt M.T.E. Chandler[1] formerly of U.S.A. (Vols') residing H st near 1st next to Govmt Printing office give you these notes. You will see that the notes are made payable to the (*Rev*) W. B. Matchett who made that infamous proposition to me, to inform John H. Surratt then in Jail under my medical treatment if he (Surratt) would only indicate someone high in authority who prompted him to this crime he (Surratt) would *save* his *life*, *liberty*, and *enrich* himself.

Also that he Matchett was connected with the Judiciary Commt of the House Reps and that he would put any friend of Surratt's in communication with an important personage of that Committee.

These facts I immediately communicated to you last winter when they happened.[2]

I would prefer not having my name used in the matter at present as Capt Chandler who is known to be a respectable man, gives his name as he *got them direct* from Matchet and he (Capt. C.) has *other notes* from Husties[3] to Matchett of $3 & $500 which notes with this one Matchett expects to collect. And Matchett *finds fault* at present with Husties in not being more prompt in the payment of the same.

These facts will tend to prove the character of the class of persons striving to *injure you.*

W.J.C. Duhamel

ALS, DLC-JP.
1. A native of Canada and a former enlisted man in the 103rd N.Y. Inf., Malcolm T.E. Chandler (1829–1890) settled in Washington, D.C., in late 1866 or early 1867. He was guard at the jail in 1867, which probably explains his contact with Matchett, but he resigned this job in early August when William H. Huestis became warden. After a brief stint as a clerk, he became an examiner in the patent office by 1870 and remained there until about 1885. Pension Records, Sarah E. Chandler, RG15, NA; 1870 Census, D.C., Washington, 5th Ward, 181; Washington, D.C., directories (1867–92); *U.S. Off. Reg.* (1871–85); *Washington Evening Star*, Aug. 2, 1867.
2. See Duhamel to Johnson, Feb. 26, 1867.
3. William H. Huestis.

From Edwin M. Stanton

War Department, Washington City, August 6th, 1867.

Sir:

I have the honor to return herewith the letter of *William H. Bagley, Esq.*[1] referred to this Department, making enquiry as to the appointment of Cadets to the Military Academy from Southern States with the following answer. The fourth section of the Act of Congress approved Feby 28/67 enacts as follows.

"That no part of the moneys appropriated by this or any other Act shall be applied to the pay or subsistence of any Cadet from any state declared to be in rebellion against the Government of the United States, appointed after the first day of January 1867 until such state shall have been restored to its original relations to the Union."[2]

This enactment has been regarded by the Department as precluding the appointment of Cadets from the States referred to and consequently none have been made since the passage of this Act.[3]

Edwin M. Stanton, Secy of War.

LBcopy, DNA-RG107, Lets. Sent, Mil. Bks., Executive, 58-C.
1. Bagley (1833–1886), a lawyer, served with North Carolina state troops during the war. In 1864 he became a state senator and then private secretary to Jonathan Worth, whose daughter Adelaide he married in 1866. Bagley was writing on behalf of his brother

who had actually been offered an appointment at West Point the previous year but had not been able to accept it. 1870 Census, N.C., Wake, Raleigh Twp., 144; Weymouth T. Jordan, Jr., comp., *North Carolina Troops, 1861–1865: A Roster* (11 vols. to date, Raleigh, 1966–), 6: 192–93; Zuber, *Worth*, 289; *NUC*; Bagley to W. G. Moore, July 29, 1867, OFH.

2. *Congressional Globe*, 39 Cong., 2 Sess., Appendix, p. 193.

3. Johnson's August 6 endorsement on the Bagley to Moore letter forwarded the letter to Stanton. The secretary *immediately* responded to the President that same day. On August 7 Moore informed Bagley of the War Department's ruling and expressed regret that "it is adverse to the case of your Brother." Moore to Bagley, Aug. 7, 1867, Johnson Papers, LC.

From Sam Milligan

Greeneville Tenn   August 7. 1867

Dear Sir:

Soon after the recept of your dispatch, I wrote you I would come to Washington.[1] Up to this time I have not been able to travel. When I wrote I spoke of being unwell with a pain in my side & a severe cold. Both have continued ever since. The former is a little better, and I hope the latter is beginning to give way; but I have been afraid to risk the trip. My purpose is fixed, as soon as I get able, to come at once.

No matter as I wrote you about the office you spoke off, if it is necessary to fill it at any time. My delay ought not, from whatever cause produced, to hinder the progress of public business. I want to see you any how, office or no office, and if I can render you any service, with or without office, it will be my pleasure to do so.

I have written this note by way of explanation of my conduct, in not redeeming my promise. My time since I wrote, has been almost wholly spent at home in the house, and often in bed.

Please accept this explanation.

Sam Milligan

ALS, DLC-JP.
1. Johnson to Milligan, July 17, 1867, and Milligan to Johnson, July 19, 1867.

From William B. Phillips

private.

15 East 30th   New York   August 7th 1867.

Dear Sir,

Something occurred to-day in our editorial council, which it may be interesting, if not useful, to know, and with regard to which, if you will permit me in a friendly and confidential way, I will make a few remarks.

Mr. Bennett Sr. was down at the office when we discussed the Stanton matter, and he gave an article to one of the writers, which if written in the spirit he intended will be more favorable to you than the paper has been for some time past. The writer is pretty radical and may not give exactly the right tone, but if not I think that will come. I am sorry I did not have the article, for it always gives me pleasure to say what I can favorable to your administration, notwithstanding the course of the paper. I told Mr. Bennett I was glad to hear him express the views he did. The article will be in to-morrow's (Thursday's) paper in all probability.[1]

First, then, Mr. Bennett thinks you have the constitutional power to suspend Stanton at least; and he thinks Stanton is acting discourteously and disrespectfully to the Executive. He regards his conduct as unprecedented in a cabinet officer and tending to be revolutionary in changing the established operations of the government. He says Stanton is thus defiant because he believes Congress will back him and because he wishes to be made a martyr for his own and his party's political capital. Mr. Bennett thinks it will raise an exciting issue that may enter into the fall elections, that you ought not to make Stanton the single martyr, as that might place him in the prominent position before the public he desires, but that you should change also all the generals in command in the South, that, in fact, having taken the bull by the horns you should try your own more temperate and moderate course with new agents in carrying out the reconstruction measures. He thinks the radicals have gone quite far enough or too far and it is time to check them if possible. He is particularly desirous of cutting under the Greely-radical platform of universal amnesty now that universal suffrage to the blacks has been conceded. He thinks that wing of the party could not escape from the consequences of their own doctrine if you push this generous policy—if you adopt a more liberal course under new commanders at the South than the present commanders are disposed to carry out. Acting upon this bold and broad ground, at the same time keeping within the laws passed for reconstructing the southern states, he thinks it likely you may produce such results in the South, that the conservative masses of the North will approve of your policy in this matter. In that case, that is, in case you make the issue broad enough and upon sound constitutional principles, and the results should be such at the South that the people at the North would be forced to commend your acts, he believes there would be a good chance of carrying the states of Pennsylvania and New York against the radicals next fall. He does not see how you are to escape from the issue with Stanton without degrading the office of President and making your own position worse, while in a bold and liberal course you may bring about a powerful reaction.

Although Mr. Bennett is changeable and makes the interests of his paper, as far as he can judge, the controlling object, yet he is very sagacious in political matters, and generally succeeds in falling in with the popular current.

I give Mr. Bennett's views rather than my own, because of his great experience and sagacity, and because they indicate the course the paper may take. I may say, however, that I think there is a good deal of reason in what he says, although I apprehend such a course as he recommends would incense the radicals very much. If for the want of time or other causes you should not be able to produce the anticipated reaction in public sentiment at the North by next winter they might proceed to extreme measures against you. However, you can judge best of your own position. At least, I trust you will excuse this hastily written letter for sake of the motive that prompted me to write, whatever you may think of the opinions expressed.

W. B. Phillips

ALS, DLC-JP.
    1. The editorial did appear in the August 8 edition of the *New York Herald*.

To Lovell H. Rousseau

Executive Mansion,
Washington, August 7' 1867.

Sir

You are hereby appointed agent on behalf of the United States to receive from the Agents of His Majesty, the Emperor of the Russias, the territory, dominion, property, dependencies and appurtenances which are ceded by His Imperial Majesty to the United States, under the treaty concerning the cession of the Russian possessions in North America, concluded March 30th 1867. A copy of the treaty is herewith communicated for your information and government.[1]

In witness whereof, I have hereunto signed my name and caused the Seal of the United States to be affixed.

Andrew Johnson

LBcopy, DNA-RG59, Commissions for State Dept. Employees.
    1. Rousseau conferred with Johnson on the morning of August 16. On August 31 he and the Russian commissioner, Capt. Alexy Pestchouroff, sailed from New York for San Francisco, arriving September 22. They reached Sitka on October 18. That same day Alaska was officially transferred to the United States. A week later Rousseau departed to assume command of the Department of the Columbia. *Washington Evening Star*, Aug. 16, 1867; Archie W. Shiels, *The Purchase of Alaska* (College, Alaska, 1967), 148, 150, 152–53. Other documents dealing with Alaska are Lewis V. Bogy to Johnson, Apr. 16, 1867; Johnson to the Senate and House of Representatives, July 6, 1867. See also Johnson to Rousseau, July 31, 1867, concerning the plans for the general to travel from New Orleans to Washington.

To George H. Thomas

Washington, D.C., Aug. 8th 1867

I have just received a despatch from President Nashville & Chattanooga Rail Road informing me that the Road is to be taken possession of tomorrow.[1] He earnestly asks extension of the time to the 20th instant, by which time arrangements will be made for the payment.[2] If this extension can be granted, as I think it can, without detriment to public interests, I hope you will extend the time to enable them to meet their engagements.[3]

Andrew Johnson

Tel, DNA-RG107, Tels. Sent, President, Vol. 3 (1865–68).

1. On August 7 Nashville and Chattanooga Railroad president Michael Burns informed Johnson that Col. Samuel R. Hamill had threatened to take possession of the railroad if payment was not made. At issue evidently was the $1.5 million debt owed by the railroad to the U.S. government. In addition to contacting General Thomas in Louisville, Johnson also notified Burns that he had telegraphed Thomas. Burns to Johnson, Aug. 7, 1867, Johnson Papers, LC; Johnson to Burns, Aug. 8, 1867, Tels. Sent, President, Vol. 3 (1865–68), RG107, NA; *Charleston Courier*, Aug. 26, 1867.

2. Burns testified at length in February 1867 before the impeachment investigation committee of Congress regarding the operations and financial obligations of the Nashville and Chattanooga Railroad. He indicated that the company had made purchases of equipment, buildings, and rail lines from the U.S. government in the amount of slightly over $1.5 million. According to Burns, this figure was to be reduced as the railroad was credited for transporting troops and supplies and carrying the mails. A plan was devised whereby the company would pay the government over a period of time. To add to the complicated story, Burns further testified that the government itself was indebted to the company in the amount of over $3.7 million. See *House Reports*, 40 Cong., 1 Sess., No. 7, "Impeachment Investigation," pt. 2, pp. 170, 1128–32 passim.

3. Burns immediately sent another telegram to Johnson to inform him that matters had been arranged satisfactorily. Likewise, General Thomas informed Johnson that it was a mistaken idea that the railroad would be taken over. Thomas indicated that he had been instructed to enforce the company's payment of debts and that Burns had been admonished to "take immediate steps to liquidate the indebtedness." Burns to Johnson, Aug. 8, 1867; Thomas to Johnson, Aug. 9, 1867, Johnson Papers, LC.

From William A. Wright[1]

Wilmington N.C   August 8th 1867

My dear Sir

About the 10th of June last, soon after my visit to the City of Raleigh in our State where I then had the honor of meeting with your Excellency, I addressed a letter to your Excellency[2] asking your favorable consideration of the petition of John N Maffitt[3] a citizen of this State, praying for a pardon for his participation in the late most unhappy civil war. The letter referred to was written in conformity with a suggestion made by your Excellency during our parting interview, and as there are peculiar reasons connected with the restoration to Mr. Maffitt of his rights of person and property which make him extremely solicitous to be relieved from the disabilities under which he now labors, I have ventured again to address you on this subject.

The petitioner Mr. Maffitt is in a really dependent condition, living in this city with his daughter who married one of my nephews.[4] His Petition is commended to your favorable action by the commandant of the

United States forces at this military Post,[5] by the Mayor of this city[6] and by his Excellency Jonathan Worth the Governor of our State. I believe the facts set forth in the petition of Mr. Maffitt are true in letter and in spirit, that he is at this time and has been since the close of the war in all respects loyal to the government of the United States, and that he is a most proper subject for that executive clemency which will restore him to all the rights of an American citizen.[7]

Wm. A Wright

ALS, DNA-RG94, Amnesty Papers (M1003, Roll 41), N.C., John N. Maffitt.

1. Wright (1807–1878) was a Wilmington lawyer and for many years chairman of the county court. He served as president of the Bank of Cape Fear and also as attorney for a railroad company. *Cyclopedia of Eminent and Representative Men of the Carolinas of the Nineteenth Century* (2 vols., Spartanburg, 1972–73 [1892]), 2: 211–12.

2. See Wright to Johnson, June 10, 1867, Amnesty Papers (M1003, Roll 41), N.C., John N. Maffitt, RG94, NA.

3. Maffitt (1819–1886) was a career navy man who entered the Confederate navy when the war began. He achieved recognition for running the coastal blockade. After the war he commanded a British ship. The petition referred to was Maffitt's letter to Johnson of June 1, 1867. Ibid; *Historical Times Illustrated Encyclopedia of the Civil War* (New York, 1986), 467.

4. Mary Florence "Florie" Wright (1842–1883), who was married to Joshua G. Wright (b. c1840), a former Confederate lieutenant and Wilmington railroad clerk. 1870 Census, N.C., New Hanover, Wilmington, 330; James Sprunt, *Chronicles of the Cape Fear River, 1660–1916* (Raleigh, 1916), 367–68; Emma Martin Maffitt, *The Life and Services of John Newland Maffitt* (New York, 1906), 56, 205, 356, 360, 425.

5. Royal T. Frank (1836–1908) was an 1858 graduate of West Point and a career army officer. He saw a variety of duties during the Civil War and continued in the regular army afterwards, including service in the Spanish-American War. *Who Was Who in America*, 1: 422; *New York Tribune*, Mar. 16, 1908.

6. John Dawson (b. c1803) was a dry goods and hardware merchant in Wilmington. 1860 Census, N.C., New Hanover, Wilmington, 115; (1870), 207.

7. Upon the President's recommendation, Maffitt was pardoned on September 5, 1867. See Amnesty Papers (M1003, Roll 41), N.C., John N. Maffitt, RG94, NA.

From Samuel W. Beall[1]

Washington   August 9th 1867

Mr. President

I was appointed Sutler at Fort Kearney by the Secretary of War.[2] Very recently my store was burned down and I lost all I possesed.

I have had a Son shot before my eyes at the battle of Shiloh and another terribly wounded in the assault on Petersburg.[3] I have been wounded myself and now carry a bullet under my hip.[4]

Governer Randall[5] the Postmaster Genl. will apprise you Mr. President of my character and qualifications.

I respectfully request that I may be appointed as Secretary of Idaho or Montanna.[6]

W. S. Beall[*sic*]

Copy, DNA-RG59, Lets. of Appl. and Recomm., 1861–69 (M650, Roll 4), W. S. Beall.

1. Beall (1807–1868) was involved in the early settlement of Wisconsin as receiver for the land office, prominent member of the state conventions, Indian agent, and lieutenant governor. He also helped to found Denver, Colorado. *DAB.*

2. Beall was appointed on June 30, 1866, upon the recommendation of his good friend Gen. U. S. Grant. Louis H. Pelouze to O. P. Morton, Mar. 16, 1867, Lets. Sent *re* Military Affairs (M6, Roll 58), RG107, NA; Simon, *Grant Papers*, 16: 440–41.

3. The son shot at Shiloh would have been either John (b. *c*1834) or Roger (b. *c*1846) but no information on military service has been found for either of them. Lewis Upton Beall (1844–1868), a first lieutenant in the 37th Wisc. Inf., was wounded on July 30, 1864, during the attack following the explosion at the Crater. After spending about eight months in the Armory Square Hospital in Washington, D.C., he was discharged from the service. CSR, Lewis U. Beall, RG94, NA; Volunteer Services Div., File B-3333-1864, Lewis U. Beall, RG94, NA; *Fond du Lac (Wisc.) Commonwealth*, Mar. 11, 1868; burial record for Taycheedah Cemetery.

4. As lieutenant colonel of the 18th Wisc. Inf., Beall was wounded at Shiloh and Vicksburg. He resigned his post, apparently because he was disabled, in August 1863 and became a major in the Veteran Reserve Corps. *Off. Army Reg.: Vols.*, 190; Simon, *Grant Papers*, 441; *DAB.*

5. Alexander W. Randall.

6. Beall was not appointed secretary of either territory but he did soon move to Montana, where he ran afoul of George M. Pinney, manager of the *Montana Post*, who printed some articles insulting to Beall, and, in an argument over the articles, shot and killed Beall. Ibid.; *New York Times*, Oct. 13, 1868. The articles, entitled "S. W. Beall on a Splurge" and "About to Depart," are found in the weekly *Montana Post*, Sept. 25, 1868.

From Charles F. Fisher

August 9, 1867, New Orleans, La.; ALS, DNA-RG56, Lets. Recd. from President.

Having learned, by way of a published telegram, that William P. Kellogg, collector of customs at New Orleans, will soon be dismissed, Fisher seeks to inform Johnson of the collector's flaws. Fisher first refers to the Congressional committee's visit to New Orleans to investigate the riot of July 1866. Representative Samuel Shellabarger asked Kellogg if he understood that he was not to appoint ex-Rebels to office, to which the collector replied in the affirmative. Fisher proceeds then to note instances wherein Kellogg knowingly appointed persons who could not legitimately take the oath. One such was the appointment of Eugene Lacoste, a man who was employed at the customhouse prior to the war and who registered as an enemy of the U.S. government in 1862 and left the city the following year. Yet upon his return in 1865, Lacoste was appointed as an inspector by Kellogg. The collector dealt similarly with Hortaire Andry, a prewar inspector who resigned in order to join the Confederate army. Upon Andry's return to New Orleans in September 1865, Kellogg again appointed him as an inspector. Subsequently, in Kellogg's absence, the deputy collector, Sidney A. Stockdale, named Andry as bonded warehouse keeper. Fisher took it upon himself in November 1865 to lay out the facts about Andry's past to Kellogg and in the process complained that he, Fisher, who had been loyal to the U.S. government had held only an inferior position at the customhouse. Kellogg's response was that Fisher was too old for another appointment and that the secretary of the treasury would not approve such an elevation. Fisher assures Johnson that he could point out additional wrongs committed by Kellogg. Fisher also notes that he had been dismissed from the customhouse in 1863, when Cuthbert Bullitt became collector, in order to make room for some of his "former know nothing friends."

From William Thorpe

Private.

Washington, August 9, '67.

Dear Sir:—

Permit me, with all due respect, to suggest that, if it be your intention to releive Mr. Stanton from the War Office the delay in so doing will *now* only intensify the bitterness and hostility of the radicals; whereas prompt action will convince them that you mean something more than threats, and are not to be intimidated, as they boast you are. A radical Representative yesterday declared to me that his party had "so effectually cowed" the President "that he dare not and could not turn Mr. Stanton out;" that they had so tied you down and surrounded you as to render you powerless "which fact is now acknowledged by Johnson's rebel friends, and they are now abandoning him with all the rest." In the eyes of the radicals the War Office does not appear to be so very important for *immediate practical* purposes as some other of the Departments, and they still cherish the hope of being able to maintain their present position in the Treasury, which is now full of them—from cellar to garrett. The last remaining administration official there now says that: "Johnson is 'played out';" and he avows his intention of supporting Mr. Chase for the Presidency.

The foregoing is intended to be strictly confidential. I have no desire to suppress names if you wish to verify these statements.

William Thorpe.

ALS, DLC-JP.

From William J.C. Duhamel

Augst 10th 1867.

Mr. President:

Yesterday after leaving the Secty of the Navy Capt Chandler communicated an important fact[1] viz

In speaking of the business followed by Matchett[2] as a broker for offices and the wages he gets from the Judiciary Commite; he, Capt C said that Matchett had informed him why he took so much interest in getting Husties[3] confirmed as Warden of the Jail because Husties would be their man (the impeacher's man) in aiding them *to work up the cases of Surratt & Dunham against the President.*[4] I think I will be able to furnish you with proof soon of how prodigal the U.S. funds are used by this Judiciary Commte for their nefarious purposes.

I hope Mr. President care will be taken to keep my name out of this matter as much as possible as a Mr. Bell[5] guard at Jail (who is often at

Black & Lamons office[6] being a relative of Lamon) reports Judge Black as Saying that in his interview with the President in behalf of Dr. Young;[7] the President said Dr. Duhamel had given him important information. This might do me a professional injury as I attend persons of all shades of politics.

I have been your personal friend for many years since (1857) and in years past often met you with mutual respected friends some of whom are dead and gone. This feeling of friendship strengthened me to give you information from time to time of things that were going on to injure you not from any obligation as to position. As you know in position or out of position I have always been true to friends.

I dislike the reputation of informer but my nature will not allow me remain silent and witness this *murder* for it is nothing else but murder. These assassins and conspirators are plotting against you and *I will* expose them whenever it is in my power.

W.J.C. Duhamel M.D.

The Rev Father Wiggett,[8] Mrs. Surratts spiritual adviser recvd. several notes from Hon B Butler and Hon Ashley M.C.[9] requesting an interview with him. Father Wiggett called to see the Hon B Butler and during a long conversation Genl Butler said in substance that he could go before the country with what evidence he had and prove "*that man*" meaning President Johnson—guilty of being implicated in the conspiracy to kill President Lincoln in an indirect manner viz by hinting to others in the lower walks of life viz if President Lincoln were out of the way and he were President he could pardon whom he pleased and if Father Wiggett could induce John H Surratt to make a clean breast of it; *he (Butler) would insure* Surratt as a member of Congress thro congress he would be delivered from further penalties and restored to liberty.

Mr. Ashley said nearly the same in different interviews.

They told Father Wigget they knew he was with Mrs. S. in her last moments and they felt as he did that she had been unjustly hung and Johnson was to blame for it. This was during Extra Cess'n Congrs in Summer of 1867.

ALS, DLC-JP.
1. Apparently both Duhamel and Malcolm T.E. Chandler visited Gideon Welles on August 9, leaving some papers with him about the Charles A. Dunham (Sanford Conover) perjury case which Welles gave to Johnson on the 10th. Beale, *Welles Diary*, 3: 165.
2. William B. Matchett.
3. William H. Huestis.
4. John H. Surratt and Charles A. Dunham. See Duhamel to Johnson, Feb. 26, 1867, and Dunham to Johnson, July 26, 1867.
5. John Bell (c1818–fl1890), a native of Virginia, apparently retained his job at the jail the rest of his life. 1870 Census, D.C., Washington, 4th Ward, 36; Washington, D.C., directories (1867–91).
6. Jeremiah S. Black and Ward H. Lamon.
7. Probably Noble Young (1808–fl1883), who practiced medicine in Washington, D.C., and taught the theory and practice of medicine at Georgetown University for twenty-

five years. When Duhamel was removed from his post as jail physician on July 26, 1867, Young succeeded him and held the position for at least six years. Atkinson, *Physicians and Surgeons*, 537; *Washington Evening Star*, July 26, 1867; Washington, D.C., directories (1878–84).

8. Bernardin F. Wiget (*fl*1872), a native of Switzerland, was a Jesuit priest who served several Washington, D.C., congregations at various times. President of Gonzaga College in the capital for several years, he was a hospital chaplain (1862–65). Having known Mary Surratt for ten or eleven years, he served as a character witness for her at her trial and accompanied her to the scaffold. Benn Pitman, *The Assassination of President Lincoln and the Trial of the Conspirators* (New York, 1865), 135–36; Weichmann, *Assassination of Lincoln*, 471; Powell, *Army List*, 828; Washington, D.C., directories (1862–73); *Washington Evening Star*, July 21, 1869.

9. Benjamin F. Butler and James M. Ashley.

From J. Henry Wilkins [1]

New York   Augt. 10th, 1867.

Dear Sir

If you have any Government Bonds, sell them at once, as you can buy them much cheaper very soon.

A friend of yours a few days ago informed me that it was no use to say a word to you, in urging you to act in your own defence or to protect your honor and reputation as chief magistrate of the United States. I do not agree with the gentleman, and in direct opposition to his views I now say to you that if you will suspend McCulloch, and appoint some such man as old Judge Ewing of Ohio,[2] or John E. Williams[3] of this City, or Freeman Clark[4] of Rochester New York, to institute a strict examination of the Printing Bureau and the whole Treasury Department, you will break up the most gigantic ring of swindlers and speculators that ever existed in any nation. You will at once put Chase, Fessenden, McCulloch and all your leading enemies on the defensive, and save yourself from the impending ruin which hangs over your head.

At present there is not a paper in the Nation bold enough to expose the duplication of Bonds, the over-issue of notes, Fractional Currency, and every obligation which the Government has made. If this corruption is continued in the Treasury the repudiation of the Government debt is inevitable. A few patriotic friends of yours have determined to start a paper in this City, for the purpose of laying before the people the true condition of their interest, now confided to such faithless and incompetent hands. When this paper makes its appearance you will be compelled to take sides with the people, or with the corrupt officials, who are wasting their substance, and piling up for themselves fortunes mountain high, who have degraded their high office by a system of stock gambling and Gold speculations.

I know your feelings will be on the side of the people, but whether you have nerve enough to assert your prerogative, and have the Augean Stables cleaned, will soon be tested.

The weak point in the fortification of your enemies is their corrupt squandering of the public money, and making the money in the Treasury Building. Strike them there, and down they go. Let me inform you what you ought to know, that McCulloch is the tool of Chase, and a more fatal enemy to you than Stanton. Stanton is an open enemy. McCulloch hides his hypocracy "with smiles and affability." He has placed his whole army of subordinates, scattered like devouring locusts through the land, in deadly hostility to your "truly wise policy," and aided the insane Congress to spancel and handcuff you. If you will not for your own sake, do for your Country's sake, make a demonstration in this case, that will prostrate your enemies, and raise you above the position you now occupy in the public mind.

Where did Chase get his Seven hundred thousand Dollars income per annum from, where did Harrington,[5] now in Switzerland, get his fortune from, where did McCulloch get his enormous fortune from, with their host of associates roling in wealth? From the people, and you as a faithful guardian of the people, are bound to stop them.

Should you neglect this imperative duty, mark what I tell you, that you will be implicated with them, and be charged with being in the ring.

I would advise you to send for Harvey Waterson[6] show him this letter and take his advice.

J. Henry Wilkins

P.S. Since writing the above I have heard that Mr. Weed has deserted you, and gone over to that tyrant Stanton. If so he is not a proper person to consult. Harvey Waterson is your friend and a man of sense. See him.

J.H.W.

ALS, DLC-JP.
1. Not identified.
2. Thomas Ewing, Sr.
3. Probably John Earl Williams (1804–1877), president of the Metropolitan Bank in New York. New York City directories (1867–77); *NUC*.
4. Clark (1809–1887), a banker from Rochester, New York, had replaced Hugh McCulloch as comptroller of the National Currency Bureau in 1865. He also served on the finance committee during New York's 1867 constitutional convention. Rochester directories (1866–75); *U.S. Off. Reg.* (1865); *NUC*.
5. George Harrington, minister to Switzerland and former Treasury Department clerk.
6. Wilkins had originally written "Thurlow Weed," but crossed the name out and replaced it with Watterson's.

From George V. Cross[1]

Chicago, Aug 12th 1867.

Dear Sir.

I have looked with breathless silence upon your course in the present crisis and have had unshaken confidence in your firmness and ability to engineer the "great ship of state" through this alarming political hurri-

cane which seems to threaten her destruction, but I notice recently a disposition on your part to resign the office—which you have filled with so
much credit to your self, and all Lovers of Liberty in our land. I sincerely
trust the report is groundless.[2]

George V. Cross

ALS, DLC-JP.
   1. According to the letterhead of Cross's letter, he was a general commission merchant
who traded hides and furs. Beyond that, he is not further identified.
   2. Some newspapers were reporting that Johnson was considering resigning the presidency. See *Chicago Tribune*, Aug. 11, 12, 1867; *New York Herald*, Aug. 11, 1867.

From James Dixon

Hartford Ct   Aug 12th, 1867

I congratulate you on your prompt and decided action in removing
Stanton & appointing Steedman.[1]

James Dixon

Tel, DNA-RG107, Tels. Recd., President, Vol. 6 (1867–68).
   1. Four days earlier Dixon had urged the appointment of General Steedman to replace
Stanton. He subsequently pushed Johnson for "prompt action." Dixon to Johnson, Aug. 8,
10, 1867, Johnson Papers, LC.

From William Driver

Nashville Tennessee   August 12th 1867

Sir

You remember the Board of Claims which sat at this Capitol nearly all
the time you was our military Governour. The Books and papers of that
Board wer sent to War Department 10th of Decr. 1864, all evidence Bills
&c. among which is many Voucher Receipts, memorandums &c given to
Claimants by Forage masters, Federal officers &c. These in many Cases
Constituted the entire proof and in a very large number part proof of
Claims wer filed with same by Advise of Court, with an "understanding"
that they should be returned if the Claims wer not approved. Much dis-
satisfaction is manifested here on this account, and we feel justly, as those
papers seem to be the Property of Individuals, not of Government, which
seems to have reppudiated the action of the Board.

If you would deem it expedient to order the return of those Papers
placeing them in the hands of some honest person for distribution among
their owners it would do much toward reconcileing a dissatisfied People
and insure you many friends.[1] The Docket with list of Claims status of
Claimants &c can be kept in Washington if necessary, as I have Duplicate

which will be Cheerfully loand to the person who is honored with charge
of the Claims and distribution thereof.

William Driver

ALS, DLC-JP.
1. Evidence of Johnson's actions in response to Driver's letter has not been uncovered.

To Ulysses S. Grant

Washington, D.C.   Aug. 12th 1867

Sir:

The Honorable Edwin M. Stanton having been this day suspended as
Secretary of War, you are hereby authorized and empowered to act as
Secretary of War ad interim, and will at once enter upon the discharge of
the duties of that office.

The Secretary of War has been instructed to transfer to you all records,
books, papers, and other public property now in his custody and charge.[1]

Andrew Johnson

LS, DNA-RG108, Lets. Recd. *re* Military Discipline, File 96-W (E)-AUS-1867.
1. See Johnson to Stanton, Aug. 12, 1867. It is impossible to know whether this letter
to Grant or the letter to Stanton was penned first. It is known, however, that the delivery
was to Stanton first and then Grant. Thomas and Hyman, *Stanton*, 551.

To Ulysses S. Grant

Washington, D.C.   Aug. 12th 1867.

Dear Sir:

I will be pleased to have you present at one o'clock to-day, at which
time several questions in reference to the newly-acquired Russian territory will be considered.

Andrew Johnson

LS, L. W. Smith Col., Morristown National Historical Park, Morristown, N.J.

From Lovell H. Rousseau

Washington D.C.   Aug 12., 1867.

The President;

On to day during an interview with General Grant, I told him I understood that Major General Sheridan had written him a letter in which he
had charged me with assailing him and his administration of affairs in his
District during my late visit to New Orleans, and asked him for a copy of

that letter if it was official. He said in reply he had recieved a letter from General Sheridan in which allusion was made to me: but that it referred to other matters, and had been immediately forwarded to the President, and was now in his possession.[1]

I have the honor, therefore, to respectfully request a copy of so much of that letter as refers to myself.[2]

Lovell H. Rousseau
Brig & Bvt Major Genl   U.S.A.

ALS, DNA-RG107, Lets. Recd., Executive (M494, Roll 100).
1. The letter from Sheridan to Grant, dated August 3, 1867, discussed the registration of voters in Louisiana and the problems caused by the continuous newspaper reports that Sheridan was about to be removed from his post. Grant forwarded it to the secretary of war on August 8 requesting "that it be laid before the President, and his attention called to the unofficerlike conduct attributed to Gen. L. H. Rousseau." Simon, *Grant Papers*, 17: 253.
2. See Johnson to Rousseau, Aug. 21, 1867.

From Nathaniel P. Sawyer

Republic Office Pittsburgh   Aug 12th 1867

My Dear Sir

We leave here this P.M. for Philadelphia where our State Committee meet to morrow morning at the Girard House at 10 oclock.[1] If You have any suggestions I can be found at the Girard.

Our friends are delighted with your action in regard to Black Bull Stanton, and hope if he will go no other way, that You will kick him out. Nothing has done You so much harm as Your Cabinet has. If Your Cabinet was composed of Your friends, You would to day be what You deserve to be, the Nations favourite.

Let Your action be quick and decisive. The people like a brave bold man. God is on Your side. Do not go back on him. "He that would be free himself must Strike the blow." Hoping that You will rout Your enemies and save the Country.

N. P. Sawyer.

ALS, DLC-JP.
1. No information concerning the Philadelphia meeting has been found.

To Edwin M. Stanton

Washington, D.C.   Aug 12th 1867

Sir;

By virtue of the power and authority vested in me, as President, by the Constitution and Laws of the United States, you are hereby suspended from office as Secretary of War, and will cease to exercise any and all functions pertaining to the same.

You will at once transfer to General Ulysses S. Grant, who has this day been authorized and empowered to act as Secretary of War ad interim,[1] all records, books, papers, and other public property now in your custody and charge.

(signed) Andrew Johnson

Copy, DLC-JP.
1. See Johnson to Grant, Aug. 12, 1867.

From Edwin M. Stanton

Washington City. August 12, 1867

Sir:

Your note of this date has been received informing me that by virtue of the power and authority vested in you as President, by the Constitution and Laws of the United States, I am suspended from Office as Secretary of War, and will cease to exercise any and all functions pertaining to the same, and also directing me at once to transfer to General Ulysses S. Grant, who has this day been authorized and empowered to act as Secretary of War ad interim, all records, books, papers and other public property now in my custody and charge.

Under a sense of public duty I am compelled to deny your right under the Constitution and Laws of the United States, without the advice and Consent of the Senate, and without legal cause to suspend me from Office as Secretary of War, or the exercise of any or all functions pertaining to the same, or without such advice and consent to compel me to transfer to any person the records, books, papers and other public property in my custody as Secretary of War.

But inasmuch as the General commanding the Armies of the United States has been appointed Secretary of War ad interim, and has notified me that he has accepted the appointment,[1] I have no alternative but to submit, under protest, to superior force.

Edwin M. Stanton   Secretary of War

LS, DLC-JP.
1. Grant to Stanton, Aug. 12, 1867, Simon, *Grant Papers*, 17: 268.

From Perez Dickinson

Knoxville Tenne.   Augt. 13. 1867

Sir

I have just read the telegraphic announcement of your removal of Stanton—and appointment of Genl. Grant.

This move is in the right direction. The country will sustain you. Your administration will be strengthened. Your friends are rejoiced.

P Dickinson

ALS, DLC-JP.

From Henry Liebenau

No: 4, Hamilton Place   West 51st Street
New York   Augt. 13, 1867.

Mr President

Permit me to congratulate you on the great event of the season, namely the just and righteous discharge of Edwin M. Stanton, from the post, he never should have been placed in, and the confidence of a generous public, which he has continued to abuse. I hail this act of yours with sincere delight, and can assure you, it meets as it richly merits the approbation of the public in this quarter.

I hoisted my Flag, (The Stars & Stripes) upon my house as soon as I see its announcement in the papers this morning, and it is proudly floating from my flag staff now, while pening this expression of my gratification and delight.

May you have the prayers of the patriot and the protection of our Heavenly Father. May your days be numerous and happy, as I feel confident they will be, by following out the course you have so nobly begun. *After Washington, This City* needs the pruning operation of your removing power, for honesty has, for sometime past, been at a discount, while corruption— Fraud and duplicity appears to enjoy a premium in high places and unless the hand of correction is speedily applied our glorious Country will become a bye-word and a reproach. Honesty and Capacity for Official position has been rendered a secondary consideration to Dollars and Cents, and your patriotic order to give soldiers a preference for position, has been transformed into a means of destroying the character of the soldier for the benefit of the scheming politicians, who see in your order, if strictly enforced, that like Othello, their occupation would be gone.

Henry Liebenau.

P.S. Permit me here to assure Your Excellency, the sentiment of approval in the Address of the Constitutional Union Association when you last visited this City,[1] were the sincere expression of my heart, and not the empty soundings of the deceptive modern politician. Had I occupied an official position, this City would have this day reverbrated to the sound of *one hundred guns*.

ALS, DLC-JP.
1. Liebenau delivered a formal welcome address when Johnson stopped in New York on June 21 during his tour of the East. *New York Tribune*, June 22, 1867.

From Thomas S. Piggot[1]

New York, August 13th 1867

Sir:

If you desire some information concerning Mr. E. M. Stanton's administration of the War Department during the Civil War, I think it could be obtained from either Mr. W. Garrett Esq,[2] President of the B & ORR, or Wm. Prescott Smith Esq, late of the same Corporation, but now Collector of Internal Revenue in Baltimore. I do not desire my name used in the premises but as I do not shrink from anything I do or say, I subscribe myself . . .

T. S. Piggot of Baltimore Maryland.

It is possible Mr Smith may know somewhat of Chief Justice Chase's operations during his term of office as Secretary of the Treasury. I am known to Col L. A Whiteley & Mr Coyle,[3] of the National Intelligencer.

ALS, DLC-JP.

1. Piggott (c1829–1868) was associated with several newspapers, including the *Baltimore Sun*, of which he was one of the editors. Baltimore directories (1864–66); *Baltimore Sun*, Mar. 17, 1868.

2. John Work Garrett.

3. Lambert A. Whiteley and John F. Coyle. Before becoming an editor of the *National Intelligencer*, Whiteley (1825–1869) was associated with several newspapers, including the *Baltimore Clipper* and the *New York Herald*. He also served as a clerk in the sixth auditor's office in Washington in the early 1860s. *Washington Evening Star*, July 21, 1869; Washington, D.C., directories (1862–69); *U.S. Off. Reg.* (1861).

From John B. Clark

Fayette Mo   August 14 1867

Sir

At a term of the United States Circuit Court held at Jefferson City, (the seat of Government of the State of Missouri) during the first or second year of the late war, a great many of the Citizens of this State were indicted by the grand jury of that Court for *conspiracy* and treason against the government of the United States; their crime in every instance as far as I have heard consisted in opin avowed acts, and sympathy with, and aid of the rebellion then being organized in Missouri.

The most of those indicted never took up arms, or entered the confederate service in any way, some did, and some returned to their origninal *allegiance* during the war, and done service in the Militia of the State in various forms, under the orders of the State, and National authorities while others remained in the confederate army until that army surrendered, and accepted their parole as surrendered Troops.

Those indictments were never acted on by the Court during the war, and the understanding has been very general with the bar, and those connected with that branch of the government, that upon the surrender, and the declaration of peace they had been ordered to be dismissed by the Attorney general of the United States or that they would be at the earliest convenience of that officer.

Whether the Attorney general has ever taken any action in the matter, or even his attention with that of your excellency called to the subject I know not, but presume it has as a matter of course, and if there has not been an order from that officer directing all such indictments dismissed that there will be one *issued* and *enforced without delay*—so that the same rule will be applied in this as in other States in such cases.

I would not address the Attorney general through your excellency on the subject if it were not that steps are now being taken to arrest, and bring to trial many of the persons thus indicted[1] contrary to what is understood to be the settled policy, if not the positive orders of the government as indicated immediately upon the surrender. I am in no wise personally interested or in any way involved in the proceedings sought to be corected. But I make this communication to your excellency, and through you to the law department of the government in order that the action of the government in reference to all of its people may be uniform, and that no incroachment upon its policy may obtain for mere partisan purposes. I hope your excellency will have this communication presented to the Attorney general of the United States with a respectful request that he take the necessary action in the premises, and that he give me his answer at his earliest convenience.[2]

John B. Clark.

ALS, DNA-RG60, Office of Atty. Gen., Lets. Recd., President.

1. Attempts to indict and try former Confederates for war-related offenses were very common, not only in Missouri, but also in Tennessee, Arkansas, and Kentucky at this time. Dorris, *Pardon and Amnesty*, 241; William E. Parrish, *A History of Missouri, 1860–1875* (Columbia, Mo., 1973), 139.

2. An endorsement stated that Clark should be sent a copy of a "letter of instructions on this point" recently written to the district attorney of western Missouri. That communication to Bennett Pike indicated that Pike should have considerable discretion and concluded with the statement that difficulty of procuring evidence was sufficient reason for not pursuing an indictment. A second letter to Pike, dated October 7, authorized him to dismiss all cases that merely involved political wrongdoing. John M. Binckley to Bennett Pike, Aug. 15, 1867; M. F. Pleasants to Pike, Oct. 7, 1867, Office of Atty. Gen., Lets. Sent, Vol. F (M699, Roll 11), RG60, NA.

From Joshua L. Foster[1]

States & Union Office, Portsmouth N.H.
August 14, 1867

Honored Sir,

I understand that Mr Alanson J. Shorey[2] of this city recently held a brief conference with your Excellency in relation to certain official changes in this vicinity.

I wish to say to you, Sir, that so far as I am advised, Mr Shorey, is acting in good faith and if you shall see fit to put confidence in him and grant his requests, I think your true friends and all opponents of radicalism in this section will approve your course. Certain changes among government office holders here have long be needed and earnestly hoped for. We feel that those changes are imperatively demanded if we are to hope for political success and the salvation of our country.

Your change in the War Department meets with a response of universal acclaim among all our truly patriotic people. Let the good work go on and you will have a party at your command that will in good time redeem and save our now distracted country. Hoping for your favorable consideration of the requests of our friend Mr S . . .

J. L. Foster   Editor States & Union.

ALS, DLC-JP.
   1. Foster (1824–1900) enjoyed a career as a successful architect before he launched his newspaper business in 1863. He edited and published the *Weekly States and Union* until 1868, in which year he began the *Daily Times*. Ezra S. Stearns, ed., *Genealogical and Family History of the State of New Hampshire* (4 vols., New York, 1908), 4: 1663–64.
   2. Not identified.

From Henry W. Hilliard
Unofficial.

Augusta, Georgia. August 14, 1867.

My dear Sir,

I am sure that you will appreciate the feeling which prompts me to express my great gratification at your removal of Mr. Stanton. When I knew you in Congress, I admired you for your independence and courage.

Your course in regard to the late Secretary of War is in my judgement, every way creditable to you. It will result too in great good. Independent of the relief that you must experience in ridding yourself of a most odious person, the manliness and courage of the *act* will do great good in the country.

With my best wishes, for the success of your Administration, and for your personal welfare . . .

Henry W. Hilliard.—

ALS, DLC-JP.

To Hugh McCulloch

Washington, D.C.   Aug 14, 1867.

Sir.

In compliance with the requirements of the eighth section of the Act of Congress of March 2 1867 entitled "An Act regulating the tenure of certain civil offices,"[1] you are hereby notified that on the 12" instant, the Honorable Edwin M. Stanton was suspended from office as Secretary of War, and General Ulysses S. Grant authorized and empowered to act as Secretary of War ad interim.

(signed)   Andrew Johnson

LBcopy, DLC-JP.
   1. *Congressional Globe*, 39 Cong., 2 Sess., Appendix, pp. 198–99.

From Thomas G. Davidson[1]

Amite City   August 15th, 1867

Honoured Sir

I desire to apply to you for a Pardon being a citizen of the state of Louisiana where I was raised. I am included in proscribed incurred as the penalty of the sessession of my state. I was a member of Congress, as you may recollect at the time Louisiana seceded but remained until my time was out.

I was allways opposed to secession but when the fight commenced as a matter of loyalty to my people I remained with them taking their fate.

I did all I could to ameliorate the hard ships of our people for they had made me what I was. I went to Baton Rouge & took the oath by order of Genl. Lawler[2] the day before your proclamation was published.

I send you here with this letter of John M Moore[3] the old Tennessee friend of yours who knows my possition and gives you information thereof. I hope for a pardon at your hands.[4]

I am Sir most respectfully your ardent will wisher that you fully succeed in your patriotic effort to preserve the Constitution of our common Country.

Thomas Green Davidson

ALS, DLC-JP.
   1. Davidson (1805–1883), a Louisiana lawyer, had been a register of the U.S. land office, member of the state house of representatives, and U.S. House (1855–61) before the war. After the war he returned to the state house. *BDUSC*.
   2. A native of Ireland, Michael K. Lawler (1814–1882) was an Illinois farmer and storekeeper. Rising from captain of the 18th Ill. in 1861 to brigadier general, Lawler fought at Fort Donelson, Port Gibson, and Vicksburg before commanding the District of East Louisiana at the end of the war. Warner, *Blue*.

3. Moore (c1832–fl1870), formerly of Lawrence County, Tennessee, and a political supporter of Johnson, was a physician. In his letter he informed Johnson that Davidson was requesting a pardon because he had not been permitted to register to vote, even though it was well known that during the war Davidson had opposed Jefferson Davis at great personal risk and had lost "all he had." 1860 Census, Tenn., Lawrence, 10th Civil Dist., Lawrenceburg, 100; 1870 Census, La., Tangipahoa, Amite City, 1; John M. Moore to Johnson, Aug. 15, 1867, Johnson Papers, LC.

4. There is no indication of a response from Johnson or that Davidson received an individual pardon.

From Hugh McCulloch

Treasury Department. August [ca. 15] 1867.[1]

Sir:

I have carefully read Mr. Martin's letter,[2] and return it herein.

Inclosed I hand you statement from our appointment office,[3] showing the circumstances under which, and on whose recommendation, Mr. Englebert[4] was appointed Assessor. I also hand you a letter from the acting Commissioner of Internal Revenue,[5] showing the number of changes of assistants that were made on the recommendations of Mr. Martin, and those made on the recommendations of Mr. Englebert, from which you will perceive that Mr. E. was recommended most strongly by the Martins[6]—father and son—and by Mr. Edward [sic] Cooper, of Tennessee, the former secretary of the President. It will be perceived that fewer changes of assistant assessors have been made under Mr. Englebert than were made by his predecessor.

If you will read carefully the statement in regard to the appointment of Mr. Martin, you will see that if any error has been committed it has not been by the Secretary of the Treasury. I had supposed, until I saw Mr. M's letter, that Mr. Englebert was what Mr. M. recommended him to be, a friend of the Administration, and that his appointment was necessary in order to carry out the conservative programme. Unless I have been misinformed, Col. Moore[7] will advise you that Mr. M. came to Washington and strongly urged the appointment of Mr. Englebert.

There are many complaints in regard to removals, as there must necessarily be. I desire the President, however, to understand that it is the aim of the Secretary to so act in regard to all appointments as to promote the interests of the Administration and of the public service.

In order that we may be advised precisely as to how Mr. Martin stood in relation to the appointment of Mr. Englebert, I inclose his letter to you under date of February 15, 1867.[8]

H MCulloch

P.S. The ruling of the First Comptroller,[9] to which Mr. M. takes exception, is undoubtedly the correct one under the statute, and was approved by the Solicitor of the Treasury[10] to whom the question was referred. I regretted that these officers could not come to a different conclusion; they were, however, called upon to interpret the law and not to make it. If their decision works hardship to Mr. M's son, and to other officers similarly situated, the lawmaking power and not the executive officer should be complained of.[11]

H MC

LS, DNA-RG56, Appts., Internal Revenue Service, Assessor, Pa., 7th Dist., J. Lee Englebert.

1. Because of McCulloch's references to other documents, it is likely that his letter was written on August 15.

2. See Robert L. Martin to Johnson, Aug. 10, 1867, Appts., Internal Revenue Service, Assessor, Pa., 7th Dist., J. Lee Englebert, RG56, NA.

3. See statement, July 31, 1867, ibid.

4. J. Lee Englebert.

5. The reference here is undoubtedly to the August 12 letter from Thomas Harland, acting commissioner, who has not been further identified. See Harland to McCulloch, Aug. 12, 1867, ibid.

6. Robert L. and Archer N. Martin.

7. William G. Moore.

8. See Robert L. Martin to Johnson, Feb. 15, 1867, ibid.

9. Robert W. Taylor.

10. Edward Jordan (1820–1899), originally of New York, moved to Ohio in 1844 where he taught school before embarking on a career in law. He served as solicitor of the treasury from 1861 until 1869 and afterwards practiced law in New York City. Evans, *Scioto County*, 287–88.

11. On August 15 the President attached an endorsement to Martin's August 10 letter in which Johnson indicated to the secretary of the treasury that he had carefully read the documents. He contended that the Treasury Department should have been wary of removals by Englebert and should not have approved them. The President wondered if these persons could be reinstated.

From Robert Q. Pinckney

August 15, 1867, Charleston, S.C.; LS, DNA-RG60, Office of Atty. Gen., Lets. Recd., President.

Pinckney of Charleston, the owner of a store and a lot in Jacksonville, Florida, reports that the store was seized by the U.S. marshal in November 1865 under a libel for confiscation. Pinckney went to Florida in January 1866 to attend the U.S. district court, but it never convened due to the absence of the judge. In any event, the marshal released Pinckney's property upon his pledge of abiding by the court's eventual decree. Although the district court opened in March 1866 at St. Augustine, Pinckney's oath of amnesty did not reach the court in time to be presented. Afterwards, the U.S. district attorney declined to dismiss Pinckney's libel, because he doubted that he had such authority. Then in May the marshal again seized Pinckney's property and continued to hold it; meanwhile the owner received no rents yet was obligated to pay taxes and insurance costs on the store. The district court did not meet again until June 1867, at which time Pinckney appeared in person; but the district attorney refused to acquiesce to the discontinuance of the case, despite having assured Pinckney that he would do so. The district attorney argued that Pinckney's oath of amnesty was insufficient and the judge concurred, even though Pinckney maintained that he did not need a special presidential pardon. Moreover, Pinckney was required to pay a bill of costs in the amount of $740, as well as bear the expense of a court appeal. In the meantime the marshal collected rents (possibly in excess of $2,000) on the use of the store that would more than cover costs now assessed to Pinckney. The store owner asks Johnson to intervene to require the court to accept Pinckney's oath, taken in compliance with the President's Amnesty Proclamation, and thereby discontinue the confiscation proceedings.

From Joseph E. Snodgrass

184 East Broadway, New York, Aug 15, 1867.

Mr President:

Early in July, and as soon as the committee of arrangements for the dedication of the Antietam National Cemetery had fixed the day for the same (September the 17th the Anniversary of the great and decisive [battle] whose name it wears[)] a special committee of three,[1] of which the undersigned had the honor of being chairman ex-officio, called on Your Excellency, to tender an invitation to attend on that interesting occasion. Not finding you at leisure, the committee addressed you a communication[2] conveying their wish and that of the Board of Trustees— which represents the States having dead on the field of Antietam and now buried in the Cemetery—that you would signify, at any early date, Your Excellency's purpose to be present on the occasion referred to.

Having recieved no response I again communicate the wishes of the committee of arrangements, and urge upon you the acceptance of their invitation, in view of the proximity of the Cemetery to Washington.[3]

Assuring Your Excellency—as perhaps it is superfluous to do—that your early assurance that you *will attend* would insure every facility for your doing so pleasantly, that your exalted station would give Your Excellency a right to anticipate at the hands of the management . . .

J E Snodgrass, Chairman, Comm of Arr.

ALS, DLC-JP.
1. The committee was composed of Snodgrass, chairman, Thomas A. Boullt, and Gibson L. Cranmer. Boullt (b. c1818) was listed as a silversmith in Hagerstown, Maryland. Cranmer (1826–1903) was a lawyer who had served as secretary of the Wheeling convention in 1861. He was president of the Antietam National Cemetery Association when the national government took responsibility for the cemetery. Cranmer was judge of the municipal court in Wheeling. 1860 Census, Md., Washington, Hagerstown, 12; *Who Was Who in America*, 1: 273; George W. Atkinson and Alvaro F. Gibbens, *Prominent Men of West Virginia* (Wheeling, 1870), 339.
2. See Snodgrass et al. to Johnson, July 8, 1867, Johnson Papers, LC.
3. The President replied to the committee that he would attend the ceremonies at Antietam on September 17. Johnson to Snodgrass et al., Aug. 20, 1867, ibid. For Johnson's speech at the site on the 17th, see *Washington Evening Star*, Sept. 18, 1867.

From J. McClary Perkins

Washington   Aug. 16" 1867.

Sir:

As a citizen of the United States much interested in whatever pertains to the real welfare and progress of the newly enfranchised freedmen of this country I desire to call your attention to the present course and policy of Major General O. O. Howard, the commissioner of the Freedmen's Bureau, which seems to be mainly directed to using the men and resources at his command to gratify and enhance his own personal interests and ambition.

This letter is directed to The President because the undersigned believes that, by the Constitution and laws of the United States, on The President rests the final responsiblity for the acts and conduct of this commissioner—whom The President virtually appoints or removes at pleasure.

It is well-known and acknowledged by the friends of the Freedmen's Bureau (of whom I claim to be one and to know their general feeling) that its "occupation is gone"—that there is nothing whatever for it to do—and that the only pretext which can be urged for its continuance beyond its present limit of existence—July 16" 1868—will be its usefulness in conducting the presidential campaign next year—and to which high office (the second if not the first) the commissioner and his friends even openly profess hopeful aspirations.

As usual, "Satan finds mischief for idle hands to do."[1] Anticipating the impending "military necessity" last fall, the commissioner took twelve thousand dollars (which he had no shadow of right to do) from a sum under his control known as the "irregular fund," and appropriated this money to the purchase of an old tavern stand and three acres of land at the head of the street and just beyond the boundary of Washington City.[2]

Then he caused an Act of Congress to be passed chartering an institution under the pompous name of "Howard University."[3] This "university" was born, instanter, like the fabled Minerva from the brain of Jupiter, full-grown and clad in the complete panoply of war. It has its Theological, its Medical, its Law, its Collegiate, its Normal, and its Scientific Department for the education of the southern freemen. In its fustian pretension it finds no rival in America, and continental Europe, with its institutions of learning centuries old, can hardly hold a torch to the "Howard University." The "Howard University" has a board of trustees,[4] of course. They all belong to the same religious sect with the "commissioner" and are his personal friends and relations. This no doubt was based on the scriptural doctrine that "charity begins at home." The friends of the educational interest of the blacks who had been working, for years before the existence of the Freedmen's Bureau, for the cause, on hearing of this wicked and unauthorized "flank movement" of the "commissioner" for his own personal aggrandizement, were naturally indignant at such an outrage on the cause he professed to serve. (This "irregular fund" is the unclaimed back-pay and bounty of certain black soldiers from Virginia and North Carolina.)[5] Complaint was made to Congress of these "tactics" of the "commanding general."[6] Redress was promptly and generally promised. But the "commissioner" joined issue with these malcontents and went to Congress, using his personal and official influence in his own favor, and succeeded in getting the resolution so modified that the whole fund was placed under the control of the "commissioner" by law![7] So the "commissioner" won again there. Now it is understood that he has taken this whole fund for "Howard University" and has since bought fifty acres instead of three—the original purchase.[8] And ten thousand dollars has been given to the complainants for "hush money"—to use the words of those receiving the money.[9] The "commissioner &c. &c." is free in his boasts that he intends to make "Howard University" "the richest institution in the United States." Not long since he made this brag in the presence of the new commissioner of education.[10]

It should have been stated that the "resolution" above referred to will be found on page 545 (ch. 186) of Statutes at Large of last Congress.

By means of a contract with Mr. S. J. Bowen,[11] postmaster of Washington, who seems to be the ruling spirit of the board of three trustees of colored schools under Act of Congress of July 11" 1862,[12] the Freedmen's Bureau has acquired a right to control the colored schools of Washington, although a plain and solemn Act of Congress is thereby nullified. Under the authority thus acquired from Mr. Bowen the Freemen's Bureau steps into one of the most advanced colored schools in Washington and takes out eight of the most advanced pupils and transfer them to "Howard University," although this modest "University" is outside the limits of the city of Washington. The avowed reason assigned to the teacher for such unreasonable conduct is that "Howard University" will be a failure unless this course is taken to fill its departments!

Good God! and has it come to this? Must the superintendents and chaplains of Freedmen's Bureau in Virginia and North Carolina be cashiered because their farming interests interfere with the proper discharge of their official duties,[13] and will the overpaid "commissioner" of Freedmen's Bureau be allowed to indulge in such "speculations" and ambitious projects as this? It is not the fortune of ordinary philanthropists to be allowed the modest privilege of building a name and monument for themselves. Posterity has heretofore performed this labor of love. But as the cockney said of Shakespeare—"he was not up to these times"—so do these modern philanthropists say of our ancestors.

It will be seen that the removal of the "commissioner" of Freedmen's Bureau would cure all the evils growing out of his official misconduct.

Several months since I was told by one of the higher officers of Freedmen's Bureau that all their work would hereafter be directed to school matters here and in the south. This is evidently done in order to create a pretext for continuing their lease of life next year and to use their official power and influence to build up "Howard University."

J. McClary Perkins.

P.S.

I desire here to communicate to The President that, after my interview with him on July 31, I saw the Sec. of Interior[14] who, after deliberation, decided that he had no legal power to remove a trustee of colored schools. He expressed regret that he had no power to do so. I then explained to him how the board would be changed if I was on it, and told him that Mr. Hall[15] would immediately resign if I could have any assurance that I could be appointed to the vacancy. His reply was that the vacancy could not be filled until it was made. Mr. Hall immediately put his resignation in my hands. It is now before me. In writing the Sec. of Interior (on 10th inst.) for some of my papers I informed him that I had Mr. Hall's resignation and was authorized to use it. But I have had no reply.

J. McC. Perkins

ALS, DLC-JP.

1. From *Divine Songs*, XX, by Isaac Watts. "For Satan finds some mischief still/ For idle hands to do."

2. A large three-story red building and lot were acquired through Generals O. O. Howard and George W. Balloch of the Freedmen's Bureau, who later reminisced that the building had previously been a saloon and dance hall. Evidence of this fact is inconclusive, however. Purchased for $12,000, it was situated north of the boundary between Washington city and county (now Florida Ave.) on Seventh Street (now Georgia Ave.), south of Pomeroy Street (now W Street). Rayford W. Logan, *Howard University: The First Hundred Years, 1867–1967* (New York, 1969), 26–27, 34.

3. See "An Act to Incorporate the Howard University in the District of Columbia," Mar. 2, 1867, *Congressional Globe*, 39 Cong., 2 Sess., Appendix, p. 201.

4. At its first official meeting the board adopted a resolution stating that "Every person elected to any official position in Howard University shall be a member of some Evangelical Church." The board was almost entirely, if not completely, made up of Congregationalists. Logan, *Howard University*, 28.

5. Supposedly the money was taken from the Veterans Bounty Fund established to pay black soldiers recruited in the northern and middle states, but at least one local newspaper denied the allegation. Ibid., 27; *Washington Evening Star*, Aug. 24, 1867.

6. Not found.

7. See "An Act to regulate the Disposition of an Irregular Fund in the Custody of the Freedmen's Bureau," Mar. 2, 1867, *Congressional Globe*, 39 Cong., 2 Sess., Appendix, p. 238.

8. There is no evidence of a fifty-acre purchase. However, 150 acres were purchased in late May 1867. *House Reports*, 41 Cong., 2 Sess., No. 121, pp. 28, 60–63.

9. Apparently a reference to the $10,000 given to the National Theological Institute (Baptist). See *Washington Evening Star*, Aug. 24, 1867.

10. Henry Barnard.

11. Sayles J. Bowen.

12. See "An Act relating to Schools for the education of Colored Children in the Cities of Washington and Georgetown, in the District of Columbia," *Congressional Globe*, 37 Cong., 2 Sess., Appendix, p. 396.

13. See Oliver O. Howard to Johnson, Aug. 22, 1866, *Johnson Papers*, 11: 108–18.

14. Orville H. Browning.

15. Albert G. Hall (*c*1832–*fl*1901), a wealthy native of Maine, served on the Board of Trustees for Colored Schools for Washington and Georgetown from late 1867 to 1869. 1870 Census, D.C., Washington, 2nd Ward, 110; Washington, D.C., directories (1866–1901).

From Ulysses S. Grant

Washington, D.C.   Aug. 17th 1867.

Sir:

I am in receipt of your order of this date[1] directing the assignment of Gen. G. H. Thomas to the command of the 5th Military District; Gen. Sheridan to the Dept. of the Mo. and Gen. Hancock[2] to the Dept. of the Cumberland. Also, of your note of this date, (enclosing these instructions,) saying: "Before you issue instructions to carry into effect the enclosed order I would be pleased to hear any suggestion you may deem necessary respecting the assignments to which the order refers."[3]

I am pleased to avail myself of this invitation to urge, earnestly urge, urge in the name of a patriotic people who have sacrificed hundreds of thousands of loyal lives, and Thousands of millions of treasure to preserve the integrity and union of this country, that this order be not insisted on.

It is unmistakably the expressed wish of the country that Gen. Sheridan should not be removed from his present command. (This is a Republic where the will of the people is the law of the land. I beg that their voice may be heard.)

Gen. Sheridan has performed his civil duties faithfully and intelligently. His removal will only be regarded as an effort to defeat the laws of Congress. It will be interpreted by the unreconstructed element in the South, those who did all they could to break up this Government by arms, and now wish to be the only element consulted as to the methods of restoring order, as a triumph. It will embolden them to renewed opposition to the will of the loyal masses, believing that they have the Executive with them.

The Services of Gen. Thomas in battling for the Union entitle him to some consideration. He has repeatedly entered his protest against being assigned to either of the five military districts, and especially to being assigned to relieve Gen. Sheridan.

Gen. Hancock ought not to be removed from where he is. His Department is a complicated one which will take a new commander some time to become acquainted with.

There are military reasons, pecuniary reasons, and, above all, patriotic reasons why this order should not be insisted on.

Cartoon depicting the controversy over Johnson's
removal of Stanton and Sheridan.
Harper's Weekly, August 24, 1867

I beg to refer to a letter, marked private, which I wrote to the President when first consulted on the subject of the change in the War Department.[4] It bears upon the subject of this removal and I had hoped would have prevented it.

U. S. Grant
Gen. U.S.A. & Sec. of War ad int.

ALS, DLC-JP.
1. Johnson order, Aug. 17, 1867, Johnson Papers, LC.
2. George H. Thomas, Philip H. Sheridan, and Winfield S. Hancock.
3. Johnson to Grant, Aug. 17, 1867, Johnson Papers, LC.
4. Grant to Johnson, Aug. 1, 1867.

From Fisher A. Lewis [1]

August 17th 1867

Dear Sir

"How long will you halt between two opinions, if the Lord be God serve him, if Baal (Radicalism) serve him."[2]

In removeing Secretary Stanton you have done well. Go boldly forward in the Lord. Stop the execution of the civil rights bill & the registration law (so called). They are dignified with the name of Law & that is all. They are not Laws & you are not bound to execute them, but you are bound by your Oath of Office to resist their execution. They are not Law for this reason, the right of making voters belongs to the States & not to Congress or the General government. The States never delegated that right but reserved it to themselves. A majority of Congress may constitute a quorum to do business & why, because a majority can pass an act, but not a minority, but a majority of a quorum cannot pass any act, for this reason, that if they could you make the less rule the greater. To illustrate suppose there are 36 states each state is entitled to two senators, that would make the sennate consist of 72 members. A majority would be 37 & that would be a quorum. If they undertook to pass a bill even if 36 voted for it & one against it, it would not be law, because it would not be passed by a majority of the senate (which is 37) but would be by a majority of the quorum, which is not a majority of the senate & therefore not law. There is a way provided for each house to fill itself, & each house or both houses have no authority to proscribe a way. If they do it is illegal or not law & you are not bound to enforce it. If they undertake to impeach you resist it, with the Army & Navy & if that is not sufficient call on the people. You say you have confidence in the people now prove it by doing these things, & you will hear a shout go up from the British possessions on the North to Mexico on the South & from the Atlantic on the East to the Pacific on the west, that will make yours & Genl. Grant's heart leap for joy. You will also hear a wailling & nashing of teeth but never mind it that is the privilige of the Devil & his followers.

I was acquainted with Genl. Meigs.[3] We were classmates at West Point & I always esteemed him as a kind an Christian gentleman. I hear various rumors. Tell him for me that I hope he has not deserted the Banner of Christ for that of the Devil.

The negro is no more a part of our Government than mud is a part of water & who ever undertakes to make mud a part of water, befouls the water & makes a fool of himself & so it will be with these radicals. I do not speak of the negro thus because I despise him, for I do not despise anything that God has made, but I want everything in it's proper place.

F. A. Lewis

ALS, DLC-JP.
1. An 1836 graduate of West Point, Lewis (c1813–1883) saw no military duty other than a brief involvement in the Florida Indian war. From 1838 until his death he was a prosperous farmer in Charleston, Jefferson County, Virginia, which became part of West Virginia during the Civil War. 1860 Census, Va., Jefferson, Charleston, 160; *West Point Register*, 226; George W. Cullum, *Biographical Register of the Officers and Graduates of the U.S. Military Academy at West Point, N.Y., From Its Establishment, March 16, 1802, to the Army Re-organization of 1866–67* (2 vols., New York, 1868), 1: 497.
2. A loose rendering of Elijah's statement in 1 Kings 18: 21.
3. Montgomery C. Meigs.

From Thomas W. Scott[1]

Adamsville Tennessee   Aug. the 18th 1867

Your well merited Honer will please excuse and pardon one in so low and humble a station as myself for addressing you knowing from your public and private character that you are a friend of those in humble life as well as the great. I am encouraged to send you this letter in order to make known to you in my imperfect way the high regard and esteem myself and friends entertain for you for the unwavering corse you have taken and pursued in vindication of our constitutional rights in opposition to the proceedings of a jacobin congress. I read with eager interest all your public speaches and messages, and heartily indorse the principals set forth, and ardently desire that you may suceed in restoreing the liberties and freedom of our once happy and united, but now devided country, with the assistance of the honest but downtroden masses of the people. It is not my desire to troble you with a long letter hopeing that this may fall in your hands at a time you are comparatively at leasure so as not to disturbe you while ingaed in business of much more importance. You will please excuse a letter of this kind from a stranger from the fact it is only to express my high regard and approval of your corse at this critical time and informe you of my willingness to serve you or my country in any capacity that I can, and will willingly accept any position or appointment that your Honor may choose to confer on one occupying as humble a station as I do. I shall deem it a great honer to serve you or my Government eather in the United States, Mexico or Russia America.[2] I have ever been a constitutional union man, and was compelled to leave my home in Texas (on account of my union proclivitis) and went in to Mexico where I learnd the spanish language and the manners and customes of the people, afterwards returned to my native county and state, and as I was seclected as the conservative candidate of this county (as you can see by refering to the inclosed circular)[3] as this is one very radical co. in Brownlows dominoun I was badly beaten. In Reference to my qualfications &c. I will refer you to L. Pearce Counsel at Matamoras Mexico, John W. Letwich Congresssm., Franklin Chase counsel Tampico Mex. Standfor L Warren Legislator Tenn, Dorsa B. Thomas Ex. Member Congress Jas. Warren Ex member legislature.[4]

T W Scott.

The writer of the within only asks your attention when at leasure.[5]

ALS, DNA-RG59, Lets. of Appl. and Recomm., 1861–69 (M650, Roll 43), T. W. Scott.

1. Scott (1829–1902) served as postmaster at Adamsville, McNairy County, for a time. *U.S. Off. Reg.* (1867); Charles Whitlow and Myrlee Wright, *150 Years of Growth and Progress in McNairy County* (Jackson, Tenn., 1973), 59.

2. Scott was immediately given a recess appointment as consul at Matamoras. By November he was established at his post. Johnson's formal nomination of Scott went forward to the Senate in early February 1868; the Senate, however, rejected Scott's appointment in March. *U.S. Off. Reg.* (1867); Ser. 6B, Vol. 2: 314, Johnson Papers, LC; Scott to Johnson, Nov. 17, 1867, Johnson Papers, LC.

3. The circular is not found enclosed.

4. Leonard Pierce, Jr., John W. Leftwich, Franklin Chase, Stanford L. Warren, Dorsey B. Thomas, and James Warren. Pierce, not further identified, served as consul at Matamoras in the early 1860s. Chase (c1806–1890) was consul general at Tampico in the late 1860s. He had lived there for a number of years prior to that assignment. Stanford Warren (1837–1883) served several different terms in the Tennessee legislature in the postwar years. He was a lawyer and newspaper editor and publisher. President Johnson appointed him as U.S. district attorney for the Western District of Tennessee in 1867. James Warren (1810–1895) represented McNairy County in the Tennessee legislature in the 1840s and again in the 1880s. Father of Stanford L., he served as sheriff of the county and was a farmer with one of the largest landholdings. *U.S. Off. Reg.* (1861–63, 1867); Albert Brown, *Cemeteries, 1824–1984, McNairy County Tennessee* (Bethel Springs, Tenn., 1993); *BDTA*, 1: 762–73; 2: 954–55; Ser. 6B, Vol. 4: 228, Johnson Papers, LC; *New York Tribune*, Dec. 28, 1890.

5. This sentence appeared on a separate sheet.

To Ulysses S. Grant

Washington, D.C.   Aug. 19 1867

General.

I have received your communication of the 17th instant, and thank you for the promptness with which you have submitted your views respecting the assignments directed in my order of that date. When I stated, in my unofficial note of the 17th, that I would be pleased to hear any suggestions you might deem necessary upon the subject, it was not my intention to ask from you a formal report, but rather to invite a verbal statement of any reasons affecting the public interests which, in your opinion, would render the order inexpedient. Inasmuch, however, as you have embodied your suggestions in a written communication, it is proper that I should make some reply.

You earnestly urge that the order be not insisted on, remarking that "it is unmistakably the expressed wish of the country that General Sheridan should not be removed from his present command." While I am cognizant of the efforts that have been made to retain Genl Sheridan in command of the 5th Military District, I am not aware that the question has ever been submitted to the people themselves for determination. It certainly would be unjust to the army to assume that, in the opinion of the nation, he alone is capable of commanding the States of Louisiana & Texas, and that were he for any cause removed, no other General in the military service of the United States would be competent to fill his place. Genl Thomas, whom I have designated as his successor, is well known to the country. Having won high and honorable distinction in the field, he has since, in the execution of the responsible duties of a department commander, exhibited great ability, sound discretion, and sterling patriotism. He has not failed, under the most trying circumstances, to enforce the laws, to preserve peace and order, to encourage the restoration of civil authority, and to promote as far as possible a spirit of reconciliation. His administration of the Department of the Cumberland will certainly compare most favorably with that of Gen'l. Sheridan in the Fifth Military District. There, affairs appear to be in a disturbed condition, and a bitter spirit of antagonism seems to have resulted from Genl. Sheridan's management. He has rendered himself exceedingly obnoxious by the manner in which he has exercised even the powers conferred by Congress, and still more so by a resort to authority not granted by law, or necessary to its faithful and efficient execution. His rule has, in fact, been one of absolute tyranny, without reference to the principles of our government or the nature of our free institutions. The state of affairs which has resulted from the course he has pursued has seriously interfered with a harmonious, satisfactory, and speedy execution of the acts of Congress, and is alone sufficient to justify a change. His removal, therefore, cannot "be regarded as an effort to defeat the laws of Congress," for the object is to facilitate their execution, through an officer who has never failed to obey the statutes of the land, and to exact, within his jurisdiction, a like obedience from others. It cannot "be interpreted by the un-reconstructed element in the South—those who did all they could to break up this Government by arms, and now wish to be the only element consulted as to the method of restoring order—as a triumph;" for, as intelligent men, they must know that the mere change of military commanders cannot alter the law, and that General Thomas will be as much bound by its requirements as

General Sheridan. It cannot "embolden them to renewed opposition to the will of the loyal masses, believing that they have the Executive with them," for they are perfectly familiar with the antecedents of the President, and know that he has not obstructed the faithful execution of any act of Congress.

No one, as you are aware, has a higher appreciation than myself of the services of Genl. Thomas, and no one would be less inclined to assign him to a command not entirely consonant with his wishes. Knowing him, as I do, I cannot think that he will hesitate for a moment to obey any order having in view a complete and speedy restoration of the Union, in the preservation of which he has rendered such important and valuable services.

General Hancock, known to the whole country as a gallant, able, and patriotic soldier, will, I have no doubt, sustain his high reputation in any position to which he may be assigned. If, as you observe, the Department which he will leave is a complicated one, I feel confident that, under the guidance and instruction of General Sherman, General Sheridan will soon become familiar with its necessities, and will avail himself of the opportunity afforded by the Indian troubles for the display of the energy, enterprise, and daring which gave him so enviable a reputation during our recent civil struggle.

In assuming that it is the expressed wish of the people that General Sheridan should not be removed from his present command, you remark that "this is a Republic, where the will of the people is the law of the land," and "beg that their voice may be heard." This is, indeed, a Republic, based, however, upon a written Constitution. That Constitution is the combined and expressed will of the people, and their voice is law where reflected in the manner which that instrument prescribes. While one of its provisions makes the President Commander-in-Chief of the Army and Navy, another requires that "he shall take care that the laws be faithfully executed." Believing that a change in the command of the Fifth Military District is absolutely necessary for a faithful execution of the laws, I have issued the order which is the subject of this correspondence, and in thus exercising a power that inheres in the Executive, under the Constitution, as Commander-in-Chief of the military and naval forces, I am discharging a duty required of me by the will of the Nation, as formally declared in the supreme law of the land. By his oath, the executive is solemnly bound, "to the best of his ability, to preserve, protect, and defend the Constitution," and although, in times of great excitement, it may be lost to public view, it is his duty, without regard to the consequences to himself, to hold sacred and to enforce any and all of its provisions. Any other course would lead to the destruction of the Republic; for the Constitution once abolished, there would be no Congress for the exercise of legislative powers; no Executive, to see that the laws are faithfully executed; no judiciary, to afford to the citizen protection for life, limb, and property. Usurpation would inevitably follow, and a despotism be fixed upon the people, in violation of their combined and expressed will.

In conclusion, I fail to perceive any "military," "pecuniary," or "patriotic reasons" why this order should not be carried into effect. You will remember that in the first instance, I did not consider General Sheridan the most suitable officer for the command of the 5th Military District. Time has strengthened my convictions upon this point, and has led me to the conclusion that patriotic considerations demand that he should be superseded by an officer who, while he will faithfully execute the law, will at the same time give more general satisfaction to the whole people, white and black, North and South.

Andrew Johnson

LS, DNA-RG94, Lets. Recd. (Main Ser.), File P-869-1867 (M619, Roll 575).

From Hugh McCulloch
Personal & private

Washington   Aug. 19 1867

Mr President

It is not often that I pay any attention to the articles, abusive of myself, with which some of the public journals are teeming, but the enclosed slip from the "New York Tribune"[1] written by its Washington Correspondent, is of such a character, and is so well calculated to prejudice me in your estimation, and the estimations of all honorable men that I feel called upon to notice it.

Although not directly asserted it is clearly intimated, that I am warring against your Administration, by distributing the patronage of the Treasury Department, among your enemies, for the purpose of strengthening myself and my financial policy with Radicals. Nothing can be more unjust than this Statement or insinuation. In the discharge of my duties, as Secretary of the Treasury, I have had no other aim, than to sustain your Administration and promote the interest of the people. The charge, in whatever form it may be put, that I have sought to Serve myself, at your expense, or at the expense of the political opinions of which you are the representative, is false if not malicious. I have not done as much as I have desired to do, for you and the Country, but I have done what I could, under the embarrassments which have surrounded me, and only regret that I could do no more. I want you to believe this, Mr President, because in my contests with Distillers, Gold Speculators, Bank Note Companies, and plunderers of all discriptions, it is of the utmost importance that I should have the confidence of the President, to whom I, as Secretary of the Treasury, am primarily responsible for the manner in which I perform my official duties.[2]

H McCulloch

ALS, DLC-JP.
   1. See the *New York Tribune*, Aug. 16, 1867.
   2. Gideon Welles mentioned in his diary that McCulloch and conservative and radical Republicans had been friendly and that McCulloch had been persuaded to compromise and bargain with them regarding patronage. Welles, however, believed McCulloch had good intentions. Beale, *Welles Diary*, 3: 152–53.

From John G. Parkhurst

(Confidential)

Detroit   Aug 19, 1867

Mr President

   My great anxiety for your success in saving our country is my apology for writing this letter.

   Presuming that a change will be made in Genl Sheridans command, & knowing your well deserved confidence in Genl. Geo. H. Thomas, I feel it my duty to you, to say, that Genl W. D. Whipple A.A.G. & Chief of Staff for Genl Thomas is one of the rankest radicals in the country, & would delight in exhibiting his radical propensities as Chief of Staff in the N.O. district & in attempting to give direction to Genl Thomas administration. I believe if Genl Thomas should be sent to relieve Genl Sheridan, Whipple should be detailed on some other duty.[1]

J G Parkhurst

ALS, DLC-JP.
   1. Winfield Scott Hancock, rather than Thomas, ultimately relieved Sheridan in the Fifth Military District. For other correspondence pertaining to the replacement of Sheridan with Thomas, see Ulysses S. Grant to Johnson, Aug. 17; Johnson to Grant, Aug. 19; and, especially, Johnson to Grant, Aug. 26, 1867.

From R. King Cutler

No. 27 Indiana Ave., August 20, 1867.

Mr. President:

   With deep regret I am compelled to notice the fact that in the evening papers of this day General Grant has bid you defiance. The fifth section of his order releiving Gen. Sheridan[1] is, in the estimation of military men, your friends, an indirect disobedience of your orders.[2] Mr. President, what does this mean? Does it mean, sir, that General Grant is to command and rule, and to make you subservient to his will; or does it mean that when Grant *does* a thing you will submit? If you please, what is the benefit of the removal of Gen. Sheridan, if Gen. Thomas—a man of whole soul, an independent, honorable man, a man of energy, nerve and education, a man who is thoroughly skilled in military affairs—is to be dictated to by your Secretary-of-War, or by the General commanding, when the Law of Congress gives the commander of the District "discretionary powers"? Is this to be the result of the change of commanders? If so, God save us from the dilemma. Just as well have Sheridan—just as well have Napoleon or any other tyrant!

If General Grant is to be President, General of the Armies, Secretary of War, and Commander of the Fifth Miltary District, then for God's sake, make no change. Let Sheridan remain! Let the worst come! Let the Devil reign!

Mr. President, does not he who issued the order releiving Gen. Sheridan have the exclusive power to dictate to the commander who is to succeed him? The laws of Congress give that power—the rules of common sense say so. Then, Mr. President, the fifth section of the order of Gen. Grant, not only in my humble judgment but in the judgment of all your friends whom I have had an opportunity of speaking with to-day, are clearly of the opinion that the act removing Gen. Sheridan is totally futile, unavailable and worse than nothing unless you at once revoke this special, dictatorial mandate of your Secretary of War. Why, sir, Flanders,[3] a notorious scoundrel, a man who would steal Six Millions of Dollars from a State Government under the cloak of his title as Governor, a man who opposes reconstruction under the Act of Congress unless it be with negro predominancy—exclusively partizen—he to be retained as Governor at the will of him your—it does seem—would-be Master, General Grant. Again, is Mayor Heath[4]—a scoundrel, who has just received $30,000 as a bribe, a man who opposes reconstruction upon any basis except universal negro suffrage and universal holding of office by negroes, a man unprincipled and without character—to be retained in office under your would-be superior, General Grant?

Gen. Thomas sent to the Fifth Military District! Of what avail? Radical he may be. Just as well leave Sheridan, if all his most damnable, cursed, wicked, unheard-of orders are to be carried out. Let him stay! Let him rule! Let him reign upon a throne! Why disturb him if his orders are to be carried out?

Mr. President, where did General Grant, your Secretary of War, get the power to "alter, change or modify" *your* positive order? Sir, is it by Toleration of you, or is it by his own will? If by his own will, am I not right when I say that it is an implied violation of your direct order? By what other reason than that of obstinacy, and like the leech to the fungus flesh Grant holds on to Sheridan?

Congress is not in session, nor did Congress when in session last, make any such proviso for the Secretary of War or the General Commanding the Army. Therefore, sir, not only myself but your friends most humbly and respectfully request you to see to the interests of the good people of Louisiana and Texas.

Why, sir, for what reason did you remove Gen. Sheridan? Was it not for his participation in civil affairs as a partizan, and for his disobedience to his superior commanding officer. Then, why allow yourself to be thwarted in the very object which you had determined should be accomplished for nobler purposes? God save me and my people from such a dilemma! May the iron will which you have manifested in the removal of Stanton and in releiving Sheridan again manifest itself in the issued raised by General Grant, and may that justice which heaven demands at your hands be immediately granted.

Permit me to see you to-morrow. I will then explain to you parts of personal conversations of myself and others with General Grant, which may surprise you, the truth of which you need not take my word for, as I will refer you to the witnesses by name.

R. King Cutler

ALS, DLC-JP.
1. The fifth section of General Orders No. 77, dated August 17, 1867, ordered that Gen. George H. Thomas, when he relieved Sheridan, "will continue to execute all orders he may find in force in the Fifth Military District at the time of his assuming command of it, unless authorized by the General of the Army to annul, alter, or modify them." *Washington Evening Star*, Aug. 20, 1867.
2. Johnson's order of August 17, quoted in Grant's order, merely assigned Thomas to the command of the Fifth Military District, Sheridan to the Department of the Missouri, and Winfield Scott Hancock to the Department of the Cumberland. Ibid.
3. Benjamin F. Flanders.
4. Edward Heath.

From C. F. Condrey[1]

Abberdeen, Miss   Aug 21d 1867

Dr sir

I have the honor to interagate you on a political question. The loyal League as they stile themselves in this country, when they first organised in this country, they renounced you and your administration in the vilest terms. After having enlisted all of the ignorant class of whites and blacks, they are now trying coax and induce the more respected classes into that political dogma, by telling and assuring them that you the president of the U.S are the head and sholders of that party. Now sir to enable me to prove the assertions that I have made in denying your connection with any such secret organization I wish you to forward me a certifficate of denial forthwith, that I may be enabled to set the respected classes right here, before it may be too late.

C. F. Condrey M.D.
Abberdeen Miss

ALS, DLC-JP.
1. Not identified.

From William J.C. Duhamel

Augst 21 1867.

Mr President:

Excuse me for writing to you so often; but I think it my duty to inform you of everything I may hear of connected with *that conspiracy* against you.[1]

Mr. T. B. Brown former Warden has just returned from Boston and he says whilst there he met Gen'l Butler[2] and he Brown wrote an article for a Boston journal.[3]

In which article Brown exhonorates Butler and says Butler never visited Conover[4] at Jail &c.

The statement of Capt Chandler[5] who is a relative of Brown's and formerly an officer at the Jail proves that Mrs. Conover[6] visited Butler at his request and she was paid money in Capt C's presence by Butler to go on certain missions in N.Y.[7]

He also defends Mr. Ashley[8]—saying Mr. Ashley *asked* Conover in his (Brown's) presence to *only tell what was true* in President Johnson's case.

You were right in your estimate of T. B. Brown as I did not think he had so much *perfidy* in his character and he has more cause to defend himself thant to attempt to defend others.

I have just returned from Cape May and met there many persons & heard their comments on this Ashley plot (and Mr. Stantons removal did not occasion near as much remark). I heard Gen'l Webb Gov Ward N.J. Hon Nem'h Perry N.J. Dr. Blake Wash't and Ex President Buchanan[9] (with whom I took supper) express their astonishment at such an atrocious plot being possible, and they hoped you would be still able to expose them in their schemes.

These gentlemen believe a day of reckoning is approaching and with it a financial or commercial disaster is not far distant; and your views so vigorously and courtously put forth in your state papers exposing the inconsistencies of Congress will triumph. As the love of country will take the place of party passion and the petty despots these theorist *traders* and *conspirators* will be overthrown. And the *United* States will take its proper place amongst the great nations of the world and the administration of Andrew Johnson as President thereby vindicated.

Wishing you health and prosperity.

W.J.C. Duhamel M.D.

ALS, DLC-JP.
1. See Duhamel's letters to Johnson of Feb. 26, Mar. 27, Aug. 6, and Aug. 10, 1867, as well as Charles A. Dunham to Johnson, July 26, 1867.
2. Benjamin F. Butler.
3. Not found.

4. Sanford Conover, alias Charles A. Dunham.

5. Malcolm T.E. Chandler.

6. Ophelia Dunham (alias Conover) (*fl*1868) had apparently been one of her husband's false witnesses in 1866. She frequently served as his intermediary, especially in his pardon negotiations. *OR*, Ser. 2, Vol. 8: 922; Randall, *Browning Diary*, 2: 153; Carrie [Dunham's cousin] to Charles A. Dunham, Oct. 19, 1868, Pardons and Remissions, Vol. 9 (T967, Roll 4), RG59, NA.

7. No other evidence of money paid to Mrs. Dunham by Butler, for any purpose, has been found.

8. James M. Ashley.

9. Alexander S. Webb, Marcus L. Ward, Nehemiah Perry, possibly John B. Blake, and James Buchanan. Webb (1835–1911) graduated from West Point in 1855 where he soon became an instructor in mathematics. At various times during the Civil War he commanded a brigade, was involved with artillery, and served as chief of staff to General Meade. In 1870 he resigned from the army and then held the post of president of the College of the City of New York for thirty-three years. Ward (1812–1884), a New Jersey manufacturer and lawyer, was involved in a number of civic cultural groups. As governor of the state (1866–69) he was a reformer and later was elected to the U.S. House of Representatives (1873–75). Perry (1816–1881), a Newark, New Jersey, cloth and clothing manufacturer, had served two terms in the state assembly, one on the common council, and two in the U.S. House (1861–65). He later became mayor of Newark (1873). Blake (1800–1881) was a medical graduate of the University of Maryland but apparently never practiced medicine. A banker, he was also commissioner of public buildings in Washington, D.C., and held several other municipal offices. Warner, *Blue*; Sobel and Raimo, *Governors*, 3: 1022; *BDUSC*; Allen C. Clark, "James Heighe Blake, The Third Mayor of the Corporation of Washington [1813–17]," *Records CHS*, 24 (1920–21): 162–63.

To Lovell H. Rousseau

Washington, D.C.   Aug 21st 1867

The following is the charge made by Genl. Sheridan against you.[1]

"I regret that I have to make the charge against Brigadier General L. H. Rousseau, U.S.A, of visiting my command recently, and without exhibiting any authority, interfering with my duties and suggesting my removal."

(Signed) P. H. Sheridan,
Maj. Gen. U.S.A."

This in a letter addressed Genl. Grant, dated Head Quarters 5th Military District New Orleans, La, August 3d 1867.[2]

Andrew Johnson

Tel, DNA-RG107, Tels. Sent, President, Vol. 3 (1865–68).

1. See Rousseau to Johnson, Aug. 12, 1867.

2. On August 22 Rousseau wrote a lengthy letter to Grant denying Sheridan's charges and insisting that he had only gone to Louisiana to visit relatives before traveling to a distant assignment. He sent a copy of this letter to Johnson requesting him to see that it was published in the newspapers. Rousseau to Grant, Aug. 22; Rousseau to Johnson, Aug. 22, 1867, Johnson Papers, LC.

From William Brazelton, Jr.

New Market [Tenn]   22d August [1867][1]

As a "Companion Royal Arch Mason" I aske your attention to this letter. In October or November 1865, I forwarded a Petition for a Special Parden Accompanied by The Amnesty Oath which I had taken. Also a reccommendation on said petition by Gov. W. G. Brownlow.[2]

I learned from a Friend that you refused to grant said Parden. Also that you had receid some communication in reference to granting said Parden.

The following are the Facts in referece to my self on the 4th March 1865. Genl. Vaughn[3] sent me from Bristol in Charge of Flag of Truce with Dispatches to Federal Authoraties. I arrivd at New Market on the evening of the 8th having only 5 men with me. On the mornig of the 9th just as we were ready to proceed to Strawbery Plains I was arrested by Maj Hoffman[4] in command of *150 Federals*. He informed me that a Dispatch had been frwd to Knoxville that a "Bogus Flag of Truce["] was at New Market with about 75 men commitg all sorts of depridatns. It so happend that one of two *Undoubted Union* men was with me from Grenville and informd Maj Hoffman of the fact that no depridation could have been commited by those with the Flag of Truce.[5] Upon their statement He frwd a Communicatn to the Commanding officer at Knoxville exhenerating me and those with me from any blame. The Gentleman who sent the Dispatch was a bitter Personal enemy of mine. I allude to J. Monroe Meek a man I had the pleasure of defeating in this County for Rep. On my return to this County I was indicted in Two Cases for Robbery Two for Larceny—one for Murder. I have been tried in all and Honerably Acquited. In the *Murder* case after the evidence had gone to the Jury the *Atty Genl. J. M. Meek* refused to prosecute it saying to the Jury the state Had failed to make out a Case—for 18 months I have been Harrassed and persecuted & Prosecuted as no innocent man ever was before. And I attribute it to the Hatred of the Atty Genl. of this Dist. J M Meek. But thank God I am clear of all indctments except those for Treason. If I thought a Petition of Hundreds of "Radicals["] as well as Hundreds of Conservativs would have any influence with Your Excellency in granting my Parden I could frwd. it. But I believe after The Honerable acquital of all that has been charge to me, by Juries of the Loyal men of Jefferson County, Your Excellency will reconsider your determinatn and granted me the Parden asked for. In addressing you this communicatn I do so without consultng any one. I address you this letter as a Companion Royal Arch Mason and aske your considerate of it as such. If charges had been preferd against me and reason give you why a Parden ought not to be granted to me if you can consitently with your duties as President grant me a Copy I should like to have them so that I may know what they are and from whence they come. In conclusion allow me to say this that when the Excitement was at its highest point in 1861, in the City of Nashville, in a personal difficulty I was the true friend of Col Robt Johnson your son and was often denounced for taking the part I did, but I refer you to him for Particulars, not that I claim anything on that score but to only show that Rebel as I was I *did not forget or fail* my Personal friends in time of need. I will close this lengthy letter, once more asking that if not inconsistent with your duty that you grant me a Special Parden.[6]

W. Brazelton Jr

ALS, DLC-JP.

1. The year has been assigned by the Library of Congress. Given what is known about Brazelton's pardon story, this date seems plausible.

2. An examination of Brazelton's pardon files reveals that on October 3, 1865, he forwarded a request for a pardon to Johnson; Governor Brownlow supported this request in his transmittal letter of October 6. Brazelton had earlier taken the oath of allegiance on June 29, 1865. Amnesty Papers (M1003, Roll 48), Tenn., William Brazelton, Jr., RG94, NA.

3. John C. Vaughn.

4. Daniel W. Hoffman (c1840–1875) of Ohio served in the 2nd Rgt., Ohio Heavy Art., and was mustered out at Nashville in August 1865. After the war he practiced law in Ohio and Kansas. *Off. Army Reg.: Vols.*, 5: 26; CSR, Daniel W. Hoffman, RG94, NA; Pension File, Daniel W. Hoffman, RG15, NA.

5. For additional comments about Brazelton's situation in East Tennessee during the war, see Thomas A.R. Nelson to Johnson, June 4, 1868, Amnesty Papers (M1003, Roll 48), Tenn., William Brazelton, Jr., RG94, NA.

6. According to Brazelton's files, he evidently was pardoned initially in November 1865; it is unclear what happened to that presidential pardon. In any event, Brazelton was subsequently pardoned on June 13, 1868—evidently in response to Thomas A.R. Nelson's letter of early June. Ibid. See also *House Ex. Docs.*, 39 Cong., 2 Sess., No. 116, p. 33 (Ser. 1293).

From Darwin G. Fenno[1]

Brownsville Texas   August 22d 1867

Sir:

I respectfully request an appointment as Brigadier General or any thing lower above the rank of orderly Sergeant in the Regular Army of the United States. For testimonials as to service and so fourth, see letter of col. T. C. Berrett[2] 62" U.S. C Infantry endorsed by Generals A. Baird and O. O. Howard, now on file in the War Department Washington D.C. I entered the service in the 1st Wisconsin Cavalry as a private Sept 16, 1861, and was mustered out as 1st Lieut and Adjutant 62" U.S. Colored Infantry March 31, 1866.[3] I never particularly distinguished myself on any occasion that I remember of. I am twenty three years old, of good moral character, and a member of the finance committee of the conservative Union Club of Cameron County Texas. I am a firm believer in the Presidents Reconstruction Policy, and am glad that Secretary Stanton has been removed for two reasons, the first is on account of his politics the second is because he has not acted on my former application for a commission in the army.

I should have brought political influence to bear but from the fact that I have none to bring. The Congressional District in which I live in Wisconsin[4] is so radical that there is no prospect of any of my Democratic friends ever reaching Congress, at least for the present.

Hoping the above will convince you of my fitness for a position in the army, and assuring you that I would bring lots of influence if I could, and relying on your sympathy for your friends, though unfortunate in not belonging to the dominant party.[5]

D. G. Fenno
Late 1st Lieut & Adjt   62" U.S. C Infantry

ALS, DNA-RG94, ACP Branch, File F-95-CB-1868, D. G. Fenno.

1. Fenno (1844–1914) eventually became a successful journalist, working for twenty-six years (1876–1902) for the *Philadelphia Times* and then until his death as managing editor and then chief editorial writer for the *Harrisburg Patriot. Harrisburg Patriot*, May 6, 1914, in Pension File, Lillie E. Fenno, RG15, NA.

2. Theodore H. Barrett (1834–1900), a civil engineer, surveyor, and farmer, was a captain in the 9th Minn. Inf., colonel of the 62nd USCT, and was brevetted brigadier general in March 1865 for faithful and meritorious service. Hunt and Brown, *Brigadier Generals*.

3. Fenno served as private, sergeant, and first sergeant in the 1st Wisc. Cav. until December 7, 1863, when he became first lieutenant in the 62nd USCT. Powell, *Army List*, 307.

4. At the time of his enlistment Fenno was a resident of Appleton, which was in the Fifth District. Pension File, Lillie E. Fenno, RG15, NA; Stanley B. Parsons, William W. Beach, and Michael J. Dubin, *United States Congressional Districts and Data, 1843–1883* (Westport, Conn., 1986), 145.

5. Johnson referred the letter to Grant asking him to have Fenno appointed a second lieutenant. He received such an appointment in the 17th Inf. in September 1867 and served with it in Texas, Virginia, North Carolina, and the Dakota Territory. In September 1871 Fenno was cashiered as a result of his conviction by a courtmartial of embezzlement, betting on games of chance, and several other infractions. After serving a little more than a year of his five-year sentence at the Minnesota State Prison, he was pardoned by President Grant in December 1872. Pension File, Lillie E. Fenno, RG15, NA.

Interview with Boston Post *Correspondent*[1]

[Aug. 22, 1867][2]

In a pleasant conversation of some length, to-day, with President JOHNSON, I remarked that he was charged with having removed Mr. STANTON in order to obstruct the execution of the Reconstruction Acts of Congress. He asked what Mr. STANTON had to do with the execution or non-execution of these acts? These acts centred the power in the hands of Gen. GRANT, and he had placed GRANT over the War Department. He could not understand how this change could be construed into a purpose to defeat the proper execution of the Reconstruction Laws. The President further remarked that at one time Gen. GRANT strongly intimated that unless Mr. STANTON was removed he should be compelled to leave here, as he could be of no possible use in view of Mr. STANTON's overbearing and dictatorial conduct. The President advised him to have a talk with the Secretary of War and perhaps they would understand each other better. He agreed, however, with the General, that Mr. STANTON ought to be removed, and he then inquired of Gen. GRANT if he would take charge of the Department in the event of a change? The latter promptly expressed his entire willingness to do so.[3] I referred to the rumor that the General had eventually protested against the removal, and the President frankly said such was the case; that the General had written him a very kind, but earnest private note, in which he had intimated his fears of anarchy, if not revolution, should Secretary STANTON be superseded.[4] Yet as he could not appreciate the General's fears on this score, he had directed the change. I then told him that the same charge was made against him for removing Gen. SHERIDAN, and that many supposed his purpose was to prevent a due execution of the law. This he thought was quite as absurd as the other, as the law was the same whether THOMAS or SHERIDAN was in command. What difference could it make who executed the law? Could any one question the ability or the patriotism of Gen. THOMAS? I then asked why Gen. SHERIDAN was removed? Mr. JOHNSON said there were two good causes, but only one had been considered: the first one was rather of a personal character, and had been overlooked. The telegram of the 23d of June,[5] which was so disrespectful to the Executive, had been claimed by Gen. GRANT to be a private telegram to himself and that no official notice of its existence had ever yet reached the President. But the second ground for the removal of Gen. SHERIDAN was the exercise of powers he did not possess, and the exercise of his legitimate powers in an arbitrary and offensive manner. I asked if he would be kind enough to designate what acts he included under the latter clause. He said the removal of Gov. WELLS was entirely uncalled for and unjustifiable. Gov. WELLS had placed at Gen. SHERIDAN's disposal the whole civil machinery of the State to aid him in the execution of the Reconstruction Acts. Nor had the latter ever indicated or pointed out a single act or word of the Governor which was calculated to embarrass him in the proper execution of his duty. On the other hand, Gen. SHERIDAN had endeavored to execute the law as a partisan and had adopted Radicalism as the only true test of loyalty. His sole purpose seemed to be to secure negro supremacy and degrade the whites, and for such conduct I deemed it my duty to relieve him from that command. I inquired if he did not think Gov. THROCKMORTON had attempted to thwart the General in a proper execution of the law. He answered emphatically, "No, sir; the records prove the reverse. The Governor of Texas also placed the whole civil machinery of his State at the disposal of the military power, and aided it in every way possible except in the manufacture of a Radical majority of voters and in securing negro supremacy. This was Gov. THROCKMORTON's

sinning, and for which he was arbitrarily removed by Gen. SHERIDAN."[6]
I said to the President that his views as to the proper execution of the
Reconstruction acts were not clearly understood by the people, and that I
would like to hear them. He answered that he could express them in a few
words. He desired a fair registration of all qualified voters without regard
to race or color. He did not wish to give any advantage to the white men,
but much less was he disposed to make them the slaves to the negroes.
Where the negroes had the majority, as in South Carolina, he wished
them to exercise the power; where the white vote was in the majority, as
in Texas, he desired that white majority to control. He wanted only the
law to be fairly executed with equal chances to all. This was being denied
them by Gen. SHERIDAN, and his manner and mode of acting was fast
familiarizing the people with the tyranny of despotic government. I remarked that the public would not be able to understand why he struck
down despotism in one department and yet suffered it to continue in another. He replied that other changes would be likely to follow very soon.
A proper investigation was now being made into the conduct of one or
two other Commanders who, it was charged, were playing the autocrat.
The President expressed the greatest apprehension as to the future of our
Government, yet said he still relied on the good sense and patriotism of
the people. In his speech in the United States Senate, in December,
1860,[7] Mr. JOHNSON said he had denounced the party who would break
up the Government in order to preserve Slavery, and he had also denounced those who would destroy the Government in order to abolish
Slavery; he was equally opposed to both extremes now, and his only wish
was for a speedy return of fraternal relations among the States.

New York Times, Aug. 24, 1867.
    1. Unknown.
    2. The *New York Times* preceded this interview by explaining that it was sent to the *Post*
under date of August 22.
    3. Gideon Welles, in his diary, remarked on June 15, 1866, that during discussions over
possible cabinet changes Johnson had thought to assign General Grant as secretary of war
ad interim and that Grant had agreed. Beale, *Welles Diary*, 2: 529.
    4. See Grant to Johnson, Aug. 1, 1867; Beale, *Welles Diary*, 3: 154–57, 174–75.
    5. The telegram was actually dated June 22, 1867, and voiced Sheridan's opinions and
actions regarding the extension of the voter registration period in Louisiana and his opposition to the ideas of the administration on this subject. For the text of the telegram and cabinet reaction, see the *New York Tribune*, June 24, 1867; Simon, *Grant Papers*, 17: 198–99;
Beale, *Welles Diary*, 3: 117–18, 125–27.
    6. Throckmorton was removed on July 30. For a general discussion of Sheridan's
removal of Wells and Throckmorton and his other actions which irritated Johnson, see
Morris, *Sheridan*, 286–96. Wells protested his own removal in Wells to Johnson, June 4,
1867.
    7. Speech on Secession, Dec. 18–19, 1860, *Johnson Papers*, 4: 3–51.

From George G. Meade

Philadelphia, Pa., Aug. 22 1867.

Sir,

I am advised that the friends of Mr. Duncan S. Walker[1] recently Maj. Genl. of Volunteers, have presented his name to you for the vacant mission to Mexico, and it gives me very great pleasure to add my recommendation to those of other gentlemen.

Altho Genl. Walker never served under my immediate command yet I am satisfied from the reports of others, that he is a gallant and distinguished officer, who rendered most mereterious services during the recent war, and that based on these services he has a great claim to the conciliation and favor of the Government, which I shall be glad to hear the exigencies of the the pubic services & the calls of others on you, have permitted you to recognise by the appointment asked for.[2]

Geo. G. Meade   Maj. Genl. U.S.A.

ALS, DNA-RG59, Lets. of Appl. and Recomm., 1861–69 (M650, Roll 50), Duncan S. Walker.

1. Walker (1814–1912) served at various times on the staffs of Generals Banks, Emory, and Hancock during the war. He was brevetted brigadier in March 1865. He enjoyed a career as a lawyer and a newspaper editor. Hunt and Brown, *Brigadier Generals*.

2. General Hancock wrote a letter in behalf of Walker's appointment. Walker did not get the assignment to Mexico; Marcus Otterburg did. See Hancock to Johnson, n.d., Lets. of Appl. and Recomm., 1861–69 (M650, Roll 50), Duncan S. Walker, RG59, NA; *Register of the Department of State*, 64.

From William H. Seward

Department of State   August 23d 1867

My Dear Sir

I hereby resign the office of Secretary of State and pray you to accept my sincere acknowledgment of the consideration and confidence with which you have honored me while performing the duties of this responsible trust.[1]

With an earnest desire for the success of your arduous labors in conducting the public affairs of the country in this important crisis and for your personal welfare and happiness . . .

William H. Seward

ALS, DLC-JP.

1. After the dismissal of Stanton, Johnson was pressured to make other changes in his cabinet, especially in the cases of Seward, McCulloch, and Randall. Seward was the only one to formally offer to resign. Johnson, however, did not accept the resignation. Castel, *Presidency of Johnson*, 144.

From Frank Smith
Private

No. 48 Pine Street   New York   Aug 23/67

My Dear Sir

I expected to leave for Washington tonight but find myself unable to do so. Mr Courtnay[1] has not yet received the papers in my case and is unable to give any opinion unless he has them.[2] He has received a *confidential* letter from Mr McCulloch *requesting him* to pursuade me to delay the matter until Mr Chandler[3] returns to Washington—and Courtnay replied that I was not willing to delay the matter longer—and requested him to send the papers. As a matter of course Courtnay is desireous of having the *papers* come to him in an official way. You have all my papers and I wish you would *urge* Mr McC or send them to Courtnay yourself.[4] I have been quite sick since I saw you. Hope to see you in a few days. Your action in *killing* your *enimies* is approved here by your friends. Thurlow Weed has been heard to say that if you removed Sheridan—*he Weed* would support him for the Presidential nomination. I hope this will find you in good health & spirits.

Frank Smith

ALS, DLC-JP.
1. Samuel G. Courtney.
2. In his August 12 letter Smith indicated that he was awaiting Courtney's opinion before he could return to Washington to confer with the President. See Smith to Johnson, Aug. 12, 1867, Johnson Papers, LC.
3. William E. Chandler, assistant secretary of the treasury.
4. For resolution of the "cotton cases," see Johnson to McCulloch, Dec. 8, 1865, *Johnson Papers*, 9: 497–98; Smith to Johnson, June 17, 1867.

From A. Toomer Porter et al.[1]

Charleston   Aug 24th 1867

Sir.

We have seen it stated in the public prints, that the volunteer officers of the Army, are soon to be mustered out of service. If this be true, & if the Freedmens Bureau is to continue, we have deemed it important to the general interest of this state, to respectfully request your Excellency, to retain Major Genl R K Scott the Asst Com in this state, untill the end of the year. His general administration has been beneficial, & it would be unfortunate to place a new officer in his position at this particular Season of the Year. If the rule adopted by your Excellency is not inexorable, your granting this request we believe will be beneficial to the Community.

[Signatures appear here.]

We could procure any number of names upon this paper if deemed necessary. The general sentiment of this community is as expressed above.[2]

A Toomer Porter

ALS (Porter), DNA-RG105, Records of the Commr., Lets Recd. from Executive Mansion.

1. In addition to Porter, seven other Charleston citizens signed the letter, including William Aiken, James B. Campbell, and Theodore D. Wagner.

2. In early December another group of prominent South Carolinians requested that Johnson retain Scott as assistant commissioner. William Whaley et al. to Johnson, Dec. 4, 1867, Records of the Commr., Lets. Recd. from Executive Mansion, RG105, NA.

From Joseph R. Flanigen

Philadelphia, Augt 25, 1867

My dear Mr President

I enclose you the financial article from the *News* of yesterday.[1] I am thoroughly out of patience, and indeed *disgusted* with your Secretary of the Treasury, and whilst I do not of course pretend to dictate what ought to be done in a matter of so much delicacy, I cannot forbear saying to you, that I think if another—and *a truer man* were placed in that Department great (*very great*) *good* would accrue to your administration.

I sought to see you on Wednesday last, and much regret that I could not do so. I wanted to say this much to you, and one or two other things which I prefer not to write. I hope I may be more successfull on my next visit.

J R Flanigen

ALS, DLC-JP.
1. The newspaper has not been found.

From James W. Nesmith

Rickreall Polk County Oregon,   August 25th 1867.

Dear Sir,

At the request of many of your supporters and friends in Washington Territory I forward the enclosed petition[1] together with a letter from Mr T F McElroy,[2] and also a slip from the "Pacific Tribune"[3] The Radical Organ of that Territory.

It is within my own knowledge that Garfield the Surveyor Genl,[4] P D Moore the collector of Internal Revenue, Wilson the collector of customs and A R Elder Indian Agent[5] all pretended to be supporters of your Administration and of your policy up to the time of the passage of the tenure of Office bill. Since that time they have all been loud in your abuse.

Under the infamous legislation of the last Congress it is beyond your power to disturb theirs in the Enjoyment of their offices. Their present appointments will soon all Expire, and I join in the prayer of the conservative men of Washington Territory that none of those persons shall be reappointed by you.[6]

J W Nesmith

ALS, DNA-RG56, Appts., Customs Service, Collector, Puget Sound, Philip D. Moore.

1. Nineteen adherents of the Conservative party complained that while Moore, Wilson, and Elder had proclaimed their conservative allegiance prior to the passage of the Tenure of Office Act, since then they had worked to elect the radical candidate for congressional delegate, and, therefore, they should not be reappointed. Conservatives of Olympia, Washington Territory, to Johnson, July 25, 1867, Appts., Customs Service, Collector, Puget Sound, Philip D. Moore, RG56, NA.

2. Thornton F. McElroy sent Nesmith the petition and newspaper clipping (from the *Seattle Pacific Tribune*) to forward to Johnson, July 26, 1867, ibid.

3. The article, entitled "Johnson's Last Pardon" and allegedly written by Philip D. Moore, was published on June 22, 1867. It suggested that Johnson had at least some foreknowledge of Lincoln's assassination. In particular, it castigated Johnson for his "arbitrary exercise of the pardoning power," especially in pardoning G. W. Gayle, who had at one time offered a reward to anyone who would assassinate Lincoln. The article suggested that the problem could be remedied by impeaching Johnson. Ibid.

4. Selucius Garfielde (1822–1881), a lawyer, settled in California in 1851 and served in its state legislature. In 1857 he moved to the Washington Territory and at various times served as the receiver of public monies (1857–60), surveyor general (1866–69), congressional delegate (1869–73), and collector of customs at Puget Sound (1873). *BDUSC*.

5. Philip D. Moore, Frederick A. Wilson, and Alfred R. Elder. Moore (c1826–fl1880), a native of New Jersey, was a lawyer and miner. Wilson (c1825–1876) settled in the Washington Territory about 1856. After his stint as collector of customs he moved to California and operated a sash, door, and blind factory. A less complete identification of Wilson can be found in *Johnson Papers*, 11: 568. Elder (c1807–fl1880), a farmer and eventually Christian Church minister and justice of the peace, was appointed to the Puyallup Indian Agency in 1863 and to the Tulalip Agency in 1865, thereafter serving them both. 1870 Census, Washington, Thurston, Olympia, 236, 239; (1880), 110; Chehalis, 2nd Div., 14; *Seattle Pacific Tribune*, Jan. 22, 1877; Bancroft, *Washington, Idaho, and Montana*, 366; Hill, *Indian Affairs*, 199; *San Rafael Herald*, Jan. 4, 1877.

6. Moore was apparently removed as collector of internal revenue and replaced by Hazard Stevens in February 1868. Elder's term expired and Charles S. King was nominated, confirmed, and commissioned to replace him in March 1868. Wilson was renominated as collector of customs in March 1869 but apparently no action was taken on the renomination. Garfielde remained surveyor general until 1869 when he became territorial delegate. Johnson Papers, Ser. 6B, Vol. 4: 389–90; *BDUSC*.

From John F. Coyle

N. York   26" Aug 1867

Your letter to Grant universally approved.

Herald says Grant felt the necessity of placing himself right with the Radicals & thus unwillingly gave you the opportunity of writing the strongest state paper you have written.[1] Yet it says your letter is full of Executive ability & the whole Common sense of the Country will sustain you.

Herald says you can challenge impeachment & win.[2]

Jno. F. Coyle

Tel, DLC-JP.
    1. See the *New York Herald*, Aug. 26, 1867, essay, "Rapid and Startling Progress of Our Great Revolution."
    2. On the following day Coyle informed the President that the *Herald* had taken a stand against Grant. Coyle to Johnson, Aug. 27, 1867, Johnson Papers, LC. See also the *New York Herald*, Aug. 27, 1867, essay, "Singular Position of General Grant."

To Ulysses S. Grant

Washington, D.C.   Aug 26th 1867.

Sir

    In consequence of the unfavorable condition of the health of Major General George H. Thomas,[1] as reported to you in Surgeon Hasson's[2] despatch of the 21st instant,[3] my order dated August 17, 1867, is hereby modified, so as to assign Major General Winfield S. Hancock to the command of the Fifth Military District created by the Act of Congress passed March 2d, 1867, and of the Military Department comprising the States of Louisiana and Texas. On being relieved from the command of the Department of the Missouri by Major General P. H. Sheridan, Major General Hancock will proceed directly to New Orleans, Louisiana, and, assuming the command to which he is hereby assigned, will, when necessary to a faithful execution of the laws, exercise any and all powers conferred by Acts of Congress upon District commanders, and any and all authority pertaining to officers in command of Military Departments.

    Major General P. H. Sheridan will at once turn over his present command to the officer next in rank to himself,[4] and, proceeding without delay to Fort Leavenworth, Kansas, will relieve Major General Hancock of the command of the Department of the Missouri.

    Major General George H. Thomas will, until further orders, remain in command of the Department of the Cumberland.[5]

Andrew Johnson.

Copy, DLC-JP.
    1. Thomas was being treated for a liver problem and, according to his surgeon, "it would be a great risk for him to go South at this time." Since his ailment had been relieved by taking medicine, Thomas used it as an excuse to keep from having to go to the deep South. Alexander B. Hasson to Ulysses S. Grant, Aug. 21, 1867, Tels. Sent, Sec. of War (M473, Roll 47), RG107, NA; Freeman Cleaves, *Rock of Chickamauga: The Life of General George H. Thomas* (Norman, Okla., 1986 [1948]), 296.
    2. Alexander B. Hasson (*c*1826–1877) became an assistant surgeon in the U.S. Army in 1849 and a surgeon in 1861. During the war he served as medical director of cavalry in the field and in a variety of other positions behind the lines. Alexander B. Hasson to Lorenzo Thomas, July 1, 1849; Hasson to C. H. Morgan, Apr. 15, 1866; Abiel W. Nelson, certification of attendance on Hasson during his last illness, Apr. 3, 1877, ACP Branch, File H-295-CB-1849, Alexander B. Hasson, RG94, NA; Powell, *Army List*, 361.
    3. Hasson to Grant, Aug. 21, 1867, Tels. Sent, Sec. of War (M473, Roll 47), RG107, NA.
    4. Charles Griffin.
    5. Johnson also sent an order to Thomas instructing him to remain in the Department

of the Cumberland. Johnson to Thomas, Aug. 23, 1867, Tels. Sent, President, Vol. 3 (1865–68), RG107, NA.

From Ulysses S. Grant

Washington, Aug. 26th 1867.

Sir:

I have the honor to acknowledge the receipt of the following letter, to wit:

[Johnson to Grant, Aug. 26, 1867]

To it I have the honor to submit the following reply. General Thomas has not yet acknowledged the receipt of the order assigning him to the command of the 5th Military District.[1] My recommendation to have the order assigning him to that command suspended, was based principally on the fact that the yellow fever had become epidemic, and some time since orders were issued, at the suggestion of General Sheridan,[2] authorizing all officers then absent from the 5th Military District, on application to the Adjutant General of the Army, to remain absent until the 15th of October. A copy of the dispatch on which this order, or circular, was based, and the circular itself, were forwarded with my recommendation for the suspension of General Thomas' order. Before substituting General Hancock, or any one else, for General Thomas to the 5th Military District, his objections, if he makes any, should be heard, or else the order for the change should be based on other grounds. Unless there are very grave public reasons, no officer should be sent to Louisiana now.

Your letter quoted above will leave the 5th Military District without a commander of the rank required by law, during the period necessary to effect the contemplated change of commanders. In fact, it orders General Sheridan to turn over his command to an officer absolutely incompetent by law, to fill it.[3] I assume that you will change this part of your instructions so as to admit of General Sheridan remaining where he now is, until relieved by an officer of the requisite rank.

The Act of Congress of July 19th 1867 throws much of the responsibility of executing faithfully the reconstruction laws of Congress, on the General of the Army. I am bound by the responsiblity thus imposed on me. I approve all General Sheridan's orders, to this date, and therefore must insist on instructing his successor to carry out those orders, so far as I am authorized to do so by Acts of Congress.

Having the responsibility placed on me that I have, in regard to the execution of the laws of Congress, in the districts composing the States not represented in Congress, I claim that I ought to be consulted as to the agents who are to aid me in this duty. But the right existing with the President to name District commanders, I can not decline to publish the order so far as it affects change of commanders. I do protest, however, against the details of the order; I do more; I emphatically decline yielding any of the powers given the General of the Army by the laws of Congress.

In the present changes the country sees but one object, no matter whether it interprets the objects of the Executive rightly or not. The object seen is the defeat of the laws of Congress for restoring peace, union and representation to the ten States now not represented. This course affects the peace of the whole country, North and South, and the finances of the country, unfavorably. The South is the most affected by it, and, through the South, the whole country feels the agitation which is kept up. It is patent to every one that opposition to Congress has induced the measures which now stand on the statute books as the laws of the land, and has induced the loyal people of this country to sustain those measures. Will not further opposition necessarily result in more stringent measures against the South? The people had come to look upon the reconstruction policy of the country as settled, whether it pleased them or not. They acquiesced in it, and at heart the great mass of people, irrespective of political creed, desired to see it executed and the country restored to quiet, ready to meet the great financial issue before us.

I would not venture to write as I do, if I was not greatly in earnest; if I did not see great dangers to the quiet and prosperity of the country in the course being pursued.[4]

U.S. Grant   Sec. of War   *ad int.*

LS, OClWHi.

1. Johnson order, Aug. 17, 1867, Johnson Papers, LC; Grant's Gen. Orders No. 77, Aug. 17, 1867, *New York Times*, Aug. 21, 1867.

2. Philip H. Sheridan to Grant, Aug. 10, 1867, and memorandum by Edward D. Townsend, Aug. 10, 1867, in Simon, *Grant Papers*, 17: 288.

3. The Third Military Reconstruction Act required the commander of a military district to be an officer no lower in rank than a brigadier general. Charles Griffin had been a brigadier general and brevet major general of volunteers, but after the war he held the regular army rank of colonel in the 35th Inf. Surely Grant was merely using this as an excuse, because he and Sheridan had already used Griffin's brevet rank to cause him to supercede Samuel P. Heintzelman as commander in Texas. *American Annual Cyclopaedia* (1867), 657; Warner, *Blue*; William L. Richter, *The Army in Texas During Reconstruction, 1865–70* (College Station, Tex., 1987), 73.

4. Upon receiving Grant's letter, Johnson responded, "You will, without further delay, issue the necessary instruction to carry into effect the order to which you communication refers." Johnson to Grant, Aug. 27, 1867, Johnson Papers, LC. See also Johnson to Grant, Aug. 28, 1867.

From Middle Tennessee Citizens[1]

August 26th 1867

Dear Sir

We your old friends in Tennessee are suffering under a Turkish tyranny. Gory headed patriots who fought under our beloved Jackson in the war of 1812 are denied and deprived of the right of *voting*. Negros fresh from the Penitentiary for Larceny and other infamous Crimes are enfranchise and exercise this right of sovingity [sovereignty]. Is there no remedies for these great evals? Will you sustain the people in electing delegates to Change the Constitution so as to let all both black and white vote. In this election for delegates will you sustain all white and black men over the age of 21 years in voting. By answering these interogatories you will confer an everlasting favor upon your very much oppressed country men.[2]

Pet, DLC-JP.
    1. The document was signed by dozens of persons, a number of whom were from Sumner County.
    2. Appended to the list of signatures is a later note, dated September 20, to President Johnson from Lawrence Kirby then in Louisville, Kentucky, in which Kirby indicated that he had traveled to Washington to present the petition to Johnson in person but had been prevented from doing so by Patterson (presumably Johnson's son-in-law). In his note Kirby concluded with a plea for the President's assistance—for the love of the country and the hatred of Brownlow.

Order re Military Assignments

Washington, D.C.   Aug. 26—1867.

Brevet Major General Edward R.S. Canby is hereby assigned to the command of the Second Military District created by the Act of Congress of March 2d, 1867, and of the Military Department of the South, embracing the States of North Carolina and South Carolina. He will as soon as practicable relieve Major General Daniel E. Sickles, and, on assuming the command to which he is hereby assigned, will, when necessary to the faithful execution of the laws, exercise any and all powers conferred by Acts of Congress upon District commanders, and any and all authority pertaining to officers in command of Military Departments.

Major General Daniel E. Sickles is hereby relieved from the command of the Second Military District.

The Secretary of War ad interim will give the necessary instructions to carry this order into effect.

Andrew Johnson.

Copy, DLC-JP.

From Rolfe S. Saunders

Memphis, Aug. 26, 1867.

Since the time we came together in 1860 to fight Secession, I have been your friend. As an evidence of your kind feeling toward me, you have conferred upon me a position of honor and trust; and in appreciation of this mark of your confidence, I have endeavored, with all the ability I possess, to discharge the duties of my office in a manner worthy the Administration of ANDREW JOHNSON,—as high an honor as I ask. As to the manner in which I have thus far discharged my duties as an officer, I have the honor of referring to every Agent of the Government who has visited Memphis and investigated my books.

I have commenced a war upon a set of understrappers here in the Revenue service, who are incompetent and unworthy to fill any position in the Government. They belong to *the other side* and are of course backed by their party who want to fill *all the offices* and monopolize the spoils, and they want no man in their way who is not "one of them." I intend to drive them to the wall, or be driven to the wall myself. As they are destitute of principle & ready to do anything that will serve their end; and not knowing what representations they may make before you and the Department, I wish merely to let you know the facts in the case, while I am at all times ready to meet any and all charges they may prefer, crush them and vindicate myself. I know how eagerly they have been watching my every move since my confirmation[1] and referring to my official conduct, I defy them, one and all.

May God bless you and give you yet many days on earth. I am one of those who yet have faith in the people; and as sure as God rules, the time is not distant, when the Administration of Andrew Johnson will rank second only to that of Washington, and when the American people and the enlightened world will accord you that honor and justice which your masterly statesmanship and unselfish & patriotic course, so justly merit.

Rolfe S. Saunders.
Collector   8th Dist. Tenn.

ALS, DLC-JP.
1. Given a recess appointment in the fall of 1866, Saunders's nomination as collector was submitted to the Senate in January 1867. He was approved and commissioned in March 1867. See John W. Leftwich to Johnson, Sept. 22, 1866, *Johnson Papers*, 11: 256–57.

From Benjamin B. French
Confidential

Washington, Aug 27 '67

My Dear Sir,

It is almost humiliating to me to be under the necessity of laying before you my necessities, but, I have striven hard to make a living by my profession since I have been out of office, & have, thus far, found it an utter failure.[1]

I have intimated to you once or twice that I should like to be remembered by you when an opportunity might offer to place me in some official position.

I have stood firmly by you, because I believed you to be an honest man, a true patriot, a warm friend of the People, and a stern and uncompromising defender of the American Constitution.

For this I have been sacrificed on the Altar of Radicalism, and I glory in the sacrifice; but I do feel as if I wanted the world to see that I am not forgotten!

I hope you may feel confidence enough in me to offer me some position where I can serve my country & yourself faithfully.

I have never yet, as I believe, accepted a position the duties of which I did not faithfully perform, and I never will, and I have the vanity to believe that I understand the workings of the machinery of our Government sufficiently well to perform the duties of almost any office with which I might be intrusted.

Should you favor me with your confidence in placing me in any position, be assured I will try to perform its duties faithfully, and to your satisfaction, and the moment I find that I do not, I will resign.

I beg of you to bear me in mind.[2]

You have known me well for twenty years, and know exactly what I am, & there is not a man living in whom I have greater reliance for justice than yourself.

B. B. French

ALS, DLC-JP.
1. Ever since French left the position of commissioner of public buildings, he had practiced law in the District of Columbia with K. V. Whaley and Ezra L. Stevens, his partners. Benjamin B. French to Johnson, Mar. 7, 1867, *Washington Evening Star*, Apr. 1, 1867.
2. In February 1868 French was given a clerkship in the Treasury Department, which he resigned in the summer of 1870. Cole and McDonough, *Benjamin Brown French*, 556–57, 617.

From Charles G. Halpine

New York, Augt. 27th 1867

My Dear Sir:

Allow me to introduce to your most favorable notice my friend Mr. John Griffin[1] of this City,—one of the best & strongest representative Irishmen that I know. He was for forty years an intimate friend of Prest. Buchanan, & on friendly terms (personally,) with Presidents Jackson, Polk and all our other Democratic lights. If you want to know who & what he is, ask your friend Col. Florence[2] who has known "Old John Griffin," as we call him, for many years. Griffin is an old Custom House Officer and I think Smythe should restore him to the very humble place—that of Weigher—which, he wants, and which he held before. At any rate, I think he should have something, for he is popular with all classes, strong in the Catholic Church and a devoted friend of President Andrew Johnson and his Administration. By the way, it may interest you to hear that old Mr. Bennett of the *Herald* has been converted from the error of his ways, and now feels inclined (since your demolition of Grant's letter,) to run your name again for the Presidency.[3] He told me yesterday that you would most probably be impeached by the Radicals, & that this would insure your Election by a perfect tornado of public opinion.

Chas. G. Halpine

ALS, DLC-JP.
1. Griffin (b. *c*1795) served as an inspector in the New York City customhouse during the 1850s. 1860 Census, N.Y., New York, New York, 4th Ward, 3rd [1st] Div., 156; *U.S. Off. Reg.* (1851–59); New York City directories (1850–59).
2. Thomas B. Florence.
3. See John F. Coyle to Johnson, Aug. 26, 1867.

From John McGinnis, Jr.

New York, Aug. 27th 1867.

My dear Mr. President:

Through Mr. Coyle, I took the liberty of conveying to you my feelings and convictions with regard to a change *now*, in the head of the Treasury department. Since that time I am greatly gratified to notice that some of the leading journals of this City express the same view taken by me, and I hear similar expressions from many of the leading financial men in this City.

There have been an unholy, wicked and bitter crusade inaugurated upon Mr McCulloch, by the whiskey fraud clique[1] of N.Y. and they are ready to resort to any means which calumny, falsehood and large sums of ill-gotten money will further, to traduce and malign Mr. McC. This is owing to the fact that Mr. McCulloch has inaugurated a vigorous warfare upon this whiskey fraud clique, the increased revenues of the past four weeks showing that he has struck in the right direction and ought to prosecute the good work with all the energy and support at his command. The N. York Herald has made an assault[2] upon the Secretary of the Treasury—but that paper is utterly devoid of principle & its present course can only be explained as a desire on their part to levy black mail, or that it is already paid and in the service of the whiskey fraud clique.

That Mr. McCulloch holds a high place in the confidence of capitalists in Europe, I know from my own observations, as well as from conversations had with some of the most prominent financial men of England, France and Italy. That a change in the head of the Treasury department at this time would be productive of disastrous results, I am most sincerely convinced. In no other branch of the Government, auxiliary to its head, would the financial pulse be so greatly disturbed as by a change in the head of the Treasury department, and I am convinced that the Radicals would seize upon such a moment with a determined purpose to bring about a financial panic—not because of their sympathy with Mr. Mc-Culloch, but with malice towards you.

With the constant and diverse stories spoken and written to you, it must be, in the honesty of your desires and purposes, difficult to determine the genuine from the spurious. So many would-be advisers are actuated by ulterior motives—and you have been so repeatedly deceived.

As for me, I have only your interest and that of our country at heart. I am not connected with any of the New York or Washington cliques—and have naught but an honest purpose in giving you my humble views. I bear in my heart a sincere affection for you—coupled with a debt of gratitude for the kindness recd. at your hands. In discharge of that debt, I have the hope of serving you, in some manner, faithfully and acceptably—& *honestly*. With this feeling I beg that you will give my views the benefit of the belief that they are honest, earnest and dictated by the best motives.

By every consideration, then, I do most earnestly hope that you will not accept the resignation of Mr. McCulloch at this time.

Jno: McGinnis Jr.

ALS, DLC-JP.

1. In May and June, *New York Times* investigations revealed that whiskey manufacturers and importers were defrauding the government of millions of dollars through elaborate systems of fraud and bribery. An investigation by the Treasury Department revealed weaknesses in the bonded warehouse system and exposed corruption among the department's assessors and collectors in New York City. In September the collector of New York's Third District, Theophilius C. Callicott, and his deputy, John Allen, were arrested for malfeasance in office. *New York Times*, June 2, July 6, 10, 13, 1867; *House Reports*, 40 Cong., 2 Sess., No. 24, pp. 1–8 (Ser. 1357); *New York Tribune*, Sept. 10, 1867.

2. On August 26 the *New York Herald* charged that McCulloch refused to reimburse certain New York importers for excessive duties, even though a federal court had upheld the firms' claims to the refunds.

From J. L. Tiffany [1]

Utica, N.Y.   Aug. 27. 1867

Dear Sir

Because I have watched your anxiety to preserve the Constitution of our once happy Country I am emboldened to appeal to you in behalf of Lieut. John C. Brain,[2] late of the Confederate navy now in prison in the Penitentiary at Brooklyn, N.Y. sick and destitute, without proper food for a sick man & in need of clothing, dying by inches. It will be a year next month since he was imprisoned, it would seem undergoing punishment without trial or conviction. Should this be so?

Although a northern man myself I feel that he is my Countryman, and in the language of our Saviour *he is my neighbor* for whom I am bound to do all a Christian should, and accordingly being informed that he was sick & in prison, suffering for food & clothing I instituted inquiry through my friends & learning the facts, sent him some money which his keeper[3] refuses to let him have, and under an unfounded suspicion or wicked accusation keeps him confined closely in his cell where he will soon die. I have caused particular investigation to be made & the keeper has not the least particle of evidence to justify the severity adopted, & I fear that he is influenced by some vindictive & bloodthirsty politicians of which I know there are many about.

From the observation of fifty years past I have formed the opinion that the southern people have been more sinned against than sinning & I judge from your indignant & truthful denunciation of John Brown when you were in the Senate,[4] of which I have a vivid recollection, that you can view with impartiality & charity & even kindness & pity the sufferings of a man, brave & noble in his nature, incurred it may be in mistaken views of the rights of his section.[5]

Is it not time that these cases of individual oppression & persecution were brought to an end, that those who have once loved & been proud of their country may again look with hope for a restoration of peace & the fruits of peace?

I trust the subject of my letter may be my excuse for addressing you.

J. L. Tiffany

ALS, DNA-RG60, Office of Atty. Gen., Lets. Recd., President.

1. Not identified.

2. Braine (b. c1839), a one-time resident of Nashville, Tennessee, saw service in the Civil War in a variety of locations and positions. Arrested in Indiana in 1861 as a rebel spy, he was released in 1862 when authorities learned he was a British citizen. In 1864, nevertheless, Braine received a commission in the Confederate navy and went on to seize several federal steamships. *OR-Navy*, Ser. 1, Vol. 3, pp. 231–47, 393–95; Francis X. Holbrook, "A Mosby or a Quantrill? The Civil War Career of John Clibbon Braine," *American Neptune*, 33 (1973): 200–208.

3. Francis McNeely, not otherwise identified. Brooklyn directories (1866–68).

4. See Johnson's "Speech on the Harpers Ferry Incident," *Johnson Papers*, 3: 318–52.

5. Although arrested in September 1866 for piracy and imprisoned for two-and-a-half years, Braine was released in early 1869—on the grounds that he had held a naval commission at the time of the ship seizures. Holbrook, "Civil War Career of Braine," 210–11; *New York Herald*, Sept. 19, 1866; *New York Tribune*, Mar. 1, 1869.

To Ulysses S. Grant

Washington, D.C.   Aug. 28 1867

Sir

I have received your communication of this date,[1] and, in compliance with your request, return herewith your letter of the 26th instant.[2]

Andrew Johnson

LS, OClWHi.

1. Grant asked to withdraw his previous letter. Grant to Johnson, Aug. 28, 1867, Johnson Papers, LC.

2. Grant to Johnson, Aug. 26, 1867. Not only had Grant sent this letter, but he also

had expressed similar sentiments rather vigorously during the cabinet meeting on August 27. On the next day, at Johnson's request, Grant and Johnson had a discussion during which Johnson allegedly convinced Grant of the error of his opinions, and thus Grant withdrew his letter. In fact, he took the letter with him and the letter printed here was merely a formality. Card, Johnson to Grant, Aug. 28, 1867, Adam Badeau Papers, LC; Beale, *Welles Diary*, 3: 185–89.

From James H. Hoblitzell [1]

Baltimore   August 28/67

Sir,

You will excuse my perseverance, but you, and above all, our glorious Country is in peril.

In all Mr. McCullohes reports—he uses the words, "*as reported to me*," or "as appears in the books."

Now it is possible, he may not be aware of the irregular operations of the Assistant Treasurer at NY.[2] Report says the later is interested in the speculation of [sustating?] the price of our Bonds abroad. Be this as it may—there can be no doubt that since Aug 1866, sales of gold have been made on account of unmatured interest, but not deducted from the amount on hand.

From a careful estimate I make in the Treasury	$70,000.00
less outstanding certificates	19,500.00
	$50,500.00

The Radical Papers keep constantly before the People Mr. McCullohs purpose to commence specie payment. In one of his reports, you will recollect he proposed to do so in *Eighteen months*.

Unmask this deception at N York, and you will see such a change in Public Sentiment North that will surprise Every Radical in the Country.

J. H Hoblitzell

ALS, DLC-JP.

1. Hoblitzell (c1816–*fl*1870), a resident of Baltimore between 1858 and 1870, was at various times an importer and jobber of dry goods and a contractor. He continued to write Johnson about this and related topics until the end of Johnson's administration. 1860 Census, Md., Baltimore, Baltimore, 14th Ward, 153; Baltimore directories (1858–70); J. H. Hoblitzell to Johnson, Mar. 17, June 25, Sept. 17, 1868; Feb. 29, 1869, Johnson Papers, LC.

2. Henry H. Van Dyck.

From Paul Bagley [1]

Washington D.C.   Aug. 29th 1867

Sir:—

You are aware that upon the evidence of witnesses who have since sworn that they were false that a proclamation[2] was made by the President charging Jefferson Davis with complicity in the assassination of

President Lincoln and offering a Hundred Thousand Dollars for his arrest—that he was two years in prison and sometime in chains—that he is now only released on bail to answer at Court in November next.

In the efforts of myself and others to induce Jefferson Davis to apply for pardon, permit me to say, Sir, as a result of our labors that it appears to be in the nature of the case *impossible* that Jefferson Davis could apply for pardon so long as the above proclamation stands out against him without admitting that charge to be true which those who made it have sworn to be false.

The Executive is therefore hereby prayed to cause a *nolle prosequi* to be entered in the case of the said Jefferson Davis in order to remove the wrong done by those false witnesses; for it is declared in the Law of God "If a man smite the eye of his servant or the eye of his maid that it perish; he shall let him go free for his eye's sake. And if he smite out his man servants tooth or his maid servants tooth he shall let him go free for his tooth's sake (Exodus 21: 26–7).["]

Now, Sir, if God will let the servant go free for his tooth's sake shall not the Executive of a great nation let a man go free for his two years imprisonment and for his chains' sake?

Should the blood of Jefferson Davis seem to be demanded because he was engaged in a rebellion which shed much blood—*that* was the blood of war. *This* is a time of peace. Because Joab "shed the blood of war in a time of peace" Soloman was charged to "bring down his hoar hairs to the grave with blood."[3]

Blackstone declares that "any law which is contrary to the Law of God is null and void."[4]

Therefore God will honor the President in acting according to the spirit of His Law in entering a *nolle prosequi*.

Paul Bagley   Missionary

ALS, DLC-JP.

1. Not identified. Bagley wrote other letters to Johnson in behalf of Davis. See, for example, Bagley to Johnson, June 14, Aug. 31, 1867, Johnson Papers, LC.

2. See Proclamation of Rewards for Arrest of Sundry Confederates, May 2, 1865, *Johnson Papers*, 8: 15–16.

3. Loose quotations from 1 Kings 2: 5–6.

4. There are many instances where Blackstone writes in this vein, though this direct quotation has not been found. For example, see Sir William Blackstone, *Commentaries on the Laws of England*, ed. by Thomas M. Cooley, 2nd rev. ed. (Chicago, 1872 [1870]), 41.

From James Blair[1]

Columbus Mississippi   Augst. 29th 1867

Dr. S.

You will please pardon my presumption for this letter.

We are on the eve of a *war of races*, anarchy and ruin stares us in the face. You & *you* alone can arrest and save the south *ruin, ruin*. At once declare a *general amnesty* & *Pardon* for *all*, and if possible enfranchize *all*.

Your name then will be blessed beyond any of your predecessors. May the choices blessing of Allmighthy God rest on you.

Jas. Blair

ALS, DLC-JP.
1. Blair (c1815–*fl*1870) was a native of Virginia and a wealthy druggist. 1860 Census, Miss., Lowndes, Columbus, 131; (1870), 58.

From John W. Hunter

Brooklyn N.Y.   August 29, 1867

Sir

A few days since I had the honor of addressing a note to you on the subject of a change in the head of the Treasury Department.[1]

At this peculiar juncture, the danger of a financial *discredit* both at home & abroad is very great, and great care should be taken *not* to give color to the charges against Mr McCulloch (for they affect not *him more* than our *National Credit*[)].

I believe these charges to be unfounded & gotten up here to break down the Secretary, and to secure your favor for a *Wall Street broker*, of the smallest possible capacity, and entirely unworthy of the place, or of your confidence or consideration.

I know your desire to stand by the *man* who may be falsely accused—and I beg for the honor of the Country which you have so much at heart that you will give to the public some evidence of your continued confidence in the present Secy. of the Treasury, and thus give comfort to the many thousands who look *now* to this point as the one of the greatest danger.

J W Hunter
3d Dist. N.Y.

ALS, DLC-JP.
1. See Hunter to Johnson, Aug. 25, 1867, Johnson Papers, LC. In this letter, Hunter endorsed McCulloch and urged his continuation in office.

From M. Richard Leverson [1]

New York   August 29/67
108 W 19th St.

Excellency

Permit me respectfully again to address you on the present aspect of political affairs.[2] Nor would I venture to do so but for the fact that I do not remember a single instance in which my political previsions have been falsified by events.

An ardent lover of American institutions I declared my intentions to become a citizen within a few hours from landing on these shores, bearing with me a letter from Mr. Adams[3] the U.S. minister at London, of which I formerly sent you a copy, testifying to my constant adherence to the Cause of the Union in its darkest hour in England!

I was one of those who afforded the opportunity to the people of the United Kingdom of declaring their will during the Civil struggle here, & thereby prevented the governing class in England from recognizing the South which almost to a man that class desired to do; & altho supported by a powerful press they were forced *even in England* to yield to the popular voice, which your Excellency in the U.S. is attempting to defy!

I do not urge you to change your policy for fear of impeachment—a man of courage like yourself—*once sure he was in the right*—would but persist the more for such a threat even tho the persistce. in his policy should make it a certainty; but I would ask you respectfully whether allying yourself with the acts the policy *& the men* who Caused the late war, seeking from the Executive Mansion to overturn the decision of that war, is not enough to make you suspect you are in the wrong? & I would ask you to hold, from dread of the Execration of every Citizen which will pursue you to your grave if your present course be persisted in.

I think if I had the pleasure of a few hours conversation with you I could induce you to make a complete volte face from a policy, destructive to yourself & most hurtful to your native & my adopted Country; & on the smallest encouragement from you I would come on at once to Washington. I repeat emphatically I do not remember any time within the last 15 years in which I have been mistaken in my political anticipations tho' I have never been noisy as a politician but for this I would not intrude my views upon your Excellency.

M Richard Leverson

ALS, DLC-JP.
1. Leverson (*fl*1892) was a New York lawyer. New York City directories (1869–72); Leverson to Grover Cleveland, Sept. 11, 1892, Grover Cleveland Papers, LC.
2. In an earlier letter, Leverson had urged Johnson to support the Reconstruction bill how that it had become law. Leverson to Johnson, Mar. 6, 1867, Johnson Papers, LC.
3. Charles Francis Adams.

From James W. Scully

Vicksburg, Miss.   August 29th 1867.

Sir:

It is impossible for me to express, in writing, the gratitude I feel towards you for your action in my late trouble,[1] and the thanks due you for the justice you have rendered me when all else seemed bent on my destruction. Believe me, Sir, when I say *justice*, for I have been subjected to a most infamous persecution; and to prove to you that it was so, the same spirit still prevails. The Order[2] releasing me from arrest and restoring me to duty had been received at the District Head Quarters *eight days ago*, and I have not yet been notified of it nor released from arrest. This, I understand, is done to please the Acting Chief Quartermaster,[3] who openly proclaims that *I cannot go on duty here*, and that he has telegraphed to the Quartermaster General[4] to have me removed. To this I have no objection, but I consider it very wrong to keep me in arrest until my removal is accomplished.

It is far from my desire, Sir, to be making complaints, but it seems that with a certain party, to be *your* friend is considered a crime, even with men who derived the little authority they have, from you, and who hold it entirely at your hands.

I hope and trust, sir, that you will overcome all your enemies, political and private, and I believe you have many friends, and *know* you have one who will stand by you to the last extremity.

J. W. Scully

ALS, DLC-JP.

1. Scully had been courtmartialed and found guilty of malfeasance in office. He was sentenced to dismissal from the army and to a fine of five dollars (or imprisonment until the fine was paid). See Scully to Johnson, July 2, 1867.

2. On August 13 the President disapproved of both the findings and the sentence in the Scully trial and ordered him to be returned to duty. On November 16 Scully was made a brevet colonel. Gen. Court-Martial Order No. 48, Aug. 13, 1867, RG94, NA; A. K. Long to Scully, Nov. 16, 1867, Tels. Sent, President (Special Reel), RG107, NA.

3. Probably Charles W. Folsom.

4. Gen. Montgomery C. Meigs.

From Thomas R. Shankland

Brooklyn N.Y.   Augt. 29. 1867

The public announcement that the Asst. Secy. of the Treasury Wm. E. Chandler, would soon return from his leave of absence, and extensive tour over the Plains, and insist upon the prompt acceptance of his Resignation, based upon a prearranged bargain, that he should name or appoint his Successor, is such a monstrous announcement,[1] as if by auction that I am surprised that the President and the Public Press of the Country, have not come down upon it, and characterised as it deserves an open sale in market of a public office in the U.S Treasury. Chandler is a Radical Friend of the writer, whose heart bleeds for a suffering People plundered and pillaged by such sales of their public offices. Has the decline of the Roman Empire come upon us, as an avalanche, at this early day?

Ths R Shankland

ALS, DLC-JP.
    1. In poor health during the spring months, Chandler had offered his resignation to Secretary McCulloch, who refused it and urged instead that Chandler take an extensive vacation. The press carried reports that Chandler would still resign upon returning to Washington after his summer travels. It was also reported that he was to choose his own successor. This did not happen, but in November Chandler did finally resign. Leon B. Richardson, *William E. Chandler, Republican* (New York, 1940), 72, 73; *New York Herald*, Aug. 26, 1867; *New York Tribune*, Aug. 26, 1867; *Washington Evening Star*, Nov. 30, 1867.

From William Thorpe

Private.

[Philadelphia]   August 29, 1867.

Dear Sir:

A friend of mine (a gentleman of wealth and position in Philadelphia), who has just returned from the extreme North-west reports that a reaction is setting in against Radicalism among the farmers and tradespeople throughout Michigan, Wisconsin and Minnesota. They are complaining about the enormous taxation, and think that Congress is to blame for making them pay the cost of supporting lazy, vagabond negroes, and maintaining a large army in the South, to *subjugate* the whites.

This gentleman also says that the revenue officials throughout those States are working for Judge Chase[1] for the next Presidency; and he believes most of them to be engaged in unlawful practices, the proof of which can be easily obtained if any one will take the trouble to look it up.

Wm. Thorpe.

ALS, DLC-JP.
    1. Salmon P. Chase.

From James H. Birch [1]

Prairie Park [Mo.], Aug. 30, 1867.

Dear Sir:

Having apprised General Shields of the liberty I had taken in presenting his name for the War Office,[2] it is perhaps no less appropriate that your Excellency should be placed in possession of his reply.[3] With such a man to do you justice through *the Army*, your friends could at least carry *Missouri*; and with a similar Cabinet, throughout, we would still hope to carry the Country. I but add, with the sincerest good will, that you have probably not a friend in this Congressional District[4] who is not hoping for such a change in the Department of the Treasury, and the Post Office, as will at least prevent Van Horn[5] from filling all the places with *your enemies*—but having confidence that you will continue to *do the best you can*, I will continue (if necessary) to *excuse* all I can.

James H. Birch.

ALS, DLC-JP.

1. Probably Judge James Harvey Birch (1804–1878), who was a lawyer, newspaper editor, Missouri state senator, register of the U.S. land office, and judge of the state supreme court (1849–52). Howard L. Conrad, ed., *Encyclopedia of the History of Missouri* (6 vols., New York, 1901), 1: 275; Walter Williams, ed., *A History of Northwest Missouri* (3 vols., Chicago, 1915), 1: 111–13, 219.

2. Birch recommended Gen. James Shields in a letter to Johnson of Aug. 15, 1867, Johnson Papers, LC.

3. James Shields to James H. Birch, Aug. 24, 1867, ibid.

4. Although the town of Prairie Park was in Nodaway County and in the Seventh District, Birch was a resident of Plattsburg, Clinton County, in the Sixth District. Parsons et al., *Congressional Districts and Data*, 122–23; Conrad, *Encyclopedia of Missouri*, 1: 275.

5. Robert T. Van Horn (1824–1916), a lawyer, was postmaster of Kansas City before the Civil War and served two terms as its mayor during the war. He was also colonel of the 27th Mo. Inf. (USA). Long-time editor of the *Kansas City Journal*, Van Horn, a Republican, served five terms in the U.S. House of Representatives (1865–71, 1881–83, 1896–97). Birch, the Democratic candidate for the Sixth District in the election of November 1866, challenged Van Horn's victory on technicalities. Congress permitted Van Horn to retain his seat, however. *BDUSC; House Misc. Docs.*, 40 Cong., 1 Sess., No. 48, pp. 1–56 (Ser. 1312).

From Edmund Cooper

Shelbyville Tenn.   August 30th 1867.

My Dear Sir:

Watching as I do, from the quiet of private life, the further progress of the mighty drama, in which you are playing such a prominent part, I cannot forbear expressing to you my hearty approval, of the vigor, with which you are now disposing of the annoying and harassing perplexities, with which your administration is surrounded.

Your letter to General Grant, in answer to his remonstrance against the removal of General Sheridan,[1] has the ring of the true metal in it, and will perpetuate your memory, in the hearts of your countrymen, whenever reason assumes its sway over minds, now blinded by passion, and distorted by prejudice.

Surely, when the people come to reflect upon the dangers and difficulties, of your administration, and calmly contemplate your actions, controlled as they are by a firm adherence to the constitution, and a livid determination to maintain at all hazards the unity of Executive Department of the Government, they will, forget the calumnies that are now being heaped upon you, by a corrupt and venal press, subsidized as it is by a revolutionary party organization, and only remember you as having served your country faithfully and laboriously during your years of vigor and maturity, as having earned a right to their confidence and respect.

Whoever contemplates with a patriotic mind not soured by political antagonisms, the evolutions of the great problems of national destiny, in which you have been compelled to play a conspicuous part, and bring the experience of the politician, to modify the inclusions that hope would anticipate, cannot but admire the achievements of the last few weeks, demonstrating the wisdom and virtue of one who has "fought the good fight," striven earnestly through the "angry tempest," and who can calmly look with scorn upon the struggles of the discomfited, who endeavoured to impede his progress.

On the other hand, there are fewer sadder spectacles than that presented by the politician, cast out from power, unable to accept his fate, and sitting unreconciled, mourning, and resentful amid the ruins of his former greatness.

Such is Mr Stanton—who in one short year has fallen from the pinacle of political power, to the depths of disgrace, and soon to the retirement of complete neglect. And as he has relished unlimited authority more readily perhaps than befited a statesman, so he will now feel his disgrace more bitterly than becomes a wise man.

Persevere in the good work. Make your power known and felt. Compel obedience in your Executive orders. Do not hesitate. You have gone too far to retrace your steps. The more boldly you fight it out in the time now adopted, the better for the country, and the more certain your reputation. Remove from out of your pathway, by the exercise of your constitutional authority all obstacles that in any manner, oppose your policy. Be firm, decisive yet conciliatory; but be the "Commander in chief of the Army and Navy of the United States."

The crisis is upon you. Your time for action has arrived. Have unity in your counsels! Let your own mind direct and control, and require obedience otherwise resignation.

In the midst of the unexampled venality and corruption which surrounds the political atmosphere of your enemies, remain *stainless*;—amongst the profligate and selfish, remain *conscientious*;—while every one else is excited and intemperate, remain moderate and self possessed—and from the "stern stuff" of which you are made.

I believe I know you—and this contest will evoke the stronger and more powerful traits of your character—and will cause your administration to be respected by your enemies, and admired by your friends.

Pardon me for this long letter. At home in the midst of professional labors, I yet take a deep interest in the welfare of the country, indisputably connected as I believe it is with the success of your present efforts to maintain the Union of the States, under the Constitution.

Edmd Cooper

ALS, DLC-JP.
1. Grant raised his objections to the removal of General Sheridan in his letter to the President of August 26; this was in response to Johnson's letter to Grant of the same date. The letter to which Cooper refers here may be Johnson's of August 27 in which he ordered Grant to carry out the instructions regarding the changes in assignments of Sheridan and others. See Johnson to Grant, Aug. 26, 1867; Grant to Johnson, Aug. 26, 1867; and Johnson to Grant, Aug. 27, 1867, Johnson Papers, LC.

From Robert J. Ker

New Orleans   August 30th 1867

As a citizen of Louisiana permit me to congratulate you upon the success which has attended your efforts to maintain the constitution under difficulies greater than have fallen to the lot of any president.

The assignment of general Hancock to this military district, will be attended by the best results I have no doubt, as he will have in his hands, the same unlimited powers as his predecessor, which he can exercise with enlightened Judgement and patriotic motives, for the restoration of harmony concord and union among our people.

It might be in my power, by my Knowledge of men and things in this community to be of some service to general Hancock in his administration and subserve your policy by placing in his possession, the information and experience that I possess, and if you will favor me with a letter of introduction to him, as having taken great interest in the rehabillitation of the constitutional relations between the state of Louisiana and the Federal government, and who visited you as the representative of the Democratic party of Louisiana with that view, what I might say to him would possess greater weight, as coming from one, who is known by you to be friendly to your administration.[1]

Robert J. Ker

ALS, DLC-JP.
1. No recommendation of Ker has been found.

From Ellis Malone[1]

Louisburg N.C.   August 30th 1867

Mr. President

I know you must be almost overwhelmed with business & hence I dislike to tax your time even to read a letter. I am no politution, never have been. I have always kept myself posted in relation to the affairs of the Country. I am 62 years old, have practiced medicine all my life untill some 10 years ago when I retired from the active duties of my profession. I thought I had enough of this worlds goods for me & my four children & my wife[2] which should have been named first.

The accursed war has robed me of nearly all I had made & I am now practicing physic to help me support my family. I am a mason—R.A.M have been master of the lodge in this place for 8 or 10 years consectitively— am now high priest of the R A Chaper of this place & have been for many years. I am glad to see that you too are a Mason and as a mason & as the President of the U.S. address you. I have no one in Washington City to refer you to for my standing in my Community & hence the above statement. Genl. Howard the head of the Negro Beaureau, knows me, was at my house and partook of my hospitality & knows my loyalty to the Constitution & the laws of the U.S.

I was as much opposed to Cesession & every thing that contributed to the late unhappy & wicked war as any man could be & yet having been a magistrate 38 years ago & having furnished a son a horse to join the Cavalry Service during the late war, to which he volunteered to save himself from Conscription[3] I am disfranchised—but enough of this. There is an impending Crisis hanging over us of which I am satisfied you nor any of the people north are Conizant. The negroes though they worked badly yet behaved themselves remarkably well untill some few months ago. Emisaries black and white, from the north & some meaner white men in our midst have been at work with them and have excited them, by inflamatory speeches & teachings with promises of confiscation of lands for their benefit joining into leagues & swearing them to support only radical leaders & to other things dangerous to the peace and harmony of the Country. Untill now & for some time back they have become bold defiant impudent & threatening to such an extent that all thinking men here see that a conflict of races is inevitable. Two months ago young Holden[4] Son of W W Holden came out here and addressed a large Crowd of the Coloured people. I with several respectable gentlemen went out to hear him. His speech was a most inflamatory & incendiary one & from the begining to the end calculated if not intended to so excite the negro against the white man as necesarily to bring on a conflict between them. I am as satisfied as I can be of any thing that has not already transpired that if thing go on as now existing & has been going on for some months that a bloody strife is before us, such an one as no good man can contemplate without horror. What adds to the certainty of this thing is that in every conflict now between the white & black which occur the military & the freedmans Beaureau protect the black & fine & imprison the white man. This is obliged to embolden the negro in outrage. I could if this paper would allow of it give you cases that I know would arrouse your indignation. And I assure you upon the honor of a man and a Mason—that the white people so far as I know are willing to give to the negro all the rights he is entitled to under the law. Thousands of people like myself are disfranchised, who had no part in Cecession or the war & unfortunately many who could register will not do it. Whats the use they say, we are ruined. The north intends to keep us so & they have the power & will do it. I know this ought not to be so & so do you, but they cant be reasoned out of it & the registration now going on in the County (the board consisting of two negroes and one white man. One of the negroes an illiterate blacksmith) shows that they (the negro) will have a majority of probably 230 to 300 majority when if all could register & vote the negro would be in the minority—& they are almost every one sworn to support the radical ticket & Holden for the next Govourner. Should that ever happen, a worse fate than that of Tennesse is [ours?]. I fear you will think my fears are father to my thought. The Lord grant it may be so. No Yankee that comes among us will believe such a thing as a war of races can happen. Every intelligent and thinking man I met an converse with think as I say to you above. We feel that we are standing upon a volcano—& most of us would get away if we could—but those who have a little left cant sell & can not get money to move away. I assure you that if I could get one half the real worth of what property I had left me in cash I would not stay here any longer than was absolutely necesary to get away. Where would you go? Any where to get away from a negro rule a negro insurection the negro encouraged by the milatary & freedmans Beaureau and the northern emisaries white & black who are here fanning the flame of prejudice & hate & revenge as well as some whites among us for self aggandisement & for bitter revenge.

Excuse me Mr. President I have written to you personaly—but what I have written are the words of truth & soberness—what I know and honestly believe. I dont know what you can do to save us and our wives & children the fate refered to above. If any thing can be done humanity requires it should be done & done quickly or it will be too late.

                                                            Ellis Malone M.D.

ALS, DLC-JP.
    1. Malone (c1805–fl1870) was both a physician and a farmer according to census reports. 1860 Census, N.C. Franklin, Louisbourg, 78; (1870), 32.
    2. Malone's wife, Martha C. (c1824–fl1880) and children, Celestia C. (b. c1840); Charles D. (c1845–fl1870); Mary E. (c1850–fl1870); and James E. (c1852–fl1880). 1860 Census, N.C., Franklin, Louisbourg, 78; (1870), 26, 32; (1880), 96th Enum. Dist., 42.
    3. Charles D. Malone was a private in the 1st N.C. Cav. (CSA). Louis H. Manarin et al., comps., North Carolina Troops 1861–1865: A Roster (11 vols. to date, Raleigh, 1966–), 2: 49.
    4. Joseph W. Holden (c1844–1875) was taken prisoner during the Civil War, released, and returned to Raleigh. He attended the University of North Carolina for one year during the war years. He soon thereafter began working with his father at the Raleigh Standard, which he did until 1868. At that latter date he was elected as a Republican to the state legislature and became speaker of the house. Subsequently, he was elected mayor of Raleigh in 1874. Raper, Holden, 209–10, 259.

From Thomas W. Egan

                                         New York City, August 31/67
Dear Sir:

In view of the many changes to be made in this city, I would suggest that unless you have undoubted reasons for listening to Fernando Wood's recommendations, you decline to appoint or remove any one upon his suggestion.[1]

I need not remind you of his widely known character as a man void of principle or honor. I beg to inform you that there is no doubt whatever that he has sold himself body and soul to the radicals in a compact to divide the Democratic party at the next election, and secure the triumph of the Radical Candidates. The Tammany or War Democrats of this city are unswervingly the friends of your policy, but no man or party occupying the position during the war that Mr. Wood and his friends held can possibly act with good faith toward you.

In making these suggestions to you, Mr. President, I assure you that I am moved by an unqualified desire to serve you. Not only so, but I have been requested to make them by many of the most prominent genuine Democrats of this city, a committee of whom will have the honor of waiting upon you in the course of next week.[2]

I beg to urge, as forcibly as permissible, that you hesitate in making any changes until this committee has conferred with you.

T. W. Egan.

·ALS, DLC-JP.
  1. In May 1867 Wood had withdrawn his support for the nomination of Egan, who had been trying for months to secure a revenue position. See Sickles to Johnson, Mar. 5, 1867; Wood to Johnson, May 13, 1867.
  2. No evidence regarding this particular meeting has been found.

From Alfred Kershaw[1]

New York   Aug. 31/67

Respet Sir

Observing Several Articles in the Radical Journals against *General Amnesty* as not *Absolving* the Parties from the *Penalties* and *Disabilities* made by the Reconstruction Acts of Congress I would *Sojest* as said Acts where pased by Congress *after* the Acts where committed for which the *Penalties* and *Disabilities* are imposed they Clearly come under the head and make them *Ex post facto* Laws and therefore as Clearly *unconstitutional* as it is Posible for Congress to make Laws. I take the Liberty to make this Sojestion for your Consideration. Your takeing the *wind* out of Gen Grants Sails has given you greatly the advantage of Position in forceing him to Change his Base or Line. Follow up the advantage and fight the Battle on *that Line* if it take you all winter. The People though Silent are watching the mooves with much anxiety forward and a Bold front and Success is shure. Allow me to Caution you of the Dangerous Effect of making Removals and appointment *Except for cause. Dont* be influenced to make them for *Political* Partisans for that alway looses public Confidence and Creates a *Distrust* in the mind of the People as to the *Honest intention* of your Actions. Avoid this and you are Safe. That was the Great *Error* of *John Tyler* Administration.

Alfred Kershaw

ALS, DLC-JP.
   1. Kershaw (c1808–fl1872), a New York native, had been a tailor and a flour merchant before entering the coal business. 1870 Census, N.Y., New York, New York, 16th Ward (1st Enum.), 14th Elec. Dist., 583; New York City directories (1854–72).

From Jonathan Nayson [1]

Amesbury, Mass   Aug. 31, 67

As a friend of your administration from the start, allow me to express the fervent hope that the current rumors of the intended removal of that notorious radical *pimp, Com. Rollins*,[2] will prove true. In God's name let him slide—for a worse enemy to you, personally and politically, does not exist. Coming from a little "one horse" town some 40 miles back in N. Hampshire, he has got into a station he never deserved, and which, *through his thousands of revenue officials*, he is ever working against you. Two worse enemies of your administration then Rollins & Chandler,[3] both rabid N. Hampshire radicals, cannot be found. They ought to follow in the train of the crowd of decapitated officials which we all hope soon to see marching by the order of the *Constitutional* "Commander in Chief." In this—the 5" Mass Revenue District—(Ben. Butlers) *every Administration man has been swept out of office by Stone, Butlers own Assessor*,[4] and Rollins, while rabid Butler *impeachers* have taken their places! The Secretary of the Treasury—an honest and honorable man— has *unwittingly* sanctioned this outrageous proceedure. And although the facts have been stated to the Secretary, no notice has been taken of it—and Stone Butler and Rollins, are yet "masters of the situation." Although one of the "Johnson men" thus proscribed, I have no desire for reinstatement—I only hope that others more desiring and needy, may be. Among these is Nathaniel Greely Esq.[5] of Newburyport, a worthy man and competant officer and a *Royal Arch Mason*. He was summarily turned out and a *rabid radical abolitionist* put in his place. *Gen. Cushing*[6] knows all about this and other cases, and as he was instrumental in getting Stones name to your Excellency, in place of Mr. Binney,[7] he ought to see to it that Mr. Greely is restored.

We are all inspired with new zeal and courage by the recent glorious manifestations of the past few days. There is *some* hope of our country yet, thank God and President Johnson!

The scene of the *casting out of the Temple* needs re-enacting. The country requires it—and thus will the cursed work described by old Thad. Stevens—as "out-side of the Constitution, and therefore nothing but usurpation," be met and successfully resisted.

Jonathan Nayson

I can refer to Col. Greene[8] of the Boston Post, Mr. Spofford[9] of Newburyport, J. C. Tucker[10] of Boston—and last but not least, to Perkins Cleaveland Esq[11] of Connecticutt and N. York. for anything concering me.

ALS, DLC-JP.

1. Nayson (b. *c*1809) was an apothecary and at one time a justice of the peace. Nayson evidently served for a short time as a weigher and gauger at the Boston customhouse in the late 1850s. 1870 Census, Mass., Essex, Amesbury, 63; Boston directories (1861–64); C. A. and J. F. Wood, *Essex County History and Directory* (Boston, 1870), 29, 205; *U.S. Off. Reg.* (1859).

2. Edward A. Rollins.

3. William E. Chandler.

4. Eben F. Stone (1822–1895), a Newburyport lawyer, state senator before the war and state representative afterwards, served in the Union army. He was later in the U.S. House for three terms (1881–87). *BDUSC*; *U.S. Off. Reg.* (1867).

5. Perhaps the Greely (*c*1822–*fl*1870) listed in the 1860 census as a tailor. Evidently he also served as a justice of the peace. 1860 Census, Mass., Essex, Newburyport, 17; Wood, *Essex County*, 30, 438.

6. Caleb Cushing.

7. William C. Binney (*c*1823–*fl*1870) was an attorney in Amesbury and a justice of the peace. Originally nominated in December 1866 by Johnson as assessor of the Fifth District, Binney was approved in January; the Senate reconsidered and subsequently rejected his nomination in March. 1870 Census, Mass., Essex, Amesbury, 50; Wood, *Essex County*, 29; Ser. 6B, Vol. 4: 24, Johnson Papers, LC.

8. Longtime publisher and editor of the *Boston Post*, Charles G. Greene (1804–1886) had twice served as naval officer at Boston. *NCAB*, 4: 445.

9. Richard S. Spofford, Jr.

10. Perhaps John C. Tucker (*fl*1870), who had worked at the Boston customhouse in the 1850s and into the early 1860s as a weigher and gauger. *U.S. Off. Reg.* (1853–55); Boston directories (1857–70).

11. Cleveland (*fl*1877) had also served in the Boston customhouse and was later a clerk of the county court in New York City. Boston directories (1859–60); New York City directories (1867–78).

From David T. Patterson

Greenville Tennessee   August 31st 1867.

Henderson[1] is here today and is anxious to make some arrangements about his farm. He proposes to Execute his note with undoubted security for the amount of the purchase money & also for the balance due you and in addition he proposes to give a mortgage on the property for the payment of the whole debt.[2]

This is the proposition & I await instructions.

Dan'l [*sic*] T. Patterson

Tel, DNA-RG107, Tels. Recd., President, Vol. 6 (1867–1868).

1. Joseph Henderson. For an earlier reference to dealings with Henderson, see Charles Johnson to Johnson, Jan. 1, 1861, *Johnson Papers*, 4: 110–11. For a recent discussion of Henderson's financial situation that eventuated the sale of his farm, see Robert Tracy McKenzie, "Civil War and Socioeconomic Change in the Upper South: The Survival of Local Agricultural Elite in Tennessee, 1850–1870," *THQ*, 51 (1993): 177.

2. Initially Patterson telegraphed Johnson requesting that the President send $17,600 for the Henderson farm. In reply, Johnson asked Patterson: "Does Henderson refuse to secure the payment of the debt in a reasonable time?" Patterson then responded with the statement that Henderson had "made no proposition or arrangement." Patterson to Johnson, Aug. 29, 30, 1867, Tels. Recd., President, Vol. 6 (1867–68); Johnson to Patterson, Aug. 30, 1867, Tels. Sent, President, Vol. 3 (1865–68), RG107, NA.

To David T. Patterson

Washington, D.C.   Aug. 31 1867

If it meets your judgment, close the transaction upon the conditions indicated in your despatch.[1]

I hope Martha will make some arrangement for the improvement of our old home, as it ought to be.

Andrew Johnson

Tel, DNA-RG107, Tels. Sent, President, Vol. 3 (1865–68).

1. Patterson acknowledged doubts about whether Joseph Henderson could meet the terms of the arrangements offered by him. Nevertheless, since Henderson believed that he could do so, Patterson agreed to wait until Tuesday, September 3. The President responded, however, by urging Patterson to close the transaction on any conditions that he thought best. On the following day, September 2, Patterson notified Johnson that Henderson had indicated that he could not meet the terms as previously outlined. "Nothing now remains to be done but to pay the purchase money and take a deed." In reply, the President instructed Patterson: "Make Henderson a present of the debt and that will close it to his satisfaction at least." Patterson to Johnson, Aug. 31, Sept. 2, 1867, Tels. Recd., President, Vol. 6 (1867–68); Johnson to Patterson, Sept. 1, 2, 1867, Tels. Sent, President, Vol. 3 (1865–68), RG107, NA.

From Benjamin C. Truman

SAN FRANCISCO,   AUG 31, 1867.

MY DEAR FRIEND:

Understanding that there is a vacancy in the "pay department," and that you are still holding the nomination in reserve, I take the opportunity of joining Messrs. Nesmith and Harding,[1] and others of your true friends of Oregon, in earnestly presenting the claims of Major Jo. DREW[2] of that State, now holding the position of "paymaster" in the Volunteers' Corps. Major Drew is one of the first friends I made upon this coast, and I want to urge his claims, my good friend, because he is the truest, most earnest, and steadfast, friend and supporter, personally and politically, you have in the army upon this coast. The slightest mention of my friend will suffice. He came here in 1849, and from that time to the breaking out of the war held high positions in the Democratic party, and like yourself was a strong Breckinridge man. Immediately upon the great issue, Major Drew took National grounds, and went uncompromisingly for the Union, like yourself. At the close of the war he took strong Constitutional grounds, conscientiously and fervently, battling with you against the warplots and new school of Secessionists. Major Drew and myself have many a little chat about you personally and politically, and I find he is really the truest friend you have upon the Pacific slope in a Federal position, an endorsement of which you will have from Senator Nesmith and others. He is at this time laboring with Nesmith and Harding in overcoming the obnoxious political complexion of Oregon, all of whom feel sure of carrying that State against the Radicals next Spring, reducing, as you may recollect, the vote during the war, which was very strong, to less than 500 last year. I hope you will give Major Drew this vacancy, for, as I stated above, he is your *truest* friend upon this coast in the army, an endorsement of which you will receive from Senator Nesmith and others by a subsequent mail.[3]

Ben C. Truman.

ALS, DNA-RG94, ACP Branch, File D-414-CB-1864, J. W. Drew.

1. James W. Nesmith and Benjamin F. Harding. Harding (1823–1899), a lawyer, served as clerk and member of the territorial legislature, U.S. district attorney, territorial secretary, and state legislator in Oregon. A Republican, he was elected in 1862 to complete the remainder of the deceased Edward D. Baker's U.S. Senate term. Although no letter of recommendation from Harding has been found, Nesmith wrote several, including Nesmith to Col. Morrow, Mar. 9, 1867, and Nesmith to Johnson, Aug. 25, 1867, ACP Branch, D-414-CB-1864, J. W. Drew, RG94, NA; *BDUSC*.

2. Joseph W. Drew (c1825–fl1882) went to Oregon with an exploring expedition and then settled there. He worked both as an Indian agent and with the Customs Department and later served in the territorial and state legislatures. During the war he was commissioned an additional paymaster of volunteers in 1864. Washington, D.C., directories (1882); Hubert H. Bancroft, *History of Oregon, 1848–1888* (San Francisco, 1888), 2: 161, 176, 181, 638; *U.S. Off. Reg.* (1861); ACP Branch, D-414-CB-1864, J. W. Drew, RG94, NA.

3. Apparently there was actually no vacancy for a paymaster in the regular army on the west coast and Drew's name was added to the waiting list, to no avail, however, as he was mustered out of the service early in 1869. He thereafter lived in Nevada and Washington, D.C. Benjamin C. Truman to Johnson (and endorsements), Nov. 13, 1867, ibid; Pension File, Joseph W. Drew, RG15, NA; Washington, D.C., directory (1882).

Appendix I

ADMINISTRATION OF ANDREW JOHNSON (1865–1869)

[Adapted from Robert Sobel, ed., *Biographical Directory of the United States Executive Branch, 1774–1971* (Westport, Conn., 1971).]

Office	Name
Secretary of State, 1865–69	William H. Seward
Secretary of the Treasury, 1865–69	Hugh McCulloch
Secretary of War, 1865–68	Edwin M. Stanton
Secretary of War ad interim, 1867–68	Ulysses S. Grant
Secretary of War ad interim, 1868	Lorenzo Thomas
Secretary of War, 1868–69	John M. Schofield
Attorney General, 1865–66	James Speed
Attorney General, 1866–68	Henry Stanbery
Attorney General ad interim, 1868*	Orville H. Browning
Attorney General, 1868–69	William M. Evarts
Postmaster General, 1865–66	William Dennison
Postmaster General, 1866–69	Alexander W. Randall
Secretary of the Navy, 1865–69	Gideon Welles
Secretary of the Interior, 1865	John P. Usher
Secretary of the Interior, 1865–66	James Harlan
Secretary of the interior, 1866–69	Orville H. Browning

*from March 13, 1868, when Stanbery resigned, until July 20, 1868, when Evarts assumed office, Browning discharged the duties of attorney general in addition to his functions as head of the Interior Department.

Appendix II

VETOES, PROCLAMATIONS, AND SELECTED EXECUTIVE ORDERS AND
SPECIAL MESSAGES (FEBRUARY-AUGUST 1867)

[Asterisks indicate documents printed in Volume 12; all are printed in
James D. Richardson, comp., *A Compilation of the Messages and Papers
of the Presidents* (10 vols., Washington, D.C., 1896–99), Volume 6.]

Date	Veto Messages	Richardson, *Messages*
Mar. 2	*Tenure of Office Act	492–98
Mar. 2	*First Military Reconstruction Act	498–511
Mar. 23	*Second Military Reconstruction Act	531–35
Jul. 19	*Third Military Reconstruction Act	536–45
	Proclamations	
Mar. 1	Admission of Nebraska into the Union	516–17
Mar. 30	Call for special meeting of the Senate	521–22
	Executive Orders	
Aug. 12	*Suspension of Sec. of War Stanton	556
Aug. 12	*Appointment of Grant as secretary of war *ad interim*	556
Aug. 17	Transfers of Generals Thomas, Sheridan, and Hancock	556–57
Aug. 26	*Modifications *re* above transfers	557
Aug. 26	*Replacement of Sickles with Canby in the Second Military District	557
	Special Messages	
Feb. 18	*Violations under the 1866 Civil Rights Act	468
Mar. 2	Report of attorney general on pardon of former Confederates	471–72
Mar. 2	*Protest of Army Appropriations Act	472
Mar. 30	Johnson's approval of funding for the Military Reconstruction acts	521
Mar. 30	Treaty between Russia and U.S. for cession of Alaska	521
Jul. 8	Additional report on pardon of former Confederates	524

Index

Primary identification of a person is indicated by an italic *n* following the page reference. Identifications found in earlier volumes of the *Johnson Papers* are shown by providing volume and page numbers, within parentheses, immediately after the name of the individual. The only footnotes which have been indexed are those that constitute identification notes.